游说、竞选捐款与
美国政治腐败

Lobbing, Campaign Contributions, and U.S. Political Corruption

韦 佳 著

中国社会科学出版社

图书在版编目（CIP）数据

游说、竞选捐款与美国政治腐败 / 韦佳著. -- 北京：中国社会科学出版社，2024. 7. -- （中国社会科学博士后文库）. -- ISBN 978-7-5227-3733-1

Ⅰ. D771.234

中国国家版本馆CIP数据核字第2024YL1431号

出 版 人	赵剑英	
责任编辑	高　歌	
责任校对	王佳玉	
责任印制	李寡寡	

出　　版	中国社会科学出版社	
社　　址	北京鼓楼西大街甲158号	
邮　　编	100720	
网　　址	http://www.csspw.cn	
发 行 部	010-84083685	
门 市 部	010-84029450	
经　　销	新华书店及其他书店	
印　　刷	北京君升印刷有限公司	
装　　订	廊坊市广阳区广增装订厂	
版　　次	2024年7月第1版	
印　　次	2024年7月第1次印刷	
开　　本	710×1000　1/16	
印　　张	23	
字　　数	385千字	
定　　价	128.00元	

凡购买中国社会科学出版社图书，如有质量问题请与本社营销中心联系调换
电话：010-84083683
版权所有　侵权必究

第十一批《中国社会科学博士后文库》编委会及编辑部成员名单

（一）编委会

主　任：赵　芮

副主任：柯文俊　胡　滨　沈水生

秘书长：王　霄

成　员（按姓氏笔划排序）：

卜宪群　丁国旗　王立胜　王利民　王　茵
史　丹　冯仲平　邢广程　刘　健　刘玉宏
孙壮志　李正华　李向阳　李雪松　李新烽
杨世伟　杨伯江　杨艳秋　何德旭　辛向阳
张　翼　张永生　张宇燕　张伯江　张政文
张冠梓　张晓晶　陈光金　陈星灿　金民卿
郑筱筠　赵天晓　赵剑英　胡正荣　都　阳
莫纪宏　柴　瑜　倪　峰　程　巍　樊建新
魏后凯

（二）编辑部

主　任：李洪雷

副主任：赫　更　葛吉艳　王若阳

成　员（按姓氏笔划排序）：

杨　振　宋　娜　陈　莎　胡　奇　侯聪睿
贾　佳　柴　颖　焦永明　黎　元

《中国社会科学博士后文库》
出版说明

为繁荣发展中国哲学社会科学博士后事业，2012年，中国社会科学院和全国博士后管理委员会共同设立《中国社会科学博士后文库》（以下简称《文库》），旨在集中推出选题立意高、成果质量好、真正反映当前我国哲学社会科学领域博士后研究最高水准的创新成果。

《文库》坚持创新导向，每年面向全国征集和评选代表哲学社会科学领域博士后最高学术水平的学术著作。凡入选《文库》成果，由中国社会科学院和全国博士后管理委员会全额资助出版；入选者同时获得全国博士后管理委员会颁发的"优秀博士后学术成果"证书。

作为高端学术平台，《文库》将坚持发挥优秀博士后科研成果和优秀博士后人才的引领示范作用，鼓励和支持广大博士后推出更多精品力作。

《中国社会科学博士后文库》编委会

摘　要

任何设计不完善且由竞争利益各方组成的系统都会滋生腐败风险。从规范上讲，公共政策旨在促进公共利益，然而在当今的美国，巨大的经济资源转化为政治影响力的进程中，公共政策往往不完全是由公共利益决定的，而是被个人、公司或特殊利益团体的导向所影响。过去的一个多世纪里，公司一直被视为竞选财务的特殊问题，对公司竞选支出的监管是美国竞选财务法律的中心思想。20世纪80年代以来，美国政府对反托拉斯监管的逐渐放松，使得大公司在全球化趋势下不断合并扩张，并以更为强大的经济实力参与到政治活动中。2010年"联合公民案"后，公司被赋予了事实上的言论自由权，不受限的支出通过越来越活跃的影子游说活动与超级政治行动委员会，将公司对政治进程的影响不断放大。同时，大公司背后个人财富的高度集中也投射着其对民主的威胁。尽管游说和竞选捐款不能直接设定立法结果，却是一种显著的加权机制，使得出资方的偏向更加重要。通过游说与竞选捐款这两种重要的政治活动形式，0.01%的美国人在选举的议题与结果上发挥着不成比例的重要作用。在当前暗钱加速渗透美国政治选举的背景下，本书立足于大量文献、数据、案例与庞杂的监管法律法规，对比联邦竞选财务系统的理想与现实图景，继而以"阿片危机"中的大制药商和大规模监禁中的私营监狱公司为透视点，探究大公司、大捐款者和特殊利益集团如何通过滥用游说、旋转门、超级政治行动委员会和暗钱组织，与候选人构建实质上的协调并实现利益交换，剖析其对立法、司法行政决策乃至民主代议制和联邦主义产生的深刻影响。本书还在公司势力与保守主义崛起的场景中，对"联合公民案"时代即2010年以来发布的相关法律和法案进行解读，从中归纳竞选财务和游说法律在反腐败方向上的发展逻辑，探寻未来相关规则的发展趋势和所面临的挑战，以期获得竞选乃至政治反腐败的法律和制度改革路径。最后，本书立足于作为政治资金腐败新工具的暗钱和加密货币这两大前沿视角，提出以区块链和人工智能作为补充的反腐败新技术路径，弥补美国当前的法律制度和社会结构缺陷。区块链技术不仅可以跟踪和披露竞选中的资金，还可以用于移动投票系统，维护选举的公正性；由大数据和人工智能支持的腐败预警系统也被证明是有效的。此外，尽管存在审查争议，但互联网社交媒体仍能够鼓励更多的普通选民参与政治，稀释大公司和特殊利益集团过于强大的政治影响力，促进平等原则的实现。

关键词：美国政治腐败；游说；竞选捐款；暗钱；技术路径

Abstract

As a proposition, any system that is imperfectly designed and populated with parties holding competing interests incubates the risk of corruption. Normatively, public policy is intended to advance a common public interest. However, in practice, policy is shaped by preferential influence that is bought and sold by individuals, corporations, special interest groups, and their lobbyists. Such parties deploy enormous economic resources to advance their respective interests. Illustratively, following the era of the early 1980's and its high cost of capital and inflation, the subsequently low (er) cost of mergers and acquisitions facilitated an explosive increase in the size of US corporations, a phenomenon further enabled by accelerating globalized capitalism and increasingly faster circulation of international capital flows. Elsewhere, for more than a century, corporate contributions were a special source of election campaign finance regulated by American campaign finance laws. This dynamic was affirmed in the US Supreme Court's 2010 decision in Citizens United v. Federal Election Commission, 558 U. S. 310, on grounds of protecting the US Constitution's First Amendment right to free speech. The resulting proliferation of Super PACs further amplified the influence of corporations in American political processes. Hence, while accounting for 30% of the dollars in general elections, this small 1% of 1% of the American electorate yields disproportionately significant impact on election issues and their outcomes. Concentration of wealth projects a threat to western liberal democracy rather than protecting it. The phenomenon of increasingly active shadow lobbying together with larger campaign contributions from mega corporations, are becoming the two of the primary methods of exerting influence over legislative outcomes. These methods do not purchase outcomes directly but do create a weighting system in which money and communication elevate in perceived importance the particular issues that concern donors. The thesis satisfies its research objective of assessing the gap between the normative ideal of the U. S. federal election system and its realpolitik, by drawing on literature, data, federal court cases, and federal electoral laws and regulations. Using two phenomena as illustrative media, namely, the roles of private prisons in mass incarceration and of pharmaceutical manufacturers in the opioid crisis, the thesis' research appraises the corrupting impact of abused lobbying, campaign contributions and campaign finance on American political systems and by extension, contemporary American society. Dissecting the evolution of US campaign finance laws between 2010 – 2023 together with their challenges in the Supreme Court over the past century, the thesis explores the need to balance freedom of speech with the legal principle of equity that follows law and identifies possible approaches to reducing the corrupting impact of lobbying and campaign contributions. Through the lens of dark money and cryptocurrencies, new political corruption tools in the post-*Citizens United* era, the research urges more innovative approaches to anti-corruption. Thus, the thesis' last chapter offers supplementary approaches to anti-corruption in U. S. campaign finance and its broader political arena. The approach to strengthening law enforcement is to elaborate the enforcement rules of campaign disclosure. It dictates out-of-box thinking by proposing that the well-established and independent US Securities and Exchange Commission oversee corporation's campaign spending, and that the current anti-trust regulation in the context of financial capitalism be reshaped. Further, technology-wise innovation should be employed. Blockchain technology can not only track and disclose money in campaigns but be employed in mobile voting systems to defend the integrity of the election. A warning system built by artificial intelligence detecting potential government corruption in procurement has also proved effective. Moreover, despite concern about campaign advertising online and censorship by social media monopolies, further use of social media may enable more ordinary voters to participate in politics and thereby lessen the political influence of big donors and corporations. Only with every vote's being equally weighed in political designation and government decision-making can the idea of popular sovereignty survive.

Keywords: Political Corruption in the U. S. , Lobbying, Campaign Contributions, Dark Money, Technical Approaches

目 录

绪 论 ……………………………………………………………… (1)
  第一节　研究背景 ………………………………………… (3)
  第二节　文献综述 ………………………………………… (5)
    一　政治腐败：系统性腐败路径解构 ………………… (6)
    二　政治腐败研究中的游说：研究路径与普遍
       结论 ……………………………………………… (10)
    三　竞选捐款与政治腐败：代表观点与核心争议 ……… (17)
  第三节　研究方法、结构、创新及贡献 …………………… (37)

第一章　游说、竞选捐款与美国政治腐败：历史到
       现实 ……………………………………………… (39)
  第一节　游说与竞选捐款的内在联系 …………………… (41)
    一　游说与竞选捐款的逻辑关系 ……………………… (42)
    二　游说与竞选捐款的监管核心 ……………………… (43)
    三　游说与竞选捐款对立法进程的协同影响机制 …… (44)
  第二节　游说与竞选捐款在美国政治中的历史轨迹 …… (47)
    一　游说在美国政治中的历史轨迹：边缘到扩张 …… (47)
    二　竞选捐款在美国政治中的历史轨迹：冲突与
       规制 ……………………………………………… (58)
  第三节　游说与竞选捐款语境下的政治腐败 …………… (75)
    一　政治腐败：从贿赂法到竞选财务法的释义 ……… (75)
    二　政治腐败下的不平等政治参与和民主代议制
       迷思 ……………………………………………… (85)
  本章小结 …………………………………………………… (93)

第二章　游说、竞选捐款与美国政治腐败：危机四伏的民主体制 (95)
第一节　精英决策取代民主决策 (96)
第二节　特殊利益集团垄断发声 (97)
第三节　技术专制蚕食立法裁量权 (99)
第四节　国会议员面临竞选筹款压力 (100)
第五节　司法公正被拍卖 (102)
本章小结 (104)

第三章　暗钱涌入政治选举：美国政治腐败的新阶段 (106)
第一节　暗钱组织的前身：527组织 (107)
第二节　"联合公民案"激发暗钱组织 (110)
一　暗钱组织的类型识别 (111)
二　暗钱组织掩体：超级政治行动委员会 (118)
第三节　暗钱组织侵蚀选举 (132)
第四节　暗钱捐款者隐匿身份 (136)
第五节　联邦选举委员会监管陷入僵局 (139)
本章小结 (141)

第四章　"联合公民案"时代竞选财务法律重塑：反腐败与言论自由的博弈 (143)
第一节　关键案例对竞选财务法律的重塑：公司政治影响力的扩张 (144)
一　联合公民时代的开启：松绑公司政治支出 (144)
二　"联合公民案"变革透视：公司与保守主义崛起 (149)
第二节　"联合公民案"时代竞选反腐败法律动态 (153)
一　2010年以来联邦竞选反腐败立法动态 (154)
二　州竞选反腐败法律改革前沿 (176)
本章小结 (179)

第五章　制药巨头游说与竞选捐款的腐败影响：以阿片危机为透视点 (182)

第一节　阿片危机成因：变相贿赂与过量处方 (186)
第二节　阿片危机的加剧：制药巨头游说与竞选捐款的腐败影响 (188)
　　一　阻挠阿片类药物法律监管 (192)
　　二　维持阿片类药品高定价 (199)
第三节　阿片危机的未来：制药巨头游说对药品监管政策的塑造 (202)
本章小结 (206)

第六章　私营监狱公司滥用游说与竞选捐款：大规模监禁的腐败循环 (208)

第一节　寄生于大规模监禁的私营监狱产业 (209)
第二节　私营监狱公司竞选捐款影响立法决策 (212)
　　一　捐款押注有望当选的议员与政府官员 (216)
　　二　以捐款换取政府合同中的不合理条款 (217)
　　三　捐款支持惩罚性移民政策下的营利模式 (220)
第三节　私营监狱公司游说活动侧面影响监禁政策 (225)
　　一　阻击移民改革与管制私营监狱法案 (228)
　　二　利用人脉关系搭建旋转门 (232)
　　三　借助非政府组织网络起草示范性法案 (234)
本章小结 (237)

第七章　美国游说与竞选捐款反腐败前瞻：系统透明与配套技术 (240)

第一节　"联合公民案"时代竞选反腐败挑战 (241)
　　一　加密货币竞选捐款难以监管 (241)
　　二　公司竞选支出权利被无限扩大 (244)
　　三　旋转门法律催生隐形游说者 (249)
　　四　限制问题倡导引发争议 (251)

第二节 美国游说与竞选捐款反腐败的制度优化 …………… (252)
　　一　精确披露执行规则 ………………………………… (252)
　　二　联邦证券交易委员会协助监管 …………………… (253)
　　三　推广竞选公共筹资 ………………………………… (254)
　　四　重塑公司反托拉斯监管 …………………………… (257)
第三节 美国游说与竞选捐款反腐败的技术路径 …………… (260)
　　一　区块链构建透明选举系统 ………………………… (260)
　　二　互联网媒体扩展选民政治参与维度 ……………… (268)
第四节 竞选财务制度改革的未来 …………………………… (271)
　　一　竞选财务法律改革的局限性 ……………………… (272)
　　二　竞选财务法律改革趋势 …………………………… (275)
　本章小结 ……………………………………………………… (280)

结　论 ………………………………………………………… (282)

参考文献 ……………………………………………………… (284)

索　引 ………………………………………………………… (338)

案例索引 ……………………………………………………… (342)

后　记 ………………………………………………………… (344)

Contents

Introduction ··· (1)
  Section 1 Background and Context ·· (3)
  Section 1 Literature Review ··· (5)
    1. Political Corruption and its Institutional Approaches ················ (6)
    2. Lobbying and Political *Quid Pro Quo*: Indicators and Findings ··· (10)
    3. Campaign Contributions and Political *Quid Pro Quo*: Opinions
       and Issues ·· (17)
  Section 3 Methodology, Outlines, Purpose of Research and
              Contribution ··· (37)

Chapter 1 Historical Development of Lobbying and Campaign
            Contributions ··· (39)
  Section 1 Interaction between Lobbying and Campaign
              Contributions ··· (41)
    1. Links between Lobbying and Campaign Contributions ·············· (42)
    2. Regulating Lobbying and Campaign Contributions ··················· (43)
    3. Coordinated Impact of Lobbying and Campaign Contributions
       on Legislation ··· (44)
  Section 2 History of Lobbying and Campaign Contributions
              in the U. S. ··· (47)
    1. Lobbying: Transition from Unlawful to Systemic ····················· (47)
    2. Campaign Contributions: Issues and Regulations ····················· (58)
  Section 3 Political *Quid Pro Quo* in Lobbying and Campaign
              Contributions ··· (75)

1. Definitions: From Bribery to Campaign Finance Laws ……… (75)
2. Unequal Participation in Representative Democracy ………… (85)
Summary ……………………………………………………………… (93)

Chapter 2　Policy Making and Campaign Finance: Democracy Fraught with Crisis ………………………………… (95)
　Section 1　Policy Making Dominated by the Elites ………… (96)
　Section 2　The Veto held by Special Interest Groups ……… (97)
　Section 3　Technocracy Diluting Lawmaking ………………… (99)
　Section 4　Lawmakers' Dependency on Campaign Financing ……………………………………………… (100)
　Section 5　Donations effect on Judicial Outcomes ………… (102)
　Summary ……………………………………………………………… (104)

Chapter 3　Dark Money in Elections: A New Era of Political Quid Pro Quo ……………………………………………… (106)
　Section 1　527 Groups: Predecessors to Dark Money ……… (107)
　Section 2　*Citizens United* Facilitating Dark Money Groups …… (110)
　　1. Types of Dark Money Groups ……………………………… (111)
　　2. Super PACs: A New Path for Dark Money ……………… (118)
　Section 3　Dark Money's impact on Fairness and Transparency in Elections ………………………… (132)
　Section 4　The Hidden Donors of Dark Money ……………… (136)
　Section 5　Federal Election Committee: Ineffective through Partisan Deadlock ………………………………… (139)
　Summary ……………………………………………………………… (141)

Chapter 4　Reshaping Campaign Financing After *Citizens United*: Anti-Corruption v. Free Speech ……………… (143)
　Section 1　Expansion of Corporate Influence: Key Cases …… (144)
　　1. Unlimited Corporate Election Spending …………………… (144)
　　2. Rise of Corporations and Conservatism …………………… (149)

Section 2　Legislation Modifying the Election Process .... (153)
　1. Federal Legislation .... (154)
　2. State Legislation .... (176)

Chapter 5　The Pharmaceutical Industry and the Opioid Crisis ... (179)
　Section 1　Major Causes of the Opioid Crisis: Bribery and
　　　　　　Over-Prescription .... (182)
　Section 2　The Role of Big Pharma Lobbying and Campaign
　　　　　　Contributions in Worsening the Crisis .... (186)
　　1. Blocking Regulations of Opioid Drugs .... (188)
　　2. Maintaining High Pricing of Opioid Drugs .... (192)
　Section 3　The Future of the Opioid Crisis .... (199)
　Summary .... (202)

Chapter 6　The Private Prison Industry and Mass Incarceration ....
.... (206)
　Section 1　The Private Prison Industry: Dependence on Mass
　　　　　　Incarceration .... (208)
　Section 2　Influencing the Legislative Process with Campaign
　　　　　　Contributions .... (209)
　　1. Backing Aspiring Representatives .... (212)
　　2. Securing Favourable Contracts .... (216)
　　3. Promoting Criminalization and Detention of Undocumented
　　　Immigrants .... (217)
　Section 3　Lobbying to Change Policies in Imprisonment ...... (220)
　　1. Suppression of Immigrant Reform Laws and the Regulation of
　　　Private Prisons .... (225)
　　2. Building Revolving Doors and Industry-Government
　　　Networks .... (228)
　　3. Drafting Model Acts through NGO Networks .... (232)
　Summary .... (234)

Chapter 7　Future for Anti – Corruption in Lobbying and Campaign
　　　　　Contributions: Transparency and Techniques ………… (237)
　　Section 1　Challenges in Disclosures and Regulations Post –
　　　　　　　Citizens United ……………………………………… (240)
　　　　1. Cryptocurrency Campaign Contributions …………………… (241)
　　　　2. Expansion of Corporate Spending ……………………………… (241)
　　　　3. The "Shadow Lobbying" of Corporate and Government
　　　　　 Employees ………………………………………………………… (244)
　　　　4. Lobbying Masquerading as "Issue Advocacy" …………………… (249)
　　Section 2　Proposed Modification to the Systems in
　　　　　　　Lobbying and Campaign Contributions …………… (251)
　　　　1. Full Disclosure of Donors ……………………………………… (252)
　　　　2. Security and Exchange Commission Assists Disclosure ………… (252)
　　　　3. Promote Public Funding of Election Campaigns ………………… (253)
　　　　4. Reform Antitrust Laws ………………………………………… (254)
　　Section 3　Technology based Approaches to Reform ………… (257)
　　　　1. Blockchain to Sustain Election Transparency ………………… (260)
　　　　2. Use of Social Media to Broaden Citizens' Participation ………… (260)
　　　　3. Artificial Intelligence to Scrutinize Government Contracts ……… (268)
　　Section 4　The Future of Campaign Finance Reform …………… (271)
　　　　1. Political and Legal Limits in Reforms ………………………… (272)
　　　　2. Trends in Reforms ……………………………………………… (275)
　　Summary ……………………………………………………………… (280)

Conclusions and Findings ……………………………………………… (282)

Bibliography …………………………………………………………… (284)

Index …………………………………………………………………… (338)

Cited Cases …………………………………………………………… (342)

Postscript ……………………………………………………………… (344)

绪　论

阿克顿勋爵说："权力具有腐败的天性。"[1] 只要掌握公共权力者利用其权力谋取私人目的，就会发生腐败。西塞罗相信，包含君主制、贵族制和民主制在内的各种类型的善政"都有一条通向纯粹邪恶的湿滑道路"。[2] 罗马历史学家波利比乌斯扩展了这一思想，认为所有政府都会经历"成长、顶峰和衰落"过程的永恒循环：以腐败为衰落的开始，君主制可能滑向暴政，贵族制演变为寡头统治，民主制则倾向于被暴民利用。[3] 休谟更预言："在设计任何的政府体制时，都必须把政府里的每个掌权者设想为无赖之徒，并设想他的一切作为都是为了谋求私利，别无其他目标。"[4] 上述论断均提示了预防腐败对国家本身的普遍必要性。因而在制宪会议（Constitutional Convention）期间，美国的开国元勋们针对腐败的影响就数十项宪法条款进行了辩论，乔治·梅森（George Mason）甚至直接将这些辩论的目的归结为"防止腐败"。[5] 观察制宪者们的设计，可以发现其在某种程度上是把美国作为一个共和国而非民主国家建立的[6]，宪法中并未提到过"民主"（democracy）一词。麦迪逊在《联邦党人文集》中提到，政

---

[1] John E. E. Dalberg-Action, "Letter to Bishop Mandell Creighton", in J. N. Figgis & R. V. Laurence, eds., *Historical Essays and Studies*, London: Macmillan, 1887, April 5, p. 1907.

[2] Marcus T. Cicero, *On the Commonwealth and on the Laws*, Cambridge: Cambridge University Press, 2017, p. 20.

[3] Polybius, *The Histories of Polybius* (Vol. 1 & 2), London: MaCmillan and Co., 1889, p. 461.

[4] David Hume, "Of the Independence of Parliament", in E. F. Miller, ed., *Hume's Essays: Moral, Political and Literary*, Indianapolis: Liberty Classics, 1985, (A) 1741 (8), p. 79.

[5] Robert Yates, "Notes of the Secret Debates of the Federal Convention of 1787", Yale Law School (May 30, 1787), https://avalon.law.yale.edu/18th_century/yates.asp.

[6] Yascha Mounk, "America Is Not a Democracy: How the United States Lost the Faith of its Citizens-and What It Can Do to Win Them Back", The Atlantic (Mar., 2018), https://www.theatlantic.com/magazine/archive/2018/03/america-is-not-a-democracy/550931/.

府通过设置分支机构即国会做出立法和决策，而国会"仅取决于人民"。[1] 而现今在很大程度上影响美国政治走向的，是来自美国民众中1%的最少数人群，后者也是人民的一部分，只是并非从99%的人群中随机选择的，而是拥有最多财富和最大影响力的最少数。讽刺的是，亚历山大·汉密尔顿恰恰希望通过将最富裕的少数者阶级转变为国家利益的调解人来发展经济。[2] 他所提倡的制度要求偏爱这一特定的少数群体，以强化市场中的货币地位、建立金融基础设施，刺激经济发展的多元化并最终为所有人带来财富。尽管曾对少数特别利益群体的影响发出担忧，麦迪逊认为汉密尔顿的计划在原则上或多或少具有合理性，只是市场收益应更广泛地在社会范围内分配，富人的统治不能代替人民主权。因为向社会的某个特定派系提供特殊利益，会腐蚀共和政府内部的权力关系，这些派系很可能不顾公众利益，寻找被个人野心和贪婪支配的立法者作为其代理人，以最大限度地从政府行为中受益。麦迪逊虽然认识到经济利益与政治权力之间存在动态关系，也仍坚信共和国的本质之一在于"选举出的代表应具备为人民的国家辨别真正利益的智慧"[3]。直接选举固然有其缺陷，但这种代议制却可能直接削弱人民可能影响政府决策的程度，促使利益分化，也意味着美国所建立起的民主制度（或许）并非真正的民主：代表们决策与行动的动机可以被依次归类为"野心"（ambition）、"个人利益"（personal interest）与"公共利益"（public good）。[4] 这种冲突印证了美国宪法秩序核心存在的悖论，因为宪法同时提倡自由主义、共和主义和国家主义的概念。[5] 而"我们人民"（We the people）在组成强化国家力量的各种政策联盟的同时，

---

[1] James Madison, "The House of Representatives from the New York Packet", *The Federalist Papers*: No. 52, Feb. 8, 1788, New York: Signet Classics, 2003.

[2] Jay Cost, *The Price of Greatness: Alexander Hamilton, James Madison, and the Creation of American Oligarchy*, New York: Basic Books, 2018, p. 295.

[3] James Madison, "The Union as a Safeguard Against Domestic Faction and Insurrection from the New York Packet", *The Federalist Papers*: No. 10, Nov. 23, 1787, New York: Signet Classics, 2003.

[4] James Madison, "Vices of the Political System of the United States", in R. A. Rutland & W. M. E. Rachal, eds., *The Papers of James Madison*, Vol. 9, 9 April 1786 – 24 May 1787 and supplement 1781 – 1784, Chicago: The University of Chicago Press, 1975, pp. 345 – 358.

[5] Jay Cost, *The Price of Greatness: Alexander Hamilton, James Madison, and the Creation of American Oligarchy*, New York: Basic Books, 2018, p. 311; Morton J. Horwitz, "Republicanism and Liberalism in American Constitutional Thought", *William & Mary Law Review*, No. 29, 1987, pp. 57 – 74.

也可能削弱政府的共和主义特征，直接表现在富裕者不平等地从政治活动中受益上。反过来，这种不平等通过金钱与政治权力互换获得其原本不会拥有的权力，借由立法者在面临利益冲突时做出基于派系利益而非人民利益的决策，使腐败得以合法的形式发生。最终，麦迪逊对党派斗争的担忧成为现实，只要可能，总统做出的决策总是最先服务于其所属政党或其他利益的集合体，其可支配的行政权力越大，越有可能将资源分配至腐败决策下的狭隘利益团体。此时，政府也随之成为一台受动机器，其受制于相互矛盾的利益之间的平衡。[①] 而由于政府平时的行政活动往往因机构雇员众多、组织臃肿，难以受到有效监督，议员往往只在接受利益团体有争议的捐款或好处被披露时，才受到审查。至此，腐败似乎成为美国"不纯粹的"现代民主制度所带来多种副作用的共同结果。共和政府必须时刻克服自身权力发生扭曲，以不至于沦为极少数"精英阶层"追求利益的专属工具。

第一节 研究背景

腐败在一定程度上影响了当今美国政治图景的塑造。诚然，美国法律制度继承了保护私有财产和尊重个人权利的英国法传统，新闻自由亦使得政治腐败丑闻几乎总是能得到及时曝光。但在其大部分历史中，美国比大多数西欧国家更腐败，只是政府的权力分立使其不至于出现拉丁美洲式的总统腐败现象。[②] 因为只要有资源和意愿去影响选举和民选官员，就不必冒着暗中交易的风险而触犯法律，公司和特殊利益集团可以通过游说和竞选捐款等活动不成比例地深入影响公共政策。因而在尚缺乏真正有效的公共选举资金体系的情况下，腐败与民主相互交织于一个简单前提——钱。当今美国政治中，金钱的影响仍旧是最具争议的问题。经济增长扩大了金

[①] [美] C.赖特·米尔斯：《权力精英》，尹弘毅、法磊译，新华出版社2004年版，第206页。
[②] 尽管美国总统拥有对立法的否决权，但与拉丁美洲国家的总统相比对法令的授权能力非常有限，对立法也没有排他性的制定权。总统限制立法行动的独立权力越大，以私人谋利代替公共利益的空间就越大。

钱在美国政治生活中的影响力，[1] 在一定时期内甚至产生了金钱与政治共生的奇特现象：经济实力不断结构化和集中化，[2] 几个行业在过去的一个世纪里迅速积累财富，以资本主义特有矛盾[3]为契机，经济优势转化为损害民主的巨大政治影响力。19世纪末期经济增长催生的一批大型垄断公司和超级富豪，如拥有标准石油公司的洛克菲勒，在当时就能够影响其业务所在州的立法者。这一系列连锁现象导致了政治腐败丑闻在美国历史上定期反复出现，并且触及政府的三个权力分支。自1872年以来，美国每50年就发生一次全国性的重大政治丑闻，[4] 1872—1873年的信贷莫比里尔丑闻[5]、1923—1924年的茶壶山丑闻[6]（Teapot Dome Scandal）和1972—1974年发酵的"水门事件"即是证明。实际上，金钱购买选票一直是一种政治惯例，只是方式时有不同。[7] 在过去三十年的经济全球化进程中，美国创造了一种激励富人、维护稳健的货币政策和多样化经济的机制，每个人都从中或多或少地得利；而随着工业结构性集中的继续，经济实力也越来越倾向于随阶层递增，少数家族拥有大部分的金融财富，其提供的政治资金在联邦和地方竞选活动支出中占据很大一部分，随之而来的是影响更为广泛和更强大的政治权力。现今，在经济全球化中迅速崛起的跨国大公司的常见操作是，

---

[1] 详见第一章第二节与第四章第一节。经济增长并不必然带来金钱在政治领域的影响力扩张。如透明国际组织将瑞士列为世界上最不腐败的国家之一，其拥有较为完善的反腐败法律框架，在许多部门领域都享有高度廉洁机制。但各国由于历史发展与政治制度的特性差异，腐败的程度和滋生领域必然不尽相同。据瑞士联邦审计办公室2018年发布的报告，廉洁如瑞士也有着十分腐败的银行体系，且在打击金融中介机构洗钱、隐匿腐败赃款、私营部门和体育界腐败以及保护举报人等方面都存在着重大缺陷。

[2] Charles H. Ferguson, *Predator Nation: Corporate Criminals, Political Corruption, and the Hijacking of America*, New York: Crown Publishing Group, 2012, p.644.

[3] 详见第四章第一节。

[4] Larry J. Sabato, L. J & Glenn R., Simpson, *Dirty Little Secrets: The Persistence of Corruption in American Politics*, New York: Times Books, 1996, p.16.

[5] 信贷莫比里尔（Crédit Mobilier）成立于19世纪60年代初，旨在建造一条跨洲铁路。该公司在19世纪50年代从法国投资者处诈骗了数百万法郎。副总裁杜兰特（Thomas Durant）与合谋者侵吞了数百万美元，为了防止国会介入调查，杜兰特向某些国会议员赠送了该公司的股票和一些礼品。副总统舒勒·科尔法克斯（Schuyler Colfax）也收到了礼物，这些非法操作持续了许多年。

[6] 茶壶山丑闻是1922—1923年曝光的贿赂案件。时任内政部长收受石油公司贿赂，在未经公开招标的情况下将茶壶山和其他两处油矿低价让予石油公司承租。

[7] Shannon Furtak, "Citizens United and Its Impact on Campaign Financing: A Brief Overview Current Events", *HeinOnline Blog*, Mar. 8, 2018, https://home.heinonline.org/blog/2018/03/citizens-united-and-its-impact-on-campaign-financing-a-brief-overview/.

支付巨额酬劳雇佣游说团体协助起草法案，以追求弱化现有法律对公司的规制或是商业计划的政策阻碍；向"社会福利"组织①汇款，以帮助议员支付竞选广告费用，议员则例行公事地批准这些几乎完全由企业游说团体制定的议案。美国前副总统戈尔将此种现象总结为财富和公司权力对政府行动的制度化支配和控制。② 这一说法或许过于绝对，金权政治并不意味着只要有钱就能够操控政治，但其无疑是政治角力中的重要构成因素。③ 美国的核心问题仍是"数以亿计的美元集中在华盛顿，试图对立法与选举过程产生影响"④。游说和竞选捐款对应的言论自由不仅被视为个人权利，还被特殊利益集团拔高为促进公共利益的手段。在这种情况下，法律法规往往是选票政治交易的结果，⑤ 足以使代议制政府的核心遭到严重破坏。

因而如何遏制金钱在竞选中滥用言论自由及其触发的不良民主趋势，俨然成为竞选财务改革甚至宪法学上一个复杂而困难的任务。需要具体回答的问题包括，如果政治腐败是政府对于联邦公共资源的不当分配，那么游说和竞选捐款活动如何以及在多大程度上对政府决策施加影响？不断修改的相关法律是否能够制止其腐败影响？本书中所列举的相关腐败现象大多未进入司法程序，也从侧面说明美国民主政治必须探索更多的治理维度，能够在为政治竞选筹集资金的同时，又不鼓励政客向游说者和捐款者出售权力。

第二节　文献综述

作为腐败问题的分支，政治腐败及其对政治进程的影响问题几乎与对政

---

① 依据美国税法第501（c）（4）款下的社会福利组织身份注册，不受联邦选举委员会监管，无须披露捐款者身份。详见第三章第二节。
② Al Gore, *The Future: Six Drivers of Global Change*, New York: Random House Publishing Group, 2013, p.320.
③ 这也解释了前纽约市长布隆伯格（Mike Bloomberg）未能凭借亿万富翁的身份获得民主党候选人的提名。1992年参选的亿万富翁罗斯·佩罗（Ross Perot）也未能赢得大选，但其展示了在没有两党强大的政治资源而仅靠雄厚竞选资金支持的情况下，候选人也历史性地走到了作为第三名总统候选人参加电视辩论这一步。
④ Paul Volcker & Christine Harper, *Keeping at it: The Request for Sound Money and Good Government*, New York: Public Affairs, 2018, p.286.
⑤ ［美］苏珊·罗斯-阿克曼、邦妮·J.帕利夫卡：《腐败与政府：根源、后果与改革》，郑澜译，中信出版社2018年版，第359页。

治本身的研究一样古老。如果对政治的研究实际上是对权力的研究，那么与合法政治权威相结合的政治腐败当然地成为其中心主题。相当一部分研究将政治腐败同时视为经济、法律和道德问题，① 这也预示了该主题文献的多学科跨度。鉴于腐败研究主题和文献数量的庞大，本综述将在简要回顾政治腐败相关研究后，重点切入游说、竞选捐款与政治腐败关系的文献梳理。文献范围覆盖了120名学者和研究机构的130余部最具代表性的权威著述。出版时间跨度为1910—2023年，学科以政治学为主，少数经济学和法学等学科的相关文献作为必要补充。文献主要构成为美国国会图书馆馆藏的美国政治研究主题专著、论文集以及互联网线上搜集的美国政治科学期刊论文、政府官方网站报告、智库研究机构报告、联邦法院案例判决、法庭之友（amicus brief）记录和《纽约时报》《华盛顿邮报》等权威报章。文献语言主要为英文，少部分期刊和会议论文为德文，还有数部美国学者经典研究的中文译本和国内美国研究领域权威学者的中文经典著作。但本综述的目的并非进行全面归纳，而是为了确定不同视角考虑游说与竞选捐款腐败的核心问题以及各研究者的独特观点或其常用的论证模式结构。通过上述方式，寻找对上述问题真正有价值的认识，以及该主题在当代研究的潜在缺陷与局限性，力图为更精细的游说和竞选财务②反腐败实践提供参考。

一 政治腐败：系统性腐败路径解构

水门事件后，政治学家对政治腐败产生了新一波的研究兴趣，以加德纳、伦奎斯特、斯科博和伯格等人为代表，涌现了一批对政治腐败的系统批判性研究。③ 他们提供的定义政治腐败的方法是将腐败研究与美国政治

---

① Andrew J. Wilson, *Comparative Political Corruption in the United States: The Florida Perspective*, M. A. Thesis, University of South Florida, 2013.
② 本书统一采用《纽约时报》《经济学人》和维基百科等国际报刊及网站的中文翻译，将"campaign finance"一词译为"竞选财务"而非"竞选资金"。
③ John Gardiner, *The Politics of Corruption: Organized Crime in an American City*, New York: Sage, 1970; Harry Scoble, "Systemic Corruption", A paper presented at the annual meeting of the American Political Science Association, New Orleans, 1973; Barry S. Rundquist, Gerald S. Strom, G. S. & John G. Peters, "Corrupt Politicians and Their Electoral Support: Some Theoretical and Empirical Observations", *American Political Science Review*, No. 71, 1977, pp. 954 – 963; Larry L. Berg, Harlin Hahn & John R. Schmidhauser, *Corruption in the American Political System*, Morristown, NJ: General Learning Press, 1976.

主流研究相结合，把腐败理论置于美国政治信仰和政治行为的背景下进行理解，同时还提供了一种以比较和国际视角研究政治腐败的方法。[1] 但即使如此，直到20世纪90年代后期，政治学和相关学科研究政治腐败的兴趣仍非常有限。[2] 正如该领域最著名的政治学家迈克·约翰斯顿所言："美国政治学作为一种制度化的学科，世代以来始终对腐败不感兴趣"。[3] 1992—2006年，该学科的顶级期刊《美国政治学评论》总共仅刊发了两篇有关政治腐败的文章。[4] 直到近年来认识到政治腐败概念的学术空白，相关问题的讨论才日趋激烈。但政治腐败的识别难度并未随着讨论的加深而降低，事实证明，很难在对政治的"投资"中划定一条清晰准确的分界线，以将合法的政治动员和通过金钱权力对政治施加非法影响区分开来。例如，如果制药公司直接向国会议员付款以换取其投票行为，这显然会被视为政治腐败，但是如果其工会通过向政党捐款来支持候选人，并以工会所期望的立法获得通过作为交换条件，那么情况就不那么清楚了：许多人会争辩说这并非腐败，而是"言论自由"或行使政治参与的权利。

（一）认识政治腐败：法律、公共利益与民意

围绕政治腐败的多角度定义间接显示了这一概念的复杂之处，要回答的问题很多。如政治腐败是否仅限于直接贿赂、竞选资金和不当影响选民？是否需要具有明确的动机、意图和明确的交换条件？实际上，这些问题的主要症结在于不同群体对政治腐败有不同的观察视角。基于公民的不同身份和认知，斯科特将现有对政治腐败的定义标准分为三种：法规规范（legal norms）、公共利益和民意（public opinion）。[5]

第一，法规规范路径所体现的法律主义标准对政治腐败的定义是，政

---

[1] John G. Peters & Susan Welch, "Political Corruption in America: A Search for Definitions and a Theory, or If Political Corruption Is in the Mainstream of American Politics. Why Is It Not in the Mainstream of American Politics Research?" *American Political Science Review*, Vol. 72, No. 3, 1978, pp. 974–984.

[2] 需要说明的是，本节的政治腐败定义综述来源集中于政治腐败主题的政治学文献，其中几乎所有文献都没有在语义上严格区分腐败与政治腐败，而是将腐败置于政治活动的场景中进行剖析，故下述引用的政治学家观点中，腐败与政治腐败几乎是混同使用的，如未做特别说明，二者均指政治腐败。

[3] Michael Johnston, "From Thucydides to Mayor Daley: Bad Politics, and a Culture of Corruption", *Political Science and Politics*, Vol. 39, No. 4, 2006, pp. 809–812.

[4] Bo Rothstein & Aiysha Varraich, *Making Sensing of Corruption*, New York: Cambridge University Press, 2017, p. 8.

[5] James C. Scott, *Comparative Political Corruption*, Englewood Cliffs: Prentice-Hall, 1972, pp. 3–5.

治行为违反了政治制度为其公职人员设定的某种正式标准或行为规则。约瑟夫·奈同意此种观点。① 但这种路径最明显的缺陷是，其本身无法逃避法律总是不够完善、无法穷举的缺陷，不可能涵盖许多会被公众判断为政治腐败的案例。道格拉斯和约翰·约翰斯顿等更多的学者也认可政治腐败的范畴不限于违法。依靠法律来识别政治腐败存在硬伤：纯粹基于法律规范的政治腐败定义范围同时太窄和太宽。② 第二，公共利益路径。在某种程度上，法律与公共利益两种路径的定义是相互补充又部分重叠的，但后者大大拓宽了涉嫌腐败行为的范围。以此为前提，海登海默和麦克·约翰斯顿等人将打击腐败的焦点放大到了任何可能破坏政治体系的行为。但约瑟夫·奈则主张明确排除对公共利益的考虑，因为并非所有的腐败行为都会损害公共利益。③ 第三，民意路径。作为腐败问题最早的研究者之一，森图里亚认为对腐败一词的理解取决于各观察者的意见以及当时主流的政治和公共道德。④ 由于民意对政治腐败的解释十分宽泛，其不确定的本质给定义带来了许多困难。并且，公众观点早已作为要素被嵌入了法律与公共利益的范畴。

最终，对政治腐败的定义问题都可以归结为两种范围之间进行选择：贿赂和直接等价交换（quid pro quo）的狭窄定义，以及上述超越法律规范的宽泛的腐败定义。后者以"违反并破坏了被认为是维持政治民主所不可或缺的公共秩序体系的规范"为政治腐败的标志。研究腐败历史的贝里和泽穹教授等人都同意，接受贿赂当然是政治腐败，以投票或执行某项目为交换的竞选捐款也在此列；⑤ 竞选者在穷人身上花费极少的竞选资金以及任何非法压制选民的行为亦包括在内。⑥

---

① Joseph S. Nye, "Corruption and Political Development: A Cost-Benefit Analysis", *American Political Science Review*, No. 61, 1967, pp. 417 – 427.
② Larry L. Berg, Harlin Hahn & John R. Schmidhauser, *Corruption in the American Political System*, Morristown, NJ: General Learning Press, 1976, p. 6.
③ 至少存在一种行为可能被认为是腐败且为法律所禁止，但有利于公共利益，例如篡改非法外籍公民的证件，这些外籍劳工所提供的低廉劳动力和技能将为经济发展做出贡献。
④ Joseph A. Senturia, "Corruption, Political", *Encyclopedia of the Social Sciences*, No. 4, 1930, pp. 448 –452.
⑤ Paula Baker, Marry Berry & others, "Interchange: Corruption Has a History", *Journal of American History*, Vol. 105, No. 4, 2019, pp. 912 – 938.
⑥ Marry Berry, *Five Dollars and Porkchop Sandwich: Vote Buying and the Corruption of Democracy*, Boston, MA: Beacon Press, 2016, p. 148.

(二) 系统性腐败理论

麦克·约翰斯顿提出了用于定义腐败并理解其原因和后果的分析框架。该框架从三个角度理解腐败，分别是"人格的"（personalistic）、"制度的"（institutional）和"系统的"（systemic）。他认为最能解释政治腐败的是最后一种，因为其能解释腐败长期深植的根源，即政府与社会互动。[①] 系统性腐败与以贿赂和类似的违法行为为代表的个人腐败不同。[②] 第一，系统性腐败利用了合法的制度惯例，竞选捐款就是这种合法制度惯例的产物。第二，系统性腐败是非人格化的，腐败的个体行为者以机构角色行事，并且参与等价交换时并不一定具备腐败动机。[③] 接受竞选捐款并为选民提供帮助的政客在某种程度上出于自己的政治利益行事，但同时也促进了民主进程的竞争和其他价值观。第三是普遍性，不仅在政府中，而且在许多其他类型的组织机构和行业中也发现了腐败。汤普森将传统的腐败概念称为个人腐败，如贿赂行为，而选举、竞选捐款相关的腐败则属于系统性腐败。[④] 后者破坏了民主进程，立法者所获收益是政治利益而非个人收益。总的来说，提出系统性腐败的学者也试图将腐败与民主理论原则联系起来，构建一个扩大法律和道德规范的体系以评价腐败，挑战当今美国联邦最高法院将腐败缩限为等价交换的观点，从而继承早期立国者和法律思想家对腐败的更广泛定义。[⑤] 并且由于"合法与非法影响力之间可能很难找到一条清晰而精确的分界线"[⑥]，系统性腐败理论可以更好地解释非个人的机构腐败难以被识别和承认的原因，以此促使立法机关决定是否公开披露未经国会批准的秘密资金捐款，或决定禁止某些类型的公司捐款。其引发了对政治体系的基本缺陷和弱点的反思，即政治腐败显然是政治过程本

[①] Michael Johnston, *Political Corruption and Public Policy in America*, Monterey, CA: Brooks/Cole Publishing, 1982, p.199.

[②] Susan Rose-Ackerman & Bonnie J. Palifka, *Corruption and Government: Causes, Consequences, and Reform*, Cambridge: Cambridge University Press, 2016, pp.7-11.

[③] Dennis F. Thompson, "Theories of Institutional Corruption", *Annual Review of Political Science*, No. 21, 2018, pp.495-513.

[④] Dennis F. Thompson, "Two Concepts of Corruption", *George Washington Law Review*, No.73, 2005, pp.1036-1069.

[⑤] Zephyr Teachout, *Corruption in America-From Benjamin Franklin's Snuff Box to Citizens United*, Cambridge, MA: Harvard University Press, 2014, pp.32-55, 227-259.

[⑥] Bo Rothstein & Aiysha Varraich, *Making Sensing of Corruption*, New York: Cambridge University Press, 2017, p.15.

身的缺陷，而不是"偶然的恶人"崛起的结果。[1]

二 政治腐败研究中的游说：研究路径与普遍结论

与竞选捐款多维度的丰富研究相比，游说的经典研究多集中在20世纪八九十年代，文献引用交叉重叠程度极高，研究路径高度相似。游说研究最鲜明的特点是循证方法的应用，从政治经济学角度收集数据，通过大量的数学建模来验证对利益集团的行为假设。目前，对游说的权威研究主要来自奥斯坦-史密斯、莱特、格罗斯曼和赫尔普曼等人。[2] 本节回顾了数位权威学者的代表性实证研究，研究者多为经济学或理工科背景，研究思路大致为在权威学者此前的假设上附加变量，然后建模验证。对于游说与政治腐败关系的剖析，主要有游说的本质、游说的政治影响力以及游说与竞选捐款的相互作用与策略选择三个方面。

（一）游说的本质

几乎所有的游说研究都表明，说客的作用之一是说服政府官员或公众相信其所传递信息的正确性。政治学家莱特等人认为，游说本质上是一种信息活动。[3] 普林斯顿大学的格罗斯曼和哈佛大学的赫尔普曼两位经济学家也都同意，游说及其所代表的利益集团在政治参与中的价值就是提供信息。[4] 凭借其信息本质，游说在代议制中发挥着重要的作用。因为在代议制中，公众意见往往不太成熟，政党也存在诸多分歧，立法者无法仅通过这些机制获得充分的信息，自己所掌握的资源和专业知识往往也不能完全处理这些事项，但又必须处理大量复杂和高度技术性的问题。作为决策者的信息来源之一，利益集团通晓许多技术问题，可以向议员们提供各

---

[1] Larry L. Berg, Harlin Hahn & John R. Schmidhauser, *Corruption in the American Political System*, Morristown, NJ: General Learning Press, 1976, p.72.

[2] David Austen-Smith, "Interest Groups: Money, Information, and Influence", in D. C. Mueller, ed., *Perspectives on Public Choice: A Handbook*, New York: Cambridge University Press, 1997, pp.296-321; Gene M. Grossman & Elhanan Helpman, *Special Interest Politics*, Cambridge, MA: MIT Press, 2001.

[3] John R. Wright, "Contributions, Lobbying and Committee Voting in the US House of Representatives", *American Political Science Review*, No.84, 1990, pp.417-438; Lester W. Milbrath, *The Washington Lobbyists*, Chicago: Rand McNally, 1963.

[4] Gene M. Grossman & Elhanan Helpman, *Special Interest Politics*, Cambridge, MA: MIT Press, 2001, chapter 4-5.

种各样的技术信息，包括议员所在选区将受到有关政策影响的评估，以及其他议员支持或反对的可能性等。此外，利益集团及其游说团体通常还十分熟悉现有的法律和项目，能在法案措辞方面提供协助，对法案的起草者尤有价值。

莱特最有说服力地阐述了游说的信息提供本质。其假设国会议员有三个相互依存的目标：连任、良好的公共政策、在国会内部的影响力。首先，立法者想要连任；其次，立法者需要制定对其选民有利的公共政策；最后，立法者希望在立法机构内发挥影响。[1] 莱特指出，除非立法者在其政府部门内拥有一定的权力，否则无法实现自己的政策目标。行使立法权力的最好途径是提出立法并使之通过，或是帮助他人通过立法。议员们必须在充满不确定性的环境中达到目标，此时就需要说客为其提供信息，以减少立法过程中的不确定因素；在此过程中，利益集团通过加强甚至改变立法者的政策，从而对立法过程施加影响。[2]

(二) 游说的政治影响力

上述游说的本质已经涉及其对政治进程产生的影响问题。诺恩斯将游说视为一种非独立的活动，是一系列旨在影响政府行为的离散活动的集合。在过去的几十年中，许多政治学家都致力于以可量化的方式验证利益集团是否对政治决策产生了不当影响。尽管对影响力本身尚无单一完整的明确概念，[3] 但利益集团"并非在真空中运作，而是与政党、公务员和选民等其他政治行为体争夺权力和影响力"[4] 的叙述，提供了一种对游说影响力的形象理解。

皮尔森和塔贝里尼证实了奥尔森等人在传统文献中的一个观点，[5] 即有组织的游说团体通过资助竞选活动，使得候选人将政策纲领向前者所偏

---

[1] John R. Wright, *Interest Groups and Congress: Lobbying, Contributions, and Influence*, Needham Heights, MA: Allyn and Bacon, 1996, p. 82.

[2] John R. Wright, *Interest Groups and Congress: Lobbying, Contributions, and Influence*, Needham Heights, MA: Allyn and Bacon, 1996, p. 75.

[3] Marie Hojnacki & others, "Studying Organizational Advocacy and Influence: Reexamining Interest Group Research", *Annual Review of Political Science*, No. 15, 2012, pp. 379-399.

[4] Adam J. Newmark & Anthony Nownes, "It's All Relative: Perceptions of Interest Group Influence", *Interest Groups & Advocacy*, Vol. 6, No. 1, 2016, pp. 66-90.

[5] Mancur Olson, *The Logic of Collective Action: Public Goods and the Theory of Groups*, Cambridge: Harvard University Press, 1965.

好的方向倾斜。① 他们还发现，在某一政策中拥有最大利益的群体更有可能组织起来，因而富人和底层穷人比中产阶级更有可能形成游说团体，从而对政策施加影响。而富人与穷人谁更容易组织游说，则是显而易见的。公司通常有额外的资金来雇佣合同游说者，竞选捐款又使他们更可能接触到立法者。游说者可以利用其在立法机关的关系来帮助实现公司的目标。② 这是纽马克和诺恩斯的观点，也符合通常的认知。利益集团影响力的权威学者吉伦斯和佩吉也主张，商业利益在华盛顿占主导地位，即使面对其他非商业利益组织的反对，他们也经常赢得立法政策的斗争。③

而经典研究《游说与政策变革》作者得出的结论是，尽管商业利益在数量和资源上具有优势，但它们在政策斗争中并不占主导地位；海因茨关于利益集团和说客影响力的多年综合性研究也得出了类似结论。④ 这也是合理的，因为虽然商业利益在华盛顿的立法斗争中占主导地位，但利益集团太多，现实情况总是较为复杂，因此说客并不会因为资金优势而自动达到目的。

但无论利益集团是否在政治进程影响力中占据主导地位，政治权力对外部影响力输送的接受程度都比想象的要高。利益集团参与政治的普遍性使其能够在政治体系中发挥巨大的杠杆作用。在最大规模的对利益集团影响力的研究之一中，鲍姆加特纳检视了98个存在利益团体活跃的国会政策制定案例，发现政策结果有利于政治行动委员会捐款和游说支出更多的一方。⑤ 现今，顶级承包商仍然是游说和联邦竞选捐款的最大支出者，因为更多的游说意味着更多的政府合同。⑥ 其他学科研究也提供了越来越多

---

① Torsten Persson & Guido Tabellini, *Political Economics: Explaining Economic Policy*, Cambridge, MA: MIT Press, 2000, pp. 61.
② Adam J. Newmark & Anthony Nownes, "It's All Relative: Perceptions of Interest Group Influence", *Interest Groups & Advocacy*, Vol. 6, No. 1, 2016, pp. 66 – 90.
③ Martin Gilens & Benjamin I. Page, "Testing Theories of American Politics: Elites, Interest Groups, and Average Citizens", *Perspectives on Politics*, Vol. 12, No. 3, 2014, pp. 564 – 581.
④ Anthony Nownes & Burdett A. Loomis, "Lobbying and the Balance of Power in American Politics", in A. J. Cigler, B. A. Loomis & A. J. Nownes, eds., *Interest Group Politics* (10th Ed.), Lanham, MA: Rowman & Littlefield, 2019, p. 284; John P. Heinz & others, *The Hollow Core: Private Interests in National Policy Making*, Cambridge, MA: Harvard University Press, 1993.
⑤ Frank R. Baumgartner, Jeffrey M. Berry & others, *Lobbying and Policy Change: Who Wins, Who Loses, and Why*, Chicago: University of Chicago Press, 2009, pp. 233, 235. 当然，也有许多研究持相反观点；一些研究则未发现利益集团游说影响立法投票的直接证据。
⑥ Andrew J. Taylor, "The Revolution in Federal Procurement, 1980-Present", *Business and Politics*, Vol. 21, No. 1, 2019, pp. 27 – 52.

的证据，肯定了游说背后带来的巨大商业价值。如财政部于2008年底推出的旨在减轻当年金融危机对公司造成损害的"问题资产救助计划"（TARP）项目。项目支出的数据表明，进行游说的公司获得项目资金支持的概率比没有游说的公司高42%，且在获得支持的公司中，进行游说的公司所获支持资金总额比没有游说的公司多2.02亿至51.4亿美元。[1] 不仅如此，游说活动和捐款可以显著减轻政府机构的监管。对证券交易委员会（SEC）的一项审计研究发现，更多的商业游说和竞选捐款会减少证交会的执法行动。[2] 政治上大量支出的公司在执法行动中受到的处罚比政治上不活跃的公司要轻。游说和捐款影响证交会执法行动的确切机制尚不清楚，但研究指出，在雇用此前与证交会有工作联系的游说者后，企业会更善于避免处罚。另一项管理学研究也发现，与不游说的银行相比，从事游说活动的银行"将被面临严厉执法行动的可能性降低了44.7%"[3]。

面对游说所产生的政治与决策影响，诺恩斯仍认定政府官员和选民才是推动政府和政治变化的动力，只是因为公众时常忽视政府的行为，游说者才得以对政府决策施加实质性的影响，而对于这种现象，公众只能责怪自己和所选举的政客。[4] 游说的作用范围比通常所认知的要广泛，往往为公众所忽略：竞选捐款就是在竞选活动中的"游说"；被游说的对象也不仅仅是立法者，还有政府官员，乃至在最高法院的提名中，游说竞争也十分激烈。[5] 他的研究还强调大多数说客都是诚信的，只有很少数会使用贿赂或敲诈勒索等非法手段，现有研究只是尚未确定说客游说成败的决定因素。

（三）游说与竞选捐款的相互作用和策略选择

利益集团是游说与竞选捐款的连接点，其对于竞选捐款以及游说信息

---

[1] Benjamin Blau, Tyler J. Brough & Diana Thomas, "Corporate Lobbying, Political Connections, and the Bailout of Banks", *Journal of Banking and Finance*, Vol. 37, No. 8, 2013, pp. 3007-3017.

[2] Maria M. Correia, "Political Connections and SEC Enforcement", *Journal of Accounting and Economics*, Vol. 57, No. 2, 2014, pp. 241-262.

[3] Thomas Lambert, "Lobbying on Regulatory Enforcement Actions: Evidence from U.S. Commercial and Savings Banks", *Research Briefs in Economic Policy* (Jul. 13, 2018), https://www.cato.org/research-briefs-economic-policy/lobbying-regulatory-enforcement-actions-evidence-us-commercial?queryID=3d1e4dca7fddb5cd4c434a0b3e55636e.

[4] Anthony Nownes, *Total Lobbying: What Lobbyists Want (and How They Try to Get it)*, New York: Cambridge University Press, 2006, pp. 217, 218.

[5] Anthony Nownes, *Total Lobbying: What Lobbyists Want (and How They Try to Get it)*, New York: Cambridge University Press, 2006, p. 22.

的战略性使用影响决策一直是学术界兴趣和研究的主题所在。[①] 从利益集团形成的问题开始,近40年来的文献都着眼于游说如何在利益竞争的环境下影响政策选择。[②] 为了影响政治决策,利益集团面临着向决策者提供信息、通过捐款进行游说,或二者兼而有之的选择。麻省理工学院的斯奈德教授在研究了说客对持不同立场的立法者进行的捐款后,得出的结论是:利益集团要么花钱影响选票,要么花钱左右决策。[③] 本内德森和费德曼在比较利益集团作出游说与竞选捐款的动机后,发现了游说团体之间的竞争对选择的影响机制,并证实了利益集团可以通过竞选捐款形式的经济激励来影响决策者的选择。[④] 他们的研究表明,在不允许竞选捐款时,竞争会激励游说团体的信息搜集活动。

游说与竞选捐款相互作用与利益集团对二者使用的选择机制关系紧密。奥斯坦-史密斯关于游说和选举之间相互作用的一系列研究是具有较大影响力的早期文献之一。以此为基础,随后有巴伦、格罗斯曼和赫尔普曼、本内德森以及利兹曼等人建立了游说和选举之间的互动模型。[⑤] 哈斯塔德和斯文森将游说通常采用的方式归纳为两种,即战略性的信息提供和竞选捐款。二者既可以影响决策者的立法行为,又可以为其提供竞选帮助,使其赢得选举。[⑥] 在对特殊利益影响力的研究中,格罗斯曼和赫尔普曼直接将游说视为说客到政客的资金转移,并认为这种模式与竞选捐款和

[①] Kay L. Schlozman & John T. Tierney, *Organized Interests and American Democracy*, New York: Harper & Row, 1986; Torsten Persson & Guido Tabellini, *Political Economics: Explaining Economic Policy*, Cambridge, MA: MIT Press, 2000, pp. 58 – 64.

[②] Mancur Olson, *The Logic of Collective Action: Public Goods and the Theory of Groups*, Cambridge: Harvard University Press, 1965.

[③] James M. Snyder, "On Buying Legislatures", *Economics and Politics*, No. 3, 1991, pp. 93 – 109.

[④] Morten Bennedsen & Sven Feldmann, "Informational Lobbying and Political Contributions", *Journal of Public Economics*, Vol. 90, No. 4 – 5, 2006, pp. 631 – 656.

[⑤] David, P. Baron, "Electoral Competition with Informed and Uninformed Voters", *American Political Science Review*, No. 88, 1994, pp. 33 – 47; Gene M. Grossman & Elhanan Helpman, "Electoral Competition and Special Interest Politics", *Review of Economic Studies*, No. 63, 1996, pp. 265 – 286; Morton Bennedsen, "Vote Buying Through Resource Allocation in Government Controlled Enterprises", *Rivista di Politica Economica*, SIPI Spa, Vol. 93, No. 1, 1998, pp. 49 – 78; Raymond Riezman & John D. Wilson, "Political Reform and Trade Policy", *Journal of International Economics*, No. 42, 1997, pp. 67 – 90.

[⑥] Bard Harstad & Jakob Svensson, "Bribes, Lobbying, and Development", *American Political Science Review*, Vol. 105, No. 1, 2011, pp. 46 – 63.

绪　论

贿赂的资金转移并无不同。① 哈斯塔德教授甚至认为游说是腐败的替代路径，如果贿赂的成本对利益集团来说过于高昂，开展游说以放松对相关利益行业的管制更合理。② 企业的发展水平较低时，会偏向于贿赂，而在更富裕时则会展开游说。但这种腐败到游说的推演还不能完全确定。格罗斯曼和赫尔普曼更直言，游说者代表的特殊利益集团，在立法过程中的几乎每个阶段都有广泛参与，③ 因而"捐款和立法者行动之间的联系不需要明确"。④ 尽管大多数立法者不认可用自己的立法支持来换取竞选捐款，但通过与说客的反复互动，立法者很可能会认识到二者之间存在这样的联系。格罗斯曼和赫尔普曼还确认了在许多情况下，尽管议员们不会承认捐款是其与说客会面的严格先决条件，但各利益集团仍将其捐款视为增加获得会面进而游说可能性的一种手段，只是他们宣称竞选捐款是为了购买访问权而非影响力，对立法者来说，捐款可能决定了其与游说者会见的时长分配。⑤ 格罗斯曼和赫尔普曼在对利益集团一系列的游说、竞选捐款与竞选者行为模式的关联建模后，总结到：更有可能获胜的政党会吸引倾向于帮助其获胜的捐款，同时利益集团也会诱使选举中占优势的候选人更多地迎合特殊利益集团的导向。⑥

　　游说与竞选捐款的策略选择也与游说的信息本质相关。奥斯坦-史密斯和莱特教授在研究游说与腐败的关系时指出，游说并不总是采取贿赂或者竞选捐款的形式。因为在许多情况下，说客拥有立法者所没有的专业知识，其可以通过战略性地分享这类知识来影响立法决策。⑦ 但考虑到说客的利益不一定与立法者利益一致，他们认为讨论说客在多大程度上能够说

---

① Gene M. Grossman & Elhanan Helpman, *Special Interest Politics*, Cambridge, MA：MIT Press, 2001, chapter 5.
② Bard Harstad & Jakob Svensson, "Bribes, Lobbying, and Development", *American Political Science Review*, Vol. 105, No. 1, 2011, pp. 46 – 63.
③ Jeffery Birnbaum, *The Lobbyists：How Influence Peddlers Get Their Way in Washington*, New York: Times Books, 1992.
④ Gene M. Grossman & Elhanan Helpman, *Special Interest Politics*, Cambridge, MA：MIT Press, 2001, p. 13.
⑤ Gene M. Grossman & Elhanan Helpman, *Special Interest Politics*, Cambridge, MA：MIT Press, 2001, p. 188.
⑥ Gene M. Grossman & Elhanan Helpman, *Special Interest Politics*, Cambridge, MA：MIT Press, 2001, pp. 361, 362.
⑦ David Austen-Smith & John R. Wright, "Counteractive lobbying", *American Journal of Political Science*, Vol. 38, No. 1, 1994, pp. 25 – 44.

服议员以利益集团的利益导向行事是没有意义的,因为利益集团施加政治影响力的方式并非只是单纯的支付金钱,还有提供立法者所需要的信息。[1] 这种信息不仅体现在日常的游说活动中,还发生在选举过程中向候选人提供选民所关注问题的信息,以帮助其选举。在选举阶段进行竞选捐款支持,和立法决策阶段开展游说之间,掌握关键信息的利益集团会倾向于后者,以有策略地操作对其有利的政策。[2] 与此同时,对于选民不了解的问题,利益集团可以通过竞选捐款发挥更大影响。[3] 此时,利益集团会使用游说和竞选捐款对竞选者和选民产生相互呼应的引导。奥斯坦-史密斯和莱特也肯定游说活动的确会影响立法者对法案的投票结果,只是这种影响不需要通过捐款奖励或威胁政客达成。[4] 鲍尔等人认为,说客影响政客的方式是"走捷径",即只在政客中寻找天然盟友进行游说。[5] 这与奥斯坦-史密斯和莱特的观点相反,他们认为进行游说恰恰是因为不同意立法者的投票倾向。

上述提及的利益集团之间的竞争也会影响对游说与竞选捐款的选择。如果在一个议题上同时存在很多不同的利益集团,那么每个集团对政策结果的利害关系就会相对变小,从而有更小的动机去给予政党利益。当对两党都进行捐款时,利益集团的动机是讨好更有可能获胜的政党。[6] 娄曼分析了多种利益集团,发现观点与决策者相似者可以零成本获得访问决策者的机会,传达需要传达的信息,此时就可以选择只游说,不捐款或少捐

---

[1] Richard A. Smith, "Advocacy, Interpretation and Influence in the US Congress", *American Political Science Review*, No. 78, 1984, pp. 44 – 63; John R. Wright, "Contributions, Lobbying and Committee Voting in the US House of Representatives", *American Political Science Review*, No. 84, 1990, pp. 417 – 438; John M. Hansen, *Gaining Access: Congress and the Farm Lobby, 1919 – 1981*, Chicago: University of Chicago Press, 1991.

[2] David Austen-Smith, "Interest groups: Money, Information, and Influence", in D. C. Mueller, ed., *Perspectives on Public Choice: A Handbook*, New York: Cambridge University Press, 1997, p. 321.

[3] David Austen-Smith, "Interest groups: Money, Information, and Influence", in D. C. Mueller, ed., *Perspectives on Public Choice: A Handbook*, New York: Cambridge University Press, 1997, p. 310.

[4] David Austen-Smith & John R. Wright, "Competitive Lobbying for a Legislator's Vote", *Social Choice and Welfare*, Vol. 9, No. 3, 1992, pp. 229 – 257.

[5] Raymond A. Bauer, Ithiel de Sola Pool & Lewis A. Dexter, *American business and public policy*, New York: Atherton Press, 1963.

[6] Gene M. Grossman & Elhanan Helpman, *Special Interest Politics*, Cambridge, MA: MIT Press, 2001, p. 344.

款;而观点较极端、与决策者观点相差较大的利益集团则会积极地竞选捐款,以获得与决策者接触的机会。①

三 竞选捐款与政治腐败:代表观点与核心争议

美国竞选捐款研究探讨的时间跨度和问题维度远远超过游说,不仅有上述与游说作用关系的实证研究,还有在竞选财务领域腐败定义的核心争论,更有依附于竞选财务法律的理论连贯性探索,乃至金钱被视为言论的宪法问题。具体涉及现有竞选财务理论框架与法律实践的一致性匮乏,反腐败法益与言论自由权的边界等许多棘手问题,且这些问题的研究难度随着最高法院在竞选财务判例中所持观点的持续变化而不断增大。总的来说,竞选捐款的文献数量要比游说多得多,② 更新也更快,探讨争议更多并且涉及领域更广泛。因而在本综述甚至研究的整体上,竞选捐款的篇幅都较游说的稍长。

美国宪法赋予了公民参与政治的权利,但行使这种权利恰恰要花费大量金钱。对于利益集团来说,这种花费主要体现在政治竞选捐款与游说两个方面。前者是指"(合法和非法)地为以政治候选人、政党以及第三方的选举活动提供资金",③ 毫无疑问,利益集团在竞选融资中发挥的作用巨大,且这种作用日益增长。后者尽管不仅仅存在于竞选活动中,但往往利用大量竞选捐款的杠杆作用影响政府决策:作出符合游说者所代表利益集团决策的立法者,反过来也会从游说者处得到更多的捐款支持。早在1910年,布鲁克斯在《美国政治与生活中的腐败》一书中就将财富集中与政治的高昂花费相联结,指出竞选捐款是腐败的根源。④ 100年后,联邦最高

---

① Susanne Lohmann, "Information, Access, and Contributions: A Signaling Model of Lobbying", *Public Choice*, Vol. 85, No. 3 - 4, 1995, pp. 267 - 284.
② Dennis C. Mueller, *Public Choice II: A Revised Edition of Public Choice*, Cambridge, MA: Cambridge University Press, 1989, chapter 11; Stephen G. Bronars & John R. Lott, Jr., "Do Campaign Donations Alter How a Politician Votes? Or, Do Donors Support Candidates Who Value the Same Things That They Do?" *Journal of Law and Economics*, Vol. 40, No. 2, 1997, pp. 317 - 350.
③ Elin Falguera, Samuel Jones & Magnus Ohman, eds., *Funding of Political Parties and Election Campaigns. A Handbook on Political Finance*, Stockholm: International Institute for Democracy and Electoral Assistance, 2014.
④ Robert C. Brooks, *Corruption in America Politics and Life*, New York: Dodd, Mead & Co., 1910, p. 309.

法院在"联合公民案"判决中部分推翻了过去一个世纪的竞选财务立法成果,肯定了大公司向竞选倾注巨额捐款、疑似购买政治影响力的行为,并导致美国政治竞选进入了史无前例的金钱权力对决。而游说、竞选捐款与政治腐败关系的相关研究也因此进入了更为激烈的辩论,从反腐败是否属于足够重要的国家利益,公司是否具有言论自由的人格权,甚至什么是腐败这类根本问题,几乎都没有共识。

(一)代表观点

耶鲁大学的苏珊·罗斯-艾克曼是美国腐败研究学者中的翘楚。在其关于美国政治腐败的数本专著中,影响力最大的是1999年出版的《腐败与政府——根源、后果与改革》,首次从经济学视角阐释腐败的经济机理,解读政府与政治腐败的动机、成本、运作方式和所引发的社会经济后果。其对竞选捐款与政治腐败的联系态度时有转变,早期认为竞选捐款是一种合法腐败,后期则在其他论著中持相反结论,观点不甚统一。在最新的研究中,她将"非法腐败"(illegal corruption)分为三类,即大腐败、小腐败和选举欺诈,认为这些类别为公共权力和私人财富之间的接口设立了广泛接受的边界。[1] 其中选举欺诈包括购买选票和操纵选举的行为,其与政治腐败有重叠的地方,但后者的范围更广,是一个特别模棱两可的类别。政治腐败既可以指代明确的条件交换,也可以指代私人财富影响选举和政策选择的更广泛途径,如竞选捐款、游说、偏袒和利益冲突在某些情况下都包括在其中。[2] 她认为政客们完全可能出于获取更多资金的动机,围绕捐款者的利益来制定政策立场,从而形成捐款者利益与竞选资金的反馈回路。不能否认,向具有相似政策立场的人单纯捐款的行为并没有构成腐败,只是在实践中,很难区分哪些政客是为了支持捐款者而改变立场,哪些只是与捐款者的立场恰好相似。但她肯定的是,即使捐款只能购买到与政客的接触机会,其也会影响立法结果。

提绍特从美国的腐败历史出发,延伸至对竞选腐败的现代形式——竞选捐款以及不受约束的外围支出的解读。与罗斯-艾克曼同样具有法学学科背景的提绍特不同意前者的部分观点,认为对腐败的经济学视角阐释并不能厘清竞选捐款的合法性。她从法律的角度分析最高法院对腐败的核心定义即条件交换,试图分析近100年来条件交换概念在最高法院的使用频

---

[1] Susan Rose-Ackerman, "Corruption & Purity", *Daedalus*, Vol. 147, No. 3, 2018, pp. 98 - 110.
[2] Susan Rose-Ackerman, "Corruption & Purity", *Daedalus*, Vol. 147, No. 3, 2018, pp. 98 - 110.

率，强调其在不同时空背景下所联系的语境导致自身含义发生的变化，并对现代竞选财务规制与腐败的界分提出质疑。尽管承认第一修正案是近年来许多不良法律的根源，但提绍特不同意宪法制定者默认腐败问题的存在，而是认为宪法本身包含了打击腐败的结构性承诺。[1] 如果将腐败的范围限制于条件交换的表面定义，即双方间关于直接说明条件交换的话语，将造成对多数涉嫌收受贿赂行为的取证困难并加剧证明难度，从而使得竞选中出现的多数腐败行为仅停留在受新闻媒体的道德质疑，但却缺乏法律上的制裁措施。

"依赖腐败"理论的提出者莱西格将美国竞选财务系统作为系统性腐败的标准模板。他指出政府依赖竞选捐款，迫使政客为其竞选筹集资金，从而形成依赖关系，因而"允许为竞选活动提供资金的方式本身就破坏了平等"。[2] 如果政客接受竞选捐款，就必然参与腐败的制度。捐款者所制造的政治人物会逐渐使得自我审查的行为变得普遍，因而国会中存在的腐败不是犯罪行为。[3] 实践中，甚至很少有人将接受合法竞选捐款的行为称为"丑闻"，即使他们也认为这种制度是腐败的。[4] 竞选活动更巧妙地创造了一种"影响力经济"，政客们越来越依赖竞选资金来进行越来越昂贵的选举。与个人腐败不同，莱西格认为这种制度腐败不必涉及非法或当前不道德的行为。他提出，包括政治竞选者在内的"好人"可以创造并维持一种系统性腐败的影响力体系。政治腐败的系统性有助于解释为什么公民总是倾向于谴责国会腐败而不是谴责代表自己选区的议员。[5] 在政治依赖的情景中，当官员不得不依赖其唯一应忠诚的人民之外的他人时，就发生了政治腐败。国会本应该只依靠人民，但当议员们依赖为竞选活动做出捐款的一小部分支持者时，这种宪政关系就会遭到破坏。因而政治竞选活动中的

---

[1] Zephyr Teachout, "Gifts, Offices, and Corruption", *Northwest University Law Review Colloquy*, Vol. 107, No. 30, 2012, p.36.

[2] Peter Overby, "Beyond Quid Pro Quo: What Counts As Political Corruption?" NPR（May 4, 2015）, https://www.npr.org/sections/itsallpolitics/2015/05/04/404052618/beyond-quid-pro-quo-what-counts-as-political-corruption.

[3] Lawrence Lessig, *Lesterland: The Corruption of Congress and How to End It*, New York: Ted Conference, 2013, p.63.

[4] Nick Baumann, "Cure for Campaign Finance Ruling?" Mother Jones（Feb.11, 2020）, https://www.motherjones.com/politics/2010/02/dems-reveal-response-citizens-united-decision/.

[5] Lawrence Lessig, *Republic, Lost: How Money Corrupts Congress-and a Plan to Stop It*, New York: Hatchette, 2011, p.17, 235.

腐败可以归因于金钱的影响，这些钱被用于支付游说和不断增加的竞选活动费用，并流入政府倾向补贴的受益人手中。① 莱西格认为这种依赖也可能违反沃伦提出的包容性理想及其涉及的平等原则，但也为制宪者所预见。在针对美国竞选系统缺陷的理论中，依赖腐败理论是相对简单的，因为不同于其结果，依存关系的存在是很容易确定的，因而相应的改革措施也可以有较为明确的方向。尤其是这种依赖关系以竞选捐款的形式体现时，莱西格相信相应的竞选财务改革措施可以根除有问题的捐款，或者至少增加其来源的广泛性。② 但同样因为简单化，该理论无法处理竞选财务实践中许多被推定为腐败的操作。比如，一些政客可能并不依赖为其支付旅行费用或与之频繁来往的游说者为其竞选活动带来捐款，但是这些游说者在实质上比其他公民拥有更多对立法者施加影响力的机会，此时立法者与游说者的接触应在多大程度上受到监督？行政部门的利益冲突规则与立法部门的利益冲突应该有哪些区别？立法者如何依据依赖腐败理论区分其服务对象或群体？依赖腐败概念也许并不能充分解决系统性腐败活动在竞选财务领域的相关问题。

和莱西格类似，方德伯克也对分析那些已经合法化和制度化，但可能被视为政治腐败的行为有着浓厚的兴趣，尤其是大额的竞选捐款，以及通过立法将资金用于特定狭窄领域的项目。他认为当立法者开始为特殊利益引入专用资金时，资金往往会以上述方式流动："找到众议员和参议员腐败的例子并不难，他们总是以专门用于特殊需要的立法作为幌子。"③

汤普森强调竞选捐款与贿赂的性质是不同的，因为竞选捐款是政治进程的必要组成部分。不仅如此，他认为在一定范围内追求竞选捐款等政治利益的行为值得鼓励。但当竞选捐款影响民选代表改变立场时，竞选捐款就破坏了协商民主（deliberative democracy）。④ 汤普森将金钱影响作为腐败

---

① Larry L. Berg, Harlin Hahn & John R. Schmidhauser, *Corruption in the American Political System*, Morristown, NJ: General Learning Press, 1976, p.62.
② Lawrence Lessig, *Republic, Lost: How Money Corrupts Congress-and a Plan to Stop It*, New York: Hatchette, 2011, pp.273-307.
③ Jim Hannah, "Political Science Experts Team Up for Book on Corruption", Wright State University News Room (Feb. 28, 2013), https://webapp2.wright.edu/web1/newsroom/2013/02/28/political-science-experts-team-up-for-book-on-corruption/.
④ Dennis F. Thompson, *Ethics in Congress: From Individual to Institutional Corruption*, Washington, DC: Brookings Institution, 1995, p.117.

的衡量标准，承认试图影响选举的竞选捐款对民主进程至关重要，但那些试图影响议员决策的竞选捐款却是对民主进程的破坏。

斯坦福大学的坎恩（Bruce Cain）教授认为政治腐败是一个有限的概念，无法完全涵盖人们对竞选财务系统的担忧。由于竞选财务法律总体上对腐败巨大的规制压力，因此总是存在一种将腐败的概念更广泛地涵盖其他与之部分相关的倾向。① 正如在审理1990年奥斯汀诉密歇根商务委员会案②时，联邦最高法院援引了一种非常宽泛的理论解释腐败。该案判决指出，当竞选捐款不能反映民意时，政治制度将被破坏，即为腐败。但如果腐败仅仅是所谓"不平等"的代名词，它的许多意义就被浪费掉了。腐败的概念在竞选财务法律中占据重要地位，如果法院选择承认竞选监管中的其他利益，则更不应否定或损害反腐败这一利益。坎恩认为汤普森将金钱作为政治腐败衡量的标准未能解决竞选财务中的许多问题，特别是竞选捐款不均在选举系统中造成的不平等，而且美国竞选财务系统在许多方面都有缺陷，难以认定一个统一的腐败标准，因此在竞选财务方面讨论腐败的概念可能是根本没有意义的。

伯克则肯定政治腐败的概念至少可以应用于竞选财务中的主要问题之一，即捐款者对民选代表行为的影响。③ 对于最高法院在一些案件中援引了腐败对金钱的影响标准，但司法机关在处理腐败问题上却步履蹒跚的现象，他总结了这种矛盾性：在某些情况下，法院将腐败定性为投票权交换和条件交换，并乐观地认为"包括公司支出在内的独立支出不会增加腐败或引起腐败现象的出现"④；而在其他时候，法院则又扩大腐败的定义和利益，表示"没有理由怀疑巨额捐款将使我们的政治体系遭受实际上的腐败"⑤。

康教授预测了"联合公民案"引发的法律改革趋势，认定该案对政治腐败的教义性缩限解释导致了对独立支出整体上的完全放松管制。"联合公民案"本身仅放开了对公司的独立支出管制，但该判决的逻辑也迅速扩

---

① Thomas F. Burke, "The Concept of Corruption in Campaign Finance Law", *Constitutional Commentary*, No.1089, 1997, pp.127–149.

② Austin v. Michigan Chamber of Commerce, 494 US 652, 660 (1990).

③ Thomas F. Burke, "The Concept of Corruption in Campaign Finance Law", *Constitutional Commentary*, No.1089, 1997, pp.127–149.

④ Citizens United, 130 S. Ct. at 909.

⑤ Nixon v. Shrink Missouri Government PAC, 528 U.S.395 (2000).

展到了对非公司主体的独立支出以及对仅独立支出的非公司实体的捐款。[①]联邦最高法院在本案中对腐败的定义,在实质上推翻了现代联邦竞选财务法自过去数十年以来对独立支出的监管,"联合公民案"的关键是,法院缩小了政府在预防腐败方面的利益。自巴克利诉瓦莱奥案[②]以来,这种对预防非法交换腐败的利益一直是抗辩宪法第一修正案,从而对竞选资金进行监管的价值基础。尽管承认政府在预防腐败方面具有足够重要的利益,但法院一贯以公允的观点拒绝将此种政府利益作为政府监管的依据。康还预计,联邦选举委员会和各级法院将依据"联合公民案"对腐败的定义,审查其他业已长期存在的竞选财务法规,从而使得对竞选资金的管制进一步放松。基于法院认定"独立支出是面向选民展示的、不与候选人协调的政治言论"[③],在缺乏这种协调或实际交流的情况下,即使法院也承认"独立支出在实际上是助长腐败的"[④],国会也不能禁止独立支出,因为其与"在防止条件交换腐败方面的利益是不相称的"[⑤]。

(二) 腐败的等价交换之争:围绕"联合公民案"的评价分歧

2010年的"联合公民案"极大地改变了美国竞选财务规制生态,有关竞选捐款的问题分歧再一次爆发。简言之,"联合公民案"判决认定公司不受限制的支出不构成腐败,并在实质上将腐败限定于交易者说出"等价交换"的话语,否则竞选捐款就不是违反竞选规则的腐败行为。由此引发的直接问题是:大量的竞选捐款的正当性何在?其是否会对候选人的独立性产生腐败影响?

1. 否定金钱在政治中的腐败作用:金钱即言论

许多学者倾向于将腐败有限地解释为包括贪污贿赂的不道德利益交换在内的条件交换,而非一种持续关系和间接压力的产物,这种结论完全否定了金钱在选举中可能产生的腐败影响。

持赞同意见的是美国首都大学法学院教授布拉德利·史密斯。作为前联邦选举委员会主席,史密斯的研究显然具有更深厚的实践经验基础,对选举中参与各方的动机与心态有着更透彻的洞悉,因而需要对其观点作出更详细的介绍。其在代表性著作和论文中,多将少数人操控竞选活动的观

---

① Michael S. Kang, "The End of Campaign Finance Law", *Virginia Law Review*, Vol. 98, No. 1, 2012, pp. 1 – 65.
② Buckley v. Valeo, 424 U. S. 1 (1976).
③ Citizens United, 130 S. Ct. at 910.
④ Citizens United, 130 S. Ct. at 911.
⑤ Citizens United, 130 S. Ct. at 911.

点作为阴谋论，以竞选中的金钱为中心，发散讨论金钱、言论自由和腐败的边界与关系。① 首先，史密斯不同意巴克利案中法院肯定政府反腐败利益的观点，认为国家没有必要防范以大笔捐款交换特定立法行为的腐败，并进一步推论，国家不具有通过规制游说与竞选支出来保护言论自由、预防政治腐败的利益出发点。而该利益出发点正是捐款和竞选支出限额法律的正当化依据。史密斯指出，尽管所谓的腐败得到了"零碎得只能作为轶事的证据和有限程度的常识支持"，② 但其尚未经过投票记录系统相关研究的证实。不仅如此，其还列举了20世纪80年代末至90年代中期的8项此类研究的结果，③ 这些研究均发现竞选捐款与立法投票记录之间几乎没有任何关联，并认为立法投票的主导力量是个人意识形态、所属政党和议程以及各自所在选区选民所持的观点。对于游说活动的性质，布拉德利认为其就像个人聘请律师或公司聘请发言人一样，个人当然有权通过与志趣相投的个人合并资源聘请顶尖的广告人才或更善于表达、更具感染力的信使，从而提高其所需要的政治通讯的效率。在2010年"联合公民案"后，史密斯在参议院委员会作证时为"联合公民案"的判决背书，认为如果国会和州立法机关使用反腐败利益抗辩宪法《第一修正案》，将能够阻止出版商出版或公司资助的书商出版包含任何主张或反对选举政治候选人的话的书籍；有权禁止在亚马逊的 Kindle 电子阅读器上销售政治类书籍；政府还可以阻止联合公民这样的非营利组织或其他的营利性公司制作如《华氏9/11》这样的纪录片。显然，这种政府立场是荒谬的。对于报刊与民调结果显示出对"联合公民案"的反对声音，史密斯认为受访者是受到了语言误导而带有偏见，即便如此，也未出现任何民众上街游行反对本案判决的

---

① Bradly A. Smith, "Before the United States Senate Committee on the Judiciary: We the People? Corporate Spending in American Elections after Citizens United", Testimony of Bradley A. Smith, Mar. 10, 2010, p. 13; Bradly A. Smith, "The Myth of Campaign Finance Reform", *National Affairs*, No. 6, Winter 2010; Bradly A. Smith, "President Wrong on Citizens United Case", National Review (Jan. 28, 2010), https://www.nationalreview.com/corner/president-wrong-citizens-united-case-bradley-smith/.

② Bradly A. Smith, *Unfree Speech: The Folly of Campaign Finance Reform*, Princeton, NJ: Princeton University Press, 2001, pp. 126 – 127; Sanford Levinson, "Electoral Regulation: Some Comments", *Hofstra Law Review*, No. 18, 1989, pp. 411 – 412. 研究的现象如1/4的民主党人在1989年10月的投票中赞成"丑闻性"的资本收益减税。

③ Bradly A. Smith, *Unfree Speech: The Folly of Campaign Finance Reform*, Princeton, NJ: Princeton University Press, 2001, pp. 243 – 244.

现象。在公司支出引发的腐败争议问题上，史密斯也同样对公司支出构成腐败的观点提出质疑。他指出，一些研究表明各州独立支出委员会的前十名出资者其实很少涉及公司资金。同样，他也质疑对软钱规制的必要性。在参议院委员会作证时其表示，在软钱的顶峰时期即20世纪90年代，民众对政府的信心反而要比《两党竞选改革法》通过以来的任何时期都要高。史密斯还认为，对公司支出作出规定的立法初衷，其实是为了防止外国公司参与竞选支出，而这点却被忽略了。此外，公司具有作为"人"的宪法权利，其与自然人权利的区别仅仅是后者仅在个人的基础上行使，而前者通过团体联合行使。全美的超级政治行动委员会（super PAC）仅有2000家，对比起成千上万的公司数量，公司的言论权利显然不仅没有被放大，反而还受到了限制。他批评道，即使金钱确实引起人们对平等和腐败的关注，但是改革方法却往往更糟。且有大量证据表明，高额政治支出可以帮助选民确定候选人，因此不应对其加以更严格的限制。[1]

对于近年来的竞选财务改革，史密斯总结了对私人捐款与开支限制问题的错误认识：一是政治竞选花费了太多钱；二是大笔捐款资助的竞选无法代表公众意见，无法解决选民关注的问题；三是候选人的花费很大程度上决定了选举结果，金钱腐蚀了选举。[2] 对于上述观点，史密斯一一驳斥。第一，竞选活动并不算特别昂贵，每两年国会在竞选活动上的总支出大约仅相当于每个选民租用一部家庭录像带的成本。第二，更高的支出能更好地帮助选民了解选情和议题，其实公众作为纳税人，也并不愿意通过小额捐款活动再为竞选活动提供资金。并且，小额捐款往往对新兴从政者不利，因为小额捐款的选民往往只对其熟悉的名字更敏感。竞选财务法律对竞选人的支出和捐款限制也对挑战者更不利，因为其需要更多的支出来弥补知名度与人脉等的不足，即使有公共筹资的政府补贴也最终是由纳税人掏腰包，为何不让财大气粗的大公司来承担支出。出于上述原因，寻求连任者在现行的竞选财务系统中受益更大，捐款与支出限制反而在实质上减少了选举竞争并巩固了现状，且更有利于富人当选。[3] 第三，竞选支出不

---

[1] Zócalo Public Square, "Do We Really Need Campaign Finance Reform?" Time (Jan. 19, 2016), https://time.com/4182502/campaign-finance-reform/.

[2] Bradly A. Smith, *Unfree Speech: The Folly of Campaign Finance Reform*, Princeton, NJ: Princeton University Press, 2001, pp.39–64.

[3] Bradly A. Smith, "Faulty Assumptions and Undemocratic Consequences of Campaign Finance Reform", *The Yale Law Journal*, No.105, 1996, pp.1049–1091.

会腐蚀选举，因为大笔支出不可避免地会导致边际效益递减，尤其是对谋求连任的现任者而言。如果选民不喜欢竞选活动所传达的信息，那么大笔支出就无法"购买"公职。而且大捐款者参与影响选举的方式有两种：一种是大力支持已明显占据优势的候选人，以在其当选后获取政策倾斜；另一种则是在参选者势均力敌的情况下，大力扶持与自身利益相符的候选人，通过竞选捐款让更多选民支持该候选人，帮助其成功当选。实际上，无论哪种方式都不必然得出巨额捐款会收买选举的结论。"事实是，竞选捐款与选民投票模式之间的因果关系似乎被改革者高估了，并且这种联系尚未得到实证研究的支持。对我们系统的民主的更大威胁，不是来自竞选支出的增长，而恰恰是来自基于这些错误假设的不正确的法规。"[1] 因而史密斯坚称，金钱在政治中的存在仍然是必要的，也是必然的。人民更多地担心资金进入政治体系的途径及其对政府的影响和可能引发的不公正现象。但他不相信一个简单根除政治腐败的解决方案的存在，甚至对定义和革除所谓政治腐败的可能性表示怀疑，因此得出的结论是："很难确定我们应该采用哪种改革方案，这些改革是否有效，甚至是否应该继续推行更多的此类改革。"

纽约大学法学院的皮尔兹教授也围绕"联合公民案"分析了赞同本案判决的原因。他否定该案会为本已不受控制的竞选捐款带来更多负面改变，反而认为这只是之前立法与判例压力不断累积而产生的质变。皮尔兹主张，如果"联合公民案"的判决对竞选财务改革的影响是负面的，那么《麦凯恩·费因戈德法》（McCain-Feingold Campaign Reform Act）即《两党竞选改革法》（Bipartisan Campaign Reform Act，BCRA）带来的负面影响与其不相上下，后者甚至更大程度地放大了非政党实体在当今选举中的作用。[2] 在该法颁布后的第一次选举即 2004 年，各政党成功从更多的个人那里筹集到了更多资金，从而成功弥补了被阻塞的软钱造成的资金缺口，部分原因是该法抬升了个人向政党捐款的上限。[3] 且《两党竞选改革法》还意外造成了外围团体支出的急剧增加。从 2002 年该法案获得通过以来至

---

[1] Bradly A. Smith, *Unfree Speech: The Folly of Campaign Finance Reform*, Princeton, NJ: Princeton University Press, 2001, pp. 63 – 64.
[2] Richard H. Pildes, "Romanticizing Democracy, Political Fragmentation, and the Decline of American Government", *The Yale Law Journal*, No. 124, 2014, pp. 839 – 845.
[3] Richard H. Pildes, supra note 1, at 144 – 145.

2008年，非党派实体的独立支出爆炸式增长了1122%，而这些都发生在2010年1月"联合公民案"的判决之前。[1] 皮尔兹的观点与史密斯不谋而合，他举例根据《国内税收法》（Internal Revenue Code）第527条设立的、不受捐款限制的政治团体"527"组织，认为其是《两党竞选改革法》造成漏洞的结果。[2] 皮尔兹指出，"联合公民案"在非政党团体近年来的资金激增中起到的作用很小，真正的祸根是1976年巴克利诉瓦莱奥案判决肯定了第一修正案，禁止对仅从事独立选举支出的非政党实体规定收受捐款的上限。他认为，是巴克利案与《两党竞选改革法》强烈地激发了民主力量的分裂。现实是，影响选举结果的潜在资金池实际上是无限的，因为巴克利案判定任何形式的支出限制都违宪，对候选人和竞选活动资金流向的限制将不可避免地导致资金流向其他渠道，"联合公民案"只是为快要决堤的资金洪流打开了闸门。因此，皮尔兹提出的方案是提升对政党捐款的上限，并转向互联网等小额公共资助选举，帮助政党而非外围团体在选举中发挥作用，即通过政党为选举提供大量资金，而不是让单个候选人排他性或压倒性地收受捐款。因为政党的捐款来源于支出至少更具有可监督性，至少能够在更大程度上减少暗钱（dark money）[3] 腐败。但他也承认，互联网碎片化的小额捐款不可避免地进一步凸显了美国社会的利益分歧与政治两极化问题。[4] 皮尔兹谈到了对美国文化中"人民主权"的独特理解，其称之为"浪漫主义的个人主义民主观"，即将公民与政府之间的组织中介（例如政党）视为真正民主的腐败。[5] 他提醒人民不应被过于浪漫和个人化的民主观念所迷惑，如果必须容忍各方利益，那么就必须尽可能地将

---

[1] Open Serects, "Total Outside Spending by Election Cycle, Excluding Party Committees", Open Serects (n. d.), https://www.opensecrets.org/outsidespending/cycle_ tots.php [http://perma.cc/V4DH-4DUE].

[2] Brookings, "Event Summary: Political Corruption in the United States and Around the Globe", The Brookings Institution (Apr. 28, 2004), https://www.brookings.edu/opinions/event-summary-political-corruption-in-the-united-states-and-around-the-globe/.

[3] 根据响应性政治中心（Center for Responsive Politics）的定义，暗钱是指未披露资金来源的非营利组织的捐款和支出，还包括作为空壳公司运营的有限责任公司注入政治活动的资金。详见第三章。

[4] Richard H. Pildes, "Small-Donor-Based Campaign-Finance Reform and Political Polarization", *The Yale Law Journal Forum*, Vol. 129, No. 18, 2019, pp. 150-170.

[5] Richard H. Pildes, "Romanticizing Democracy, Political Fragmentation, and the Decline of American Government", *The Yale Law Journal*, No. 124, 2014, pp. 839-845.

其置于"人民"的控制之下，成为"履行民主制度核心职责的、适当形式的公共物品"。美国政党的独特之处和民众对政党特有的不信任感，也正是其提倡加强政党在选举中地位，以防止腐败在更难以监督的外围团体中滋生的原因。

威斯康星大学的施威德尔教授等人也认为，对"联合公民案"所产生的潜在负面影响评估是没有根据的，外部支出具有一定的积极作用。他研究发现，由独立支出赞助的广告有时关注的问题并不同于竞选广告。因此，政治支出的增加"极大地增加了政治言论的多样性"①。2010年"联合公民案"后，参与政治发言的外部团体的意识形态并未日趋统一，排名前十位的赞助商在发行广告支出中所占的比例比2002年的比例要小。他承认外部资金组织力量累积的事实，但也认为外部支出只是暴露了政治进程中本来会被忽略的其他问题。对金钱在政治中影响的担忧实际被夸大了，因为共和党和民主党之间存在相对的资金"平衡"。而且并非是外部支出团体，反而是两党在主要捐款者利益方面意识形态的统一更令人不安，显然对民主的健康发展不利。

尽管庞大的捐款在政治竞选活动中引发了严重的问题，竞选财务与选举改革专家赫伯特·亚历山大和哈罗德·迈耶斯仍深信披露的作用："如果需要进行任何改革，不是要限制候选人实际需要的大笔捐款，而是要使披露更加全面。"② 他们建议让候选人以免费或减价的方式获得更多的电视和广播广告资源。

归根结底，上述学者观点的核心是，不应通过是否存在等价交换的腐败来断定美国代议制民主的健康与否。"联合公民案"对竞选财务系统的负面影响被夸大了，真正需要改善之处是披露与公共筹资系统，竞选财务法律制度也历史性地存在系统性漏洞。他们不约而同承认的现实是，美国民众的意识形态两极化已经成为竞选中最大的不确定因素，大捐款者对竞选的影响并没有批评者长期以来想象的巨大。在肯定现行竞选捐款和支出规定的前提下，金钱可以用来影响政策，这样行贿就变得毫无必要。联邦最高法院并非认识不到或纵容腐败，早在1853年就对有偿游说活动及其

---

① Kenneth Goldstein, David A. Schweidel & Mike Wittenwyler, "Lessons Learned: Political Advertising and Political Law", *Minnesota Law Review*, No.96, 2012, pp.1732-1754.

② Herbert E. Alexander & Harold B. Meyers, "A Financial Landslide for the G.O.P", *Fortune*, Mar. 1970, pp.104-105.

不正当的影响表示关注,因为这一行为容易通过"在高利润强烈诱惑下的激烈党派斗争创造和运作不正当的影响,污染政治机构的廉洁性"①。甚至可以说,最高法院对政治活动中可能发生的腐败是极其敏感的。

2. 肯定金钱在政治中的腐败作用:腐败不限于等价交换

早在1969年,前耶鲁大学校长小布鲁斯特(Kingman Brewster, Jr.)就发出担忧:"经济权力、舆论资源和政治权力的集中形成了一种闭环,政客必须从公司筹集资金,才能支付电视广告的巨额费用。媒体与公司则必须向成功的政客们示好,以确保他们的专营权。开放的社会似乎正以相互依赖的方式逐渐关闭。"②设法控制金钱在政治和经济上腐败影响的尝试很多,并且普遍集中在竞选捐款和政治决策中的商业利益两个方面。许多州都在努力改革选举制度,尤其是候选人和整个选举系统的经费筹措规则,以减少腐败发生的可能。这些应对措施都反映了一种忧虑:由于选举成本的急剧增加,越来越多的候选人都不得不接受"附加条件"的捐款。"联合公民案"判决的反对者认定:"最普遍的腐败形式是将钱转移到竞选资金中。"③加州大学选举法专家哈森批评最高法院对腐败的狭义定义,认为如果将不受限制的公司支出合法化,那么禁止贿赂、回扣和酬谢的法律显然也不再具有意义。④"联合公民案"后竞选支出的激增,也使得越来越多的学者将竞选捐款可能涉及的政治腐败视为一个系统性问题。

提绍特认为即使是在18世纪,腐败也不仅仅限于贿赂,其还有着更广泛的含义:"早期世代的腐败意味着过多的私人利益影响了公共权力的行使。"⑤她对上述史密斯等人对金钱在政治中的充分信任表示反驳,认为识别政治腐败的关键在于内容与意图,而非表面行为的形式。⑥利益交换

---

① Marshall v. Baltimore & Ohio Railroad, 57 U. S. 314, 333 – 334 (1853).
② Morton Mintz & Jerry S. Cohen, *America, Inc.: Who Owns and Operates the United States*, New York, NY: Dial Press, 1971, p.151.
③ Larry L. Berg, Harlin Hahn & John R. Schmidhauser, *Corruption in the American Political System*, Morristown, NJ: General Learning Press, 1976, p.90.
④ Richard L. Hasen, *Plutocrats United: Campaign Money, the Supreme Court, and the Distortion of American Elections*, New Haven, CT: Yale University Press, 2016; Lawrence Lessig, *Republic, Lost: How Money Corrupts Congress-and a Plan to Stop It*, New York: Hatchette, 2011.
⑤ Zephyr Teachout, *Corruption in America-From Benjamin Franklin's Snuff Box to Citizens United*, Cambridge, MA: Harvard University Press, 2014, p.38.
⑥ Zephyr Teachout, *Corruption in America-From Benjamin Franklin's Snuff Box to Citizens United*, Cambridge, MA: Harvard University Press, 2014, p.374.

绪 论

并不能为腐败划清明确的界限，因为它本身也是"一个具有多重含义的争议性概念"①。而且在某些情况下，没有任何条件附加的竞选捐款，可能比有明确条件交换的贿赂给市民社会带来更多的不确定性甚至损害。因此提绍特显然对"联合公民案"持反对态度。执笔"联合公民案"多数意见的肯尼迪大法官对腐败的认识是基于芝加哥经济学派的角度，将腐败缩小到简单利益交换的范围②，并以霍布斯战争状态下的世界观重新解释美国当代政治生活，即公民利用金钱等资源在公共领域获取个人利益。③ 提绍特则指出，竞选捐款的内核动机才是决定其是否属于腐败的关键，其外在表现可能游离于法律的规制之外，游说与竞选捐款法律制度在本质上不过是围绕利益交换、有组织贿赂的腐败规则。提绍特和瓦利斯都强调，制宪者们致力于预防和消除的是一种宽泛的系统性的腐败，而不是狭义的贿赂腐败④。他们认为，前者正以一种早已有之却又前所未有的趋势侵蚀着民主，即使法律意义上的腐败更少，但现实中的行贿或腐败却越发频繁地发生。公司通过"联合公民案"被赋予了事实上的言论自由权，显然是与公民话语的力量不成比例的。提绍特指出，如今的谷歌、油管、脸书等互联网巨擘已凭借其经济上的主导地位成功重塑了美国的公共政治生活，它们的影响力和控制力无处不在，控制着大部分上传的信息流和公共话语的方式，如脸书对政治广告的事实审查政策甚至可以比联邦选举委员会的裁决有更直接的监管作用，前者能够立即影响潜在的政治广告赞助者、现有候选人和政党的行为。⑤ "联合公民案"显然造成了进一步放大公司政治影响力的后果。

哥伦比亚大学的布瑞福特教授着重从"联合公民案"赋予公司言论权

---

① [美] 泽菲尔·提绍特：《美国的腐败——从富兰克林的鼻烟盒到联合公民胜诉案》，冯克利、苗晓枫译，中国方正出版社2015年版，第8页。
② 这也与法学界近几十年来越来越多地引入经济学概念有关。
③ 在霍布斯所描述的"自然状态"（state of nature）下，由于资源总是不足的，如果没有一个掌握社会契约"利维坦"，"所有人对所有人的战争"状态永远不会结束。其中所包含的社会达尔文主义也与芝加哥学派的思想路径相呼应。如果将此种观点推演到极致，最终得出的结论将是政治腐败在现代自由经济社会中是一个毫无意义的概念。
④ John J. Wallis, "The Concept of Systematic Corruption in American History", in E. Glaeser & C. Goldin, eds., *Corruption and Reform*, Chicago: University of Chicago Press, 2006, p.37.
⑤ K. Sabeel. Rahman & Zephyr Teachout, "From Private Bads to Public Goods: Adapting Public Utility Regulation for Informational Infrastructure: Dismantling Surveillance-based Business Models", Knight First Amendment Institute at Columbia University (2020), https://knightcolumbia.org/content/from-private-bads-to-public-goods-adapting-public-utility-regulation-for-informational-infrastructure.

的角度分析了法院对金钱腐败影响的认识产生变化的原因。"联邦最高法院在1830年代到2010年之前都坚持着两个限制公司参与选举的理由:一是公司财产的财富聚合可能对民主产生威胁,二是公司不应以不符合其股东利益的目的使用自有资金。在奥斯汀案中被认为可能是腐败根源的上述理由都被"联合公民案"推翻了。"联合公民案"判决在将腐败的定义范围缩小到了以利益交换为目的的贿赂行为的同时,还摒弃了对股东利益的重要保护。"① 与史密斯相对,他也以"联合公民案"推演出一种"理想选择":享有言论自由等人格权的公司成为完整的法律意义上的人,并作为候选人参选。② 可见该案结论带来的后果之荒谬。比较特殊的一点是,布瑞福特承认,即使以无视长期以来对公司参与政治的担忧为代价,"联合公民案"的判决消除了此前关于公司言论判例中明显的异常现象,该案的结论即使是不正确的,也有其合理性,因为其使得巴克利案以来的竞选财务学说更具连贯性了。③

不同于以往的理论争辩,亚利桑那大学的罗伯森等人进行了高度现实的模拟法庭实验,测试民众对腐败的认知是否只限于"联合公民案"所划定的等价交换。④ 实验通过受试者模拟陪审员的形式进行了两项研究。第一项研究模拟大陪审团审议起诉。⑤ 45名受试者在接受相应培训后组成大陪审团,聆听经验丰富的检察官现场陈述,并听取两名证人的证词。检察官指控一名国会议员和大捐款者直接共谋贿赂,案件事实完全模仿国会全体535名议员几乎每天都要从事的接受游说和竞选捐款行为,然后受试者现场讨论是否同意签发起诉书。令人惊讶的是,绝大多数陪审员都选择依据联邦贿赂法规,对议员和大捐款人(megadonor)的日常竞选

---

① Richard Briffault, "Statement of Richard Briffault", Columbia University, FEC "Forum: Corporate Political Spending and Foreign Influence"(Jun. 23, 2016), http://www.fec.gov/members/weintraub/CorporatePoliticalSpendingandForeignInfluence.shtml.
② Richard Briffault, "Corporations, Corruption, and Complexity: Campaign Finance after Citizens United", *Cornell Journal of Law and Public Policy*, Vol. 20, No. 3, 2011, pp. 643 – 671.
③ Richard Briffault, "Corporations, Corruption, and Complexity: Campaign Finance after Citizens United", *Cornell Journal of Law and Public Policy*, Vol. 20, No. 3, 2011, pp. 643 – 671.
④ Christopher Robertson & others, "The Appearance and the Reality of Quid Pro Quo Corruption: An Empirical Investigation", *Journal of Legal Analysis*, Vol. 8, No. 2, Winter 2016, pp. 375 – 438.
⑤ 除了少数州规定起诉任何刑事案件都需要提请大陪审团审议外,美国多数州的法律规定仅重大刑事案件需经大陪审团同意起诉。另外,所有在联邦法院起诉的重罪都需要提供大陪审团的起诉书。在审议起诉会议中,仅需检察官与证人出席,供大陪审团聆听和询问。

捐款交流进行起诉。第二项研究模拟审判的定罪阶段。遴选出的1276名模拟陪审员被告知，在竞选财务法律中腐败的定义是交易者明确说出"等价交换"，同时法庭陈述的案件事实都在"联合公民案"认定的腐败狭义范围之外。在聆听律师的总结陈词后，2/3的陪审员在线投票赞成有罪指控。罗伯森的实验虽然存在局限性，但也表明，最高法院通过"联合公民案"重塑的竞选财务监管体系中，政治人物和大捐款人的竞选筹款互动实际上是对腐败的替代，[1] 这也为坚持预防性的竞选资金限制法律提供了新的依据。

显然，最高法院在"联合公民案"后取消了主要的腐败预防措施，明确了"等价交换"的贿赂将成为其唯一的监管对象。对此，波斯特在《分裂公民》中警告说："从国家的利益出发，对竞选财务改革进行概念性的（限制）设计，将导致宪法上的一条盲目的死胡同。"[2] 他指出，从历史上看，存在三个重大的国家利益来支持政治中的资金监管，即促进平等、消除曲解和防止腐败。他同意提绍特和莱西格的观点，认为法院在巴克利案与麦卡琴案[3]中对腐败的不同定义是错误且混乱的。哈佛法学院教授劳伦斯·却伯将联邦最高法院缩小腐败行为的认定范围以保护言论自由的做法评价为："允许政府控制谁可以花钱在更大空间上发表意见，只会使得言论自由变得虚幻"[4]，"'联合公民案'轻描淡写地否认了美国政治中腐败的残酷性，其所导致的贿赂行为正因为其合法而真正可悲"[5]。已退休的前联邦最高法院大法官史蒂文斯也在其著作《六项修正案》中，敦促将竞选资金的监管与宪法第一项修正案所提供的保护分离开来。[6]

---

[1] Christopher Robertson & others, "The Appearance and the Reality of Quid Pro Quo Corruption: An Empirical Investigation", *Journal of Legal Analysis*, Vol. 8, No. 2, Winter 2016, pp. 375 – 438.

[2] Robert C. Post, *Citizens Divided: Campaign Finance Reform and the Constitution*, Cambridge, MA: Harvard University Press, 2014, p.58. 书名分裂公民（Citizens Divided）与"联合公民案"（Citizens United）相对，具有讽刺意味。

[3] McCutcheon v. FEC, 572 U.S. 185 (2014).

[4] Laurence Tribe & Joshua Matz, *Uncertain Justice: The Roberts Court and the Constitution*, New York: Picador, 2015, p.210.

[5] Laurence Tribe, "Dividing 'Citizens United': The Case v. The Controversy", *Constitutional Commentary*, Vol. 30, No. 2, 2015, pp. 463 – 494.

[6] Steven G. Calabresi, "Book Review: 'six Amendments' by John Paul Stevens-Justice Stevens argues that we need six new amendments. Among them: ending the death penalty and taking away the right to bear arms", *The Wall Street Journal*, Jul. 14, 2014.

游说、竞选捐款与美国政治腐败

众多学者也主张金钱使得政治家丧失独立性，杰出的候选人只有通过"共同利益的结盟"①才能在政治竞争中存活，②否则很可能由于缺乏资金而被迫放弃政治竞选。也正因为如今私人利益对公职人员的腐败形式更加微妙，公职人员逐渐失去了对公众的使命感，从而转向对私人捐款者的忠诚，并否认所获得的恩惠与其决策之间的关系。③伯格等人提出了以下问题：当国会议员的许多投资和利益都在他们可以直接或间接施加影响的领域（如担任该领域的国会委员会主席），这真的是一个巧合吗？④政治学家奥威莱克在1932年就已经设想到了美国民主通过政党私人筹资和削弱民选而变为财阀统治（plutocracy）的可能性⑤，她将资助政党者和为政党投票的人区分开来分析，预言美国选举的私人资金将使立法程序遭到破坏并偏离民主原则。⑥许多前游说者、前任和现任国会议员以及总统候选人都将游说者及其代理的捐款者与竞选者之间的互惠关系称为"合法贿赂"。⑦20世纪50年代的前民主党参议员保罗·道格拉斯就特殊利益与政府之间密切的重叠关系，列举了一些极具腐败可能性的典型例子：政府签下大合同时，某些合同条款可以让承包商获取巨大利润；政府向个人和公司收取巨额税款，从而诱惑行贿以换取减税政策。⑧尽管通常不将其称为腐败，但利益冲突问题与特殊利益和政府之间的互动并没有本质上的区别。前《华盛顿邮报》记者杰弗里·伯恩鲍姆（Jeffrey Birnbaum）表示，捐赠者

---

① 共同利益联盟与传统的不法收受利益（graft）是有区别的，前者更加隐晦间接，往往不违反法律。
② Larry L. Berg, Harlin Hahn & John R. Schmidhauser, *Corruption in the American Political System*, Morristown, NJ: General Learning Press, 1976, p.65.
③ Paul H. Douglas, *Ethics in Government*, Cambridge, MA: Harvard University Press, 1952, p.44.
④ Larry L. Berg, Harlin Hahn & John R. Schmidhauser, *Corruption in the American Political System*, Morristown, NJ: General Learning Press, 1976, Chapter 5.
⑤ Louise Overacker, *Money in Elections*, New York: MacMillan Company, 1932, p.vii.
⑥ Thomas Stratmann, "The Market for Congressional Votes: Is Timing of Contributions Everything", *Journal of Law & Economics*, Vol.41, No.1, 1998, pp.85–114; Thomas Stratmann, "Can Special Interests Buy Congres- sional Votes? Evidence from Financial Services Legislation", *Journal of Law & Economics*, Vol.45, No.2, 2002, pp.345–373.
⑦ Robert G. Kaiser, *So Damn Much Money: The Triumph of Lobbying and the Corrosion of American Government* (1st ed.), New York: Knopf, 2009; Fred Wertheimer, "How Chief Justice Roberts and Four Supreme Court Colleagues Gave the Nation a System of Legalized Bribery", *The Huffington Post*, Oct.6, 2015.
⑧ Paul H. Douglas, *Ethics in Government*, Cambridge, MA: Harvard University Press, 1952, p.22–23.

和支出者"委婉地眨眨眼,就同一想法点头同意,无管如何实施,事实就是事实,利益集团就是通过金钱购买了选票"。① 历史学家博斯汀也同意,正是因为许多政治和社会科学家未能认识到美国政治中腐败的系统性根源,因而才倾向于采用相对狭窄的方法来处理金钱在美国政治中的不当影响。② 腐败所涉及的绝对不仅是公职人员的个人财产增加、直接贿赂或利益冲突等现象。

芝加哥大学的施特劳斯教授则指出,腐败被错误地理解为游说和竞选捐款派生的问题,但竞选财务改革根本不是要消除腐败,担心腐败的人实际上是对不平等现象和民主政治的本质发出忧虑。③ 他认为从某种程度上说,相同条件下对腐败的担忧将持续存在,实际上这是对任何代议制政府固有的某些倾向的关注,如民主政治沦为利益集团之间的斗争,这些倾向只是在"等价交换"的竞选捐款中表现得更为明显,因此,如果能够以某种方式实现适当的平等,那么担心腐败的诸多理由将不复存在。④ 康奈尔大学法学教授安德库弗勒也持较为中立的态度。她将腐败更多地视为一种道德和宗教观念,相比起现代更具有中世纪的特征,因此在现代法律中的地位会引发诸多困扰,针对其制定的政策也十分糟糕。⑤ 她论证试图消除腐败的措施就像试图消灭宗教上的罪恶一样徒劳,认为这也是竞选财务司法如此混乱的原因之一。虽然政治活动中不受管制的金钱侵蚀了公众对政府的信任。但永远不可能将金钱与政治分割,她因此敦促公众应对政府保持信心,相信法律必须比任何东西都强大得多。

3. 改革措施及局限性

许多文献最终都提到了对于竞选捐款活动中政治腐败的预防或补救措施。一般提出的补救措施有法律法规威慑和司法执法行动,组织变革和改

---

① Jeffrey Birnbaum, "The End of Legal Bribery How the Abramoff Case Could Change Washington", *Washington Monthly*, No. 38, 2006, p. 21.
② 参见 Daniel J. Boorstin, "Effects of Watergate", *The Congressional Quarterly*, 1973, pp. 1796 – 1797。但博斯汀在1973年的采访中将水门事件与早期的美国丑闻区分开来,他认为这些腐败事件是相对孤立的,因为它们都只是出于个人的贪婪和欲望。
③ David A. Strauss, "Corruption, Equality, and Campaign Finance Reform", *Columbia Law Review*, No. 94, 1994, pp. 1369 – 1389.
④ David A. Strauss, "Corruption, Equality, and Campaign Finance Reform", *Columbia Law Review*, No. 94, 1994, pp. 1369 – 1389.
⑤ Laura S. Underkuffler, *Captured by Evil: The Idea of Corruption in Law*, New Haven, CT: Yale University Press, 2013, pp. 59, 248.

革决策方式。

  首先是立法震慑。以严重违反竞选法的腐败行为为例，现有的惩罚机制主要依赖罚金、三倍赔偿金和类似执法措施，对此伯格等人建议实行强制性最低刑期（mandatory minimum prison sentences）制度，该强制性刑期应最低为六个月，法官可依自由裁量权判处最长两年的刑期。[①] 他们认为，在公司和个人因违反《联邦竞选法》行为而所得利益大幅增加的情况下，对公司及其高管仅处以数千美元的罚款无法阻止选举活动中的违法行为。要发挥有效的威慑作用，罚款必须达到一定数额。当然，只有对隐瞒报告大量款项捐赠的重大罪行才能判处有期徒刑。对于轻微或一般违反竞选法律的行为，例如未列出正确地址和电话号码等类似错误，则应采用与现有其他处理轻罪行为类似的方式进行处理。总之，应实施强制最低刑期并保证监督和执行的及时有效性，刑期不需要太长，但不可转换成其他刑罚。[②]

  为数不少的学者甚至呼吁在必要时通过宪法修改对竞选财务系统进行根本的改革。[③] 如弗曼相信坚持金钱的影响在美国的政治和法律中已根深蒂固，唯一的适当解决方案就是修改宪法。[④] 为了解决美国竞选财务结构中固有的系统性腐败问题，宪法必须停止赋予竞选捐款与政治言论等同的法律地位。但由于美国宪法的刚性本质[⑤]，在法律上的确很难通过常规立法修宪来纠正此问题，只能由联邦最高法院推翻既往判例实现，但由保守

[①] Larry L. Berg, Harlin Hahn & John R. Schmidhauser, *Corruption in the American Political System*, Morristown, NJ: General Learning Press, 1976, pp. 180 – 182.

[②] 自18世纪贝卡利亚时代至20世纪70年代，司法、执法机关与公众普遍认为严刑峻法的威慑力对预防犯罪最有效。但过去30年的犯罪学与刑法学实证研究表明，以威慑作用为代表的严厉刑罚无法对犯罪的预防起到作用，二者甚至并不呈相关关系。伯格等人在20世纪70年代所提出的刑罚威慑措施，恰恰是在法学循证方法得出上述结论之前提出的，因此也具有一定的时代和专业局限性。从奥巴马政府时期至今，强制最低刑法律在刑事司法改革中受到了很大的冲击。

[③] Ian Ayres & Jeremy Bulow, "The Donation Booth: Mandating Donor Anonymity to Disrupt the Market for Political Influence", *Stanford Law Review*, No. 50, 1998, pp. 837 – 891; John C. Nagle, "The Recusal Alternative to Campaign Finance Legislation", *Harvard Journal of Legislation*, No. 37, 2000, pp. 69 – 103.

[④] Conrad Foreman, "Money in Politics: Campaign Finance and Its Influence Over the Political Process and Public Policy", *UIC John Marshall Law Review*, Vol. 52, No. 185, 2018, pp. 185 – 256.

[⑤] 有两种修改宪法的方法。其一，可以由国会发起修宪，参议院和众议院2/3多数投票来修改宪法；其二，2/3的州即34个州发起制宪会议以提出修正案，如果3/4的州即38个批准该修正案，则将其纳入宪法。可见，在美国修改宪法并非易事。修改难度大的宪法称为刚性宪法，与之相对的则是柔性宪法。

绪　论

派掌控的后者也不太可能在近期扭转其观点。

采用政治经济学作为研究方法的学者也提出了许多改革建议：第一是通过使腐败决策的预期成本超过预期收益并减少机会来减轻腐败。惩罚应与腐败行为的预期收益成正比，但前者必须与实际相符，不宜过高而导致无法执行，如 1925 年的腐败法（Corruption Practices Act of 1925）对竞选捐款和支出的上限设置得过低，导致严重违反该法的候选人反而无法被起诉。[①] 此外，应加强调节政府官员离任后就业的旋转门规则以防止个人和系统性腐败。与防止特定机构的官员实施腐败相比，机构角色和私人生活之间的界限通常是多孔的，官员可以辞职，但仍继续影响留任者，并分享他们利用特权以伺机寻租的经验。打破这些联系，至少可以降低腐败行为的发生频率，从而减轻根深蒂固的利益盘踞对改革施加的阻力。

第二是进行组织改革。国会内部的改革行动已经表明，国会不愿意"进行急需的内部重组"，"议员们面临一系列严峻的道德问题，但未采取任何行动来收紧有关财务披露的规定或公开所有联邦官员的外部收入、财产和礼物账目"[②]。因而面对腐败，道德委员会已成为"国会山上最无用的机构之一"。罗斯－艾克曼教授提出，应通过设置重叠的管辖权并建立监督机构以加剧腐败的行政成本，防止权力集中。但他也承认恐怕没有一种组织形式能保证完全与腐败隔绝。[③] 谢尔曼则认为对内部决策和组织结构的重组还需要得到外部主导力量的支持，有时是一场巨大的丑闻，有时是建立内部问责制的主导政党。[④] 当然，政治环境的变化对于改善国会道德标准更不可或缺。[⑤] 只有政治环境得到改变，廉洁的官员得到任命，才能提高政治领域的道德标准。因此改革工作应针对的是系统或制度腐败，这

[①] Susan Rose-Ackerman, *The Economics of Corruption: An Essay in Political Economy*, New York: Academic Press, 1978, p. 187.
[②] Larry L. Berg, Harlin Hahn & John R. Schmidhauser, *Corruption in the American Political System*, Morristown, NJ: General Learning Press, 1976, pp. 172–173.
[③] Susan Rose-Ackerman, *The Economics of Corruption: An Essay in Political Economy*, New York: Academic Press, 1978, p. 180.
[④] Naomi Caiden, "Shortchanging the Public", *Public Administration Review*, Vol. 39, No. 3, 1979, pp. 294–298.
[⑤] George Benson, *Political Corruption in America*, Lexington, MA: Lexington Books, 1978, pp. 273–290.

样方能最大限度地减少个人腐败行为。①

第三是改革决策方式。决策过程更清晰可见和更充分地公开决策者信息能够减少腐败机会。随着现代政府职能的更多外包,以及越来越多的官员在公职和私人组织之间来回流动,政府决策受到外部因素影响的可能性递增,现代美国政府的决策越来越倾向于在"影子政府"中做出。在这个由"影子精英和影子游说者"决策的世界中,腐败"比贿赂官僚或海关官员更加微妙也更难以发现"。② 因此,加迪纳提出,决策的过程和内容应更加透明,要明确规定政策目标和标准,并提供有关制定法规决策者的更多信息,政策决定应接受审查。同时如果条件允许,应使用外部认证代替官僚式的许可程序。③ 罗斯-艾克曼则将解决方式简化为提高政府合同招标程序的竞争力和透明度,并扩大披露,认为及时和完整的披露就可以直接让选民将过于依赖特殊利益捐款的议员淘汰掉。④ 她还强调民间社会必须参与反腐败工作,公民社会团体可以选区为单位,通过社交媒体平台组建民间监督机构,提供鼓励举报和调查的手段,以便监督利益集团和律师等占据经济和政治力量交界处关键位置的主体,同时保护举报人。

总之,腐败和反腐败的措施与现代政府决策的本质息息相关。也正因为如此,反腐败措施都或多或少地存在制度上的局限性,这种局限性被托克维尔看作是一种民主制度的内在瑕疵或必然代价。托克维尔在《论美国的民主》中提到,平民因经商而富裕起来后,"金钱的影响开始见于国务……商业成为进入权力大门的新阶梯,金融家结成一个既被人蔑视又受人奉迎的政治权力集团"⑤。时至今日,其对于特殊利益集团在美国所具有巨大影响力的评论似乎仍是准确的。但他也指出,"民主不能给予人民以最精明能干的政府",民主优势的彰显并不能寄希望于选举制度的完美,而是基于其选举出的政府的缺陷,激发出政府本身与市民社会的独立性和创造力。罗斯-艾克曼也认同民主选举不一定能治愈政治腐败,相反,选

---

① George Benson, *Political Corruption in America*, Lexington, MA: Lexington Books, 1978, pp. 273-291.
② Janine R. Wedel, "Rethinking Corruption in an Age of Ambiguity", *Annual Review of Law & Social Science*, No. 8, 2012, pp. 453-498.
③ John Gardiner & Theodore R. Lyman, *Decisions for Sale*, *Corruption and Reform in Land-use and Building Regulations*, New York: Praeger, 1978, pp. 186-188.
④ Susan Rose-Ackerman, "Corruption & Purity", *Daedalus*, Vol. 147, No. 3, 2018, pp. 98-110.
⑤ [法] 托克维尔:《论美国的民主》,高牧译,南海出版公司2007年版,第660页。

举制度的某些部分比其他体制下的选举制度更容易受到特殊利益的影响，竞选财务系统对捐款和支出的严格限制本身，就会助长未报告的非法交易行为。① 她提议通过缩短竞选时间来直接减少政治竞选的成本。

第三节 研究方法、结构、创新及贡献

在现有的游说和竞选财务体系下，美国立法和选举政治已经形成了一个微妙的当代贵族制堡垒：公职竞选者实际上仅限于拥有巨大个人财富或可以筹措大笔资金的个人，政治影响力几乎完全由富裕阶层以及与富人有联系的人支配。针对腐败多年生草本植物似的难以根治属性，应该更加重视将经济影响力转化为政治权力手段的实证研究；并且仍有必要扩展政治腐败概念及其在竞选财务实践中的释义，还要继续寻求竞选财务理论与立法实践的连贯性。针对游说购买访问权、旋转门现象的更多领域案例研究，也有利于拓展对公私交汇领域中政治腐败的认识。基于上述研究的已有成果与不足，本书整体上呈现总分结构，思路由历史、现状、新发展、具体场景透视和解决路径层层递进，其中联合公民时代产生的政治暗钱和加密货币政治资金成为新的政治腐败工具，阿片危机和大规模监禁的案例透视以及区块链和人工智能技术的改革路径，都展现了本研究的前沿视角。对两个案例的选择有其原因，前者是广为人知的阿片危机，大制药商对立法和政策的不当影响规模最大、且持续多年，引发了最多的腐败争议；而大规模监禁危机则鲜为人知，又是公权力私营的独特领域，笔者利用专业背景优势，作出了深入的跨领域分析。两个案例既形成鲜明对比，又存在诸多相似之处，从中可以发现竞选捐款与游说在不同领域腐败模式的一致性。研究的重点之一也即另一贡献是，基于对过去一个世纪中细致烦琐的竞选财务和游说法律发展的梳理和阶段划分，对联合公民时代即2010—2023年提出的法律和法案进行了解读，从中归纳竞选财务和游说法律在反腐败方向的发展逻辑，最终对该领域在未来的发展趋势及改革难以克服的局限性提出预测。

---

① Susan Rose-Ackerman, "Political Corruption and Democratic Structures", in A. K. Jain, ed., *The Political Economy of Corruption*, London: Routledge, 2001, pp. 35-62.

本书分为七部分，第一章从理论与实证角度阐释了游说与竞选捐款的内在关系及其对美国政治进程的协同影响机制。本章也对游说与竞选捐款在美国的发展历史进行了梳理和归纳，游说经历了边缘、萌芽到扩张与规制阶段，而对竞选捐款的规制则似乎在不断制造漏洞。第二章是游说、竞选捐款对美国社会影响的总体现实观察。从精英决策取代民主决策、特殊利益集团垄断发声、技术专制蚕食立法裁量权、国会议员面临巨大竞选筹款压力以及司法体系腐败五个方面，透视当代美国立法司法机构的政治腐败。第三章以"联合公民案"后暗钱肆虐选举为背景，对暗钱组织进行了类型识别，揭示其以超级政治行动委员会为渠道掩藏大捐款者身份、放大后者对竞选的资金影响的运作方式，以及联邦竞选委员会对暗钱监管不力的原因。第四章剖析并预测了"联合公民案"时代竞选财务和反腐败法律改革的方向。大量的改革法案将规制游说旋转门、披露公司竞选支出，堵塞暗钱与外国影响漏洞作为重点，但近十年中通过的法律数量寥寥无几，尚无一种更为全面的竞选资金改革方案。第五章、第六章则具体展现了游说与竞选捐款相关政治腐败在制药与私营监狱两个行业的运作场景，以了解特殊利益团体运用巨额资金影响立法与执法机关的模式。二者都涉及立法与执法机构的腐败动因，其影响覆盖了从普通公众到底层监狱的广大社会人群，有差异又相互呼应。最后的第七章是对美国竞选财务法律与政治反腐败的改革探索，分为法律制度与技术创新两个路径，在法律部分，以证券交易委员会作出跨领域规制为代表；而在技术创新部分，应运用区块链、人工智能技术和互联网社交媒体监督竞选等政府和政治活动，预防腐败的产生。在未来，改革仍将长期在党派斗争中艰难行进，且面临加密货币捐款带来的新挑战，但小额捐款人影响力的与日俱增也带来了希望。

第一章　游说、竞选捐款与美国政治腐败：历史到现实

关于政治腐败，美国前总统吉米·卡特曾在2015年总结道："美国已成为寡头而非民主政治，无限制的政治贿赂是赢得州长、参众议员、总统提名乃至选举的关键。我们的政治系统已形成对大捐款者的回报，他们期待着在选举结束后能得到好处。"[①] 2004年民主党总统候选人约翰·克里也认为"金钱对政治的腐蚀是腐败的一种形式"。[②] 高昂的竞选花费带来了巨额的竞选捐款需求，而游说正是连接政客与捐款者的重要管道。无论是公众、学者还是司法界都一直对竞选捐款及游说活动在立法决策中的影响表示担忧。怀疑竞选活动有助于某些政治参与者从立法决策者处获得特别关注的理由显而易见：金钱可以购买价格不菲的竞选广告，从而增加议员的连任机会。[③] 议员似乎也因此意识到金钱是其连任的重要影响因素，因而每天花费数小时、有时甚至与游说者合作筹集竞选经费。[④] 自然地，资金对候选人越重要，游说者和大捐款者对他们来说就越重要。当候选人在对某问题做出决策时，不得不在满意的选民和满意的捐款者之间做出取舍。[⑤] 一位

[①] Eric Zuesse, "Jimmy Carter Is Correct That the U. S. is No Longer a Democracy", *The Huffington Post*, Aug. 3, 2015.

[②] Seth Cline, "Retiring Senators Lament Money in Politics: Senators Kerry, Harkin, and Levin All Decried the State of Campaign Finance in Retiring Remarks", U.S. NEWS (Mar. 8, 2013), https://www.usnews.com/news/articles/2013/03/08/retiring-senators-lament-money-in-politics.

[③] Alan S. Gerber & others, "How Large and Long-Lasting are the Persuasive Effects of Televised Campaign Ads? Results from a Randomized Field Experiment", *American Political Science Review*, Vol. 105, No. 1, 2011, pp. 135–150.

[④] Ryan Grim & Sabrina Siddiqui, "Call Time for Congress Shows How Fundraising Dominates Bleak Work Life", *The Huffington Post*, Dec. 06, 2017.

[⑤] Thomas Stratmann, "What Do Campaign Contributions Buy? Deciphering Causal Effects of Money and Votes", *Southern Economic Journal*, Vol. 57, No. 3, 1991, pp. 606–620.

华盛顿的游说者甚至根据自身经验总结道:"我们已经到了立法者仅从自己或对手所获得捐款的角度来考虑如何做决定的地步。"[1] 2016 年《美国政治科学杂志》刊登的一项实验研究发现,当国会议员办公室仅被告知要求会面者是他们的选民时,会面者很少有机会能接触到议员;而当研究者向办公室透露会面者此前曾为其竞选捐款时,议员们同意会面的概率就会提高三倍到四倍。[2] 该研究被认为证明了竞选捐款与政策有直接的因果关系。[3] 类似的例子其实早已存在。1995 年,《华盛顿邮报》报道了前众议院多数党鞭汤姆·德莱(Tom Delay)国会办公室接待处桌上的一本册子,上面罗列着"友好"与"不友好"的公司、行业和协会。[4] 游说者会使用这本册子确定德莱是否会与他们见面,德莱也根据这本册子决定对游说者的态度,而得以被保留在"友好"之列最简单方式,就是竞选捐款。有观点认为,相对不受欢迎的行业为竞选人提供了更多的捐款,这是因为竞选人在与不受欢迎的行业(如银行业、烟草和博彩业)相关联时会失去选民的支持,竞选人可能会要求这些行业向支持其的竞选广告投放更多资金,即更大额的捐款,来抵消这种不受欢迎带来的选票损失。[5] 批评者则说,游说与竞选捐款制度在实质上"鼓励了立法者将有限的时间更多地花在了游说者和捐款者及其背后所代表的利益上,故而不再有时间去听取别人的话了"。[6] 2017 年一项研究得出的结论是,竞选中用于支持或反对竞选人的大部分资金来自美国极少部分的富人和特殊利益集团,[7] 而该群体对立

---

[1] Elizabeth Drew, *Politics and Money, the New Road to Corruption*, New York: Macmillan Publishing Company, 1983, p.3.

[2] Joshua L. Kalla & David E. Broockman, "Campaign Contributions Fcilitate Access to Congressional Officials: A Randomized Field Experiment", *American Journal of Political Science*, Vol. 60, No. 3, 2016, pp. 545–558.

[3] 华盛顿邮报、赫芬顿邮报、加州大学伯克利分校和哈佛大学网站等均在针对该研究的报道中论及此观点。

[4] David Maraniss & Michael Weisskopf, "Speaker and His Directors Make the Cash Flow Right", *The Washington Post*, Nov. 27, 1995, Page A01.

[5] Thomas Bassetti & Filippo Pavesi, "Electoral Contributions and the Cost of Unpopularity", *Economic Inquiry*, Vol. 55, No. 4, 2017, pp. 1771–1791.

[6] Alexander Fouirnaies & Andrew B. Hall, "The Financial Incumbency Advantage: Causes and Consequences", *Journal of Politics*, Vol. 76, No. 3, 2014, pp. 711–724; Lynda W. Powell, "The Influence of Campaign Contributions on Legislative Policy", *The Forum: A Journal of Applied Research in Contemporary Politics*, Vol. 11, No. 3, 2013, pp. 339–355.

[7] Joshua L. Mitchell & others, *The Political Geography of Campaign Finance: Fundraising and Contribution Patterns in Presidential Elections, 2004–2012*, New York: Palgrave Macmillan, 2015, p. 113.

法和政策的喜好和优先事项通常与大多数美国人背道而驰,[1] 无论民主党还是共和党的捐款者都在意识形态上比包括中产阶级在内的主要选民更极端。[2] 这就决定了游说与竞选捐款影响下的立法和政策并非以大部分选民的利益为优先。主宰佛罗伦萨数个世纪之久的美第奇（Medici）家族的座右铭"金钱获得权力，权力保护金钱"[3]，似乎与今天的美国政治有诸多相似之处。游说与竞选捐款的腐败现实侵蚀了权力在人民心中的神圣感，赢家制定规则似乎已成为美国政治活动的核心要义。

第一节　游说与竞选捐款的内在联系

游说和竞选捐款对于代议制民主至关重要。游说可以帮助民选官员获取制定立法或监管所需的信息，评估政府行为将如何影响特定利益、行业、选区乃至整个社会，确定不同的群体对特定政策选择的态度。反过来，受政府政策影响或寻求政府援助以解决政治、经济或社会问题的个人、组织或团体也可以参与游说，向决策者提供他们所支持立场的事实和论据。与游说类似，竞选捐款也涉及信息和交流。竞选捐款使候选人、政党或利益集团有资金向选民表达意见，为选民提供决定其投票选择所需的关键信息，从而影响选民对公职人员任免的决定或其观点倾向的知情情况。鉴于二者在实现民主自治中的关键作用，游说和竞选支出均受到宪法第一修正案关于对请愿权、言论自由和结社自由的具体保护。

然而，游说和竞选捐款也因对财富不均和利益团体对政治进程的不当影响引发了人们的普遍关注。二者在很大程度上都取决于对资金的使用，但财富在美国社会中根本上是分配不均的。诚然，财富不均等不能完全决定游说或选举结果，游说者和捐款者只是获取了影响决策的权力，支持者

---

[1] Benjamin I. Page & Jason Seawright, What Do US Billionaires Want from Government? Paper presented at the annual meeting of the Midwest Political Science Association, 2014.

[2] Seth J. Hill & Gregory A. Huber, "Representativeness and Motivations of the Contemporary Donorate: Results from Merged Survey and Administrative Records", Political Behavior, Vol.39, No.1, 2017, pp.3–29.

[3] Beatrice Walton, "The American Ruling Class", Harvard Political Review, Harvard Politics, Sep.6, 2011, https://harvardpolitics.com/books-arts/the-american-ruling-class/.

的数量、组织能力以及在具体议题上的实质性立场仍会影响选举和立法结果。但资金充沛的个人、组织和利益集团在收集分析信息以及向政府决策者提供事实和论据方面占据优势,它们所支持的候选人可以更轻松地与选民直接沟通,在竞选中也更可能获胜。无论是游说还是竞选捐款,都通过对抗公民的法定政治平等,为超级富豪以及大公司这两大政治权力市场上的参与者不成比例地攫取了巨大优势。

一 游说与竞选捐款的逻辑关系

作为政治活动的两种重要形式,游说与竞选捐款在本质上是同一个硬币的两面,通过把资金和言论交流结合在一起,极大地影响了民主进程。尽管通常隶属于不同的法律或规定,但二者往往彼此影响、相互加强,无论是个人、组织还是利益集团都会动用游说者和竞选资金来推进各自的目标。金钱在政治中的作用从来不仅仅体现在竞选支出上,还体现在数十亿美元的游说行业中。那些希望影响立法程序的个人或团体可以选择如何使用他们的政治支出:或是在竞选捐款和游说之间二选其一,或是两者兼而有之。在实践中,许多顶级游说组织在选举中的支出也是最高的。[①] 竞选捐款在很大程度上为游说提供接触政客的机会,而得以进行游说的机会反过来又会使捐款者受益,[②] 这两种活动都通过与个人、组织和利益团体的互动得到强化。

游说和竞选捐款都可以成为寻求影响力的工具,当二者叠加,可能会加剧各自带来不当影响的风险,因此必须共同分析两者对国会议员投票倾向的影响。多数情况下,游说活动的影响力来自游说者所代表的客户,而不是游说者本身。因此真正的问题不在于游说者,而在于其所代表的利益集团。尽管政治活动中的金钱并非都构成寻租腐败,但商业团体和行业协

[①] 参见 Open Secrets, "Top Organization Contributors", Open Secrets (n. d.), https://www.opensecrets.org/orgs/top-donors? topdonorcycle = 2020; Open Secrets, "Top Lobbying Spenders", Open Secrets (n. d.), www.opensecrets.org/lobby/top.php? showYear = 2018&indexType = s.

[②] Lynda W. Powell, "The Influence of Campaign Contributions on Legislative Policy", *The Forum: A Journal of Applied Research in Contemporary Politics*, Vol. 11, No. 3, 2013, pp. 339 – 355. 这是学界的主流观点。也有部分学者认为,立法者可以从游说者处了解政策问题,但不会受其影响,参见 John M. De Figueiredo, "Lobbying and Information in Politics", *Business and Politics*, No. 4, 2002, pp. 1 – 7.

会显然主导着游说领域,与之捆绑的竞选资金可以成为对候选人和在任者的影响力来源。企业组建的政治行动委员会(political action committee,简称 PAC)[1] 通常使用捐款达到立即与议员接触、对其进行游说进而获得支持的目的,在实质上对政策是有影响的。在一些情况下,游说者的活动甚至也可能为游说者本人提供超越其客户利益的特殊影响。因而某种程度上,游说和竞选捐款中的大量金钱与公民的政治平等存在一种紧张关系。二者对利益集团特殊保护的寻求往往还会造成政府或私人资源的错配。政府官员可能会根据自己的个人利益需求做出决定,此时公共利益很可能被放置于官员职位连任或物质追求的对立面。就政府资源而言,可能是稀缺的政府预算被用于发放特殊补贴,而不是投资于对整个社会更为有利的基础设施;对私人经营者而言,这种错配则会削弱竞争,易形成卡特尔循环。因此竞选资金和游说活动在发挥其法定的功能之外,显然也引起了大众对不正当影响或腐败的担忧。

二 游说与竞选捐款的监管核心

鉴于上述二者对选举可能产生的腐败影响,对游说和竞选资金监管的核心都是控制其对政治进程的不当影响。同时,对游说者竞选资金活动的监管也日益成为二者相互融合的领域。2007 年,国会通过《诚实领导和政府公开法》(Honest Leadership and Open Government Act)明确规范游说者的竞选捐款活动,即首次在法律上将竞选捐款与游说活动相联结。国会要求竞选委员会披露实质上与游说者捆绑的捐款。同年的联邦选举委员会诉威斯康星州生命权案[2]中,法院为公司和工会的竞选支出提供了例外保护,以确保竞选财务法律不限制公司和工会的游说支出。正如该案所论述的,游说受到的控制往往比竞选捐款少,说明这两种活动涉及的法益是不同的,但本案也是二者监管逐渐交叉融合的证明。许多州也对游说者的竞选捐款、捆绑和其他形式支持候选人竞选的活动实施了直接限制。如纽约州

---

[1] 政治行动委员会是联邦竞选活动的传统主要参与者之一,是由企业、工会、个人或其他特殊利益团体设立的,旨在筹集和支出资金以直接帮助选举联邦和州候选人的独立私人实体,是上述主体出于政治目的集中资源的一种形式。据联邦选举委员会统计,截至 2023 年 12 月 31 日,全美的政治行动委员会已达 7857 个。
[2] FEC v. Wis. Right to Life, 551 U.S. 449 (2007).

公共道德联合委员会（Joint Commission on Public Ethics）于2016年通过了一份对州游说法和竞选财务法的修正案。[①] 修改后规定，任何在该州游说活动中花费到达一定数额的游说实体或游说客户，都必须披露其游说活动的大额捐款者，并且披露门槛也大大降低。新修正案显然将游说实体与竞选捐款者联系在一起，以便同时进行监督。

游说和竞选捐款在监管结构上也仍存在一些差异。二者通常适用不同的法律，有不同的规则与执行机构。竞选捐款通常受到比游说更为严格的监管。尽管竞选活动和游说活动都有披露要求，在联邦政府层面，竞选财务报告的门槛比游说报告的门槛要低，对于竞选捐款和竞选支出的信息披露要求比游说支出更多、更频繁。但一个共同的趋势是，游说与竞选捐款者都通过对其所在行业的前雇员或未来的雇员施加金钱影响来调节监管利益，以获得更宽松的监管。

三　游说与竞选捐款对立法进程的协同影响机制

作为政治互惠文化的关键部分，游说者通过使用法律允许的各种工具与立法者及其工作人员建立关系，尤其是为立法者筹集竞选捐款，那些提供最大资助的游说者可能获得最多的促进客户特定利益的机会，而竞选捐款则"可以帮助游说者促使议员了解并突出这些利益"[②]。游说与竞选捐款的联系不仅仅停留于逻辑或理论假设上，还被众多实证研究所证明。已有研究确认了竞选捐款可以购买到与政客接触的权利，并且这种接触权利与游说活动是系统地衔接在一起的。[③]

第一，游说支出和竞选捐款的团体高度重合。最新的研究绕开了统计游说和竞选捐款团体数量的传统研究模式，而是通过分析团体游说支出和捐款数量的重合程度，确定了竞选捐款和游说支出之间的紧密联系。在计

---

① 法案详见 https://jcope.ny.gov/system/files/documents/2018/02/advisory-opinion-16-01.pdf.
② Heather K. Gerken & Alex Tausanovitch, "Lobbying, Campaign Finance, and the Privatization of Democracy", *Election Law Journal*, No. 13, 2014, pp. 75–90.
③ Amy M. McKay, "Buying Amendments? Lobbyists' Campaign Contributions and Microlegislation in the Creation of the Affordable Care Act", *Legislative Studies Quarterly*, Vol. 45, No. 2, 2020, pp. 327–359; Joshua L. Kalla & David E. Broockman, "Campaign Contributions Fcilitate Access to Congressional Officials: A Randomized Field Experiment", *American Journal of Political Science*, Vol. 60, No. 3, 2016, pp. 545–558; Laura I. Langbein, "Money and Access: Some Empirical Evidence", *The Journal of Politics*, Vol. 48, No. 4, 1986, pp. 1052–1062.

算在华盛顿拥有政治行动委员会的利益团体从事游说联邦政府活动的比例后,研究发现同时具有说客和政治行动委员会的利益团体支出占所有利益团体游说支出的70%和所有政治行动委员会捐款的86%。[1] 不仅在联邦层面,针对卫生领域的州政治行动委员会和游说团体研究发现,尽管只有14%的组织拥有政治行动委员会并同时进行游说,但这些团体向议员捐出了其从上游的政治行动委员会获得的76%的捐款。[2]

第二,从游说和竞选捐款背后的利益集团角度来看,在政治活动中最活跃的公司,从有利的公共政策中也获利最大。[3] 二者的协同作用可以通过公司的纳税结果说明。《美国政治科学杂志》2009年刊载的一项研究指出,增加游说支出能够有效地让政府降低公司的税率:游说支出每增加1%,次年公司税率将降低0.5%—1.6%,普通公司每花费1美元进行有针对性的税收优惠游说,其回报在6美元和20美元之间;[4] 而对48个州相关数据进行的另一项研究发现,公司每花1美元用于竞选捐款就可以为其减税6.65美元。[5] 类似的影响还体现在公司的直接盈利上,2011年的一项研究显示,向联邦候选人提供更多资金的公司也在随后获得了更多合同。[6] 上述研究至少都证明了,这种协同作用并非偶然。利益集团的竞选捐款策略往往取决于其对游说的重视程度,反之,如果捐款可以购买游说的渠道,那么游说成功也必然会增加竞选捐款。因为在某种程度上,游说可以极大地促进被代表方的利益。麻省理工学院2020年的实证研究表明,

---

[1] Micky Tripathi, Stephen Ansolabehere & James M. Snyder, "Are PAC Contributions and Lobbying Linked? New Evidence from the 1995 Lobby Disclosure Act", *Business and Politics*, Vol. 4, No. 2, 2002, pp. 131 - 155. 没有政治行动委员会的团体往往在游说上花费很少,或者在法律上被禁止捐款。

[2] David Lowery & others, "Understanding the Relationship between Health PACs and Health Lobbying in the American States", *Publius*, No. 39, 2008, pp. 70 - 94.

[3] Matthew D. Hill & others, "Determinants and Effects of Corporate Lobbying", *Financial Management*, No. 42, 2013, pp. 931 - 957; David M. Hart, "Why Do Some Firms Give? Why Do Some Give a Lot?: High-Tech PACs, 1977 - 1996", *The Journal of Politics*, Vol. 63, No. 4, 2001, pp. 1230 - 1249.

[4] Brian Kelleher Richter, Krislert Samphantharak & Jeffrey F. Timmons, "Lobbying and Taxes", *American Journal of Political Science*, Vol. 53, No. 4, 2009, pp. 893 - 909.

[5] Robert S. Chirinko & Daniel J. Wilson, "Can Lower Tax Rates Be Bought? Business Rent-Seeking and Tax Competition Among U. S. States", *National Tax Journal*, Vol. 63, No. 4, 2010, pp. 967 - 993.

[6] Thomas Bassetti & Filippo Pavesi, "Electoral Contributions and the Cost of Unpopularity", *Economic Inquiry*, Vol. 55, No. 4, 2017, pp. 1771 - 1791. 对此问题也有相反的结论,芝加哥大学与西北大学的研究认为,没有证据表明向候选人捐款的公司会从候选人的获胜中获得任何金钱利益。

竞选捐款能够系统地提高游说的成功率，从而为利益集团制造更为集中有效的回报。①

第三，游说和竞选捐款共同影响政党与候选人。一个政党或候选人要在选举中获胜，无疑需要选民的支持。选民的倾向通常受到两种方式的影响：一方面，政党在政治光谱上的立场和选民自己的立场越接近，选民就越有可能投票给该政党；另一方面，政党相对于另一个政党的竞选支出越高，选民投票给该政党的可能性就越大。② 因而充足的竞选资金也是必要的。以 2022 年为例，平均而言，每名国会众议员需要筹集约 279 万美元来竞选并赢得席位，而成功竞选参议员则需要约 2653 万，相比 2012 年已经翻倍。③ 而游说者是竞选资金的重要组成部分，游说活动的主要重点之一就是帮助国会议员筹得竞选资金。出于竞选财务法律的各种限制规定，隶属于特殊利益的公司不能直接向国会议员提供资金，但他们可以把资金给游说者，由游说者为议员组织筹款活动。然后，资金筹集所得将捐赠给议员，同时保证了整个交易的合法性。如在 2012 年大选中，六名与竞选资金捆绑的游说者为共和党参议员罗姆尼（Mitt Romney）的总统竞选活动筹集了超过 1700 万美元；民主党参议员哈里·里德（Harry Reid）则从捆绑游说者那里筹集了 14% 的竞选资金。④ 获得捐款的代价是，每个政党或候选人都要与某些游说团体达成共识，在政治光谱中的某个主题选定立场，但可能的后果是其立场与选民的立场产生更大的偏差。对游说团体来说，一种让政党或候选人偏离选民意愿的立场会降低该党赢得选举的概率，从而也会降低确保其所代表的利益集团获得较有利政策的机会，但这

---

① In Song Kim, Jan Stuckatz & Lukas Wolters, Strategic and Sequential Links between Campaign Donations and Lobbying, MIT, 2020.

② Francisco R. Ruiz, Lobbying, Campaign Contributions and Political Competition, Department of Economics Working Papers 55/16, University of Bath, Department of Economics, 2016.

③ Open Secrets, "Election Trends", Open Secrets (n. d.), https://www.opensecrets.org/elections-overview/election-trends; Jay Costa, "What's the Cost of a Seat in Congress?" Maplight (Mar. 10, 2013), https://maplight.org/story/whats-the-cost-of-a-seat-in-congress/. 实际上不同议员竞选花费相差巨大，如马萨诸塞州参议员伊丽莎白·沃伦（Elizabeth Warren）赢得选举的花费为 4250 万美元，而前美属萨摩亚已故众议员埃尼·法莱奥玛瓦加（Eni Faleomavaega）筹集的资金最少，约为 11 万美元。2022 年的参议院选举则再次创下了竞选支出新高。

④ Michael Beckel, "Obama Bundlers Closely Tied to Influence Industry", The Center for Public Integrity (Mar. 8, 2013), http://www.publicintegrity.org/2013/03/08/12279/obama-bundlers-closely-tied-influence-industry.

种影响可以通过增加对该党或候选人的竞选捐款来部分抵消或补偿。

通过游说和竞选捐款这两种成熟的法律机制产生政策成果,金钱对民主自治所施加的巨大影响迎合了经济精英群体的利益。官员被说服花更多时间听取出资者对某些政策的特殊关注,并更有可能基于这种互动作出对出资者有利的决定。[1] 无论是对政党、候选人、游说者、政治行动委员会还是其背后代理的利益集团,竞选捐款与游说之间都存在着某种战略互补的作用机制,故有必要共同研究这两项活动,以充分理解影响力构成的复杂关系。

第二节 游说与竞选捐款在美国政治中的历史轨迹

腐败与美国历史紧密相连。制宪者将英国不公正的贵族世袭和"无代表征税"(taxation without representation)的统治体系视为腐败,最终成为美国独立的催化剂。[2] 新生的民主也伴随着腐败,无论是贿赂、购买选票,还是游说和竞选财务,其中蕴含不断变化的腐败问题都有其历史。[3]

一 游说在美国政治中的历史轨迹:边缘到扩张

在美国脱离英国建立独立新政府的过程中,政治领导人需要为政府选择的民主形式提供正当化的理由。被称为"宪法之父"的詹姆斯·麦迪逊所提

---

[1] Richard L. Hasen, "Lobbying, Rent-Seeking, and the Constitution", *Stanford Law Review*, No. 64, 2012, pp. 191 – 253; Joshua L. Kalla & David E. Broockman, "Campaign Contributions Fcilitate Access to Congressional Officials: A Randomized Field Experiment", *American Journal of Political Science*, Vol. 60, No. 3, 2016, pp. 545 – 558.

[2] Andrew J. Wilson, *Comparative Political Corruption in the United States: The Florida Perspective*. M. A. Thesis, University of South Florida, 2013. "无代表,不纳税"(No Taxation without Representation)源自美国独立战争前夕的政治口号,用来抗议英国政府对美洲殖民地征税而不给予殖民地在英国议会中的代表权。现今能在许多华盛顿特区的车牌上看到,因为特区居民必须缴纳联邦税,却没有在国会中投票的代表。

[3] Michael Johnston, *Syndromes of Corruption: Wealth, Power, and Democracy*, Cambridge, UK: Cambridge University Press, 2005, p. 64.

出的新政府架构不仅能够支撑联邦制和三权分立等基本统治原则，还容纳了团体或"派系"在政治进程中的参与。他所理解的派系"无论是公民的多数还是少数，都是出于某些共同的热情或利益冲动而团结起来促成的，这些利益冲淡了其他公民的权利甚至是社区的永久和整体利益"。① 制宪者所创建的错综复杂的分层政府体系，为有组织的团体提供了多种机会来影响政府的运作。理想的情况下，每个具有野心的团体都有一定的伸展空间，彼此之间互相牵制抵消，不会有任何一个派系取得压倒选民意愿的优势。② 基于此，麦迪逊提出了将政府部门划分为三个平等但独立实体的想法，派系在后来则被称为利益集团，并为游说思想提供了重要的历史象征意义。

政治学家托马斯·戴伊曾说："政治就是政府资源的分配，即谁得到什么，何时，何地，为什么以及如何获得。"③ 由于社会资源的天然稀缺，利益集团政治和游说活动几乎存在于所有西方民主政治社会。游说是指，公民以外的其他人将信息数据或意见传达给政府决策者以影响特定决策，游说者作为联络人与重要的政府决策者接触。美国历史上对游说的态度与法律定性经历了不同时代背景下的变迁，通过近200年的发展，当今的游说已经同竞选捐款一样，成为金钱对政治影响不可或缺的一环（见图1-1）。不同于19世纪被认定为非法，现在的游说活动可能已成为便利的腐败替代品，既可以在影响立法决策的同时将腐败指控挡在门外，又可以使贿赂更有机可乘。如今主持重要委员会并担任领导职务的国会议员也最有可能在游说行业获得高薪职位，光明正大地成为游说者。尽管投入巨大，但游说公司对前政府官员的投资带来的回报显然更可观，雇佣更多前政府官员的游说集团在63%的情况下会取得胜利，为客户带来数十亿美元的利益。④ 对于政府官员来说，其政治职业生涯可以以潜在未来雇主的利益为出发点，即将离任的议员们之间也可能为了讨好雇主相互竞争，从而将游说活动的潜在影响进一步推向使企业和富人利益最大化的方向。

---

① James Madison, "The House of Representatives from the New York Packet", *The Federalist Papers*: No. 52, Feb. 8, 1788, New York: Signet Classics, 2003.
② Nick Allard, "The Law of Lobbying: Lobbying Is an Honorable Profession: The Right to Petition and the Competition to Be Right", *Stanford Law & Policy Review*, No. 19, 2008, pp. 23-68.
③ Thomas R. Dye, *Politics in America*, Englewood Cliffs, NJ: Prentice Hall, 1995.
④ Lee Drutman, supra note 261, 转引自 Conrad Foreman, "Money in Politics: Campaign Finance and Its Influence Over the Political Process and Public Policy", *UIC John Marshall Law Review*, Vol. 52, No. 185, 2018, pp. 185-256.

第一章　游说、竞选捐款与美国政治腐败：历史到现实

图 1-1　游说：一个资本游戏

注：1949年的棋盘游戏大亨米尔顿·布拉德利（Milton Bradley）推出的桌游，玩家扮演众议员或参议员，在各种特殊利益集团的帮助或阻挠下，引领国会通过相关法案。

资料来源：作者摄于美国国家历史博物馆。

（一）边缘时期：游说的非法定性与行为界分

早在19世纪初，"游说"一词就以口语的形式流行，指的是某些团体将自己的利益压在当权者身上。[①] 安德鲁·杰克逊（Andrew Jackson）时代，法院就对"游说代理人影响和促成法律通过"的腐败影响表示了关切，[②]

---

① Gregory R. Bordelon, "History and Evolution of Lobbying Regulation", in A. Handlin, ed., *Dirty Deals? An Encyclopedia of Lobbying, Political Influence, and Corruption*, Santa Barbara, CA: ABC-CLIO, LLC, 2014, pp. 29–63.

② Trist v. Child, 88 U.S. 441, 451 (1874).

认为游说不仅是一种以有偿代理非法影响政府决策的腐败活动，还是个体对于自己公民身份的一种背叛。从 19 世纪 30 年代到 20 世纪 30 年代初，出售个人影响力都被视为法律上的民事不法行为（civil wrong）①，因为公民无权支付他人来推进其立法意图的达成。最早出现在联邦最高法院的游说案例印证了这种观点。1847 年 11 月，巴尔的摩和俄亥俄铁路公司的官员收到了一封信，信中提议铁路公司说服立法机关授予铁路公司一定的通行权，来信者亚历山大·马歇尔（Alexander Marshall）自称是弗吉尼亚州一位经验丰富的游说组织成员。② 马歇尔在信中强调，铁路公司需要对立法机关施加一种"积极而有组织的影响力"，因此应雇佣"诚恳而渴望成功"的经纪人从事该活动，如果失败了，经纪人没有报酬，但若成功了则应重金奖励。③ 马歇尔的计划是组织代理团队积极参与党派活动，在此计划下，除非公司想要的法律得到通过，否则铁路公司无须支付任何费用。在评估了此项工作的困难程度后，马歇尔提出铁路公司若接受该要约，需要先支付 5 万美元（约合 2024 年的 187 万美元）雇佣代理人团队。马歇尔保证不使用任何不正当的手段，而是通过立法机关周边受人尊敬和具有影响力的代理人来达到游说目的，但一切安排都会保密。随后，马歇尔声称铁路公司同意了这一安排，他按计划为铁路公司赢得了立法胜利后，因铁路公司未按合同支付费用而提起诉讼。联邦最高法院最终驳回了马歇尔的要求，认为该合同在公共政策下是无效的。法院裁定"尽管任何人的利益都可能受到立法机关公共或私人行为的影响，毫无疑问地有权亲自或由代理的律师敦促其主张和论点，但对法院来说，马歇尔对自己作为铁路公司代理人角色的隐瞒令人不安：一名雇用的拥护者或代理人，以不同的身份行事，对立法机关进行欺骗"。④ 1843 年宾夕法尼亚州高等法院警告道"在总政府所在地和其他地方已经出现了一类人，这些人将促使立法机关的法案通过作为一种业务"，他们"以工作职责为途径误导立法机关议

---

① Matt Stoller, "Lobbying Used to Be Illegal: A Review of Zephyr Teachout's New Book on the Secret History of Corruption in America" [*Matt Stoller Blog*], Nov. 17, 2014, https://medium.com/@matthewstoller/in-america-lobbying-used-to-be-a-crime-a-review-of-zephyr-teachouts-new-book-cff14d1c0326.
② Gustavus Myers, *History of the Supreme Court of the United States*, Chicago, IL: Charles H. Kerr & Company, 2015, p.269.
③ Marshall v. Baltimore & Ohio R. Co., 57 US 314 – 1854.
④ Marshall v. Baltimore & Ohio R. Co., 57 US 314 – 1854.

员",即使尚无证据表明立法者实际上已因此从事不当行为。[1] 同样在1864年曲思特诉柴德案中,联邦最高法院认为,"并不存在一个明确的方法来将秘密进行的不适当游说与付费的适当游说进行区分"[2]。和前例相似,游说在本案中被认为是违反公共政策的,因此游说合同也无法得到执行。不仅如此,有偿游说还会使个人、立法者、游说者乃至整个社会的诚信受到折损。内布拉斯加一所法院也评价游说服务"在本质上是腐败并有悖于公共政策的"。[3]

即使到了随后的进步时代(Progressive Era)[4],改革者仍时常将政治腐败的现象归咎于游说者。[5] 1877年佐治亚州的宪法草案甚至将游说定义为一种犯罪,因为向政府上诉请愿和与政府官员分享意见是公民的个人权利,该权利是不可出售的。纽约高等法院在1893年将公民的政治参与和游说活动进行了较为严格的区分:"对任何拟议的立法有兴趣的每个公民,都须有权雇用代理人并向其支付酬劳、起草法案并向委员会解释。"其强调指出,仅起草和向立法者解释法案并要求将其引入法案,其本身并不涉及要求立法者实际对这些法案进行表决,只要原告"不是游说者"并与立法机关的任何成员都没有熟识或影响,他便没有任何特殊的手段来促成立法,因此此类活动不涉及法院"违背公共政策"的"游说服务"。[6] 判断游说活动正当与否的另一关键特征是个人服务和专业服务之间的区别。马萨诸塞州法院在1920年的一项判决中认为:"为确保立法而进行的招揽或个人影响,与为使立法者理解其所要求采取措施的优点而提供的合法服务,存在明显的区别。"[7] 这些判决观点也在美国早期游说活动的图景中画定了一条分界线,分界线的一侧是促进利益相关公众的立法、法规或政策建议的准备或解释行为,即所谓的"良好"政治参与游说;另一侧则是使

---

[1] Clippinger v. Hepbaugh, 5 Watts & Serg. 315, 320-321 (Pa. 1843).
[2] Trist v. Child, 88 U. S. 441, 452 (1874).
[3] Richard Briffault, "The Anxiety of Influence: The Evolving Regulation of Lobbying", *Election Law Journal*, Vol. 13, No. 1, 2014, pp. 160-193.
[4] 进步时代是指1890—1920年美国社会的政治改良时代,其间涌现大批进步运动者和社会活动家,提倡以科学为工具对社会进行大刀阔斧的改革,科技、教育、医疗、人权、金融、工业等各个领域随之得到了长足发展,政府内部的政治利益集团被削弱,腐败问题得到改善。
[5] Elisabeth S. Clemens, *The People's Lobby: Organizational Innovation and the Rise of Interest-Group Politics in the United States, 1890-1925*, Chicago, IL: University of Chicago Press, 1997.
[6] Chesebrough v. Conover, 140 N. Y. 382, 387 (1893).
[7] Adams v. East Boston Co., 127 N. E. 728, 631 (Mass. 1920).

用秘密的影响力，以特殊手段措施篡改立法者的意向，即"不良"游说。而游说的相关法律就来源于这两种游说之间的紧张关系：游说既可以是腐败行为，又可以是合法行为，其在受到宪法保护的同时也需要监管。

（二）萌芽时期：游说的合法化与规制的开始

在今天的美国，游说被认为是受宪法第一修正案保护的言论活动，但其被联邦最高法院所赋予的这种法律地位，实际上也仅有几十年的历史——直至1941年，联邦最高法院才将符合特定条件的游说活动认定为合法。在马歇尔诉铁路公司案败诉近一个世纪后，联邦巡回法院在一份判决中对游说做了如下评述："为了支持国会的权力，有人认为游说是为国会的监管权力所涵盖的，即对公众舆论的影响就是一种间接的游说，因为公众舆论会影响立法。因此，影响公众舆论的企图受到国会的管制。被确切定义的游说活动因而受到国会的控制，……无论是语义学还是三段论都不能阻碍人们通过书籍和其他公共著作影响他人的自由。……据说游说本身是一种邪恶和危险。我们同意，通过私人的接触进行游说可能是一种邪恶的行为，并且可能对立法程序构成潜在危险。据说公共舆论构成的间接游说对国会施加的压力可能是邪恶的，并具有潜在危险，但那并非邪恶，而是民主进程良好、健康的精髓。"[①] 至此，游说活动被认为是受宪法保护的言论、新闻、结社和请愿自由的一个方面：游说者可以向政府官员表达有关特定行业、地理区域、政府部门或社会经济团体状况的建议，拟议现行法律法规的成本、收益或政府行动的后果以及受这些立法政策决定潜在影响的民众可能持有的观点。它不仅是政治表达的手段，还是民众参与政府的一种形式，更是指导政府决策的有用工具。

鉴于州和联邦法律开始对游说进行规范而不再是一味禁止，契约精神下合同的日益神圣化和游说行业的专业化，也使得游说合同得不到执行的情况逐渐消失。但游说行业的合同化也导致政治决策形成了一个封闭市场，个人影响力在其中出售。之所以说其是封闭的，正是因为其与公开市场对消费者的普遍准入不同——在这里，只有金钱和人脉才是敲门砖。决策者为游说者提供了一种产量无法满足公共需求的产品信息，但这也导致游说对市场经济的负面影响，因为其无形中鼓励生产者投资购买政治权力而非改善产品（如为商品减税以提高市场竞争力进行游说而不是通过技术创新提高质量或降低

---

① Rumely v. United States, 197 F.2d 166, 173–174, 177 (D.C. Cir. 1952).

产品成本）。① 1972 年的《伯德修正案》（Byrd Amendment）禁止使用国会拨发的资金来游说联邦合同、捐款、贷款和合作协议②，显示出立法机构对于资助游说活动始终存在的担心，也从侧面印证了游说可能带来的负面影响。20 世纪中叶以来，尽管联邦最高法院在多个判例中不时放开或收紧游说的相关规定，但不变的是其强调游说受到第一修正案保护的法律现实，这也在一定程度上体现了司法机构看待游说的矛盾心态。

（三）扩张时期：旋转门与游说规制的今天

游说的一项基本功能是，为决策者提供有关拟议政策将如何影响各个相关利益团体的翔实信息，并反过来为利益团体提供关键的政治情报。对于大多数捐款者而言，巨额的政治支出只是讨价还价的生意，雇佣游说者使其得以约见制定法规和进行监督的机构及其代理人，并通过游说者将大笔资金用于竞选捐款作为回报。无论引发多么激烈的争议，联邦法院赋予游说的合法性使之在过去的几十年间以惊人的速度增长，自 1975 年第一个专开展游说业务的专门公司——华盛顿游说公司成立至今，美国已有超过 1.2 万名注册游说者，③ 仅对纽约州政府的游说支出每年就超过两亿美元④。但游说产生的影响远不止于说客游说的内容本身。很多时候，游说行业对政策的最大影响可能并非说客真正说服了立法者，相反其影响主要来自问题的另一面——所有高级公职人员都知道，只要表现"得当"，他们都可以在离开政府后找到比现在薪酬高五倍以上的游说工作。响应性政治中心的统计表明，自有记录以来，共有 447 名前国会议员成为注册游说者。⑤ 1998—2004 年，参议院有 50% 的参议员在离职后成为游说者，众议院则为 42%。⑥ 2007 年以来，越来越多的国会议员平均在任时间从数十年

---

① Richard Briffault, "Lobbying and Campaign Finance: Separate and Together", *Stanford Law & Policy Review*, No. 19, 2008, pp. 105 – 129.
② 13 U. S. C. x 1352.
③ Statista, "Total Number of Registered Lobbyists in the United States from 2000 to 2022", Statista (Nov. 3, 2023), https://www.statista.com/statistics/257340/number-of-lobbyists-in-the-us/; Christopher DeMuth, "Our Corrupt Government", *Claremont Review of Books*, 2015, August 1.
④ New York State Joint Commission on Public Ethics, "2012 Annual Report", 2013, https://jcope.ny.gov/news/joint-commission-public-ethics-releases-2012 – annual-report.
⑤ Open Secrets, "Former Members", https://www.opensecrets.org/revolving/top.php?display = Z.
⑥ Russell Berman, "An Exodus from Congress Tests the Lure of Lobbying", The Atlantic (May 1, 2018), https://www.theatlantic.com/politics/archive/2018/05/lobbying-the-job-of-choice-for-retired-members-of-congress/558851/.

缩短到只有区区数年。① 2012 年一项研究解释了这种现象发生的可能原因：研究所追踪的 12 名国会议员在离任后平均工资增长了 14.5 倍。② 公共公民团体（Public Citizen）的最新研究更发现，2019 年有近 2/3 的前国会议员进入了寻求影响联邦政府政策的游说公司、咨询公司、贸易团体或商业团体工作。③ 国会议员卸任后转为说客仿佛已成为既定安排。

毫无疑问，游说行业与政府雇员之间的"旋转门"对腐败有着不可忽视的助推作用。华盛顿的"政策倡导者"中有很大一部分从未注册为说客④，因为他们声称其仅仅是给予立法者和官员"历史性建议"。以国会前众议院拨款委员会主席鲍勃·利文斯顿（Bob Livingston）为例，其在 1999 年因婚外情指控离开国会一周后，便成立了一个名为利文斯顿集团的游说商店。尽管利文斯顿仍在"冷静期"（cooling-off period）中，即被法律禁止对前同事进行游说，但冷静期并不限制前议员指令和管理其他说客，利文斯顿便充分利用了这种自由。该游说商店开业的第一年就净收入 110 万美元，六年后被列为华盛顿特区第 12 大非律所游说公司⑤；1999—2004 年的 5 年间，该公司盈利近 4000 万美元。⑥ 2003 年美国入侵伊拉克期间，由于在土耳其领土内行动的要求遭到土耳其当局的拒绝，国会随即取消了对土耳其的 10 亿美元拨款。相关记录显示，在补充投票前的几天里，利文斯顿利用他的影响力和人脉指挥其说客和助手，联系了其曾经主持的众议院拨款委员会成员和工作人员，还接触了与众议院国际关系委员会、参议院拨款委员会、参议院军事委员会和众议院筹款委员会的成员。利文斯顿与众议院议

---

① Congressional Research Service, Congressional Careers: Service Tenure and Patterns of Member Service, 1789 – 2019, Jan. 3, 2019, p. 13; Victor Reklaitis, Market Watch & Katie Marriner, "Newcomers? Congress is Still All About Longtimers-And One Party Has More of Them", Market Watch (Jan. 29, 2019), https: //www. marketwatch. com/story/newcomers-congress-is-still-all-about-longtimers-and-one-party-has-more-of-them-2019-01-09.
② Brad White, *Congressional Revolving Doors: The Journey from Congress to K Street*, Washington D. C: Public Citizen's Congress Watch, 2005, p. 1 – 2.
③ Alan Zibel, "Revolving Congress: The revolving door class of 2019 flocks to K Street", Public Citizen (May 30, 2019), https: //www. citizen. org/article/revolving-congress/.
④ Tim LaPira & Herschel Thomas Ⅲ, "Just How Many Newt Gingrich's Are There on K Street? Estimating the True Size and Shape of Washington's Revolving Door", *SSRN Electronic Journal*, Apr., 2013.
⑤ 游说公司可以分为律所（law firms）和非律所游说公司（non-law firm lobbying firms）两种。律所提供的服务范围广泛，不仅包括法律咨询和诉讼代理，还有游说。
⑥ Brad White, *Congressional Revolving Doors: The Journey from Congress to K Street*, Washington D. C: Public Citizen's Congress Watch, 2005, p. 3.

长丹尼斯·哈斯特（Dennis Hastert）的外交政策顾问取得了联系，其后甚至与副总统切尼（Dick Cheney）和负责政治事务的副国务卿谈话，最终在就美国政府是否取消对土耳其补充拨款的议案投票表决中，利文斯顿所代表的利益集团取得胜利，也因此从土耳其方获得 180 万美元酬金。①

由于报酬丰厚，与利文斯顿类似的行为在退休国会议员中并不鲜见。如在 2000 年初期和中期选举中，民主党和共和党两党的前众议院议长和前参议院多数党领袖都以说客的身份现身。但 2005 年的阿布拉莫夫丑闻推动了改革，针对该丑闻颁布的《诚实领导和政府公开法》推出新限制，直接导致了注册人数减少。国会延长了为期一年的"冷静期"，将参议员游说前同事的冷静期定为两年，增加了对游说者的披露要求和处罚力度。奥巴马于 2009 年当选总统后也签署了一项行政命令，禁止说客在入职政府后从事其之前游说事项的相关工作，并禁止前白宫官员离任后游说白宫。特朗普在总统任期的首日就签署了一项关于游说的行政命令，要求被任命者签字承诺不接受游说者的礼物，并在离开政府五年之内不会游说其之前任职的机构或代理外国政府进行游说。

尽管这类限制可能在某种程度上达到了限制旋转门的目的，但其也进一步激发了所谓的"影子游说"（shadow lobbying）——前国会议员加入大型律所或游说公司担任顾问，组织整个游说活动，确定需要联系的人和要传达的信息，然后由游说团队中的其他人进行联系。这样既不会违反冷静期的规定，又可以避免游说者的污名。如 2001 年的参议院多数领袖汤姆·达施勒（Tom Daschle）声称自己的游说活动仅是"战略顾问"，在幕后制定游说策略，但不与决策者直接接触。② 在 2011—2012 年的一场竞选辩论中，前众议院议长金里奇就辩称自己没有从事游说，只是为房地产巨头房地美提供了与抵押贷款危机有关的"历史性建议"，以此获得了 30 万美元的报酬。③ 此外，至少在联邦一级，即使是注册的游说者也不必对影响更广泛的政治媒体支出或社交媒体活动进行报告，这种政策倡导风格的影子游说俨然成为美国当代游说活动的主导形式。游说与国会间的"旋转

---

① Wikipedia, "Turkish Lobby in the United States", https：//en.wikipedia.org/wiki/Turkish_ lobby_ in_ the_ United_ States.
② Thomas B. Edsall, "The Shadow Lobbyist", *The New York Times*, Apr. 25, 2013.
③ Clea Benson & John McCormick, "Gingrich Said to be Paid about ＄1.6 Million by Freddie Mac", *Bloomberg*（Nov. 17, 2011）, https：//www.bloomberg.com/news/articles/2011-11-16/gingrich-said-to-be-paid-at-least-1-6-million-by-freddie-mac.

门"以及各式各样以"政策倡导"为名义的游说者与打着"咨询建议"旗帜进行的边缘游说活动,都为利益寻租者带来了可乘之机。随着游说支出的逐年递增,水涨船高的说客薪酬与公务人员的微薄收入进一步拉开差距。尤其对在竞选连任中失败的议员来说,游说更是一种颇具吸引力的选择,他们比自愿退休的议员更有可能留在华盛顿成为游说者。①

不仅仅是国会议员,政府雇员也同样进入了游说旋转门。自克林顿政府以来,就一直有高盛的前雇员在财政部担任高级职务;② 联邦通信委员会(FCC)自 2009 年以来的三位全职主席都来自大媒体公司;2001—2010 年,约有超过 1/4 负责审查抗癌和血液药物的食品药品监管局(FDA)员工进入制药行业工作。③ 许多公司甚至直接表明其与国会的联系。如以游说为主要业务的卡温顿与伯灵律师事务所(Covington & Burling LLP)就公开宣称其雇员为前国会议员,甚至前白宫内阁秘书长也是其工作人员。旋转门不仅是个人在行业和监管机构之间来回流动的一种模式,它的本质是公司直接参与监管机构的任命,监管机构又反过来监管这些公司。由此可见,旋转门现象不仅仅是单向的人事流动,而是双向的;它不仅在国会议员及办公室雇员之间施加影响,还广泛渗透到政府各个监督机构中。这类广泛存在的旋转门现象间接加剧了政治腐败。

显然,对于旋转门现象,现行法律只能在一定程度上加以规制,而不应将其完全禁止。首先,阻止前议员担任游说者将在很大程度上损害游说行业的合法职能。诚然,在 K 街④游说公司工作的前国会议员是整个旋转门现象的不体面代名词,其在离任后的高薪职位也往往被认为是在任时为特殊利益服务的腐败证据。但特殊利益集团在立法过程中发挥如此巨大影响力的主要原因之一,不仅仅是其拥有的大量财富,更是其掌握的有关议题的宝贵信息。这些专业性的信息经游说者及时传达,可以帮助议员理解

---

① Open Secrets, "Revolving Door: Former Members of the 114th Congress", Open Secrets (n. d.), https://www.opensecrets.org/revolving/departing.php?cong=114.
② Katya Wachtel, "The Revolving Door: 29 People Who Went from Wall Street to Washington to Wall Street", Business Insider (Jul. 31, 2011), https://www.businessinsider.com/wall-street-washington-revolving-door-2011-4.
③ Sydney Lupkin, "A Look at How the Revolving Door Spins from FDA to Industry", National Public Radio (Sep. 28, 2016), https://www.npr.org/sections/health-shots/2016/09/28/495694559/a-look-at-how-the-revolving-door-spins-from-fda-to-industry.
④ K 街位于美国华盛顿特区,因是许多游说公司和政治组织总部所在地,而成为美国政治游说活动的象征和中心。

甄别收到的各种决策建议。由于许多立法领域涉及的专业知识范围狭窄,技术性要求也很高,现任者需要依靠富有经验的前议员和高级员工的知识和经验,来获取信息并对具体问题进行考量。因而限制国会议员成为游说者将破坏国会获得专业资讯的重要网络。其次,旋转门能为较小的利益团体提供影响决策的机会。游说团体往往更有可能在较为集中的行业形成,大公司通常也更愿意进行游说,但完全杜绝旋转门是一种"一刀切"的做法。富有的利益集团仍然很有可能为前国会议员提供高薪工作。可以想象,像脸书、摩根大通、埃克森美孚这些大公司的首席执行官,无论是否有前任议员引荐,让国会议员接听电话都不会很难。而较小的公司可以从游说活动获得更多的好处,因为它们通常对政治机构的直接影响较小。[1] 因为游说支出有限,其往往只能依赖以前国会议员的宝贵人际关系,而旋转门禁令很可能让这些小团体的声音更难被听到。再次,旋转门是公私部门交流的有效渠道。在美国,公共部门和私营部门之间的技术和经验交流是互惠互利的,并可以为整个社会带来巨大利益。具有丰富政府任职经验者能够帮助管理公司,而政府也可以依靠那些了解私营部门运作方式者的专业知识,这种人员的流动性能够使双方从中受益。最后,对前议员终身禁止游说可能触及宪法赋予公民的言论自由权,此前也的确存在相关关闭旋转门的法律在法庭上得不到法官支持的先例。相比之下,法律应当以更加实际的改革方式有效管理和调节旋转门,如给国会提供更多的预算,向议员支付更多薪水从而高薪养廉,或为竞选活动提供合理数量的公共资金,使议员不至于浪费大量时间在打电话和向捐款者索款上,也将给议员们更多时间专注于本职工作。这样还能减少特殊利益集团过多接触议员的机会,既能在最大限度上为社会带来收益,也更能遏制腐败。总之,试图推行一个毫不透气的禁令将产生诸多不利后果,如果完全禁止旋转门这种腐败的减压阀,腐败将可能以贿赂等更严重和难以监管的隐藏形式频繁出现。

在不会完全禁止旋转门的前提下,对游说的法律规制总体上呈现四种目标或趋势:(1)保护个人、团体和组织向立法和行政部门官员陈述事实和观点的游说权利;(2)防止游说对政府行为的不当影响;(3)提高游说活动与官员间互动的透明度。换言之,尽管游说的核心即向官员陈述事

---

[1] Nauro F. Campos & Francesco Giovannoni, "Lobbying, Corruption and Political Influence", *Public Choice*, Vol. 131, No. 1/2, 2007, pp. 1–21.

实和论点的权利受到宪法保护，但规则严格限制游说者给予官员物质利益（如礼物、酬金和免费旅行待遇等），前政府官员参与游说活动即"旋转门"行为受到限制，说客被要求在更大限度上披露其收入和支出。在过去的10年中，由于受到联邦最高法院颠覆性的判例判决影响，改革与规制游说的注意力已转移到游说者在竞选财务中所扮演的角色上：一些司法管辖区或是对说客提供或筹集竞选捐款作出限制，或是要求对这些活动进行更大限度和更频繁的披露。从目前游说法律在联邦最高法院的判例演变趋势来看，游说活动与竞选财务法规之间的联系越发紧密，二者都已被最高法院纳入第一修正案言论自由权的保护项下。对游说的监管范围和力度都在增加，以向竞选捐款规制逐渐靠拢，这与长期以来对于游说和竞选捐款共同构成政治腐败的担忧相呼应，而这种担忧在未来短期内仍将继续存在。

二 竞选捐款在美国政治中的历史轨迹：冲突与规制

竞选捐款是美国民主选举制度中极具特色的制度，与政治参与和言论自由权利息息相关，直接显示了社会利益集团的政治立场和政府内部力量的利益分割。长期以来，美国以其花费昂贵的选举尤其是总统大选在全世界独树一帜。众所周知，在过去的几十年中，美国的政治竞选活动正变得越来越昂贵，尤其在21世纪以来的20年中，动辄上亿的政治资金充斥着竞选活动。纵观竞选支出在一个世纪以来的发展变化，不难发现政治竞选事实上从一开始就充斥着大笔的金钱，且在早期颇有明目张胆行贿受贿的腐败之嫌。

1828年肯塔基州长竞选中，一名候选人就索取了单笔高达1万美元（约合2024年的33万美元）的捐款。[1] 1922年，参议院就曾正式宣布对共和党所领导的参议院初选所花费的19.5万美元（约合2024年的356万美元）表示谴责，认为其"与现有的合理政策相悖，有损参议院的荣誉与庄严，且对自由政府的不可转让性产生了危险"。在1972年的大选中，保险巨头美国联合保险公司董事长克里蒙·斯通（Clement

---

[1] Victor W. Geraci, "Campaign Finance Reform Historical Timeline", Connecticut Network (n.d.), https://ct-n.com/civics/campaign_finance/Support%20Materials/CTN%20CFR%20Timeline.pdf.

第一章　游说、竞选捐款与美国政治腐败：历史到现实

Stone）向尼克松捐款约200万美元（约合2024年的1468万美元）；梅隆金融公司（Mellon）继承人、石油巨头理查德·梅隆亦向尼克松捐款100万美元；通用汽车（General Motors）继承人斯图尔特·摩特（Stewart R. Mott）则向两名候选人分别捐赠40万美元。① 同年，公共公民团体联合房屋制造商联合会以及哥伦比亚特区消费者协会，向尼克松总统提起诉讼，指控其接受了奶农合作社的捐款，以换取农业部对牛奶价格的补贴优惠待遇。② 三家组织迫使合作社披露与选举有关的交易，尼克松总统也不得不披露了其接收的500万美元捐款来源。③ 民主党人虽然历来不太依赖公司捐款，但也严重依赖少数商人的个人财富来筹集资金。1893年，民主党众议员卡特·哈里森（Carter H. Harrison）在芝加哥市长的竞选中花费50万美元（约合2024年的1704万美元）④，最终再次任职。历史学家罗伯特·卡洛曾描述20世纪五六十年代时任参议院多数领袖的林登·约翰逊的超级现金机器：助手们从得克萨斯飞回华盛顿特区时口袋里塞满了石油大亨赞助的现金，随后将钱分发给约翰逊的支持者。⑤ 乔治·华莱士曾担任四届亚拉巴马州长，其在任期间是种族隔离的忠实支持者。白人至上主义团体密西西比公民委员会（Mississippi Citizens' Council）在华莱士1968年竞选总统时为其筹集了25万美元资金，为隐匿身份，该团体将捐款交由300名个人，分别写了1000美元左右的支票给华莱士。华莱士最终筹集到约45万美元（约合2024年的397万美元），竞选财务总监不得不命令一名前橄榄球运动员用力踩踏大堆的支票和现金，以便将其塞入12个超大号袋子内。⑥

巨额的竞选捐款使得相应的竞选总支出急剧上升，呈现每十年至少翻倍的趋势：1956—1968年，竞选支出从1.55亿美元增加到3亿美元，1992年的大选支出达2亿美元，是1980年的两倍，2008年奥巴马和麦

---

① Frank J. Sorauf, *Money in American Elections*, Glenview, IL: Scott, Foresman, 1998, p.33.
② Ciara Torres-Spelliscy, "Got Corruption? Nixon's Milk Money", Brennan Center (Oct. 21, 2013), https://www.brennancenter.org/our-work/analysis-opinion/got-corruption-nixons-milk-money.
③ Louise Overacker, *Money in Elections*, New York: MacMillan Company, 1932, p.1.
④ Bradly A. Smith, *Unfree Speech: The Folly of Campaign Finance Reform*, Princeton, NJ: Princeton University Press, 2001, pp.21–22.
⑤ Robert A. Caro, *The Years of Lyndon Johnson: Master of the Senate*, New York: Alfred A. Knopf, 2002, pp.403–413.
⑥ Dan T. Carter, *The Politics of Rage: George C. Wallace, the Origins of the New Conservatism, and the Transformation of American Politics*, New York: Simon & Schuster, 1995, p.335.

凯恩的大选支出则高达10亿美元。① 因而长期以来，竞选财务法律的目标主要集中在限制竞选捐款和支出以降低竞选成本，或通过建立广泛的竞选公共资金制度减少特殊利益在选举和立法过程中的影响上，从而在整体上构建一个对变革更开放的政治制度。从19世纪中期至今，以限制竞选捐款、支出和促进相关披露为主要任务的竞选财务法律，依次经历了从几乎真空、执行薄弱、制造漏洞，到21世纪初的短暂胜利，再到"联合公民案"至今的低谷期几个阶段。竞选捐款相关法律的规制起落也从侧面反映了美国政治竞选腐败偶尔受到短暂压制，但总体上持续加剧的现实。

（一）现金自由交易：1867年以前的监管空白年代

竞选捐款在美国早期的竞选活动中就已十分盛行，在20世纪上半叶及之前的大多数时间里，竞选资金都是以现金交易（cash-and-carry）的形式流动的。② 资金不需经过报告，也不存在支出限制，公众更无从对其进行审查。竞选支出的相关记载最早可以追溯至1755年：乔治·华盛顿在弗吉尼亚议会（House of Burgesses）选举中失败，他认为失败的原因在于竞选的宣传不力，因此两年后，他在选举前花费约195美元（约合2024年的9970美元）为391位选民购买了35加仑③宾治酒和45加仑烈性苹果酒以及准备了丰盛的晚餐，最终得以成功当选④。立法机关随后通过了一项法律，禁止竞选人或代表他们的个人向选民提供"金钱、肉食、饮料、娱乐场所……任何礼物、奖励或招待等，以使之当选"。⑤ 作为美国历史上第一位有组织的政治竞选人，安德鲁·杰克逊于1828年第二次竞选公职，上任后他将政府机构内的美差授予竞选捐款

---

① Max Galka, "The History of Campaign Spending", Metrocosm (Aug. 02, 2015), http://metrocosm.com/the-history-of-campaign-spending.
② Dennis W. Johnson, *Democracy for Hire: A History of American Political Consulting*, New York: Oxford University Press, 2017, p.130.
③ 一加仑约为3.8升。
④ BallotPedia, "History of Campaign Finance Regulation", BallotPedia (n. d.), https://ballotpedia.org/History_of_campaign_finance_regulation; Ronald Collins & David Skover, *When Money Speaks: The McCutcheon Decision, Campaign Finance Laws, and the First Amendment*, Oak Park: Top Five Books, LLC, 2014.
⑤ Lobby Seven, "Campaign Finance: The Best Government Money Can Buy", Lobby Seven (Jul. 26, 2017), https://www.lobbyseven.com/single-post/2017/07/26/Volume-17-Campaign-Finance.

第一章　游说、竞选捐款与美国政治腐败：历史到现实

者，以表示回报。① 这也成为明目张胆的权钱交易在美国历史上发生的证据之一。② 1839 年，一项由众议院任命的委员会通过对纽约海关大楼员工进行的政治评估，对纽约港收藏家塞缪尔·斯沃特威特（Samuel Swartwout）展开了首个关于竞选经费的调查。③ 1838 年，花费 22 美元（约合 2024 年的 725 美元）就可以从选民处买到一张纽约市长选举的选票。④ 针对愈演愈烈的贿赂式索取竞选捐款和公然买卖选票现象，林肯曾在 1864 年的一封信中警告道："危机即将来临……公司已经尾随内战的结束登场，大肆的腐败将随之而来。金钱将通过掠夺民意来延长其统治，直到所有财富都集中在少数人手中、共和国被摧毁为止。"⑤

（二）法律初次介入：1867—1935 年的监管执行乏力年代

在 19 世纪末和 20 世纪初，竞选财务法律首次介入竞选资金监管，其规制的重点包括保护雇员和工会成员免于被迫参与政治竞选捐款、披露竞选资金、限制公司捐款资格和建立公共竞选筹资系统等。但出于种种原因，这些法律或缺乏执行力，或在制定时留下监管漏洞，最终导致美国正式开启了竞选捐款的腐败时代。

1867 年，《海军拨款法案》（Naval Appropriations Bill）获得共和党领导的国会通过，成为第一部竞选财务法，该法案明令禁止联邦官员向海军船坞工人索取竞选捐款。1883 年，由于当时许多政府工作者为保住工作而被迫捐款，俄亥俄州参议员乔治·彭德尔顿发起了《彭德尔顿法》（Pendleton Civil Service Reform Act），禁止以竞选捐款换取联邦政府职位或

---

① Beth Rowen, "Campaign-Finance Reform: History and Timeline", InforPlease (n. d.), https://www.infoplease.com/history/us/campaign-finance-reform-history-and-timeline. 也有说法认为杰克逊总统并未寻求竞选捐款，而是将公制委任予其政治支持者。参见 Shannon Furtak, "Citizens United and Its Impact on Campaign Financing: A Brief Overview Current Events", [HeinOnline Blog], Mar. 8, 2018, https://home.heinonline.org/blog/2018/03/citizens-united-and-its-impact-on-campaign-financing-a-brief-overview/.
② 参见周琪、袁征《美国的政治腐败与反腐败——对美国反腐败机制的研究》，中国社会科学出版社 2009 年版，第 180 页。
③ Elisha J. Edwards, "Tammany: Early Spoilsism and the Reign of the Plug-Uglies", McClure's Magazine, Vol. 4, No. 1, 1985, pp. 574 - 575.
④ Victor W. Geraci, "Campaign Finance Reform Historical Timeline", Connecticut Network (n. d.), https://ct-n.com/civics/campaign_finance/Support%20Materials/CTN%20CFR%20Timeline.pdf.
⑤ Gerald Sussman, Global Electioneering (1st ed.), Lanham, MD: Rowman & Littlefield Publishing Group, 2005, p. 215.

就联邦政府财产征集竞选捐款，以将《海军拨款法案》的保护对象扩大适用于政府工作人员，因而获得了公众的广泛支持。这两部法律也成为联邦政府正式介入竞选资金监管的标志。

19世纪70年代开始，政府监管逐渐与公司扩张形成了共生关系。南北战争伴随而来的北方工业化加速创造了大型国有公司的新景象，战时政府合同以及对铁路公司日益普遍的补助为许多此类企业奠定了发展的基础。① 共和党国会的高关税政策为国内多个行业提供庇护，公司也从中受益。② 但日益扩张的州与联邦政府权力使得大公司逐渐意识到需要增加自身的政治参与，于是开始选举支持公司利益的候选人。随着大量利益集团的出现，尤其是工商利益团体日益积极地介入总统选举，巨额竞选资助首次出现在美国总统选举中。③ 1888年，共和党全国竞选资金中约有40%来自宾夕法尼亚州的制造业和商业利益团体。④ 同年，首个有官方记录的正式竞选捐款由美国百货商店之父约翰·沃纳梅克（John Wanamaker）作出，他为本杰明·哈里森（Benjamin Harrison）的总统竞选活动捐款5万美元（约合2024年的161万美元）⑤，其后哈里森顺利当选。1896年的大选创下了竞选资金的新纪录，共和党开始发布政治广告，定期举行新闻发布会、宣讲、印制海报、传单、徽章和广告牌。当时罗斯福的竞争对手威廉·麦金莱（William McKinley）从大公司处筹集了约700万美元（约合2024年的2.5亿美元），这些公司显然利用了当时《彭德尔顿法》禁止以竞选捐款来换取联邦政府职位所留下的法律空白。⑥ 最终赢得大选后，麦金莱政府的立法与政策都十分亲商业。

---

① Lloyd J. Mercer, "Railroad Land Grants", in K. L. Bryant, Jr., ed., *Encyclopedia of American Business History and Biography*: *Railroads in the Age of Regulation, 1900 – 1980*, New York: Bruccoli Clark Layman, Inc. and Facts on File Publications, 1988, p. 353.
② Daniel K. Tarullo, "Law and Politics in Twentieth Century Tariff History", *UCLA Law Review*, No. 34, 1986, pp. 285 – 370.
③ 林宏宇：《美国总统选举政治研究》，天津人民出版社2018年版，第28页。
④ Bradly A. Smith, "Faulty Assumptions and Undemocratic Consequences of Campaign Finance Reform", *The Yale Law Journal*, No. 105, 1996, pp. 1049 – 1091.
⑤ James T. Bennett, *Stifling Political Competition*: *How Government Has Rigged the System to Benefit Demopublicans and Exclude Third Parties*, New York: Springer, 2009, p. 57.
⑥ History Commons, "1896: Presidential Campaign Criticized as Corrupt, Public Begins Demanding Campaign Finance Reform", History Commons (n. d.), http://www.historycommons.org/context.jsp? item = a1896mckinleydouglas.

第一章　游说、竞选捐款与美国政治腐败：历史到现实

麦金莱的竞选负责人、前共和党全国委员会主席马克·汉纳（Mark Hanna）在对充满着不平等和政府腐败惊人的19世纪末概括时甚至说："民主国家的所有问题都是关于钱的问题"①，"政治里有两件重要的东西，第一是金钱，第二个我想不起来了"②。因此，1896年也被认为是美国金钱腐败政治的元年。

　　随着公司在选举中支出的增加，限制公司参与选举的运动也开始兴起。为了驯服逐渐壮大的公司权力，国会扩大了联邦法规的控制范围，试图将公司纳入竞选监管。国会于1881年成立了州际贸易委员会（Interstate Commerce Commission）调整州际贸易活动，后又通过了1890年《谢尔曼反托拉斯法》（Sherman Antitrust Act）。同时扩大对铁路票价、商业竞争和工作条件等的普遍监管，以约束公司的垄断地位，从而为限制公司垄断竞选资金铺垫。1891年，肯塔基州成为第一个禁止公司为政治选举捐款的州。1894年5月至9月举行的纽约州制宪会议期间，后来成为美国国务卿和战争部长的以利胡·罗脱（Elihu Root）试图禁止公司为选举捐款，但未能成功；1897年，内布拉斯加、密苏里、田纳西和佛罗里达四个州通过立法，禁止公司为竞选捐款；1901年，新罕布什尔州参议员威廉·钱德勒（William E. Chandler）提出了第一个禁止公司向政治委员会捐款的法案，但法案也未获通过。1905年，共有五个州立法禁止公司竞选捐款。③ 时任总统罗斯福在向国会致辞时表示，总统竞选活动在金钱和政治问题上"凝聚了民众的情绪"，并呼吁采取"强有力的措施来消除政治上的腐败"，他还建议"法律禁止公司向任何政治委员会或出于任何政治目的捐款"，并为政治候选人提供公共资助，④ 但他并没有禁止公司经营者捐款。事实上，罗斯福前一年大选的成功恰恰得益于其从各大公司处筹集的200万美元（约合2024年的6972万美元）捐款。⑤ 罗

---

① Jack Beatty, "A Sisyphean History of Campaign Finance Reform: A look at how we ended up back where we began", The Atlantic（Jul., 2007）, https://www.theatlantic.com/magazine/archive/2007/07/a-sisyphean-history-of-campaign-finance-reform/306066/.
② Michael Kazin, "The Nation: One Political Constant", The New York Times, Apr. 1, 2001.
③ Louise Overacker, Money in Elections, New York: MacMillan Company, 1932, p.294.
④ John Nichols, "Teddy Roosevelt Was Right: Ban All Corporate Contributions", The Nation（Jan. 21, 2010）, https://www.thenation.com/article/teddy-roosevelt-was-right-ban-all-corporate-contributions/.
⑤ Earl R. Sikes, State and Federal Corrupt-Practices Legislation, Durham, NC: Duke University Press, 1928, pp.127-128.

斯福在1907年签署《蒂尔曼法》（Tillman Act），该法以南卡罗来纳州参议员本·蒂尔曼的名字命名，首次禁止公司和国家特许（州际）银行向联邦候选人直接捐款，但当时并没有一套良好的执行制度来真正实现上述规定，甚至没能成为对竞选者收受大公司捐款进行谴责的道德依据。由于没有任何执法规定，政客们能够轻易逃脱资金监管，因而该法在实质上是无效的。

与此同时，要求国会和总统候选人公开竞选捐款也成为美国最早和最具争议的针对性透明制度之一。1908年，时为总统候选人的威廉·塔夫脱（William Taft）承诺公开他的全部捐款人名单。但在1910年《联邦腐败行为法》（The Federal Corrupt Practices Act，也称为 Publicity Act 即《宣传法》）通过之前，披露都还只是出于展示政治上清廉的必要。《联邦腐败行为法》是由总统罗斯福所倡导的第一部竞选活动财务披露法律，被认为是针对大企业在政治上发挥影响的一剂"解毒剂"[1]。该法确定了众议院选举中各政党的竞选开支限额，并要求众议院候选人在竞选后对支出进行披露，但未能得到执行。次年8月，《联邦腐败行为法》修正案通过，要求对参议院候选人采取同样的约束，并且对所有国会候选人的开支都施加了限制，规定众议员和参议员的选举支出限额分别为5000美元和1万美元。亨利·福特于1918年在美国参议院竞选中输给商人杜鲁门·纽伯里（Truman Newberry）后，试图援用该法律击败后者。福特声称纽伯里为竞选筹集了超过10万美元（约合2024年的203万美元）的资金，违反了支出限额规定。纽伯里在1921年被定罪，但随即向联邦最高法院提起上诉。法院最终支持纽伯里的告诉，并取消了支出限制。[2] 但竞选资金的监管也不总是失败的，1925年经修订的《蒂尔曼法》被并入《联邦腐败行为法》修正案，首次正式建立了竞选资金的披露制度，法定提交披露报告的人员范围被扩大，所有超过100美元的捐款都需要按季度报告，同时为参议员制定了2.5美元的竞选支出上限。到1928年，有18个州禁止了所有类型的公司捐款，另外9个州禁止了某些类别公司的捐款，如银行、公用事业和保险公司。这在立法层面至少是一种胜利。尽管同样因为缺乏执行机制而导致公司和银行捐款的禁

---

[1] Archon Fung, Mary Graham & David Weil, *Disclosing Campaign Contributions to Reduce Corruption*, Ash Center for Democratic Government and Innovation, Harvard Kennedy School, 2007.

[2] Newberry v. United States, 256 U.S. 232 (1921).

令在很大程度上被忽略，这些法律自此专门负责监管美国的竞选资金活动，直至水门事件的发生。

另外值得一提的是，公共筹资制度在20世纪初的竞选捐款改革中被创立。为了抵制竞选捐款可能带来的腐败现象，罗斯福总统首次提出了针对所有联邦候选人的公共筹资体系，呼吁通过政党为联邦候选人提供公共资助。科罗拉多州曾于1909年通过一项法律，规定竞选活动的费用只能由州和候选人本人支付。候选人花费不得超过其所竞选公职预期第一年薪水的40%，他人捐款或候选人接受他人捐款都是重罪。根据该法案的规定，在选举中，科罗拉多州的财政部长必须为每张政党州长提名的选票支付给每个政党州主席25美分（约合2024年的8.4美元），其中一半用于竞选活动目的，一半分配给该州各县党主席。但当两党州主席要求财政部长兑现资助时均遭到拒绝，司法部长对该强制性付款请求提出了抗辩，州最高法院随后判决该法案违宪，但是没有提供书面意见或相关裁决解释。[①] 因此，对竞选捐款进行公共资助的第一次州试验最终以失败告终。

（三）公司规制扩张：1935—1974年的政治行动委员会年代

20世纪初期开始，一系列的竞选财务立法都着力于限制竞选捐款的主体资格，即谁有权或不得为竞选活动捐款。但是在试图限制公司、工会和行业协会不成比例的强大政治影响力时，立法者无意间创造了现代政治中最强大的竞选机器之一：政治行动委员会，它逐渐将美国的政治腐败推向高峰。

为了约束联邦雇员的政治竞选活动，进一步推动选举清廉并维护选举自由，1939年《哈奇法》明文禁止恐吓或贿赂选民，规定不得将任何指定用于救济或公共工程的公共资金用于选举目的，以联邦资金作为工资的官员不得使用工作承诺、晋升、经济援助、合同或任何其他好处来强迫选民的竞选捐款或政治支持。但无论是之前的《联邦腐败行为法》还是这部《哈奇法》，都因为规定缺乏惩罚机制等诸多漏洞而很容易被绕过。捐款者可以成立多个委员会，一次向每个委员会捐献小于100美元的金额，即使不提交报告也没有相关的处罚规定。作为受到竞选财务改革主要影响的政府机构，国会甚至也缺乏监管的动力，并未采取任何行动来加强执法。

直接导致的结果是，20世纪30年代工会以会费为名义收取竞选捐款

---

① Earl R. Sikes, *State and Federal Corrupt-Practices Legislation*, Durham, NC: Duke University Press, 1928, pp.144–145.

的现象逐渐开始大行其道。20世纪40年代,这种竞选融资活动更是进入了繁荣时期。① 针对工会利用竞选捐款左右选举的操作,国会于1943年通过了《史密斯—康纳利法》(Smith-Connally Act),将对公司的竞选捐款禁令扩大至工会。同年,名为美国劳工联合会(Congress of Industrial Organization)的工会组织成立了美国第一个政治行动委员会,由工会成员自愿捐款,以支持民主党候选人。由于政治行动委员会本身不是工会,因此可以在不触犯捐款资格禁令的前提下向候选人捐款。更重要的是,政治广告和支出限制法律仅适用于候选人,而政治行动委员会不受这种束缚,因此后者可以花费尽可能多的钱来独立地向公众宣传特定候选人和议题。尽管在1947年国会通过了《塔夫脱—哈特利法》(Taft-Hartley Act),对联邦选举中的工会支出设置了更多限制,如禁止在公司和工会在联邦竞选中独立支出,并规定候选人只有承诺在大选竞选期间不动用公司的法人资金或收取私人捐款,才可以用公共资金进行竞选。但直到今天,利益集团通过政治行动委员会影响竞选活动的运作方式仍与彼时大致相同,并未受到立法规制的太多影响。

1967年,在竞选财务法律实施将近50年后,国会终于开始接收竞选财务报告,之前通过的竞选财务法律才得以真正执行。同时,一个多世纪的立法试验证明,竞选财务法律过于广泛或过于模糊,甚至常常无法通过诉讼向联邦最高法院申请法益保护。因此,国会终于在1971年做出了真诚的尝试,针对早先法律的漏洞以及金钱在政治活动中日益增长的影响,《联邦腐败行为法》被修订为《联邦竞选法》(Federal Election Campaign Act,简称FECA)。该法构建了全国性的竞选资金公开制度,从而使竞选财务法发生了根本性的变化。这为工会和公司建立的政治行动委员会提供了立法框架,允许工会和公司使用自有资金来建立、运营和征集自愿捐款,以供其政治行动委员会在联邦竞选中使用。《联邦竞选法》要求完整报告竞选活动的捐款和支出,精确地规定了候选人在竞选期间可以花多少钱,并要求国家公职的竞选者在季度报告中披露100美元及以上的捐款,而在选举年中,5000美元或以上的捐款必须在48小时内报告,并在报告后48小时内向公众披露,该法被普遍认为是一部规制"硬钱"(hard money)② 的法律。该

---

① Jaime Fuller, "From George Washington to Shaun McCutcheon: A Briefish History of Campaign Finance Reform", *The Washington Post*, Apr. 4, 2014.
② "硬钱"是个人或政治行动委员会赠与特定竞选人的政治捐款,由联邦选举委员会根据《联邦竞选法》管理和限制,需要按规定进行披露。详见第一章。

法还对捐款数目和媒体支出作出了限制。441b条规定，在某些特定的选举中，禁止公司和组织在任何形式的媒体上动用其自有资产"直接捐款"和进行"明确宣传"支持或反对某候选人的独立支出。① 其中一项限制是：电视广告的支出上限为在上次选举中投票人数乘以每人10美分，最高为5万美元。可以想象，在当时执行这样一条规则非常困难，因为国会没有任命执行机构来执行该法律。

1972年的水门事件导致国会在1974年修改了《联邦竞选法》，建立了竞选资金监管的新体系，扩大了披露要求，并针对长期以来竞选财务法律得不到执行的顽疾，成立了独立于两党的联邦选举委员会，赋予后者法规编撰权和民事执法权。委员会由6名专员领导，其中属于同一个政党的专员不能超过3个，负责接收已披露的信息并向公众公开，委员会至今仍在负责对竞选财务法律的监督与执行。

（四）改革受阻：1976—2002年的软钱泛滥年代

20世纪70年代后期的一个重要节点是，逐渐相近的立法和随之带来的各种法律争议，使得国会将竞选财务法律规范连同堕胎、枪支管控等重大事项的解释权交给了法院，同时为日后最高法院从宪法层面一再推翻竞选捐款限制埋下了伏笔。

彼时，联邦政府和几乎所有州都要求公开披露竞选捐款和有关竞选捐款者的信息，未与候选人协作的竞选活动的独立支出也同时被要求进行披露。1975年，联邦通信委员会（FCC）进一步澄清了其披露要求，规定广播公司应"完全公平地披露在电视和广播中为政治广告付费者的真实身份"。在此之后，联邦最高法院基本控制了所有关于竞选财务法规的解释与发展。1976年，在具有里程碑意义的巴克利诉瓦莱奥一案中，最高法院通过撤销《联邦竞选法》做出的一些限制，改变了竞选财务在美国宪法框架下的地位。最高法院从合众国诉奥布莱恩案②对言论的定义出发，将竞选经费真正纳入了第一修正案的保护范畴。判决虽然肯定了上述披露要求的合宪性，认为这是"收集数据以检测违反捐款限额的重要手段"，公开披露大额捐款和支出有助于"威慑现实中的腐败现象，避免了腐败现象的

---

① Brian Duignan, "Citizens United v. Federal Election Commission", Britannica (Sep. 6, 2019), https://www.britannica.com/event/Citizens-United-v-Federal-Election-Commission.
② United States v. O'Brien, 391 U.S. 367 (1968).

出现",并"阻止了那些在选举中将金钱用于不正当目的的行为"。① 但法庭认定《联邦竞选法》关于竞选捐款与支出的部分条款违宪,指出公司只要不在竞选宣传广告中使用支持或反对某候选人的用语,就可以使用法人财务进行捐款。该规定打开了巨大的竞选财务监管空白,公司与工会在这些广告上得以开始花费数亿美元的"软钱"(soft money)。

"软钱"是与"硬钱"相对的概念。"硬钱"是个人或政治行动委员会赠与特定竞选人的政治捐款,由联邦选举委员会根据《联邦竞选法》管理和限制,需要按规定进行披露。例如在2019—2020年选举周期中,捐款者受到以下限制:捐款人在每次选举中对每位候选人捐款限额为2800美元,未与竞选人关联的政治行动委员会具有支持多个候选人的资格。若向候选人提供的捐款超过联邦限额,则可能会面临刑事指控,后果为支付罚金与监禁刑。"软钱"则是在联邦选举监管框架之外,为政党或政治行动委员会筹集和支出的捐款,只能用于"政党建设",例如提倡某法律的通过或敦促选民进行登记,没有金额限制,但不能用于支持或反对特定的候选人。软钱可以像"硬钱"一样可以来源于个人、政治行动委员会甚至公司等,并可以对联邦选举产生间接的影响。1978年,联邦选举委员会更改了政党筹款的管理规则,规定竞选财务法律的捐款规则仅适用于政治竞选,不适用于"政党建设"活动。这意味着州一级的政党被允许接受来自公司和工会捐献的、用于政党建设的软钱,且金额不设限,而此前《联邦竞选法》禁止这两种资金作为政治捐款来源。尽管接受这种"软钱"必须有与"硬钱"的账户区分开的独立银行账户,并根据《联邦竞选法》的要求和限制进行支出,但由于其捐款不在联邦法律的涵盖下,因此没有金额限制。

---

① Buckley v. Valeo, 424 U.S.1 (1976). 本案还指出了披露竞选捐款的一个例外,即对于自证披露捐款会导致威胁、骚扰或报复的合理可能的少数派政党,政府不得强制其进行披露。在这种情况下,法院在结社自由和言论自由与对政治腐败的关切之间取得了平衡,这种平衡主要受到政党规模的影响。由于少数派政党候选人不太可能赢得选举,因此对于少数派政党,政府在阻止选举被"购买"方面的总体利益减少了。而对主要政党,这种平衡倾向于控制腐败。基于本案的结论,1982年,联邦最高法院判决少数党"社会主义工人党"豁免披露,因为对捐款者进行报复的威胁意味着强制披露将限制该党筹集资金的能力。在此案中,地方法院发现了骚扰的大量证据,证实了该党对捐款者可能会受到骚扰的担忧,包括威胁性的电话和仇恨内容的邮件、焚烧该党书籍、破坏党员财产,警察骚扰党内候选人并在政党办公室开枪等。还有证据表明,在审判前的12个月中,有22名该党成员因其党员身份而被解雇。此外,法院还发现了政府骚扰的证据,包括联邦调查局的监视计划和旨在削弱该党行使职能的其他活动。详见 Brown v. Socialist Workers' 74 Campaign Committee, 450 US 87 (1982).

第一章　游说、竞选捐款与美国政治腐败：历史到现实

起初，软钱进入竞选系统的速度缓慢，但在之后的几个竞选周期中暴增。在1988年的总统竞选中，民主党和共和党人都发现了该裁决所造成的漏洞，由于软钱不受选举法律的约束，公司、工会和个人都可以政党建设为目的向政党捐款，两党随即通过政治行动委员会展开了"软钱竞赛"。1980年，民主党和共和党的软钱总额仅为1900万美元，1984年为2100万美元，1992年增至8600万美元，1996年则达到2.63亿美元。① 这是由于当时联邦选举委员会也并未详细定义政党建设，只是将其解释为没有明确告诉人们投票或不投票给特定候选人的活动，故各政党以政党建设为名，大肆投放包括教育选民等有关选举问题的广告，这些广告只需遵守不向选民建议投给或不投给某候选人的规定即可。如果候选人甲在投放的广告中说："我是个好人，而候选人乙是坏人，请在选举日为我投票。"由于该广告明确指出了"为我投票"，就是一则政治广告，花销必须算入"硬钱"。但如果候选人乙也投放了一则广告："候选人甲有着可怕的过去，如果任由这种情况发展下去，总有一天会有人就会闯进您家里拿走所有的钱。请务必在选举日投票。"由于该广告通过提供有关某个问题的信息"教育"人们，而并没有建议投票给特定候选人，因此这笔钱就可以归入所谓的政党建设范畴，并以软钱来支付（见图1-2）。但实际上对选民来说，上述由软钱支付的广告实质上与硬钱资助的广告在并没有多大差别，二者政治观点的倾向性都十分明显。

同时，无论是民主党人还是共和党人都开始积极寻求公司和大捐款人的资金作注入软钱账户，因此政治行动委员会变得更加普遍，成为实质上的快速筹资机器。1972年，位于北卡罗来纳州莱利市（Releigh）的全国国会俱乐部（National Congressional Club，简称NCC）轻松帮助刚刚当选参议员的杰西·赫尔姆斯还清了10万美元竞选债务，在随后的几十年中，NCC和其他政治行动委员会一样急速扩张，成为20世纪80年代全国最大的同类组织，动辄筹集数百万美元资金。②

尽管后来在1990年的奥斯汀诉密歇根商会案中，法院认为"公司财

---

① Dennis W. Johnson, *No Place for Amateurs: How Political Consultants Are Reshaping American Democracy*, New York: Routledge, 2001, pp.177-193.
② William A. Link, *Righteous Warrior: Jesse Helms and the Rise of Modern Conservatism*, New York: St. Martin's Press, 2008, p.364.

· 69 ·

游说、竞选捐款与美国政治腐败

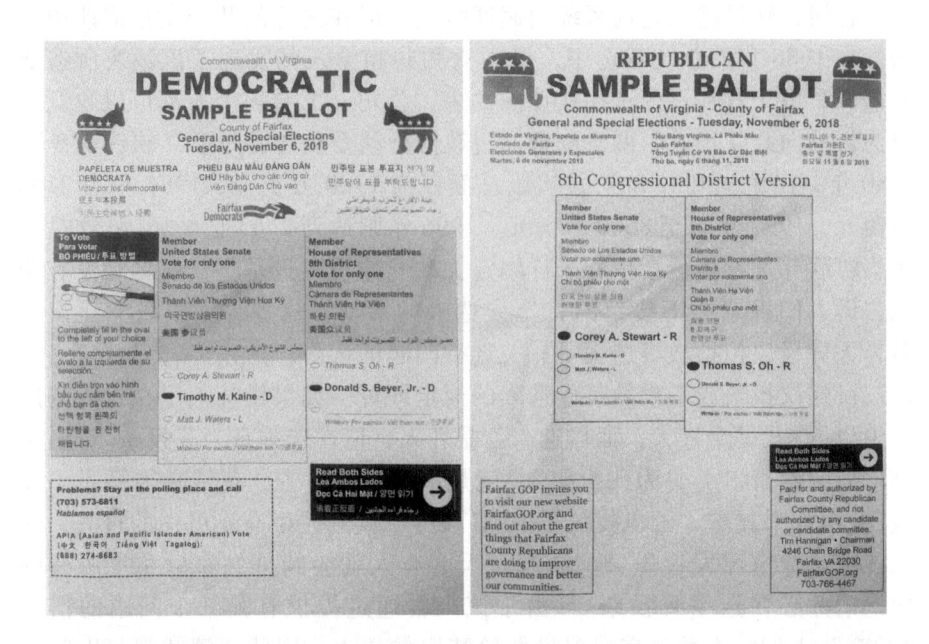

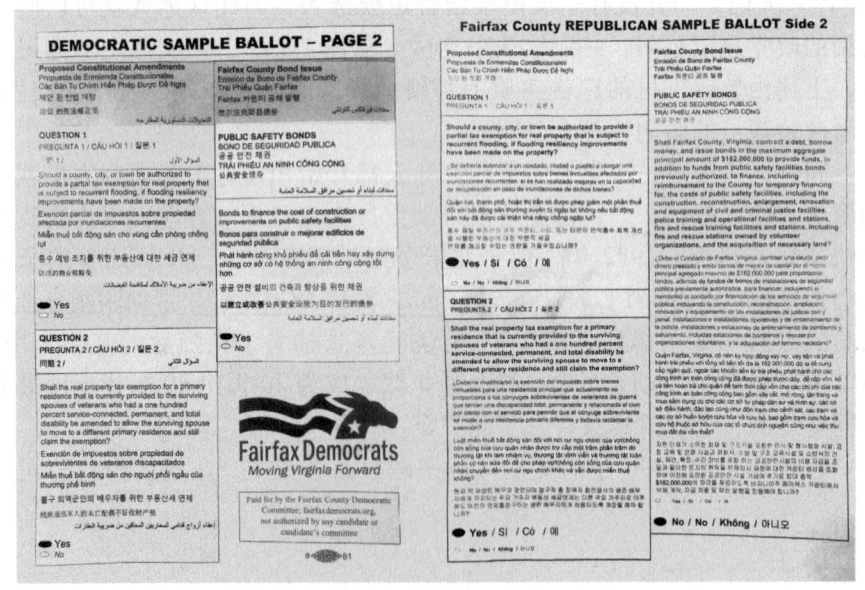

图 1-2　弗吉尼亚州费尔法克斯县 2018 年选举投票样本

资料来源：作者摄于麦克莱恩（McLean）市一投票站。

第一章　游说、竞选捐款与美国政治腐败：历史到现实

富会不公平地影响选举"①，裁定《密歇根州竞选财务法》禁止公司使用其自有资产作为独立支出支持或反对候选人参加选举，未违反宪法第一和第十四修正案（平等保护权），维持了对公司言论的限制。但密歇根州法律仍然允许公司从隔离基金②中支出此类费用，因而该案未能对巴克利案制造的竞选资金监管漏洞进行补救。

巴克利案使得公司和协会长期以来不得利用自身资产投入竞选支出的限制被打破，公司和组织实际被部分赋予了传统法意义上自然人才享有的人格权——言论自由。③法院认定打破这种捐款限制所带来利益集团影响公正竞选的腐败可能，不及第一修正案所保护的言论表达自由重要。自此，以言论自由为名，无限额的软钱闸门被打开，涌入政治选举活动施加腐败影响。

（五）短暂胜利：2002—2006年的阻击软钱年代

直至2002年，参议员约翰·麦凯恩三世和罗素·费因戈德推出《麦凯恩·费因戈德法》即《两党竞选改革法》，禁止为全国性政党和政治广告发行提供无限的软钱，竞选捐款与支出监管体系首次在联邦层面得到较为全面的改革，25年前巴克利案造成的监管漏洞方被堵塞。该法律的颁布标志着国会再次收紧政治支出限制并加强了披露监督，并将此前《联邦竞选法》禁止公司和团体组织使用其自有资产从事政治行为的范围从"明确宣传"扩展到"选举性传播"④，其主要目的是弥补之前允许候选人及其支持者使用"软钱"规避竞选支出限制的法律漏洞。由于软钱包括用于资助宣传特定候选人的发行广告资金，作为监管工作的重要部分，国会要求赞助特定候选人广告的组织披露捐款者的姓名及此类广告的明确支出，且任何"明知且故意"违反披露规定的人将面临最高5年监禁的刑事处罚。在2003年麦康奈尔诉联邦选举委员会一案中，最高法院再次维持了对《两党竞选改革法》披露要求的合宪性判断⑤，以此作为保证软钱及政治广

---

① Austin v. Michigan Chamber of Commerce, 494 U.S. 652 (1990).
② 隔离资金是指公司为特定目的而设立并保持独立于其他财务的资金。该基金常见于保险公司和投资管理领域，其设置旨在确保资金的安全，防止这部分资金被用于非指定用途。
③ 在其后的 First National Bank of Boston v. Bellotti（1978）中，肯尼迪大法官强调争议点并非公司是否像自然人一样拥有言论自由，而是"立法是否剥夺了第一修正案所保护的表达"。
④ Brian Duignan, "Citizens United v. Federal Election Commission", Britannica (Sep. 6, 2019), https://www.britannica.com/event/Citizens-United-v-Federal-Election-Commission.
⑤ McConnell v. FEC, 540 U.S. 93 (2003).

告限制规定得到实际执行的重要基础。

《两党竞选改革法》固然取得了规制软钱捐款的重要胜利，但仍为其后暗钱组织的爆发留下了漏洞。由于软钱漏洞被阻塞，巨额资金在税法中找到了新的突破口——"527组织"和"501组织"。"527组织"（527 organization或527 group）是根据美国税法第527条成立的、没有"明确主张"选举或击败候选人（或政党），而不受州或联邦竞选财务法律监管的组织。大公司和利益集团根据税法501（c）条成立的慈善机构、基金会、社会福利组织和行业协会则被称为"501组织"。两种组织都参与从事政治选举，并在选举中投入大量资金。"527组织"往往以其活动不包含以政治目的为由规避公开捐款者身份的义务，并常涉嫌与候选人及其政党非法协作，但由于联邦选举委员会的相关规定缺乏执行力，其逐渐成为暗钱输入"501组织"和干涉选举的重要上游渠道。尽管被禁止在初选和选举之前投放广告，以及为候选人提供直接宣传，但这些组织都得到了软钱禁令的豁免，完全不受捐款限制的约束，其背后的资金规模远超过软钱的顶峰时期，在《两党竞选改革法》生效短短数年后以意想不到的腐败力量侵蚀了美国政治竞选。

（六）监管持续松动：2006年至今在最高法院的接连挫败

2003年，《两党竞选改革法》在肯塔基州参议员米奇·麦康奈尔（Mitch McConnell）、加州民主党和全国步枪协会联合提起的诉讼中首次受到挑战，理由是该法律对于竞选捐款的规定过于广泛，并且限制了原告第一修正案的权利，法院判决支持该法律。但随后最高法院和上诉法院的一系列案件大大侵蚀了《两党竞选改革法》。2006年，最高法院在兰德尔诉索瑞尔案[①]中裁定，佛蒙特州对竞选捐款的严格上限规定因违反了第一修正案而无效。紧接着在2007年，最高法院在联邦选举委员会诉威斯康星州生命权案中推翻了麦康奈尔案的判决，称对非营利组织发行议题广告等竞选支出进行限制是违宪的。在2010年"联合公民案"前，共有24个州禁止公司支出来支持或反对选举候选人。但"联合公民案"最终推翻了奥斯汀与麦康奈尔两案的判决，废除了《蒂尔曼法》《塔夫脱—哈特利法》和《两党竞选改革法》等法律一个世纪以来对公司捐款的相关限制，赋予了公司和组织自然人格上的言论自由权，使其得以利用自有资产无限制地

---

① Randall v. Sorrel, 548 U.S. 230 (2006).

进行竞选通讯，发表政治观点。总之，"联合公民案"与2014年废除向政治行动委员会捐款总支出上限的麦卡琴胜诉案一起，在相当程度上破坏了近一个世纪以来竞选捐款规制体系所建立的有效性与完整性。

追溯近代美国竞选捐款制度的简短历史，不难发现围绕竞选捐款规制的争议已经持续多年。反对规制竞选捐款者引用宪法捍卫其立场，认为相关法律是违宪的。反对者提出，对竞选捐款或支出的法律限制甚至剥夺了《第一修正案》关于人民言论自由和向政府申诉的权利。他们认为选举对经费的高需求加上竞选财务法律对政党及候选人不现实的低捐款限制，才是导致大量金钱流向超级政治行动委员会和其他资金来源不透明团体的主要原因之一，因而反对竞选活动的公共补贴和对私人资金的限制，认为限制个人对政治竞选活动的捐款数额本质上是对其可能从事政治活动的限制：限制候选人支出不仅是对其本人政治言论的侵蚀，还影响了因此受到限制的捐款者政治言论自由权的行使。无论言论自由还是结社权，它们都是用来保护政治活动参与的，而对竞选支出和捐款的限制人为设定了公众能够参与政治活动的上限。① 联邦最高法院在1961年的一项判决常被引用来支持这一立场，布莱克大法官（Hugo Black）在此案中的多数意见中表达了对竞选财务规制法律的反对。布莱克法官说：人们希望法律行为对自己有利而对竞争者不利，这既不罕见也不违法。……剥夺人们为与其有经济利益关联的事务担任公职的资格，将使政府失去宝贵的信息来源……此时人民的请愿权就被剥夺了。② 最近的例子是，2010年的"联合公民案"中联邦最高法院对监管特殊利益集团竞选资金的自由主义态度，似乎也表明了其在政府预防竞选腐败与言论自由两种利益之间的取舍。该案生效至今已逾十年，却毫无被推翻的迹象，也许至少在未来十年内，对竞选捐款的松绑和竞选财务法律规制有效性的逐渐瓦解将成为一种趋势。

然而，如果仅据此将腐败行为升格为受到宪法保护的地位，似乎也较为牵强，目前仍有充分的理由认为这并非最高法院在此案或任何其他案件中的立场。主张竞选财务法规构成对《第一修正案》权利否定的观点忽视了过去数十年的判例和法律：最高法院选择不对1907年1月颁布

---

① Ralph K. Winter, *Money, Politics, and the First Amendment*, Washington, D.C.: American Enterprise Institute for Public Policy Research, 1971, p.60.
② Eastern Railroads Presidents Conference v. Noeer Motor Freight Co., 365 US 126 (1961).

的公司捐款禁令进行宪法释义；1947年6月通过的禁止工会捐款的法律；1940年7月批准（并于1970年修改）了个人捐款限制；1971年通过的对候选人及其候选人家属捐款的限制。[1] 巴克利案也重申了对候选人捐款限额的合宪性，因为这对于处理"允许无限制捐款制度中固有的现实或腐败现象是必要的"。[2] 一系列的判例间接表明了，如果判定禁止或规范私人竞选捐款的法律违宪，甚至将私人竞选捐款提高到宪法秩序的特权地位，将只会帮助强大的利益集团维持甚至提升其特权地位。从宪法价值体系考虑，大规模或无限量的竞选捐款对选举结果不成比例的影响否定了法律的平等保护，这可能使本身就具有缺陷的政治制度永久地偏向于既定利益，而这些利益反过来还会进一步巩固私人资金在美国政府中的腐败影响。因此，大法官们不可能无视公民提高选举平等影响力的宪法要求，以言论自由受到侵犯而将某一规制竞选捐款的法律整体判定违宪。1975年，上诉法院以遏制"金钱对政治的腐蚀影响"的必要性为由，维持了1974年《联邦选举改革法》的主要规定。法官们对引述第一修正案反对该法主张的答复是，在权衡言论自由和公平选举的两个价值时，与竞选活动无关的支出是受到高度保护的言论形式，而竞选活动的捐款是一种间接的言论形式，并可以构成腐败或腐败的"外观"，因此受到的宪法保护较少。[3] 而且选举过程中防止滥用权力和重建公众信心的利益比"对第一修正案权利的附随限制"更重要，[4] 这些限制构成了对侵犯政治结社自由的充分抗辩，因而在更广泛的意义上，对确保联邦选举的正当性是必要的。总之，围绕法律的平等保护主张完全可以对抗可能受到限制的言论自由。无论如何，围绕竞选捐款法律规制的争论预示着，在未来短期内，"政府对经济不平等的接受与其对政治平等的承诺之间的冲突"[5] 将一直存在于美国的政治选举中，这也是超越现行竞选捐款乃至整个竞选财务制度的更大范畴的问题。

---

[1] Larry L. Berg, Harlin Hahn & John R. Schmidhauser, *Corruption in the American Political System*, Morristown, NJ: General Learning Press, 1976, pp. 184–185.
[2] Buckley v. Valeo, 424 U.S. 1 (1976).
[3] Elizabeth Drew, *The Corruption of American Politics: What Went Wrong and Why*, Secaucus, NJ: Carol Publishing Group, 1999, p. 50.
[4] Shelton v. Tucker, 364 U.S. 479 (1960).
[5] Gunnar Myrdal, *An American Dilemma: The Negro Problem and Modern Democracy*, New York: Harper & Brothers Publishers, 1944.

第三节 游说与竞选捐款语境下的政治腐败

一 政治腐败：从贿赂法到竞选财务法的释义

在政治学中，恐怕没有比"腐败"一词出现频率更高的词汇了。[①] 任何有关腐败的研究都应对该主题的性质和范围有一个明确的概念。尽管腐败真实普遍地存在着，但与对民主确切属性的理解一样，对腐败这一社会现象的定义至今未能达成共识。从确定腐败行为与非腐败行为之间的界限意义上讲，这种概念应该是精确的，但对政治腐败这一社会现象的论述确实需要在特定语境下才能带来一些共同的理解，方才具有实践指导意义。游说与竞选捐款便为理解政治腐败提供了一个经典场景。因为游说、竞选捐款与政治腐败的交织问题是民主制度设计的基本问题。作为民主威胁的腐败与民主的实现之间，具有天然的矛盾纠缠。受到第一修正案的保护，游说和竞选捐款也为政治腐败的滋生提供了空间。腐败虽然在一定程度上可以作为政治和社会的融合手段或连接机制，同时也是重新分配社会财富的一种方式，但美国革命的理论基础决定了腐败的政府将不具备统治的合法性。而选举中的腐败则不仅扰乱政府统治，也是对公民身份的威胁。对游说和竞选捐款中发生的政治腐败进行定义，需要从其最狭窄的刑事法概念出发，发散至政治学概念甚至广义的道德观念，再结合现行的竞选财务法规确定其涵盖的范围。

（一）政治腐败的狭义理解：贿赂

为官员提供物质利益以影响其职务行为是不正当的，广泛存在的关于贿赂和非法酬谢的刑事禁令就反映了这种观念。刑法的重点聚焦在私人利益与特定官方行为紧密勾连在一起的情况。鉴于刑法谦抑的本质，对这种特定行为的范围设定必然十分狭窄。《联邦贿赂法》规定："联邦官员不得'腐败地'接受或索取，任何人不得腐败地提供或给予任何有价值的东西

[①] Robert C. Brooks, "The Nature of Political Corruption", *Political Science Quarterly*, Vol. 24, No. 1, 1909, pp. 1-22.

'以换取……'任何官方行为的影响。"① 交易的腐败本质是认定腐败意图存在的一部分，也是"贿赂"的特征。"这种犯罪元素——腐败的协议或交易——被描述为要求在交易中涉及一些明示或暗示的利益交换条件，即用某物交换另一物。"② 在政治腐败的情况下，贿赂可能涉及支付给政府官员以换取其使用官方权力的款项。联邦最高法院曾在1991年的麦考密克诉合众国案中裁定③，只有在"付款是为了换取官员对其执行或不执行官方行为的明确承诺而支付的款项"时，才能将竞选捐款视为贿赂。

基于类似的理由，莱西格认为，从政府官员或公共机构的范畴看，政治腐败的一般含义是非常清楚的——腐败意味着贿赂，以贿赂换取政府的特别恩惠或特权，即利益的等价交换。④ 从这种最狭隘的政治腐败定义角度来看，2006年的杰克·阿布拉莫夫（Jack Abramoff）案展示了一个围绕游说和竞选捐款与国会议员的腐败场景，并指出相关因素如何助长了制度化的腐败。阿布拉莫夫和他的合伙人都曾是活跃的共和党人，在华盛顿颇具影响力，可以轻易打入白宫和国会大楼的领导层。他们打包大型体育赛事的包厢门票，陪同有影响力的官员打高尔夫并支付全部费用，为豪华晚宴埋单。由于内政部对印第安部落事务具有联邦监管权力，2000—2003年，六个印第安部落向阿布拉莫夫支付了超过8000万美元的游说费用，⑤由阿布拉莫夫代表部落客户向前布什政府内政部副部长格里尔斯（J. Steven Griles）的女友领导的"共和党环境倡导委员会"（Council of Republicans for Environmental Advocacy）组织捐款50万美元，并多次要求格里尔斯以内政部名义对国会审议的赌博立法进行干预。⑥ 另据《华盛顿邮报》

---

① 18 U.S.C. § 201.
② Jack Maskell, *Lobbying Congress: An Overview of Legal Provisions and Congressional Ethics Rules*, CRS Report for Congress, Washington D.C.: Library of Congress, 2007, p.31.
③ McCormick v. United States, 500 U.S.257 (1991), p.273.
④ Lawrence Lessig, *Republic, Lost: How Money Corrupts Congress-and a Plan to Stop It*, New York: Hatchette, 2011; Martin Gilens, *Affluence and Influence: Economic Inequality and Political Power in America*, Princeton, NJ: Princeton University Press, 2011, p.226.
⑤ Susan Schmidt & James V. Grimaldi, "The Fast Rise and Steep Fall of Jack Abramoff", *The Washington Post*, Dec.29, 2005, p.A01.
⑥ Department of Justice, "Italia Federici Sentenced for Evading Taxes and Obstructing Senate Investigation into Abramoff Corruption Scandal", DOJ (Dec.14, 2007), https://www.justice.gov/archive/opa/pr/2007/December/07_crm_1005.html.

报道，2005年，阿布拉莫夫的游说公司买下了时任众议院行政委员会主席的前俄亥俄州共和党议员鲍勃·内伊（Bob Ney）的办公室，其所支付的对价则是海外旅游、使用华盛顿地区的运动场地、免费用餐、演唱会门票以及伦敦赌场中价值数千美元的赌博筹码。内伊在2002年批准了一家以色列电信公司为众议院安装天线的许可证，该公司后来向阿布拉莫夫支付了28万美元的游说费用，并向其名下的"501"慈善组织"首都体育基金"（Capital Athletic Foundation）捐赠了5万美元。[1] 通过建立运营"首都体育基金"等多个非营利组织、游说公司以及政治智囊团，阿布拉莫夫向与该组织无关的接收者输送了数百万美元捐款或贿赂。2006年1月，阿布拉莫夫对共谋、欺诈和逃税行为认罪，与其有牵涉的其他21名白宫、国会官员、国会议员助手和游说者也被定罪。[2] 格里尔斯承认曾在接受参议院针对其与阿布拉莫夫关系的调查期间撒谎，因伪证罪于2007年被判处10个月监禁和3万美元罚金；[3] 鲍勃·内伊则因接受数万美元的非法礼物、利用其立法影响力来帮助其竞选捐款者而被判入狱30个月，并处以6万美元罚金。[4] 另一个例子是国会议员兰迪·坎宁安（Randy Cunningham），其因收取国防承包商ADCS 240万美元以换取国防部合同而被判处八年零四个月监禁，随该案曝光的还有一张坎宁安为自己影响力标价的"菜单"（见图1-3），菜单标明每5万美元能得到何种服务，其将联邦资金集中到特定项目上，把专项拨款直接拨给自己选择的项目，以换取说客的酬劳。[5] 众议员威廉·杰斐逊（William Jefferson），2000—2005年从涉及石油、制糖、通信和其他行业的公司那里共计索取40万美元的贿赂，作为回报，利用自己在众议院筹款委员会（Ways and Means Committee）的职位便利，

---

[1] James V. Grimaldi & Susan Schmidt, "Lawmaker's Abramoff Ties Investigated", *The Washington Post*, Oct. 18, 2005, p. A01.

[2] Dan Froomkin, "Jack Abramoff, In New Book, Decries Endemic Corruption in Washington", *The Huffington Post*, Oct. 28, 2011.

[3] Department of Justice, "Former Interior Deputy Secretary Steven Griles Sentenced to 10 Months in Prison for Obstructing U. S. Senate Investigation into Abramoff Corruption Scandal", DOJ (Jun. 26, 2007), https://www.justice.gov/archive/opa/pr/2007/June/07_crm_455.html.

[4] Philip Shenon, "Ney Is Sentenced to 30 Months in Prison", *The New York Times*, Jan. 19, 2007.

[5] Randal C. Archibold, "Ex-Congressman Gets 8-Year Term in Bribery Case", *The New York Times*, Mar. 4, 2006.

游说、竞选捐款与美国政治腐败

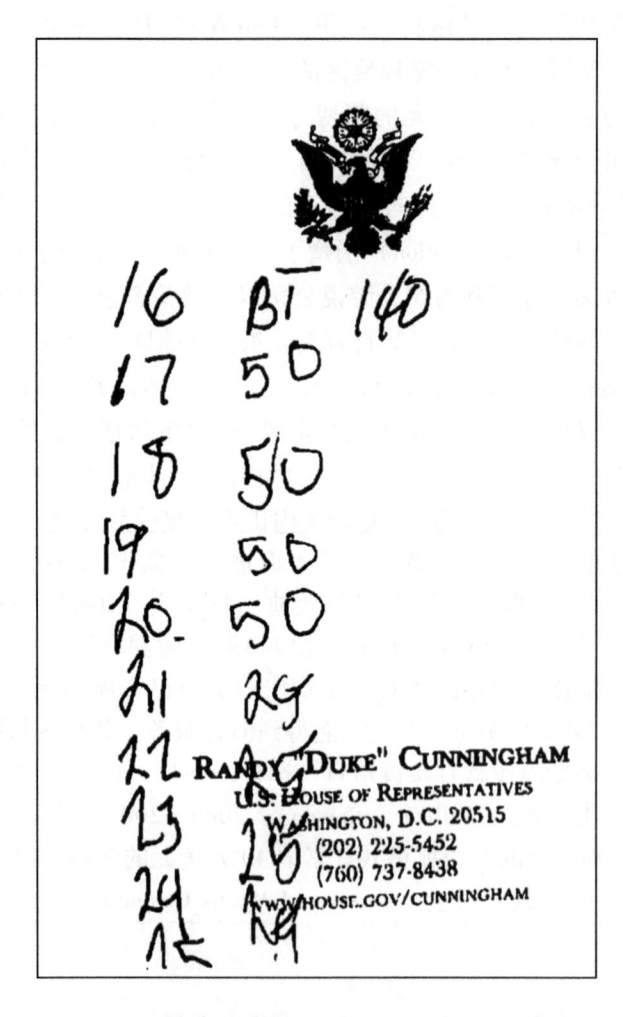

图 1-3　前国会议员兰迪·坎宁安名片上的"菜单"

注：这份菜单是对保证获得政府合同的报价。左列为标的额，以百万美元为单位，右列为收费，以千美元为单位）。如承包商要想获得一份价值 1600 万美元的合同，收费为一艘价值 14 万美元的游艇（BT）。合同标的额每增加 100 万美元，贿赂金额就会增加 5 万美元。一旦合同标的额超过 2000 万，每增加 100 万仅加收 2.5 万美元。

资料来源：Wekipedia, "Duke Cunnningham", https：//en.wikipedia.org/wiki/Duke_Cunningham.

推动这些公司的经营项目。① 杰斐逊因而成为美国国会历史上第一位被联邦调查局搜查办公室的议员，并被判处国会议员史上最长的13年监禁刑罚。2011年，伊利诺伊州民主党前州长罗德·布拉戈耶维奇因试图"出售"奥巴马原来在参议院的席位而入狱。②

（二）竞选财务法视角下政治腐败释义的扩张和缩限：从腐败的外观到等价交换

当将游说与竞选捐款场景中的政治腐败置于竞选财务法律中加以识别时，情况远比上述阿布拉莫夫案所代表的刑事贿赂现象复杂。私人在游说与竞选捐款中对政府的不当影响场景往往十分模糊，缺乏必要且明确的构成要素，因而多数超出了刑事腐败概念能够衡量并明确覆盖的范围。当私人利益（例如免费用餐、娱乐、旅行或盈利可能性巨大的投资机会）与特定的官方行为无关，而仅旨在促进机会的获取或良好关系的建立时，就可能发生游说者及其代表的利益不当影响决策者的情形。即使与特定的职务行为无关，这些好处仍可以使政府决策者从公共利益中分散注意力，并形成公共政策的倾斜，从而可能构成一种不正当影响的腐败形式。③ 显然，对于政治腐败概念的争论就在上述两者之间来回摇摆。政治腐败到底是什么？是贿赂式的等价交换，还是对政府官方行为的不当影响？施特劳斯将竞选活动中的腐败理解为"竞选捐款对官员的隐性或显性交换"④，但类似这样的定义并不能解决实践问题。因为从竞选实践来看，需要对腐败下定义从而回答竞选捐款等操作是否至少具有腐败的外观的问题。这种对政治腐败认识的摇摆冲突最终体现在联邦最高法院对具体案例的处理变化上。

1. 政治腐败的扩张释义时期：腐败的外观与不当影响

早自巴克利诉瓦莱奥案起，拥有对竞选财务法律释义权的司法机构就一直在同腐败和腐败的外观概念与后果作斗争。⑤ 联邦最高法院对腐败的

---

① David Stout, "Ex-Louisiana Congressman Sentenced to 13 Years", *The New York Times*, Nov. 13, 2009.
② Kim Bellware, "Rod Blagojevich is Out of Prison Thanks to a Kind of Mercy He Rarely Showed as Governor", *The Washington Post*, Feb. 20, 2020.
③ Richard Briffault, "The Anxiety of Influence: The Evolving Regulation of Lobbying", *Election Law Journal*, Vol. 13, No. 1, 2014, pp. 160 – 193.
④ David A. Strauss, "Corruption, Equality, and Campaign Finance Reform", *Columbia Law Review*, No. 94, 1994, pp. 1369 – 1389.
⑤ Richard Briffault, "Corporations, Corruption, and Complexity: Campaign Finance after Citizens United", *Cornell Journal of Law and Public Policy*, Vol. 20, No. 3, 2011, pp. 643 – 671.

定义由宽到窄。1976年巴克利诉瓦莱奥案裁定，有且仅有腐败及其外观可以证明限制竞选资金是合理的①："在一定程度上，为确保现任和潜在任职者的政治条件交换而做出的巨额捐款，将损害我们民主代议制度的完整性"②"公众意识到对巨额竞选捐款存在所构成的腐败外观几乎与实际的等价交换一样危险"③。对于为何不仅仅惩罚那些以贿赂形式提供和接受捐款的行为，法庭指出，等价交换表示捐款人以向候选人捐款的意向为条件，换取该候选人承诺当选后利用其公职使捐款人受益的承诺，或者类似贿赂之类的事情。尽管贿赂已经是非法的，但其仅仅是"有钱人影响政府行动的最公然和具体的尝试"④，并不能涵盖所有的竞选捐款腐败行为。相对的，"利用金钱影响政府行为"是一个比贿赂更宽泛的概念，并且可以支持政府对竞选资金施加更多管制。此后，腐败的概念一直游离于贿赂和对政府行为的广泛影响之间。

在9年后的联邦选举委员会诉国家保守党政治权利委员会案中，法院强调，腐败的狭义含义类似于贿赂式交易，"腐败的标志是财务上的等价交换，即以金钱争取政治利益"⑤。在审理1990年奥斯汀诉密歇根商务委员会案时，联邦最高法院更是采用了一种非常宽泛的理论解释腐败，维持了密歇根州对公司独立支出发布支持或反对州政府候选人广告的花费上限。瑟古德·马歇尔（Thurgood Marshall）大法官将腐败的范围扩大到"以公司形式积累起来的巨大财富聚集的腐蚀和扭曲效应，其与公众对公司政治思想的支持几乎或根本没有相关性"⑥。由此逻辑推知，当公司或企业使用其巨大的财富集合试图让人们偏离自身判断的基线时，就会出现腐败。自然地，该观点也并不支持公司在宪法上的言论自由权⑦。此后，法院进一步采用了更为宽泛的腐败概念。2000年的杰瑞米亚·尼克松诉"缩减密苏里政府"政治行动委员会案⑧判决意见认为，

---

① Buckley v. Valeo, 424 U.S.1 (1976), at 67.
② Buckley v. Valeo, 424 U.S.1 (1976), at 26 – 27.
③ Buckley v. Valeo, 424 U.S.1 (1976), at 27.
④ Buckley v. Valeo, 424 U.S.1 (1976), at 28.
⑤ FEC v. National Conservative PAC, 470 U.S.480 (1985).
⑥ Austin v. Michigan Chamber of Commerce, 494 U.S.652 (1990).
⑦ 马歇尔并非认为所有的公司都应该受到言论限制。在马歇尔的定义中，一旦公司获得了政府的特别许可，就可以"腐败"，如纽约时报、华尔街日报、美国全国广播公司（NBC）、美国广播公司（ABC）以及其他新闻公司。
⑧ Nixon v. Shrink Missouri Government PAC, 528 U.S.377 (2000).

腐败问题不限于贿赂公职人员，其广泛威胁还扩展到迫使政客按照大捐款者的意愿行事。

2003年麦康奈尔诉联邦选举委员会案[①]虽然聚焦于国会对软钱捐款的限制规定，但却使关于腐败及其外观概念的矛盾问题达到了顶峰。软钱的存在让富人、公司和工会的捐款在实际上大大超过了通常适用于个人捐款的金额限制，违反了当时仍然有效的公司和工会向联邦捐款的禁令。而软钱逃避联邦捐款限制的概念基础是，捐款不是流向特定候选人或直接支持特定候选人的政党，而是用于资助政党的一般活动或支付支持该党所有候选人的政党活动，例如对选民登记和投票的推动宣传、政党广告或问题倡导[②]。软钱的支持者认为，在捐款者与特定候选人之间没有直接关系的情况下，软钱并没有引发腐败问题，因而也不应受到限制。但麦康奈尔案的判决结论是，即便联邦职位的竞选连任者和政党领导人无法在自身的竞选中使用这些进入政党账户的捐款，仍有充分的证据表明他们狂热地追求软钱。同样，富裕的个人、公司和工会为确保对联邦官员的影响力捐献软钱，无论后者是否采取可识别的立法或投票行为。对此，审理麦康奈尔案的法官坚信，对于腐败的构成，既没有必要在捐款人与候选人之间建立明确的关系，也无须在捐款与接受者的特定立法或其他政府目标之间建立联系。因而最终法院采用了更为广泛的解释，认为国会可以合理地得出以下结论：向政党委员会捐款能够使捐款人获得政府官员的优惠待遇，并广泛地影响政府决策，这就可能构成"腐败"，因而限制竞选捐款是有正当理由的。

2. 政治腐败的缩限释义转向：等价交换

联邦最高法院对于腐败的宽泛解释在2010年联合公民诉联邦选举委员会案[③]发生了转向。安东尼·肯尼迪大法官在2010年该案判决中指出，腐败只能局限于公职人员同意明确履行特定行为或条件交换。判决多数意见所提到的"条件交换"，即"quid pro quo"一词出自拉丁文，翻译成英文是"this for that"，即"以此换彼"，最早作为合同法上的传统术语，用来描述合同当事人之间相对平等的交换。因此，条件交换在历史上并非一开始就作为腐败的法律术语出现。1976年以前所有联邦与州的贿赂和勒索

---

① McConnell v. FEC, 540 U.S. 93（2003）.
② 详见第七章第一节第四部分。
③ Citizens United v. FEC, 558 U.S. 08-205（2010）.

案件中,"条件交换"出现的次数加起来总共不到100次。① 直到法院判决巴克利诉瓦莱奥案取消对竞选支出的限制时,才在判决中使用了"条件交换"短语。莱西格也指出,在制宪会议及草案辩论期间,腐败问题曾被提出数百次,但只有少数几次即约1%的情况下腐败被等同为条件交换,此种腐败出现的频率与现今相同,并不频繁。② 瓦利斯与提绍特也共同强调,制宪者们致力于预防和消除的是系统性的腐败,而并非条件交换的贿赂腐败。③

然而"联合公民案"的多数意见法官坚持使用条件交换来缩小腐败的定义。他们将制宪者们的假设理解为,公共利益可以通过公众的个人道德和精确的系统性激励来构建,在该体制下,广义上的政治腐败问题微不足道,是可以用系统性的法律约束的。这种对市民政治自律的崇高信心源于保守派大法官对芝加哥法律经济学派的信仰,这种信仰最终通过"联合公民案"等判决被制度化,并得以在联邦制社会中实践。基于人性自私和效率优先的假设模型,这种霍布斯式的经济政治观是抽象的,而非植根于美国200多年来的立法活动、判例与普遍政治经验,这也是"联合公民案"违背市民对腐败朴素认知的原因。

无论如何,最高法院对政治腐败的狭义解释转变所产生的后果是,国会制定的竞选财务法律现在只能规制一种该种特定类型的腐败,对腐败更小的限制也意味着更大的操作空间,无形间增强了游说利益集团和竞选捐款者操控法律与政策的能量。在"联合公民案"时代,政府无权干涉公司的政治广告,对竞选捐款的限制也并不能对竞选支出构成显著影响,以利益交换为限制的腐败行为成为竞选支出的唯一底线。在该底线之上,游说、竞选捐款与立法机构三者构成的惯常场景就是,说客作为中间关系的代理人与国会议员共同推动了一种送礼经济。这种经济中没有非法的礼物,但每一方都为另一方的工作提供补贴,游说者通过向议员保证筹集到竞选资金,议员则通过为游说者的客户获得重大利益来保证自身利益。这种相互补贴可以在没有任何

---

① Stephen K. Medvic, "The U. S. Political System is Flawed But not Corrupt", *The Washington Post*, May 5, 2017.
② 参见 Lawrence Lessig, "McCutcheon v. FEC: Supreme Court Amicus Brief of Professor Lessig in Support of the FEC", Campaign Legal Center (2014), p. 12, https://campaignlegal.org/document/mccutcheon-v-fec-supreme-court-amicus-brief-professor-lessig-support-fec.
③ John J. Wallis, "The Concept of Systematic Corruption in American History", in E. Glaeser & C. Goldin, eds., *Corruption and Reform*, Chicago: University of Chicago Press, 2006, p. 37.

人直接进行任何交换的情况下发生,只要不直接交换礼物,联合公民时代的竞选财务法律系统和制度就允许这些礼物合法地存在。最轻描淡写的表达是,尽管依照该系统行事的人没有违反法律,但这种礼物交易和上述阿布拉莫夫等人的贿赂腐败行为,在普通人看来显然没有多大区别。

不过,如果将游说和竞选捐款转化为政治权力的唯一方法简单认定为刑事贿赂,或者将政治腐败局限于受贿赂法管制的腐败,那么就不会有如此之多围绕本文主题的论证和著述。因此在司法判例与学理领域,这两种腐败还是被加以区分。肯尼迪大法官在"联合公民案"中也引述自己早先的观点,对二者做出了模糊的分割:"在传统的(贿赂)腐败之外,还有腐败可能与金钱在我们政治体系中的特殊影响有关。民选代表的性质是支持某些政策,必然的结论是其支持同样肯定这些政策的选民和捐款者。"[1]从过往判例来看,尽管以往条件互换的腐败仍然普遍存在,但新的问题已不在于涉及条件交换的游说、竞选捐款与腐败的界限日益模糊,而是它们在法律上的距离越来越相互排斥。联邦最高法院在解决重大政治冲突,尤其是对腐败的定义方面往往发挥着巨大作用。但自20世纪70年代保守派法官掌管该最高司法权力机构以来,其许多决定都有助于扩大游说制度的不民主因素,"联合公民案"就是力证。"联合公民案"的意义不仅仅在于对于公司人格权的赋予和对腐败的最狭义解释,还在于保守派法官开启了对腐败狭义概念广泛适用,因而深刻影响竞选财务法律的时代。

当然,"联合公民案"对政治腐败的认识转向也不能被片面理解为大公司和特殊利益的胜利,它还反映了对政府权力的天然不信任。这种不信任基于的假设是:在革除"腐败"的名义下,政府被赋予了可怕的广泛权力,政府有权决定谁可以说话,说话的声音大小以及可以说的内容,以防止民众"误信"。但这种受到"规范"的民主更可能是不完整的、被破坏了的民主,因为真实的民主往往是混乱的。竞选捐款的合法性基础在于,公民会基于理性判断选择候选人。但竞选捐款可以有多个来源并通过各种渠道就位,而其中诸多渠道都可能被用来故意掩饰私人或利益团体的联系。如果法律禁止公司直接捐款,那么他们的员工就会提供个人捐款。公民为他们所支持政策的候选人捐助资金,在无法确定捐款者真实动机的情况下,很难确定腐败是否存在。

---

[1] Citizens United v. FEC, 130 S. Ct. 676, 910 (2010).

游说、竞选捐款与美国政治腐败

更棘手的是,无论是个人、公司还是其他利益团体,通过游说管道所捐献的资金在多大程度上影响民选官员的决策,都无疑是一个充满争议的问题。游说活动通过将私人关系与个人影响力标价出售,在利益集体与政府官员之间搭建桥梁,以肯定后者某种过去的公务行为或换取后者对未来行为的隐含承诺,虽然其中的竞选捐款不可能不涉及利益交换,但这些行为通常也不属于联邦最高法院所定义的、以"条件交换"(quid pro quo exchanges)为核心的腐败。①

因此政治游说与捐款中的腐败完全可能游离于竞选财务法律之外,以多种形式出现,甚至在缺乏利益交换前提的情况下,以牺牲公共利益为最终代价,使少数人、特定团体甚至多数人获利。此时,表面不存在利益交换的政府赞助、立法减税或者疏于法律监管执行等的作为或不作为,都可能构成腐败。只是现实法律中为其合法性划分了较为清晰且宽容的界限,这种界限是非道德的,意味着其接受竞选捐款与做出对捐款者有利的立法决策合法性之间存在政治腐败的现实可能性,但又为现有法律体制所容忍:即遵守游戏规则(法律)的腐败不是犯罪,而仅受到行业委员会、联邦选举委员会的规制以及国会、公众和媒体道德审查的监督。显然,竞选捐款与游说一样,作为受宪法保护的言论自由权利,带来的腐败影响也在后联合公民时代,成为第一修正案公民权利必须容忍的副作用。

总之,在政治腐败的广义语境下,刑事司法体系中的腐败犯罪也仅仅是本文所讨论的众多政治腐败现象之一,本书的主要研究对象在于游说活动与竞选捐款对美国政府的腐败影响,这类腐败现象只有少数是直接违法的,多数则为合法或处于法律监控执行不力的灰色地带。这也是公众对美国的腐败现象虽有所认知,却鲜少听闻官员因涉嫌重大贪污腐败犯罪而被起诉的原因之一。但这并不能抹杀美国政治腐败的普遍性,上述因贿赂国会议员被判入狱的前游说者阿布拉莫夫曾说:"除了所犯下的违法行为,我参与的是合法的贿赂制度,所有的一切都是贿赂,所有的一切。"② 这种说法并非毫无依据。2013年12月,莫兰德反腐败调查委员会在被纽约州长科莫关闭前,发布了一份长达98页的报告,描述

---

① 参见 Citizens United v. FEC, 558 U.S. 310 (2010).
② Lawrence Lessig, *Republic, Lost: How Money Corrupts Congress-and a Plan to Stop It*, New York: Hatchette, 2011; Martin Gilens, *Affluence and Influence: Economic Inequality and Political Power in America*, Princeton, NJ: Princeton University Press, 2011, p.8.

了该州的"公共腐败流行病"。报告指出:"自1999年以来,平均每11名议员中就有一个在道德或刑事违法行为的阴影下离职","合法才是真正的丑闻"①。系统性的政治腐败正以一种早已有之却又前所未有的趋势侵蚀着民主,法律意义上的腐败越来越少,但现实中政治学意义上的行贿或腐败却越发频繁地发生。现代的立法者与数百年前的制宪者所面临的挑战并没有不同:不是如何消除政府内部的永久性问题——贿赂或直接交换的交易,而是建立一个每个部门都足够独立,不受系统性腐败侵害的政府。

换言之,当今美国社会的政治事实是,尽管竞选捐款中真正涉及的腐败问题并不是传统的贿赂腐败问题,②但狭义的"条件交换"却取代了更广泛的传统腐败观念,正式成为法律上的定义。从判例法中获得了巨大权力的游说者,被允许堂而皇之地运用竞选捐款和与立法者之间的旋转门来获取并施加影响力。从技术上来说,只要游说者在与议员对话时没有直接说出"交易"的相关话语,前者对后者的竞选资金支持就不能被解释为腐败。此外,由于腐败交易的对价大小往往取决于政治家的议价能力,无论是行业规则还是以刑事贿赂法为最后底线的立法规范都难以对其进行精确衡量。联邦最高法院对竞选财务中腐败定义解释的限制倾向,在重塑美国的法律和政策的同时,也将导致公民失去捍卫民主文化的重要法律工具。

二 政治腐败下的不平等政治参与和民主代议制迷思

(一)不平等政治参与:少数人主导的竞选捐款

长期以来,竞选捐款都被视为最不平等的政治参与形式。③ 美国的主要产业惯于利用政治选举体系这一关键弱点来削弱甚至规避外来竞争。从20世纪80年代开始,美国制药、军火、私人监狱公司等各大行业高管争相聘请前政府官员作为公司董事会成员或说客以增加影响力,通过政治行

---

① Jill Lepore, "The Crooked and the Dead: Does the Constitution Protect Corruption?" *The New Yorker*, Aug. 18, 2014.
② David A. Strauss, "Corruption, Equality, and Campaign Finance Reform", *Columbia Law Review*, No. 94, 1994, pp. 1369 – 1389.
③ Kay L. Schlozman, Sidney Verba & Henry E. Brady, *The Unheavenly Chorus: Unequal Political Voice and the Broken Promise of American Democracy*, Princeton: Princeton University Press, 2012.

动委员会向选举注入大量竞选捐款，并聘请专家学者在反托拉斯案件中作证，最终通过彼此合并，完成了削弱政府反托拉斯法的执行力、将生产转移到海外、削减员工的工资福利、获得对环境法规的豁免、税收减免、宽松的会计准则以及要求国会限制外国竞争影响等一系列举措，甚至从实际上将不法操作可能带来的刑事起诉风险降到了最低程度。与此同时，党派关系分化也在这一时期更加普遍，变得尤为妥协和教条主义。[1] 针对20世纪70年代以来软钱支出的爆炸式增长，20世纪90年代的国会做出了诸多修改《联邦竞选法》的尝试，在此期间，参议院的竞选财务改革议程经历了29次听证会、522位证人出席、17次冗长辩论和113次投票，但所有尝试均以国会无法达成多数意见而失败告终。[2] 直至2002年通过的《两党竞选改革法》终于禁止为全国政党提供无限的软钱，大批暗钱随即流向"527组织"。2004年选举中，保险巨头克里蒙·斯通与通用汽车继承人斯图尔特·摩特向527组织投入了近1.5亿美元资金[3]，大肆攻击候选人，试图影响选举结果。在外围资金的压力下，竞选支出也随着竞选捐款水涨船高（见图1-4）。1974年，所有参议院与众议院候选人的竞选总支出分别为2840万和4400万美元，而2010年参众两院竞选支出则分别激增至5.68亿与9.29亿美元，是同年英国议会选举支出的80倍；[4] 十年后的2020年，参众两院竞选总支出已达99亿美元。[5] 2014年麦卡琴诉联邦选举委员会案取消了向政治行动委员会捐款的总支出上限。由于受资助者接受捐款的政治行动委员会数量没有限制，竞选捐款数额进一步抬升一个层级。最明显的资金变化体现在总统大选中，在2012总统选举年里，包括政治行动委员会和所谓超级政治行动委员会在内的联邦、州和地方竞选活

---

[1] Barry Hessenius, *Hardball Lobbying for Nonprofits: Real Advocacy for Nonprofits in the New Century*, New York: Palgrave Macmillan, 2007, pp. 22, 41.

[2] Dennis W. Johnson, *Democracy for Hire: A History of American Political Consulting*, New York: Oxford University Press, 2017, p. 133.

[3] Open Secrets, "'527s' Advocacy Group Spending", Center for Responsive Politics (n. d.), http://www.OpenSecrets.org/527s.

[4] Lisa Rosenberg, "U. S. Political Finance: Americans spend more on elections, but they lead from behind", Sunlight Foundation (Nov. 10, 2014), https://sunlightfoundation.com/2014/11/10/u-s-political-finance-americans-spend-more-on-elections-but-they-lead-from-behind/.

[5] Open Secrets, "Cost of Election", Open Secrets (n. d.), https://www.opensecrets.org/elections-overview/cost-of-election.

动的广告总支出已超过50亿美元，①由于金融服务和其他大型行业的结构变得越来越集中，单个广告的支出也水涨船高，加之广泛的游说行为制造了许多难以受到挑战的"安全席位"，②选区有了更为明显的党派分化，本应由选民投票决定的结果实质上变成了党派间和候选人间竞选支出的博弈。公民联合案判决后的十年中，不仅每个选举周期的选举支出显著上升，而且透明度大大降低，富裕的大捐款者的政治影响力不断提高。③ 2020年的国会选举结果显示，高达88%的席位是由支出最多的候选人赢得的。④因而无论是连任者还是挑战者都不得不筹集大笔经费应对竞争升级，反过来又进一步刺激了竞选捐款和外围支出。在这种压力下，候选人和政党拒绝捐款者的可能性越来越低，此即验证了莱西格所说的"依赖腐败"⑤。在这种依赖下，政治话语必须转变为反映最活跃捐款者的要求和观点的方式：捐款者可以向候选人提供的资金越多，依靠这些资金上任或连任公职的候选人出售法律政策决定、以作为利益交换的风险就越大。⑥

竞选捐款与支出激增的同时，候选人依赖的捐款者也发生了变化：金钱政治兴起与收入不平等加剧同时发生并相互加强，使得政治竞选捐款来源变得高度集中。据阳光基金会统计，在"联合公民案"胜诉后的第一个选举周期即2010年，占美国人口总数不到0.01%的人（近2.7万人）的竞选捐款高达7.74亿美元，占竞选捐款总额的24%；2012年，3.1人捐

---

① Charles H. Ferguson, *Predator Nation: Corporate Criminals, Political Corruption, and the Hijacking of America*, New York: Crown Publishing Group, 2012, p.575.
② Paul Harris, "America is Better Than This: Paralysis at the Top Leaves Voters Desperate for Change", The Guardian, Nov.19, 2011.
③ Karl Evers-Hillstrom & Brendan Quinn, "Open Secrets Looks Back at 2020, a $14 Billion Year", Open Secrets (Dec.22, 2020), https://www.opensecrets.org/news/2020/12/2020-opensecrets-year-in-review/.
④ Eliana Miller, "Despite Some Big Losses, Top Spenders Won 88 Percent of 2020 Races", Open Secrets (Nov.20, 2020), https://www.opensecrets.org/news/2020/11/top-spenders-won-88-percent-of-2020-races/.
⑤ Bruce E. Cain, "Is 'Dependence Corruption' the Solution to America's Campaign Finance Problems?" *California Law Review*, Vol.102, No.1, 2014, pp.37-47.
⑥ Daniel I. Weiner & Ian Vandewalker, *Stronger Parties, Stronger Democracy: Rethinking Reform*, New York: Brennan Center, 2015, p.2, https://www.brennancenter.org/sites/default/files/publications/Stronger_Parties_Stronger_Democracy.pdf.

(亿美元)

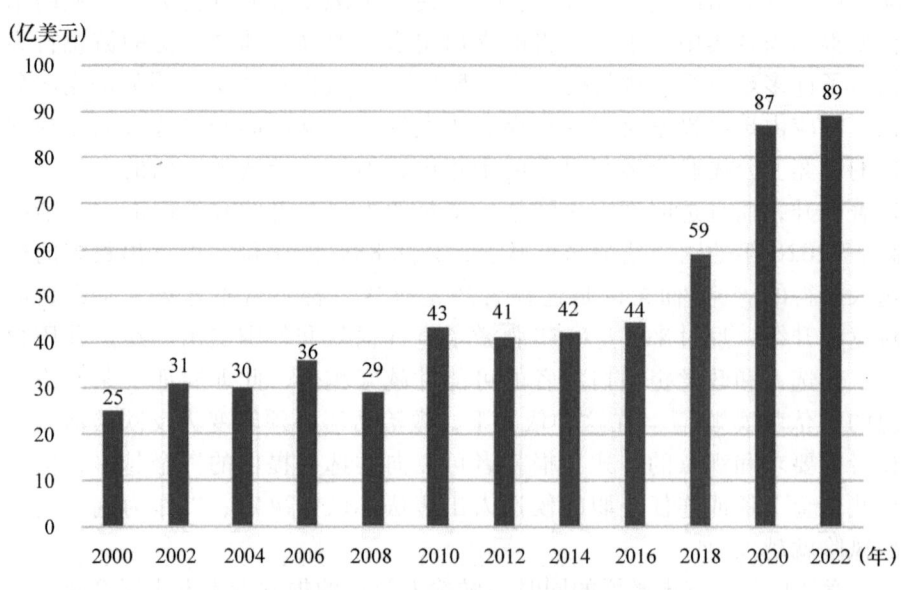

年份	支出
2000	25
2002	31
2004	30
2006	36
2008	29
2010	43
2012	41
2014	42
2016	44
2018	59
2020	87
2022	89

图1-4 2000—2022年参众两院候选人竞选支出

资料来源：Open Secrets, "Cost of Election", Open Secrets (n. d.), https://www.opensecrets.org/overview/cost.php, 不含总统大选支出。

献了超过15亿美元，占总捐款比例的28%，达到历史最高点。[①] 这些"1%中的1%"美国人捐款的中位数甚至远超过平均美国家庭年收入的中位数，依靠巨额的竞选捐款，他们成了美国政治的"守门人"——在无数次游说和竞选筹款活动中为自身利益植入优先级，并为美国公众确定"应讨论"的政治议题和"应采取"的政治立场范围，甚至能在很大程度上确定可以接受的政府人选。政治学家本杰明·佩吉和拉里·巴特尔斯等人在2013年的一项著名研究中将这一结论进一步延伸，他们发现富人与其他人的差异不仅仅在于财富的数量，还有其政治事项的优先级，尤其是在经济和政府支出问题上，富人与普通公众的意愿时常相悖。[②] 越来越多的证据表明，完全不代表公众利益的捐款者观点对政策决策产生了巨大的影响，

[①] Lee Drutman, "The Political 1% of the 1% in 2012", Sunlight Fundation (Jun. 24, 2013), https://sunlightfoundation.com/2013/06/24/1pct_of_the_1pct/.

[②] Benjamin I. Page, Larry M. Bartels & Jason Seawright, "Democracy and the Policy Preferences of Wealthy Americans", *Perspectives on Politics*, Vol. 11, No. 1, 2013, pp. 51–73.

中产阶级与工人阶级选民最终会发现自己被排除在决策过程之外,这也是造成公众舆论倾向与立法政策结果之间不一致的重要原因。主导美国政治选举的"1%中的1%"人群利用经济优势带来的权力,扭曲政治系统、保护自身或给予自身特权的现状也从侧面表明,美国社会中阶层鸿沟与贫富差距带来的不平等正通过政治参与扩大。有评论认为,金钱的影响总体上已经"改变了美国政治"[1],这种巨大财富聚集形成的扭曲效应正通过每次选举一步步侵蚀着美国的民主制度。

(二) 政治平等与民主代议制权力寻租的矛盾

既然来自少数人的巨额捐款破坏了选举的代表完整性,那么在面对可能为民众改善选举不平等状况的替代方案时,国会是会选择维持现状还是会制定立法以约束公司等特殊化利益集团的政治力量扩展?这个问题涉及对政治参与和代表权的理解。共和党和民主党的历史和思想根源都表明,特殊利益对公共政策的影响与民主本身一样古老。[2] 麦迪逊在《联邦党人文集》中曾谈到经济利益中的政治参与动机:"在文明国家中,有土地的利益、制造的利益、商业的利益和金钱的利益。相对于其他更小的利益,这些利益在文明国家中逐渐变得必要,乃至被分为不同的类别,由不同的情感和观点驱使。对这些各自不同又相互干扰的利益进行监管即为现代立法的主要任务,其涉及政党和派系的精神以及政府的必要日常运作。"[3] 由于立法的主要任务是对上述各种利益及其相互干预进行规范,因此各个有关方面的利益方会不可避免地参与制定或通过此类立法。而今,利益相关方通过游说、竞选捐款和资助政策研究(如智囊团或智库)等渠道在立法过程中注入金钱和自己想表达的信息、观点,以实现自身所代表的利益。因此尽管选民总是可以投出代表自己观点或利益的一票,但富人和高利润产业却更能够以自己的方式影响政府的作为与不作为。[4] 根据政治学家

---

[1] Robert G. Kaiser & Alice Crites, "Citizen K Street: How Lobbying Became Washington's Biggest Business-Big Money Creates a New Capital City. As Lobbying Booms, Washington and Politics are Transformed", *The Washington Post*, Sep. 6, 2011.

[2] Lance Selfa, *The Democrats: A Critical History*, New York: Haymarket Books, 2008, pp. 39 - 42.

[3] James Madison, "The Union as a Safeguard Against Domestic Faction and Insurrection from the New York Packet", *The Federalist Papers*, No. 10, Nov. 23, 1787, New York: Signet Classics, 2003.

[4] Jane Mayer, "Covert Operations: The Billionaire Brothers Who are Waging a War Against Obama", *The New Yorker*, Aug. 23, 2010; Alice O'Connor, "The Privatized City", *Journal of Urban History*, Vol. 34, No. 2, 2008, pp. 333 - 353.

谢茨施耐德的冲突范围理论（scope of conflict theory）①，民主体制中的政策变化是"由公众参与冲突的范围决定的"②，而议员等政治参与者则使用政策措辞来扩大或缩小决策者的数量和类型范围。也即，政治参与者们可以扩大他们认为必要和正当的政府干预范围，也可以减少或取消其认为缺乏根据或适得其反的政府干预范围。希尔与胡柏也认为竞选捐款并不仅仅停留在"投入产出"的层面，而是一种公民在选举风险的激励下试图扩大其参与范围的途径。③ 谢茨施耐德乐观地认为，由善于竞选且负责任的政党组成的民主政府可以扩大冲突，即使得冲突社会化，从而解决重要的经济和社会问题。但"作为冲突社会化工具的民主政府，其有效性取决于其权力和资源的振幅"④，从而为冲突提供相互缓冲的空间。这就意味着政党必须有足够的资源，由于政党优先考虑的是解决冲突并制定政策替代方案，此时为政党提供资源者，即游说或捐款者的动机变得尤为重要。正如谢茨施耐德所言，"对替代方案进行定义乃权力的至高手段"⑤。如果某人向解决社会问题的人付费或捐款，那么就可能在决定所谓的社会问题上拥有发言权。由于政府对其资源产生依赖，可能无法使冲突社会化，从而选择将决策权更多地置于私人或利益集团手中而非选民手中。在这一点上，冲突范围理论与"依赖腐败"理论对腐败的认识也是相互呼应的。

冲突社会化失败的后果之一是，民众抱怨金钱带来的不平等政治影响力破坏了其所信仰的人人平等和一人一票原则（one person/one vote），这种观点不难理解。民主政治不仅取决于公开竞争，还取决于制度化的平等

---

① "冲突理论"即"冲突范围理论"，其描述的范围即"冲突的规模和程度"。这可能涉及各种类型和层次的私人或公共组织。一般来说，战争中的弱势方会寻求将冲突范围扩大到新的参与者，以获得优势。一旦冲突范围停止升级，最终的输家将由政策决定。例如，一名房主抱怨工厂太吵，业主无法降低工厂的噪声水平，因此参与到当地政府关于"噪声条例"的公共决策中，然后通过新的更严格的噪声法规获胜。而工厂则通过州立法扩大了冲突的范围，通过影响州立法，以更高一级却更宽松的噪声法规获胜。

② Elmer E. Schattschneider, *The Semi-Sovereign People: A Realist's View of Democracy in America*, New York: Thomson Learning, 1975, p.5.

③ Seth J. Hill & Gregory A. Huber, "Representativeness and Motivations of the Contemporary Donorate: Results from Merged Survey and Administrative Records", *Political Behavior*, Vol.39, No.1, 2017, pp.3-29.

④ Elmer E. Schattschneider, *The Semi-Sovereign People: A Realist's View of Democracy in America*, New York: Thomson Learning, 1975, p.16.

⑤ Elmer E. Schattschneider, *The Semi-Sovereign People: A Realist's View of Democracy in America*, New York: Thomson Learning, 1975, p.66.

假设。① 从历史上看，美国的政治平等取决于每个选民有权获得单一的、平等的投票权。也就是说，平等权意味着每个人在投票箱面前都是平等的。基于美国平等权的演进历史，通过宪法修正案和法律变更，这种平等使国家在过去的一个多世纪逐渐取消了对选举权的限制：非裔美国人、妇女、年轻人和无产者都有投票权，不应有任何原因使一票应然地比另一票更有价值。在这种历史背景下，政治平等几乎等同于选民们平等地站在投票箱前投出自己的一票。尽管民主竞争是在私人利益的驱动下进行的，但公民们期待民主竞争是公平的，并默认将这些利益的表达方式汇合到广泛接受的公共政策中。

但也许制宪者从来没有打算让每个人都具有平等的"政治影响力"。竞选与投票本身是两个不同的概念，平等的投票权并不能改变竞选活动中政治影响力的大小。公民可以自由地运用自己的能力和财力来或多或少地活跃于政治生活中，并试图说服他人以特定的政治主张投票。而且正如贝维尔所指出的那样，"平等政治影响力"② 本身的含义就模糊不清：如果说"政治平等"意味着人们并不能合法地获得或行使政治影响力，那么在实质上不同程度的政治参与意味着什么？有效参与政治辩论与"不适当的政治影响"的边界在哪里？但与此同时，基于每个人都有平等投票权的政治平等传统观念，如果人人都拥有相同的政治影响力，那么"政治影响力"概念的存在本身就是多余的。故从此种角度来看，只要金钱可以合法地购买与之对应的影响力，"平等政治影响力"的概念就是自相矛盾的。

一个被频繁讨论的例子是税收改革。税收是一个国家财富分配方式的最直接体现之一。皮尤研究中心2023年的调查显示，超过2/3的美国人认为公司和最富有人士所缴纳的实际税款少于其应缴税款③，对二者的减

---

① Michael Johnston, "The Definitions Debate: Old Conflicts in New Guises", in A. K. Jain, ed., *The Political Economy of Corruption*, London: Routledge, 2001, pp. 11 - 32.

② Lillian BeVier, "Money and Politics: A Perspective on the First Amendment and Campaign Finance Reform", *California Law Review*, No. 73, 1985, pp. 1045 - 1090; Lillian BeVier, "Campaign Finance Reform: Specious Arguments, Intractable Dilemmas", *Columbia Law Review*, No. 94, 1994, pp. 1258 - 1280.

③ J. Baxter Olophant, "Top Tax Frustrations for Americans: The Feeling that Some Corporations, Wealthy People Don't Pay Fair Share", Pew Research Center (Apr. 7, 2023), https://www.pewresearch.org/short-reads/2023/04/07/top-tax-frustrations-for-americans-the-feeling-that-some-corporations-wealthy-people-dont-pay-fair-share/. 类似的调查很多，此前5年盖洛普和布鲁金斯学会（Brookings Institution）的调查也都得到了类似的结论。

税政策也并没有使普通美国人受益。[1] 尽管民众普遍支持提高富人的税率，但为富人减税仍然是两党政府的行动准则。布什总统签署的对富人和企业实施大规模减税政策，在其离任后也得到了奥巴马政府的支持，从而使之成为永久法律。随后在共和党人入主白宫的2017—2020年，国会又通过了使大公司和富人受益的新减税法案，公司税率由35%进一步降至21%。[2] 主要的税收负担从公司和富人到普通美国人的转移以及工薪阶层工资的增长停滞，成功地将国家财富的很大一部分从工人阶层二次分配给了经济精英阶层，为最有钱的人提供了最大的利益。巧合的是，这种从下至上的财富重新分配在巴克利诉瓦莱奥案判决后尤其明显。[3] 在政治游戏中，金钱的影响迫使政党与候选人不得不迎合捐款者所属的利益集团，因此无论是选择民主党还是共和党，精英政客或是流量明星，普通美国人都无法通过一人一票的方式维护自己的经济利益。

不仅是税收在内的财富，政府腐败与政治腐败的本质手段其实就是"对联邦公共资源的不当分配"。[4] 作为政府的代理人，总统与国会议员负责对公共资源进行分配。政治参与被冲突理论解释为特殊利益集团购买"替代方案"，从而重新进行公共资源分配的途径。这种利益集团利用政府的强制力，以有利于该集团的优先性重新分配资源或财富的运作方式，被经济学家称为"寻租"，这也是大捐款者的捐款对公共政策决策过程的腐蚀机理。于是政治金钱影响立法政策的以下场景变得更容易理解[5]：参议

---

[1] Conrad Foreman, "Money in Politics: Campaign Finance and Its Influence Over the Political Process and Public Policy", *UIC John Marshall Law Review*, Vol.52, No.185, 2018, pp.185-256.

[2] 参见Tax Cuts and Jobs Act of 2017。但随后的拜登政府采取了不同于前任政府的税收政策，调整了税制以缩小贫富差距，主张对富人增税，对穷人减税。2023年1月1日生效的《通胀削减法》（Inflation Reduction Act），旨在打击特殊集团的利益，促进经济增长，因而2023年个人所得税扣除额大幅提高7%。在2023财年预算案中，拜登政府计划通过对亿万富翁和公司增税，以降低政府赤字。

[3] Nicholas Confessore, Sarah Cohen & Karen Yourish, "Small Pool of Rich Donors Dominates Electing Giving", *The New York Times*, Aug.1, 2015.

[4] Jay Cost, *A Republic No More: Big Government and the Crisis of American Political Corruption*, New York: Encounter Books, 2015, p.1.

[5] Michael J. Cooper, Huseyin Gulen & Alexei V. Ovtchinnikov, "Corporate Political Contributions and Stock Returns", *Journal of Finance*, Vol.65, No.2, 2010, pp.687-724; Ahmed Tahoun, "The Role of Stock Ownership by US Members of Congress on the Market for Political Favors", *Journal of Financial Economics*, Vol.111, No.1, 2014, pp.86-110; Lawrence Lessig, *Republic, Lost: How Money Corrupts Congress-and a Plan to Stop It*, New York: Hatchette, 2011; Martin Gilens, *Affluence and Influence: Economic Inequality and Political Power in America*, Princeton, NJ: Princeton University Press, 2011.

院通过的立法通常符合富人的政策偏好；国会委员会在竞选活动参与者关心的问题上更积极地参与，如修正提案、质询和出席听证；股票价格根据公司的竞选捐款而波动（这也侧面证明了股票交易者在判断公司的盈利能力时知道政治支持的价值）；竞选筹款和联系捐款演说占据了国会议员的大部分时间；游说破坏了公众对立法机构的信任。还有观点将游说视为对立法的一种"补贴"形式，即"向经过立法者精心挑选的企业提供价格昂贵的、与之需要匹配的政策信息、政治情报"[1]。有人脉的游说者与国会议员联系，为其撰写的法案提供建议。竞选捐款通过为竞选者提供急需的资金获得对决策的影响准入和对其有利的公共政策，捐款者与受赠者相互依赖彼此所提供的信息与利益。2010年"联合公民案"的判决导致流入政治竞选的资金陡增，言论自由权利的边界被扩大，选民个人与小利益团体的声音却越发微渺。谢茨施耐德的冲突范围似乎正在缩小而非扩大，美国政治民主似乎正通向一条"财阀统治之路"[2]。这也说明，游说活动与竞选捐款及其在政府选举中对政府代理人和周边团体的巨大腐败影响力，已逐渐成为政府背离公共利益的重要原因，二者共同描绘了美国当今政治腐败生活的主要图景。

本章小结

对腐败概念认识的局限性，与将其几乎等同于贪污受贿等不道德的直接等价交换有关。不道德或不正当的腐败行为通常都被描绘为直接和即时的交易，即立法者立即采取特定的行为，以换取金钱报酬。基于这种认识，法律禁止公职人员与政策的受惠者以贿赂和回扣等形式进行串通。但在现代美国政治生活中，这种支付钱款买通决策的形式并没有在议员中形成一种普遍的盈利模式，因此禁止直接贿赂的立法在应对腐败方面也不甚有效：直接贿赂发生的频率很低，而且由于其行为总是保密的，随之而来

---

[1] Richard L. Hall & Alan Deardorff, "Lobbying as Legislative Subsidy", *American Political Science Review*, Vol.100, No.1, 2006, pp.69–84.
[2] Walter, D. Burnham, *Democracy in Peril: The American Turnout Problem and the Path to Plutocracy*, Working Paper, No.5, The Roosevelt Institute, 2010.

的调查和执法成本也会很高，往往要依赖内部知情人士罕见的举报。而若涉及举报，政府还需要向"吹哨人"支付巨额酬劳，这种执法辅助方式的激励成本也相当高。① 尽管狭义的等价交易仍然存在，但当今政治腐败的最普遍形式仍是将钱转移到竞选捐款中。决策者通过与利益集团相连来满足其竞选资金或谋求连任晋升的需求。许多政客公开否认其与某些利益集团的直接关系，但游说和竞选捐款实际上已成为他们与富人及其代言人之间联系的合理化手段。这种取代直接贿赂的腐败行为已经不再符合个人收益、直接付款和立即满足条件等早期的腐败行为特征了。对于那些希望通过滥用游说和捐款影响政府决策的人来说，这种合法的关系不仅远比直接贿赂安全，成本更低，利润还往往更大。巨额私人资金在政治生活中的影响就是当今美国系统腐败的主要根源。而对竞选资金日益增长的需求以及经济和政治利益之间的密切联系，也迫使政客与大捐款人建立关系，反过来进一步推动了腐败可能性的蔓延。不仅如此，公职人员和利益集团代理人之间的持续密切关系还带来了一种间接压力，使得利益交换对公职人员的腐败影响更加微妙，甚至超过了竞选捐款的表面范畴。在竞选捐款之外，利益相关人还可以通过一系列的优待，使立法者在决策时逐渐将所谓的私人友谊而非公众利益放在首位，并且确信其做出的决策完全是基于对选民的使命感而客观公正的。因为即使"捐钱时没有附带条件，收款人迟早也会心存感激"②。

对美国当代政治腐败的另一个误解是，不作为形式的腐败几乎被忽略了。一些学者与公众对有组织利益集团的运作目标有种误读，往往倾向于将腐败默认为一种作为，如接受大额捐款或贿赂并通过相应的有利于特殊利益集团的法案等。但事实恰恰相反，利益集团的首要目标是维持现状以自我保护。如专栏记者罗伯特·谢里尔所指出："国会议员与业界之间利益重叠的主要形式是无所作为。大多数行业并不是派游说者去华盛顿寻求有利可图的立法。华盛顿游说团体的主要目标不是通过立法，而是维持现状，即阻止对其不利的立法通过。从这个方面来看，他们做得相当成功。"③

---

① 根据联邦《虚假陈述法》（False Claims Act）、《多德—弗兰克法案》（Dodd-Frank Act）以及联邦证券交易委员会和国税局等的相关规定，涉案金额超过100万美元时，政府通常给予"吹哨人"追回款项的10%—30%作为奖金。截至2021年，联邦证监会累计向207名吹哨人发放超过10亿美元奖金。
② Al Martinez, "Portrait of a Lobbyist: Power or Myth", *The Los Angeles Times*, May 26, 1974, p.3.
③ Robert Sherrill, *Why They Call It Politics* (2nd ed.), New York: Harcourt Brace Jovanovich, 1974, p.128.

第二章 游说、竞选捐款与美国政治腐败：危机四伏的民主体制

"任何一种基于美国例外主义的自大言论都无法掩盖人们对腐败日益增长的普遍印象，美国正因缺乏政府的有效治理而使其自身经济前途陷入危险之中。"[①] 政治腐败对民主共和提出了尖锐的问题：如果国家是民主的，为什么还会有系统性的腐败滋生，并成为共和背景下的民主现实？麦迪逊认为尽管腐败根植于人类的天性中，但即使是多数人的暴政也无法为精英领导共和政府体制下的腐败提供合理化解释，政府、政治腐败与公众道德或社会风气在一定程度上是互不相干的。[②] 因而其致力于构建一个坚实强势的政府，以对抗腐败的侵蚀，但这也导致政府权力不断扩张，直至逾越18世纪制宪者为其制定的权力边界。[③] 同时宪法制度本身的结构性缺陷也造成了政治腐败在美国独立后蓬勃发展的资本主义带动下发端，并在其后以多种形式不断实现自我延续。

共和的题中之义，乃持不同观点的各党派或各派系的联合，但当国会和行政部门在技术专制的影响下设立各种各样的委员会，获得越来越多的权力，超出了宪法起草者当初为二者设计的框架时，这些权力难以

[①] Thomas E. Mann & Norman J. Ornstein, *It's Even Worse than It Looks: How the American Constitutional System Collided with the New Politics of Extremism*, New York: Basic Books, 2016, p.101.

[②] James Madison, "The House of Representatives from the New York Packet", *The Federalist Papers*: No.52, Feb.8, 1788, New York: Signet Classics, 2003.

[③] 正如美国历史学家理查德·霍夫斯塔德（Richard Hofstadter）在《美国政治传统及其缔造者》（*The American Political Tradition and the Men Who Made it*）中所言，美国宪法的基础是霍布斯哲学和加尔文主义，即认为人类的天然状态是战争，世俗大众的心智与上帝相抵触。美国传统价值的基础是基督新教，相信人类的原罪性，因此需要依赖制度（法律和秩序）乃至政府管理以避免战争状态。而政府也是由人组成，因此其权力也需要约束。美国政府是在此基础上，借鉴洛克的有限政府概念与孟德斯鸠的三权分立概念建立而来，因此早期的美国政府权力与欧洲政府相比是较小的。

被合理剪裁分配，直接的消化途径为通过派系（斗争）分而食之。这里产生的两个问题是，其一，扩张的过剩权力难以被监管，易滋生腐败；其二，作为消化过剩权力手段的派系斗争，其本身也与腐败紧密相连。这些问题与其他诸多原因一起，将共和体制逐渐推向腐败的危机边缘。诚然，派系斗争获得的权力可以通过合法手段被游说团体所代表的利益集团分解，最终以资源分配的形式体现。在理想情况下，游说是民主参与政治的形式之一，各个游说团体是社会各种意志的表达集合体，保护公共利益的政府决策可以代表多数人的意志，通过谨慎分配资源实现民主。但在现实中，游说团体更可能也更频繁地代表着各个领域的狭隘利益集团。两党斗争促成了一个以说客为中心的华盛顿经济体，向有可能从国会立法与政策中受益的利益集团出售游说与竞选捐款服务。当今游说系统参与人数之多与竞选花费之巨，足以说明美国政治的高度货币化和权力寻租化，其表现形式多种多样，并不限于传统认识中收受贿赂的犯罪行为。联邦政府已经濒临"精致的盗贼统治者"[1]的边缘：政治服务于财富，而财富的扩大则通过购买政府服务达成。联邦最高法院多数大法官对金钱在政治中的腐蚀力视而不见，不仅加深了经济精英阶层和特殊利益集团与普通选民政治影响力之间的鸿沟，还为国会议员与司法体系工作者的职务行为蒙上了腐败的阴影。

第一节　精英决策取代民主决策

美式民主的矛盾在于，政治家、学者和所谓精英都信任专家的治理模式，他们自认为知道什么是"最好的"，并且不希望受到民众干涉。因此无论是在哪里，人民都不乏对权力的杠杆失去控制的担忧。"自私的"，抑或"自以为是"的民主通过富裕的捐款者所资助的游说智囊团和研究机构，将其意识形态以专家和科学的形式包装，通过"分享"某项专业领域知识影响从政者的立法和政治决策，为接受捐款的政客提供看似正当的理由，以制定有利于利益集团的决策并左右选民的意愿。

---

[1] Christopher DeMuth, "Our Corrupt Government", *Claremont Review of Books*, 2015, August 1.

第二章　游说、竞选捐款与美国政治腐败：危机四伏的民主体制

最直接的问题是，当代游说与竞选捐款体制下的美式民主制度是否挤压了民主，抑或这种民主是否甚至会滋生暴政？有研究试图回答这个问题。在普林斯顿大学的吉伦斯和西北大学的佩吉教授的著名研究中，通过跟踪各个群体的偏好预测国会和行政部门在20多年间对1779个政策问题所采取的行为方式，并将收入排在美国前50%的美国人与排在前10%的美国人的政策偏好与主要游说或商业团体进行比较，结果表明无论是在共和党还是民主党政府下，政府决策在更多时候都是遵循后者的偏好。[1] 也即，美国并非依照多数选民的意志所统治的。从前民主党总统竞选人伯尼·桑德斯到共和党参议员特德·克鲁兹都相信政府正在努力争取"1%"的精英阶层的支持而非一般人的支持。[2] 这至少表明了经济精英和狭隘的利益集团在政府决策中的影响力非同一般。这些阶层、集团在超过半数的情况下取得了有利于他们的政策，并且几乎每一次都能成功阻止对其不利的立法通过；与此同时，以公众为基础的利益团体对公共政策影响不大，至于普通公民的意见，更是几乎没有任何独立的影响。[3] 对此结果，研究者承认："当经济精英的偏好和有组织的利益集团的立场掌握局面时，普通美国人的倾向或意见对公共政策的影响微不足道，几乎为零，在统计上无显著影响。"[4]

第二节　特殊利益集团垄断发声

现今，身份是在美国政治中利益分割的标准，能够轻易超越一人一票

---

[1] Martin Gilens & Benjamin I. Page, "Testing Theories of American Politics: Elites, Interest Groups, and Average Citizens", *Perspectives on Politics*, Vol.12, No.3, 2014, pp.564–581.

[2] Jay Cost, "The Swamp Isn't Easy to Drain: Corruption has been Inherent to American Government Since the Founding Fathers-and Acknowledge that is the First Step Toward Containing It", The Atlantic (Jul. 14, 2018), https://www.theatlantic.com/ideas/archive/2018/07/the-swamp-isnt-easy-to-drain/565151/.

[3] 对该研究得出的结果也有很多争议，如密歇根大学的Stuart Soroka教授与得克萨斯州大学的Christopher Wlezien教授都认为根据Gilens和Page针对数据的分析不成立，中等收入的美国人和富裕的美国人实际上在绝大多数议题上意见相同。

[4] Martin Gilens & Benjamin I. Page, "Testing Theories of American Politics: Elites, Interest Groups, and Average Citizens", *Perspectives on Politics*, Vol.12, No.3, 2014, pp.564–581.

的民主原则。在当今的华盛顿，五花八门的游说组织正在努力寻求影响力的扩张，高度多样性的游说组织似乎代表了美国公民生活的方方面面，从各类商会到工会，都充满着不同的意识形态色彩，但这并不代表所有人都被代表，游说代理人与广大公众之间的鸿沟是存在的。流行于华盛顿的一句现代谚语揭示了这种代表背后的残酷性："如果你不在桌子旁，那么就在菜单上。"根据一项对1981—2006年活跃于华盛顿的3.7万余个游说团体、政治行动委员会和其他活动团体的调查统计[1]，这些团体所代表的利益大幅度地向富裕者的方向倾斜：超过一半的团体以各种形式为企业的利益代言，其中仅有约5%代表着广泛的公共利益（如荒野保护、汽车安全、国土安全、外国人人权、降低税率、生育和教育权利等），4%的团体代表少数族裔或性别身份特殊的边缘人群，而不到1%的人代表经济困难或需要社会服务的群体。无论是离异的单身母亲、仅以小费为收入的酒保和侍者，还是洗衣店杂工、货车司机或是无薪实习生，都没有代表其利益的组织。当理想主义的小政府倡导者们削减美国的社会服务预算时，没有一个代表低收入者的团体发出声音，缺乏代表、被决策者忽视的底层公民在金钱铸造的竞选扩音器面前声若蚊蝇。在2018年皮尤研究中心发布的调查中，41%的受访者表示在过去5年中没有做出过任何竞选捐款，同时高达72%的民众认为"向民选官员提供大量金钱的人比其他人有更大的影响力"。[2] 在过去的10年中，大公司和特殊利益团体的游说与竞选捐款得到第一修正案的进一步授权，而普通公民的言论自由与平等保护权却遭受侵蚀，选举中大量特殊利益支出进一步削弱了公众对政府的信心。"民主项目"2018年的一项调查显示，美国公众将政治中的金钱视为民主制度中的最大问题，77%的受访者表示："如今国家政府制定的法律主要反映了强大的特殊利益及其游说者想要的东西。"[3]

---

[1] Kay L. Schlozman, Sidney Verba & Henry E. Brady, "The People With No Lobby in Washington", Boston Globe (Aug. 26, 2012), https://www.bostonglobe.com/ideas/2012/08/25/the-people-with-lobby-washington/cJds8XhPRwgJUCt3MgUYhO/story.html.

[2] Pew Research Center, "The Public, the Political System and American Democracy", Pew (Apr. 26, 2018), https://www.pewresearch.org/politics/2018/04/26/the-public-the-political-system-and-american-democracy/.

[3] Democracy Project, "The Democracy Project: Reversing a Crisis of Confidence", Democracy Project (2018), https://www.democracyprojectreport.org/report.

第二章 游说、竞选捐款与美国政治腐败：危机四伏的民主体制

第三节 技术专制蚕食立法裁量权

游说与竞选捐款对美国政坛的腐败侵蚀还表现在其与技术专制（technocracy）的结合上。在许多特殊政策领域，国会的诸多立法工作已被所谓的独立机构取代，如联邦通信委员会、证券交易委员会、环境保护局、消费者金融保护局和职业安全与健康管理局等。这些机构往往被指定负责解决技术上复杂且在政治上极具争议性的问题，一经国会设立便可以在各自领域制定绝大多数的联邦法规，这也意味着这些机构拥有前所未有的、有时甚至包括刑事执法权在内的自由裁量权。以 2007 年为例，国会在该年度共颁布了 138 项公法，同时各个独立的联邦机构制定了 2926 条规则。[1] 因此，在讨论美国政治腐败时应当注意到，联邦各独立机构和委员会实质上的独立立法地位分割了国会一部分的立法权，无形中进一步分散并削弱了选民参与管理国家的权利。与此同时，由于在很大程度上不受立法监督，这些独立委员会也难以在大利益集团的游说与竞选捐款活动中独善其身，反而往往成为政府与特殊利益集团之间的旋转门突破口。

国会立法权力下放形成的技术专制与腐败紧密相连，甚至可能构成腐败的空位链。[2] 以环境保护署为例，斯科特·普伊特（Scott Pruitt）于 2017 年由特朗普政府提名出任署长，截至 2018 年 7 月，普伊特已身陷政府问责署、白宫预算管理办公室、白宫特别顾问委员会和国会下设两个委员会等主导的 14 项调查，调查内容涉及利益冲突、不当保密和公务支出等。[3] 担任环保署长期间，普伊特出差时频繁乘坐飞机头等舱和军用机，并从一

---

[1] Yascha Mounk, "America Is Not a Democracy: How the United States Lost the Faith of its Citizens-and What It Can Do to Win Them Back", The Atlantic (Mar., 2018), https://www.theatlantic.com/magazine/archive/2018/03/america-is-not-a-democracy/550931/.
[2] "空位链"（vacancy chain）最初是一个生物学概念，用以描述寄居蟹丢弃的蟹壳总有下一只寄居蟹接手。该概念随后被引入社会学与犯罪学理论。以腐败犯罪为典型，在犯罪空位链假设中，如果腐败的源头未被切除，无论如何更换腐败权力位置上的主体，都无法根除腐败现象：随着腐败链条的移动，因前任腐败失职而空缺的职位总会有下一任来接替腐败。
[3] Lisa Friedman, "The Investigations That Led to Scott Pruitt's Resignation", The New York Times, Jul. 13, 2018.

名加拿大能源公司说客处以远低于市场平均的价格租赁了一套位于华盛顿特区的公寓。普伊特的助手为其在官方日程上保留了"秘密"的时间,以隐瞒其与行业代表的24次秘密会见①。其前任丽莎·杰克逊(Lisa Jackson)与前前任卡罗尔·布朗纳(Carol Browner)也因欺诈、腐败和销毁文件等违反《信息自由法》(The Freedom of Information Act,简称FIOA)的行为离任。2019年1月,特朗普任命前煤炭能源行业说客安德鲁·惠勒(Andrew Wheeler)接任普伊特。惠勒曾为受煤炭生产巨头穆雷能源(Murray Energy Corp)和美国铀钒矿业公司(Energy Fuels Inc)等依赖于环保署政策的公司游说,故其与化石燃料利益集团之间的关系以及可能涉及的利益冲突,也引发了广泛争议。

第四节 国会议员面临竞选筹款压力

盖洛普2015年的一项民调显示②,52%的美国人认为国会是"腐败的",69%的民众指出国会议员们倾向于迎合特殊利益团体的需求而非听取各自选区选民的意愿,高达79%的被调查者指出议员们脱离了普通选民,这与国会议员花费大部分时间在从富裕捐款者处筹集资金的事实相符。2004年民主党总统候选人约翰·克里曾表示:"我们面临着另一项挑战,就是竞选公职所必需的巨额资金带来的腐败力量。"③ 资金带来的优势不仅仅是增加候选人在竞选中的竞争力,还直接与竞选结果相关,拥有雄厚资金支持的候选人往往就会赢得国会选举。在2010—2016年,众议院选举的90%席位都被比对手花费更多的候选人赢得。④

---

① Scott Bronstein, Curt Devine & Drew Griffin, "Whistleblower: EPA's Pruitt kept secret calendar to hide meetings", CNN (Jul. 3, 2018), https://edition.cnn.com/2018/07/02/politics/scott-pruitt-whistleblower-secret-calendar/index.html.
② Andrew Dugan, "Majority of Americans See Congress as Out of Touch, Corrupt", Gallup (2015), https://news.gallup.com/poll/1600/Congress-Public.aspx.
③ Seth Cline, "Retiring Senators Lament Money in Politics: Senators Kerry, Harkin, and Levin All Decried the State of Campaign Finance in Retiring Remarks", U.S. NEWS (Mar. 8, 2013), https://www.usnews.com/news/articles/2013/03/08/retiring-senators-lament-money-in-politics.
④ Maggies Koerth-Baker, "How Money Affects Elections", FiveThirtyEight (Sep. 10, 2018), https://fivethirtyeight.com/features/money-and-elections-a-complicated-love-story/.

第二章 游说、竞选捐款与美国政治腐败：危机四伏的民主体制

议员不仅必须为自己的席位筹集更多资金，而且还不得不为自己的政党筹集更多资金，但四处筹款往往以牺牲了解与其立法工作最相关的政策细节为代价。以华盛顿特区民主党新任国会议员的标准指导日程为例：议员每日工作9—10小时起步，4小时用于与捐款者的通话，两小时作为国会议员的实际工作如参加听证会、投票，其会见的选民也可能是捐款者（见表2-1）。议员紧凑的工作安排时常迫使许多听证会被安排在同一时间，有时一些委员会成员甚至要同时参加两三个听证会，这显然影响了立法决策的准确性。即使在听证会上投票时，也需要考虑在没有沟通联络的情况下做出决策而冒犯了超级政治行动委员会的秘密捐款者，从而引发大量的攻击广告，这种潜伏的恐惧毫无疑问会影响立法者的政策决定。即使刚刚在上一次选举中竞选成功，也不得不尽快投入到为下次选举筹集资金的活动中去。国会甚至关闭了供议员就餐的餐厅，因为几乎所有人都把时间花在了竞选筹款上，没人有时间在那里吃午餐。虽然在竞选筹款之外，国会议员还有公共财政支持选举作为第二选择，但往往没有议员愿意选择这个选项——向捐款者筹措资金、获取政治支持才是其政治生涯发展的可持续策略。即使国会的开会时间已经比过去的几十年大大缩短，但听证会仍难免和筹款活动日程经常发生冲突。不过国会议员并不需面临艰难选择，与其坐在座位上聆听听证事项，提出棘手的问题惹怒潜在的捐款人，不如直接与听证所涉及行业人士联系筹集资金，之后以更令捐款者愉悦的方式投出自己的一票。

表2-1　　　　　　　华盛顿特区民主党新任国会议员标准日程

时长（小时）	事项
4	致电捐款者
2	议会/委员会开会
1—2	会见选民
1	战略推广（用餐，媒体会见）
1	修整

资料来源：Allison Klein, "The Most Depressing Graphic for Members of Congress", *The Washington Post*, Jan.14, 2013.

来自政党的压力也是因素之一。每个政党都会敦促其议员筹集资金，以

帮助政党维持在国会的多数党地位或是重新获得多数席位。立法者被下达了筹款指标，为共和党全国国会委员会或民主党国会竞选委员会筹集资金，位置越高者筹款压力越大。这些筹款要求使立法者无法从事代表人民的工作，间接激励了国会议员从其监管的夹缝中寻求竞选献金。议员们花费更多的时间与选民和利益集团代表会面、交谈，也就没有多少时间研究和审议真正具有重要性的国家问题。毫不夸张地说，一些议员们已经可以被称为"筹款机器"，越来越少的国会委员会开会时间就是证明。据统计，2005—2006年，众议院委员会就审议立法开会449次，参议院委员会开会了252次，而仅仅十年后的2015—2016年，该数字分别下降至254次和69次。[①]

这种恶性循环带来的后果是，利益集团最终得以对联邦财政预算等重要议题施加符合自身利益的影响。其干预可能使联邦在州和地方问题上不当倾注资源，实质上削弱了联邦制的核心，即联邦政府在法律与政策制定上的优越性。联邦和州之间的责任区别在于，联邦政府比州政府拥有更强大的垄断地位，华盛顿能够在不受平衡预算要求的约束下负责货币供给，以相对低的成本借入资金，同时不会面临公民和投资的州际"政策竞争"。[②] 而游说与竞选捐款通过将联邦预算向地方和团体利益倾斜，使得联邦主义有陷入狭隘化之虞。

第五节　司法公正被拍卖

　　联邦最高法院的判决对立法和行政机关在选举领域的影响往往是政治选举腐败研究的重心，但其对自身所在司法领域的影响则鲜为人所关注。随着公司政治对话能力的增强，对于腐败的担忧扩展到了司法系统以及独立的司法机构。联合公民诉联邦选举委员会一案中，最高法院推翻了联邦政府多年来对公司在选举中独立支出的限制。不再受限的公司与工会支出开始对立法与行政甚至司法机构职位选举产生变革性的影响，大笔资金进

[①] Issue One & R. Street, "Why we left Congress: How the Legislative Branch Is Broken and What We Can Do About It", Issue One (Dec., 2018), https://www.issueone.org/why-we-left/.

[②] Christopher DeMuth, "Our Corrupt Government", *Claremont Review of Books*, 2015, August 1; 参见 Steward Machine Co. v. Davis. 301 US 548, 57 S. Ct. 883, 81 L. Ed. 1279-Supreme Court, 1937.

第二章 游说、竞选捐款与美国政治腐败：危机四伏的民主体制

一步扩大了其在政治选举中的影响力，立法、司法与政府行政机构的公信力均遭到不同程度的削弱。在过去的 20 年里，竞选经费的猛增使得竞选人面临筹集资金的巨大压力，这种压力并不仅仅体现在司法机构竞选中。以法官为例，根据国家州法院中心数据，全国 87% 的州法院法官需要经过竞选上任和获得连任①，而超过 97% 的州法院与地方法院法官表示需要为公职选举筹措大量资金②。如在 2006 年华盛顿高等法院法官选举中，每一支电视广告都是由独立于候选人本人的特殊利益团体支付的，这些广告支出成就了该州有史以来最昂贵的司法系统选举。竞选活动的费用不断膨胀也与外部特殊利益集团的广泛参与相吻合，而"联合公民案"使得通常作为诉讼当事人的公司或团体进一步成为司法领域竞选活动的主要资金提供者。为选举贡献大量资金的公司团体具有强烈的动机，以雄厚的资金支持其认为可能有利于它们的法官，结果必然是司法系统的独立与公正受到外部干预。2010 年就有一位西弗吉尼亚州法官在听证一起其竞选捐款者为当事方的案件时，因侵犯了另一当事方经由公正法院之公正听证的宪法权利而被联邦最高法院要求回避。一名得州法官在每次听证会前都要求律师明示他们所任职的律师事务所，然后在众人面前打开捐款册，查阅该律所是否为其职位连任做出过捐款。③ 2006 年《纽约时报》的一项研究披露，在过去的 30 年中，一名俄亥俄州法官在其审理的 91% 的案件中做出了对其有过竞选捐款的当事人胜诉的判决，而另一名州法官则在其审理的约 70% 的案件中偏向了在竞选中为其提供资金支持的当事人。④ 路易斯安那州的一个例子尤其夸张，法官在双方都没有为其捐款的情况下，在 47% 的案件中支持原告；但如果他从辩方收到捐款（或者当双方都有捐款但从辩方处收到更多钱），则只在 25% 的情况下支持原告，而在原告一方的捐款占优

---

① National Center for State Courts, "Judicial Selection and Retention", National Center for State Courts (n. d.), http：//www.ncsconline.org/WC/CourTopics/FAQs.asp?topic = JudSel; Adam Liptak, "Rendering Justice, With One Eye on Re-election", *The New York Times*, May 25, 2008.
② Greenberg Quinlan Rosner, "Justice at Stake-State Judges Poll", Brennan Center for Justice (2001), http：//www.justiceatstake.org/media/cms/JASJudgesSurveyResults_ EA8838C0504A5.pdf.
③ Lawrence Lessig, *Republic, Lost: How Money Corrupts Congress-and a Plan to Stop It*, New York: Hatchette, 2011; Martin Gilens, *Affluence and Influence: Economic Inequality and Political Power in America*, Princeton, NJ: Princeton University Press, 2011, p.230.
④ Adam Liptak & Janet Roberts, "Campaign Cash Mirrors a High Court's Rulings", *The New York Times*, Oct.1, 2006.

的情况下,判决原告胜诉的案件比例达90%。[1] 美国律师协会主席对这一现象评价为:"当司法系统要求法官从出庭者处索取捐款,蒙住正义女神双眼的纱布也随之被除去了。"[2] "联合公民案"的判决使公司、工会和其他特殊利益集团这群盘踞于司法系统上空的秃鹫有了更多将资金转化为权力的机会,以在立法、行政领域之外进一步扩张其政治影响力。正如一位前俄亥俄州工会官员曾指出的:"我们很久以前就意识到,选举7名法官要比选132名立法者要容易得多。"[3] 就像指南针因磁场干扰而偏离指向,在司法独立性受到捐款和特殊集团势力影响的情况下,司法系统的公正性受到了干扰甚至破坏。

在竞选腐败之外,法官司法腐败的例子也不鲜见。因为司法独立主要防范的是上级机关的行政干预,对于当事人向上干预则缺乏管束。此外,司法腐败的原因也与大多数时候对法官的相应监督与惩戒措施都十分宽松有关,因为其使得司法腐败行为的成本相应降低。根据路透社于2020年进行的首个全美司法不端行为统计,2008—2018年发生的3613起法官违法案件中,涉案法官均受到纪律处分,但其个人身份和犯罪行为的关键细节都被隐瞒,在因不当行为受到制裁后,每10名法官中就有9名被允许重返法官席。[4]

本章小结

美国民主体制危机四伏:掌握财富的"精英"购买技术专制下的政府服务,使得联邦利益大幅向地方倾斜,导致利益分配的不均衡;立法机构试图通过增设专门委员会以加强专业领域的监管,反而促使政府与商业利

---

[1] Adam Liptak & Janet Roberts, "Campaign Cash Mirrors a High Court's Rulings", *The New York Times*, Oct. 1, 2006.
[2] Carolyn B. Lamm, "Let's Leave Politics Out of It", *ABA Journal*, Vol. 96, No. 3, 2010, p. 10.
[3] Bert Brandenburg & Roy A. Schotland, "Keeping Courts Impartial Amid Changing Judicial Elections", *Dædalus*, Fall 2008, Fall, pp. 102 – 109.
[4] Michael Berens & John Shiffman, "Thousands of U. S. Judges Who Broke Laws or Oaths Remained on the Bench", Reuters (Jun. 30, 2020), https://www.reuters.com/investigates/special-report/usa-judges-misconduct/.

第二章 游说、竞选捐款与美国政治腐败：危机四伏的民主体制

益的结合日益紧密；立法与司法工作者都在为竞选捐款奔波，其立法与司法行为的公正性时常受到质疑，变相贿赂亦不鲜见。种种现象表明，美国的代议制民主"既不是真正的代议制，也不是非常的民主，因为公民自治已经让位于公司、特殊利益集团和富人的统治"。[①] 虽然美国建国至今尚未出现专制独裁者，但占总人口0.01%的顶级富人为维护既得利益，仍在持续与华盛顿的建制派和华尔街的金融精英结成利益共同体，不断培养在美国政界的代理人来满足自己的诉求。因而被游说者缠绕的国会与被金钱大肆操纵的选举制度所引发的腐败担忧，无疑是真实存在的。即便如此，美国的政治决策与选举仍不应被理解成一场纯粹的金钱游戏。诚然，宪法第一修正案赋予人民言论自由权利，延伸为游说和竞选捐款的合法基础，而随之涌入政治领域的巨额竞选资金却也造成了公民言论自由与政治平等之间根本的对立紧张关系。精英阶层和利益集团在三权分立和竞选法律制度的制约下不断试探，力求深度左右立法决策以实现利益的维系或再分配。但即使其发声被金钱不成比例地放大，产生超过一人一票的影响，仍没有任何一方能够在政治上拥有完全的确定性。正如屡创新高的竞选支出仍然无法完全保证赢得选举甚至买到选票，选举人团制度也更增加了选举制度的不确定性，2016年大选结果即是力证。四年一次的大选虽耗费巨额资金，但也使得市民与精英阶层和大公司的矛盾在对变革机会的展望和决定中，得到阶段性的纾解和妥协。2020年总统大选的焦灼与争议正是美国社会潜藏各种矛盾和不确定性爆发的集中表现，积压已久的反智主义和极端政治正确，在新媒体时代正以近乎民粹式的浪潮席卷美国社会。同时，互联网搜索引擎、社交媒体巨头审查和"黑人命贵"（Black Lives Matter）运动都在以一种前所未有的形式深度影响着美国的未来走向。随着对政府的信任度徘徊在历史低点，政治分裂已成为美国政治生活的最显著特征。无论是黑人平权、堕胎立法、非法移民居留、互联网媒体言论审查还是对社会主义意识形态的态度，各种辩论无一不在考问着每一个美国人：是继续美式民主的一路向西，坚持全球化进程，开放包容新的意识形态，还是因循250年前建国伊始的传统框架，回归保守的基督教信条，抑或抛弃盟友，万事以美国为优先？在将来，无论是民主党还是共和党入主白宫，美国人民都时刻站在通向截然不同未来的十字路口，面临着关键选择。

[①] Roger Cohen, "Germany's Lessons for China and America", *The New York Times*, May 22, 2020.

第三章　暗钱涌入政治选举：美国政治腐败的新阶段

　　现代民主国家要求政党组织和候选人在选举中必须具备强大的竞争政治力，这需要大量的资金。为了保持选举系统的正常运转，各政党和候选人需要募集大量资源来成功开展竞选活动，这也对资金披露的范围与及时性提出了很高要求。而美国以候选人为中心的独特选举制度决定了捐款主要不是经过政党，而是围绕候选人流动，又进一步增加了竞选资金的披露难度。[①] 在政党内部选举（初选、预选会议和选举大会）中，政党通常是中立的，这意味着候选人须依赖于利益团体和一群支持者来为其竞选活动筹集资金。每个候选人组成自己的竞选委员会，阐明自己的议题，无论党首是否赞成，都可以自由地宣传政策并为个人和团体争取特殊利益，同时从个人和利益集团那里建立自己的财务支持网络。若是支出屡创纪录的总统大选，则会使竞选财务披露管理面临更为严峻的挑战。

　　对竞选资金的不充分披露很可能直接导致选举甚至民主政体的腐败。一方面，政党和候选人都必须获取庞大的竞选资源；另一方面又必须避免在法律上触碰选举腐败的红线。这种矛盾与一直试图影响政府决策的特殊利益集团一拍即合。操控政治的利益驱动力过于强大，以至于政府不愿或无法有效地通过法规加以全面制止。法律所允许的向政治输送金钱的新渠道层出不穷，合法可查的竞选捐款和游说都有诸多限制，催生了难以规制的软钱、影子游说活动和旋转门现象；软钱管道被堵塞后，有组织的利益

[①] Clyde Wilcox, "Transparency and Disclosure in Political Finance: Lessons from the United States", Paper prepared for presentation at the Democracy Forum for East Asia Conference on Political Finance, Sejong Institute, Seoul, Korea, 2011, p. 20; Richard H. Pildes, "Romanticizing Democracy, Political Fragmentation, and the Decline of American Government", *The Yale Law Journal*, No. 124, 2014, pp. 839–845.

集团在美国选举中的作用却持续增强，亿万富翁借由"联合公民案"制造的漏洞，通过超级政治行动委员会无限制地向竞选活动注入资金；随着披露义务要求的下降，巨额暗钱以"501非营利组织"、有限责任公司和超级政治行动委员会为载体掩盖捐款者身份，如洪流般涌入政治选举。2010年"联合公民案"后，暗钱组织在州和联邦选举中的作用随着每个选举周期逐渐增加。在2020年大选中，政治暗钱以史无前例的规模影响了两党的白宫角逐。超过10亿美元的暗钱资助了两党在白宫和国会竞选活动，将近1.74亿美元的匿名资金支持了拜登，远超特朗普的2520万美元。[1] 深度影响选举的资金如此之巨，却往往能够游离于法律的监督之外，无疑加剧了绝大多数无力为竞选活动做出大额捐款的美国人所处的不平等地位。如今，3/4的美国人认为"美国政府制定的法律主要反映了强大的特殊利益群体想要的东西"，[2] "华盛顿的腐败是最严重的腐败问题"[3]。

第一节 暗钱组织的前身：527组织

理论上，几乎所有政治委员会，包括州、地方和联邦候选人委员会、传统政治行动委员会、超级政治行动委员会和政党都是527组织。但在实践中，527组织的定义通常仅适用于因没有"明确主张"选举或击败候选人（或政党）而不受州或联邦竞选财务法律监管的组织。在2002年国会通过《两党竞选改革法》前，软钱的捐赠方式几乎不受监管，该法通过后，为全国政党提供无限软钱的行为被禁止，州政党委员会也受到限制。但在《两党竞选改革法》禁止公司、工会、个人和其他组织匿名捐款的条

---

[1] Anna Massoglia & Karl Evers-Hillstrom, "'Dark Money' Topped $1 Billion in 2020, Largely Boosting Democrats", Open Secrets (Mar. 17, 2021), https://www.opensecrets.org/news/2021/03/one-billion-dark-money-2020-electioncycle/.

[2] James Hohmann, "The Daily 202: A Poll Commissioned by Bush and Biden Shows Americans Losing", *The Washington Post*, Jun. 26, 2018.

[3] Ashley Kirzinger & others, "Kaiser Health Tracking Poll-Late Summer 2018: The Election, Pre-Existing Conditions, and Surprises on Medical Bills", Kaiser Family Foundation (Sep. 5, 2018), https://www.kff.org/health-reform/poll-finding/kaiser-health-tracking-poll-late-summer-2018-the-election-pre-existing-conditions-and-surprises-on-medical-bills/.

文生效后,竞选财务律师在《税法》第527条中找到了一条25年前的规定,该规定允许政党、委员会或协会组成的政治团体接受捐款而无须为其缴税,使它们实质上成为一种政治组织,或宣扬一种理念,或与工会、公司相联系并被允许接受无限捐款。这种免税组织在后来被称为"527组织",国税局将其定义为"由政党、委员会、协会、基金或其他组织(无论是否成立)组织运作,以直接或间接接受捐款为主要目的的政治组织"。著名的共和党州长协会就是527组织的一员。在法律允许的范围内操作时,对527组织的捐款数额没有上限,也没有捐款主体限制,更不存在支出限制,只是不能向候选人捐款或与之协调支出。其在接受无限资金的情况下可以保持捐款者匿名,因而成为那些希望影响选举但又不留下身份信息人士的首选捐款对象。不难发现,527组织在实质上是政党、候选人和超级政治委员会对选举不受限制地施加影响的工具,只要不与候选人协调或明确主张选举或反对特定的候选人,几乎所有政治委员会如州、地方和联邦候选人委员会、传统政治行动委员会、超级政治行动委员会以及政党委员会都不受联邦选举委员会的监管。仅当527组织的选举支出超过一定数额门槛时,才需要在联邦选举委员会注册,并选择是以政治行动委员会还是以超级政治行动委员会的形式成立。因此,受联邦选举委员会监管的所有政治委员会均为527组织,但并非所有527组织都是政治委员会。但即使所有527组织都须在美国国税局注册并公开披露其捐款者,定期提交捐款和支出报告,它们对国税局的报告也要比政治行动委员会和超级政治行动委员会向联邦选举委员会的报告要慢得多。

2002年《两党竞选改革法》通过之后,政党先前进行的许多由软钱资助的活动转由527组织接管。这些团体在2004年的总统大选中筹集了约6亿美元资金,[1] 并因资助发行了许多广告,目标明确地大肆攻击竞选人而声名狼藉,被称为"现代政治的攻击犬和挑衅者"[2],且常被投诉与候选人有非法协调之嫌疑。尽管越来越多的软钱涌入数字政治广告,互联网在很大程度上仍旧是监管真空地区,作为美国选民获取信息的最普遍平台,互联网信息披露要求却远低于电视甚至露天政治广告牌,资金监管漏

---

[1] Dennis W. Johnson, *Democracy for Hire: A History of American Political Consulting*, New York: Oxford University Press, 2017, p.134.
[2] Albert W. Alschuler & others, "Why Limits on Contributions to Super PACS Should Survive Citizens United", *Fordham Law Review*, Vol.86, No.5, 2018, pp.2299–2358.

第三章 暗钱涌入政治选举：美国政治腐败的新阶段

洞持续扩大。针对527组织在2004年选举中政治活动不遵守规范的情况，联邦选举委员会在同年8月发布了新规则，要求527组织若利用筹集资金明确主张选举或不支持此候选人，则必须在委员会处注册为"政治委员会"。政治委员会必须遵守规定，以硬钱方式支付选举支出并禁止接收不受监管的软钱。此外，出资播出广播广告的527组织也被要求用硬钱支付其一半的管理费用。但由于选举法律介入的滞后性，该新规定在2004年大选之后才生效，最终仅对违规的527组织罚款了结，而后者对选举结果造成的不当影响已难以消除。新规定使得527组织必须向国税局注册并公开披露其所收捐款和支出，这也导致后来暗钱大量由527组织流向税法501节项下的组织。部分超级政治行动委员会也不再选择注册为527组织，而是以税法501（c）（4）项下的社会福利组织身份注册，从而避免在联邦选举委员会注册为需承担诸多披露义务的政治行动委员会。这些社会福利组织同样可以筹集不限数量的资金，但不必披露捐款者名单。"联合公民案"使个人直接向候选人、政党和政治行动委员会的捐款演变成了一种系统，允许匿名的个人和组织将数十万甚至数千万美元的庞大资金分配给参与政治活动的团体用于选举，这也为后来暗钱组织的爆发埋下了隐患。

　　527组织也可以被视为超级政治行动委员会的早期版本。从历史上看，527组织可以选择注册为政治行动委员会，并在联邦选举委员会的限制下直接向候选人捐款；或者可以专注于对枪支或堕胎等具体问题的倡导，而不直接支持或攻击候选人，从而被允许筹集和花费不限量的资金。在2004年的选举中，曾有527组织因模糊了倡导问题与候选人之间的界限，直接支持或批评候选人而被法庭处以罚金。527团体对于竞选资金的主导作用仅限于21世纪头十年中期，[①] 2010年的一系列关键判决使得527组织能够组成超级政治行动委员会，如今527团体的角色已部分被超级政治行动委员会所取代，后者既可以筹集无限量的资金，又可以支持候选人。

[①] Drew DeSilver & Patrick Van Kessel, "As more Money Flows Into Campaigns, Americans Worry About Its Influence", Pew Research Center（Dec. 7, 2015）, https：//www. pewresearch. org/fact-tank/2015/12/07/as-more-money-flows-into-campaigns-americans-worry-about-its-influence/.

游说、竞选捐款与美国政治腐败

第二节 "联合公民案"激发暗钱组织

美国政治系统尤其是竞选财务系统"一直面临着公开性的压力"[①],而政治暗钱就是一种讽刺性的存在。在美国政治与法律语境下,暗钱是指被未披露捐款者或资金来源未知的非营利组织或有限责任公司,所用以影响政治选举活动的金钱。[②] 1976年联邦最高法院对巴克利诉瓦莱奥一案的判决为暗钱渗入美国政治选举系统开了先例。在该案判决中,法院虽然肯定了各州有权限对公职候选人的捐款进行限制,但也根据宪法第一修正案指出,只要在广告中或政治通讯中没有提及"投票给"(vote for)、"选"(elect)、"支持"(support)、"投选票给"(cast your ballot for)、"某某进入国会"(Smith for Congress)、"vote against"(反对)、"defeat"(打败)"或"拒绝"(reject)这八个"魔法词"中的任意一个,就认为发出广告的团体或个人没有与任何候选人协作,因此其投入的资金不受《联邦竞选法》关于财务披露、捐款限制等规定的约束。此后在2008年联邦选举委员会诉威斯康星生命权公司案中,最高法院裁定在大选期间或大选开始前的几个月内,不得禁止发布广告。而在联合公民诉联邦选举委员会案的判决中,最高法院首次允许包括有限责任公司与特定非营利性公司在内的公司主体公开资助播放(呼吁人们投票赞成或反对联邦候选人的)政治广告。尽管判决声明禁止根据美国税法501(c)(3)条款组织的、可以接受免税捐款的慈善机构和基金会参与从事政治选举,但仍允许税法501(c)(4)条款的"社会福利"组织和501(c)(6)款的行业协会这两种非营利组织在选举中投入大量资金。判决为暗钱组织的爆发敞开了大门。与政治候选人、政党或政治行动委员会,以及527组织不同,这些非营利组织通常不需要披露其捐款者。这意味着公众对试图影响选票的广告、海报和广播背后的资金提供者无从知晓。显然,暗钱与捐款披露是对立的,

---

① [美]塞缪尔·亨廷顿:《美国政治:激荡于理想与现实之间》,先萌奇、景伟明译,新华出版社2017年版,第316页。
② Open Secrets, "Dark Money Basics", Open Secrets (n.d.), https://www.opensecrets.org/dark-money/dark-money-basics.php.

后者可以对捐款人施加向特定候选人、政党和团体施加捐款或不捐款的压力，暗钱则能使其完全摆脱这种压力。

一　暗钱组织的类型识别

根据依法成立团体的性质不同，暗钱组织大致可分为两类，这两类组织既可以购买政治广告、打宣传电话，也可以选择向同样发布政治广告的其他团体如超级政治行动委员会捐款，同时避免公众、捐款公司的股东或客户知道捐款人对有争议话题所持的立场。在2020年联邦选举中，暗钱支出高达10亿美元，其中6.6亿美元由不透明的政治非营利组织和空壳公司向外部团体捐出。[①]

（一）501组织

作为暗钱组织的代表类型，501组织既可以从公司、个人和工会那里收受无限捐款，又可以从不受公开要求的非营利组织和空壳公司处筹集无限捐款。501组织可以分为三类：一是依据税法501（c）（4）条款成立的非营利社会福利组织，以促进社会福利为目的，向这类组织捐款不可减税，如全国步枪协会、计划生育行动基金、全国有色人种促进协会（NAACP）和塞拉俱乐部（Sierra Club）等；二是依据税法501（c）（5）条款成立的工会；三是依据税法501（c）（6）条款成立的非营利、不参与企业利润分配的商业联合组织，通常包括商业联盟、商会、房地产委员会、贸易委员会和职业橄榄球联盟等，如美国商会（U.S. Chamber of Commerce）、美国人工作安全会、美国医学会以及美国制药研究与制药商协会（PhRMA）。501组织因成立依据的税法501节编号得名，可以合法地从（富裕的）个人、公司、工会和倡导团体处筹集无限的资金，并从事某些与候选人选举相关的活动。即使501组织实际以影响联邦、州或地方的议题、政策、任命或选举结果为目的，只要用于政治活动的预算不超过其总预算的49%，即每年在竞选活动中的花费小于自身花费的一半，则其不被视为以从事政治活动为主要目的，因而不需披露捐款者。尽管因为这些规定，501组织参加选举活动时比政治委员会受到更多限制，但实际上其受

[①] Anna Massoglia & Karl Evers-Hillstrom, "'Dark Money' Topped $1 Billion in 2020, Largely Boosting Democrats", Open Secrets (Mar. 17, 2021), https://www.opensecrets.org/news/2021/03/one-billion-dark-money-2020-electioncycle/.

到的监管并不严格。国税局从未对"主要目的"的"主要"下过定义，或者规定应如何计算总活动支出的百分比。以依据税法 501（c）(4) 条款成立的免税组织为例，其收入必须限于"慈善、教育或娱乐目的"，但其实际具有游说立法、参加政治活动和选举的"无限潜能"。法律允许 501（c）(4) 团体"自行宣布"为免税组织，意味着其自身可以决定，以是否属于"社会福利"组织，或是否应注册为从事政治活动的 527 组织（因此必须披露其捐款者）为理由，在受到国税局审查之前不透明地合法运作近两年（见表 3-1）。

表 3-1　501（c）(3) 组织[①]、501（c）(4) 组织和 527 组织对比

性质	501（c）(3)	501（c）(4)	527
税法地位	免税；对其捐款可抵税，其收受捐款无须缴纳联邦赠予税	免税；对其捐款不可抵税；政治支出须征税	免税；对其捐款不可抵税，其收受捐款无须缴纳联邦赠予税
相关组织	可组建 501（c）(4) 组织	可组建 501（c）(3) 或 527 组织	可由 501（c）(4) 组织组建
游说活动	有支出限制；含投票措施和司法提名	无支出限制；含投票措施和司法提名	允许很少的游说支出，若非出于促进政治的目的，则要征税
政治活动	禁止参加党派政治活动；可以进行无党派选民参与活动；禁止为政治活动建立 527 组织。处罚：撤销组织及其管理者免税地位	可根据联邦和州竞选财务法进行党派政治活动；必须是组织的"次要"目的而非"主要"目的	总支出无限制；遵守联邦和州竞选财务法律，包括捐款限制
国税局申报要求	年度报税	年度报税；申报政治支出	以具体组织类型为准
国税局对不可抵税捐款的披露要求	无要求	对于捐款，须通过书面、电视、广播或电话公开（有例外）；对于业务支出抵税，须披露用于游说和政治活动支出的百分比	对于捐款，须通过书面、电视、广播或电话公开；其他披露和要求适用联邦或州竞选法律
对捐款者的披露义务	无要求；申报国税局但不向公众公开	无要求；申报国税局但不向公众公开	有要求；申报国税局并依照联邦或州竞选法律申报

① 仅针对公共慈善组织，私人基金会须遵守更多限制性规定。

第三章 暗钱涌入政治选举：美国政治腐败的新阶段

　　这些组织每年可以各自在独立开支上花费数亿美元，暗中影响着选举而不会像其他组织一样面临国税局的重重审查。如在2016年的选举中活跃的暗钱组织，可以到近两年后的2017年底申报税款时才透露资金款项来源。不仅如此，共和党人在2015年秋末预算法案中附上了一项规定，该规定阻断了税务机构制定法规追查此类组织的途径。自2008年以来，随着这种在政治手腕上十分精明并具有高度党派性的所谓社会福利组织的出现，竞选融资体系发生了质变。根据2010年3月的SpeechNow.org诉联邦选举委员会案①裁定，进行独立支出（即未与候选人竞选活动协调或不接受候选人命令）的政治委员会可以接受无限制的捐款。基于该案的判决和联邦选举委员会法规的监管漏洞，大量暗钱通过非营利性的501（c）社会福利团体和商业协会，向联邦选举注入了大量的秘密捐款。数据显示，2004—2012年，501（c）组织的支出增长了近500%，从不到6000万美元增长到3.34亿美元；同期，527组织的总支出下降了65%，从4.31亿美元下降至1.51亿美元。② 无疑，这些从527组织流失的金额流向了501（c）组织，其中一部分流向了超级政治行动委员会，二者在2014年共计筹集了6.09亿美元。③

　　联邦选举委员会公布的数据显示，2018年选举周期中最大的暗钱支出者为"多数向前"（Majority Forward）组织，这是一个自由主义派别的501（c）（4）非营利组织，其在2018年选举中花费超过4600万美元④，该组织资金来源至今不明，因为它仅仅将支出用于"发行广告"（见图3-1），而并没有明确支持或反对候选人，并且不会将广告投放在初选前30天或大选前60天内。这些广告全部用来攻击"摇摆州"的共和党参议员。尽管最近的联邦选举委员会指南⑤要求所有的外部支出团体必须披露在过去一年中所有超过250美元的独立支出，以及出于"政治目的"的超过200

---

① SpeechNow.org v. FEC, 599 F.3d 686（D.C.Cir.2010）.
② Francis Barry, "Forget the Dictionary, Super PACs aren't New", Bloomberg View（Mar.21, 2021），https：//www.bloomberg.com/opinion/articles/2014-03-21/forget-the-dictionary-super-pacs-aren-t-new.
③ Francis Barry, "Forget the Dictionary, Super PACs aren't New", Bloomberg View（Mar.21, 2021），https：//www.bloomberg.com/opinion/articles/2014-03-21/forget-the-dictionary-super-pacs-aren-t-new.
④ Anna Massoglia & Karl Evers-Hillstrom, "Liberal 'Dark Money' Group Gets an Early Start Targeting GOP Senators ahead of 2020", Open Secrets（Jan.31, 2019），https：//www.opensecrets.org/news/2019/01/lib-dark-money-group-majority-forward-targeting-gop-senators-2020/.
⑤ FEC, "FEC Provides Guidance Following U.S. District Court Decision in CREW v. FEC, 316 F.Supp.3d 349（D.D.C.2018）", FEC（2018），https：//www.fec.gov/updates/fec-provides-guidance-following-us-district-court-decision-crew-v-fec-316-f-supp-3d-349-ddc-2018/.

· 113 ·

游说、竞选捐款与美国政治腐败

```
                                                              Approved
                                                              1/18/19
   NAB Form PB-18 Issues

              AGREEMENT FORM FOR
           NON-CANDIDATE/ISSUE ADVERTISEMENTS

   Station and Location:                    Date:
   WRAZ-TV, Raleigh, NC                     1/18/19

   I, Mike Furman - authorized media buyer
   do hereby request station time concerning the following issue:

   Majority Forward
                   Anti Thom Tillis


   Does the programming (in whole or in part) communicate "a message
   relating to any political matter of national importance?"
        ■ Yes                              □ No

   For programming that "communicates a message relating to any political matter of
   national importance," list the name of the legally qualified candidate(s) the programming
   refers to, the offices being sought, the date(s) of the election(s) and/or the issue to
   which the communication refers (if applicable):

   Thom Tillis  —  US Senate, Nov 3 2020


   I represent that the payment for the above described broadcast time has been furnished
   by (name and address):
   Majority Forward
   700 13th Street NW, Suite 600
   Washington, DC 20005
```

图 3-1　"多数向前"组织在美国广播电视协会 2019 年 1 月的登记记录

注："多数向前"组织计划于 2020 年 11 月在北卡罗来纳州播放攻击共和党参议员汤姆·提利斯（Thom Tillis）的广告。

资料来源：Anna Massoglia & Karl Evers-Hillstrom, "Liberal 'Dark Money' Group Gets an Early Start Targeting GOP Senators ahead of 2020", Open Secrets（Jan. 31, 2019），https：//www.opensecrets. org/news/2019/01/lib-dark-money-group-majority-forward-targeting-gop-senators-2020/.

美元的捐赠者身份。但"多数向前"组织自称"不接受指定用于特定政治目的的捐款",因而仍无须透露背后的资助者。这也是多数501组织规避联邦选举委员会监管的惯用说辞,而该指南也未对"政治目的"进行明确定义,因此在实际操作中基本没有约束力。另外,虽然国税局规定禁止501(c)(4)非营利组织以政治活动为主要目的,但与其他很多501组织一样,"多数向前"组织除了十分明显的政治活动之外,其社会福利工作活动都难以查询追溯。501(c)(4)社会福利组织在特朗普执政期间规模扩大了两倍,[1] 成为美国政治中最强大的资金力量之一。如与参议院共和党领导层保持"一致"的501(c)(4)非营利组织"一个国家"(One Nation),其在2020年选举周期中向联邦选举提供的资金比任何其他暗钱组织都要多,其中约有1.02亿美元用于竞选捐款和广告。[2]

根据501(c)(6)条款成立的商业联合组织也是特殊利益集团影响选举结果的理想工具之一。这些利益集团通常会建立自己的非营利组织来支付选举广告的费用,但如果资金庞大或工作量巨大,其也会选择与已经存在的众多第三方暗钱组织合作。例如在2020年中游说支出高达5930万美元的501(c)(6)非营利组织"美国商会"[3] 以为捐款者保密为营销策略,实际出售的服务则是一种政治掩护。对不想将自身形象与负面攻击广告挂钩的保险公司、制药商和医疗设备制造巨头来说,美国商会就像是一位乐于助人、专替人干"脏活"的好帮手。事实证明,501组织正作为一种新型的政治手段,不断扩大控制巨额竞选资金的富人对选举的匿名影响。

(二)有限责任公司

有限责任公司(LLC)在法律上具备许多必要的业务功能,但因缺乏透明度且组成结构独特而很容易被滥用。与英法澳等发达国家相比,美国在公司透明度问题上十分松懈,根据"公开公司"组织发布的公司注册数据,在全球范围内,美国在公司透明度方面排名第43位,以33/100的得

---

[1] Scott Bland, "Liberal Dark-money Behemoth Raised Nearly $140M Last Year", *Politico*, Nov. 20, 2020.
[2] Anna Massoglia, "'Dark Money' Groups Find New Ways to Hide Donors in 2020 Election", Open Secrets (Oct. 30, 2020), https://www.opensecrets.org/news/2020/10/dark-money-2020-new-ways-to-hide-donors/.
[3] Open Secrets, "Top Spenders", Open Secrets (n.d.), https://www.opensecrets.org/federal-lobbying/top-spenders.

分落后于俄罗斯、所罗门群岛和许多东欧国家。① 资金来源不明的有限责任公司幕后往往涉及数十亿美元的非法活动,如洗钱、信用卡欺诈和恐怖分子融资。作为"最黑暗"的暗钱组织,以政治活动为目的成立的有限责任公司可以帮助掩盖捐赠者身份或政治候选人的资金来源。由于隶属州法律管辖,成立有限责任公司提交公司章程所需的信息往往很少。尽管大多数州都要求登记有限责任公司的名称、地址和注册代理人或创始成员,但在特拉华州或怀俄明州等地,州法公共记录既不需识别注册代理人或控制人,也不必由首席执行官和其他 C 级高管②组成公司董事会,甚至不必组织营利活动。由于公司被允许在实际所有者匿名的情况下成立,因而一部分会在实际上成为所谓的空壳公司。凭借对直接的创始人所有权和对公司结构的极少要求,有限责任公司成为暗钱组织转移政治资金的传输工具,同时保护了捐赠者身份或资金来源的隐秘性。

1997 年,一家名为"三人管理"(Triad Management)的空壳公司花费 300 万美元发布了针对 26 名众议院和 3 名参议院民主党参选人的攻击性广告。参议院经调查发现,超过一半的广告资金来自"经济教育信托基金"(Economic Education Trust),而该信托基金由工业巨子查尔斯和大卫·科赫兄弟投资。③ 科赫家族出资设立的许多政治机器都以 501 组织或有限责任公司的形式隐名运作。又如 2012 年的 W Spann 有限责任公司案,W Spann 公司成立于 3 月,于同年 7 月解散,所有法律手续由一名波士顿的房地产律师完成,其间没有任何股东、高管或业务活动的记录。在其存在的短短四个月中,唯一的业务活动就是向由三名罗姆尼的前助手创立的超级政治行动委员会"恢复我们的未来"捐款 100 万美元。④ 另外,River Birch LLC 和 Willow LLC 两家有限责任公司自 2015 年以来已向名为"美国新视野"(New Horizons USA)的超级政治行动委员会捐款 30 万美元,但二者向州监管机构报告的 20 万美元捐款没有出现在联邦竞选财务文件中,⑤ 两份报告本应

---

① OpenCorporates, "The Open Company Data Index", OpenCorporates (n. d.), http://registries.opencorporates.com.
② 如首席财务官(CFO)、首席运营官(COO)和首席营销官(CMO)等。
③ Jane Mayer, "Covert Operations: The Billionaire Brothers Who are Waging a War against Obama", *The New Yorker*, Aug. 23, 2010.
④ Dan Eggen, "Short-lived Firm's $1M Donation to GOP Fund Raises Concern Over Transparency", *The Washington Post*, Aug. 04, 2011.
⑤ Michael Beckel & Amisa Ratliff, "Mystery Money", Isssue One (Jul. 29, 2020), https://www.issueone.org/wp-content/uploads/2020/07/Mystery-Money-Report-Tipsheet.pdf.

第三章　暗钱涌入政治选举：美国政治腐败的新阶段

该相同，而向联邦选举委员会提交虚假竞选财务报告显然是违法的。

上述仅仅是在过去十年中向各个超级政治行动委员会提供巨额捐款而被披露的极少数空壳公司。响应性政治中心发现，取消对竞选捐款的限额管制与匿名捐款者捐款的大幅增加相对应。[1] 自联邦最高法院2010年的"联合公民案"改变超级政治行动委员会的捐款上限以来，有限责任公司开始更加有效地掩盖大量竞选捐款来源，暗钱捐款数量激增。2016年大选中就有超过4000家有限责任公司向各类政治团体捐款[2]，金额接近2000万美元（见图3-2）。而在2020年大选中，有限责任公司和非营利暗钱组织向外部团体提供了创纪录的4.3亿美元外部资金。[3] 2022年，三名政府承包商高管在哥伦比亚特区被起诉，起诉书显示，由于法律禁止政府承包商在联邦选举中捐款，被告创建了一个空壳公司，并利用该空壳公司向超级政治行动委员会提供非法捐款，委员会则利用该资金支持某参议院候选人选举。[4]

由于缺乏透明度和问责制，超级政治行动委员会越来越依赖匿名空壳公司的捐款，每个选举周期都有数百万美元的政治支出来源被掩盖，这也使得有限责任公司成为暗钱集团中最黑暗的一种组织。对于这类空壳公司的泛滥与监管之缺位，甚至有研究机构这样评论道："在美国，申办一家空壳公司所需要登记的信息甚至比办理一张图书馆借阅卡所需的个人信息还少。"[5] 此外，美国法律禁止外国政府和外国公民直接或间接从事影响美国选举的活动，外国人可以在美国设立有限责任公司，但不能通过其为选举捐款。可是从技术上来看，只要这类公司不主动披露捐款者，就几乎无

---

[1] Gabbi Fisher, "Limited Liability Donations: Corporate Dark Money Remains a Glaring Problem in the US", Sunlight Foundation (Aug. 5, 2014), https://sunlightfoundation.com/2014/08/05/limited-liability-donations-corporate-dark-money-remains-a-glaring-problem-in-the-us/.

[2] Sue Halpern, "Filling the Empty Seats at the F.E.C. Won't Fix America's Corrupt Elections", The New Yorker, Aug. 04, 2011.

[3] Anna Massoglia, "'Dark Money' Groups Find New Ways to Hide Donors in 2020 Election", Open Secrets (Oct. 30, 2020), https://www.opensecrets.org/news/2020/10/dark-money-2020-new-ways-to-hide-donors/.

[4] Department of Justice, "Former Government Contractor Executives Indicted for Unlawful Campaign Contributions", DOJ (Feb. 20, 2022), https://www.justice.gov/opa/pr/former-government-contractor-executives-indicted-unlawful-campaign-contributions.

[5] Global Financial Integrity, "The Library Card Project: The Ease of Forming Anonymous Companies in the United States", Global Financial Integrity (Mar. 21, 2019), https://secureservercdn.net/50.62.198.97/34n.8bd.myftpupload.com/wp-content/uploads/2019/03/GFI-Library-Card-Project.pdf?time=1648218825.

法确定捐款的来源，不仅如此，外国人还可以利用有限责任公司等商业实体（外围团体）逃避反腐败法律。因此，空壳公司已经成为外国政治暗钱流入的重要媒介，美国政治选举也因此被外国势力干预的疑云所笼罩。

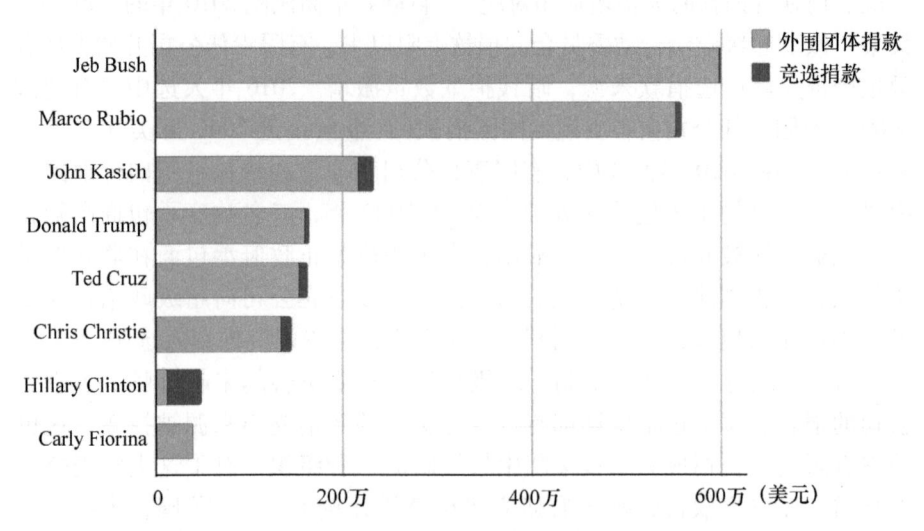

图 3-2　2016 年有限责任公司向总统候选人捐款情况

资料来源：Ashley Balcerzak, "Surge in LLC Contributions Brings More Mystery about True Donors", Open Secrects（Apr. 27, 2017）, https：//www.opensecrets.org/news/2017/04/surge-in-llc-contributions-more-mystery/; Open Secrets, "Cost of Election", Open Secrets（n. d.）, https：//www.opensecrets.org/overview/cost.php.

二　暗钱组织掩体：超级政治行动委员会

联邦政治行动委员会是在一个日历年内筹集或花费超过 1000 美元，用于支持联邦选举中的候选人或议题的组织。其主要目的是从其成员和捐款者处汇集资金，以支持特定的候选人或政治议题。联邦政治行动委员会受到每次选举可直接为候选人捐款 5000 美元等来自联邦选举法律的约束，并须在联邦选举委员会进行注册接受监管。超级政治行动委员会是政治行动委员会的一种，由于超级政治行动委员会不能直接向候选人捐款，因此也不受常规政治行动委员会必须遵守的筹款和支出限制，其可以从个人捐款者那里筹集无限量的资金，只要这些捐款者位于美国境内即可。尽管不能直接为特定候选人捐款，并且被禁止将其活动与候选人的竞选活动进行

第三章　暗钱涌入政治选举：美国政治腐败的新阶段

协调，超级政治行动委员会可以无限制地在诸如广告等外部活动上花费大量资金，以支持政治候选人或问题，因而在技术上也被称为"仅独立支出委员会"（independent expenditure-only committee）。2010 年"联合公民案"以来，超级政治行动委员会已经成为暗钱组织的有效掩体，作为后者资金的上下游制造监管障碍；同时联邦法律中的漏洞也使其利用从暗钱组织处获得的资金与候选人建立实质上的协调，并帮助大捐款人进一步放大巨额暗钱在政治活动中的影响。

（一）超级政治行动委员会与暗钱组织相互依附

自 2006 年公开秘密网站开始追踪暗钱以来，未披露捐款者的暗钱组织在联邦选举中的直接支出已超过 10 亿美元。① 尽管暗钱组织在"联合公民案"前已普遍存在，但"联合公民案"判决直接为暗钱组织提供了新的输送渠道——超级政治行动委员会。2010 年 1 月起，暗钱组织可以不受限制地从支持其的公司财产中支取政治开支，用以支持或打压政治候选人，从而影响选举结果。

超级政治行动委员会在暗钱组织资金网络中起到的掩护作用是双向的。一方面，可以作为暗钱组织的资金下游，制造多一层资金结构，使得法定披露的层级无法触及源头（见图 3-3）。虽然超级政治行动委员会在法律上必须披露其捐款者，但其可接受不需披露捐款者的暗钱组织（如从事政治活动的 501 非营利组织和没有披露其捐款者的空壳公司）的无限捐款，而无法追溯原始捐款者。此时它们也被视为暗钱组织。如公司和个人可以向 501 组织捐款，无须公开披露资助者，然后 501 组织向超级政治行动委员会捐款，数额不限。随后超级政治行动委员会报告其接受了 501 组织的捐款，但后者的原始捐款者无须公开。这不只是假设，实际上就是超级政治行动委员会"美国十字路口"（American Crossroads）和 501 组织"十字路口 GPS"（Crossroads GPS）的合作模式。如果暗钱组织要在电视上播放自己的议题广告，就必须在大选前 60 天之内披露其捐款者。② 相

---

① Anna Massoglia, "State of Money in Politics: Billion-dollar 'Dark Money' Spending is Just the Tip of the Iceberg", Open Secrets (Feb. 21, 2019), https://www.opensecrets.org/news/2019/02/somp3-billion-dollar-dark-money-tip-of-the-iceberg/.

② 不能说"魔法词"但也不需要披露广告发布者身份的是议题广告，可以由暗钱组织资助；能说"魔法词"且需要披露发布者身份的广告属于独立支出（independent expenditure），往往由超级政治行动委员会资助。在初选前 30 天和大选前 60 天内播放的议题广告被视为竞选通讯（electioneering communications），需要像独立支出一样披露资助者。但披露仅限于电视和广播，互联网或社交媒体上的政治广告不在披露之列。2002 年《两党竞选改革法》曾禁止工会和特定公司为此类竞选通讯支出其法人或组织自有资金，但该规定被 2010 年"联合公民案"推翻。

反，如果暗钱组织向超级政治行动委员会捐款，大捐款者可以有效地在竞选中花费无限的金钱播放同样的广告，同时向公众隐瞒自己的身份。在2020年的选举中，暗钱团体通过广告支出和对超级政治行动委员会等政治委员会的捐款达到了创纪录的7.5亿美元。[①] 在创下支出纪录的同时，暗钱的披露程度也降到了最低。2020年的所有暗钱支出中，向联邦选举委员会报告的直接外部支出仅为9560万美元，低于2010年"联合公民案"裁决以来的所有选举周期。[②] 不透露其捐款者的501组织将暗钱转移到与其关系密切的超级政治行动委员会上，并将更多的现金转用于未向联邦选举委员会报告的"发行广告"。

同时，超级政治行动委员会也可以作为暗钱组织的资金上游，成为后者的资金来源（见图3-3）。暗钱组织依法不需要披露其捐款者，而超级政治行动委员会也可以利用披露的滞后性带来的时间差，无须在选举前披露其支出明细。当前竞选财务法律的披露规则是在1974年制定的，当时竞选活动组织的财务主管用打字机打字，然后将报告邮寄给联邦选举委员会，报告的时效较为滞后。现在竞选活动团体都拥有捐款和支出的电子数据库，能够很快捷地提交报告，但是披露时效规则并未更新以适应技术变化。

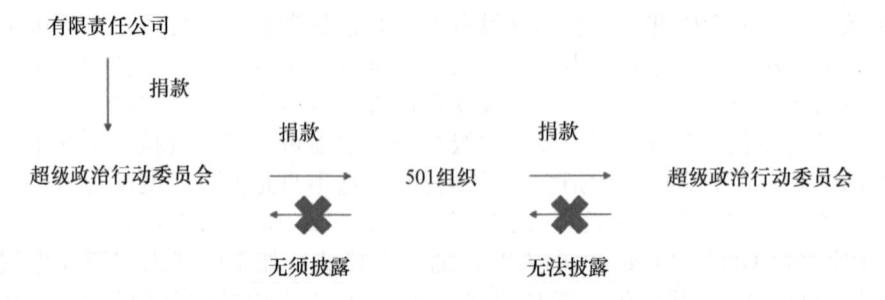

图3-3 暗钱组织、有限责任公司与超级政治行动委员会配合掩盖资金来源模式

[①] Anna Massoglia, "'Dark Money' Groups Find New Ways to Hide Donors in 2020 Election", Open Secrets (Oct. 30, 2020), https://www.opensecrets.org/news/2020/10/dark-money-2020-new-ways-to-hide-donors/.

[②] Anna Massoglia, "'Dark Money' Groups Find New Ways to Hide Donors in 2020 Election", Open Secrets (Oct. 30, 2020), https://www.opensecrets.org/news/2020/10/dark-money-2020-new-ways-to-hide-donors/.

超级政治行动委员会也可以依附于暗钱组织,使得后者得以在与其共享实体的情况下维持匿名运营。同一个人或团体可以同时创建超级政治行动委员会和非营利组织,并结合使用二者,从而使得原始资金来源更难以追溯。近年来新成立的暗钱组织越来越多地选择注册为非营利性质的501组织,而这些组织都与其支持的超级政治行动委员会紧密相关(见表3-2)。事实上,这些暗钱组织中有许多与其资助的政治委员会共享人员、办公空间和其他资源,因此许多超级政治委员会都是暗钱组织的附属组织。如上述的"多数向前"组织与由数个亿万富翁捐款设立的"参议院多数党"[①] 超级政治行动委员会就有紧密联系,二者共享雇员和办公空间。选举中这类操作的普遍程度甚至已经到了涉嫌合法化洗钱的地步,因此大多数外围开支都由暗钱组织所提供。此外还有一种模式是超级政治行动委员会向附属其的501非营利组织捐款。由于后者本身就是暗钱组织,在其接受捐款后,资金来源也较为隐秘。

表3-2　　　　　暗钱组织与超级政治行动委员会对比[②]

	超级政治行动委员会	暗钱组织
实体性质	选举委员会	非营利组织
监管机构	联邦选举委员会	国税局
披露捐款者义务	有	无
披露支出义务	有	次年报税时申报
捐款限制	无	无
政治性	完全政治性	政治活动支出≤50%
与候选人协作	不允许	不允许

另一种与暗钱组织相互依附的是混合型政治行动委员会(Hybrid

[①] 这类行动委员会与政党高层有着紧密的联系,因此对独立支出的非政党实体的巨额捐款正流入这类民主党"替代物",而不是进入党组织本身的机关(如民主党参议院竞选委员会),因为现行法律不允许政党接受仅用于独立支出的无限制捐款。
[②] 在某些情况下,超级政治行动委员会也可以被视为暗钱组织。尽管这些超级政治行动委员会在法律上必须披露其捐款者,但它们可以接受政治性非营利组织和未披露其捐款者的空壳公司的无限捐款,此时它们也被视为暗钱组织。详见下节。

PAC）。混合型政治行动委员会同样受到联邦选举委员会监管，必须公开报告其财务状况以及捐款者的身份。混合型政治行动委员会既可以作为传统的政治行动委员会运作，如向候选人委员会捐款，又可以作为独立支出的超级政治行动委员会。与超级政治行动委员会的不同之处在于，混合型政治行动委员会不仅可以直接向选举和委员会提供有限的资金，同时仍可以无限制地独立支出。因此从本质上讲，混合政治行动委员会相当于在同一屋檐下同时运行的传统政治行动委员会和超级政治行动委员会。但其必须为两种相应支出保留两个单独隔离的银行账户，并向联邦选举委员会报告这两个账户的所有收支。其独立支出账户可以募集并接受个人、公司、工会和其他政治委员会的无限制捐款，以资助独立支出及其他涉及联邦候选人或鼓励选民投票的广告，但不得将这些资金用于另一个账户，即用于传统政治行动委员会的捐款。混合型政治行动委员通常也与501组织结合紧密。如"美国未来前进"（Future Forward USA）是一个新成立的混合型政治行动委员会，直到2020年才第一次向联邦选举委员会报告与选举相关的广告，该组织花费了近1亿美元支持拜登，同时在广播中攻击特朗普总统，它的大部分资金来自未透露捐款者的组织。根据联邦选举委员会发布的文件，"美国未来前进"在10月的前两周从附属其的501（c）（4）非营利组织"美国未来前进行动"（Future Forward USA Action）处获得了高达2900万美元的捐款。[①] 仅在2018年选举周期中，超级政治行动委员会和混合型政治行动委员会就从暗钱组织处总计获得约1.76亿美元的捐款。[②]

以上数字并不包括"弹出式"超级政治行动委员会（pop-up super PACs）的支出。超级政治行动委员会可以自行选择每月或每季度向联邦选举委员会报告其捐款者，但由于报告时间的滞后性，其很可能滥用该规定，选择在选举后披露捐款者，以帮助后者在投票结束前隐瞒身份。这数个月的时间差，就给了"弹出式"超级政治行动委员会匿名活动的机会。其通过在联邦选举委员会申报日期截止之后战略性地提交编队文书，然后

[①] Karl Evers-Hillstrom, "Pro-Biden Super PAC Funds $100 Million Ad Campaign with 'Dark Money'", Open Secrets (Oct. 23, 2020), https://www.opensecrets.org/news/2020/10/pro-biden-super-pac-darkmon/.

[②] Karl Evers-Hillstrom, "'Dark Money' Groups Funneled Millions to Powerful Super PACs During 2018 Midterms", Open Secrets (Jan. 3, 2019), https://www.opensecrets.org/news/2019/01/dark-money/.

迅速投入数百万美元参加竞选，以此将捐款者的身份掩藏直至选举日前一天。在2020年大选中，民主党和共和党的弹出式超级政治行动委员会同时在9月1日成立，随后的一个月各自在电视和广播广告上花费1亿和9000万美元，占当时竞选支出的80%，为特朗普和拜登竞选发挥了重要作用，最终2020年总统大选再次打破电视和广播广告支出纪录。①

通过与超级政治行动委员会合作，暗钱组织史无前例地向2020年选举输送了无限的秘密政治支出，导致选举深受国内寡头与境外势力干涉的影响。越来越多的资金来源披露结果表明，暗钱组织作为超级政治行动委员会的主要捐款者之一，不但没有随着越发严格的规制有所削减，反而通过超级政治行动委员会和其他外部支出团体进行资金二次集中；越来越多由个人紧密控制的有限责任公司取代个人身份，成为超级政治行动委员会的最大捐款者。超级政治行动委员会与有限责任公司在实际捐款者及其资金支出的团体与候选人之间增加了一层隔离，并利用对下游捐款者身份的披露来制造资金来源公开的假象。

（二）超级政治行动委员会与候选人建立实质协调

超级政治行动委员会与传统政治行动委员会的不同之处意味着，前者可以接受无限制的资金作为软钱，但被禁止直接向候选人或政党捐款或与之协调。此限制旨在防止超级政治行动委员会在竞选活动期间与其支持候选人的竞选活动相互合作补充，如就某些战略信息或行动时机进行沟通，或参与可能导致捐款人与候选人进行利益交换的谈判，仅候选人和超级政治行动委员会经理通过媒体或其他公共领域讨论竞选策略是合法的。但实际上，超级政治行动委员会完全可能支持特定的候选人，某些超级政治行动委员会正是由候选人的前员工或同事进行管理或提供咨询。政治行动委员会也可以选择设置一个账户作为内部超级政治行动委员会，接受无法直接捐赠给候选人的无限捐款。

相较于领导力即支持多个候选人的政治行动委员会②，专门针对单个

---

① Ben Kamisar, "Meet the Press Blog: Latest News, Analysis and Data Driving the Political Discussion", NBC News (Jan. 6, 2021), https://www.nbcnews.com/politics/meet-the-press/blog/meet-press-blog-latest-news-analysis-data-driving-political-discussion-n988541/ncrd1245783#blogHeader.

② 也称为领导型政治行动委员会（leadership PACs）或多候选人政治行动委员会。其创建目的是为国会领导人筹措资金以资助其他候选人，受到与传统政治行动委员会相同的限制，允许向每位候选人提供最高5000美元的捐款，但可以通过民意调查和支付旅费等方式来使其支持的候选人受益。据联邦选举委员会统计，截至2023年12月31日，这样的委员会数量已达753个。

候选人的超级政治行动委员会是各类超级政治行动委员会中特别可能滋生腐败的一种形式：其只是帮助捐款者和候选人绕过个人在每次选举中至多能给单个联邦候选人2500美元捐款限额的工具。该限制由国会于1974年制定，被视为抵制选举腐败的重要壁垒。单一候选人的超级政治行动委员会仅支持一名候选人，但它们实际上也是候选人所支持的竞选活动所创制的一部分。这类超级政治行动委员会筹款的活动，有时是由候选人的竞选助手和政治同僚，有时甚至是由候选人本人参加，其往往能无上限地筹集数十万到数千万美元的资金，同时不受限制的支出也直接使得候选人受益，因而从效果上看，与给候选人直接供款并无二致。

2012年总统候选人罗姆尼的竞选团队和他的超级政治行动委员会"恢复我们的未来"（Restore Our Future）就选择了同一家政治咨询公司和活动策划公司，并在同一家酒店租用了房间，依靠的是同一批来自纽约的筹款人。但从法律上看，罗姆尼的超级政治行动委员会仍然保持"独立"。不仅如此，禁止协调的规定自身还存在一些明显漏洞：禁止将超级政治行动委员会的支出与候选人的支出进行协调的规则，只限制了候选人向超级政治行动委员会的经理提供建议，而并不限制候选人与超级政治行动委员会的捐款者间的交流。候选人仍然可以告知捐款者他们希望如何使用超级政治行动委员会的资金，只要捐款者不在法律上以候选者代理人身份将候选人的意愿传达给实际决定资金用途者，就可以充当候选者的事实代理人。而且只要遵守一定限制，候选人也同样可以建议捐款者如何使用其公司自有资金，如提议捐款给特定的超级政治行动委员会等。① 自2012年的选举周期开始，所有主要的共和党总统候选人都有超级政治行动委员会的支持，一些民主党人如奥巴马总统也有自己的超级政治行动委员会"美国优先行动"（Priorities USA Action），2020年拜登与特朗普的竞选也是如此。

如果候选人被发现指示政治行动委员会或超级政治行动委员会播放消息或电视广告，其花费将计入硬钱，同时也构成对竞选财务法律的违反。但在实践中，超级政治行动委员会与候选人或政党的违规协作触发刑事诉讼的可能性极小，甚至连民事处罚都很少见。选举委员会的处罚也没有及时性，往往是在大选结束之后很久才会实施。1999—2011年，联邦选举委员会对候选人委员会与独立开支的个人或组织之间的协作开展过三项调

---

① FEC, "Advisory Opinion 2011 - 12", FEC（Jun. 30, 2011）, https：//saos. fec. gov/saos/searchao; jsessionid = A07F1B8AF176F6344186DE1729A7D398? SUBMIT = continue&PAGE_ NO = 0.

第三章　暗钱涌入政治选举：美国政治腐败的新阶段

查，其中两次调查结果显示违规协作，罚款总额仅为2.6万美元，金额完全是由两党6名议员组成的选举委员会决定的。[①]

(三) 大捐款人通过超级政治行动委员会放大政治影响

2010年联合公民的胜诉并未直接涉及超级政治行动委员会，但其判决公司和工会有权自由使用自有资产进行支出（如用于播放政治广告），其既可以是独立支出，也可以是竞选通讯（即在选举前提及候选人的广告，但不一定明示支持或反对候选人当选）。此前，此类广告通常必须通过附属于工会或公司等的传统政治行动委员会筹集捐款资助。2010年3月，哥伦比亚特区上诉法院在SpeechNow.org诉联邦选举委员会案中裁定，仅用于独立支出的捐款并非竞选捐款，不受宪法的限制。联邦法官认为"无限制的独立支出会导致腐败的论点是无效的"，这种观点"在'联合公民案'后显然没有任何价值"。[②]该判决催生了超级政治行动委员会，其可以从非外国的公司、工会、协会和个人处筹集无限量的资金，进行独立政治活动，如无限量地将资金花费在购买政治广告或选票调查等相关服务上，以公开支持或反对政治候选人。在超级政治行动委员会产生之前，只有拒绝公司和工会捐款的个人、政党委员会、传统政治行动委员会和非营利组织才能进行独立支出，而随着2010年"联合公民案"和SpeechNow案对捐款限制的取消，超级政治行动委员会数量迅速增加，在2022年竞选周期中已达到2476个，[③]其主导的独立支出与其他形式的外部支出呈指数增长（见图3-4）。在2020年大选中，超级政治行动委员会筹集捐款总额高达创纪录的34.2亿美元，几乎是2016年17.9亿美元的两倍，2020年总支出约21.3亿美元[④]。

[①] Rachael Marcus & John Dunbar, "Punishment for Coordination between Candidates and Outside Groups is Rare", The Center for Public Integrity (May 19, 2014), https://publicintegrity.org/federal-politics/rules-against-coordination-between-super-pacs-candidates-tough-to-enforce/.

[②] 599 F.3d 686 (D.C. Cir. 2010).

[③] Open Secrets, "2022 Outside Spending, by Super PAC", Open Secrets (n.d.), https://www.opensecrets.org/outside-spending/super_pacs. 竞选结束之后数量会有所回落，下次选举前又会增加，循环往复，但总体上每个选举周期数量都在增加。据该网站统计，截至2023年12月25日，Super PAC的数量为1799个。

[④] Open Secrets, "Super PACs", Open Secrets (n.d.), https://www.opensecrets.org/outside-spending/super_pacs/2020?chrt=2022&disp=O&type=S; Open Secrets, "2016 Outside Spending, by Super PAC", Open Secrets (n.d.), https://www.opensecrets.org/outside-spending/super_pacs/2016?chrt=2022&disp=O&type=S.

游说、竞选捐款与美国政治腐败

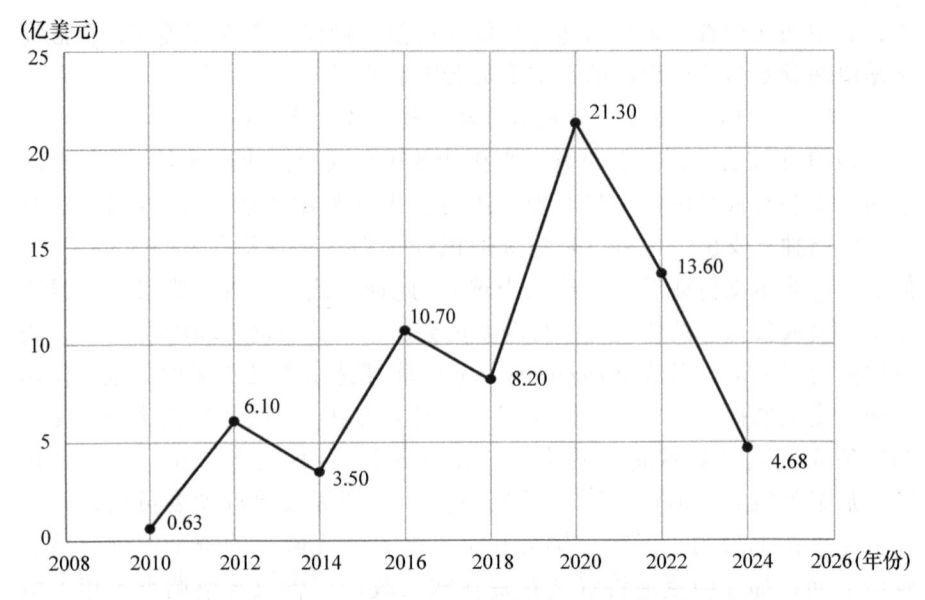

(亿美元)

图 3-4　2010—2024 年选举周期超级政治行动委员会支出

资料来源：Open Secrets, "Outside Spending", Open Secrets (n. d.), https://www.opensecrets.org/outsidespending/; Open Secrets, "Super PACs", 数据截至 2024 年 2 月 25 日。

大捐款者的影响也随着超级政治行动委员会的资金规模不断放大。在与总统竞选和国会竞选活动相关的支出中，1/5 以上来自资金来源与支出均不受限制的委员会和团体。[①] 同时，这些团体的资金来源也变得越发集中，越来越依赖于少数大捐款人所提供的资金。2010—2015 年，几乎所有超级政治行动委员会支出中的 60% 都可追溯到 195 名个人捐款者及其配偶名下。[②] 2016 年大选中，向超级政治行动委员会捐款排名前 100 者捐款总额约为 11 亿美元，占全部捐款的 67.8%，平均每个人或机构捐款者捐出约 1100 万美元；[③] 对比在 2020 年大选中，向超级政治行动委员会捐款总

[①] Bob Biersack, "8 Years Later: How Citizens United Changed Campaign Finance", Open Secrets (Feb. 7, 2018), https://www.opensecrets.org/news/2018/02/how-citizens-united-changed-campaign-finance/.

[②] Daniel I. Weiner, "Citizens United Five Years Later", Brennan Center for Justice (Jan. 15, 2015), https://www.brennancenter.org/publication/citizens-united-five-years-later.

[③] Open Secrets, "Super PACs: How Many Donors Give", Open Secrets (n. d.), https://www.opensecrets.org/outside-spending/donor-stats/2016?type=B.

第三章 暗钱涌入政治选举：美国政治腐败的新阶段

人数逾 80 万，而前 100 名大捐款者却占据了 69.7% 的更高比例资金，平均每人捐款激增至 2140 万美元①（见图 3-5）。超级政治行动委员会收到捐款大部分来自富人的事实从侧面证明了其正是最富裕的 1% 甚至 0.01% 的美国人的政治代理人。这类资金来源特定、与竞选人往往存在实质关联的外部组织，在庞大经济资源的加持下进行政治活动，只要其中有一名捐款者为暗钱组织，都可能破坏选举的透明度乃至公正性。

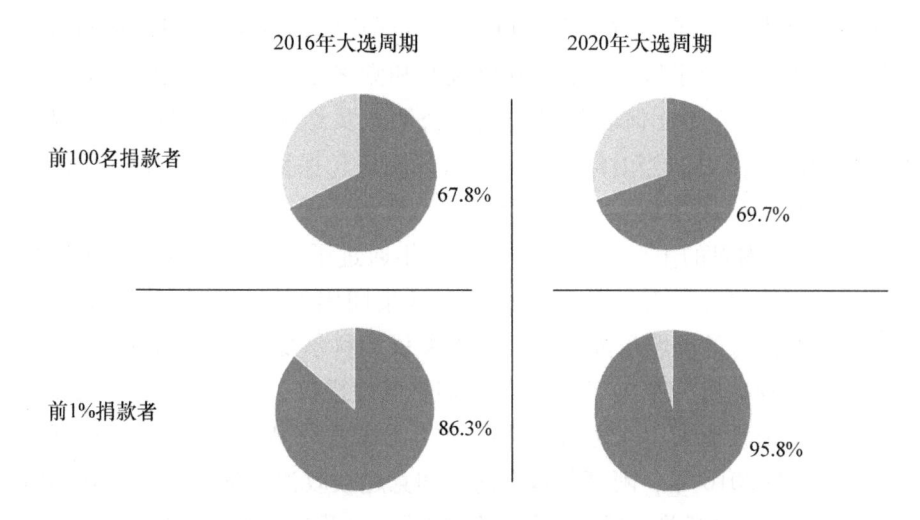

图 3-5 2016 年与 2020 年超级政治行动委员会大捐款人捐款比例

资料来源：Open Secrets, "Super PACs: How Many Donors Give", Open Secrets (n.d.), https://www.opensecrets.org/outside-spending/donor-stats/2016? type = B.

不言而喻，当捐款者向候选人的超级政治行动委员会捐款 1000 万美元时，通过超级政治行动委员会的媒介作用，捐款者默认可以购买到与捐款价值同等或更高的影响力。2010 年的"联合公民案"判决不仅造就了超级政治行动委员会，也为腐败提供了可乘之机。在许多人看来，"不受约束的超级政治行动委员会捐款已成为美国严重腐败的象征"②。与 40 年前水门事件时不同，"联合公民案"时代的国会议员们已经几乎没有必要

---

① Open Secrets, "Super PACs: How Many Donors Give", Open Secrets (n.d.), https://www.opensecrets.org/outside-spending/donor-stats/2020? type = B.
② Albert W. Alschuler & others, "Why Limits on Contributions to Super PACS Should Survive Citizens United", *Fordham Law Review*, Vol. 86, No. 5, 2018, pp. 2299 - 2358.

在暗地里筹款或秘密交接捐款。① 当年在水门事件期间因违反竞选财务法律而被判有罪的公司高管，现在可以直接将支票写给实质与议员协作的超级政治行动委员会。这种现象之普遍，使得一些亿万富翁捐款者也将无限制的超级政治行动委员会捐款视为腐败。如金融大鳄唐纳德·萨斯曼（Donald Sussman）在2016年向民主党超级政治行动委员会及其同盟组织捐款3900万美元后②，对《华盛顿邮报》表示其目标"实际上是从政治中赚钱"③。又如"国会领导基金"（Congressional Leadership Fund）在网站声称其为"专门致力于保护和加强众议院共和党多数派的超级政治行动委员会"，并且"独立于任何联邦候选人或公职人员运作"。据"政客"网站披露，2018年5月，当时即将卸任的众议院议长保罗·瑞恩（Paul Ryan）与美国"赌王"谢尔顿·阿德尔森会面，后者也是2018年共和党最大的捐款者。④ 在瑞恩的主导下，众议院前一年通过了一项1.5万亿美元的减税计划，阿德尔森所有的拉斯维加斯金沙集团因此得以减税7亿美元。⑤ 瑞恩和与其同行的前明尼苏达州共和党参议员科尔曼（Norm Coleman）一起向阿德尔森提出一个关于保护众议院利益的提议，然后瑞安离开房间，科尔曼提出捐款要求，阿德尔森随后向"国会领导基金"捐款3000万美元。⑥ 此前在2016年，阿德尔森在向共和党超级政治行动委员会及其同盟组织捐赠了7800万美元后⑦接受采访时表示："我反对富人尝试影响选举，

---

① Dan Eggen, "Post-Watergate Campaign Finance Limits Undercut by Changes", *The Washington Post*, Jun. 16, 2012.

② Open Secrets, "2016 Top Donors to Outside Spending Groups", Open Secrets (n. d.), https://www.opensecrets.org/outsidespending/summ.php?disp=D.

③ Matea Gold, "Hedge Fund Manager S. Donald Sussman Gave $21 Million to Pro-Clinton Super PAC Priorities USA", *The Washington Post*, Oct, 20, 2016.

④ Jake Sherman & Alex Isenstadt, "Sheldon Adelson Kicks in $30M to Stop Democratic House Takeover: The Donation to the Congressional Leadership Fund is a Big Boost to Republicans Facing a Tough Midterm Environment", *Politico*, May 10, 2018.

⑤ Jim Tankersley & Michael Tackett, "Trump Tax Cut Unlocks Millions for a Republican Election Blitz", *The New York Times*, Aug. 18, 2018.

⑥ Thomas B. Edsall, "After Citizens United, a Vicious Cycle of Corruption: Unconstrained Outside Spending on Elections is Corrosive to Our Democracy", *The New York Times*, Dec. 6, 2018.

⑦ Open Secrets, "2016 Top Donors to Outside Spending Groups", Open Secrets (n. d.), https://www.opensecrets.org/outsidespending/summ.php?disp=D.

第三章　暗钱涌入政治选举：美国政治腐败的新阶段

但只要可行，我也会这么做。"① 2010 年以来最高法院的一系列关键判决使得政治资金大爆发，候选人与暗钱组织和不受限制的超级政治行动委员会之间隔绝腐败的壁垒成为危墙，超级政治行动委员会俨然已成为富人从政治中赚取回报的投资产品。《哈佛法律评论》曾在 2015 年对此总结道："超级政治行动委员会为协助候选人而进行的筹款活动已经突破了法律规定的独立性界限，此种形式已构成利益交换的腐败威胁。"②

（四）独立支出团体组成竞选资金黑洞

独立支出也叫外部支出（outside spending）或外围支出，是指团体或个人独立于候选人的委员会且未与后者协同的政治支出。从常规的党委委员会、政治行动委员会、领导力政治行动委员会到颇具争议的超级政治行动委员会、527 组织和 501 暗钱组织均可能涉及独立支出（见表 3 - 3）。与候选人有联系的独立支出团体能够吸引最多的资金。2015 年筹款超过 1000 万美元的 10 个独立支出团体全部与其支持的候选人有联系，而筹款超过 100 万美元的 28 个独立支出团体中只有 4 个没有与其支持者有表面上的联系。③ 在 2016 年总统大选中，独立支出团体所筹集的 2.85 亿美元资金有 2.7 亿美元，即 95% 来自不受捐款限制的组织。④ 尽管如此，独立支出团体的真实筹资规模仍可能被低估，因为至今为止暗钱组织仍未被法律要求披露其收入。自"联合公民案"以来，由于可以接受无限捐款，超级政治行动委员会、527 组织和 501（c）（4）暗钱组织已成为候选人在联邦选举中获得超大份额竞选资金的渠道。撇开候选人之间的区别，在由候选人和支持单个候选人的团体筹集的总统竞选资金总额中，竞选委员会、传统政治行动委员会和领导力政治行动委员会等受捐款限制的实体筹集到的 1.43 亿美元与无限额捐款组织所筹集到的 2.7

---

① Steven Bertoni, "Billionaire Sheldon Adelson Says He Might Give $100M to Newt Gingrich or other Republican", Forbes (Feb. 21, 2012), https://www.forbes.com/sites/stevenbertoni/2012/02/21/billionaire-sheldon-adelson-says-he-might-give-100m-to-newt-gingrich-or-other-republican/.

② "Working Together for an Independent Expenditure: Candidate Assistance with Super PAC Fundraising", Harvard Law Review, No. 128, Mar., 2015, pp. 1478 – 1499.

③ Ian Vandewalker, "Shadow Campaigns: The Shift in Presidential Campaign Funding to Outside Groups", Brennan Center for Justice (2015), https://www.brennancenter.org/sites/default/files/analysis/Shadow_Campaigns.pdf.

④ Ian Vandewalker, "Shadow Campaigns: The Shift in Presidential Campaign Funding to Outside Groups", Brennan Center for Justice (2015), https://www.brennancenter.org/sites/default/files/analysis/Shadow_Campaigns.pdf.

亿美元相形见绌。① 换言之，2016年总统大选筹集的4.12亿美元中，几乎有2/3来自无限额的独立支出团体。随着独立支出闸门的进一步敞开，2020年总统大选中的独立支出达到史无前例的32亿美元，为2016年的两倍（见图3-6）。无捐款限制的团体在筹集资金方面有着显而易见的优势，其可以从富有的捐款者处得到写着数百万金额的支票。

表3-3　　　　　　　政治委员会与各竞选团体组织对比②

	是否被FEC认定为政治委员会	是否必须向FEC披露捐款者	能否向联邦候选人捐款	捐款金额上限（每候选人每次选举，单位：美元）	联邦候选人能否为该实体筹集对联邦选举的捐款	收受用于联邦选举支出的捐款有否限制（每捐款人每年，单位：美元）
全国政党委员会	是	是	是	5000	是 受FECA限制	41300 每个政党单独账户等限制
候选人委员会	是	是	是	2000	是 受FECA限制	3300 每个候选人每次选举等限制
传统PAC	是	是	是	5000	是 受FECA限制	5000 及其他限制
超级PAC	是	是	否	0	是 受FECA限制	否
527组织	否	否 除独立支出和竞选通讯	否	0	—	否
501（c）4/5/6组织	否	否 除独立支出和竞选通讯	否	0	—	否

---

① Ian Vandewalker, "Shadow Campaigns: The Shift in Presidential Campaign Funding to Outside Groups", Brennan Center for Justice (2015), https://www.brennancenter.org/sites/default/files/analysis/Shadow_ Campaigns.pdf.
② 仅限于联邦选举。"FEC"为联邦选举委员会，"FECA"为《联邦竞选法》，金额以2023—2024年竞选周期为准。

第三章 暗钱涌入政治选举：美国政治腐败的新阶段

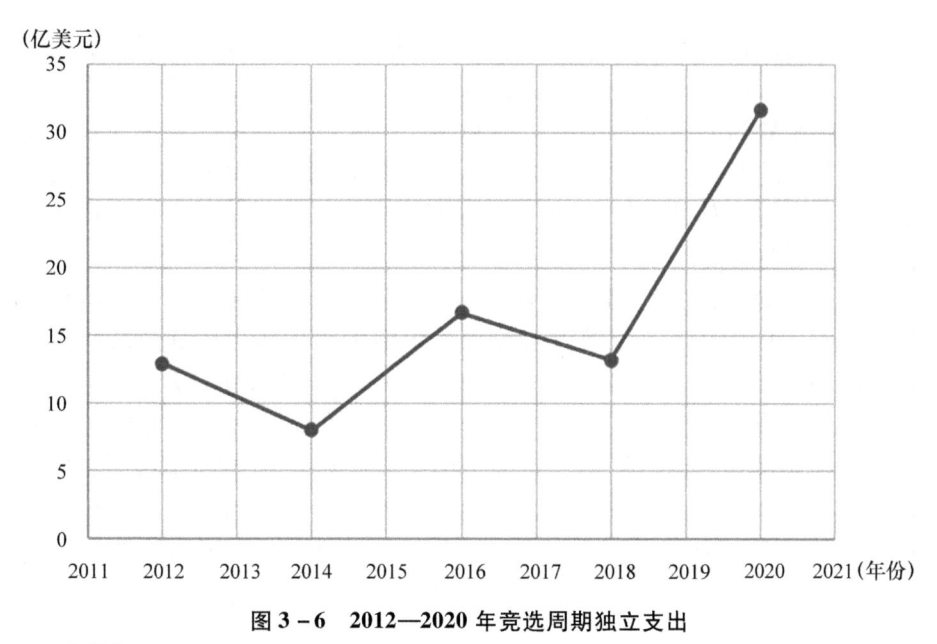

(亿美元)

图 3-6　2012—2020 年竞选周期独立支出

资料来源：Eliana Miller, "Outside Spending in 2020 Races Reaches Record ＄3.2 Billion", Open Secrets（Dec. 21, 2020）, https：//www.opensecrets.org/news/2020/12/outside-spending-reaches-record-in-2020.

自 2010 年"联合公民案"判决打开暗钱组织和超级政治行动委员会无限开支的闸门以来，该类独立支出团体不断违反规则，允许富有的特殊利益与候选人进行系统性地协调，以逃避反腐败法律的约束。而负责执法的联邦选举委员会自 2010 年以来从未就违规协调开出罚单，这更使得联邦选举法律禁止候选人与外部团体进行协调的规则变得毫无意义。竞选委员会在初选阶段对同一候选人的捐款上限仅为 3300 美元[①]，虽然在理论上这样的数额不可能帮助候选人与独立支出团体协调，但是由于禁止协调规则几乎没有任何强制力，候选人实质上可以选择与支持其的独立支出团体密切合作，对后者施加控制，甚至指派关系密切的顾问进行管理。由大捐款者支持选举特定候选人的团体数量激增的情况并非首创。在水门事件之前的时代，候选人就组成了许多所谓的独立委员会，每个委员会都可以对外捐款。1971 年的《联邦竞选法》通过将候选人与单个授权的委员会捆

---

① 以 2023—2024 年竞选周期为准。

绑到一起来制止这种做法，但联合公民的胜诉使得对独立支出组织的监管失效，这种波动带来的结果正逐渐显现：候选人表面上仍然选择与必须遵守捐款限制规则的政治行动委员会和领导力政治行动委员会保持紧密联系，但其实际上与超级政治行动委员会甚至暗钱组织等独立支出团体的关系也十分密切，而捐款者现在可以合法地向候选人提供远远超过候选人捐款限额的财政支持。

在"联合公民案"时代，无数巨额资金通过各种独立支出团体绕过收支限制，以无孔不入之势逃避监管、包围选举、围剿竞争者的情况已形成美国政治选举的新常态。2020年选举中，花费超过1亿美元的顶级外部团体没有一个完全披露其捐款者；在所有外部支出中，只有30%来自完全披露其捐款者的团体，达到了历史最低水平。① 仅部分披露其捐款者的"灰钱"（grey money），在2020年选举开始的一周内支出就超过了16亿美元，是2016年大选的八倍。② 毫不夸张地说，美国政治选举已进入了一个"无法无天、巨额秘密金钱泛滥和特殊利益集团贩卖影响力的新镀金时代"③。

第三节 暗钱组织侵蚀选举

作为美国最大的商业游说团体，"美国商会"是自2010年"联合公民案"以来支出最高的暗钱组织（见图3-7）。2010年1月—2016年12月，"美国商会"花费了约1.3亿美元用于宣传和攻击候选人的政治广告，并通过其政治行动委员会直接向候选人提供了竞选捐款。美国商会在政治广告上的花费约占所有暗钱集团在政治广告上花费总和的1/6。研究机构Issue One的报告显示，支出排名前15位的暗钱组织在选举中秘密花费了超

---

① Anna Massoglia, "'Dark Money' Groups Find New Ways to Hide Donors in 2020 Election", Open Secrets (Oct. 30, 2020), https://www.opensecrets.org/news/2020/10/dark-money-2020-new-ways-to-hide-donors/.

② Anna Massoglia, "'Dark Money' Groups Find New Ways to Hide Donors in 2020 Election", Open Secrets (Oct. 30, 2020), https://www.opensecrets.org/news/2020/10/dark-money-2020-new-ways-to-hide-donors/.

③ 徐彤武：《"外围团体"对2012年美国大选的影响》，《美国研究》2012年第3期。

过6亿美元的资金，占暗钱资金流的75%。① 在这些暗钱组织中，只有极个别能被追溯到其半数资金的来源，但对于其余暗钱组织来说，其账户中只有不到2%的资金能够与捐款者或捐款组织联系起来。在排名前15的暗钱组织中，有14个在提交联邦选举委员会的报告中表示，其有一半的政治支出花费在负面攻击候选人的广告上，其中有6个更是将90%的政治支出花费在负面政治广告上。② 以北卡罗来纳州为例，2014年该州境内播放的政治广告多达2.5万余条，是2010年的100倍。③ 且选民还会看到看起来像政治广告的广告，例如某广告提及某个候选人，但没有明确主张支持或反对该候选人，且不在符合"竞选通讯"的时间点播出，有些频道一年四季都在播放这类广告，其发布者也没有向联邦选举委员会或国税局报告的义务。2018年由暗钱资助的电视政治广告甚至比过去两个选举周期都多，占所有广告的38%，暗钱组织还在脸书、"X"（原推特）和其他数字平台上花费了数百万美元。④ 脸书仅要求网页数字广告购买者在获得批准后，以美国政府颁发的身份证明进行身份确认，但这种外部审核很有限，无法阻止外国利益使用美国关联公司的身份或聘用具有美国身份的广告购买者。这些听起来名称完全无害甚至并不真实存在的非法人实体实质上可以花费无限的资金发布网络政治广告，且因其未在联邦选举委员会登记备案，监管者几乎不可能发现这些广告的幕后主导人或实际资助者。2012年，注册为501"慈善组织"的"十字路口GPS"在油管网站上反复播放一则关于奥巴马总统的广告，⑤ 内容是一位妇女凌晨3点醒来，对着镜头说："我经常睡不着，担心我们的工作、房子，所有开支都在上升，连我母亲的医疗费用也是。我什么时候才能退休？最近我也非常担心我的孩子，担心他们的未来会怎样。我支持奥巴马总统，因为他把话说得如此好听，但从那以后情况就变得越来越糟。"最后，这名妇女看着自己熟睡的

---

① Michael Beckel, "Dark Money Illuminated", Issue One (2018), https：//www.issueone.org/wp-content/uploads/2018/09/Dark-Money-Illuminated-Report.pdf.
② Michael Beckel, "Dark Money Illuminated", Issue One (2018), https：//www.issueone.org/wp-content/uploads/2018/09/Dark-Money-Illuminated-Report.pdf.
③ Ashley Parker, "Outside Money Drives a Deluge of Political Ads", *The New York Times*, Jul. 28, 2014.
④ Wesleyan Media Project, "Digital Spending Dominates in Early 2020 Presidential Race：Candidates Have Spent ＄61 Million on Facebook and Google and Just ＄11 Million on TV", Wesleyan Media Project（Sep.19，2019），http：//mediaproject.wesleyan.edu/releases-091919/103018/.
⑤ Thomas B. Edsall, "Who Needs a Smoke-Filled Room?" *The New York Times*, Sep.9, 2014.

游说、竞选捐款与美国政治腐败

孩子说："一定有可以阻止奥巴马总统开空头支票的办法。"财力雄厚的暗钱组织通过各种媒介高调地发布难以追溯幕后操纵者的负面攻击在线政治广告,使之既能在政治选举中引导舆论,又可以把正面信息留给其支持的候选人传达,使得被支持者远离主动的政治话语攻击,从而在选民面前保持良好的形象。美国政府问责署(Government Accountability Office)在2020年的一份报告中得出结论,在线政治支出和试图掩盖来源的暗钱,加剧了竞选财务法律未能充分规制的竞选支出不透明带来的新风险。[①]

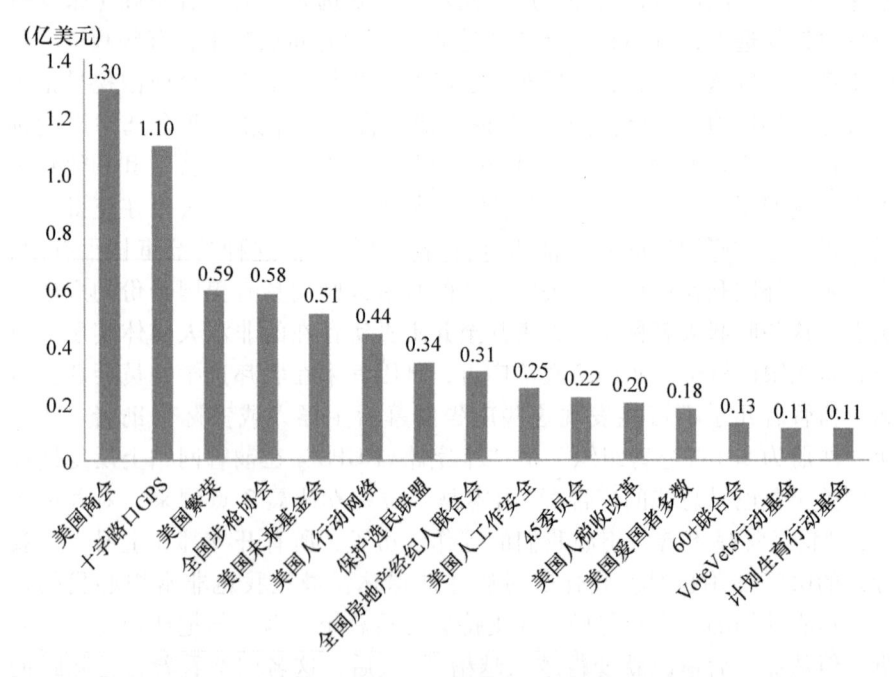

图 3-7 2010—2016 年美国前 15 大暗钱组织政治支出

资料来源:Michael Beckel,"Dark Money Illuminated",Issue One (2018), https://www.issueone.org/wp-content/uploads/2018/09/Dark-Money-Illuminated-Report.pdf.

政治支出排名前 15 的组织中,"美国商会"是全国最大的商业游说组织;"十字路口 GPS"是一个与前总统乔治·W. 布什的顾问卡尔·罗夫

---

① Amy Klobuchar, "Campaign Finance: Federal Framework, Agency Roles and Responsibilities, and Perspectives", U.S. Government Accountability Office (Feb. 3, 2020), https://www.gao.gov/assets/710/704228.pdf.

· 134 ·

第三章 暗钱涌入政治选举：美国政治腐败的新阶段

(Karl Rove)相关联的共和党统一组织；"倡导生育健康"的"美国繁荣"由工业巨子科赫兄弟出资，科赫家族与布什家族是姻亲；"保护选民联盟"旨在选举倾向于环保主张的民主党候选人；"全国步枪协会"为美国最大的枪支游说团体，是支持第二修正案的共和党政客的忠实拥护者；"美国爱国者多数"则是由政府前雇员联合会领导的组织，其与民主党参议员哈里·里德（Harry Reid）和查尔斯·舒默（Charles Schumer）有密切联系；"计划生育行动基金"则倾向于选举支持生育选择权的候选人，以反对反堕胎者。

不仅资金来源不明，暗钱组织还经常在向联邦选举委员会报告时隐瞒竞选支出。无党派团体 Issue One 的调查显示，根据"美国人税收改革"在 2010 年和 2012 年选举周期中对联邦选举委员会的报告，其在支持竞选或反对联邦候选人上的费用比在向国税局申报的"直接或间接的竞选活动支出"少了 800 万美元；2012 年，"全国步枪协会"向联邦选举委员会报告其上述花费为 700 万美元，而在向国税局申报时则称其没有进行直接或间接的竞选活动。[1] 此外，在 2006 年知名说客阿布拉莫夫对国会议员的贿赂案中，包括"美国人税收改革"在内的非营利组织扮演着博彩业捐款者洗钱工具的角色。而像"十字路口 GPS"和"美国人税收改革"这样运营和融资不完全透明的暗钱组织，也仅仅是科赫兄弟在 2012 年耗资 4 亿美元所组成的秘密竞选资金网络中较为人所知的成员[2]，该网络还有另外 15个十分低调的倡导性组织和有限责任公司，彼此间紧密协作。大卫·科赫甚至毫不讳言其"主要兴趣不是参加竞选活动而是决策"[3]。

从秘密的"社会福利"、不透明的有限责任公司，到超级政治行动委员会，暗钱可以多种形式流入政治领域并为改变其格局发力。不仅是"美国繁荣"这样资金充裕的组织，即使是一些不知名的新设暗钱组织，也可能拥有左右选情的能力。2011 年，一个名为"自由之路"（Freedom Path）的非营利团体横空出世，在犹他州播出支持时任共和党参议员奥林·哈奇（Orrin

---

[1] Michael Beckel, "Dark Money Illuminated", Issue One (2018), https://www.issueone.org/wp-content/uploads/2018/09/Dark-Money-Illuminated-Report.pdf.
[2] Matea Gold, "Koch-backed Political Network, Built to Shield Donors, Raised $400 Million in 2012 Elections", *The Washington Post*, Jan. 5, 2014.
[3] Jacob S. Hacker & Nathan Loewentheil, "How Big Money Corrupts the Economy", Democracy Journal (Winter, 2013), https://democracyjournal.org/magazine/27/how-big-money-corrupts-the-economy/.

Hatch）的广告，同时播出关于其民主党对手的广告，在此期间无人知晓广告背后真正的发布者，后哈奇成功连任，直至一年之后才有调查显示美国制药研究与制药商协会在2011年为"自由之路"提供了近90%的资金。而这家由安进、葛兰素史克和辉瑞公司等主要药品生产商组成的游说巨头与哈奇长期保持着"友好关系"。但犹他州的选民在投票时并不知道这一点，因为"自由之路"是根据税法501节（c）（4）条款成立的非营利性社会福利组织，在联合公民赢得联邦最高法院的支持后，这类组织在无资金来源披露义务的同时，可以自由支取公司财产影响选举结果。另一个支持民主党的暗钱组织则以有限责任公司的形式出现。2014年，新罕布什尔州共和党人斯科特·布朗（Scott Brown）与时任民主党参议员珍妮·沙因（Jeanne Shaheen）就该州参议院席位展开了激烈争夺。选举日临近时，一家名为"美国就业增长理事会"的公司花费70万余美元发布了支持沙因的广告，以推动后者连任。而对于该有限责任公司的所有已知信息仅仅是其与另一个501非营利组织有关联，资金来源完全不明。利用"联合公民案"后产生的法律漏洞，暗钱组织得以隐藏在法律照射不到的阴影下，暗中影响甚至控制关键选战中的话语权，而最终出价最高者即能赢得政治选举。

第四节　暗钱捐款者隐匿身份

艾克曼指出："在所有的民主政体中，即使筹款的法律限制看起来比较宽松，但某些给予政客的捐款仍是违法的，因而政客们和那些财大气粗的支持者可能仍倾向于使用匿名捐款。"① 参议员约翰·麦凯恩曾作为共和党总统候选人在2008年参加大选，之后其在采访中感慨道："我们的所作所为让捐款限制成了笑话。一定会发生巨大的丑闻，因为周围有太多洗钱现象和与之相连的腐败，我们甚至不知道是谁是幕后操纵者。"② Issue One 在对2010—2016年近1200笔汇款、注册游说者向国会提交的报告、工会

---

① ［美］苏珊·罗斯-阿克曼：《腐败与政府：根源后果与改革》，郑澜译，中信出版社2018年版，第175页。
② Alina Selyukhn, "John McCain Predicts 'Huge Scandals' in the Super PAC Era", *The Huffington Post*, Mar. 27, 2012.

提交劳工部的年度报告和公司文件进行交叉比对后,最终曝光了超过400名暗钱捐款者的身份(见表3-4)。而调查结果公布前,这些捐款者从未与暗钱组织联系到一起过。分析暗钱捐款者的身份发现,公司、工会与基金会构成了暗钱的主要捐赠者。以"美国商会"为例,其主要捐款者是健康保险公司 Aetna、石油巨头雪弗龙公司以及陶氏化学公司;枪械制造商斯特姆·鲁格(Sturm, Ruger & Co., Inc.)近年来为"全国步枪协会"捐款超过1200万美元;烟草公司雷诺兹美国(Reynolds American Inc.)近年向"美国税收改革""美国繁荣"和"美国商会"秘密进行了捐款;美国排名前20的贸易组织或行业协会,如美国石油学会(API)、美国电影协会(MPAA)和美国制药研究与制药商协会各自捐助了支出排名前15的暗钱组织中的至少5个。在此期间,美国制药研究与制药商协会仅对"美国人行动网络"就捐出了1200万美元;由亿万富翁投资者沃伦·巴菲特建立的巴菲特基金会向"计划生育行动基金"捐款2600万美元。

尽管已有调查披露暗钱组织的部分捐款者,但更普遍的情况则和对"十字路口GPS"这类组织的调查结果一样,可追溯来源的资金仅占其所筹集到资金的2%。多数暗钱组织的资金来源仍无法识别,足以证明肯尼迪大法官在"联合公民案"中所设想的"有效披露"情景至今仍难以实现。"联合公民案"后,501非营利组织和其他公司实体的披露义务变得极低。2020年5月,国税局和财政部发布规则,允许501(c)(4)等免税组织在其年度信息申报表(IRS form 990)中隐瞒捐款者信息,在此之前,虽然这类捐款者的信息是不公开的,但申报者必须向国税局进行披露。[1] 同时,这些组织与超级政治竞选委员会协同运作,相互之间的资金流动几乎不受法律监管。此外,暗钱组织赞助的成千上万无法查询来源的互联网在线广告为来自美国境外的非法竞选支出敞开了大门,竞选尤其是总统大选变得极易为外国势力干涉。暗钱组织已成为服务于站在经济金字塔顶端阶层谋取自身利益的工具,操纵着美国的政治选举。在现有判决塑造的选举披露法律下,将政治暗钱的来源与去处向公众公布,不仅需要更新已经过时的规则使其更具系统性透明度,还需要在技术上引入更先进的数据公开工具,从而为第三方外部监督提供支持。

---

[1] Department of the Treasury, Internal Revenue Service, "Guidance Under Section 6033 Regarding the Reporting Requirements of Exempt Organizations", *85 Federal Register 31959*, May 28, 2020.

表 3-4　　2010—2016 年排名前十的暗钱捐款者[①]

捐款方	身份类别	捐款总数（万美元）	受益方数量	受益方
自由合伙人商会	501（c）(6) 贸易协会	18134.5	6	60+联合会、美国未来基金会、美国繁荣、美国税收改革、全国步枪协会、美国商会
全国步枪协会基金会	501（c）(3) 公共慈善	10645	1	全国步枪协会
美国安可 (原病人权利保护中心)	501（c）(4) 社会福利组织	10484	6	60+联合会、美国未来基金会、美国人工作安全、美国繁荣、美国税收改革、全国步枪协会
十字路口草根政策 (十字路口 GPS)	501（c）(4) 社会福利组织	4092.5	7	60+联合会、美国人行动网络、美国未来基金会、美国人工作安全、美国税收改革、全国步枪协会、美国商会
美国计划生育联邦	501（c）(3) 公共慈善	2877	1	计划生育行动基金
苏珊·汤普森·巴菲特基金会	501（c）(3) 私人基金会	2592	1	计划生育行动基金
陶氏化学公司	公司	1374	2	美国人行动网络、美国商会
美国制药研究和制药商协会	501（c）(6) 贸易协会	1333	5	美国人行动网络、美国未来基金会、美国税收改革、美国商会
斯特姆·鲁格公司	公司	1205	1	全国步枪协会
选民教育保护联盟基金	501（c）(3) 公共慈善	947.5	1	保护选民联盟

[①] 资料来源：Michael Beckel,"Dark Money Illuminated", Issue One (2018), https://www.issueone.org/wp-content/uploads/2018/09/Dark-Money-Illuminated-Report.pdf.

第三章　暗钱涌入政治选举：美国政治腐败的新阶段

第五节　联邦选举委员会监管陷入僵局

正如美国竞选财务法律的发展轨迹所证明的那样，执法不力阻碍了有效监管。作为负责监督和执行竞选财务法律的唯一机构，联邦选举委员会在监管中发挥着关键作用。① 联邦选举委员会也是少数领导权均分的联邦机构之一，6名委员中，来自同一政党的不得超过3人，委员会在包括决定调查涉嫌违法行为等任何重大事项上采取行动，都需要4票。但是长期以来，由于党派政治僵局、缺乏领导力和行政资源不足等问题，联邦选举委员会的执法能力受到了极大限制，甚至对基本的人员编制和预算等行政事项都无法达成共识。2018年，由于白宫和参议院未能通过竞选规章制度和经费改革方案，对联邦选举委员会6个专员职位的签署任命只完成了4个。而即使在达到法定列席人数的情况下，联邦选举委员会也一直处于监察长、首席顾问律师、人事主任空缺，而不得不跛脚运作的窘境。作为委员会的内部监督机构，监察长和副监察长位置的长期空缺更使得委员会的内部审计、调查报告及对不当行为的监督工作陷入停顿。如前所述，委员会必须在投票中获得4票赞成才能对决议事项作出决定，而专员职位的长期空缺迫使该机构剩下的4名专员必须一致投票通过以批准新法规。如果四名委员中的任何一位辞职或不能工作，委员会将因未达到法定人数而无法进行投票或行使其他职务行为。委员会的一项重要职责是执行竞选财务规则，但是由于专员们无法达成一致同意，其甚至无法对严重的违规行为展开调查。2020年，该机构仅在案件执法中收取了70万美元的民事罚款，而2006年为560万美元。② 由于同样的原因，委员会在"联合公民案"后的10年中都未能完成一项重大新规则的制定工作，其制定的规则中，至

---

① 联邦选举委员会负责执行联邦选举法的民事责任部分，刑事条款则由司法部（DOJ）执行，委员会可以将涉嫌犯罪的违法行为提交给司法部。
② FEC, "Status of Enforcement-Fiscal Year 2021, Second Quarter (01/01/21 – 03/31/21)", FEC (Apr., 2021), https：//www.fec.gov/resources/cms-content/documents/2nd_ Quarter_ Status_ of_ Enforcement_ 2021.pdf; FEC, "OGC Enforcement Statistics For Fiscal Years 2003 – 2008", FEC (Jan., 2009), https：//www.fec.gov/resources/cms-content/documents/enforcestatsfy03-08.pdf.

· 139 ·

今都没有出现过超级政治行动委员会一词，更不用说对超级政治行动委员会与候选人和政党的实际违规协调做出规制。

此外，由于现有联邦竞选财务法中"协调"的定义无法制止候选人与其在名义上独立的支持者之间进行大量合作，加之委员会对二者非法协调的执行监管不力，进一步为暗钱流入选举制造了漏洞。面对暗钱组织对选举的腐败侵蚀，作为选举监督者的联邦选举委员会曾有成员提出要求针对部分暗钱组织展开调查，以确定其活动时是否具有政治行动委员会性质和登记披露捐款者的义务，但由于其是联邦政府同类机构中唯一由双数成员组成的机构，委员会终因投票无法达成一致意见而将该提议搁置。党派对立造成的决策僵局长期存在于委员会事务执行中，这也是委员会监管滞后的主要原因之一。任何执法决定都需要4张赞成票，即使在专员均列席的情况下，委员会也常常以3∶3的票数陷入僵局：民主党人主张进行调查，而共和党人则投票驳回该案。在1999—2011年，委员对协作问题作出了数个调查和罚款决定；但在"联合公民案"后的14年里，尽管与政治候选人密切合作的影子竞选团体大量涌现，导致投诉源源不断，但委员会仅发起过几次调查，且仅有一起处罚。[①] 可见在后公民联合时代，委员会无法打击暗钱组织以及候选人与巨资外部团体之间的广泛协调。显然，联合公民的胜诉也进一步凸显了联邦选举委员会在案件执法和规则制定方面的功能失调。暗钱在每次选举周期中不断增长，很大程度上也与联邦选举委员会在投票决议甚至基本运作中长期遇到的行政与政治瓶颈有关。如今捐款人可以大胆地通过有限责任公司将暗钱注入选举，因为其已经预知不会遇到来自选举委员会的阻碍，没有4票赞成的选举委员会几乎等于不存在。这也表明，联邦机构已无法有效应对暗钱组织对选举的影响。在暗钱肆虐的2020年大选周期的大部分时间中，联邦选举委员会都无法正常运行，直至投票日1个月后的12月，参议院终于确认了3名候选人，方才使得该机构有足够的专员来执行竞选财务法律，但其未来的执法能力仍具有很大的不确定性。这种缺乏执行力的问题在2024年的总统大选期间再次成为讨论的焦点。不仅如此，随着国会开始关注人工智能发展可能引发的竞选经费问题，委员会又面临着新的考验，2023年8月，委员会发布了一份《可用性通知》（Notice of Availability），

[①] Daniel I. Weiner & Owen Bacskai, "Owen Bacskai The FEC, Still Failing to Enforce Campaign Laws, Heads to Capitol Hill", Brennan Center for Justice（Sep. 15, 2023），https：//www. brennancenter.org/our-work/analysis-opinion/fec-still-failing-enforce-campaign-laws-heads-capitol-hill.

征集公众意见，以决定是否需要为人工智能生成的政治广告特别制定一套规则来禁止"欺诈性虚假陈述"（fraudulent misrepresentation of campaign authority）的行为。未来，人工智能有可能彻底改变政治竞选，因而或许亟须制定新的规则。

本章小结

随着政治反腐败浪潮与对大捐款者及其捐助暗钱的质疑逐渐走入公众视线，反对巨额竞选捐款或支出已逐渐成为民主政治中的推动力量。在2020年党内初选中，数十名民主党人考虑重新规划其竞选团体和资金来源，一些知名候选人明确表示放弃或拒绝超级政治行动委员会提供的资金，以期在初选中获得基层捐款者的支持。然而随着两党竞争的白热化，民主党人随即将对暗钱的担忧丢到一边，开始争取暗钱的资助，最终政治暗钱以史无前例的规模注入了大选活动。在2020年的竞选周期中，联邦法律将总统初选的捐款上限设定为2700美元[1]，超过3.2亿美元的暗钱通过无接受捐款限制的超级政治行动委员会赞助了民主党竞选。[2] 拜登的最终当选也再次证明了，超级政治行动委员会是当代美国政治中最有力的竞选机器之一。但同时，管理这些筹款委员会的法律很复杂，它们并非由候选人正式创建，候选人也难以用合法的方式实际控制它们，这使得大选在一定程度上偏离了单纯的两党斗争和民选决定，而华盛顿沼泽深处的利益集团则像控制牵线木偶般，大肆操纵金钱流向，深入影响大选走势。而未来，随着暗钱相关信息的不断曝光，超级政治行动委员会带来的负面影响可能在之后的选举中被舆论逐渐放大，越来越多的候选人都将更加谨慎地对待超级政治行动委员会及其背后暗钱组织的支持，直至其从中获得的支持难以弥补因选民对暗钱捐款者和攻击性广告的厌恶而失去的选票，才会

---

[1] 由于通货膨胀，个人对联邦候选人的捐款上限在每两年选举周期中都会有所调整。2023—2024年选举周期，个人可以向每位联邦候选人（包括总统候选人）捐款的上限是每个选举阶段3300美元。这意味着在初选和大选中，个人总共最多可以捐6600美元。

[2] Fredreka Schouten, "Democrats Deride 'Dark' Money, but a New Analysis Shows it Helped Boost Joe Biden", CNN（Nov. 27, 2020）, https：//www.cnn.com/2020/11/27/politics/dark-money-democrats-joe-biden/index.html.

游说、竞选捐款与美国政治腐败

不得不自觉提高竞选资金的透明度，以争取更多小额捐款的普通选民。同时，伴随着各界对暗钱警惕意识的觉醒，已经有越来越多州逐渐推出阻击政治暗钱的立法。因此长期来看，如果候选人在将来还想单纯依靠超级政治行动委员会来在竞选中取得成功，可能会越发困难甚至会失败。但总体来看，新的问题还在持续出现，如如何评估统计由外围团体赞助的社交媒体和互联网站点广告，以及如何披露此类站点筹集的黑洞资金（blackhole money）[①] 等。联邦选举委员会也必须克服党派僵局，对不断变化的竞选资金管道做出更快和更主动的响应，这也对其内部协调性、外部执行力和披露制度的时效性提出了极高要求。

[①] 指从未在竞选财务系统中报告过的政治暗钱。据布伦南司法中心估计，暗钱集团在2020年大选期间投入了超过6.5亿美元的黑洞资金购买互联网广告。目前，技术上还没有任何对脸书和推特的赞助帖子、Hulu上的流媒体广告以及油管上播放广告等互联网广告的内容和支出做出存档和统计的办法。

第四章 "联合公民案"时代竞选财务法律重塑：反腐败与言论自由的博弈

在当今的美国，几乎每一个关于竞选财务监管的问题都充斥着争论。围绕竞选捐款的观点往往呈现两极化：有人呼吁更严格地限制捐款，并禁止向政党提供大额捐款，而另一些人则主张消除所有的捐款限制；一部分人主张为候选人提供免费或廉价媒体补助以及直接公共补贴，而另一部分人却希望直接放弃当前十分有限的总统选举公共资助系统；有些人呼吁禁止在选举前发布某些类型的广告，而另一些人则坚持竞选支出不应受到限制，因为其完全属于言论自由。相比竞选财务，对候选人、利益集团和政党是否必须披露其资金来源以及如何使用这些资金等问题，都有着较为一致的共识：披露是竞选财务监管的基石。[1] 即使那些反对竞选筹款和支出限制的人也公开支持披露，甚至在某些情况下还会赞同更严格地执行披露要求。毫无疑问，披露能够减少竞选腐败。但"联合公民案"从整体上打破了竞选捐款上限，导致大捐款人和公司竞选资金无限制地流入暗钱组织，将围绕竞选捐款与资金披露的争议推到了顶峰。竞选财务法律的规制作用不断受到蚕食，而竞选资金的腐败影响业已渗透国会，改革仍陷于党派斗争的泥沼之中，未来的改变缓慢而不明朗。

---

[1] 当然也有主张完全不披露捐款的观点。鉴于法律允许政策制定者公开索取捐款，耶鲁大学法学院的艾尔思（Ian Ayres）教授提出用匿名制度代替美国的公开制度。他设想捐款者将通过中介机构（政府机构或金融债券机构）捐款，把资金存入匿名账户，并定期向候选人转账。候选人或决策者收到捐款但无法将其追溯到特定的个人或利益集团，从而使得政治人物无法索取捐款（因为任何个人或利益集团都可以声称已经捐款），以防止政党和个人的寻租行为。哈佛法学院的莱西格教授也认为应放弃当前竞选捐款制度，代之以一种完全不同的公共资助竞选资金模式，其中捐款者和捐款信息完全匿名。参见 Ian Ayres, "Disclosure Versus Anonymity in Campaign Finance", in I. Shapiro & S. Macedo, eds., *Designing Democratic Institutions*, New York: New York University Press, 2000, pp. 19-55.

第一节　关键案例对竞选财务法律的
　　　　重塑：公司政治影响力的扩张

美国的收入不平等程度本来就高于所有欧洲国家，2016年收入最高的前1%的美国人年收入已占全国收入的近1/4，同时他们还控制着全美近40%的总财富，[①] 而在30年前，相应的比例分别为12%和33%。[②] 收入差距的扩大自然加剧了财富的不平等，而随之带来的社会不信任感，使得近年来学界对经济不平等转化为政治不平等的问题越发关注。[③] 大公司及其背后的大捐款人作为重要的政治参与者，可以通过参与竞选活动所制造的影响力来吸引决策者的注意，该假设一直是对金钱资源转化为政治权力最具争议的解释之一。[④] 以"联合公民案"为起点，近年来数个竞选财务案件判决为外围团体大开方便之门，允许其无限制地利用大量资金来影响选举，无形中鼓励了立法者花费更多时间关注代表利益集团的捐款者。同时，立法机关推动的竞选和政治反腐败法案在国会受到重重阻力，竞选财务法律几乎未能做出任何改变以应对"联合公民案"所带来的腐败风险，美国竞选与政治反腐败持续面临严峻挑战。

一　联合公民时代的开启：松绑公司政治支出

水门事件后，国会就掀起了竞选财务的改革浪潮，逐渐形成了竞选资

[①] Matea Egan, "Record Inequality: The Top 1% Controls 38.6% of America's Wealth", CNN (Sep. 27, 2017), https://money.cnn.com/2017/09/27/news/economy/inequality-record-top-1-percent-wealth/index.html.

[②] Joseph E. Stiglitz, "Of the 1%, By the 1%, For the 1%", Vanity Fair (Mar. 31, 2011), http://www.vanityfair.com/news/2011/05/top-one-percent-201105.

[③] Larry Bartels, *Unequal Democracy: The Political Economy of the New Gilded Age*, Princeton, NJ: Princeton University Press, 2009, p. 23, 235.

[④] Lawrence Lessig, *Republic, Lost: How Money Corrupts Congress-and a Plan to Stop It*, New York: Hatchette, 2011; Martin Gilens, *Affluence and Influence: Economic Inequality and Political Power in America*, Princeton, NJ: Princeton University Press, 2011, pp. 230 – 246; Martin Gilens & Benjamin I. Page, "Testing Theories of American Politics: Elites, Interest Groups, and Average Citizens", *Perspectives on Politics*, Vol. 12, No. 3, 2014, pp. 564 – 581.

第四章 "联合公民案"时代竞选财务法律重塑：反腐败与言论自由的博弈

金监管制度的基础。尽管改革取得了重大胜利，但财力雄厚的大公司和特殊利益集团通过不断向最高法院提出挑战，逐渐削弱了竞选财务法律中保障政治影响力平衡的规定，最终导致来源隐秘的资金得以无限制地流入选举。两个关键案例——"联合公民案"和麦卡琴案的法律争议都围绕捐款和支出限额展开。在联合公民胜诉案中，最高法院最终推翻了对公司在政治广告上的支出限制，判定公司将自有资金用于此类活动受到第一修正案言论自由权的保护；而在麦卡琴案中，法院判定对个人竞选捐款的总额限制违宪。两案判决对大捐款人的背书，实质上将政治选举与立法决策中可能出现的腐败操作进一步地合法化了。对此，布伦南司法中心在一份报告中总结道："我们的民主主要服务于少数富人的利益。"一小部分美国人拥有"自水门事件以来的最大权力，而其他多数人似乎正在与政治脱离"。①

（一）2010年"联合公民案"：公司团体捐款限制违宪

如果可以将金钱与政治相分离，是否应该这样做？这实际上是美国竞选财务问题中的一个根本分歧。保守派长期以来秉持的原则是，竞选捐款是一种政治言论，受到宪法第一修正案保护。基于该原则，联邦最高法院在联合公民诉联邦选举委员会案中，将此种权利的保护范围从个人扩大到了公司和工会，导致公司实体在实际上享有了人格权。在"联合公民案"之前，以宾夕法尼亚为代表的22个州曾立法严格禁止公司为选举候选人或出于任何政治目的进行竞选捐款或支出。② 其他州如亚拉巴马州和纽约州也对公司在政治选举上的支出作出了限制性规定。尽管如此，这些立法都未能将政治选举与公司等商业利益有效隔离。在这一点上，"联合公民案"无疑是竞选财务法律进程的里程碑案件，因为无论怎样理解，该案判决都赋予了富裕的个人、公司和特殊利益团体利用金钱影响选举的更大自由。《纽约时报》曾预言，"联合公民案""将使得上亿美元流入选举，并扭转总统大选的局面"。③

联合公民是一个依据税法第501（c）（4）条成立的非营利保守派组

---

① Daniel I. Weiner, "Citizens United Five Years Later", Brennan Center for Justice（Jan. 15, 2015）, https://www.brennancenter.org/our-work/research-reports/citizens-united-five-years-later.
② 禁止以公司财产为政治选举独立支出的22个州为阿拉斯加、亚利桑那、科罗拉多、康涅狄格、艾奥瓦、肯塔基、马萨诸塞、密歇根、明尼苏达、蒙大拿、北卡罗来纳、北达科他、俄亥俄、俄克拉何马、宾夕法尼亚、罗德岛、南达科他、田纳西州、得克萨斯、西弗吉尼亚、威斯康星和怀俄明。
③ Michael Luo & Jeff Zeleny, "Obama, in Shift, Says He'll Reject Public Funding", *The New York Times*, Jun. 20, 2008.

织，它出资拍摄了一部批评时任参议员希拉里·克林顿的纪录片，并计划在竞选前30天内播出。但2002年《两党竞选改革法》第441（b）条扩大了1971年《联邦竞选法》对公司和工会的捐款及支出限制，禁止公司或工会等组织在初选前的30天内动用自有资金购买"竞选通讯"（electioneering commucation），规定涵盖了以"任何广播、有线电视或卫星电视的形式向超过5万人开展任何支持或击败候选人的活动"。该规定的理由是政府根据言论主体的不同身份，即个人还是公司，来确定不同的言论自由权利。而且，无论是《两党竞选改革法》第441（b）条还是《联邦竞选法》第203条，均未禁止公司或工会通过个人向政治行动委员会捐款以进行竞选通讯与或表达主张。

但最高法院认为，上述规定压制了公司的"声音和观点接触公众并告知其哪些个人或实体与选民的利益对立"，因而构成了对政治言论自由的侵犯。撰写多数意见的肯尼迪大法官认为，《两党竞选改革法》第441（b）条所禁止的独立支出是未与候选人或竞选活动进行协调或预先安排的，因此不可能产生一种以金钱为条件的交换。尽管此类支出可能令公司"欣喜若狂，并可以增加与候选人的接触机会，但灌输和接触并不是腐败"。[1] 关于政府认为第441（b）条的目的之一是保护公司股东权益，即股东有权不资助他们不认同的政治言论，法院认为，股东的利益已受到"公司民主"（corporate democracy）制度的充分保护，而对独立支出的限制（如对公司支出的禁令）则具有令人生畏的影响，因而这种限制丧失了基于国家利益的正当性理由。根本上，联邦最高法院的判决基础是，《第一修正案》的言论自由条款禁止政府限制公司（包括非营利性组织、工会和其他协会）用于政治通讯的独立支出。

该判决在取消联邦选举中公司竞选开支禁令的同时，也使得自一个多世纪以来建立的、将公司资金排除在联邦选举之外的国家政策，与数十年来的竞选财务判例和法律被一并推翻。最高法院认定，独立支出不会导致腐败，因为其是透明的，公司的竞选支出只要独立于候选人，就不会对候选人产生腐败影响，因此也不应受到限制。富裕的捐款者和公司的无限制支出被认定不会扭曲政治进程，因为公众能够看到谁在为广告付费，并对不同的演讲者和信息给予适当的重视。但事实上，选民往往对竞选支出背后的真正势力并

---

[1] Citizens United v. FEC, 558 U.S. 310 (2010).

第四章 "联合公民案"时代竞选财务法律重塑：反腐败与言论自由的博弈

不知情。基于威斯康星州生命权案对第一修正案原则的解释，"联合公民案"还重申了政府无论何时，包括在选举前的特定时间内，都无权限制问题倡导类广告的独立支出，即无论言论主体的身份如何，都应允许其发言。至此，旨在保护选举不受公司和工会资金影响的1907年《蒂尔曼法》、1947年《塔夫脱—哈特利法》、1971年《联邦竞选法》、2002年《两党竞选改革法》、1990年奥斯汀诉密歇根商会案，以及2003年麦康奈尔诉联邦选举委员会案的判决全部被推翻。这意味着联邦法律不得再限制公司和团体在竞选通讯方面的支出，它们可以合法地支出以直接倡议支持或击败候选人的竞选通讯，而出资者也无须披露其身份，这直接导致超级政治行动委员会与501组织在该判决后的大量崛起。如前所述，以"联合公民案"为基础，SpeechNow.org案使得超级政治行动委员会成为选举中的"无限钱包"。该判决取消了联邦为独立支出团体制定的接受捐款限额。至此，在"联合公民案"后被赋予投票权的公司得以无限制地将资金投入独立支出团体，通过不断涌现的超级政治行动委员会操纵巨额资金，影响选举。

（二）2014年麦卡琴胜诉案：个人捐款总额限制违宪

麦卡琴案的核心争议是个人捐款限额，其是由过去半个世纪中颁布的一系列法律订立的。《联邦竞选法》于1971年首次通过，水门事件丑闻发生后，1974年的修正案限制了个人在特定年份内，可以向全国政党和联邦候选人作出的直接捐款总额。其旨在防止捐款者通过向多个团体捐款，绕过基本限额后将资金汇合到同一个候选人手中。1976年的巴克利诉瓦莱奥案虽然承认独立支出捐款受到言论自由的保护，但出于防止腐败的目的，仍肯定了捐款总额限制（aggregate limit）的合宪性。2002年的《两党竞选改革法》维持了对竞选捐款的两个限制：其一限制了个人、合伙企业和其他组织在内的捐款人，向指定类别的接收者的捐款限额；其二仍然限制个人在特定选举周期内的捐款总额，该限额每年都会根据劳工部确定的通货膨胀率重新校准，具体数额由联邦选举委员会在选举周期当年的年初宣布，并将个人捐款限额的期限从一年度改为两年度。在2011—2012年的选举周期中，根据不同的捐款受赠人，单个捐款人两年内的上限为：联邦候选人4.62万美元，全国政党7.08万美元，即捐款总限额为11.7万美元。[①]

[①] Noah Feldman, "Treat Millionaires Like They're Billionaires", Harvard University Weatherhead Center for International Affairs (Feb. 21, 2013), https：//wcfia.harvard.edu/publications/treat-millionaires-they're-billionaires.

游说、竞选捐款与美国政治腐败

亚拉巴马州居民麦卡琴（Shaun McCutcheon）在上述选举周期中向共和党全国委员会、共和党委员会以及多名共和党候选人捐款。这些捐款在各自的基本限额之内都是被允许的，但相加就会超过总限额，麦卡琴希望能作出更多的捐款，遂联合共和党全国委员会起诉联邦选举委员会，认为上述两年的捐款总额限制侵犯了其为第一修正案所保护的言论自由权利。地方法院的观点是，总限额的设定目的是防止腐败发生以保护政府利益，因而是合理的。① 联邦最高法院则根据"联合公民案"创设的狭义审查标准推翻了这种观点，认为限制捐款总额不仅无法达成《两党竞选改革法》预防腐败的既定目标，反而还对个人参与民主进程构成限制，因而违宪。判决并未更改个人在单次选举中对单个候选人捐款的2800美元限额，以及对单个政治行动委员会的5000美元限额规定，② 但单个捐款者（包括政治行动委员会）可以提供给候选人或党委委员会的金额上限自此无效。首席大法官罗伯茨（John G. Roberts Jr.）在判决书中写道："捐款人所支持的候选人人数或其支持的理由为何，与报纸可以为多少候选人背书一样，不应受到政府的限制。"③ 由于巴克利诉瓦莱奥案禁止州限制独立支出，但同时又允许其限制捐款，无意中造成了候选人在竞选中面临无限竞选资金的情况，这种矛盾也是巴克利诉瓦莱奥裁决被推翻的原因之一。对于竞选捐款与腐败之间颇具争议的关系，多数意见还指出，"利益交换的腐败与对（立法者的）一般影响之间的界限似乎模糊不清……但是必须尊重对其的区分，以维护基本的第一修正案权利"。④ 法院将言论自由置于反腐败的法益之前，即只有在不打击个人言论自由的情况下，才能追求与腐败作斗争的集体利益。而且判决将捐款限额的反腐败功能与限额本身彻底剥离，认为本案中捐款总额限制其实并未与预防腐败的目的紧密联系，政府应有许多其他手段与选举腐败作斗争，而不必对竞选捐款做出总限制。

大公司及其背后的大捐款者，无论其何其富裕或有怎样超乎常人的政

---

① McCutcheon v. FEC, 134 S. Ct. 1434 (2014).
② Michael Beckel, "The 'McCutcheon' Decision Explained – More Money to Pour into Political Process", The Center for Public Integrity (Apr. 22, 2014), https://www.publicintegrity.org/2014/04/22/14611/mccutcheon-decision-explained-more-money-pour-political-process.
③ McCutcheon v. FEC, 572 U.S. 185 (2014).
④ U.S. Supreme Court, "Shaun McCutcheon, et al., Appellants v. FEC (2014), majority opinion: Opinion of Roberts, C. J.", Supreme Court (n. d.), http://www.supremecourt.gov/opinions/13pdf/12-536_e1pf.pdf.

第四章 "联合公民案"时代竞选财务法律重塑：反腐败与言论自由的博弈

治远见，都应受制于个人身份，平等地行使其政治影响力，这是民主的基本原则。显然，麦卡琴案判决塑造的实际法律效果与上述民主原则背道而驰。该案造成的直接结果是，由于法律不限制政治行动委员会的数量，如果捐款者拥有足够广泛的政治行动委员会联系，则其在理论上可以通过多个政治行动委员会向特定候选人大量捐款。布雷耶（Stephen G. Breyer）大法官也对判决提出异议，认为多数意见建立在"联合公民案"对腐败的狭窄定义基础上，判定捐款总额违宪"破坏了竞选财务法律的结构，对民主进程造成了巨大伤害"。①尽管竞选捐款中的政治腐败问题不应直接归咎于钻营法律漏洞的腐败堕落者，因为制度本身应比人性的自我约束可靠，但恰恰也是司法机关对政府权力的不信任，使得本已滞后的竞选财务制度在腐败面前更陷于劣势，进一步激励了政客和政党为提供资金的特殊利益集团服务。最高法院在过去20年里的一系列判决中所表现出对宪法核心原则的偏离以及对腐败现实的漠视，将本身有缺陷的民主选举制度逐渐异化为金权政治游戏。前总统奥巴马曾评价"联合公民案""赋予了华盛顿的特殊利益及其游说者更大的权力，为特殊利益打开了限制选举支出的闸门"②。无论是麦卡琴案还是此后的竞选财务实践，都证明了这一点。

二 "联合公民案"变革透视：公司与保守主义崛起

以金钱等于言论为基础，"联合公民案"使得大公司、暗钱集团和超级政治行动委员会史无前例地成为竞选活动的主要参与者。该判决带来的改变看似十分突然，但其本质上是大公司、保守主义力量与竞选财务法律长期政治博弈的结果，同时也折射出过去的一个世纪以来二者政治影响力不断扩张积聚的社会现实。

（一）资本主义矛盾与公司崛起

纵观历史，资本主义似乎比许多其他组织经济活动的方式都更有利于政治和宗教自由，但民主资本主义意识形态的内部矛盾也一直存在，而且往往难以调和。此种矛盾背景下，公司对政治的影响力历史亦被视为工人对抗资本主义剥削的抗争史。美国公司的政治影响力始于19世纪下半叶。

---

① McCutcheon v. FEC, 572 U.S. 185 (2014).
② Bradly A. Smith, "President Wrong on Citizens United Case", National Review (Jan. 28, 2010), https://www.nationalreview.com/corner/president-wrong-citizens-united-case-bradley-smith/.

美国内战期间，随着北方工业的崛起、巨额的政府采购合同和铁路建设，公司资本获得了大量积累，经济实力显著增强。在战后的数年里，公司在美国社会生活中的作用迅速提升，其控制国会和州立法机构的能力也不可避免地随之增长。同时由于工业革命对产业的重塑，机器大生产的逐步普及使得工业事故也变得司空见惯。据统计，在1888—1908年的"强盗男爵"时代[①]，总计70万美国工人在工业事故中丧生，平均每天约有100人死亡。[②] 而即使作为过错方，公司也很少承担工人因工伤亡的赔偿责任。工厂主除了提供恶劣严酷的工作条件外，还将工资维持在尽可能低的水平。员工通过组织罢工和倡议劳动保护立法以减轻剥削的行动，在公司所有者间引起了强烈反响。试图组织工会的劳动者与警察发生激烈对峙，代表公司的游说者和律师随后涌入国会与州议会的大楼，试图对立法与政策产生影响。此时大工厂在工业革命鼎盛时期所累积的财富，使得立法中促进私人和公司利益的部分得到了迅速发展。根据政治学者约瑟夫森所记载的历史，这段时间的"立法厅被改造成了集市，选票明码标价，买卖的则是制定法"[③]。也正是在这个腐败的年代，公司参与了被称为"第二宪法"的1868年宪法第十四修正案的撰写，试图将自身纳入宪法保护范围内；[④] 1886年圣塔克拉拉县诉南太平洋铁路公司一案[⑤]中，法庭记者记录了联邦最高法院的观点，即公司享有"作为个人的权利"，这也被视为现代公司被部分赋予第一修正案、第五修正案和第十四修正案保护权的基础。[⑥] 可见，公司的大规模竞选捐款始于1880—1890年大公司经济影响力的积累。

---

① 强盗男爵（Robber Baron）时代指19世纪中叶到20世纪中叶，工厂主或实业家成为巨人般的垄断者，碾碎竞争对手、操纵市场、腐化政府的时期。垄断者在贪婪和权力的驱使下，用不道德的手段控制民主国家，不公正地积聚了大量财富。钢铁巨擘安德鲁·卡耐基、摩根大通之父约翰·P.摩根和石油大亨洛克菲勒等都被认为是强盗男爵的代表人物。
② Al Gore, *The Future: Six Drivers of Global Change*, New York: Random House Publishing Group, 2013, p.107.
③ Matthew Josephon, *The Robber Barons: Great American Capitalists, 1891–1901*, New York: Harcourt, Brace and Company, 1934, p.168.
④ Ciara Torres-Spelliscy, "The History of Corporate Personhood", Brennan Center for Justice (Apr. 8, 2014), https://www.brennancenter.org/our-work/analysis-opinion/history-corporate-personhood.
⑤ Santa Clara County v. Southern Pacific Railroad Company, 118 U.S. 394 (1886).
⑥ E. Rassweiler, "Corporate Control of Elections, Citizens United v. Federal Election Commission (2010) and Related Decisions: The History and Consequences", Corporate Control of Elections (2018), https://corporatecontrolofelections.com/#_edn21. 第一、第五和第十四修正案分别涉及言论自由权、正当程序和免于自证其罪的沉默权、平等保护权。

第四章 "联合公民案"时代竞选财务法律重塑：反腐败与言论自由的博弈

正如美国政治学家、外交官芮恩施在1907年发表的一项美国立法实践研究中所言，彼时的商业利益已经开发出了一种"比偶然腐败行为的旧方法更有效应对立法机关的新系统"。① 现今公司利益团体发起的具有高度组织性的立法游说活动即是证明。

2010年"联合公民案"与2014年"麦卡琴案"，皆以公司胜诉告终。至此，公司在法律上正式拥有了与选民几无差别的言论自由权。表面上，这两个判例进一步将金钱在实质上与言论等同，实则是公司政治影响力日渐壮大的写照。这种现象并不应让人感到意外。早在美国建国时，开国元勋们就曾对政治权力的集中，尤其是公司经济权力的过度集中对民主的影响，表示过预见性的担忧。杰弗逊总统在1816年的一封信中曾发出警告："我希望我们的国家在诞生之初，就粉碎敢于挑战我们政府、藐视法律的那些富有公司的贵族制。"② "联合公民案"提示了公司被赋予巨大影响力时可能为美国政治制度带来的挑战，引发了公众对大公司资金支配政治的担忧。

（二）保守主义者利用言论自由

对于亲公司的保守主义派别来说，对公司特殊的竞选财务限制混淆了财富或权力与公司之间的界限。尽管公司对竞选的影响可以被涵盖于私人财富在竞选活动中的作用，乃至对当代美国社会财富分配不平等的讨论范畴下，但并非所有的公司都以从事经济活动为主或因此拥有大量财富。非常富有者在选举中所扮演的角色不同，也并非所有的财富和权力都是以公司形式出现的。主张限制富人干预竞选的立法者往往将公司作为攻击目标，仅仅因为公司是在交易活动中获得私人财富的实体，可以作为获得政治权力以攫取更多私人财富的途径。

观察上述理由可以发现，无论是巴克利诉瓦莱奥案还是"联合公民案"的判决结果都并非偶然：它们都只是保守主义在过去十余年中，赢得联邦最高法院内部权力主流支持带来的胜利。这种法院内部的权力分野恰恰体现在其对争议性极高的复杂案件的决定性影响力。20世纪70年代保守派法官掌管最高司法权力机构以来，保守主义的议程已越来越多地建立

---

① Paul S. Reinsch, *American Legislatures and Legislative Methods*, New York: Century Company, 1907, p. 231.
② U.S. Supreme Court, "Citizens United: Opinion of Stevens, J.", Supreme Court (n.d.), http://www.supremecourt.gov/opinions/09pdf/08-205.pdf.

在言论自由的基础上，保守派的许多决定都有助于扩大现有制度中的不民主因素——借由第一修正案的保护，竞选活动的无限开支被合法化，对烟草、药品和枪支的管制也受到言论攻击。过去被保守主义者敌视的第一修正案已然成为其所偏爱的言论武器。"联合公民案"正是五位保守派大法官基于言论自由权利而达成的裁判：《第一修正案》保护公司不受限制的竞选开支，因而政府无权规制政治言论。随着联邦最高法院的立场逐渐发生偏移，保守派的政治立场也越发频繁地在判决中显现。《纽约时报》的一项分析发现，由首席大法官罗伯茨领衔的最高法院更倾向于接受基于自由言论的保守派而非自由派的观点。这与之前的半个世纪形成了鲜明对比。在过去的60余年中，联邦最高法院对保守派相关言论案件的审理比例呈倍数增长，胜诉比例也维持在较高水平（见图4-1）。"联合公民案"的胜诉是对大政府干预公民甚至公司言论自由担忧的结果，这种倾向由来已久。最近的例子发生在2022年5月，在联邦选举委员会诉特德·克鲁兹竞选参议员团队案①中，联邦最高法院宣布联邦选举委员会对候选人贷款偿还的限制无效。此前竞选法不允许候选人使用选举后收到的捐款来偿还选举期间个人贷款超过25万美元的部分。克鲁兹援引言论自由权，认为其通过获取捐款支持自己竞选的政治表达受到了侵犯，他的最终胜诉为大公司和富人捐款制造了又一个法律漏洞。

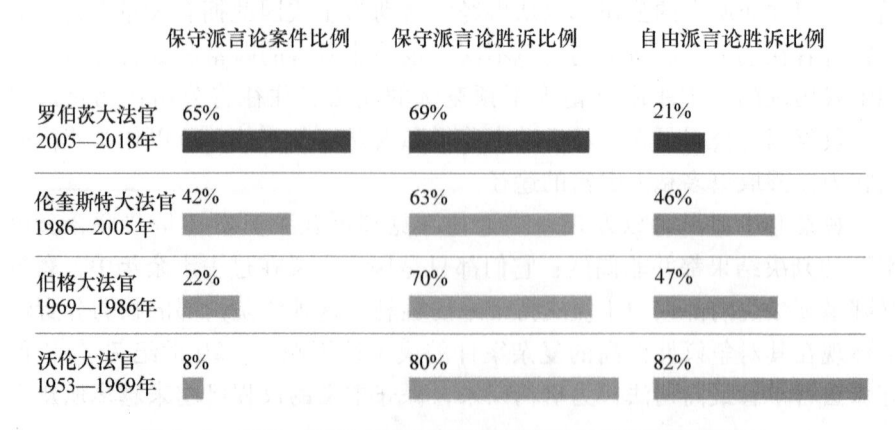

	保守派言论案件比例	保守派言论胜诉比例	自由派言论胜诉比例
罗伯茨大法官 2005—2018年	65%	69%	21%
伦奎斯特大法官 1986—2005年	42%	63%	46%
伯格大法官 1969—1986年	22%	70%	47%
沃伦大法官 1953—1969年	8%	80%	82%

图4-1　1953—2018年联邦最高法院言论相关案例判决情况

资料来源：Adam Liptak, "How Conservatives Weaponized the First Amendment", *The New York Times*, Jun. 30, 2018.

---

① FEC v. Ted Cruz for Senate, 596 U. S. 289 (2022).

第四章 "联合公民案"时代竞选财务法律重塑：反腐败与言论自由的博弈

而该案所指向的事实还不止于此，被保守派武器化的言论自由从很久以前就开始突破生活中的许多边界。在1976年的"公共联盟"（Public Union）案①中，一个名为公共联盟的消费者保护组织挑战州法，最终最高法院以侵犯商业言论自由为由，判决强制在药品广告中显示处方药价格的州法无效。此案也标志着保守主义在当代联邦最高法院中影响力的开始。对此，斯坦福法学院前院长苏利文在《哈佛法律评论》中评论道："虽然此案是由消费者保护主义组织提起的，但公司很快成为其后一系列裁决的主要受益者，无论是对处方药品的广告限制，还是强制在啤酒罐上标示酒精含量，或是限制在学校附近展示烟草户外广告的规定，都被废除。"② 随着沃伦大法官领导的自由主义派别在联邦最高法院的消退，交由右翼掌管的言论自由"并没有为弱势者提供庇护，反而成为美国权力等级最高者的一把利剑，其受害者包括竞选财务改革的拥护者、反对烟草者、L. G. B. T. Q. 群体、工会、动物权利倡导者、环保主义者以及仇恨言论的受害者和堕胎手术提供者"③。由于几乎所有的经济和监管政策都会影响或触动言论，因而大公司总是可以滥用对言论自由的保护原则，从而不断重新定义市民的政治生活。

第二节 "联合公民案"时代
竞选反腐败法律动态

随着游说者和国会公职人员越来越多地卷入游说和竞选捐款丑闻中，国会对游说、竞选捐款的不当影响和公职人员享有某些特殊利益的现象表示了进一步的关注，在"联合公民案"即2010年后的十余年中，关于信息披露和放松管制的辩论一直是国会内外反复出现的主题，国会相继讨论和通过了更严格的法律、法规与内部规定，以防治腐败。在第111届国会

---

① Virginia State Board of Pharmacy v. Virginia Citizens Consumer Council, Inc. 425 U. S. 748 (1976).
② Kathleen M. Sullivan, "Two Concepts of Freedom of Speech", *Harvard Law Review*, No. 124, 2010, pp. 143 – 177.
③ 如托马斯大法官（Clarence Thomas）在一项判决的多数意见中认为，强制反对堕胎的健康诊所告知妇女如何进行堕胎手术，是对诊所言论自由的侵犯。布雷耶大法官则对此表示异议，认为这是对第一修正案言论自由的滥用。Louis M. Seidman, "Can Free Speech Be Progressive?" *Columbia Law Review*, Vol. 118, No. 7, 2018, pp. 1 – 30.

期间，众议院通过了《披露法案》，要求提供更多关于不同捐赠者之间资金流动的信息，并在随后的几届国会中重新引入。国会还考虑了一些替代方案，包括一些披露的要素以及要求主要受《税法》第501（c）条监管的501组织进行额外披露。关于是否或如何额外披露信息的争论也延伸到了联邦选举委员会和法院。目前，数部新法律、近百部法案和数个国会内部规定总体涉及五个改革领域：（1）有偿游说者对游说活动进行更广泛和更详细的披露，尤其对于与政府政策有交集的专业游说者的活动，须更集中更频繁地披露；（2）国会议员及其工作人员对礼物和优待的收受，包括交通和旅行费用的赠与，受到更广泛的限制；（3）增加对前政府高级官员代表私人利益进行游说活动即"旋转门"的新限制，修改卸任后参与游说的国会议员的政府退休福利待遇；（4）披露空壳公司的实际受益人或控制人，减少暗钱和外国对竞选活动的干预；（5）扩大政治广告的法律定义，同时增加互联网站点对数字和互联网广告的审查责任。

毫无疑问，竞选捐款及其披露问题在过去数十年中一直都是竞选反腐败政策讨论的核心。但截至第118届国会期间，尚无任何直接与竞选资金相关的法案被立法成为法律，国会也没有对联邦竞选财务法律作出实质性修改。作为联邦竞选经费政策标志的信息披露要求，在过去的十余年中也基本保持不变，表明竞选资金政策将会是一个持续法律和政治问题。不仅如此，立法进展还受到其他阻碍。《2023财年综合拨款法案》（FY2023 Consolidated Appropriations Act）在第735条禁止将报告某些政治捐款或支出作为获得政府合同的条件，并禁止国税局针对税法501（c）（4）的规定进行某些活动，同时禁止证券交易委员会发布有关披露公司政治活动的规定[1]，无形中为竞选资金的监管制造了更多困难。但即使进步改革举步维艰，也仍会有更多的监管和诉讼案例，使竞选财务及反腐败政策法律处于实质上的动态变化中。

一　2010年以来联邦竞选反腐败立法动态

在过去的十余年中，无论是民主党还是共和党议员都为净化选举和政

---

[1] R. Sam Garrett, "The State of Campaign Finance Policy: Recent Developments and Issues for Congress", Congressional Research Service (Sep. 12, 2023), https://crsreports.congress.gov/product/pdf/R/R41542.

第四章 "联合公民案"时代竞选财务法律重塑：反腐败与言论自由的博弈

治环境做出了相当努力。国会网站数据库的检索结果显示，2010年1月—2023年10月，尽管国会仅通过了两部相关法律，① 但反腐败性质的竞选财务改革法案已有近百个。这些法案大多尚未在众议院获得通过，也仍体现出立法者对于规范游说和竞选捐款、促进竞选资金披露的反腐败改革的决心。

（一）2010年以来颁布的竞选反腐败法律

1.《K街反腐败公正法》：游说者犯罪记录登记

2007年国会通过的《诚实领导和政府公开法》对1995年《游说披露法》作出了修订，要求雇佣公司内部游说者、游说公司和自雇游说者的组织或实体在众议院书记处（Clerk of the House）和参议院秘书处（Secretary of the Senate）注册并进行报告。2019年1月3日，特朗普总统签署了《K街司法反腐败法》②（Justice Against Corruption on K Street Act/"JACK Act"）。《K街司法反腐败法》在此基础上，对报告义务作出了进一步扩充，其以披露游说者的腐败行为监察重点，要求游说者披露此前其与腐败有关的所有定罪历史③。《K街司法反腐败法》的灵感来自杰克·阿布拉莫夫腐败游说案，该案导致二十多名游说者、国会助手和政客被定罪，阿布拉莫夫因欺诈、逃税、共谋贿赂以及贿赂公职人员在联邦监狱服刑四年后，又以政治改革者的身份继续从事游说活动。为了帮助政治领导人和公司了解试图影响公共政策的游说者背景，进一步监督有腐败行为和欺诈前科的游说者对立法者公正决策和竞选活动的影响，《K街司法反腐败法》规定，所有游说披露表格与该法生效后提交的季度报告，均需包含在联邦与州法院被判犯下贿赂、勒索、挪用公款、非法回扣、逃税、欺诈、利益冲突、虚假陈述、伪证和洗钱犯罪的游说者信息，并附上定罪日期及相关罪行陈述。为了确保申报的准确性，申报人应进行内部尽职调查，以识别其所雇佣的注册游说者应报告的犯罪记录。对于违反该法规定或在收到通知后未能适当补充登记信息的，将根据《游说披露法》处以最高20万美元的民事罚款，而"明知腐败"而为之者则可能

---

① 另外还有三部修正案，仅涉及每五年延长一次联邦选举委员会对违反其规定的行为执行民事罚款权。
② Public Law No: 115-418 (01/03/2019).
③ 严格来说，犯罪历史与犯罪记录是不同的。前者为法院的有罪判决，后者则可因犯罪人年龄、犯罪类型等因素而依法或依申请封存。英国、美国、加拿大、法国、俄罗斯和中国香港等国家或地区都制定了犯罪前科消灭制度。

· 155 ·

被处以最高 5 年监禁。① 新法律的实施效果良好，政府问责署最新发布的 2019 年游说报告显示，尽管有 20% 的游说者未按照要求完整披露过去担任的全部职位，但其已识别的 161 名有犯罪记录的游说者全部如实披露了其犯罪前科。② 2019 年，有前科的游说者在华盛顿进行了至少涉及 310 万美元的游说活动。③ 根据布伦南司法中心 2015 年的统计数据，超过 7700 万即三分之一的成年美国人有犯罪记录，④ 而《K 街反腐败公正法》将有效促进对有腐败前科的高风险游说者的监督。

2. 《哈奇现代化法》：联邦雇员竞选资格和道德限制

2012 年 12 月，国会通过了对 1939 年《哈奇法》的修正法案《哈奇现代化法》（Hatch Act Modernization Act）。《哈奇法》在本质上是严格规范政治候选人利用联邦资源进行竞选的反腐败法律，在此基础上，《哈奇现代化法》一方面放宽了对联邦雇员的竞选资格和道德限制，另一方面也细化并加强了对联邦雇员违反相关规定的处罚措施。此前《哈奇法》规定，对于某些州和地方雇员，若其主要工作与全部或部分由政府或联邦机构提供的贷款或拨款的活动有关，就不得竞选公职。⑤《哈奇现代化法》放宽了公务员竞选公职的范围，规定禁令只适用于某些直接或间接的、完全由美国或联邦机构贷款或拨款支付工资的州和地方雇员。⑥ 以此为前提，包括华盛顿特区在内的多数联邦雇员都得以被允许参与大多数的党派政治活动。

---

① Robert Kelner & others, "Congress Amends LDA Forms to Require Reporting of Lobbyist Convictions", Covington & Burling LLP（Apr. 8, 2019）, https://www.insidepoliticallaw.com/2019/04/08/congress-amends-lda-forms-to-require-reporting-of-lobbyist-convictions/.

② U. S. Government Accountability Office, "2019 Lobbying Disclosure: Observations on Lobbyists' Compliance with Disclosure", Requirements（Jun., 2020）, https://www.gao.gov/assets/710/705616.pdf.

③ John Kennedy, "Sen. Kennedy's JACK Act Reveals Millions Paid to Lobbyists with Criminal Convictions", U. S. Senator for Louisiana（Feb. 20, 2020）, https://www.kennedy.senate.gov/public/2020/2/sen-kennedy-s-jack-act-reveals-millions-paid-to-lobbyists-with-criminal-convictions.

④ Matthew Friedman, "Just Facts: As Many Americans Have Criminal Records as College Diplomas", Brennan Center for Justice（Dec. 17, 2015）, https://www.brennancenter.org/our-work/analysis-opinion/just-facts-many-americans-have-criminal-records-college-diplomas; Rebecca Vallas, "Removing Barriers to Opportunity for Parents With Criminal Records and Their Children", Center for American Progress（Dec. 10, 2015）, https://www.americanprogress.org/issues/poverty/reports/2015/12/10/126902/removing-barriers-to-opportunity-for-parents-with-criminal-records-and-their-children/.

⑤ 5 U. S. C. 1501 – 1508.

⑥ Public Law 112 – 230, 5 U. S. C. 1502.

第四章 "联合公民案"时代竞选财务法律重塑：反腐败与言论自由的博弈

但须遵守以下禁止事项：使用其官方权力或影响力来干涉或影响选举结果；在党派竞选活动中竞选公职；索取、募集或接受竞选捐款；在联邦办公场所、公务期间、穿制服和使用政府车辆的情况下参加党派政治活动。① 此外，居住在马里兰、弗吉尼亚州和哥伦比亚特区附近自治市或行政区的联邦政府雇员也被允许参加哥伦比亚特区的公职选举。但是在第7323（b）（2）和第7323（b）（3）条中列出的职位或机构雇员受到更大的限制，如司法部刑事司法司和国家安全部门的雇员，除由总统任命并经参议院同意，不得参与党派政治活动。与1993年的上一版本《哈奇法》相比，《哈奇现代化法》还改变了对违反该法律的联邦雇员的处罚，前者不再被自动解职，新的处罚手段有简单的谴责、开除和执行禁止聘用期。特别检察官办公室（Office of Special Counsel）和功绩制保护局（Merit Systems Protection Board）负责执行《哈奇现代化法》，若发现有雇员违反该法律，且该行为可能导致解雇，则雇佣机构必须解雇该雇员或没收其两年薪水；如果该雇员在被解职的18个月内受雇于该州当地机构、华盛顿特区或其他州，那么该聘用机构或原离职的机构将可能失去部分联邦资金划拨。② 《哈奇法》自颁布以来，一直在为联邦雇员参与政治活动范围划定严格的界限。在联邦政府拥有和经营的场所，如国家公园等，政客的出入都可能受到限制。多名政府要员也曾因无意间违反规定发表党派政治言论，而被特别检察官办公室警告或处罚。2004年，柯特兰（Kirtland）空军基地的公共事务干事在发送电子邮件邀请员工参加布什的竞选演讲后，检察办公室收到大量举报其违反《哈奇法》的投诉。③ 2016年，一名移民法官因在主持听证会时为总统候选人希拉里·克林顿的平台宣传，而违反了《哈奇法》，随后被联邦政府禁止聘用30年，并处以1000美元的罚款。④ 2020年8月，时任农业部长珀杜（Sonny Perdue）因在宣传农业部于新冠疫情期间向农民采购粮农食品的计划时，表示支持特朗普连任，因而违反了

---

① 5 U.S.C. 7323 (a).
② U.S. Office of Special Counsel, "State, D.C., or Local Employee Hatch Act Information", Office of Special Counsel (n.d.), https：//osc.gov/Services/Pages/HatchAct-StateLocal.aspx#tabGroup51.
③ Kathleen Hennessey, "White House Memo Fuels Debate on Whether Parks, Politics Mix", *Los Angeles Times*, Aug. 30, 2004.
④ Kate Sullivan, "Judge Disciplined for Promoting Hillary Clinton's Immigration Plan", CNN (Sep. 18, 2019), https：//www.cnn.com/2019/09/18/politics/immigration-judge-hatch-act-hillary-clinton/index.html.

《哈奇法》禁止政府内阁成员在公务期间参加政治活动的规定而被罚款。①据统计，至少有25名特朗普政府官员违反了《哈奇法》，而奥巴马时期仅有两起。② 特别检察官办公室在 2014—2019 年发布了 1273 条个案相关指导意见，并在 2019 年收到了创纪录的 281 个《哈奇法》相关投诉。③ 排除其他因素的影响，《哈奇现代化法》通过细化对联邦雇员滥用权力和联邦资源的处罚措施，有效提升了特别检察官办公室的执法力度。其在很大程度上构建了对联邦雇员滥用职务权力、不当影响选举的更广泛监督体系，也为联邦政府在党派政治斗争中的中立地位提供了重要保障。

（二）2010 年以来的主要竞选反腐败法案

在"联合公民案"判决后的十余年中，包括新任议员在内的众多国会议员，已将竞选财务改革作为主要立法改革内容之一，提交了近百部竞选财务和反腐败法案。但如前所见，真正成为法律的法案屈指可数。尽管面对数届国会中的连续失败，改革倡导者仍未放弃，不断修订更新法案内容，并在新一届国会中将其提出。众议院行政委员会、参议院规则委员会以及行政委员会是负责竞选财务政策问题的主要机构。自 2010 年起，委员会审议了多个反复提出的提案，主要集中在三个方面：增强信息披露，防止外国资金干涉以及设置捐款限额或开支限制。具体而言，这些改革法案旨在规制游说活动、禁止外国干涉选举、为总统竞选提供公共资金、要求披露公司捐款、限制存在利益冲突的捐款和扩大政治通讯的范围等。④ 尽管绝大多数法案都未能获得两院投票成为法律，但它们反映了联合公民时代竞选与政治反腐败的主要改革方向，具有重要的参考价值。

1. 披露公司竞选支出

2010 年以来，规制公司竞选支出的法案都没有获得成功，因而新的改

---

① Rebecca Beitsch, "USDA's Perdue Fined for Violating Hatch Act while Promoting Food Boxes", The Hill（Oct. 08, 2020）, https://thehill.com/homenews/administration/520240-usdas-perdue-fined-for-violating-hatch-act-while-promoting-food-boxes.
② Andrew Solender, "Here's Why Trump Officials Rarely Face Penalties For Hatch Act Violations", Forbes（Aug. 26, 2020）, https://www.forbes.com/sites/andrewsolender/2020/08/26/heres-why-trump-officials-rarely-face-penalties-for-hatch-act-violations/? sh = 7a3ba64ca2d2.
③ Nicole Ogrysko, "Many Feds Do Care about the Hatch Act. But the Law Allows Others to Shrug It Off", Federal News Network（Aug. 31, 2020）, https://federalnewsnetwork.com/mike-causey-federal-report/2020/08/many-feds-do-care-about-the-hatch-act-but-the-law-allows-others-to-shrug-it-off/.
④ 许多法案都已在前几届国会中出现过，经修改后重新在近几年中提出，对于这类法案，本节仅介绍其最新版本。

第四章 "联合公民案"时代竞选财务法律重塑：反腐败与言论自由的博弈

革构想开始跳脱出传统的竞选监管系统，力图借用证券监管机构、国家问责机构甚至金融犯罪情报机构的力量来促使公司政治支出资金公开，这既是另辟蹊径的创新，也涉及更广泛行政资源的调配协作，无形中对机构执法合作提出了更高要求。

2023 年 7 月，众议员萨班斯（John Sarbanes）提出了《投票自由法案》①。法案是对 2021 年众议院投票通过的《为了人民法案》②的延续和补充，要求各州对联邦选举进行选举后审计，以保障选举安全，还涉及竞选资金，包括扩大对外国公民竞选支出的禁令，要求额外披露与竞选有关的筹款和支出，要求对某些政治广告作出额外免责声明等。虽然已有建议修改《联邦竞选法》从而向公司、工会、超级政治行动委员会及其他实体施加额外披露要求的提案，③ 但鉴于"联合公民案"以来联邦选举委员会对公司选举资金监管程度的进一步下降，许多竞选财务法专家和部分国会议员开始提出将竞选财务监管的压力向证券交易管理领域分流。2021 年 2 月，伊利诺伊州民主党众议员福斯特（Bill Foster）提议修改 1934 年《证券交易法》（Securities Exchange Act），要求公司报告其政治活动和出于其他目的的某些支出。④ 该法案与 2019 年加州民主党议员卡巴甲（Salud Carbajal）提出的《公司政治披露法案》⑤ 大体相似。法案没有涉及对现有竞选财务法律的改变，而是要求修正《证券交易法》第 13 条，规定证券发行人每年公开披露前一年的政治活动支出摘要供公众查阅，且由主管公司监管领域的联邦证券交易委员会负责发布相关法规并确保该法案得到执行。其中政治活动支出不仅包含独立支出，还包含与 501（c）免税组织交易所支付的费用或会费，广播、有线或卫星电视传输的传统竞选通讯以及其他一切以公开形式传播的互联网竞选通讯所产生的费用等。这两个法案目标明确、内容全面但又十分简明，但与其他许多法案一样，由于立法目标范围广泛而触动多方利益，显著增加了谈判妥协的难度，因此新法案在

---

① H. R. 11-Freedom to Vote Act.
② H. R. 1-For the People Act of 2021.
③ H. R. 1334-To amend the Federal Election Campaign Act of 1971 to provide for additional disclosure requirements for corporations, labor organizations, Super PACs and other entities, and for other purposes.
④ H. R. 1087 – To amend the Securities Exchange Act of 1934 to require reporting of certain expenditures for political activities, and for other purposes.
⑤ H. R. 1053 – Corporate Political Disclosure Act of 2019.

当届国会中能够取得的立法进展仍有待观察。

此前的 2019 年《公司透明法案》① 改革路径则更为激进,其试图调用刑事司法领域的司法情报系统与国家问责署的监督资源来强制公司申报竞选支出。法案要求新成立的和某些已设立的小型股份有限公司以及有限责任公司披露其受益所有人②的信息。具体来说,特定实体在申请成立股份有限公司或有限责任公司时,必须向金融犯罪执法网络(Financial Crimes Enforcement Network)③ 提交受益所有权信息,而某些已成立的股份有限公司和有限责任公司也必须在该法案实施两年内向执法网络提交上述信息。对提供虚假、欺诈性受益所有权信息或故意不更新、不提供完整受益所有权信息的行为,该法案不仅规定了民事处罚,还拟授权单处、并处罚金和 3 年以下监禁的刑事处罚。此外,政府问责署负责验证和报告其他法律实体如合伙企业的实益所有权信息的真实性,并评估本法案的实践有效性。该法案在众议院获得通过,但最终未能进入参议院投票程序。

2. 修宪禁止公司竞选捐款

对于竞选捐款的监管权力,也有议员提议直接从宪法方面进行彻底修正,从而消除"联合公民案"为竞选财务监管带来的负面影响,扭转立法机构与联邦选举委员会的被动地位。这种改革路径可以为国家监管竞选捐款提供最为有力和彻底的手段,但实现改革的难度也是最大的——参众两院都必须以 2/3 的票数通过宪法修正案。

佛罗里达州民主党众议员多以奇(Theodore Deutch)在 2021 年 1 月提案授权国会和各州,对候选人和其他人筹集和花费竞选资金影响选举设定合理的限制以达到规范目的。④ 若法案通过,国会和各州将被授权通过相应的具体立法实施该修正案的权力。公司和其他依法设立的实体将从在宪法基础上与自然人区分开来,其因"联合公民案"在事实上获得的言论自

---

① S. 1978 – Corporate Transparency Act of 2019.
② 受益所有人(beneficial owner)是指对公司或有限责任公司行使实质性控制权,合伙拥有公司或持有限责任公司 25% 及以上的权益,或从公司或有限责任公司的资产中获得实质性经济利益的个人。
③ 金融犯罪执法网络是美国财政部下属的金融情报机构,负责收集和分析有关金融交易的信息,以打击国内和国际洗钱、恐怖主义融资和其他金融犯罪。其与数十个情报机构共享信息,包括酒精烟草和火器管理局、禁毒署、联邦调查局、特勤局、国税局、海关与边境执法局以及邮政督察局等。
④ H. J. Res. 1 – Proposing an amendment to the Constitution of the United States relating to contributions and expenditures intended to affect elections.

由等人格权将被废除，从而被禁止以竞选支出的形式影响选举。俄勒冈民主党众议员施雷德（Kurt Schrader）也在两周后提出了一项与前者对应的宪法修正案，要求赋予国会规制联邦选举中竞选捐款和竞选支出的权力。[①] 国会将有权禁止、限制和以其他方式，规管对联邦选举候选人的捐款和与之等同的实物捐赠以及用于支持或购买影响联邦政府选举结果的媒体广告的支出或实物捐赠。这一修正案同样提出禁止非美国公民，包括非美国的协会、外国政府或其代理人进行捐款或捐赠。两个宪法修正提案在本质上都是为了消除公司在"联合公民案"中被实质上赋予的言论自由权，以切断选举中大量不受监管的外部支出来源。

3. 披露暗钱来源与禁止外国影响

美国大选中大量暗钱流入的现状，既有党派斗争的原因，又存在一部分外国势力的干涉因素。而联邦选举监管机构缺乏意愿或没有能力介入并执行现有规则，对暗钱监管造成了直接困难。着眼于对《税法》《联邦刑法》和《外国代理人登记法》的修订，国会议员们提出的法案主题涵盖披露501组织暗钱来源，禁止为外国资金输入成立空壳公司，外国主体向政府官员送礼以及间接禁止外国公民获取投票权。

作为对"联合公民案"的回应，《披露法案》曾于2010年6月以219票赞成、206票反对在众议院获得通过，并于2014年、2018年和2023年数次被引入众议院，但未能成功立法。作为一项以披露为核心的竞选财务综合改革法案，其主张修正1971年《联邦竞选法》，以更快地公开竞选活动的支出，并打击逐年激增的暗钱在大选中的使用。《披露法案》的披露规定有诸多进步之处，如主张适当扩大当前的报告要求范围，以获悉直接或通过将资金转移到其他外围组织而最终资助大量竞选广告的外围人员或组织；缩短报告此类支出的首次披露时间和间隔频率；向互联网企业施加更多的客户审查义务以完善广告的购买者信息，并促使企业改进当前的免责声明要求，修改电视和互联网等媒介广告的"免责声明"条款，要求在广告主体中声明赞助广告的组织及其主要出资者。但该法案随后被共和党人拖入冗长辩论，在2010年7月和2010年9月的数次终结辩论（cloture）动议表决中都未能获得必要的60票，法案最终难产。自此，参议院和众议院的民主党人每年都会将《披露法案》的新版本重新在国会中介绍。

---

① H. J. Res. 21 – Proposing an amendment to the Constitution of the United States giving Congress power to regulate campaign contributions for Federal elections.

2014年，由50个参议院民主党议员提出该法案的新版本亦未能成功。2018年版的《披露法案》提出了进一步以披露手段使暗钱组织透明化的设想①：要求501（c）（4）组织、527组织和超级政治行动委员会在24小时内向联邦选举委员会提交报告，披露其1万美元或以上的选举支出，以及在该选举周期内收到的所有1万美元以上的捐款者；要求公司、工会和其他组织的领导者在其资助或发布的政治广告中表明身份；政府应责成联邦承包商在竞标过程中披露其竞选捐款；要求进行选举支出的公司披露其真实所有者，以限制使用空壳公司作为选举资金渠道的行为。此外，该版本还提出禁止外国具有主要控制权、所有权或指示权的美国公司对选举进行支出。2023年版的《披露法案》②在原有基础上，扩大了现有的外国资金禁令范围，将用于有偿网络通信或其他数字通信以及联邦司法提名通信的费用包括在内。法案禁止外国公民向与投票倡议和公民投票有关的竞选活动捐款，并要求政府问责署在每4年的选举周期内，研究和报告联邦选举中非法外国资金的情况。该法案还特别规定，设立或利用意图隐瞒外国公民选举捐款的公司或其他实体应受到罚款和/或最高5年监禁的刑事处罚。法案还要求外围组织披露前一年向该组织捐款最多的捐款者。

2019年的两项法案旨在彻底阻塞501组织的暗钱通道。2019年1月，科罗拉多州民主党众议员克罗（Jason Crow）在竞选中击败共和党对手后，提出的第一个法案即为《终止暗钱法案》③。他提议披露向《税法》501（c）（4）"社会福利"免税团体捐款的个人或团体身份，并废除国税局调查这类组织行为的禁令，不再限制税务服务部门的资金使用，从而将这类非营利组织的政治活动透明化。同年7月，缅因州民主党众议员戈尔登（Jared Golden）向国会介绍了《打击暗钱法案》。④该法案提出的解决措施更为直接：修改1986年《税法》，禁止501（c）（4）实体将总支出的10%以上用于政治支出或其他目的。在明确《税法》对政治支出的定义基础上，法案还提出了"政治干预"概念，进行政治干预活动的组织不享有免税职能：针对联邦、州、地方和公职候选人的国外竞选活动，明确主张选任、反对、提名或罢免政治候选人；支持或反对与特定政党有联系的候

---

① S. 3150 – DISCLOSE Act of 2018.
② H. R. 1118 – D ISCLOSE Act of 2023.
③ H. R. 868 – End Dark Money Act.
④ H. R. 7525 – Crack Down on Dark Money Act.

第四章 "联合公民案"时代竞选财务法律重塑：反腐败与言论自由的博弈

选人；为候选人的竞选活动或政党捐款。

还有一些法案着眼于杜绝外国资金对选举的影响，这部分外国资金也是暗钱的主要来源之一。最新版本的《保护我们的民主法案》①由共和党参议院希夫（Adam Schiff）于2023年7月提出，与《联邦贸易法》中对外国贸易的相关规定结合试图堵塞外国利用非竞选资金干涉美国选举的漏洞。加州众议员则建议禁止外籍人士在州或地方选举以及全民公投中进行捐款，以防止外国资金影响地方选举体系。②佛罗里达州共和党众议员博西（Bill Posey）则在此前建议修改1978年《政府道德法》（Ethics in Government Act），要求国会议员披露与外国实体的业务关系。③该法案较为温和，是否能够通过还有待观察。此前在2月，有明尼苏达众议员提案修改1938年《外国代理登记法》，要求外国委托人的注册代理人披露其对官员任何有价值物的赠与，并在司法部建立一个单独部门负责该事项的调查和执法行动。④2020年提出的《空壳公司滥用法案》⑤对外国资金所采取的措施则激烈得多，其以刑法为切入点，拟将使用公司或其他实体隐瞒外国公民或实体提供竞选捐款或捐赠的行为非法化。违反者将被选处或并处罚金和最高5年的监禁。其具体提议修改《美国法典》的犯罪与刑事诉讼卷（即《联邦刑法》），规定成立公司以隐瞒外国人的选举捐款和捐赠构成犯罪，公司或其他实体及其所有人、高级管理人员、律师或公司注册代理人为隐瞒活动而成立或使用该公司的行为，均属违法。2019年《揭露外国在美影响法案》⑥同样主张从税法路径披露501暗钱组织的收入来源，并对未披露接受外国政治捐款的美国人征收消费税。具体来说，该法案对接受外国来源捐款的免税组织制定了额外的披露要求，主张修改《税收法》以

---

① H. R. 5048 – Protecting Our Democracy Act.
② H. R. 1516 – To amend the Federal Election Campaign Act of 1971 to prohibit contributions and donations by foreign nationals in connection with State or local ballot initiatives or referenda.
③ H. R. 661 – To amend the Ethics in Government Act of 1978 to require Members of Congress to disclose business ties with foreign entities, and for other purposes.
④ H. R. 1419 – To amend the Foreign Agents Registration Act of 1938 to establish a separate unit within the Department of Justice for the investigation and enforcement of such Act, to provide the Attorney General with the authority to impose civil money penalties for violations of such Act, and to require agents of foreign principals who are registered under such Act to disclose transactions involving things of financial value conferred on officeholders.
⑤ H. R. 8347 – Shell Company Abuse Act.
⑥ H. R. 703 – Uncovering Foreign Influence in the United States Act of 2019.

公开向免税组织捐款5万美元或以上的外国人姓名和地址，并要求披露所有外国竞选捐款。若美国公民提供了国外来源的政治捐款，在捐款之日起的30天内未披露该捐款的，将对其征收10%的消费税，此后每30天阶梯式提高10%税率，以100%为税率上限。披露应包括捐款数额，并指明捐款者。外国来源政治捐款被定义为联邦、州候选人，或在当地选举办公室所代表的、在美国拥有的美国身份或税收居民①以外者的资助。此处的外国人，不仅包括外国自然人，还包括外资拥有的公司、外国政府及其实体。此外，2019年提出的《对抗非法游说法案》②也要求司法部建立一个独立的部门，以调查并监督外国代理人的依法注册情况。司法部将被授予对违法行为处以民事罚款的权力，并要求外国代理人披露其外国委托人与公职人员之间的经济往来。2018年的《拒绝法案》③也致力于扩大对外国国民选举捐款的禁令：受外国国民或政府控制的公司不得捐款；禁止免税的外国附属组织向超级政治行动委员会捐款等与竞选有关的活动；外国人不得参与任何人选举活动的决策过程。法案还请求修订《外国代理人登记法》，以废除个人注册为游说者义务的例外豁免情况，并增加对与外国委托人利益相关的信息备案和标记要求。

在2020年大选的激烈争夺中，外国人投票权争议也被进一步激化。自1996年《非法移民改革和移民责任法》（Illegal Immigration Reform and Immigrant Responsibility Act）颁布以来，联邦法律禁止非公民参加联邦选举。原则上，只有美国公民才有本国选举的投票权，但近年来美国各地已在不同程度上考虑允许持有绿卡的合法永久居民、未经法律许可在美国居住的移民和学生签证持有人在学区校董事会或镇议会的地方选举中投票。如纽约市曾提出赋予绿卡持有人和持有工作签证的外国人士选举投票权的法案。而旧金山已允许作为学生家长或监护人的非公民居民在校董会选举中投票，马里兰州也有11个城市允许非公民在地方选举中投票。④ 尽管已

---

① 指持有绿卡或一日历年内在美国居留183天以上者。
② H. R. 1467 – Protect Against Unlawful Lobbying (PAUL) Act of 2019.
③ H. R. 6249 – REFUSE Act.
④ Benjy Sarlin, "San Francisco Allows Undocumented Immigrants to Vote in School Elections", NBC News (Jul. 21, 2018), https://www.nbcnews.com/politics/immigration/san-francisco-allows-undocumented-immigrants-vote-school-elections-n893221; Reuters Staff, "Maryland city approves letting non-citizens vote in local elections", Reuters (n. d.), https://www.reuters.com/article/us-usa-immigration-maryland/maryland-city-approves-letting-non-citizens-vote-in-local-elections-idUSKCN1BO242.

经存在相关法律，但科罗拉多、佛罗里达和亚拉巴马州均在 2020 年相继通过了选票提案（ballot measures）①，确认只有年满 18 岁的美国公民才能投票的州宪法规定，而在 2020 年大选之前，只有北达科他和亚利桑那州的宪法禁止非公民在州或地方选举中投票。② 2021 年 1 月，南卡罗来纳共和党议员邓肯在众议院提出了《革除选举外国干预法案》，③ 对于允许非公民在州或地方选举中投票的地方政府，法案将禁止使用联邦资金向其支付款项。

不难发现，无论是《终止暗钱法案》《揭露外国在美影响法案》还是《空壳公司滥用法案》，都旨在对选举中的暗钱釜底抽薪。这类解决方式直接、彻底的法案，往往毫无意外地无法进入委员会投票。尽管与上述难产的法案一样，《革除选举外国干预法案》也很可能无法在当届议会中通过，但其生动反映了现今两党阵营及其背后选民力量之间的艰难拉锯，对每一张选票的争夺正变得前所未有的重要。

4. 延长游说冷静期和扩大游说定义

针对游说的改革法案以大幅延长冷静期和增加惩罚性规定为主，围绕刑事法律规制和公务员退休福利的剥夺措施展开。这实质上也反映了现有冷静期规定的有效性与游说禁令惩罚性不足的问题。根据目前的法律，参议员离任后的游说冷静期为两年，众议员为一年。

2017 年在众议院提交宪法与民事司法小组委员会审议的《抽干沼泽法案》，希望通过修改《联邦刑法》，对高级行政部门官员及其雇员离职后的游说活动施加更强有力的限制，④ 并试图禁止前政治任职者在离任五年内从事游说交流，扩大了遵守旋转门禁令的人员范围，不仅包括高级政治官员、高级行政人员，还包括在例外服务中担任机密或决策的雇员。该法案主张对《外国代理人登记法》进行了修正，终身禁止前政治任职者代表外国政府或外国政党游说。继 2017 年法案闯关失败后，众议员博西于 2019

---

① 即一州或地方的全民公投。如此处科罗拉多州的选票提案是："是否对科罗拉多州宪法进行修正，要求有资格在任何选举中投票的个人，必须是美国公民？"
② Patty Nieberg, "Three States Pass Amendments that 'Only Citizens' Can Vote", Associated Press (Nov. 7, 2020), https://apnews.com/article/alabama-local-elections-constitutions-florida-voting-rights-a28936630a24030df958092834f6b2c1.
③ H. R. 93 – Eliminating Foreign Intervention in Elections Act.
④ H. R. 484 – DRAIN the SWAMP Act.

年再次提出了《结束国会旋转门法案》。① 法案拟禁止被注册游说者雇佣的前国会议员或前国会高级雇员在法案颁布后享有任何福利。这些福利包括联邦雇员退休制度中的节俭储蓄计划②，联邦雇员的健康福利方案，如联邦补助的牙科和眼科福利以及联邦雇员团体人寿保险计划。同年，科罗拉多民主党参议员本内特（Michael Bennet）向参议院国土安全与政府事务委员会宣读了旨在增加对游说的限制和相关惩罚规定的《关闭旋转门法案》。③ 该法案拟终身禁止前参众议员或当选候任的参众议员游说在任议员、官员或国会雇员以及其他立法机构的雇员。对参议员的雇员，参众议员的私人工作人员，国会委员会工作人员、领导层和其他立法机构的职员，游说禁令统一从现有的1年延长到6年。已注册的说客或外国委托人的代理人在六年内不得为与其有实质游说接触的国会议员或国会委员会雇佣。法案还要求，在单个申报期内雇佣3个以上游说者的实质游说公司实体，须按年度申报其所雇佣的所有前国会议员和高薪雇佣咨询的立法部门官员，并在增加披露要求的基础上加重了违反信息披露义务的民事处罚。

尽管该法案在提出后未在国会得到响应，但类似的努力从未停止过。2020年成功连任后，博西在2021年1月又提出法案，建议修改《联邦刑法》，为前国会议员参与游说活动制定5年的冷静期，同时将前国会官员和雇员的游说禁令期间统一为卸任后的两年内，并通过降低后者的收入门槛标准扩大禁令的适用范围。在代表外国委托人游说方面，规定前国会议员或前国会高级雇员若因此获得报酬，将失去获得退休金或某些其他联邦福利的资格。④ 明尼苏达州民主党众议员克雷格（Angie Craig）也在当天提出了与该法案类似，但改革更为激进的《谦逊法案》⑤。其提议将前任议员和国会的其他民选官员在离职后任意时间内进行的游说行为定为应受处罚的犯罪，并对公务出行开支作出了更为严格的约束。为了规避无记录在

---

① H. R. 3326 - End the Congressional Revolving Door Act.
② 联邦退休储蓄投资委员会（Federal Retirement Thrift Investment Board）通过节俭储蓄计划（Thrift Savings Plan），为超过590万前任和现任政府雇员以及军人进行个人退休金的综合投资管理。
③ S. 2622 - Close the Revolving Door Act of 2019.
④ H. R. 665 - To provide that a former Member of Congress or former senior Congressional employee who receives compensation as a lobbyist representing a foreign principal shall not be eligible for retirement benefits or certain other Federal benefits.
⑤ H. R. 459-HUMBLE Act.

第四章 "联合公民案"时代竞选财务法律重塑：反腐败与言论自由的博弈

案的私下接触游说行为，法案拟禁止众议院为前众议员提供进入众议院大厅、使用健身设施、其他可供众议员使用的设施以及国会议员餐厅和使用停车位等便利。随后在2021年2月，威斯康星州共和党众议员加拉格尔（Mike Gallagher）提出了对在联邦一级从事游说活动的前国会议员和前政府高级行政官员的5年禁令，处罚措施为终止其在联邦雇员退休制度中的进一步退休保障。[1] 伊利诺伊州民主党众议员施耐德（Bradly Schneider）也在同一时间提出了与上述法案类似的一揽子议案，拟规定前国会议员在作为受薪说客工作时，应被剥夺部分联邦退休福利以及享受某些国会服务的资格。[2] 法案要求每名国会议员在官方网站上公布个人年度财务信息披露报告的链接，并禁止使用政府拨款支付其随行配偶的官方旅行费用。施耐德也主张修订《政府道德法案》，要求高级行政部门雇员签署道德承诺书。[3] 目前，上述各项法案均已提交至相应的众议院委员会等待审议。

当前国会的游说规定并不要求受薪的议题倡导者注册为联邦游说者，除非他们代表特定客户与政府官员联系，并花费至少20%的营业时间用于游说活动，该规定被许多前国会议员和国会高级工作人员利用，因而以议题倡导者的身份从事游说。针对此种情况，2019年新入驻国会的纽约民主党人罗斯（Max Rose）提出了《关闭游说漏洞法案》。[4] 法案旨在消除该法律漏洞，要求如果有人像游说者一样活动，并且像游说者一样得到报酬；或者仅仅在策略指导层面支持游说联系，无论这些活动者是否亲自进行联

---

[1] H. R. 753 – To prohibit congressional recesses until Congress adopts a concurrent resolution on the budget that results in a balanced Federal budget by the last fiscal year covered by such resolution, to establish a 5-year ban on individuals appointed to Executive Schedule positions and Members of Congress engaging in lobbying activities at the Federal level, to provide for the termination of further retirement coverage for Members of Congress under the Federal Employees Retirement System, and for other purposes.

[2] H. R. 1078 – To provide that a former Member of Congress receiving compensation as a lobbyist shall be ineligible to receive certain Federal retirement benefits or to use certain congressional benefits and services, to require each Member of Congress to post on the Member's official public website a hyperlink to the most recent annual financial disclosure report filed by the Member under the Ethics in Government Act of 1978, to prohibit the use of appropriated funds to pay for the costs of travel by the spouse of a Member of Congress who accompanies the Member on official travel, to restrict the use of travel promotional awards by Members of Congress who receive such awards in connection with official air travel, and for other purposes.

[3] H. R. 1077 – To amend the Ethics in Government Act of 1978 to require senior Executive branch employees to sign an ethics pledge, and for other purposes.

[4] H. R. 783 – Lobbyist Loophole Closure Act.

系，都注册为游说者。此外，还有一个促进游说者披露身份的 2019 年《清晰法案》。① 在对 1971 年《联邦竞选法》修改的基础上，法案要求政治委员会、独立支出人员以及竞选通讯支出人员在向联邦选举委员会提交的报告中，披露报告所提及的个人是否为注册游说者，若已注册，则应另附声明证实其已依据 1995 年《游说披露法》注册。同时联邦选举委员会应确保，其公共数据库中关于注册游说者的信息以电子方式链接到参议院秘书处和众议院书记处网站，以实现不同机构间的游说者信息联通。

5. 促进政治通讯披露

自由公正的选举需具备透明性和完整的问责制，这要求公众有权了解政治广告的真正资金来源，以便在充分知情的前提下做出政治选择。政治广告资金的透明度对于执行其他竞选财务法律也至关重要，尤其是在禁止外国赞助竞选广告方面。针对现今互联网站点政治广告普遍不受披露监管的情况，国会提出了数项法案作为响应。法案均以扩大现有政治通讯的法律定义为途径，拟将互联网站点广告和其他数字广告纳入捐款披露范围，以提升竞选财务的透明度并有效执行问责制。尽管这些法案均未能在国会中取得立法胜利，但也为将来的综合性改革指明了努力方向。

2020 年的《司法广告法案》②旨在对联邦司法提名传播即政治广告方面做出全面规制。其试图将政治通讯涵盖所有的广播、有线或卫星电视、付费互联网和付费数字通信，付费促销、报纸、杂志、户外广告设施、群发邮件、电话银行、电话消息的传播工作，数量为 30 天内的 500 条通话或电子消息，或所有其他形式的公众政治广告。该法案要求修改 1971 年《联邦竞选法》，凡一个日历年内在联邦司法提名传播上花费超过 5 万美元的公司、劳工组织或政治委员会等组织，均须向联邦选举委员会提交一份声明。声明应包含组织名称和主要营业地点，若发行主体为公司，还需列出受益所有人清单，且对声明的时间及披露捐款人的姓名和地址等内容也有明确要求。法案还要求传播广告标记免责声明，并在声明中指出该广告的资助者。最后，拟禁止外国国民和受外国影响的公司资助联邦司法提名广告。

2019 年的《诚实广告法案》③的目的也是将传统媒体政治广告的法律

---

① H. R. 842 – CLEAR Act.
② H. R. 8459 – Judicial Ads Act.
③ H. R. 2592 – Honest Ads Act.

限制扩大适用于互联网或数字政治广告。其通过要求广告的购买和发布者向公众披露广告相关信息，提高在线政治广告的透明度和问责制，力求维护选民的充分知情权，从而在国家安全的层面上提升选举的公正性。法案为互联网和数字广告的披露声明制定了特别规则，即电视台、电台、有线或卫星电视服务的供应商和社交网站等网络平台都必须作出合理的尽职审查努力，以确保其发布的政治广告不被外国人直接或间接购买，在线平台还必须公开政治广告的购买记录。

类似的法案还有同年由加州民主党众议员洛夫格伦提出的《为实现长久民主制止对选举的有害干预法案》。[①] 法案幸运地在众议院得到通过，但最终未能进入参议院投票。其同样规定将现有的竞选广告法规应用于在线广告，并限制外国实体的政治支出和选举干扰。政治委员会必须向联邦调查局和联邦选举委员会报告涉嫌提供非法选举资助的外国联系，相关违规行为将被上升到刑事处罚的层面。法案拟规定不当干扰选举的外国人应被驱逐出境，并禁止再次进入美国。通过将政治广告和竞选通讯的现有要求全面适用于互联网和数字广告，促使广告的赞助者履行捐款的相关限制和披露义务。不仅如此，法案还要求大型在线平台负责维护政治广告的公共数据库，以禁止在选举前60天内发布欺骗性的音频或视频。相比于其他打击外国干涉选举的法案，该法案对外国实体的政治支出施加了更为具体的限制。其规定外国实体不得参加与投票倡议和公民投票有关的活动，以及涉及候选人或政治议题的网络活动支出，同时候选人也被禁止与部分外国实体共享非公开的竞选信息。

6. 限制利益冲突捐款

在第117届国会中，针对竞选捐款的最新改革提案主要围绕《联邦竞选法》的相关捐款规定展开。这些法案旨在对与候选人可能产生利益冲突的捐款进行限制或披露，具体涉及当选总统的就职委员会收受的捐款、总统的商务行为支出、政治委员会使用捐款向候选人亲属支付竞选服务报酬，以及被提名人或候任者参与的捐款与筹款活动等。

民主党十分重视监管与总统可能存在利益冲突的捐款。宾夕法尼亚州民主党众议员斯坎隆（Mary Scanlon）于2021年1月提出《就职资金诚信法案》，旨在修改《联邦竞选法》的就职大会捐款相关条目，以对向就职委员

---

① H. R. 4617 – Stopping Harmful Interference in Elections for a Lasting Democracy Act.

会捐款的行为作出规范，同时禁止部分类型的捐赠，并要求就职委员会进行报告。① 法案规定个人向就职委员会捐款总额超过5万美元将被视为违法行为，就职委员会不得接受自然人以外的组织或外国人的捐款，未使用的资金也不得赠予501组织等非营利组织。总统就职典礼后的90天内，就职委员会应向联邦选举委员会提交报告，披露所收受捐款的金额和日期、捐款人的姓名和地址，并列明所有支出的金额、日期和目的。2019年的《总统商务官方支出法案》② 则显然是民主党人针对特朗普总统提出的。法案要求各执行机构向政府道德办公室（Office of Government Ethics）提交季度报告，列出该机构因总统所有的私营公司而支出或使用联邦资金的每一个事项，包括支出的金额和公司名称，并在报告后10日内在本机构网站上公布。其实民主党议员在2018年就已经提出过类似的《腐败法案》。③ 同样拟规定联邦机构与特朗普集团控制的财产所进行交易的报告要求，范围覆盖总统本人、其亲属、行政部门负责人、特朗普集团员工控制和关联的组织或业务。2018年和2019年的这两个法案均未在特朗普政府下得到通过。

  提案的另一个努力方向是切断政治委员会对候选人亲属的利益输送。2021年2月，威斯康星州共和党众议员蒂梵尼（Thomas Tiffany）也在国会提出修改《联邦竞选法》，以禁止政治委员会就候选人的配偶为委员会提供的服务进行补偿，若委员会向候选人配偶或直系亲属支付款项，应进行申报。④ 针对超级政治行动委员会等与候选人之间普遍存在的事实协调支出问题，北卡罗来纳州民主党众议院也建议在《联邦竞选法》中，进一步说明对向候选人捐款为名进行协调支出的处置方式。⑤ 同时提交众议院的法案中，还有一部也涉及规范政治委员会的捐款事项。伊利诺伊州议员施耐德建议《联邦竞选法》规定所有政治委员会在一个日历年度内收到同一捐款者的捐款累计达1000美元或以上时，应在48小时内向联邦选举委员

---

① H. R. 422 – Inaugural Fund Integrity Act.
② H. R. 4454 – Disclosing Official Spending at Presidential Businesses Act.
③ H. R. 5182 – CORRUPT Act.
④ H. R. 856 – To amend the Federal Election Campaign Act of 1971 to prohibit certain political committees from compensating the spouse of the candidate for services provided to or on behalf of the committee, to require such committees to report on payments made to the spouse and the immediate family members of the candidate, and for other purposes.
⑤ H. R. 1172 – To amend the Federal Election Campaign Act to clarify the treatment of coordinated expenditures as contributions made to candidates under such Act, and for other purposes.

第四章 "联合公民案"时代竞选财务法律重塑：反腐败与言论自由的博弈

会报告。① 同时，亚利桑那州共和党众议员也提出《联邦竞选法》应禁止政治委员会接受来源未经证实的在线捐款。②

与被提名和候任的政治候选人相关利益冲突的捐款和参与筹款活动行为也受到了立法提案的关注。2019年《政治筹款冲突法案》③ 要求被总统任命的行政部门官员披露其是否向政治行动委员会、501组织等政治非营利组织或行业贸易协会捐款，或为其募集捐款。其提出修订1978年《政府道德法》，要求经参议院确认的提名人或候任者以及担任机密或决策职位者，应披露与上述组织的捐款或筹款活动。

7. 选举综合改革法案

选举综合改革法案主要涵盖四项内容：综合提升游说与竞选捐款的透明度，约束法官行为，推行小额捐款人众筹竞选资金，以及保障投票本身的参与度和公正性。

由于此前的数次立法努力均告失败，2018年《披露法案》被并入内容更广泛的2019年《为了人民法案》④。后者在前者基础上进一步增加了对政府成员的道德规定，要求总统和副总统候选人公开其过去十年的所得税申报表，禁止政客将纳税人税款用于支付性骚扰指控的和解协议，并为联邦最高法院制定新的道德准则，迫使大法官遵守现有的司法行为守则。该法案在2019年3月以234票赞成、193票反对在民主党控制的众议院获得通过，但最终未能在共和党控制的参议院中获得进展。作为第117届国会第一个提出的众议院法案，2021年版的《为了人民法案》⑤ 仍为竞选财务立法传递了强劲的改革信号。在2019年版的基础上，新《人民法案》同样重点关注提升透明度，减少大笔资金对选举的影响，同时致力于选举安全改革，增加美国人进入投票站的机会，并在国会建立问责制，采取廉政措施以及加强公务员的道德规范等。法案主张加强对政治行动委员会的资金来源和公司的竞选捐款行为进行源头管

---

① H. R. 1076 – To amend the Federal Election Campaign Act of 1971 to require all political committees to notify the Federal Election Commission within 48 hours of receiving cumulative contributions of $1000 or more from any contributor during a calendar year.

② H. R. 1127 – To amend the Federal Election Campaign Act of 1971 to prohibit the acceptance by political committees of online contributions from certain unverified sources, and for other purposes.

③ H. R. 812 – Conflicts from Political Fundraising Act of 2019.

④ H. R. 1 – For the People Act of 2019; S. 949 – For the People Act of 2019.

⑤ H. R. 1 – For the People Act of 2021.

理，要求只要是由公司提供的捐款，无论是否通过政治行动委员会支出，也无论公司以何形式对外承担法律责任，均应在一年内向联邦选举委员会提交证明，披露相关政治资金流向，否则将可能面临伪证罪指控。除公司外，劳工组织和其他实体均对其竞选活动的相关支出承担披露义务，须报告超过 1000 美元的竞选相关支出情况，并列明支付人姓名和地址。此外，如果竞选相关支出由参与竞选活动以外的主体使用银行隔离账户资金支付，则披露应涵盖所有相关人员的姓名、地址以及金额。作为一项综合改革方案，《人民法案》还旨在收紧有关国内外游说者游说登记的规定，支持游说的联系人咨询或其他游说咨询工作都将被视为游说，这意味着那些以"历史学家"和"顾问"名义工作的隐形游说者将承担与游说者相同的注册、披露和冷静期义务。

2020 年末，华盛顿州众议员洁雅珀（Pramila Jayapal）和马萨诸塞州参议员沃伦（Elizabeth Warren）分别在参众两院提出了《反腐败与公共诚信法案》，旨在对竞选资金、公共腐败、游说、利益冲突和道德相关的联邦法律进行广泛修改。① 法案提出进一步加强对离职后游说的限制，扩大财务披露要求，建立新的道德机构来监督联邦雇员，修改总统利益冲突法，并使得《美国法官行为守则》（Code of Conduct for U. S. Judges）适用于最高法院的大法官。洁雅珀还在公共选举资金方面建议联邦选举委员会推行代金券试点计划，使得个人使用代金券向合格候选人提供小额捐款。② 类似的还有 2019 年《立即公平选举法案》主张设立公平的选举基金，为符合特定条件并同意遵守某些限制的参议员候选人提供资金，法案还修改了有关参议院竞选广告的条款，并对部分政府合同征税。③ 此外，还有旨在修改《政府道德法》，进一步公开议员财产和旅行支出的《透明政府法案》。④

亚利桑那州共和党议员韦斯特曼（Bruce Westerman）在 2021 年 3 月

---

① H. R. 9029 – Anti-Corruption and Public Integrity Act; S. 5070 – Anti-Corruption and Public Integrity Act.
② H. R. 1572 – To direct the Federal Election Commission to carry out a voucher pilot program under which individuals may use vouchers to make small dollar contributions to qualified candidates for election for the office of Representative in, or Delegate or Resident Commissioner to, the Congress, and for other purposes.
③ S. 2257 – Fair Elections Now Act of 2019.
④ H. R. 5150 – Transparency in Government Act of 2019.

第四章 "联合公民案"时代竞选财务法律重塑：反腐败与言论自由的博弈

提案修订2002年《帮助美国投票法》(Help America Vote Act)，要求各州对联邦公职选举进行选举后审计，并对选民身份的完整性、安全性证明，以及选民登记名单维护程序做出规定。[1] 同年2月的《恢复选举信心法案》旨在通过建立统一的新标准和程序，使用互联网提升选举的公正性和安全性，以促进选民在联邦选举中登记和投票的权利。[2] 法案同样提议修改《帮助美国投票法》，在州法律允许的情况下，为联邦政府选举设计一个安全、统一且及时的邮件选票系统，选民既可以选择电子邮件方式申请邮寄提交选票，也可以同样使用邮寄方式送达邮寄请求。同时针对消除现有选民登记制度存在不准确、花费高昂、难以访问和信息模糊等问题以及因此对年轻人、残疾人以及少数族裔造成的不成比例的影响，法案提出运用互联网实现选民登记和名单维护程序的网络数字化，以提高所有资格公民获取选举信息和参与选举的完整性、准确性和效率。《清洁选举法》[3] 也于同年1月在众议院提出，其全名为《公民立法机构反腐败选举法》，旨在禁止各州使用联邦资金管理选举，以在不受党派倾向影响的前提下保证联邦初选的公开公正。该法案计划各州成立独立的无党派委员会对国会选区进行重新划分，公开州与地方公职的初选，在此前提下，以选举管理为目的使用联邦资金。此外，还有建议改革联邦选举委员会的提案，建议将成员数量从6名减少到5名，以提升该机构的监督效率。[4]

随着越来越多的选民要求候选人拒绝大捐款人的资助，竞选财务反腐败已成为主流风向。候选人意识到，若要恢复美国人民对民主进程的信念，那么必须采取比以往更加有力的措施来改革竞选财务系统。越来越多的众议员正在全面推动游说、公司竞选财务、竞选通讯与相关道德准则方面的改革。可想而知，上述大多数法案都未能在当届的国会议程中通过成

---

[1] H. R. 1529 – To amend the Help America Vote Act of 2002 to require States to conduct post-election audits for elections for Federal office and to provide attestations of the integrity and security of voter identification and voter registration list maintenance procedures, and for other purposes.

[2] H. R. 102 – Restoring Faith in Elections Act.

[3] H. R. 100 – Citizen Legislature Anti-Corruption Reform of Elections Act, aka CLEAN Elections Act.

[4] H. R. 1414 – To amend the Federal Election Campaign Act of 1971 to reduce the number of members of the Federal Election Commission from 6 to 5, to revise the method of selection and terms of service of members of the Commission, to distribute the powers of the Commission between the Chair and the remaining members, and for other purposes.

为法律，其中的主要阻力来自两党的意见分歧和富人占据的特殊利益集团等。随着民主党2021年获得参众两院的多数议席，情况或许会发生松动。但总体看来，国会对竞选改革尤其是旋转门和竞选捐款问题方面的改革态度并不坚决。堵塞暗钱通道、完全禁止旋转门或制定终身冷静期的法案，看似可以全部改革的形式革除竞选财务中的大部分腐败问题，但实际往往难以进入众议院的讨论程序。在"联合公民案"之后的10年中，这种趋势尤为明显：只有小型、局部的或与之前影响恶劣的腐败丑闻直接相关的改革方案，才能得到两党及其背后特殊利益集团的妥协支持，而上述通过的两部竞选反腐败法律即是各方政治经济利益博弈的结果。

（三）其他现行反腐败法律与行政规则

尽管"联合公民案"为竞选财务和反腐败法律带来了结构性的动摇，仍有一部分联邦法律作为竞选财务和反腐败制度的基石，继续发挥着不可替代的监管作用。

首先是作为反腐败执行底线的刑事法。《联邦刑法》有多项条文限制联邦政府机构、联邦承包商和联邦资金的受让人以游说为目的使用联邦资金。针对游说者以各种名义向国会议员以及工作人员馈赠礼物的情况，联邦法典中的反贿赂条款规定，联邦官员不得"腐败地"接受或索取，任何人不得腐败地提供或给予任何有价值的东西"以换取"任何官方行为的影响。[①] 在这种情况下，必须证明行贿是"官方行为的原动力或源头"，促使官方行为执行或同意执行。其中竞选捐款也可以是用于贿赂的"有价值之物"，因为受益人显然可以从中获得个人利益。除了有关贿赂的条款外，"非法酬金"（Illegal Gratuities）一节明确禁止因"已做或将做的官方行为"而提供或收取法律规定以外的有价值物。在公务人员收受个人礼物的情况下，非法酬金的腐败动机认定并不需要特别的腐败意图，也不存在利益交换，只要求所提供或收取的有价值物"与法律规定的不符"，而且是因"某种可识别的官方行为"而提供或收取。由于这种非法酬金不需要作为影响官方行为的动力，也不要求其是为了影响官方行为而给付，甚至可能给付于官方行为已经做出后，作为对该行为的"感谢"，因此其认定范围也较为宽泛。

其他涉及游说与竞选活动的综合反腐败法律还包括1998年修订的

---

① 18 U.S.C. § 201.

第四章 "联合公民案"时代竞选财务法律重塑：反腐败与言论自由的博弈

《海外反腐败法》（Foreign Corrupt Practices Act）与《信息自由法》等。尤其是《信息自由法》与近年来的诸多法律改革有所关联，其要求在联邦和州层面进一步开放公民与政府的联系信息，以促进政府与私人实体行为的进一步披露。由于该法涉及私营监狱等多个有争议领域的信息公开，故而与反腐败监督息息相关。

成文法上的道德准则也发挥着重要的约束作用。1978年的《政府道德法》是在水门事件后通过的，其强制公职人员以及直系亲属公开财务和工作经历，并限制公职人员在离任公职后的一段时期内不得以游说者身份开展游说工作，尤其是禁止联邦雇员两年内对此前受雇的机构进行游说。除了成文法规定，国会还会在宪法的权威下实行自我廉洁性机制，严格约束机构的议员及其他雇员的行为，以确保相关法律与规定得到遵守。例如在1929年，一位康涅狄格州参议员将一名为某贸易协会（与关税立法有关的利益团体）工作的受薪说客安排在审议相关立法委员会的工作人员中，使其能够接触到委员会的机密材料。在当时，该做法未有触犯任何法律或规定，但参议院随即声明该参议员的行为虽"没有腐败的动机，但也与良好道德和参议员伦理道德相悖"。[①] 为应对官员在游说中可能受到的不当或过度影响，参众两院引入了限制国会议员、办公室职员从私人处收受礼物和好处的内部规则。1958年，参议院订立了内部道德规则，规范了在竞选筹款活动中接受捐款的条件、用途以及财产的申报；[②] 众议院则在1968年要求众议员根据"政府服务道德规范"约束自身行为，被选举或任命的官员不得在任何可被视为影响其政府职责的情况下，收受礼品或好处。这些规则尤其着重规范前者与注册游说者、外国代理人及其客户的互动，除非各自部门的相关规则准许，议员、办公室职员和其他雇员原则上都不得收受礼物。因此，无论是微不足道的礼品，还是来自游说者及其客户邀请的会议或提供的活动差旅费，都受到国会内部规定的严格监督和限制。不仅如此，注册游说者也必须熟知这些限制送礼的规定，并向政府证明其未向上述人员提供任何礼物或好处。上述这些规则并不一定都是可执行的，但国会议员及其工作人员也不得不

[①] Richard D. Hupman, *Senate Election, Expulsion and Censure Cases from 1793 to 1972*, Washington: U. S. Government Printing Office, 1972, pp. 126 – 128.

[②] 周琪、袁征：《美国的政治腐败与反腐败——对美国反腐败机制的研究》，中国社会科学出版社2009年版，第180页。

因此进一步明确法律规定和内部书面规章，对某些边缘交易行为所可能产生的不当影响加以警惕。此外，专业游说者组织也会依据国会道德标准对游说者提出相应的道德准则和专业标准要求。

二 州竞选反腐败法律改革前沿

竞选资金包括联邦、州和地方各级选举活动所筹集的资金。在联邦一级，竞选财务法律由国会制定，依靠联邦选举委员会这一独立机构执行。① 总体上，现行的联邦竞选财务法律要求候选人委员会、政党委员会和政治行动委员会定期提交报告，以披露其筹集和花费的资金。各州也都有自己的竞选财务法律和披露制度，效力水平各不相同。② 尽管国会在竞选财务法律与制度方面尚未能做出重大改革动作，多项改革法案也难以在国会获得两党统一的支持，但各州已逐渐意识到暗钱等问题可能对民主造成的危害，并在立法上先行一步。

仅2015年一年内，各州就推出了至少125项针对竞选财务改革的立法或法案，旨在从州层面防止州一级的地方选举受到腐败侵蚀（见图4-2）。阳光基金会在对这125项立法进行分解统计后发现：18项法案涉及竞选公共融资，占据所有主题的14%，其次是定义候选人与捐款人利益冲突的法案，另有8%的法案直接涉及对暗钱的规制。③ 还有其他法案关注公司捐款人的透明度、竞选通讯规制和限制游说者捐款等，道德委员会的改革以及市政一级的选举捐款也是各州竞选财务体系改革的重点之一。

从各州情况来看，提出竞选改革法案最多的为民主党主政的夏威夷州，共提出16项法案，其中多数涉及公司透明度、大额捐款披露和超级政治行动委员会资金披露等问题；亚利桑那州提出的12项法案中，有5项涉及对暗钱的规制，包括对独立支出团体和竞选广告资助者的身份披

---

① 非联邦职位的竞选受到州和地方法律管辖，超过一半的州允许公司和工会进行一定程度的捐款。截至2010年，部分州对个人捐款的限制低于联邦选举法律的限制，而密苏里州、俄勒冈州、弗吉尼亚州和犹他州则没有限制。本书主要探讨联邦政府的竞选活动。
② Michael J. Malbin & Thomas L. Gais, *The Day After Reform: Sobering Campaign Finance Lessons from the American States*, Albany: Rockefeller Institute Press, 1988, pp. 33 - 51.
③ Peter Olsen-Phillips, "State Legislatures Taking Aim at Dark Money, Disclosure", Sunlight Foundation (Mar. 17, 2015), https://sunlightfoundation.com/2015/03/17/state-legislatures-taking-aim-at-dark-money-disclosure/.

第四章 "联合公民案"时代竞选财务法律重塑：反腐败与言论自由的博弈

露，以及有限责任公司和商业实体的加强披露；马里兰州也对规制暗钱、报告独立支出和实时披露捐款等问题进行了关注，并提出了两个关于选举州长与副州长的公共筹资法案，同时单独推出为选举公共筹资建立基金的一项法案（见图4-3）。在这125项法案中，有27项法案由共和党议员提出，10项法案由两党一致推动，其余绝大多数为民主党议员所主导。这也显示了民主与共和两党人士在公司言论自由权、捐款透明度、暗钱管制和独立支出竞选广告资助者披露等竞选财务改革问题上的不同态度。

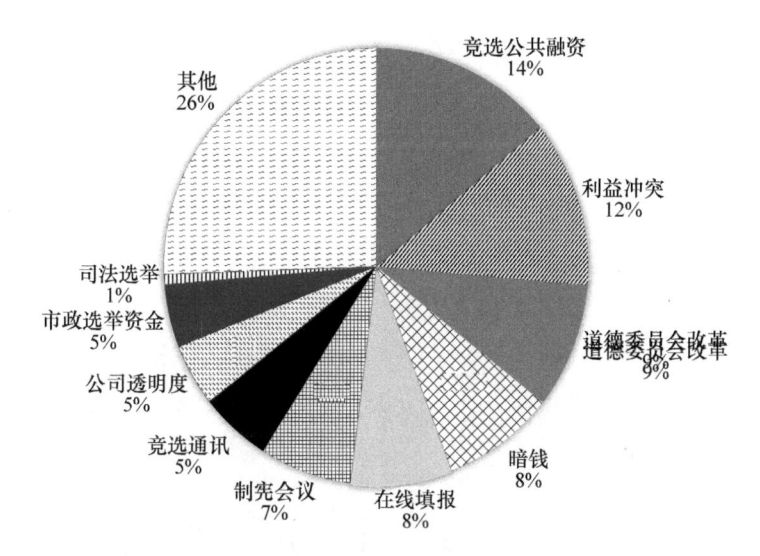

图4-2　2015年125项州竞选财务改革法律主题

资料来源：Sunlight Foundation 数据。https：//docs.google.com/spreadsheets/d/1KAflEho8zD-EAtSMXoXzhWiSKExA2d2ZLcmMw8rW9IY/pubhtml.

在提出大量的改革法案后，多个州已经取得了立法进展。蒙大拿州于2015年通过了披露竞选活动的参议院第289号法案，要求所有投放竞选广告的团体公开其最大的捐款个人、捐款公司或工会的首席执行官身份。[①] 同年在亚利桑那州，参议院1207号法案也获得了州议会通过，要求在该州竞选广告中使用"投票赞成"或"反对"等字样的独立支出团体披露其

---

① SB 289 – Revise campaign finance laws. Montana Senate Bill, https：//leg.mt.gov/bills/2015/billpdf/SB0289.pdf.

大额捐款者。① 该州通过的另一项法案还对政治委员会作出了更明确的定义，以规范竞选团体在选举中的活动。② 2017年《加利福尼亚州披露法》在两党的支持下得到通过，该法案要求政治广告列出捐款金额在5万美元或以上的前三名捐款者。③ 无论捐款者的资金通过何种隐秘渠道的竞选委员会打入，捐款者姓名都将依法列明公示，此举也可以防止捐款人利用中间人洗钱。该法律使得加州公民第一次得以在透明信息机制下审视竞选资金来源，从而做出更明智的决定。

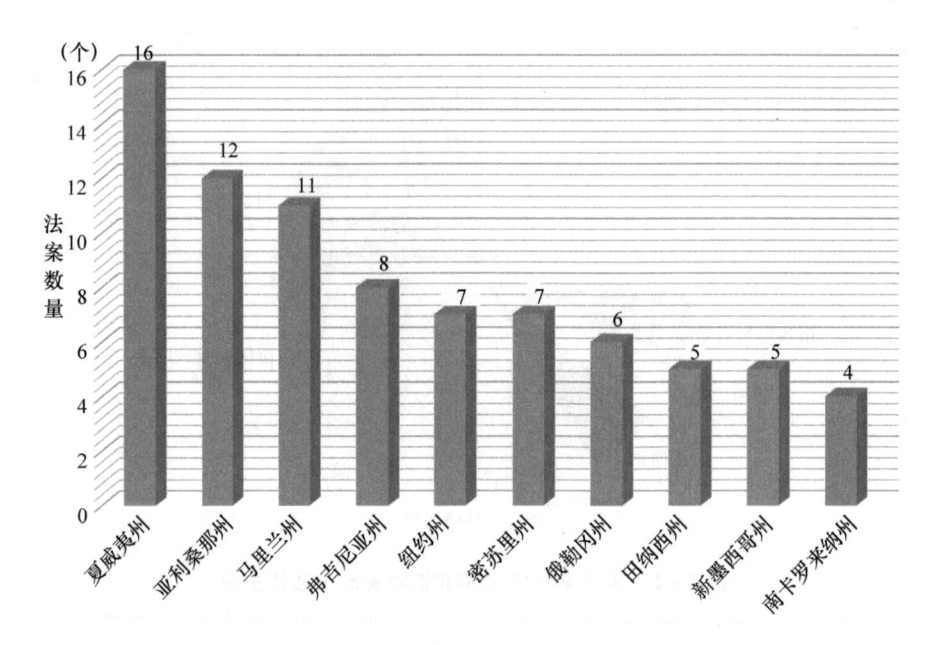

图4-3 2015年各州推动竞选财务改革法案数量统计

州	法案数量
夏威夷州	16
亚利桑那州	12
马里兰州	11
弗吉尼亚州	8
纽约州	7
密苏里州	7
俄勒冈州	6
田纳西州	5
新墨西哥州	5
南卡罗来纳州	4

资料来源：Sunlight Foundation，https://docs.google.com/a/sunlightfoundation.com/spreadsheets/d/1KAflEho8zD-EAtSMXoXzhWiSKExA2d2ZLcmMw8rW9IY/pubhtml.

---

① SB 1207 – Campaign finance disclosures; corporations; entities. Arizona Senate Bill, https://www.azleg.gov/legtext/52leg/1r/bills/sb1207p.pdf.
② HB 2407 – Referendum and recall provisions. Arizona House Bill, ttps://www.azleg.gov/legtext/52leg/1r/bills/hb2407p.pdf.
③ AB-249 – Political Reform Act of 1974; campaign disclosures. California Disclose Act, https://leginfo.legislature.ca.gov/faces/billNavClient.xhtml?bill_id=201720180AB249.

第四章 "联合公民案"时代竞选财务法律重塑：反腐败与言论自由的博弈

候选人违反相关规定的惩罚措施也趋于严厉。2017年，有23个州议会修订了竞选财务法律，其中9个州更新了对违反披露和捐款限额规定行为的刑事和民事处罚。[①] 如加州2017年的《政治改革法》（Political Reform Act）将违反某些披露规定的行为视为轻罪，以与全国范围内不断扩大的财务披露趋势保持一致。加州、马里兰州、北达科他州、俄勒冈州、得克萨斯州和犹他州将某些类型的捐款和披露失误定为刑事犯罪。在夏威夷州，未能按时提交披露声明的候选人将面临75美元的罚款，并被公布姓名。阿肯色州和爱达荷州则要求候选人以电子方式提交其披露声明，前者还与加州都通过了相关法规，要求州务卿建立可搜索的在线数据库，以供公众查看候选人和官员的捐款者。2021年，共有49个州提出了600多项竞选财务相关法案，主题包括捐款限制、竞选资金的使用、信息披露和执行、政治行动委员会及其报告义务。

本章小结

竞选财务法律改革可能本身就是一项近乎西西弗斯式的任务。"联合公民案"与SpeechNow诉联邦选举委员会案的裁决，可以说是几十年来竞选财务法最根本的变化。在某种程度上，"联合公民案"甚至已经成为近半个世纪以来联邦最高法院作出的最具民主破坏性的竞选财务法律判决。联邦最高法院的多数保守派法官选择无视巨额资金在选举中恣意操控政治活动机器的现实，同时不合理地怀疑了立法者防止腐败的动机，从而对解决目前竞选财务系统的弊端构成了严重阻碍。该判决将最阴暗腐败的资金注入了选举系统，以超级政治行动委员会式的暗钱新腐败取代了软钱的旧腐败，从而使最富有的美国人在竞选筹款活动中发挥了更主要的作用。2020年是"联合公民案"判决十周年，但其背后的隐忧不仅仅是对公司支出限制的废除，还有从立法到司法系统对腐败和竞选财务法律的认识争议。这可能为将来的宪法挑战提供基础，从而扰乱现代竞选财务法的基本要素。而新的问题使得情况更加复杂：在过去的10年

[①] NCSL, "2017 Campaign Finance Enactments", NCSL（Jan. 3, 2018）, https://www.ncsl.org/elections-and-campaigns/2017-campaign-finance-enactments.

中，不可追踪的加密货币捐款出现，其与暗钱完全有可能共同作用，进一步损害竞选财务的监管有效性。此外，尽管各方已经进行了大量的反腐败立法努力，但现有法律中仍存在着根本性的腐败因素。1977年《海外反腐败法》的主旨是应对国际贸易中政治腐败的增加，但该反腐败法律并未禁止美国企业向外国政府官员支付"疏通费"（facilitation payment）①，也就是这种行为并不在法律上被认定为腐败，而只是日常商业行为的一部分。更鲜为人知的是，《联合国反腐败公约》（United Nations Convention against Corruption）在草案商议期间，一条名为"资助政党"（Funding Political Parties）的规定曾出现在草案第7条"公共部门"的防止官员腐败项下，拟要求公约国在选举等政治活动中采取特定措施预防腐败，以避免民主选举制度遭到腐蚀。但美国拒绝了奥地利、法国和荷兰提出的旨在解决竞选资金腐败问题的提议，最终上述草案条款在第三次审议时被删除。② 这些事实也从侧面表明，无论是否能够从立法技术的角度构建"理想的"反腐败制度，任何一项法律均脱胎于各方利益的政治博弈，往往需要经历一个迂回渐进的过程。由于政党之间及其内部所各自代表的不同利益在竞选财务与选举各环节程序方面的诸多细节难以达成一致，法案的通过总是会需要多方商议妥协。尤其在竞选财务法律的反腐败层面，对现代政党的内部自律性要求更高；在巨额竞选资金的支持下，要求候选人保持（不仅仅是形式上的）政治独立性也同样十分困难。但如果成文法不切实际地严格制定行为标准并辅以严厉的刑罚，反腐败改革通常只会适得其反。因为这可能将违法行为推向地下，或鼓励向执法者行贿，最终损害法律的权威。长期以来，国会中也一直有议员极力推动竞选财务立法改革，尤以限制大公司巨额资金在竞选中的隐秘性和压倒性影响为主要目标。但无论是两党间还是各党内，仍存在不同派系集团的复杂利益冲突，这使得较为激进的突破性改革法案往往难以在短时间内获得两院通过。这造成了尽管在意识形态上，普通法国家

---

① 2010年7月生效的多德-弗兰克法（Dodd-Frank Act）旨在阻止（石油）公司与外国政府进行腐败交易。它要求埃克森美孚和雪佛龙等在美国上市的石油、天然气和采矿公司，以及巴西石油公司等国际石油巨头披露在每个项目中对各国政府的疏通费。但2012—2018年，该法律的多项相关反腐败规定和证监会制定的对应执行规则或被判决无效、或被其他新法律替代，因而未能实施。
② 本书作者采访联合国反腐败专家、香港廉政公署（ICAC）执行处前首席调查主任Michael Burley所获信息，Michael Burley曾参与《联合国反腐败公约》的起草。

第四章 "联合公民案"时代竞选财务法律重塑：反腐败与言论自由的博弈

基于对民主秩序的保护，毫无疑问地需要打击腐败，但卷帙浩繁的竞选财务法律与判例法体系不仅难以像其他部门法领域一样有效地执行，而且还具有显著的滞后性和不连贯性。因而可以想象在将来，竞选财务反腐败的立法进程与其可执行性还会遭遇来自党派和联邦最高法院等方面的诸多挑战。

第五章 制药巨头游说与竞选捐款的腐败影响：以阿片危机为透视点

腐败在文化、政治和社会语境下的多重定义反映了人们对该概念的审慎态度，也使得就其定义达成共识充满挑战。但围绕腐败定义的各种不同理解"不应使我们对某些行为在大多数甚至所有社会中都被视为腐败的事实视而不见"[1]。区分竞选捐款和贿赂之间的界限能够在理解和应对腐败方面发挥至关重要的作用。尽管腐败的法律定义已在联邦最高法院2010年联合公民胜诉案中被确定为利益交换，但当其他疑似腐败的现象出现在现实场景中时仍很难得到界分。例如，相对小的投入获得不成比例的巨额回报，如果并非发生于交易中，而是出现在政治场景下，是否构成腐败？阳光基金会的研究[2]显示，2007—2012年，美国各行业公司共花费58亿美元用于游说和竞选捐款，相应的回报则是4.4万亿美元的联邦业务订单和政府补贴。这些企业的盈利在很大程度上与政府决策密不可分，而企业在上述政治活动中投入如此之巨，也正是因为确定这种投入是有效的：在2008—2012年竞选周期捐款与游说支出最大的200家美国公司中，有174家公司最终获得了政府补贴；[3] 参与游说与竞选捐款的公司平均每花费1美元，就能获得来自政府760美元的收益（见图5-1）。例如在本调查中花费前200的公司及其员工、家属共向超级政治行动委员会捐献了300万

---

[1] Leslie Holmes, *The End of Communist Power: Anti-Corruption Campaigns and Legitimation Crisis*, Cambridge, England: Polity Press, 1993, p.63.
[2] Bill Alison & Sarah Harkins, "Fixed Fortunes: Biggest Corporate Political Interests Spend Billions, Get Trillions", Sunlight Foundation (Nov. 17, 2014), https://sunlightfoundation.com/2014/11/17/fixed-fortunes-biggest-corporate-political-interests-spend-billions-get-trillions/.
[3] Good Jobs First, "Discover Where Corporations are Getting Taxpayer Assistance Across the United States", Good Jobs First (n.d.), https://www.goodjobsfirst.org/subsidy-tracker.

第五章　制药巨头游说与竞选捐款的腐败影响：以阿片危机为透视点

美元，其中仅是与前众议院议长博约纳（John Boehner）有联系的"国会领袖"政治行动委员（Congressional Leadership PAC）就获捐250万美元。即便如此，仍有大量证据表明，目前有关竞选捐款的数据并不完整，由于税法对501非营利组织的披露保护、报告遗漏和捐款人不遵守联邦竞选财务报告法律等原因，联邦选举委员会和国税局所掌握的竞选捐款数据低于大多数行业的实际政治支出。① 尽管在"联合公民案"中，联邦最高法院认为"（竞选捐款和游说对政府决策的）偏袒与影响是不可避免的"②，此种情况看似并不能归入联邦最高法院对腐败的狭义定义，但巨大的利益回报与资金的不透明性使人无法回避游说、竞选捐款与政府决策之间腐败存在联系的可能性。显而易见，这种极易被滥用的游说与竞选捐款系统对民主制度百害而无一利，但其危害远不止对民主制度这类抽象概念的侵蚀。本章以游说与竞选捐款支出最巨的美国制药领域为例，透视游说团体与竞选捐款活动对美国政坛腐败的影响以及美国公众在公共医疗卫生领域为此付出的沉重代价。

2010年以来，以处方止痛药、海洛因③和芬太尼为主的阿片④类药物滥用危机开始严重威胁美国公共健康、社会福利与财政增长。⑤ 据估计，2018年约有250万美国人对阿片类药物成瘾。⑥ 这种公众对阿片类强力镇痛药物大规模成瘾的现象被称为阿片流行病（Opioid Epidemic）或阿片危机（Opioid Crisis）。据统计，2000—2018年约有30万名美国人死于阿片类药物或毒品吸食过量；⑦ 在2003—2013年美国禁毒署（Drug Enforce-

---

① Paul Jorgensen, "Pharmaceuticals, Political Money, and Public Policy: A Theoretical and Empirical Agenda", *Journal of Law, Medicine & Ethics*, Vol.41, No.3, 2013, pp.561-570.
② Citizens United v. FEC, 558 U.S.310 (2010), p.44.
③ 近年来英国等部分欧洲国家和加拿大将处方级海洛因用作毒品脱瘾治疗，以弥补美沙酮治疗耐药性的局限性，但不包括美国。
④ 阿片全称为阿片样物质，可以分为鸦片剂、半合成阿片与合成阿片三大类，效力以依次成数十倍或数百倍递增。鸦片剂提取自鸦片即罂粟；合成阿片则由人工合成，不存在于自然界，因此也被称为"实验室毒品"，以曲马朵和超过1400多种变体的芬太尼家族为代表；半合成阿片是对合成阿片的再处理，如将吗啡加工合成海洛因，羟考酮和氢可酮也在此列。
⑤ 美国境内首例阿片吸食过量死亡出现于1991年，但自2010年起死亡数字呈指数级上升。
⑥ Adeel Hassan, "Doctor Who Prescribed 500000 Doses of Opioids Is Sent to Prison for 40 Years", *The New York Times*, Oct.1, 2019.
⑦ Jacey Fortin, "D. E. A. Let Opioid Production Surge as Crisis Grew, Justice Dept. Says", *The New York Times*, Oct.2, 2019.

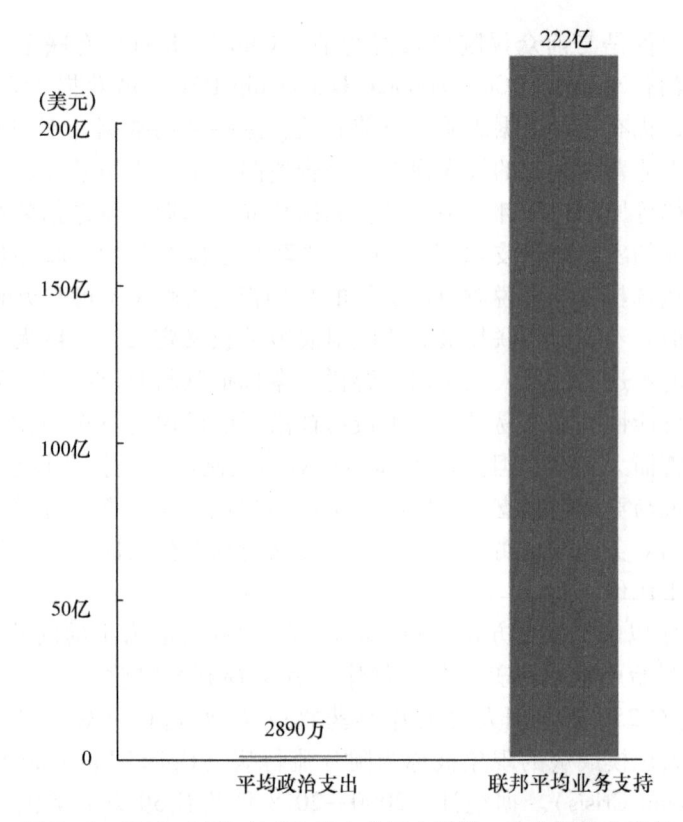

```
                                                    222亿
(美元)
200亿

150亿

100亿

50亿
                    2890万
  0
              平均政治支出              联邦平均业务支持
```

图 5-1 2008—2012 年 200 家大公司在游说、竞选捐款支出与获得联邦业务金额比较

资料来源：Bill Alison & Sarah Harkins, "Fixed Fortunes: Biggest Corporate Political Interests Spend Billions, Get Trillions", Sunlight Foundation（Nov. 17, 2014）, https://sunlightfoundation.com/2014/11/17/fixed-fortunes-biggest-corporate-political-interests-spend-billions-get-trillions/.

ment Administration）授权制药商大量生产阿片类药物的 10 年间，[①] 死亡人数的年增长率平均达到 71%，[②] 在 2021 年达到 8 万，而以芬太尼为主的

[①] 以阿片类止痛药羟考酮（药品名奥施康定）的总生产配额（Aggregate Production Quota）为例，其在 2002—2013 年由约 34 吨增长为 150 吨，增幅在 400% 以上。参见 Department of Justice, "Review of the Drug Enforcement Administration's Regulatory and Enforcement Efforts to Control the Diversion of Opioids", Office of the Inspector General（2019）, https://oig.justice.gov/reports/2019/e1905.pdf.

[②] Jacey Fortin, "D. E. A. Let Opioid Production Surge as Crisis Grew, Justice Dept. Says", *The New York Times*, Oct. 2, 2019.

第五章　制药巨头游说与竞选捐款的腐败影响：以阿片危机为透视点

合成阿片类毒品是过量死亡的主要原因，为 2015 年的 7.5 倍①（见图 5-2）。美国疾病控制与预防中心数据显示，2019 年美国平均每天有 136 人死于阿片过量，② 每年单因阿片类处方药物过量而造成的医疗救护、成瘾治疗开销、刑事司法系统介入和生产力损失高达 785 亿美元。③ 作为国家人口整体健康状况的标杆指数，美国人均寿命在 2015—2017 年连续 3 年呈下降趋势，而以芬太尼为主的阿片吸食过量导致的死亡人数大幅上升，是意外死亡率激增的两大主要原因之一。④ 2017 年 10 月，特朗普总统

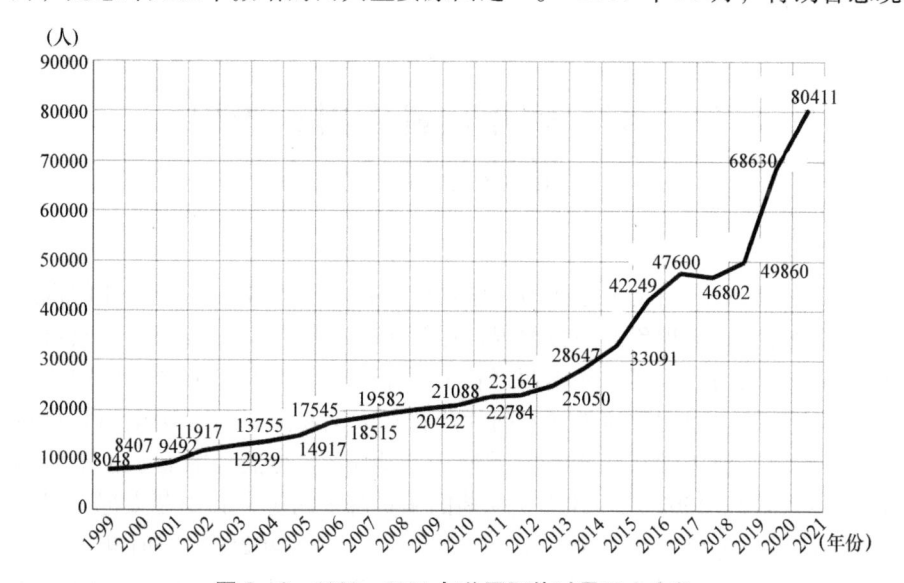

图 5-2　1999—2021 年美国阿片过量死亡人数

资料来源：Claire Felter, "The U. S. Opioid Epidemic", Council on Foreign Relations（Jul. 20, 2020）, https：//www.cfr.org/backgrounder/us-opioid-epidemic; National Institute on Drug Abuse, "Overdose Death Rates", National Institute on Drug Abuse（Jun. 30, 2023）, https：//www.drugabuse.gov/drug-topics/trends-statistics/overdose-death-rates.

---

① National Institute on Drug Abuse, "Overdose Death Rates", National Institute on Drug Abuse（Jun. 30, 2023）, https：//www.drugabuse.gov/drug-topics/trends-statistics/overdose-death-rates.
② National Institute on Drug Abuse, "Overdose Death Rates", National Institute on Drug Abuse（Jun. 30, 2023）, https：//www.drugabuse.gov/drug-topics/trends-statistics/overdose-death-rates.
③ Curtis S. Florence & others, "The Economic Burden of Prescription Opioid Overdose, Abuse, and Dependence in the United States, 2013", Medical Care, Vol. 54, No. 10, 2016, pp. 901-906.
④ Josh Katz & Margot Sanger-Katz, "'The Numbers Are So Staggering.' Overdose Deaths Set a Record Last Year", The New York Times, Nov. 29, 2018; Meilan Solly, "U. S. Life Expectancy Drops for Third Year in a Row, Reflecting Rising Drug Overdoses Suicides", Smithsonian（Dec. 3, 2018）, https：//www.smithsonianmag.com/smart-news/us-life-expectancy-drops-third-year-row-reflecting-rising-drug-overdose-suicide-rates-180970942/.

宣布阿片危机为全国公共卫生突发事件；2018年5月，其将阿片危机进一步升级为国家紧急状况，并表示将采取多项公共医疗处遇措施应对逐渐失控的阿片危机。拜登政府则提出了"国家控制毒品战略"和"团结议程"，更新了几十年的老旧联邦法规，以完善阿片类毒品治疗项目，卫生部宣布拨款用于购买可以检测非法药物中所含危险物质的地西泮（xylazine）试纸条，① 以控制阿片危机的蔓延，但2020年以来死亡人数的急剧增长仍未得到逆转。

第一节 阿片危机成因：变相贿赂与过量处方

阿片危机的成因是多方面的，昂贵的医疗保健费用和经济就业的低迷都被认为是导致该现象的间接原因，尽管美国政府指责发展中国家政府疏于毒品管控因而导致阿片从墨西哥和中国涌入美国境内，2018年的中美贸易摩擦也最终以中国政府承诺对阿片药物芬太尼物质进行立法全面管控达成初步和解，但美国疾病控制与预防中心2011年的报告则显示了不同的相关性：1999—2002年阿片类止痛药的销量翻了两番，其中芬太尼、吗啡和羟考酮的处方使用率分别增长了226%、73%和402%，同时期急诊室对三种阿片类药物的接诊率分别增加了641%、113%和346%；② 阿片药物过量死亡人数也呈同等比例增加。③ 美国食品药品监管局药品中心负责人也指出，阿片类药物危机从根本上源于医生个人的处方决定，由于监管局没有权限规范医生的医疗行为，因此只能依法强制制药商在阿片类药物

---

① Department of Health and Human Services, "Biden-Harris Administration Marks Two Years of Advancements in HHS' Overdose Prevention Strategy with New Actions to Treat Addiction and Save Lives", HHS (Feb.1, 2024), https://www.hhs.gov/about/news/2024/02/01/biden-harris-administration-marks-two-years-advancements-hhs-overdose-prevention-strategy-new-actions-treat-addiction-save-lives-press-release.html.

② Donovan Keene, "Big Pharma: The International Reach of the Opioid Crisis", Harvard Political Review (May 4, 2020), https://harvardpolitics.com/big-pharma/.

③ CDC, "Vital Signs: Overdoses of Prescription Opioid Pain Relievers-United States, 1999 – 2008", CDC (n.d.), https://www.cdc.gov/mmwr/preview/mmwrhtml/mm6043a4.htm.

外包装上添加粗体警告。① 在21世纪头十年，药物和毒品过量死亡增加了近4倍，成为美国人口意外死亡的主要原因。在很长一段时间内，处方阿片类药物杀死的美国人数甚至一度超过吸食非法毒品过量的死亡人数。② 据美国国立卫生研究院统计，2015年约两万人死于以海洛因为主的毒品吸食过量，而死于合法处方药过量者则达到近3万人。③

有研究表明④，阿片制药公司在某地的营销支出越高，当地医生开出的阿片类药物处方数量就越多，相应的阿片过量死亡人数也随之上升。美国禁毒署官员指出，"制药行业营销与医生的不当处方可被视为当前阿片流行病的根源之一"⑤。根据透明国际2016年的报告，美国制药行业每年针对医生的促销活动花费达420亿美元，相当于平均每位医生6.1万美元。⑥ 开具名牌制药商所生产高价阿片处方的医生能获得丰厚的奖励：有时是免费食品和饮品，有时则是体育赛事的私人包厢和五星级餐厅的晚餐款待。对于不积极为病人开具这些昂贵的名牌镇痛药的医生，医药公司还会派遣医药顾问以"咨询"为名义对其进行劝导。对此，一些地区如新泽西州不得不规定医生每年参与营销药物的收入不得超过1万美元。但限制直接收入并不能阻挡阿片制药企业对医生进行变相贿赂：1995—2000年，

---

① Matthew Perrone & Ben Wieder, "Pro-Painkiller Echo Chamber Shaped Policy Amid Drug Epidemic", The Center for Public Integrity（Dec. 15, 2016）, https：//publicintegrity.org/state-politics/pro-painkiller-echo-chamber-shaped-policy-amid-drug-epidemic/.

② CDC, "2018 Annual Surveillance Report of Drug-Related Risks and Outcomes-United States Surveillance Special Report", CDC（Aug. 31, 2018）, https：//www.cdc.gov/drugoverdose/pdf/pubs/2018-cdc-drug-surveillance-report.pdf; CDC, "Drug and Opioid-Involved Overdose Deaths-United States, 2013 – 2017", CDC（Jan., 2019）, https：//www.cdc.gov/mmwr/volumes/67/wr/mm675152e1.htm? s_cid=mm675152e1.

③ National Institute on Drug Abuse, "National Overdose Deaths from Select Prescription and Illicit Drugs", National Institute on Drug Abuse（Jan., 2019）, https：//www.drugabuse.gov/related-topics/trends-statistics/overdose-death-rates.

④ Scott E. Hadland, Ariadne Rivera-Aguirre & Brandon D. L. Marshall, "Association of Pharmaceutical Industry Marketing of Opioid Products with Mortality from Opioid-Related Overdoses", JAMA Network Open（Jan. 18, 2019）, https：//jamanetwork.com/journals/jamanetworkopen/fullarticle/2720914.

⑤ Tom Jacobs, "Opioid Deaths Follow Where Big Pharma Spends Money on Marketing to Doctors", Pacific Standard（Jan. 18, 2019）, https：//psmag.com/social-justice/opioid-deaths-follow-where-big-pharma-spends-money-on-marketing-to-doctors.

⑥ Jillian C. Kohler, "Corruption in the Pharmaceutical Sector：Diagnosing the Challenges", Transparency International（Jun., 2016）, p. 17, https：//www.transparency.org.uk/sites/default/files/pdf/publications/29-06-2016-Corruption_In_The_Pharmaceutical_Sector_Web-2.pdf.

普渡制药在度假村举办了40次"疼痛会议",邀请初级保健医生和专门从事癌症治疗的医生参加,该公司向安排会议上演讲的2500多名医生发放报酬。[1] 止痛药制造商对医生的不当营销造成美国3%有处方权的医生开具了55%的阿片类药物处方;[2] 在加利福尼亚州,3%的医生甚至开具了高达62%的阿片类药物处方。[3] 超处方导致2012年阿片类药物的处方量达到惊人的2.59亿次,比1999年翻了两番,平均每个成年美国人就持有1瓶剂量的阿片类药物处方。[4] 2016年全美平均阿片类止痛药处方量达到每人36片,在亚拉巴马州、阿肯色州和田纳西州甚至达到人均70片。[5] 一方面,阿片制药厂商通过过度营销和变相贿赂医生鼓励医生超处方,造成患者对阿片药物依赖;另一方面,制药厂商通过滥用游说与竞选捐款机制,以极具腐败嫌疑的争议方式使国会维持对阿片类药品上市、定价与营销的相对宽松监管,可以说是"将政府和监管机构放入自己的口袋里"[6]。

第二节 阿片危机的加剧:制药巨头游说与竞选捐款的腐败影响

在美国,某种程度上公共政策的制定并非取决于对问题本身的考量,而是由有能力购买政治影响的个人、公司基于少数利益决定的。制药巨

---

[1] Desert hope Treatment, "Who Are the Players in the Pharmaceutical Industry (Big Pharma)?" Desert hope Treatment (Oct. 2, 2019), https://deserthopetreatment.com/big-pharma/.
[2] National Women's Health Network, "Opioids and Women: From Prescription to Addiction", National Women's Health Network (n.d.), https://www.nwhn.org/prescription-addiction-opioid-epidemic/.
[3] Francie Diep, "Should We Blame Pharmaceutical Companies for America's Opioid Epidemic? Here's What the Science Says", Pacific Standard (Apr. 3, 2019), https://psmag.com/news/should-we-blame-pharmaceutical-companies-for-americas-opioid-epidemic.
[4] CDC, "Opioid Painkiller Prescribing", CDC (Sep. 26, 2017), https://www.cdc.gov/vitalsigns/opioid-prescribing/.
[5] Plan Against Pain, "An Analysis of the Impact of Opioid Overprescribing in America", Plan Against Pain (n.d.), https://www.planagainstpain.com/wp-content/uploads/2017/09/PlanAgainstPain_USND.pdf.
[6] Andrew Kitchenman, "New Jersey Tops Country in Prescribing Brand-Name Drugs", NJ Spotlight (Nov. 20, 2013), https://www.njspotlight.com/stories/13/11/19/new-jersey-tops-country-in-prescribing-brand-name-drugs/.

第五章　制药巨头游说与竞选捐款的腐败影响：以阿片危机为透视点

头、石油巨头与枪支团体等一直是美国游说产业资金的主要来源。各大巨头每年运用数百万美元支持维护其利益的政治参选人士并以此影响立法，其影响力在某种程度上可能已经超出了左右立法者牺牲选民利益的程度。作为21世纪兴起的大型工业之一，制药业对这种腐败的运作模式并不陌生，贿赂、利益冲突和欺诈等一系列非法或不道德行为使其在历史上成为石油和汽车行业之后违法行为最常见的行业。[1]《卫报》甚至在新闻标题中写道："制药业已取代了军火行业，成为行为不端的行业榜首。"[2] 阿片类药物的大规模处方逐步升级为美国历史上最大规模的毒品流行，其原因之一是监管机构被其应监管的行业所控制。众所周知，药品价格操纵、限制性的专利法规、疗效成疑的产品、重复的营销程序、虚假的广告宣传，已是美国制药行业的多年沉疴。[3] 但这些问题之所以在过去数十年里持续存在，部分原因是在游说与竞选捐款的影响下，国会在制药利益集团与公共卫生利益之间选择了前者，从而回避了其他政策选择。现在，制药巨头的主要任务是反对或推迟限制阿片类药物的新立法，维持和扩大现有的药品定价及运输的监管法律漏洞。因而对政府与制药业腐败联系的担忧主要集中在该行业的游说和竞选捐款问题上，因为制药行业是美国竞选的最主要参与者，无论是制药公司本身还是其员工都会直接向候选人、政党和政治行动委员会捐款，同时还向外围组织提供资金，或以电视广告的形式独立于候选人进行大量支出。截至2023年，占据美国医药市场份额前五的制药公司依次为：强生、礼来、艾伯维、辉瑞和默克。前十制药公司市值高达2万亿美元。[4] 长期以来，这些行业巨鳄运用庞大的资金运作对美国立法与政治决策产生了巨大影响，制药行业尤其是制药商巨头及其组织下的游说团体（统称为"Big Pharma"，以下简称为"制药巨头"），已因其围

---

[1] John Braithwaite, *Corporate Crime in the Pharmaceutical Industry*, England: Routledge & Kegan Paul Books, 1984; Graham Dukes, John Braithwaite & J. P. Moloney, *Pharmaceuticals, Corporate Crime and Public Health*, Cheltenham, England: Edward Elgar, 2014.

[2] Terry Macalister, "Pharma Overtakes Arms Industry to Top the League of Misbehaviour", *The Guardian*, Jul. 7, 2012.

[3] Martin J. Murray, "The Pharmaceutical Industry: A Study in Corporate Power", *International Journal of Health Services*, Vol. 4, No. 4, 1974, pp. 625–640.

[4] Global Data, "Top 10 Pharma Companies in the US by Market Capitalization", Global Data (Sep. 30, 2023), https://www.globaldata.com/companies/top-companies-by-sector/healthcare/us-companies-by-market-cap/#:~:text=Comprehensively%2C%20the%20top%2010%20Pharma,Inc%20is%20the%20lowest%20(%24.

绕医生、州和联邦议员进行极具争议的游说活动和提供巨额竞选捐款支持的行为引发了普遍的合法性关注，其强大的资金能力正在侵蚀着国家政治体系。

据统计，2022年美国各行业在联邦层面游说活动支出共计41亿美元，达到2010年以来的最高点①，其中制药业在游说活动中的支出达3.79亿美元，在参与游说活动的各行业中占据首位，相当于排名第二、第三位的电子制造业和保险业游说支出之和，因此也被称为最大的利益集团（见图5-3）。1999—2018年的20年间，制药巨头团体在游说活动中的直接花销近40亿美元。②（见图5-4）

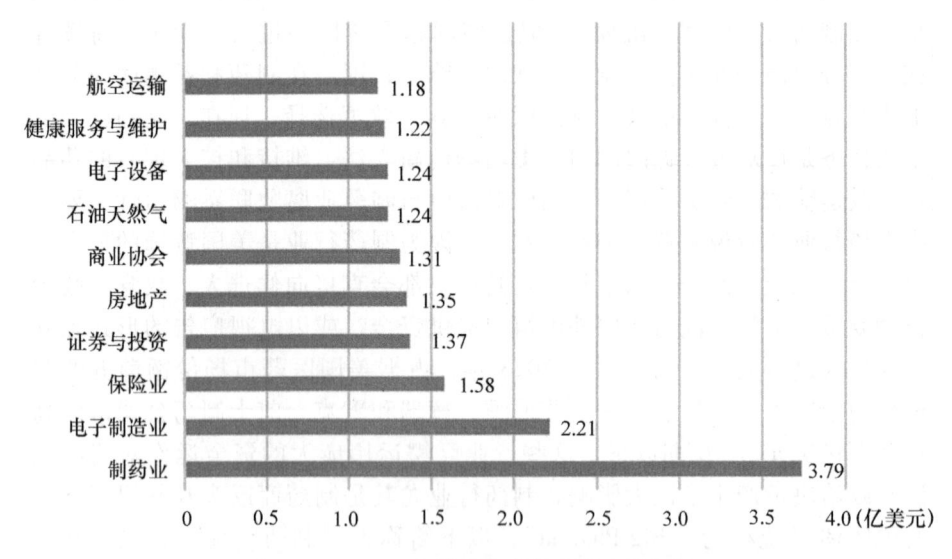

行业	支出（亿美元）
航空运输	1.18
健康服务与维护	1.22
电子设备	1.24
石油天然气	1.24
商业协会	1.31
房地产	1.35
证券与投资	1.37
保险业	1.58
电子制造业	2.21
制药业	3.79

图5-3　2022年游说支出排名前十的行业

资料来源：Statista, "Leading Lobbying Industries in the United States in 2022, by Total Lobbying Spending", Statista (Nov. 3, 2023), https://www.statista.com/statistics/257364/top-lobbying-industries-in-the-us/.

---

① Taylor Giorno, "Federal Lobbying Spending Reaches \$4.1 Billion in 2022 — The Highest Since 2010", Open Secrets (Jan. 26, 2023), https://www.opensecrets.org/news/2023/01/federal-lobbying-spending-reaches-4-1-billion-in-2022-the-highest-since-2010/.
② Open Secrets, "Industry Profile: Pharmaceuticals/Health Products", Open Secrets (n.d.), https://www.opensecrets.org/federal-lobbying/industries/summary?id=H04.

第五章　制药巨头游说与竞选捐款的腐败影响：以阿片危机为透视点

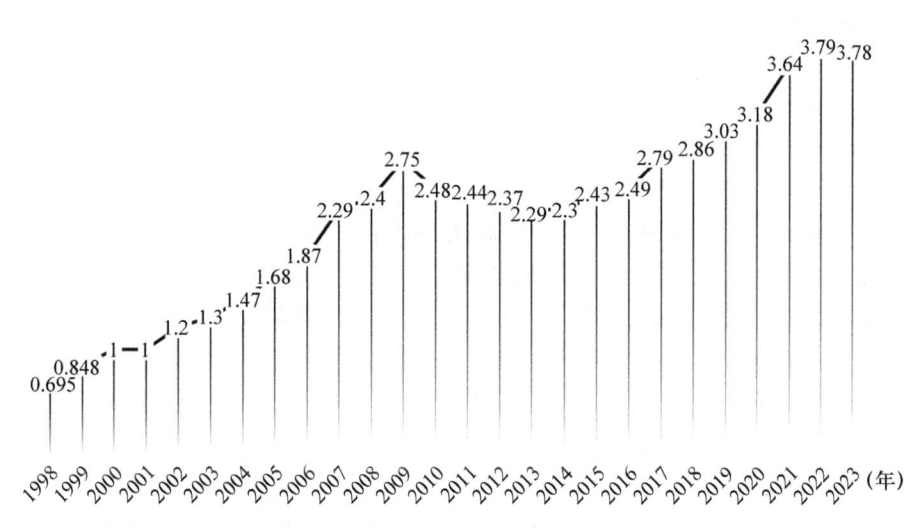

图 5-4　1998—2023 年药品保健品行业游说支出（单位：亿美元）

1999—2018 年，药品和保健产品在竞选捐款上花费了 13 亿美元，仅占全美处方药 5.5 万亿美元支出的 0.1%。① 在 2010 年通过《平价医疗法案》（又名 Obamacare 即"奥巴马医改"）后，药品和保健产品行业的竞选捐款在每个竞选周期中都大幅增长。② 在 2012 年的联邦选举中，制药商就花费了 2130 万美元，是 1990 年的 4 倍，③ 2020 年甚至达到 8900 万美元，比 10 年前增长了 170%。④

捐款大部分流向了负责决策的在任者。1990—2012 年，平均 74% 的竞选捐款都指向了多数党派人士和国会委员会成员，⑤ 而他们正是立法决

---

① Centers for Medicare and Medicaid Services, "National Health Expenditure (NHE) Amounts by Type of Expenditure and Source of Funds: Calendar Years 1960-2028", Centers for Medicare and Medicaid Services (n. d.), https://www.cms.gov/Research-Statistics-Data-and-Systems/Statistics-Trends-and-Reports/NationalHealthExpendData/NationalHealthAccountsProjected.
② 同年的"联合公民案"则使得对超级政治行动委员会和其他外部支出团体的捐款增加。
③ Paul Jorgensen, "Pharmaceuticals, Political Money, and Public Policy: A Theoretical and Empirical Agenda", Journal of Law, Medicine & Ethics, Vol. 41, No. 3, 2013, pp. 561-570. 此处比较已计入通货膨胀率。
④ Open Secrets, "Pharmaceuticals / Health Products Background", Open Secrets (n. d.), https://www.opensecrets.org/industries/background?cycle=2024&ind=H04.
⑤ Paul Jorgensen, "Pharmaceuticals, Political Money, and Public Policy: A Theoretical and Empirical Agenda", Journal of Law, Medicine & Ethics, Vol. 41, No. 3, 2013, pp. 561-570.

定向制药商或任何利益集团利益倾斜的各个环节决策者。据美联社统计，整个制药行业在 2006—2015 年为州长、州议会议长、参议员与卫生委员会主席等在内的 7100 名公务员提供了 2400 万美元的竞选捐款，[①] 平均 10 个众议员中就有 9 个接受过制药行业的竞选捐款。[②] 历史表明，所有捐款都用得其所，制药行业利润率非常高，而其利润在很大程度上取决于该行业特定的多个联邦政策。以阿片危机为例，对负责领导应对药物危机的参众两院委员会成员收到的竞选捐款调查发现，在 2016 年的中期选举中，众议院委员会 55 名成员中的 49 名与参议院委员会 23 名成员中的 15 名都收取了一些政治行动委员会的竞选捐款，而这些政治行动委员会都与因涉嫌加剧阿片危机而正被政府调查的医药公司相关。[③] 此外，国会议长和委员会主席也从该行业获得了大笔款项。

简言之，在游说与竞选捐款的影响下，联邦政府积极地为制药公司提供从药品推广、专利保护到价格保护的各种倾斜性政策，而未能将公众健康利益置于决策考量的首位。

一 阻挠阿片类药物法律监管

在行业腐败行为的历史影响下，制药行业仍在不断扩大其商业活动的范围，凭借将巨大财力投入到高昂的游说支出与竞选捐款中，获得立法与政策上的优待，同时还能消除对行业利益的威胁。通常情况下，议员从与他们利益相对一致的团体处筹集竞选资金，这当然有助于将其注意力集中在可能被忽略的问题上，但更常见的情况是，金钱使立法者及其捐款者的主张更接近。

（一）向联邦与州议会大量捐款

据"公开秘密"网站报告，在 2020 年的选举周期中，制药行业向 435

[①] The Center for Public Integrity, "Pharma Lobbying Held Deep Influence Over Opioid Pilicies", The Center for Public Integrity (n. d.), https：//publicintegrity.org/state-politics/pharma-lobbying-held-deep-influence-over-opioid-policies/.

[②] Chris McGreal, "How Big Pharma's Money – and its Politicians – Feed the US Opioid Crisis", The Guardian, Oct. 19, 2017.

[③] Matthew S. McCoy & Genevieve P. Kanter, "Campaign Contributions from Political Action Committees to Members of Congressional Committees Responding to the Opioid Crisis", The Journal of the American Medical Association, Vol. 320, No. 14, 2018, pp. 1489–1491.

名众议员中的420名提供了1510多万美元的竞选资助,平均每人至少获捐约3.6万美元,该行业还向全部100名参议员赞助了1019多万美元,平均每名参议员10万美元。① 作为制药业的长期盟友,前共和党参议员奥林·哈奇在42年的国会生涯中参与制定了许多规范非专利药品的现行法律,并制定了限制药品生产商准入的垄断保护措施。作为前参议院财政委员会主席,哈奇也被认为是民主党人和特朗普提出的降低药品价格的主要障碍。1998年以来,制药行业向哈奇竞选委员会共计捐款280万美元,比对其他非总统候选人的国会议员的捐款都多;② 当哈奇在2012年面临重大的连任挑战时,制药巨头还向支持前者的超级政治行动委员会捐款75万美元,以推动其连任。③ 当然捐款也可以在议员退休时再捐出予以答谢。制药巨头组织在2019年哈奇退休时,向他的同名基金会捐款200万美元,这个由哈奇创立的基金会智库和研究型图书馆在2017—2018年已收到前者14万美元的捐款。④

大部分州的司法委员会也都收到了来自制药巨头的捐款,制药公司的捐款也参与到各州选举与立法中,或是寻求与其利益一致的立法者支持。如制药公司曾通过游说活动与竞选捐款反对前民主党参议员克莱尔·马克卡斯基尔(Clair McCaskill)提出的法案,该法案旨在恢复禁毒署对查处可疑药物运输的执法自由裁量权,以避免药物经销商受到更严格的药物运输审查。2017年,前众议员汤姆·马里诺(Tom Marino),在华盛顿邮报和哥伦比亚广播公司报道其推动立法限制禁毒署对阿片类止痛药经销商和药店的执法权后,被迫辞职。⑤

---

① Open Secrets, "Pharmaceuticals / Health Products: Money to Congress-Summary", Open Secrets (n. d.), https://www.opensecrets.org/industries/summary.php?ind = H04 + +.
② Open Secrets, "Pharmaceuticals / Health Products: Money to Congress – Top 20 Member", Open Secrets (n. d.), https://www.opensecrets.org/industries/summary.php?ind = H04&cycle = All&recipdetail = M&sortorder = U.
③ Michael Beckel, "Drug Lobby Gave $750000 to Pro-Hatch Nonprofit in Utah's U. S. Senate Race", The Center for Public Integrity (Jun. 3, 2014), https://publicintegrity.org/politics/drug-lobby-gave-750000-to-pro-hatch-nonprofit-in-utahs-u-s-senate-race/.
④ Karl Evers-Hillstrom, "Pharma Lobby Poured Millions into 'Dark Money' Groups Influencing 2020", Open Secrets (Dec. 8. 2020), https://www.opensecrets.org/news/2020/12/pharma-lobby-poured-millions-into-darkmoney-groups.
⑤ Scott Higham & Lenny Bernstein, "The Drug Industry's Triumph Over the DEA", *The Washington Post*, Oct. 15, 2017.

(二) 游说州议会与行业协会

尽管药物管控的立法权属于联邦政府，但由于近年来阿片危机的加剧，各州在过去数年引入了数百项阿片类处方药物相关法案，州议会也随之成为止痛药制造商难以忽视的游说对象。据统计，2006—2015 年，为应对当时对阿片类药物成瘾性日益严格的审查，制药行业团体平均每年雇佣 1350 名说客开展游说活动，其中 400 名说客针对州议员，游说花费高达 400 万美元，[①] 以维持对阿片药物积极处方的合法性。以新墨西哥州为例，该州每年因阿片服用过量而导致死亡的人数在全美排名第二，仅次于西弗吉尼亚。2011 年，该州居民维斯伯克的儿子在一次摔跤比赛中锁骨骨折，在使用奥施康定镇痛药后逐渐成瘾，最终死于用药过量。[②] 维斯伯克随即向新墨西哥州议会提出将阿片的首次处方日数限制在七天以内的法案，其后州议会召开了立法听证会。制药行业团体并没有在听证会上发言，而是将 2012 年在新墨西哥州游说活动和竞选捐款的投入加倍，最终维斯伯克法案未在当年获得通过。共和党议员罗杰斯（Mike Rogers）起草了一项法律，要求食品药品监管局更改奥施康定瓶身上的标签，以将其用途限制在严重疼痛范围内。普渡制药花费巨资游说反对该法案，最终该法案甚至未能进入投票程序。制药巨头最强大的政治影响力不仅限于联邦和州立法机关，还延伸至在政治领域同样具有话语权的行业协会。尽管疾病控制预防中心的《2016 年处方指南》标明三天以内的阿片类处方药物治疗对大多数疼痛有足够的镇痛效果，但是制药行业与保险业游说团体通过对美国医学协会进行游说，使得后者坚称《2016 年处方指南》没有提出禁止性强制，并以患者依法获得药物的权利不可侵犯以及医患关系依法不受政府干预为由，明确反对旨在将首次阿片处方限制在三天以内的"卡拉 2.0"法案，[③] 以推迟法案在国会进入投票程序（见图 5-5）。同时制药行业团体

[①] Matthew Perrone & Ben Wieder, "Pro-Painkiller Echo Chamber Shaped Policy Amid Drug Epidemic", The Center for Public Integrity (Dec. 15, 2016), https://publicintegrity.org/state-politics/pro-painkiller-echo-chamber-shaped-policy-amid-drug-epidemic/.

[②] Nancy Laflin, "Local Mother Tells Story of Son's Overdose Death in Newly Released Documentary", Koat (Feb. 7, 2020), https://www.koat.com/article/albuquerque-couple-featured-in-documentary-thats-getting-lots-of-attention-in-hollywood/30801047#.

[③] 卡拉 2.0 法案（CARA 2.0 Bill）由最初版本的卡拉法案与 21 世纪疗法法案（21st Century Cures Act）合并而成，主要目的除限制阿片类药物首次处方天数外，还旨在推广丁丙诺啡（Buprenorphine）等阿片替代类药物治疗及严格监测医生处方项目。

还支持医学协会阻止《瑞恩·柯立顿法案》（Ryan Creedon Act）的通过，该法案旨在要求医生接受阿片类药物风险方面的培训。不仅如此，制药巨头还游说田纳西州议会通过了一项法律，要求医生在患者坚持的情况下开出处方阿片止痛药。①

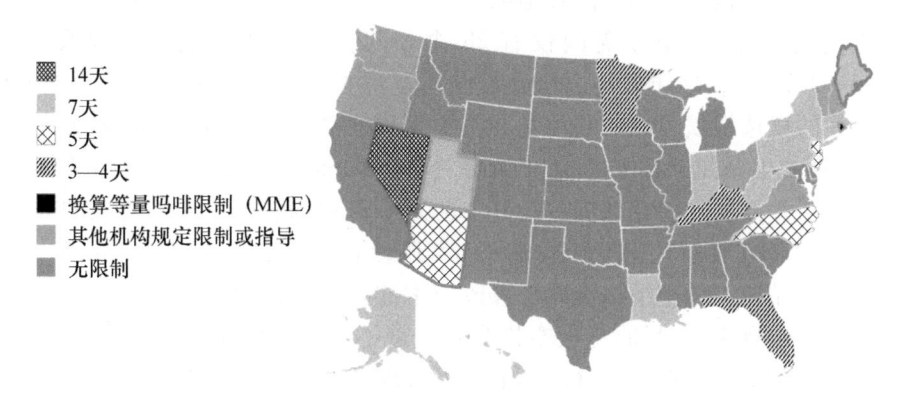

图 5-5 28 个州对阿片的首次处方日数的立法限制

资料来源：Marilyn Serafini, "The Physicians' Quandary with Opioids: Pain versus Addiction", NEJM Catalyst（Apr. 26, 2018），https://catalyst.nejm.org/quandary-opioids-chronic-pain-addiction/.

（三）资助501组织多方运作

受制于游说披露法律的限制，非营利团体成为制药巨头影响国家药品法律政策的最有力武器。501非营利团体组织在法律上与制药巨头没有直接关联，往往也不在公共记录之内，因而可以以自身名义为制药行业谋取利益进行游说或发表相关有倾向性的研究报告，而不受游说披露法律的约束。例如一家由数十个大型制药商、贸易集团以及制药行业非营利组织组成的松散民间团体"疼痛关怀论坛"（Pain Care Forum）已非公开运作十余年。该团体由奥施康定制造商普渡制药的首席说客组织牵头，负责在制药巨头的名义之外进行游说活动。疼痛关怀论坛没有实际地址，也没有自己的网站供公开查阅，但其每月定期组织招待来自白宫、食品药品监管局

---

① Jamie Satterfield, "Tennessee High Court Says Big Pharma Can be Held Liable in Opioid Epidemic", Knox News（Dec. 18, 2020），https://www.knoxnews.com/story/news/crime/2020/12/18/tennessee-high-court-big-pharma-can-held-liable-opioid-epidemic/3956216001/.

和卫生部的高级官员。2007年，论坛以慢性病疼痛患者的名义对华盛顿州医疗委员会等专业机构进行游说，以使之反对疾病预防与控制中心起草的限制阿片处方药计量医疗指南。2006—2015年，疼痛关怀论坛共计花费7.4亿美元，雇佣大量前国会办公室官员在全国50个州议会办公室进行游说，并为华盛顿特区和全国各地的民选官员提供资金，以避免阿片类药物处方受到限制。① 至今美国仅有28个州对阿片处方进行了立法限制。2006—2016年，疼痛关怀论坛会员向司法部长候选人先后提供了超过60万美元的竞选捐款，并向共和党和民主党州检察长协会捐助160万美元资金。② 亚拉巴马州检察长卢瑟·斯特兰奇（Luther Strange）从疼痛关怀论坛处获得5万美元的竞选捐款，其中两万来自辉瑞制药。大笔捐款的效果显著：2013年斯特兰奇上任后率先向美国食品药品监管局发出建议函，建议食品药品监管局不予批准无防篡改技术的新阿片仿制药物上市。除斯特兰奇外，还有47个州的总检察长联名签署了这封建议函。2013年在奥施康定的专利即将过期时，食品药品监督管理局决定不予批准新阿片类仿制药，普渡和辉瑞等制药巨头生产的名牌阿片类药物得以在至少未来几年内继续占领止痛药市场。2006年，论坛在国会上做简报时提出，羟考酮等阿片类药物是安全有效的，且对于没有吸毒史的患者来说不会成瘾。论坛还在2010年制作了一份有4000个签名的请愿书，宣称为保护患者隐私，反对阿片类药处方的实名电子登记。同年，论坛向4名参议员分别捐献800美元，这些参议员均在反对限制阿片类药物使用的《慢性疼痛阿片处方指南》投票中投出了反对票。③ 新墨西哥州的阿片类药物滥用率仅次于西弗吉尼亚地区，2006—2015年，论坛成员向该州的联邦和州议会候选人捐献了33.7万美元，捐款不分党派，民主党和共和党都从中受益。④ 对此，一

---

① Matthew Perrone & Ben Wieder, "Pro-Painkiller Echo Chamber Shaped Policy Amid Drug Epidemic", The Center for Public Integrity (Dec. 15, 2016), https：//publicintegrity.org/state-politics/pro-painkiller-echo-chamber-shaped-policy-amid-drug-epidemic/.
② Liz E. Whyte, Geoff Mulvihill & Ben Wieder, "Politics of Pain: Drugmakers Fought State Opioid Limits Amid Crisis", The Center for Public Integrity (Dec. 15, 2016), https：//publicintegrity.org/state-politics/politics-of-pain-drugmakers-fought-state-opioid-limits-amid-crisis/.
③ Geoff Mulvihil & Liz E. Whyte, "Drugmakers Fought Domino Effect of Washington Opioid Limits", The Center for Public Integrity (Sep. 21, 2016), https：//publicintegrity.org/state-politics/drugmakers-fought-domino-effect-of-washington-opioid-limits/.
④ Susan M. Bryan, "New Mexico Faces Uphill Battle with Drug Abuse", The Journal (Sep. 22, 2016), https：//nsr.the-journal.com/articles/2450.

位来自约翰霍普金斯大学的药物安全专家表示:"疼痛关怀组织人为地在减少阿片药物依赖与改善疼痛患者护理质量之间制造了冲突,其背后的既得利益才是最大受益者。"① 受制药企业资助的美国疼痛基金会②、美国疼痛学会与美国疼痛医学会也是疼痛关怀论坛的主要成员,供职于上述组织的多名专家参与撰写了"团体健康研究所"发布的评估报告,报告提出减轻1亿美国人的疾病痛苦应是最优先的考虑事项,该问题与目前的阿片类药物滥用成瘾危机无关。在获得阿片类药物制造商资助的组织中,反对疾病预防控制中心《阿片处方指南》的组织占多数。③ 部分受到资助的团体还假冒疼痛倡导组织的身份,向退伍军人、老年人和阿片成瘾者发放优惠券,大肆推销阿片止痛药。

在2020年大选中,制药巨头的游说团体继续向暗钱团体捐款,以向立法者与选民传达对该行业友好的信息。游说团体向暗钱团体"美国人行动网络"捐出了450万美元,该组织用这些资金发起了大规模反对规范处方药价格的广告活动,以对抗特朗普允许老年医疗保险(Medicare)④ 协商药品价格的提议和众议院降低药物价格的法案。⑤

(四)欺诈阻挠监管机构监管

为阻止联邦机构对阿片药物的扩大监管,制药行业还通过各种渠道将竞选捐款以合法捐赠形式嵌入以美国食品药品监管局为代表的监管机构预算中。在此种情况下,制药行业捐款所体现的作用已经超出了竞选经费及

---

① Matthew Perrone & Ben Wieder, "Pro-Painkiller Echo Chamber Shaped Policy Amid Drug Epidemic", The Center for Public Integrity (Dec. 15, 2016), https://publicintegrity.org/state-politics/pro-painkiller-echo-chamber-shaped-policy-amid-drug-epidemic/.
② 由制药与医疗器材行业捐款组成的美国疼痛基金会因误导患者和政府官员、夸大阿片止痛药疗效等问题已于2012年解散。
③ Lindsy Liu, Diana N. Pei & Pela Soto, "History of the Opioid Epidemic: How Did We Get Here?" Poison Control, National Capital Poison Center (n. d.), https://www.poison.org/articles/opioid-epidemic-history-and-prescribing-patterns-182; US Senate Committee on Homeland Security & Governmental Affairs, "Fueling an Epidemic (report two): Exposing the Financial Ties Between Opioid Manufacturers and Third Party Advocacy Groups", University of Pennsylvania (2018), https://www.law.upenn.edu/live/files/7738-report-fueling-an-epidemic-exposing-the-financial.
④ Medicare成立于1965年,是一个为65岁及以上老年人及某些残障人士提供医疗保险、支付医疗费用的联邦政府项目。
⑤ Karl Evers-Hillstrom, "Pharma Lobby Poured Millions into 'Dark Money' Groups Influencing 2020", Open Secrets (Dec. 8. 2020), https://www.opensecrets.org/news/2020/12/pharma-lobby-poured-millions-into-darkmoney-groups.

其相关活动领域，这也成为相关监管机构独立性受限的重要原因，从而引发了各界对其涉嫌利益冲突与直接贿赂的争议。

20世纪90年代初，制药巨头通过在议会的游说活动使新型强效止痛药顺利通过美国食品药品监管局审查，这类原本用于大象、长颈鹿等大型动物的镇静剂被准入人药市场，其中以阿片药物为主。这些阿片药物由人工合成，强效且廉价。最初的阿片药物用于晚期癌症患者的镇痛措施，可从人道主义角度有效减轻临终病人的痛苦。但由于阿片药物效力极强，同等剂量下产生的利益为普通镇痛药的数百至数千倍①，商业利益可观，制药巨头最终在未提供阿片药物的临床风险数据的情况下，成功使得食品药品监管局批准具备高度成瘾性的阿片处方药作为非癌症镇痛剂推向医药市场。由于对商业利益的追求甚至超过了对药物毒性尤其是成瘾性的担忧，制药巨头只公开对开发药品有利的测试结果，并不断向医生保证阿片处方的安全性，媒体也向公众宣称阿片处方药的成瘾可能性极低。截至1999年，已有86%的阿片药物使用者将阿片用于非癌症相关的日常镇痛。② 尽管阿片类药物应用于非癌症的慢性疼痛治疗也在随后被证明是导致对阿片类药物成瘾与过量死亡人数大量增加的原因之一，③ 但这并未影响阿片类药物在非癌症治疗领域的扩张。2007年，奥施康定制造商普渡制药因其药物的错误标识及其隐瞒成瘾风险而被罚款6亿美元，同时三名高管人员对欺骗性营销方面的刑事指控表示认罪，④ 引爆了阿片制药业的一系列丑闻。2009年辉瑞因对止痛药伐地考昔的误导营销而被罚款23亿美元；⑤ 因隐瞒药物风险和非法营销现已停产的罗非考昔，默克制药也在2011年同意支付9.5亿美元罚金。⑥ 然而一系列丑闻的相继爆发并未阻碍阿片类药物迅速占领美国止痛药物市场，制药巨头仍旧发挥着其巨大影响力。2020年

---

① 以芬太尼家族为例，芬太尼为吗啡效力的50—100倍，而卡芬太尼效力则为芬太尼的1000倍。
② Art Van Zee, "The Promotion and Marketing of OxyContin: Commercial Triumph, Public Health Tragedy", *American Journal of Public Health*, Vol. 99, No. 2, 2009, pp. 221-227.
③ Dora H. Lin, Eleanor Lucas & Irene B. Murimi, "Financial Conflicts of Interest and the Centers for Disease Control and Prevention's 2016 Guideline for Prescribing Opioids for Chronic Pain", *JAMA Internal Medicine*, Vol. 177, No. 3, 2017, pp. 427-428.
④ Barry Meier, "In Guilty Plea, OxyContin Maker to Pay $600 Million", *The New York Times*, May 10, 2007.
⑤ Gardiner Harris, "Pfizer Pays $2.3 Billion to Settle Marketing Case", *The New York Times*, Sep. 2, 2009.
⑥ Duff Wilson, "Merck to Pay $950 Million Over Vioxx", *The New York Times*, Nov. 22, 2011.

11月，普渡制药再次因共谋阻挠禁毒署执法、谎报信息、行贿医生以提高阿片类药物制造配额和销量等违法行为，被判处了制药业史上最高的55亿美元刑事罚金与罚没。① 长期以来，超大型制药企业广泛使用欺诈与贿赂手段推广药物营销，足以被称为"新美国黑手党"。

二 维持阿片类药品高定价

阿片危机与阿片类止痛药定价关系密切。价格高昂的处方止痛药迫使无力支付医疗费用或已因阿片处方滥用成瘾的美国人转向街头毒品。止痛药芬太尼效力极强，致死剂量仅为3毫克，约为海洛因的50倍，而同家族的卡芬太尼致死剂量为2毫克，其完全由人工合成，相比天然阿片价格低廉，因而利润空间极大。毒贩在获取芬太尼原料后，可以在家中厨房将其与其他药物混杂压制成毒品，但街头毒品并非在工业化流程控制下生产，每一粒止痛药的成分比例均不相同，往往随机的一粒就能造成过量死亡，而幸运存活的阿片成瘾者则逐渐对效力更强的街头阿片毒品成瘾。

2018年，美国在卫生保健上约花费3.6万亿美元，占其国内生产总值的17.6%，其中零售处方药3450亿美元，人均处方药支出从1999年的520美元增加到1220美元，比排在第二、第三的瑞士和加拿大高出30%。② 药品定价是制药公司及其相关利益集团政治游说活动的重要主题之一，尽管两党都将降低处方药价格列为优先事项，但大制药商的游说者和他们带来的巨额竞选捐款可能会抵消联邦和州政府为此所做的努力。不同于欧洲国家政府与制药商商议定价的情况，制药公司在美国拥有较大的自主定价权，因而一些制药公司在短短数年内将某类药品的定价提升数十倍的例子并不罕见。③

---

① Department of Justice, "Opioid Manufacturer Purdue Pharma Pleads Guilty to Fraud and Kickback Conspiracies", DOJ (Nov. 24, 2020), https://www.justice.gov/opa/pr/opioid-manufacturer-purdue-pharma-pleads-guilty-fraud-and-kickback-conspiracies.
② Oliver J. Wouters, "Lobbying Expenditures and Campaign Contributions by the Pharmaceutical and Health Product Industry in the United States, 1999 – 2018", *JAMA Internal Medicine*, Vol. 180, No. 5, 2020, pp. 1 – 10; Statista, "Pharmaceutical Spending Per Capita in Selected Countries as of 2018", Statista (2019), https://www.statista.com/statistics/266141/pharmaceutical-spending-per-capita-in-selected-countries/.
③ 如美国最大的阿片类仿制药制造商万灵科（Mallinckrodt）公司生产的H. P. Acthar抗婴儿癫痫凝胶在2000年的定价为每瓶40美元，其在2009年每瓶售价为3.9万美元，价格上涨了970倍。

制药商的竞选捐款目标十分明确。在州一级，竞选捐款遵循周期性的模式，与州参议院和市议会的选举时间，或关键法案决议时间相一致。1999—2018 的 20 年间获得医药和保健产品行业最多捐款的两个州分别为加利福尼亚州和俄亥俄州。[1] 加利福尼亚州获得 3.99 亿美元捐款，其中约 50% 和 30% 分别于 2005 年和 2016 年捐出，顺利阻击了 3 项旨在降低药物成本的法案；[2] 在俄亥俄州收到的 7400 万美元中，有 6100 万美元（约八成）用在 2017 年，旨在降低处方药开销的法案投票被成功否决。[3] 联邦层面，众议院在 2003 年试图通过《药品准入法案》（Pharmaceutical Access Act）来降低药品价格，该法案允许美国的个人或零售商从国外购买药品，价格远低于在美国销售的同类药品。该法案遭到获得制药商捐款议员的强烈反对，最终未获通过。同年的民主党议员提出《医疗保险现代化法案》（Medicare Modernization Act），该法案在老年医疗保险中增加了门诊处方药，而对竞选捐款和游说接触的分析表明，在 2002 年和 2004 年的选举周期中，支持该法案的民主党参议员和团体收到了大量捐款。[4] 通过竞选捐款，制药公司再次避免了药品高定价和高利润的立法威胁。

制药行业代笔撰写临床试验文章并以高级研究人员的身份挂名发表也已经成为一种普遍做法，尤其是在行业主导的试验中。这也能让议员们心安理得地接受捐款并支持药品的上市推广。2009—2018 的 10 年间，制药巨头们花费将近 35 亿美元对国会议员进行了强有力的游说活动，以排除联邦对药品价格的限制。[5] 2010 年通过的奥巴马医改最终将药品价

---

[1] Oliver J. Wouters, "Lobbying Expenditures and Campaign Contributions by the Pharmaceutical and Health Product Industry in the United States, 1999 – 2018", *JAMA Internal Medicine*, Vol. 180, No. 5, 2020, pp. 1 – 10.

[2] California's Legislative Analyst's Office, "The California Legislature's Nonpartisan Fiscal and Policy Advisor Proposition 61", California's Legislative Analyst's Office (Nov. 08, 2016), https://lao.ca.gov/BallotAnalysis/Proposition? number = 61&year = 2016.

[3] Kaiser Health News, "Pharma Racks up Huge Victory in Ohio as Voters Overwhelmingly Reject Drug Price Relief Act", Kaiser Health News (Nov. 08, 2017), https://khn.org/morning-breakout/pharma-racks-up-huge-victory-in-ohio-as-voters-overwhelmingly-reject-drug-price-relief-act/.

[4] Richard L. Hall & Robert P. Van Houweling, Campaign Contributions and Lobbying on the Medicare Modernization Act of 2003, Annual Meeting of the American Political Science Association, Philadelphia, PA, 2006, p. 5.

[5] Open Secrets, "Pharmaceuticals/Health Product: Lobbying, 2021", Open Secrets (n.d.), https://www.opensecrets.org/industries/lobbying.php? cycle = 2016&ind = H04.

格限制的有关内容排除在法案之外。2015 年的《可负担处方药法案》计划授权政府就药物价格福利计划与制药商谈判，并允许从加拿大等其他国家进口类似药物，还规定对制药商错误标识和非法营销药品的行为做出撤销药品专营期的惩罚。该法案进一步要求制药公司每年向政府提交报告，详细说明他们如何为产品定价并披露研发成本。对此，包括制药巨头中最有影响力的牵头组织——美国制药研究与制药商协会在内的 15 家制药企业、贸易公司、无障碍药品协会与相关非营利组织对联邦政府进行了最大范围的游说，最终该法案被搁置。此外，制药巨头平均每年花费 1990 万美元游说国会议员，[①] 在 2017 年的游说活动中成功阻止了一项提升药品定价透明度的法案通过。在 2018 年 5 月白宫发布的"蓝图"报告中[②]，特朗普政府将药品高价归咎于包含制药商、分销商、保险公司和药房管理人员在内的整个医药系统。2020 年 11 月，白宫颁布了降低药品价格的行政命令，计划使司法部得以行使监管权，并让国会有更大的权力禁止商业保险回扣，鼓励制药商让消费者直接获得药品折扣。[③] 2022 年 10 月，拜登签署了旨在降低美国人使用处方药成本的行政命令。

制药业利用游说者反对新药定价监管的另一种方式，是利用政府机构和游说公司之间的"旋转门"。制药行业与美国政府之间已经建立了快速转换的旋转门，例如，美国市场占有率第五的默克制药公司雇佣了前任众议员的前助手，在该名国会议员转任卫生与公共服务部长后，该前助手就药品定价问题对卫生部进行了游说，这些联邦前雇员开设了自己的游说公司，以之前的职业背景搭建游说桥梁。[④] 旋转门的另一种形式则是帮助前

[①] Open Secrets, "Pharmaceutical Research & Manufacturers of America", Open Secrets (n. d.), https://www.opensecrets.org/lobby/clientsum.php?id=d000000504.

[②] The Secretary of Health and Human Services, "American Patients First – The Trump Administration Blueprint to Lower Drug Prices and Reduce Out-of-Pocket Costs", HHS (May, 2018), https://www.hhs.gov/sites/default/files/AmericanPatientsFirst.pdf.

[③] James S. Brady, "Remarks by President Trump on Delivering Lower Prescription Drug Prices for All Americans", The White House (Nov. 20, 2020), https://trumpwhitehouse.archives.gov/briefings-statements/remarks-president-trump-delivering-lower-prescription-drug-prices-americans/.

[④] Wenyin Lu & Pat Dolan, "Former Price Aides Now Lobby Their old Boss on Behalf of Tobacco, Big Pharm", CREW (Jul. 31, 2017), https://www.citizensforethics.org/reports-investigations/crew-investigations/revolving-door-former-price-aides-now-lobby-old-boss-behalf-tobacco-big-pharma/.

医药行业游说者到政府的相应部门任职。据《纽约时报》报道，2017年特朗普总统聘请约瑟夫·格罗甘（Joseph Grogan）从事处方药政策制定方面的工作，格罗甘此前任职于吉利德科技公司（Gilead），是该公司在提高处方药品价格方面的首席说客。[①] 尽管特朗普总统命令格罗甘承诺"在两年内不会从事之前游说领域相关的特定事项工作"[②]，仍有媒体指出格罗甘的任职违反了白宫对于前任游说者在白宫从事相同领域工作的两年冷静期规定，认为其有关的政策建议有利于处方药品的定价提升，其中存在利益冲突。民主党参议员谢罗德·布朗（Sherrod Brown）甚至在一份给工作人员的备忘录中表示"制药巨头不需要游说"，因为"该行业已经入驻白宫"[③]。

第三节 阿片危机的未来：制药巨头游说对药品监管政策的塑造

随着近10年多个州陆续为阿片类药物制定了更加严格的处方规定，制药公司一方面尽管仍未放弃维持现有阿片类药物管理政策的竞选捐款与游说活动，另一方面也开始转向未来新一代的阿片类替代药物的推广——滥用威慑配方（abuse-deterrent formulations）阿片类药物。制药公司已瞄准特朗普价值3.5亿美元的阿片瘾癖新倡议（New Opioid-Addiction Initiative），该倡议旨在寻求阿片替代药物和治疗处遇措施。阿片制药巨头宣称其新近研发的滥用威慑配方阿片药物可以作为传统阿片类止痛药的理想替代品。新配方阿片药通过将传统吞服类止痛药压制成难以粉碎或溶解的片剂，避免患者通过鼻腔吸食从而推迟作用于大脑的药效高峰，以有效减少药物成瘾。除此之外，这类新阿片药还具备其他"优势"：价格高、严格

[①] Sheila Kaplan & Katie Thomas, "Draft Order on Drug Prices Proposes Easing Regulation", *The New York Times*, Jun. 20, 2017.

[②] Citizens For Ethics, "A Bitter Bill: How Big Pharma Lobbies to Keep Prescription Drug Prices High. Citizens for Responsibility and Ethics in Washington", Citizens For Ethics（Jun. 18, 2018）, https://www.citizensforethics.org/a-bitter-pill-how-big-pharma-lobbies-to-keep-prescription-drug-prices-high/.

[③] Julian Borger, "Industry that Stalks the US Corridors of Power", *The Guardian*, Feb. 13, 2001.

第五章　制药巨头游说与竞选捐款的腐败影响：以阿片危机为透视点

受到专利保护、[1] 尚无来自仿制药的竞争；由于受到防篡改技术的保护，在药品知识产权被侵犯时能够获得更高额的保险金赔偿。制药巨头正组织在各州与联邦游说，力图将滥用威慑配方阿片药物纳入阿片瘾癖新倡议以及未来立法中。尽管食品药品监管局在一项声明中指出，滥用威慑配方的吞服类新阿片药并不能阻止患者滥用药物，并且"该类药物并不能预防阿片成瘾，而患者对此有清晰的认识非常重要"，[2] 但这并没有阻挡"美国癌症协会癌症行动网络"（American Cancer Society Cancer Action Network）和"综合疼痛管理"（Academy of Integrative Pain Management）组织的游说团体在各州的前进步伐。由于对与行业之间的联系以及资金来源的刻意掩饰，外界通常对这些团体的阿片制药商背景不甚了解，这类团体以疼痛患者的名义鼓吹引入新阿片类药物，并对癌症患者给予特别的阿片类止痛药豁免限制。另一些团体如"患者准入联盟"（Alliance for Patient Access）和"患者崛起"（Patients Rising），则以患者代表的身份出现，却在网络平台发布广告，攻占社交媒体，而它们实际由制药公司资助。目前已有五个州相继通过了引入滥用威慑配方新阿片类药物的法律和数十个等待商议表决的相关法案，但值得注意的是，至少 21 个法律和法案使用了与说客建议草案几乎完全相同的文本措辞，几乎可以肯定这些法案版本都是由上述组织的说客直接提供的。对此有学者认为，新型阿片类药物只是制药公司逃避社会责任、利用游说法律漏洞将更多成瘾药物注入医疗系统的手段而已。[3]

还有相对上述游说团体组织更为隐蔽的匿名组织，正悄无声息地影响着阿片药品政策与立法。这些匿名组织游离于法律与公众监督之外，由超级政治行动委员会、游说公司以及其他未知主体匿名设立，被称为"幽灵船"（ghost ship）。"美国公民思想"（Citizens for American Ideas）即为幽灵

---

[1] 药品专利也是制药业确保药品高企的手段，有研究指出，若以非专利药定价，美国药品支出将是现在的1/10。参见 Dean Baker, "Issues in Trade Protectionism", *Report for the Center for Economic and Policy Research* (2009): 1-10; Richard D. Wolff & Stephen A. Resnick, *A Contending Economic Theories: Neo-classical, Keynesian, and Marxian*, Cambridge, MA: MIT Press, 2012.
[2] FDA, "Statement from FDA Commissioner Scott Gottlieb, M. D., on Agency's Efforts to Encourage the Development of and Broaden Access to Generic Versions of Opioid Analgesics that are Formulated to Deter Abuse", FDA (Jul. 20, 2018), https://www.fda.gov/news-events/press-announcements/statement-fda-commissioner-scott-gottlieb-md-agencys-efforts-encourage-development-and-broaden.
[3] Liz E. Whyte, Geoff Mulvihill & Ben Wieder, "Politics of Pain: Drugmakers Fought State Opioid Limits Amid Crisis", The Center for Public Integrity (Dec. 15, 2016), https://publicintegrity.org/state-politics/politics-of-pain-drugmakers-fought-state-opioid-limits-amid-crisis/.

船的最新极端例子,这一组织于2018年12月启动的网站上批评民主党人降低Medicare药物成本的计划,并将宣传其观点的信件材料邮寄至所在选区的选民家中,敦促选民直接与当地议员联系表达其观点,但其刻意隐藏的网络地址却无法查询到所有人。美国公民思想还伪装成基层团体组织的专家,在药品价格上与最大的处方药游说团体"美国生物技术创新组织"(Biotechnology Innovation Organization)以及美国制药研究与制药商协会联合提出相反的意见,但该组织的发起人和资助者却无人知晓。

另外,制药业对卫生监管机构的巨大影响力也超乎公众的认知。一方面,部分公务人员有时会在制药行业的压力下出售公共利益;另一方面,制药公司雇佣在监管机构有工作经验的人,以获取政府经验。阻止政府与企业之间的人员交换十分困难,这种旋转门带来的不良后果之一,是监管者和被监管者以一种共同的官僚主义心态看待对药品的监管工作。一项由纽约大学法学教授诺曼·多森(Norman Dorsen)主持的独立调查发现,食品药品监管局内部倾向于将"合作"和非对抗作为完成工作的最有效方式,那些使行业陷入困境(例如推迟批准一种新药)的监管局低级官员往往会被转移到"敏感"级别更低的职位上。① 在此期间,食品药品监管局的监管层有意识地确定和筛选了对制药行业采取合作而非与之对抗态度的员工。

针对制药巨头阿片类产品的诉讼始于21世纪初,目前已有数十个州的检察官起诉美国的多家阿片生产与销售商。2012—2015年,美国阿片止痛药制造商Insys Therapeutics开办虚假的演讲者项目,为医生发放巨额演讲费和餐旅费,宣传芬太尼喷剂等产品以扩大其在非癌症疼痛患者中的使用,雇佣开药最多的医生及医生的成年子女担任其父母所在地的医药销售代表②,并给予巨额金钱与其他物质性奖励。2019年6月,Insys Therapeutics公司因涉嫌贿赂医生给病人开出极易成瘾的芬太尼舌下喷雾止痛剂、骗取国家医保等行为认罪。制药公司隐瞒其药品的极度成瘾性并引导医生过量处方的行为助长了美国阿片危机的泛滥,该危机在过去20年里已导致约20万美国人死亡。③ 2019年4月24日,特朗普总统在一次有关药物

---

① John Braithwaite, *Corporate Crime in the Pharmaceutical Industry*, England: Routledge & Kegan Paul Books, 1984, p.301.
② Katie Thomas, Insys, "The Opioid Drug Maker, to Pay $225 Million to Settle Fraud Charges", *The New York Times*, Jun.5, 2019.
③ Katie Thomas, Insys, "The Opioid Drug Maker, to Pay $225 Million to Settle Fraud Charges", *The New York Times*, Jun.5, 2019.

第五章 制药巨头游说与竞选捐款的腐败影响：以阿片危机为透视点

成瘾的公开活动中表示其拒绝了来自制药业的竞选捐款，以提醒该行业正视自身在目前阿片危机中所起的负面作用。特朗普认为该行业"应当负起责任来"，政府开始启动对制药行业的审查，作为当前处方止痛药成瘾阿片危机的应对措施。联邦检察官也于2019年4月23日对阿片销售商罗切斯特药品公司（Rochester Drug Cooperative）及其前首席执行官提出了重罪指控。罗切斯特因涉嫌逃避政府监管，向药房提供超出规定数量的芬太尼贴片和羟考酮止痛药等阿片类处方药物，以满足超处方医生的需求，而成为美国国内首个在阿片危机中被起诉的药品经销商。同年，强生公司因在俄克拉何马州的阿片处方药相关指控中罪名成立，被判处5.72亿美元罚款。① 俄克拉何马州针对强生公司的诉讼是美国第一起直接对阿片类药物流行危机直接负责的制药公司案。2020年2月，美国最大的阿片类药物制造商万灵科（Mallinckrodt Pharmaceuticals）宣布将支付16亿美元以解决因其在阿片类药物危机中所起的促进作用而引发的诉讼。② 仅2019年就有2000余起与阿片危机相关的类似案件待审。③

观察上述针对制药巨头赔偿数额甚巨的诉讼，可以发现美国的制药行业似乎存在着一种替罪羊倾向：只要可以用钱了结，就用钱了结；只要可以将责任推卸到他人身上，就推卸到他人身上。这种制药行业的墨菲定律使得即使是作为法律底线的刑事诉讼在应对罪犯时也遇到困难，国家的这类法律干预往往具有滞后性且收效甚微。此外，这里还涉及公司犯罪的问题，对于犯罪的制药公司，除了处以天价罚金之外，被问责的直接责任人员的判决往往与罪责、公平或正义无关。一些制药公司甚至设置了专门负责坐牢的副总裁职位，以保证公司在陷入诉讼时有人能够代替实际受益的控制人为公司行为负责。加之得益于现代商法中的公司人格独立理论，实际控制人往往并不以自身财产对公司的债务负责，如果在天价的集体索赔诉讼中败诉，制药公司可以资不抵债为由宣告破产，从而在实际上将赔偿责任限于公司自有财产，实际控制人并不需要承担连带赔偿义务。因此，相对于不成比例且极其有限的刑事法律后果，制药行业滥用游说和竞选捐

---

① Chris McGreal, "Johnson & Johnson Opioid Ruling Explained – the Key Points", *The Guardian*, Aug. 26, 2019.
② Kaplan, S. & Hoffman, J., "Mallinckrodt Reaches $1.6 Billion Deal to Settle Opioid Lawsuits", *The New York Times*, Feb. 25, 2020.
③ Sheila Kaplan & Jan Hoffman, "Johnson & Johnson Ordered to Pay $572 Million in Landmark Opioid Trial", *The New York Times*, Aug. 26, 2019.

款机制腐蚀立法和监管机构以换取高额商业利益回报的行为成本是极低的。

本章小结

监管机构的权力与制药行业用财富铸成的政治影响力不成比例,是当下美国药品监管在立法层面之外面临的一大困境。相比食品药品监管局对制药行业被动且滞后的监督规制,制药公司不仅可以通过强大的财力购买民间组织和行业协会的话语权,使用欺诈、贿赂等最便捷的腐败手段,还可以向对其不利的监管者进行政治游说、捐款,选举亲行业利益的政府官员,或通过"旋转门"关系进行腐败利益输送。在这种背景下,国家与公司或行业之间联系成了一种持续损害公共利益的机制,一方面使得大公司统治精英对其利益的反对者进行识别、标记并以犯罪为名义施以惩罚[1],另一方面通过混淆手段,将影子游说、竞选捐款等可能存在利益冲突的"有害行为和可疑关系合法化"[2],以最终为决策者及与其勾连行业的共同利益服务。在新自由主义泛滥与公私领域明确二分法的影响下,政府与制药商合作制定公共卫生政策能够在更大限度上免除追究责任,不仅为腐败创造了成熟的环境,还可以掩盖其中的利益冲突、裙带关系和监管缺失以及其他与腐败相关的操作,并为二者上述有害活动提供合法化辩解。阿片危机即是制药行业长期滥用游说与竞选捐款推行腐败商业模式的顶峰现象,而并非特例,其反映的是美国金权政治背景下的社会现实:拥有财富即具备操纵政治和侵蚀法律的不当影响力。

因此,任何强制性的公共卫生政策都必须接受独立的科学质询、公开辩论和法律审查。当公共卫生政策涉及作为监管者的国家与被监管行业之间的密切合作时,尤其是被监管相关行业存在持续腐败行为的历史时,透

---

[1] Renate Bridenthal, *The Hidden History of Crime, Corruption, and States*, New York: Berghahn Books, 2013, p.4.
[2] Penny Green & Tony Ward, *State Crime: Governments, Violence and Corruption*, London: Pluto Press, 2004, p.29; Edwin H. Sutherland, *White Collar Crime: The Uncut Version*, New Haven, CT: Yale University Press, 1983, pp.45–53.

明度在决策过程中尤为重要。公共卫生保健的决策过程必须足够开放，任何相关方都应有参与协商委员会、听证会和依法开展游说的机会，无论该方代表商业、科学、专业领域还是任何其他利益。这些规定的基本要素是公开性，即必须披露游说活动正在进行以及有关各方的身份、参与游说的内容和结果。

第六章　私营监狱公司滥用游说与竞选捐款：大规模监禁的腐败循环

20世纪70年代，针对愈演愈烈的毒品犯罪，尼克松政府发动了"毒品战争"（War on Drugs）。严厉的量刑法实施40余年间，数百万人被投入监狱。1980年时仅有4万人因毒品犯罪被监禁，而至2008年已达到50万人，增加了1100%，相当于1980年全美监禁人数的总和。① 白宫经济顾问委员会2016年的监禁报告表明，美国监狱关押着超过全世界1/5的囚犯，平均每100名成年人里就有1人被监禁，而被监禁者中毒品犯罪占多数。② 从某种角度来看，制药巨头自90年代初以来对阿片药物的大肆游说和不当的市场推广，使得大量成瘾民众在无法获得处方和瘾癖加深的情况下，转向以可卡因和海洛因等阿片类毒品③为代表的网络与街头毒品，也间接导致持有、贩卖和走私毒品相关犯罪率的急剧上升，每年因毒品犯罪被捕和监禁的人数屡创新高。即使在奥巴马时期的刑事司法改革取得了显著成效，提升了多项毒品犯罪的定罪标准，并将所有毒品走私的罪名刑期缩短25%后，2019年联邦监狱中仍有高达46%的犯人因毒品犯罪入狱服刑。④ 而随着美国矫

---

① Marc Mauer, "The Changing Racial Dynamics of the War on Drugs", The Sentencing Project (Apr., 2019), https://www.sentencingproject.org/wp-content/uploads/2016/01/The-Changing-Racial-Dynamics-of-the-War-on-Drugs.pdf.
② White House Council of Economic Advisors, "Economic Perspectives on Incarceration and the Criminal Justice System", The White House (Apr., 2016), https://obamawhitehouse.archives.gov/sites/default/files/page/files/20160423_cea_incarceration_criminal_justice.pdf.
③ 海洛因为阿片类毒品的一种，属半天然半合成阿片。
④ E. Ann Carson, "Prisoners in 2019", Bureau of Justice Statistics (Oct., 2020), https://www.bjs.gov/content/pub/pdf/p19.pdf.

第六章　私营监狱公司滥用游说与竞选捐款：大规模监禁的腐败循环

正系统规模的不断扩大，年支出已高达 800 亿美元，[1] 联邦和各州财政承受了巨大负担。政府开始转向私人外包渠道以降低支出。私营监狱经营者声称其可在花费更低的情况下，提供与公立矫正设施相同水平的服务，如监禁设施、食物、医疗健康和教育项目等，从而为纳税人节约税金。在大规模监禁政策沉重财政负担的压力下，私营监狱也顺势扩张。自 1989 年以来，美国两家最大的营利性监狱公司 GEO 集团和美国矫正公司（Corrections Corporation of America，现已改名为"CoreCivic"）已向政治候选人捐出了超过 1000 万美元，并花费了将近 2500 万美元进行游说工作。[2] 同时，这些私营公司的收入和市场份额猛增。相比于制药、保险和石油行业，私营监狱的游说与捐款活动与政治决策之间的腐败联系较鲜为人知。且不同于上述行业，私营监狱行业的利润几乎完全取决于公共政策和政府资金，其客户仅为政府，而非一般民事主体。因而可以认为，私营监狱对政府人员滥用游说和竞选捐款的行为模式，在某种程度上构成了一套独特又极具代表性的美国政府与政治腐败模型。

第一节　寄生于大规模监禁的私营监狱产业

国家天然地掌握刑罚权，政府代表国家行使该权力。尽管监狱设施通常由州或联邦政府负责，但其带来的支出与周边创造的利益也同样是政府的重要关切。以公共支出为代价，现代监狱被要求以人道方式对犯人进行安置，并为其提供个人化的矫正措施，监狱的行政运作支出持续增加；反过来，由于监狱行政花费的高昂，刑事司法系统被迫向受害人以外的各方投入大量资金。有了私营监狱，许多负担就从政府手中转移到私人公司中。政府无须管理监狱的所有相关工作，而只需在进行监督的同时源源不断地提供犯人。自 2000 年以来，联邦政府和州政府都越来越依赖私有化，州立监狱部门与私人监狱承包商合作进行监狱建设和运营也变得越来越普

---

[1] Peter Wagner & Bernadette Rabuy, "Following the Money of Mass Incarceration", Prison Policy (Jan. 25, 2017), https://www.prisonpolicy.org/reports/money.html.
[2] Michael Cohen, "How For-profit Prisons Have Become the Biggest Lobby No One is Talking About", The Washington Post, Apr. 28, 2015.

遍。根据司法部的数据，2020年私营监狱和拘留设施的在押人数为1990年的20倍以上，① 这反映出美国对待囚犯的方式发生了重大变化。

尽管奥巴马总统在2010—2016年围绕联邦量刑规则进行了一系列刑事司法改革，大量释放符合一定条件的犯人，各州和联邦监狱中的犯人数量也随着改革带来的犯罪率下降而稳步减少，但旨在代替传统上由政府扮演的角色来获利的私人监狱经营者，已经在负担沉重的大规模监禁系统中牟取了大量利润，并且这种利润并没有降低的趋势。一种不准确的印象是，相对公立监狱，私营监狱便宜的运营价格是使其变得越来越普遍的原因。实际上数十年的研究表明，监狱私有化与节省矫治成本的联系尚没有根据。② 一些监狱看似为政府节省了管理成本，但实际上其每个监狱的人均花费比公共设施要高得多。③ 不仅如此，私营监狱还正在变得越来越昂贵。以佐治亚州为例，在管理相同数量犯人的情况下，其在2018财年向私营监狱支付的费用大约是12年前的两倍。④ 尽管此类监狱往往更加昂贵，但其既不能为囚犯提供足够的工作培训和教育等复归服务，也无法达到预防累犯和提升公共安全的目的。2016年8月，奥巴马政府发布了减少依赖并最终逐步淘汰私营监狱的改革政令，特朗普在次年当选后，该项政令随之被废除，拜登政府随后继续奥巴马的政策，但私营监狱并未受到太大冲击。截至2023年，美国监狱与拘留设施中关押了超过190万人，其中，13万余名囚犯被拘禁在由私营监狱公司运营的监狱或拘留设

---

① ICMA, "The Price of Private Prisons", ICMA (Nov. 22, 2011), https：//icma.org/blog-posts/price-private-prisons? gclid = CjwKCAiAl4WABhAJEiwATUnEF5qbBrXXOA4v_ 2JlPu8eDSh9195rfpg2Dquo7aXlqVWq9HNFeunJwhoCLvkQAvD_ BwE; Prison Policy Initiative, "Mass Incarceration：The Whole Pie 2020", Prison Policy Initiative (Aug. 11, 2020), https：//www.prisonpolicy.org/reports/pie2020.html.

② Kara Gotsch & Vinay Basti, "Capitalizing on Mass Incarceration：U.S Growth in Private Prisons", The Sentencing Project (Aug. 2, 2018), https：//www.sentencingproject.org/publications/capitalizing-on-mass-incarceration-u-s-growth-in-private-prisons/.

③ Associated Press, "Audit：Private Prisons Cost More than State-run Prison", Associated Press (Jan. 2, 2019), https：//apnews.com/article/af7177d9cce540ab9f2d873b99437154; Megan Mumford, Diane Whitmore Schanzenbach & Ryan Nunn, "The Economics of Private Prisons", The Brookings Institution (2016), https：//www.brookings.edu/wp-content/uploads/2016/10/es_ 20161021_ private_ prisons_ economics.pdf.

④ Megan Mumford, Diane Whitmore Schanzenbach & Ryan Nunn, "The Economics of Private Prisons", The Brookings Institution (2016), https：//www.brookings.edu/wp-content/uploads/2016/10/es_ 20161021_ private_ prisons_ economics.pdf.

施中。[1] 由于美国矫治费用十分高昂，监禁每名犯人的年平均花费在一些州可高达 8 万美元，[2] 比常青藤大学的学费更贵。而美国拥有世界上最多的私营监狱人口，[3] 因此私人监狱业务合同的标的数额与利润巨大。

随着私营监狱向公共领域的扩张，缓刑和假释制度开始朝私有化方向迈进，各种各样的矫正周边服务也被私营化：监狱医疗、药品和精神保健服务，食品、小卖部和食堂服务，运输、电话、电子邮件和汇款服务，娱乐视听和安保设备等。这些服务共同构成了巨大的私营监狱周边产业链，在给犯人及其家属造成沉重经济负担的同时，也在实质上使得监狱从社会犯罪现象与大规模监禁中不正当地获得收益——仿佛监狱本身的存在就是为了维持机构运作、创造就业，而非预防被害，这也极易导致腐败。[4] 这就提出了一个营利性监狱的目标问题。监狱系统的目标是使囚犯复归社会，但 2014 年的统计结果表明，美国监狱犯人释放后九年内的累犯率达到 83%。[5] 该数字揭示了昂贵的刑事司法系统的无效性，但如果监狱的有效率为 100%，私人监狱将很快破产。那么问题是，监狱是应该改造犯罪人，还是谋取利润？如果监狱的目标是赚钱，那么不得不承认其维持大规模监禁现状的倾向。因而，私营监狱没有改造或矫治犯人的动机，相反，犯人在私营监狱或拘留设施中停留的时间越长，再犯罪并回到监狱的次数越多，私营监狱的利润就越多。一系列研究证明了这种猜想。例如，2007 年至 2009 年在明尼苏达州进行的一项研究发现，与公立监狱相比，私营监狱中囚犯的被捕率高出 13%，而再次被定罪的可能性高出 22%；[6] 俄克

---

[1] Prison Policy Initiative, "Mass Incarceration: The Whole Pie 2023", Prison Policy Initiative (Mar. 14, 2023), https://www.prisonpolicy.org/reports/pie2023.html.

[2] California's Legislative Analyst's Office, "How much does it cost to incarcerate an inmate?" California's Legislative Analyst's Office (2019), https://lao.ca.gov/PolicyAreas/CJ/6_cj_inmatecost.

[3] Kara Gotsch & Vinay Basti, "Capitalizing on Mass Incarceration: U.S Growth in Private Prisons", The Sentencing Project (Aug. 2, 2018), https://www.sentencingproject.org/publications/capitalizing-on-mass-incarceration-u-s-growth-in-private-prisons/.

[4] 韦佳：《美国司法再投资改革实践检视》，《河南师范大学学报》（哲学社会科学版）2020 年第 1 期。

[5] 这里统计的是 2005 年从监狱中被释放后 9 年内再次被逮捕的概率。参见 National Institute of Justice, "Measuring Recidivism", NIJ (Feb. 20, 2008), https://nij.ojp.gov/topics/articles/measuring-recidivism#statistics.

[6] Grant Duwe & Valerie Clark, "The Effects of Private Prison Confinement in Minnesota on Offender Recidivism", Minnesota Department of Corrections (Mar., 2013), https://mn.gov/doc/assets/MN_Private_Prison_Evaluation_Website_Final_tcm1089-272834.pdf.

拉何马州进行了类似的研究，发现私营监狱犯人的再犯率比公立监狱高17%；[1]一项针对1996—2004年密西西比州2.7万名囚犯的研究发现，在罪行类似的情况下，私立监狱平均比公立监狱多关押犯人60—90天。[2]显然，在过去的40年，私营监狱公司已经找到了从大规模监禁中获利的方法。

私营监狱合同与定罪量刑法律都是由州和联邦政策制定者批准与订立的，受到州和联邦机构行政管理者监督，因此与政客积极建立关系是私营监狱公司的重要商业策略，在政治上花费大量资金以实现其业务目标，恰恰符合其利益最大化的需求。和政治角力游戏中的许多其他行业一样，为确保私营监狱在监禁中具有稳定且不断增长的"市场份额"，私营监狱公司通过三管齐下的策略来确保监禁政策与政府合同中的巨大盈利，即竞选捐款、游说活动以及建立关系网"旋转门"。这些策略带来的直接效果是私人监狱公司得以与政府签订包含更符合监狱公司利益条款的承包合同，在立法上通过或维持严苛的定罪与量刑法律以使得更多人入狱，并对予以配合的政府与立法机构人员给予高薪聘用等回报。因为每名犯人平均每年可以带来1万—2万美元的可观利润。凭借上述策略，自20世纪90年代起每年流向私营监狱公司的资金流激增。美国两大私营监狱巨头GEO集团与美国矫正公司2023年的收入分别为24亿美元和19亿美元。[3]

第二节　私营监狱公司竞选捐款影响立法决策

长期以来，政治影响力一直决定着营利性私营监狱的增长，并在今天

---

[1] Andrew L. Spivak, Susan F. Sharp, "Inmate Recidivism as a Measure of Private Prison Performance", *Crime and Delinquency*, Vol. 54, No. 3, 2008, pp. 482-508.
[2] Anita Mukherjee, "Impacts of Private Prison Contracting on Inmate Time Served and Recidivism", *American Economic Journal: Economic Policy*, Vol. 13, No. 2, 2021, pp. 408-438.
[3] GEO Group, "The GEO Group Reports Fourth Quarter and Full Year 2023 Results", GEO Group (Feb. 15, 2024), https://investors.geogroup.com/news-releases/news-release-details/geo-group-reports-fourth-quarter-and-full-year-2023-results#:~:text=For%20the%20full%20year%202023, for%20the%20full%20year%202022; CoreCivic, "CoreCivic Reports Fourth Quarter and Full Year 2023 Financial Results", CoreCivic (Feb. 7, 2024), https://ir.corecivic.com/news-releases/news-release-details/corecivic-reports-fourth-quarter-and-full-year-2023-financial.

第六章 私营监狱公司滥用游说与竞选捐款：大规模监禁的腐败循环

以各种方式继续存在。纵观过去一个世纪的普通法判例，最高法院曾在维持《联邦竞选法》中捐款限制的裁决中承认："为确保与现任者和竞选者达成政治等价交换而产生的大额捐款，（导致）代议制民主遭到了破坏。"[1] 美国前副总统戈尔曾在其书中写道："美国民主制度已经遭到入侵，未经公司游说机构和控制竞选资金的其他特殊利益许可，美国国会将无法通过法律。"[2] 有关再分配政治经济学的研究指出，对联邦政府相关活动的大量捐款增加了政府合同腐败的可能性，并且竞选捐款的影响主要在总统所属的执政党，而对非执政党的捐款，很大程度上并不影响政府决策。[3] 得益于公司大量捐款的从政者也能够反过来影响招标条款与评价，以使得特定的捐款公司直接获益。当高度参与政治的公司遇到系统腐败风险较高（即有过系统腐败历史的）的联邦官僚机构时，政府腐败风险明显增大。

2001—2011年，美国第二大私营监狱美国矫正公司向其所支持的政党和候选人捐献了190万美元，同时为游说活动支出1740万美元，其在2011年营收高达17亿美元；[4] 全美最大的环球监狱承包商GEO集团则在2003—2011年的联邦游说活动中花费250万美元，另将290万美元用于对州和地方官员的游说和竞选捐款，[5] GEO集团在2011年的营利为16亿美元。[6] GEO、美国矫正公司与康奈尔（Cornell，后被GEO收购）三家私营监狱公司在2010年共计竞选捐款约222万美元，是2002年的近三倍（见图6-1）。在这10年间，美国矫正公司和GEO集团的竞选捐款均增加了一倍以上，而美国矫正公司向国会议员捐献的资金中，超过1/3流向了参

---

[1] Christopher A. Anzalone, *Supreme Court Cases on Political Representation*, 1787-2001, New York: Routledge, 2002, p.435.

[2] Al Gore, *The Future: Six Drivers of Global Change*, New York: Random House Publishing Group, 2013, p.319.

[3] Mihály Aazekas & others, "Institutional Quality, Campaign Contributions, and Favouritism in US Federal Government Contracting", Government Transparency Institutes (Aug.2018), http://www.govtransparency.eu/wp-content/uploads/2018/08/Fazekas-et-al_DonationsPPcorr_US_GTI_WP_2018.pdf.

[4] Open Secrets, "Corrections Corp of America", Open Secrets (n.d.), https://www.opensecrets.org/lobby/clientsum.php?id=D000021940&year=2002.

[5] Suevon Lee, "By the Numbers: The U.S.'s Growing For-Profit Detention Industry", ProPublica (Jun.20, 2012), https://www.propxiublica.org/article/by-the-numbers-the-u.s-growing-for-profit-detention-industry.

[6] Michael Cohen, "How For-profit Prisons Have Become the Biggest Lobby No One is Talking about", *The Washington Post*, Apr.28, 2015.

众两院负责拨款的委员会成员。①

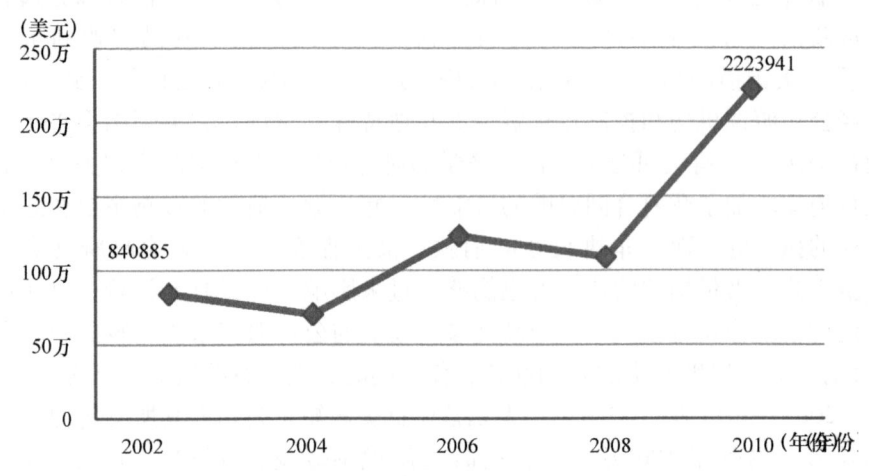

```
(美元)
250万                                                    2223941
200万
150万
100万  840885
 50万
   0
      2002      2004      2006      2008      2010  (年份)
```

图6-1　2002—2010年美国矫正公司、GEO集团和康奈尔公司竞选捐款总计

资料来源：Follow the Money, "Private Prisons: Hiding Behind a Veil of Democracy", Follow the Money (n. d.), https://www.followthemoney.org/assets/Uploads/Private-Prisons-Hiding-Behind-a-Veil-of-Democracy-Tylek.pdf.

在州一级，私营监狱公司倾向于将竞选捐款资源集中投入特定的几个州，特别是加利福尼亚、佛罗里达和佐治亚。这些州的犯人数量多，关押成本和利润也水涨船高，是私营监狱公司的主要业务所在地。2003年至2010年，美国矫正公司在这三个州的竞选捐款总额为100万美元，占其在全美捐款总额的2/3。② GEO集团则与佛罗里达州议员有着盘根错节的联系。佛罗里达众议院前议长、共和党参议员马可·卢比奥（Marco Rubio）曾在2012年因该州最大的私营监狱黑水河惩教所（Blackwater River Correctional Facility）的筹建，而与部分共和党的捐款者一起受到联邦政府的调查，该监狱由GEO集团负责设计并运营。作为共和党在佛州最大的捐款者，GEO在2006—2009年通过佛罗里达GEO集团公司（Florida Geo Group,

---

① Chris Kirkham, "Private Prisons Profit from Immigration Crackdown, Federal and Local Law Enforcement Partnerships", *The Huffington Post*, Aug. 06, 2012.
② Marie Gottschalk, *Caught: The Prison State and the Lockdown of American Politics*, Princeton, NJ: Princeton University Press, 2016, p. 315.

第六章　私营监狱公司滥用游说与竞选捐款：大规模监禁的腐败循环

Inc.）与 GEO 集团公司（Geo Group, Inc.）的两个政治行动委员会，向佛罗里达州共和党捐款 8.5 万美元；2005—2010 年，GEO 通过其政治行动委员会分别向全国共和党国会委员会和参议院委员会捐献了 1.5 万美元和 3.2 万美元，并在 2009—2010 年直接向马可·卢比奥美国参议员政治行动委员会（Marco Rubio for U. S. Senate PAC）捐献了 1 万美元；2010 年 GEO 的数名高管、分包商及其说客共向佛罗里达胜利委员会（Florida Victory Committee）捐献了 3.35 万美元，该政治行动委员会的受益人正是马可·卢比奥美国参议员政治行动委员会、全国共和党参议员委员会和佛罗里达州共和党政治行动委员会。① 作为卢比奥政治行动委员会的最大捐款人，GEO 捐出的 3.35 万美元中，有 1 万美元直接来自怀特建筑公司（White Construction Company）的首席执行官，该公司作为 GEO 的分包商获得了 2010 年开业的黑水河惩教所 1.14 亿美元的合同。卢比奥从 GEO 那里获得了近 4 万美元的竞选捐款，这也使他成为 GEO 在参议院捐款额最高的议员。② 2016 年，GEO 集团员工向卢比奥捐款 3.04 万美元，以支持其在当年的参议院竞选。此外，GEO 还向支持卢比奥的佛罗里达第一超级政治行动委员会捐赠了 5 万美元。③ 卢比奥雇佣了唐娜·阿杜因（Donna Arduin）担任其经济顾问，后者作为受托人供职于 GEO 信托基金。在卢比奥的支持下，阿杜因和参谋长罗伯特·克耐普（Robert Kneip）大力推动了新的州预算案，内容包括要求佛罗里达监狱局确认约 1350 个男性成年心理监护和医疗床位预算，并在必要时使用私人监狱床位，④ 以进一步扩大私营监狱的盈利。该预算法案的最大受益者即为 GEO 集团及其子公司。而长期以来，GEO 集团旗下的监狱设施因糟糕的医疗保健状况、涉嫌侵犯人权以及相较于其他监狱较高的死亡率而受到广泛批评。由此可见，相对于每年获取的上亿美元的政府合同与拨款，GEO 对地方立法者数百万美元的捐款并非无利可图。卢比奥的例子也表明，在现有法律下，只要双方不说出"交易"之类

---

① Beau Hodai, "Marco Rubio, GEO Group, and a Legacy of Corruption", PRWatch（Aug. 29, 2012），https：//www.prwatch.org/news/2012/08/11591/marco-rubio-geo-group-and-legacy-corruption.
② Michael Cohen, "How For-profit Prisons Have Become the Biggest Lobby No One is Talking About", *The Washington Post*, Apr. 28, 2015.
③ Alex Leary, "Behind Marco Rubio, a Powerful Ally： Private Prison Operator GEO Group", *Tampa Bay Times*, Aug. 25, 2016.
④ Beau Hodai, "Marco Rubio, GEO Group, and a Legacy of Corruption", PRWatch（Aug. 29, 2012），https：//www.prwatch.org/news/2012/08/11591/marco-rubio-geo-group-and-legacy-corruption.

的相关词语，就不会受到检察官的起诉。其支持私营监狱公司扩展营业范围的行为也许在经验直觉上会被认定为"腐败"，但并不满足联邦最高法院在"联合公民案"中对"利益交换"重新作出的定义。由此也可发现，"联合公民案"判决为特殊利益集团与有权决策者之间的腐败利益输送敞开了大门，现行法律已脱离了一般社会道德约束的框架。

一 捐款押注有望当选的议员与政府官员

私营监狱公司通过政治行动委员会及其员工向州与联邦一级的政治候选人与议员捐款，以与国会主要领导者建立紧密联系。GEO集团、美国矫正公司和康奈尔三所私营监狱公司更倾向于捐助更有可能当选的候选人，其85%的捐款都花费在了有望当选者与谋求连任者身上（见图6-2）。这种捐款模式也表明，私营监狱公司力求通过竞选捐款，尽早建立和巩固与可能当选议员尤其是其中关键决策者的正面联系，显示其对权力的追求比表达其自身政治信仰的意愿更为强烈。最值得注意的是，捐款对象涵盖了从州议会到高等法院法官候选人等所有可能影响决策的人员。当然，由于两党对待犯罪与矫正的态度不同，[1] 从20世纪90年代后期起，私营监狱公司总是将更多的捐款投入支持共和党的活动。[2] 2010年，三家私营监狱公司将超过30%的竞选捐款直接捐给了在州政府担任各种职务的连任候选人。[3] 而在2013年和2014年的选举周期中，私营监狱行业共向360名州政府候选人捐出250万美元。[4] 仅在2014年，该行业就为州长、副州长、

---

[1] 共和党长期以来都是私人监狱公司的支持者。两党在刑事政策理念方面存在差异，民主党较为相信矫治理论，认为犯罪人是可以为社会改造的，并且吸食大麻等很多行为都应非犯罪化，同时提倡非监禁的社区服务矫正和恢复性司法；共和党则倾向于强硬对待犯罪，主张监禁隔离的理论，因此支持最低刑期限制和三振出局等法律。另有研究表明，游说与竞选捐款多数情况下倾向于维某一政策而非转变，因而私人监狱公司的大部分竞选资金都投入了共和党竞选人，支持民主党并不能改变它的刑事政策。

[2] Open Secrets, "For-profit Prison", Open Secrets（Mar. 22, 2021）, https://www.opensecrets.org/industries./indus.php?cycle=2020&ind=G7000.

[3] Justice Policy Institute, "Gaming the System: How the Political Strategies of Private Prison Companies Promost Ineffective Incarceration Policies", Justice Policy Institute（Jun., 2011）, http://www.justicepolicy.org/uploads/justicepolicy/documents/gaming_the_system.pdf.

[4] In the Public Interest, "Buying Influence: How Private Prison Companies Expand Their Control of America's Criminal Justice System", In the Public Interest（Oct., 2016）, https://www.inthepublicinterest.org/wp-content/uploads/ITPI_BuyingInfluence_Oct2016.pdf.

总审计长、总检察长以及州议会的 30 名候选人每人捐款至少 5000 美元，其中 27 人在选举中获胜。[①] 同年，三家私营监狱公司的员工及其政治行动委员会共计向在任的国会议员捐款约 35 万美元。[②] 此外，与其他行业一样，由于现行竞选财务法律允许暗钱的存在，所以无法确定私营监狱行业通过所谓的"社会福利"团体和其他非营利组织向选举注入的实际资金数量。

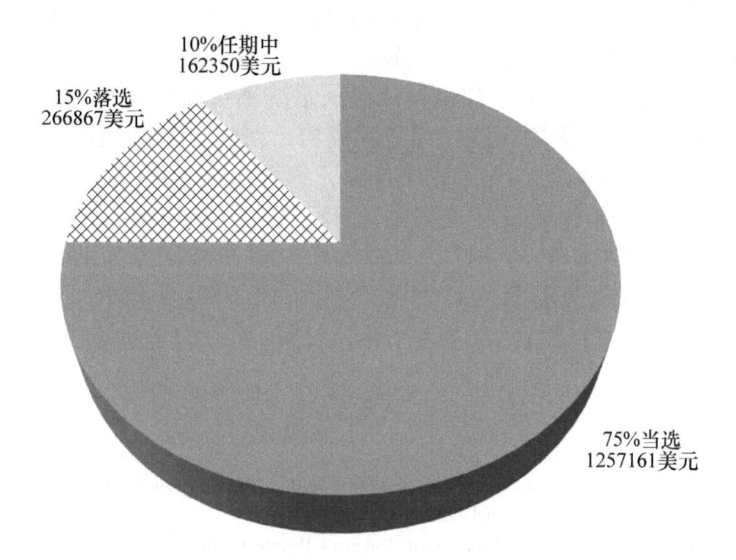

图 6-2　2003—2010 年 GEO、美国矫正公司和康奈尔公司竞选捐款对象当选比例

10%任期中 162350美元
15%落选 266867美元
75%当选 1257161美元

资料来源：Justice Policy Institute, "Gaming the System: How the Political Strategies of Private Prison Companies Promost Ineffective Incarceration Policies", Justice Policy Institute (Jun., 2011), http://www.justicepolicy.org/uploads/justicepolicy/documents/gaming_the_system.pdf.

二　以捐款换取政府合同中的不合理条款

得益于在政治竞选中的慷慨解囊，私营监狱堂而皇之地在与政府签订

---

① Davon Woodley, "Democracy Behind Bars: How Money in Politics, Felony Disenfranchisement and Prison Gerrymandering Fuel Mass Incarceration and Undermine Democracy", Democracy Behind Bars (Jul., 2018), https://democracybehindbars.org/wp-content/uploads/sites/9/2018/07/DemocracyBehindBarsWEB.pdf.
② Peter Wagner & Bernadette Rabuy, "Following the Money of Mass Incarceration", Prison Policy (Jan. 25, 2017), https://www.prisonpolicy.org/reports/money.html.

的合同中加入入住率保障条款：全美 2/3 的私营监狱都在合同中规定了政府必须输送的犯人数量以保证床位入住率。① 这意味着，如果监狱床位没有达到约定入住率，政府仍然每年要为每个床位支付 2.3 万美元。② GEO 集团和美国矫正公司在 2011 年与政府签订的合同中，均规定其各监狱设施的入住率应达到 90%；亚利桑那州的一些私营监狱甚至在政府合同中要求监狱入住率为 100%。③ 这类合同条款制造了一种倾向，即政府为遵守约定，同时不浪费床位费，将想办法输送犯人以填满各私营监狱的床位。监狱公司的利润率得到保障，却也导致司法系统不可避免地成为制造与监禁罪犯的机器。④ GEO 集团在这方面尤其成功，在其 2012 年年度报告中，其 96 个监狱与拘留设施的 7.3 万张床位中，约有 6.6 万张已正在使用；平均而言，该公司 2012 年的设施使用率为 95.7%。⑤ 2018 年，美国联邦与各州监狱中关押犯人总计达 147 万人⑥，其中私人监狱监禁的囚犯数量达 12.8 万人，约占全美监禁人口的 8.5%，⑦ 比 2000 年增长了 47%。⑧ 按 2012 年全美私营监狱总计 15.7 万个床位计算，⑨ 私营监狱床位的平均使用

---

① In the Public Interest, "Criminal: How Lockup Quotas and 'Low-Crime Taxes' Guarantee Profits for Private Prison Corporation", In the Public Interest (Sep., 2013), https://www.inthepublicinterest.org/wp-content/uploads/Criminal-Lockup-Quota-Report.pdf.
② Liberty Vittert, "The Cold Hard Facts about America's Private Prison System", Fox News (Dec. 19, 2018), https://www.foxnews.com/opinion/the-cold-hard-facts-about-americas-private-prison-system.
③ In the Public Interest, "Criminal: How Lockup Quotas and 'Low-Crime Taxes' Guarantee Profits for Private Prison Corporation", In the Public Interest (Sep., 2013), https://www.inthepublicinterest.org/wp-content/uploads/Criminal-Lockup-Quota-Report.pdf.
④ 从规范角度来看，刑事司法系统的确客观上制造了犯罪人，但当今美国刑事司法机器的运作优先考虑的是犯罪预防而非惩罚为目的刑事制裁后果，其重心也是事前预防而非事后补救。
⑤ Kendall Bentsen, "Money, Not Morals, Drives Marijuana Prohibition Movement", Open Secrets (Aug. 5, 2014), https://www.opensecrets.org/news/2014/08/money-not-morals-drives-marijuana-prohibition-movement/.
⑥ Jacob Kang-Brown, Eital Schattner-Elmaleh & Oliver Hinds, "People in Prison in 2018", Vera Institute of Justice (Apr., 2019), https://www.vera.org/downloads/publications/people-in-prison-in-2018-updated.pdf.
⑦ The Sentencing Project, "Private Prisons in the United States", The Sentencing Project (Aug. 2, 2018), https://www.sentencingproject.org/publications/private-prisons-united-states/.
⑧ Kara Gotsch & Vinay Basti, "Capitalizing on Mass Incarceration: U.S Growth in Private Prisons", The Sentencing Project (Aug. 2, 2018), https://www.sentencingproject.org/publications/capitalizing-on-mass-incarceration-u-s-growth-in-private-prisons/.
⑨ Suevon Lee, "By the Numbers: The U.S.'s Growing For-Profit Detention Industry", ProPublica (Jun. 20, 2012), https://www.propublica.org/article/by-the-numbers-the.u.s-growing-for-profit-detention-industry.

第六章 私营监狱公司滥用游说与竞选捐款：大规模监禁的腐败循环

率约为81.5%。

合同还确保私营监狱将花费最昂贵的老年犯人或患病犯人排除在其设施之外，并更多地收押有色人种。犯人的医疗支出是仅次于治安维护的最高支出项，以加利福尼亚州为例，犯人医疗支出平均占监狱总预算的31%。[1] 通常，安置一名非老年囚犯的费用为每年3.4万美元，而50岁及以上囚犯的费用约为6.8万美元。[2] 因此，美国矫正公司在与政府的合同中加入了其他不合理条款，以阻止55岁以上的老年囚犯转移到其运营的监狱中。除了老年囚犯，美国矫正公司和GEO集团与州矫正部门之间订立的合同中，都明确排除那些医疗费用"高于平均水平"的囚犯，他们不会被纳入合同。排除标准包括老年囚犯，还包括残疾、HIV阳性者、有敏感医疗状况或高风险诊断者等十多项。如GEO集团在与俄克拉何马州签订的合同中明确规定："根据疾病控制与预防中心的诊断定义，承包商可以将患有艾滋病的犯罪者交还给该州。……若接受治疗的丙型肝炎阳性犯人数超过两个，则矫正部门须把这些罪犯转移出该（私营）监狱。"[3] 亚利桑那州与私营监狱签订的合同为每个囚犯的医疗保健服务设置了1万美元的上限，当单个囚犯的医疗费用超过此上限时，将被立刻送回州立监狱，并由州政府承担与该囚犯有关的所有医疗费用。[4] 私营监狱还会排除有昂贵的牙科、眼科和心理治疗需求者。如全国第三大私营监狱公司管理和培训公司（Management and Training Company，MTC）与密西西比州矫正署签订的合同："MTC对提供咨询和心理健康计划概不负责；MTC对提供医疗、心理健康、验光、药物、牙科或类似服务概不负责。"[5]

---

[1] Gabrielle Canon, "Here's the Latest Evidence of How Private Prisons Are Exploiting Inmates for Profit", Mother Jones（Jun. 17, 2015）, https://www.motherjones.com/crime-justice/2015/06/private-prisons-profit/.

[2] ACLU, "At America's Expense: The Mass Incarceration of the Elderly", ACLU（Jun., 2012）, https://www.aclu.org/sites/default/files/field_document/elderlyprisonreport_20120613_1.pdf.

[3] Christopher Petrella, "The Color of Corporate Corrections, Part Ⅱ: Contractual Exemptions and the Overrepresentation of People of Color in Private Prisons", *Radical Criminology*, No.3, 2014, pp.69-88.

[4] Arizona Department of Corrections, "FY 2018 Operating Per Capita Cost Report", Arizona Department of Corrections（Jan., 2019）, https://corrections.az.gov/sites/default/files/REPORTS/Operating_Per_Capita/adc-percapcostreport_fy2018-final.pdf.

[5] Christopher Petrella, "The Color of Corporate Corrections, Part Ⅱ: Contractual Exemptions and the Overrepresentation of People of Color in Private Prisons", *Radical Criminology*, No.3, 2014, pp.69-88.

因此，私营监狱订立的政府合同，往往在实质上规定只能容纳最年轻、最健康也即花费较少的囚犯。这意味着私营监狱倾向于收治非裔和拉丁裔犯人，因为监禁他们比白人更便宜——少数族裔的囚犯年龄通常比白人囚犯年轻。① 在加利福尼亚州、佐治亚州、俄克拉何马州和得克萨斯州，有色人种在私人监狱中所占的比例至少比公立监狱高出12%。② 在年老和疾病犯人之外，公立监狱还必须不成比例地拘押更多高风险的罪犯，高风险也意味着更高级别和更昂贵的安全警戒配备。研究显示，安全级别为中级或最低等级的囚犯占私营监狱人口的90%，而这一比例在公立监狱为69%。③ 这无疑为公立监狱带来了更沉重的财政和管理负担。而亚利桑那州矫正署在2010年的研究发现，私营监狱的最低安全设施未能节约矫正支出，而且其中等安全关押设施也比同等公立监狱的花费更高。④ 尽管如此，亚利桑那州仍然继续与私营监狱公司签订包含不合理条款的合同。2000—2017年，该州的私营监狱犯人数量增加了约480%。⑤

三 捐款支持惩罚性移民政策下的营利模式

从根本上，私营监狱的持续营利完全依靠于国家的法律与刑事司法政策。"9·11事件"以来，国会不仅加强了基于国籍的入境筛查，还进一步扩大了被强制拘留的移民范围，并对移民犯罪进行刑事起诉，相应推动了对移民拘留设施的投资。2004年，国会颁布了《情报改革和预防恐怖主义法》（Intelligence Reform and Terrorism Prevention Act），要求国土安全部在2006—2010财年以每年增加8000个床位的速度为拘留能力扩容。2009

---

① Joshua Holland, "Higher Profits Explain Why There Are More People of Color in Private Prisons", Moyers (Feb. 7, 2014), https://billmoyers.com/2014/02/07/higher-profits-explain-why-there-are-more-people-of-color-in-private-prisons/.
② Christopher Petrella & Josh Begley, "The Color of Corporate Corrections: The Overrepresentation of People of Color in the For-Profit Corrections Industry", *Radical Criminology*, No. 2, 2013, pp. 139 – 147.
③ Curtis R. Blakely & Vic W. Bumphus, "Private and Public Sector Prisons-a Comparison of Select Characteristics", *Federal Probation*, Vol. 68, No. 1, 2004, pp. 27 – 31.
④ Charles L. Ryan, "FY 2010 Operating Per Capita Cost Report: Cost Identification and Comparison of State and Private Contract Beds", Arizona Department of Corrections, Bureau of Planning, Budget, and Research (2011), https://static.prisonpolicy.org/scans/0904prison.pdf.
⑤ The Sentencing Project, "Private Prisons in the United States", The Sentencing Project (Aug. 2, 2018), https://www.sentencingproject.org/publications/private-prisons-united-states/.

第六章　私营监狱公司滥用游说与竞选捐款：大规模监禁的腐败循环

年开始，国会又根据拨款法确定了非法移民拘留设施的配额，要求国土安全部拨款保障每天3.34万个非法移民拘留设施的床位，无论是否有足够的人被拘留；2013财年，该配额增加到3.4万个。[①] 而随着2010年奥巴马政府正式针对大规模监禁顽疾发起刑事司法改革以减少监狱人口以及部分州对保释制度的修正，私营监狱公司在联邦和各州的监狱以及地方拘留所的关押人数有所下降，私营监狱公司的利润受到冲击，开始将主要业务扩张至非法移民关押领域，其竞选捐款与游说的方向也随之转向支持对非法移民实施更严格驱逐政策的政客以及移民与边境保护局等行使关押非法移民权力机构的官员上。美国矫正公司还向超级政治行动委员会捐款，以倡导实施更严厉的刑事处罚，简化起诉程序，并取消对被指控犯下与暴力或帮派有关重罪的非法移民的保释。[②]

在此前的大选中，私营监狱公司已经比以往更加活跃。尽管GEO集团在强调对特朗普竞选活动的资助"完全出于促进公私伙伴关系，且完全不对任何具体的刑事司法、量刑或移民政策立场提出主张"。但其在联邦一级的捐款从2004年的13.9万美元一跃增加到2016年的120万美元。[③] GEO集团在2017年花费了170万美元用于游说，比2016年大幅增加了70%以上，[④] 其后向一个超级政治行动委员会捐赠了22.5万美元，花费2200万美元支持特朗普竞选，其子公司GEO矫正控股（GEO Correction Holdings Inc.）则向支持特朗普的另一超级政治行动委员会"即刻重建美国"（Rebuilding America Now）捐赠27.5万美元，[⑤] 其中10万美元是在司法部宣布削减私人监狱的次日作出的。尽管许多竞选财务专家指出其子公

[①] Kara Gotsch & Vinay Basti, "Capitalizing on Mass Incarceration: U.S Growth in Private Prisons", The Sentencing Project (Aug. 2, 2018), https://www.sentencingproject.org/publications/capitalizing-on-mass-incarceration-u-s-growth-in-private-prisons/.

[②] California's Legislative Analysts Office, "Proposition 6. Criminal Penalties and Laws. Public Safety Funding. Statute", California's Legislative Analysts Office (n. d.), http://www.lao.ca.gov/ballot/2008/6_11_2008.aspx.

[③] Livia Luan, "Profiting from Enforcement: The Role of Private Prisons in U.S. Immigration Detention", Migration Policy Institute (May 2, 2018), https://www.migrationpolicy.org/article/profiting-enforcement-role-private-prisons-us-immigration-detention.

[④] Livia Luan, "Profiting from Enforcement: The Role of Private Prisons in U.S. Immigration Detention", Migration Policy Institute (May 2, 2018), https://www.migrationpolicy.org/article/profiting-enforcement-role-private-prisons-us-immigration-detention.

[⑤] Amy Brittain & Drew Harwell, "Private-prison Giant, Resurgent in Trump Era, Gathers at President's Resort", *The Washington Post*, Oct. 25, 2017.

司违反竞选财务法律禁止联邦承包商进行政治捐款的规定，GEO辩称作出捐赠的子公司非合同法人且未与任何政府机构签订任何合同，因而可以作出捐款，而一向僵化的联邦选举委员会也未介入调查。而特朗普好友巴拉德（Brian Ballard）则与GEO集团签约成为其说客，并负责为特朗普的就职典礼筹款。特朗普当选当天，GEO与美国矫正公司股票分别大幅上扬18%和34%，[1]两家公司随后各自为特朗普的就职典礼捐赠了25万美元。[2]此次大选中，GEO和美国矫正公司向众议院拨款委员会中的众议员捐款最多，该委员会主要负责控制国土安全部拘留计划的预算。2017年2月，时任司法部长的塞申斯（Jeff Sessions）撤销了奥巴马政府逐步淘汰私人监狱的改革政令。此举被参议员伯尼·桑德斯认为是新政府对共和党竞选捐款者的奖励。同年初，特朗普总统签署了两项有利于私人监狱利益的行政命令，计划加强在美墨边境的执法，提高拘留率，迅速开展对移民的移送聆讯，并扩大拘留设施的容量。几个月后，GEO集团获得了1亿美元的合同，在得克萨斯州建立了一个新的拘留所，[3]而移民与海关执法局延长了与美国矫正公司在该州1000张床位的移民处理中心合同。[4]作为关键的执法边境州，GEO集团的大部分业务都在得州开展。获得GEO集团竞选捐款最多的三位众议员也都来自得州，分别是库伯森、奎勒和卡特。[5]这三位议员都是拨款委员会的成员，其中库伯森和奎勒同时是该委员会国土安全小组委员会的成员，该委员会决定着私营监狱产业的大部分业务。而总部位于田纳西州的美国矫正公司现金捐款的两大接收方是库伯森和田

---

[1] Hanna Kozlowska & Jason Karaian, "The First Big Winners of Donald Trump's Victory are Private Prison Companies, Whose Stocks are Soaring", Quartz（Nov. 9, 2016）, https://qz.com/832775/election-2016-private-prison-company-stocks-cca-and-geo-group-are-surging.

[2] Fredreka Schouten, "Private Prisons Back Trump and Could See Big Payoffs with New Policies", USA Today（Feb. 23, 2017）, https://www.usatoday.com/story/news/politics/2017/02/23/private-prisons-back-trump-and-could-see-big-payoffs-new-policies/98300394/.

[3] Geoff West & Alex Baumgart, "'Zero-tolerance' Immigration Policy is Big Money for Contractors, Nonprofits", Open Secrets（Jun. 21, 2018）, https://www.opensecrets.org/news/2018/06/zero-tolerance-immigration-is-big-money-for-contractors-nonprofits/.

[4] Livia Luan, "Profiting from Enforcement: The Role of Private Prisons in U. S. Immigration Detention", Migration Policy Institute（May 2, 2018）, https://www.migrationpolicy.org/article/profiting-enforcement-role-private-prisons-us-immigration-detention.

[5] Michael Sozan, "Solutions to Fight Private Prisons' Power Over Immigration Detention", Center for American Progress（Jul. 16, 2016）, https://www.americanprogress.org/issues/democracy/reports/2018/07/16/453309/solutions-fight-private-prisons-power-immigration-detention/.

第六章　私营监狱公司滥用游说与竞选捐款：大规模监禁的腐败循环

纳西州众议员弗莱希曼（Chuck Fleischmann），后者也是国土安全小组委员会的一员。①

如前所述，私营监狱公司的盈利高度依赖特朗普政府实施的惩罚性移民政策，因而2024年的总统大选对私营监狱业的利益也至关重要。民主党主张不再允许联邦与私人监狱签订合同，与特朗普主张的"零容忍"政策相比，民主党倾向于对非法移民采取更为宽松的政策。因而若该党继续执政，私营监狱前景堪忧。自选举以来，该行业进一步提高了参与政治活动的频率，力求促进对联邦犯人的遣返和对移民与海关执法局拘留设施的替代办法等议题。此前，GEO集团和美国矫正公司都在2018年的选举周期中为众议院和参议院候选人做出了大量捐款。这些努力的成果是显著的，GEO集团和移民与海关执法局签约设立了11个移民拘留所，并在得克萨斯州的卡恩斯市设有一处家庭中心②；美国矫正公司则依合同开设了8所移民拘留中心，其中包括得州迪勒的家庭中心，此类中心花费高昂，因而为公司带来了大部分收入。③ 2016—2017年，美国矫正公司实现了935%的联邦合同增长；④ 2017财年，美国矫正公司与GEO集团分别从移民与海关执法局的合同中获得了1.35亿和1.84亿美元。⑤ 私营监狱公司和移民与海关执法局签订的合同通常也包含与监狱床位使用率规定类似的"固定价格"条款，这意味着无论是否使用拘留场所，公司都将依照合同

---

① Michael Sozan, *Solutions to Fight Private Prisons' Power Over Immigration Detention*. Center for American Progress (Jul. 16, 2016), https://www.americanprogress.org/issues/democracy/reports/2018/07/16/453309/solutions-fight-private-prisons-power-immigration-detention/.

② 家庭中心是专门用于关押非法移民妇女及其未成年子女的拘留场所。这种拘留所设施较完备，居住条件好，内设教育和技能培训课程，能够依法探视，并为拘留者提供医疗、宗教和法律等服务。

③ Rob Urban & Bill Allison, "Prison Operators Could Cash in on Trump's 'Zero Tolerance' Immigration Policy", Bloomberg (Jun. 28, 2018), https://www.bloomberg.com/news/articles/2018-06-28/prison-operators-gain-as-u-s-immigration-detentions-surge; Sharita Gruberg & Tom Jawetz, "How the U.S. Department of Homeland Security Can End Its Reliance on Private Prisons", Center for American Progress (Sep. 14, 2016), https://www.americanprogress.org/issues/immigration/news/2016/09/14/144160/how-the-u-s-department-of-homeland-security-can-end-its-reliance-on-private-prisons/.

④ Alex Baumgart, "Companies that Funded Trump's Inauguration Came up Big in 2017", Open Secrets (Jan. 19, 2018), https://www.opensecrets.org/news/2018/01/companies-that-funded-trumps-inauguration/.

⑤ Freedom for Immigrants, "Detention by the Numbers", Freedom for Immigrants (n.d.), https://www.freedomforimmigrants.org/detention-statistics/.

中的床位数量获得收入。① 因而无论实际需要如何，政府政策都是鼓励过剩的拘押设施的，私营监狱的高利润正是从此处获得。2019年7月，美国移民海关总署共计抓捕了5.3万名非法移民，仅路易斯安那州每天就有1000人入狱。② 这些非法移民中的75%最后会被拘留在私营拘留所，每年花费超过35亿美元。③ 移民与海关总署、法警局（United States Marshals Service）和联邦监狱局三个联邦执法和拘留机构带来的业务利润，已经占到美国矫正公司和GEO集团2017—2018年总收入的48%，在2019年则

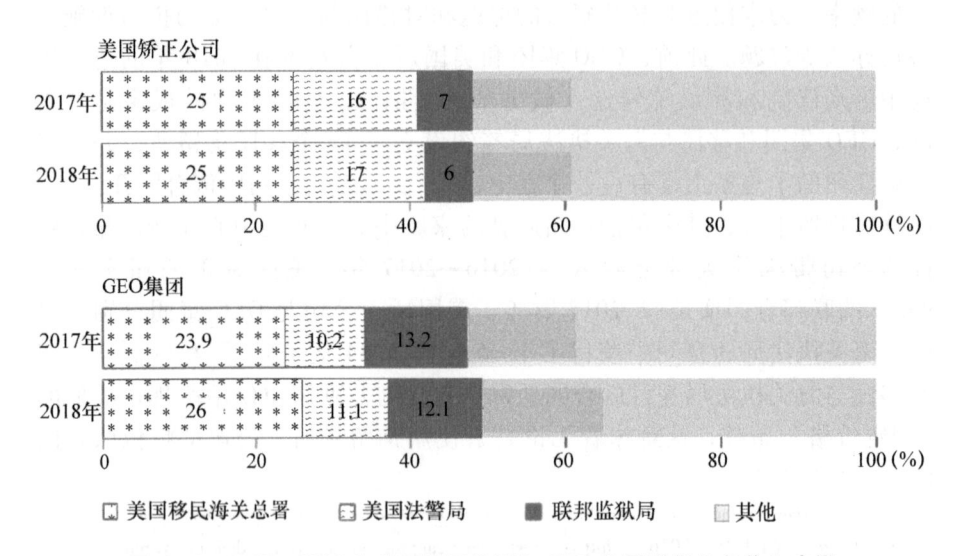

图6-3 2017—2018年美国矫正公司与GEO集团联邦业务收入来源

资料来源：美国矫正公司与GEO集团向美国证券交易委员会提交的年度财报。参见 https://sec.report/CIK/0001070985；https://fintel.io/sfs/us/geo；Hauwa Ahmed, "How Private Prisons Are Profiting under the Trump Administration", American Progress (Aug. 9, 2019), https://cdn.americanprogress.org/content/uploads/2019/08/29100331/DrivingPrivatePrisons-Brief.pdf.

---

① Chico Harlan, "Inside the Administration's $1 Billion Deal to Detain Central American Asylum Seekers", *The Washington Post*, Aug. 14, 2016.
② 由检：《年赚300亿：特朗普背后的大金主，在美国监狱做成了一份大生意》，新浪网，http://k.sina.com.cn/article_6065395581_16986977d01900i8tg.html，2019年9月3日。
③ Monsy Alvarado & others, "'These People are Profitable'：Under Trump, Private Prisons are Cashing in on ICE Detainees", USA Today (Dec. 21, 2019), https://www.usatoday.com/in-depth/news/nation/2019/12/19/ice-detention-private-prisons-expands-under-trump-administration/4393366002/.

超过50%（见图6-3）。每年纳税人缴纳的税款中至少有3.7亿美元流入私营监狱营收。[1]

当然，除了上述法定要求披露的竞选捐款，私营监狱公司也完全有可能通过暗钱组织进行与竞选活动有关的额外支出。但在现行法律下，竞选活动相关的支出仍未能得到充分公开，联邦选举委员会时常处于消极怠工的状态，而掌握更详细信息的国税局也并不会主动与前者配合，进行竞选财务调查，因此很难确定未披露部分竞选资金的流向。

第三节　私营监狱公司游说活动侧面影响监禁政策

迄今公司、团体组织游说活动在美国政治中所发挥的影响已得到充分证明。为确保监禁政策与政府合同中的巨大盈利，刑事法律必须得到严格执行，政府需要有续签合同的意愿，并且法律应能够在系统上源源不断地制造新囚犯，这都与游说息息相关。多年来，在上述动机的驱使下，私营监狱围绕着强硬对待犯罪和保持大规模监禁的主题积极进行游说。与私营监狱承包商和供应商从政府合同中赚取的数十亿美元相比，数百万的游说花费无疑是九牛一毛。与其他行业类似，私营监狱公司也雇佣游说公司和游说者，以维护其在国会和州议会中的商业利益。当今的游说者在与政府打交道时，通常有三点前提：一是用于竞选捐款的资金；二是用于接触决策者的裙带关系（cronyism）；三是对新闻媒体保密以避免公众抗议。尽管私营监狱公司多次强调自身并不参与任何量刑政策和法律的建议，但相对于公立监狱，私营监狱公司是通过关押囚犯获利的，它们有充分的动机主动与控制监狱政策和拨款的政客接触，开展的游说工作也着重于影响监禁和执法的相关法案，如近年来广泛涉及的毒品与移民犯罪等问题。这些游说工作已通过促进严格的移民法律、鼓励监禁非暴力吸毒者，以及阻止对

---

[1] Michael Cohen, "How For-profit Prisons Have Become the Biggest Lobby No One is Talking about", *The Washington Post*, Apr. 28, 2015; Equal Justice Initiative, "Mass Incarceration Costs $182 Billion Every Year, Without Adding Much to Public Safety", EJI (Feb. 6, 2017), https：//eji.org/news/mass-incarceration-costs-182-billion-annually.

私营监狱进行监督等对其不利的法案等手段，扩大了私营监狱的使用范围，成功增加了私营监狱人口。美国矫正公司甚至在文件中表示，维持毒品战争对于其业务的成功至关重要："毒品和管制药物或非法移民政策的任何变化都可能会影响逮捕、定罪和判刑的人数，从而有可能减少对收容他们的矫正设施的需求。"① 但在其所有的联邦游说报告中，均声明其不就赞成或反对决定一个人是否被监禁的政策进行游说。②

相比对政治候选人的捐款必须通过其下属员工和政治行动委员会协调作出并受到法定捐赠限制的严格约束，对于游说者的资助则没有受到任何限制。2010—2020 年，私营监狱公司在游说上的花费逾 4000 万美元。③ 2003 年以来，美国矫正公司在联邦一级的游说费用每年都在 90 万美元以上。④ 同时由于私营监狱公司目前的主要客户是州政府，对州议员的游说也未被忽略（见图 6-4）。仅在佛罗里达州美国矫正公司和 GEO 就雇佣了 30 名游说者，用以促进私营监狱的合同和政策，⑤ 协助私营监狱在刑事司法体系内的进一步扩张。然而，规制州一级别的游说活动在现实中较有挑战性，因为私人监狱公司的游说者经常与政客闭门会面，他们对谈话内容没有向公众公开的义务，此外，各州对游说者的报告义务要求也有所不同：一些州要求游说者披露游说合同的金额，可以是确切数字或特定范围；一些州仅要求游说者确定有形支出，如餐食和礼物；另一些州并不要求游说者报告其受委托游说的法案；还有一部分州不但要求提供合同金额，还要求游说者标明其活动是支持或反对某项立法。⑥ 加州的游说披露

---

① Michael Cohen, "How For-profit Prisons Have Become the Biggest Lobby No One is Talking about", *The Washington Post*, Apr. 28, 2015.
② Kendall Bentsen, "Money, Not Morals, Drives Marijuana Prohibition Movement", Open Secrets (Aug. 5, 2014), https://www.opensecrets.org/news/2014/08/money-not-morals-drives-marijuana-prohibition-movement/.
③ Open Secrets, "For-profit Prison Summary", Open Secrets (Feb. 2, 2024), https://www.opensecrets.org/industries/indus? ind = G7000.
④ Center for Responsive Politics, "Lobbying Corrections Corp of America-Summary 2010", Open Secrets (Jun., 2011), www.opensecrets.org/lobby/clientsum.php? lname = Corrections + Corp + of + America&year = 2010.
⑤ Matthew Clarke, "Study Shows Private Prison Companies Use Influence to Increase Incarceration", Prison Legal News (Aug. 22, 2016), https://www.prisonlegalnews.org/news/2016/aug/22/study-shows-private-prison-companies-use-influence-increase-incarceration/.
⑥ 关于各州对游说披露法的规定，参见 The National Conference of State Legislatures 网站, http://www.ncsl.org/default.aspx? TabID = 746&tabs = 1116, 84, 211#211.

第六章 私营监狱公司滥用游说与竞选捐款：大规模监禁的腐败循环

较为完整，以美国矫正公司在该州的游说活动为例，2001—2011 年该公司每年在对州长办公室、立法机关、惩教局、立法分析师办公室（Legislative Analyst's Office）、财务局、计划与研究办公室、青年和成人惩教署以及总务局（Department of General Services）的游说上平均花费超过 15 万美元。[①] 游说的事项包括预算、监狱建设、少年监狱设施、州外监狱计划、对法官量刑自由裁量权的限制、在将犯人转移至外州关押时是否取得犯人同意，以及对私营监狱的彻底废除。[②] 加利福尼亚州虽然只是个例，但它为私营监狱公司在州一级的游说情况提供了一定的背景信息。

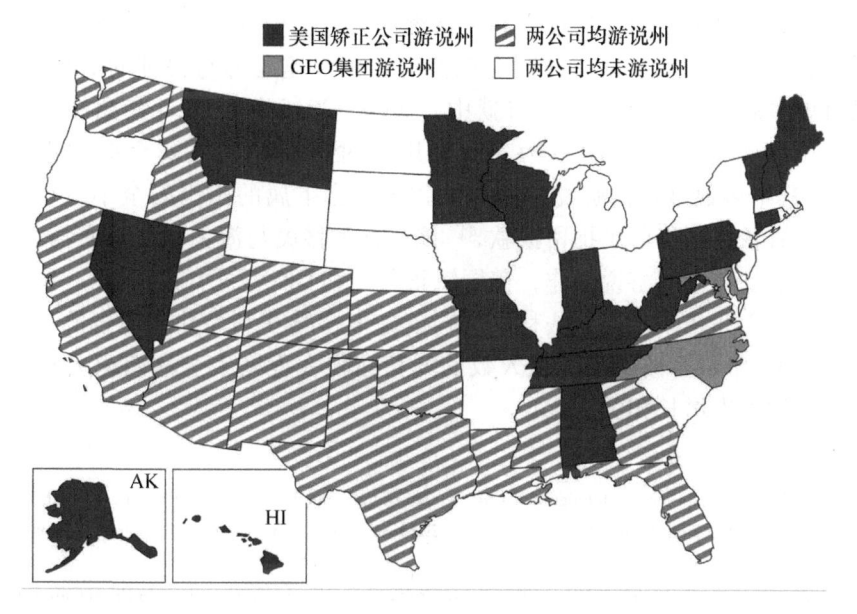

图 6-4　2003—2011 年美国两大监狱公司各州游说分布

资料来源：ACLU, "Banking on Bondage, Private Prisons and Mass Incarceration", ACLU (Nov., 2011), https://www.aclu.org/banking-bondage-private-prisons-and-mass-incarceration.

[①] Cody Mason, "Too Good to be True: Private Prisons in America", The Sentencing Project (Jan., 2012), https://sentencingproject.org/wp-content/uploads/2016/01/Too-Good-to-be-True-Private-Prisons-in-America.pdf.

[②] California Secretary of State's Cal-Access Search, "Core Civic Lobbying Activity", California Secretary of Dr. Shirley N. Weber (2019), http://cal-access.sos.ca.gov/Lobbying/Employers/Detail.aspx?id=1145409&view=activity&session=2019.

· 227 ·

一 阻击移民改革与管制私营监狱法案

奥巴马政府时期,包括拘留在内的移民执法花费高达 180 亿美元,超过了联邦调查局、禁毒署和烟酒枪炮及爆裂物管理局等所有其他联邦执法机构的总和,移民拘留所按照每人每天 166 美元向政府收费,[1] 超过 75%的拘留设施由私人监狱公司运营。[2] 这些公司倾向于将尽可能多的非法移民置于其控制之下,因而联邦拘留的立法变化会直接影响其盈利。为了确保有效的政策目标实现,私营监狱公司需要与政客保持牢固的关系,它们主要的游说目标是国会的预算和拨款委员会,受雇的游说者们利用大量竞选捐款的杠杆作用,试图使国会保持对移民快速起诉与关押的简化程序,以将更多的囚犯关押在私人监狱中。2006—2015 年,GEO 集团和美国矫正公司共计花费超过 1000 万美元,用于对国会的国土安全拨款进行游说。[3] 其中多数是直接游说众议院拨款委员会下属的国土安全小组委员会成员,后者负责为移民拘留拨款,[4] 该拨款和移民与海关执法局密切相关。通过复杂且昂贵的游说工作,美国矫正公司和 GEO 集团成功获得了国会的更多拨款,并在严格的非法移民惩罚措施中持续获利。并非巧合的是,在过去的 12 年中,被拘留移民人数的增长在很大程度上与这两家公司对国会的游说支出增长相关。[5]

---

[1] Doris Meissner & others, "Immigration Enforcement in the United States: The Rise of a Formidable Machinery", Migration Policy Institute (Jan., 2013), https://www.migrationpolicy.org/pubs/enforcementpillars.pdf.

[2] Monsy Alvarado & others, " 'These People are Profitable': Under Trump, Private Prisons are Cashing in on ICE Detainees", USA Today (Dec. 21, 2019), https://www.usatoday.com/in-depth/news/nation/2019/12/19/ice-detention-private-prisons-expands-under-trump-administration/4393366002/.

[3] Sharita Gruberg, "How For-Profit Companies Are Driving Immigration Detention Policies", Center for American Progress (Dec. 18, 2015), https://www.americanprogress.org/issues/immigration/reports/2015/12/18/127769/how-for-profit-companies-are-driving-immigration-detention-policies/.

[4] Livia Luan, "Profiting from Enforcement: The Role of Private Prisons in U.S. Immigration Detention", Migration Policy Institute (May 2, 2018), https://www.migrationpolicy.org/article/profiting-enforcement-role-private-prisons-us-immigration-detention.

[5] Sharita Gruberg & Tom Jawetz, "How the U.S. Department of Homeland Security Can End Its Reliance on Private Prisons", Center for American Progress (Sep. 14, 2016), https://www.americanprogress.org/issues/immigration/news/2016/09/14/144160/how-the-u-s-department-of-homeland-security-can-end-its-reliance-on-private-prisons/.

第六章　私营监狱公司滥用游说与竞选捐款：大规模监禁的腐败循环

　　另一个例子是美国矫正公司和 GEO 集团对 2013 年"全面移民改革"（Comprehensive Immigration Reform）的游说活动。2013 年 1 月，由马可·卢比奥和查尔斯·舒默牵头两党参议员组成的"八人帮"（gang of eight）①提出了该法案，旨在为 1100 万非法移民和临时工人开辟争取公民身份途径的同时，加强边境管控。在此立法过程中，拨款委员会、司法委员会、参议院财政委员会和众议院筹款委员会（Ways and Means Committee）发挥着关键作用。其中司法委员会负责具体定义合法与不合法，区分民事和刑事侵权。首先，全面移民改革的相关法案必须在该委员会获得通过，才有可能最终进入参议院和众议院进行全体最终投票。其次，参议院财政委员会以及众议院筹款委员会负责为实施这项改革筹集资金。最后，由拨款委员会投票决定哪些机构从各种执行费用中获得多少拨款，例如监狱、狱警、法官、律师，负责处理移民合法化案件的人员、文书、转运囚犯和公共关系等部门。依循上述决策机构的脉络，两家公司在 2012—2013 年度共花费了 295 万美元游说国会，以利用自己的金钱和影响力确保即使移民改革通过，私营拘留所关押的移民也不会减少。美国矫正公司的游说策略着眼于影响两院的领导机构，同时为上述参众两院委员会的议员提供大量竞选资金；GEO 集团则致力于游说和资助关键边境州的众议员和参议员，尤其是提出该法案的参议院"八人帮"。其雇佣的游说者和公司主要投资人向起草改革方案的"八人帮"捐款超过 40 万美元，其中一半以上流向了同为司法委员会成员和移民与边境执法小组委员会主席的舒默和卢比奥。② 舒默还从美国矫正公司的机构投资者拉扎德资产管理公司（Lazard Asset Management）处获得了 8 万余美元的捐款，在移民改革法案通过参议院投票后，拉扎德购买了超过 200 万股美国矫正公司股票。③ 尽管 GEO 已承诺不参与相关的监禁改革辩论，但其花费 12 万美元聘请了全球领航

---

① "八人帮"是美国国会八名成员组成的别称，包括 4 名共和党议员和 4 名民主党议员。情报"八人帮"由 4 名众议员和 4 名参议员组成，包括众议院议长、参众两院多数党和少数党领袖等；移民"八人帮"由 8 名参议员组成，截至 2023 年还有 6 人在任。

② Laura Carlsen, "With Immigration Reform Looming, Private Prisons Lobby to Keep Migrants behind Bars", *The Huffington Post*, Mar. 5, 2013.

③ Open Secrets, "Sen. Charles E. Schumer-New York: Contributors 2007-2012", Open Secrets (n. d.), https://www.opensecrets.org/members-of-congress/contributors?type=C&cid=N00001093&newMem=N&cycle=2012; SEC, "Form 13F-HR Lazard Asset Management Llc", SEC (Aug. 13, 2013), https://sec.report/Document/0001207017-13-000157/.

· 229 ·

(Navigators Global)公司，在2013年第一季度就移民全面改革有关的问题向国会进行游说，而该游说公司是由卢比奥的参谋长孔达创立的。[1] 作为游说者，孔达不仅将竞选活动的现金捐赠给政客，还经常为这些控制政策议程的国会领导人筹款。这类与竞选捐款资金进行捆绑的游说在私营监狱行业是一种相当普遍的操作。美国矫正公司的主要游说者之一、前众议院多数党领袖戈帕德（Richard Gephardt）也为民主党国会竞选委员会捆绑了竞选资金。[2] 在强大竞选资金的背书下，私营监狱公司对非法移民改革的游说效果可以说十分成功：改革法案被众议院搁置，而卢比奥则继续支持扩张"精简行动"（Operation Streamline），即对因非法越境被抓捕的移民，在一天内分配律师出庭，并由联邦刑事法院完成定罪和审判；卢比奥还在拟议的2014年预算中为联邦法警局增加了21亿美元预算，后者的职责包括逮捕和运输移民，其中大部分人将被运送到私营监狱中。GEO集团首席执行官佐雷（George Zoley）在与投资者举行的季度电话会议中表示，GEO集团已从华盛顿得到保证，联邦政府合同带来的预期收入增长不会受到全面移民改革法案的威胁。[3] 2019财年，移民与海关执法局共拘留了近50万人，每天被拘留者超过5万人，相比2016年的3.4万人大幅增加。[4]

可以发现，由于联邦政府对政治资金的约束有限，这种捐款与游说相互配合的运作已经形成了一种私营监狱的自我保护与利益扩张模式，并且不断被有利于其营利的立法结果印证。以2010年私营监狱行业游说推动或阻挠的法案及其结果为例（见表6-1），该行业对主张私营监狱信息公开（法案编号H.R.2450）、收缩地方政府资金规模的法案（法案编号S.

---

[1] Lee Fang, "Disclosure Shows Private Prison Company Misled on Immigration Lobbying", The Nation (Jun. 4, 2013), https://www.thenation.com/article/archive/disclosure-shows-private-prison-company-misled-immigration-lobbying/.

[2] FEC, "Schedule A: Reportable Bundled Contributions Forwarded by or Credited to Lobbyist/Registrants and Lobbyist/Registrant PACs", FEC (n. d.), https://docquery.fec.gov/cgi-bin/forms/C00000935/1224496/sa/3L.

[3] The GEO Group, "The GEO Group, Inc. Q4 2012 Earnings Conference Call Transcript", GEO (Feb. 21, 2013), http://conferencecalltranscripts.org/include?location=http://www.alacrastore.com/research/thomson-streetevents-Q4_2012_The_GEO_Grerence_Call-T5015529.

[4] Department of Homeland Security, "U.S. Immigration and Customs Enforcement Budget Overview", Department of Homeland Security (n. d.), https://www.dhs.gov/sites/default/files/publications/19_0318_MGMT_CBJ-Immigration-Customs-Enforcement_0.pdf.

251）持当然的反对态度，这些法案也都在众议院遭到了否决。例如，将私营监狱设施的运作状况纳入《信息自由法》的提案，无疑有利于刑事司法系统在矫正执行阶段的公开公正，但会促使私营监狱改善硬件设施、增加狱警数量并改善犯人人权状况，无疑增加了私营监狱公司的运营成本。该法案最终甚至未能通过众议院相关委员会的最初投票程序，与私营监狱公司对相关委员会成员进行捐款和游说的活动不无关系。又如，尽管美国矫正公司自2010年以来就没有直接游说过国土安全部，但它每年都在国会就国土安全年度拨款法案进行游说，以表达其对联邦监狱局、联邦拘留受托人办公室（Office of the Federal Detention Trustee）和移民与海关执法局等机构的拨款支持。而国土安全部负责监督全国大约200个移民拘留中心，包括由联邦、州和地方政府运营的设施以及由营利性私人监狱运营的设施。迄今这种游说活动仍十分活跃且有效，对私营监狱行业不利的法案均受到了持续阻挠。参议员伯尼·桑德斯于2015年提出了《司法不得出售法案》（Justice Is Not for Sale Act），主张禁止私营监狱，被众议院监督管理问责小组委员会否决，他于2021年2月再次在众议院提出，但仍无下文；2015年修改后卷土重来的《私营监狱信息法案》，也未能通过小组委员会审议，他于2019年底再次提请众议院犯罪、恐怖主义与国土安全小组委员会审议，也未能通过。[①]在党派分歧之外，这些法案在国会所遭遇的重重阻力，无疑展示了私营监狱行业的巨大资金杠杆和强大的政治影响力。

表6-1　　　　　　　　2010年美国监狱行业公司游说法案[②]

法案编号	法案名称	法案描述	具体游说事项	结果
H. R. 2450	《2009年私营监狱信息法案》	要求在非联邦监狱或矫正设施中关押有联邦囚犯的每个非政府实体、州或地方政府实体都必须遵守《信息自由法》的规定，发布有关非联邦监狱或矫正设施的运作信息	反对所有条款	众议院犯罪、恐怖主义与国土安全小组委员会否决

[①] 详见美国国会网站 https://www.congress.gov 立法查询。
[②] Center for Responsive Politics, "Lobbying Corrections Corp of America-Bills 2010", Open Secrets (Feb., 2011), http://www.opensecrets.org/lobby/clientbills.php?id=D000021940&year=2010; Govtrack, "Federal Legislation", Govtrack (May, 2011), Govtrack. www.govtrack.us/congress/legislation.xpd.

续表

法案编号	法案名称	法案描述	具体游说事项	结果
S. 251	《2009年安全监狱通讯法案》	禁止向州和地方政府提供联邦资金以支付债务，禁止美联储理事会向州和地方政府提供财政援助	反对所有条款	众议院犯罪、恐怖主义与国土安全小组委员会否决
S. 3607	《2011年国土安全部专项拨款法案》	国土安全部截至2011年9月30日的财年拨款	2011财年与移民和海关执法局相关的准备金和资金及拘留有关规定；2012财年预算与联邦拘留受托人办公室和海关执法局相关的拨款和资金	在司法部预算减少17%的情况下，2011财年联邦拘留受托人办公室的预算增加5.3%
S. 3636	《2011年商务、司法、科学及相关机构拨款法案》	截至2011年9月30日的财年，商务和司法部、科学和相关机构的拨款	2011财年与监狱局和联邦拘留所有关的拨款和资金；有关私人监狱的规定	在司法部预算减少17%的情况下，2011年监狱局的预算增加3.4%
H. R. 3082	《2010年军事工程和退伍军人事务及相关机构专项拨款法案》	截至2010年9月30日的财年中，为军事建设、退伍军人事务部及相关机构拨款，并用于其他目的	2011财年与监狱局有关的拨款和资金；2011财年、2012财年的预算和与联邦拘留受托人办公室、移民与海关执法局有关经费	2010年12月获两院通过，公法编号：111-332

二 利用人脉关系搭建旋转门

在竞选捐款与游说活动之外，与可能影响政府抉择的政府官员、国会议员建立关系网络也必不可少，这一点对于私营监狱公司来说尤为重要，因为其利润几乎完全取决于公共政策和政府资金。从这个角度来看，与政府官员之间搭建的广泛关系已经是私营监狱行业发展不可或缺的部分。促成有权决策者对资源进行腐败分配的关键媒介，往往以非独立官僚机构的

第六章　私营监狱公司滥用游说与竞选捐款：大规模监禁的腐败循环

形式出现，后者被视为政府与利益集团的中间人。① 中间媒介的通常形态是咨询公司，由竞选捐款方所代表的利益集团或被捐款人间接控制。建立关系的常规模式是政府官员通过设立私人咨询公司或担任利益相关行业公司的咨询顾问，以事前或事后收取可观报酬为交换条件建立联系。私营监狱公司依靠其与政府官员的关系受益，正是通过上述模式雇佣州和联邦政府的前官员。以 GEO 集团与奥巴马政府时期法警局长海顿（Stacia Hylton）的密切关系为例。作为 GEO 集团营收的重要组成部分，海顿麾下的法警局与 GEO 集团签订的合同占后者年收入的 19%。② 2010 年，海顿成立了一家名为"海顿柯克与合伙人"（Hylton Kirk and Associates）的私人监狱咨询公司。海顿从司法部退休后，其与 GEO 集团签订了一份价值高达 11 万美元的咨询合同。③ 另一个例子是佛州前参议员乔·内格隆（Joe Negron），在帮助 GEO 获得了 690 万美元的合同后，其在 2018 年直接放弃了连任竞选，转而投向年薪 40 万美元的 GEO 集团，担任总顾问职位。④

反过来，私营监狱公司利用资金支持前雇员成为政府官员，以更持久的合同关系或其他利益输送"反哺"公司，则是一种逆向的关系建立。这种先建立人际关系、再将与之相连的人脉送入政府体制中的运作方式，能使私营监狱公司占据主动权，甚至将对自身有利的主张纳入起草的新法律或政策中也成为可能。2010 年，时任新墨西哥州监狱局长的乔·威廉姆斯（Joe Williams）因拒绝对违反合同的 GEO 和美国矫正公司进行罚款，而受到该州参议员的强烈批评。新墨西哥州立法财务委员会发现，如果威廉姆斯执行该合

---

① Taylor C. Boas, F. Daniel Hidalgo & Neal P. Richardson, "The Spoils of Victory: Campaign Donations and Government Contracts in Brazil", *Journal of Politics*, Vol. 76, No. 2, 2014, pp. 415 – 429; Rasmus Broms & others, *Political Competition and Public Procurement Quality*, Gothenburg: QoG Working Paper Series No. 2017; Nicholas Charron & others, "Careers, Connections, and Corruption Risks: Investigating the Impact of Bureaucratic Meritocracy on Public Procurement Processes", *Journal of Politics*, Vol. 79, No. 1, 2017, pp. 89 – 103.
② The GEO Group, "2010 Annual Report", GEO (2011), https://www.annualreports.com/HostedData/AnnualReportArchive/t/NYSE_ GEO_ 2010.pdf.
③ Jim McElhatton, "Marshalls Service Nominee Answers Critics Conflict-of-Interest Charge", *The Washington Times*, Nov. 17, 2010.
④ Matt Dixon, "Negron making $400K Annually as General Counsel for GEO Group", *Politico*, Mar. 15, 2019.

同的违约条款，两家公司将可能面临1800万美元的罚款。① 在担任监狱局长之前，威廉姆斯曾在GEO旗下的一所监狱中担任典狱长。类似的联系还有亚利桑那州长简·布鲁尔（Jan Brewer）曾雇佣两名高级顾问，这两名顾问此前都为私营监狱公司所雇佣的说客。对于私营监狱公司而言，其在私人和公共领域之间的紧密联系，反过来也为对监禁政策有决定影响力者提供了权力寻租的机会。无论私营监狱公司如何以自身不参与刑事政策的辩论为由进行抗辩，其通过竞选捐款、游说以及与决策者建立旋转门式的广泛联系，不道德地扩大其业务规模和范围都已是不争的事实。

三 借助非政府组织网络起草示范性法案

组织网络对所有企业都极为重要，通过企业联合会，私营监狱行业也可以达到参与制定新政策乃至影响立法的目的。美国立法交流委员会（American Legislative Exchange Council，简称ALEC）是一家总部位于华盛顿特区的公共政策非营利组织，其由各州议员、企业和政府机构组成，常常为州议员示范性地草拟法案。但其提供的不仅是示范性法案，还为行业与政客编织人脉网络。通过每年以成员身份支付7000—25000美元的会费，② 或赞助立法交流委员会会议和宴席的形式，私营监狱企业或行业组织团体及其说客得以在理事会会议上与各州议员交流并建立联系，以向委员会提出对其有利的草案建议。如果再交5000美元加入委员会的特别行动组，利益集团或其说客就可以秘密起草示范性法案并就草案与议员进行不公开讨论。③ 示范性法案在美国立法程序中是普遍存在的。在协助制定强制性立法（fill-in-the-blank legislation）的团体中，影响力最大的是州政府委员会（Council of State Governments），作为无党派的非营利团体，其为州政府、法院和行政机关提供政策研究和指导。分析显示，由州政府委员会起

---

① State of New Mexico Legislative Finance Committee, "Review of Private Prison Contracts Penalty Assessment", State of New Mexico Legislative Finance Committee (2010), http：//www. privateci. org/private_ pics/NMDOCstaffing. pdf.
② Cody Mason, "Too Good to be True: Private Prisons in America", The Sentencing Project (Jan., 2012), https：//sentencingproject. org/wp-content/uploads/2016/01/Too-Good-to-be-True-Private-Prisons-in-America. pdf.
③ Ted Park, "Dirty Money: ALEC's Monopoly on American Law", The Byline (Jun. 30, 2020), https：//medium. com/thebyline/dirty-money-alecs-monopoly-on-american-law-2627ede1f2c.

草的4300多项示范性法案此前在立法机构提案,其中950项已被作为法律颁布。① 而立法交流委员会的影响力仅次于州政府委员会。今日美国公共廉政中心进行的一项调查发现,2010—2018年,立法交流委员会起草了约1万份示范法案,其中2900份通过其会员在州议会或国会中提出,600份已经通过成为法律,在联邦和州立法机关通过的概率高达20%。② 立法交流委员会参与制定的许多法案都与特殊利益的改革愿望相符,其中当然也包括了降低公司税率和扩大监狱私有化等有利于监狱公司的主张。研究还表明,由立法交流委员会支持的提案成为法律的速度要比其他提案快得多,③ 因而公司及其说客在立法交流委员会的低廉会费投入无疑获得了快速且丰厚的回报:这不仅比协调候选人的竞选捐款和直接游说的花费要低得多,还可以产生更直接和长远的立法影响。

这种强大且快速的影响立法能力,让对于因犯多多益善的私营监狱公司,不可避免地参与到起草延长刑期或民事违法刑事化的示范性立法活动中。在20世纪八九十年代,立法交流委员会提出的法案极大地影响了后来颁布的三振出局法(three-strikes laws)与真实量刑法律(truth in sentencing laws),二者分别要求对累犯判处25年有期徒刑至终身监禁,并且部分罪犯服满判决刑期的85%才能依法假释。真实量刑法已在25个州签署为州法,截至2008年,约有35个州正在事实上实践该法律。④ 刑事法律改革带来的变化是长期且巨大的,1992—2016年,被判无期徒刑或50年以上"事实无期监禁"(virtual life)的人数从近7万人增加到约20.6万人。⑤ 近年来,

---

① Rob O'Dell & Nick Penzenstadler, "You Elected Them to Write New Laws. They're Letting Corporations Do It Instead", The Center for Public Integrity (Apr. 4, 2019), https://publicintegrity.org/politics/state-politics/copy-paste-legislate/you-elected-them-to-write-new-laws-theyre-letting-corporations-do-it-instead/.

② Yonne W. Sanchez & Rob O'Dell, "What is ALEC? 'The Most Effective Organization' for Conservatives, Says Newt Gingrich", USA Today (Apr. 5, 2019), https://www.usatoday.com/story/news/investigations/2019/04/03/alec-american-legislative-exchange-council-model-bills-republican-conservative-devos-gingrich/3162357002/.

③ Molly Jackman, "ALEC's Influence Over Lawmaking in State Legislatures", The Brookings Institute (2013), www.brookings.edu/articles/alecs-influence-over-lawmaking-in-state-legislatures/.

④ Wikipedia, "Truth in Sentencing", https://en.wikipedia.org/wiki/Truth_in_sentencing#United_States.

⑤ Ashley Nellis, "Still Life: America's Increasing Use of Life and Long-Term Sentences", The Sentencing Project (May 3, 2017), https://www.sentencingproject.org/publications/still-life-americas-increasing-use-life-long-term-sentences/.

立法交流委员会开始在私营监狱行业的协助下，开始起草非法移民刑事化方面的示范法律。令人毫不意外的是，这些法律都旨在增加在移民拘留所中的人数。如要求地方执法机构执行联邦移民法律并将雇佣非法移民定罪的《禁止非法移民庇护城市法案》[①]（No Sanctuary Cities for Illegal Immigrants Act），已在23个州的议会提案宣读。[②] 尽管现有研究无法量化私营监狱行业在上述入罪化法律中起到的作用程度，但几乎已可以肯定私营监狱公司通过利用其购买的影响力，促使立法者制定了更为严厉的刑事司法政策。[③]

通过上述民间游说团体起草示范立法以及公司的竞选捐款和游说努力，私营监狱公司促使政府官员制定出让更多人入狱的刑事政策，以维持高监禁人口带来的巨额利润。而其购买的政治影响力和相应回报达到顶峰时，也正值美国监禁率达到全世界的最高点。尽管没有直接证据表明私营监狱行业加重了大规模监禁的恶性循环，但也很难排除其游说和其他影响立法的活动中对后者产生的推进作用。私营监狱业内公司曾多次在股东报告中提到对改革毒品犯罪量刑法律与政策改革的担忧，因而难以避免通过竞选捐款、游说和参与具有立法影响力协会的活动，鼓励立法者将监禁作为治理对策。这种态度又与立法者的考虑不谋而合：立法者在寻求替代性刑罚以改革现有量刑法和处遇方式时，也不得不考虑监狱人口减少或社会犯罪率降低将迫使政府为监狱空床支付更多费用，进而给联邦和地方财政预算造成压力的情况。正如一位前堪萨斯矫正局长所说："我所担心的是我们州负有维持（私营矫正机构）床位率的义务，而这种压力将微妙地影响量刑法律，使之更为严厉以增加监狱人口。"[④] 因而扩大监禁，维持高监禁率仍是最简单的选择。而同时，私营监狱获得的政府合同不断增加，相比公立监狱却不能保证任何的成本节约，尤其在最低安全级别监狱方面，

---

① 庇护城市（sanctuary city）通常指不起诉非法移民的北美城市，如纽约、费城、芝加哥、洛杉矶和旧金山等。当地政府有权禁止警察询问移民的身份，并拒绝配合海关与边境执法局对非法移民的执法行动。

② Ted Park,"Dirty Money: ALEC's Monopoly on American Law", The Byline（Jun. 30, 2020）, https://medium.com/thebyline/dirty-money-alecs-monopoly-on-american-law-2627ede1f2c.

③ Justice Policy Institute,"Gaming the System: How the Political Strategies of Private Prison Companies Promost Ineffective Incarceration Policies", Justice Policy Institute（Jun., 2011）, http://www.justicepolicy.org/uploads/justicepolicy/documents/gaming_the_system.pdf.

④ Kevin Johnson,"Private Purchasing of Prisons Locks in Occupancy Rates", USA Today（Mar. 8, 2012）, http://blog.wolfslaw.com/articles/Private%20purchasing%20of%20prisons%20locks%20in%20occupancy%20rates%20USATODAY.com.pdf.

第六章　私营监狱公司滥用游说与竞选捐款：大规模监禁的腐败循环

前者总体比后者支出浪费约30%。①

从根本上，GEO集团和美国矫正公司等私营监狱公司之所以对决策者具有巨大的影响力，是由于当前的竞选财务和游说法律无形中制造了一种按需付费的许可制度，这种制度使政策制定偏向于公司利益，并且不能公平地代表选民的观点。但腐败带来的后果不止于此。2011年宾夕法尼亚州爆出的"孩子换现金"丑闻进一步揭示了私营监狱公司与公职人员之间金钱关系的极致。路泽恩县法院的两名法官在2003—2008年的5年间，通过不公正的审判程序将超过2000名青少年送入两所私营少年监狱，以获取后者给予的超过260万美元的回扣。② 这个极端的例子凸显了司法公正因受私营监狱的腐败影响所付出的巨大代价。尽管如此，在联合公民时代公司言论自由的加持下，私营监狱利益集团仍得以利用游说与竞选捐款堂而皇之地促使立法者与之配合，维持不公平的法律以及昂贵而无效的监狱机器，以保障其商业利益。立法者主导的刑事司法系统天平在政治资金面前发生了倾斜，公共安全和社区福祉的价值亦被遗忘。而不幸的是，在美国政治和公共政策中，私营监狱行业并非金钱与政治影响力交叉的唯一领域。2021年1月，时任总统拜登签署行政命令，要求改革监禁制度，取消私营刑事拘留设施的使用，司法部也将不再与私营监狱续签现有合同。当然，若2024年共和党赢得大选，新总统理论上可以通过签署新的行政命令来推翻或修改之前的行政命令。③

本章小结

齐泽克曾这样概括现代美国的民选制度："在权力的组织和合法化方

---

① Arizona Department of Corrections, "State versus Private Prison FY 2007 Cost Comparison", Arizona Department of Corrections (2009), www. azcorrections. gov/adc/reports/ADC_ FY2007_ cost_ comparison. pdf.
② Wikipedia, "Kids for Cash Scandal", https：//en. wikipedia. org/wiki/Kids_ for_ cash_ scandal.
③ 行政命令是美国总统直接管理联邦政府运作和指导政府政策的一种工具，可以在没有国会立法的情况下实施政策变更。历史上，新上任的总统通过签署新的行政命令来改变或取消前任总统的政策并不少见。这种做法是美国政治体系中行政权力更迭的一部分，反映了新政府的政策方向和优先级的变化。

面，选举制度越来越倾向于市场竞争的模式。"[1] 类似于商业交易，选民是购买方，竞选人即潜在的政府官员为相对的卖方，交易标的是公民对维护社会制度和追诉犯罪等需求。资本主义国家市场经济下，涉及国家权力与资源分配的竞选制度自然也融入市场，成为商品供求的一部分。也正因为如此，一些国家权力的专属领域也可以被私有化，私营监狱正是写照。在过去的40年中，受到严厉的定罪量刑法律和强硬打击毒品犯罪的刑事政策刺激，美国的监禁率激增。这不仅加剧了社会的种族冲突，其高昂的花费更使得各州陷入财政困境，而私营监狱在某种程度上被视为一种节约纳税人税款和缓解预算压力的应对措施。2020年美国监狱关押的230万人中，身处私营监狱和拘留设施的人数已超过1990年的20倍。[2] 关押每名犯人的平均费用也在不断上涨，监狱行业的利润变得前所未有地诱人。在市场逐利本质的引导下，私营监狱公司已经找到了从大规模监禁中获利的途径，如通过公私领域的人员流动在政府机构与私营监狱行业之间搭建"旋转门"：前任的州监狱部门工作人员去私营监狱行业谋求职位，而前私人监狱公司职员则进入监狱部门工作。广泛的游说和大量的有对性的竞选捐款也在实质上增加了私营监狱公司获得政府合同的机会，并且使其更有可能规避监管部门的充分监督。通过向监禁率最高州的候选人有针对性地捐赠大量资金并开展游说活动，以期其在选举中连任，私营监狱公司最终获得竞选支出数十倍标的额的联邦合同。而巨额合同鲜为人知的背面是，囚犯的安全和权利更有可能被侵犯，累犯率更高，地方政府不得不签订满足犯人入住率的强制性条款。加之近年来特朗普政府惩罚性的移民执法政策，政府对拘留设施的需求持续增加，使得私营监狱公司的利益越发紧密地与国家政治交织在一起。2019年，美国两大私人监狱公司从移民和海关执法局处拿到的合同总价值约为13亿美元，占每家公司收入的各一半，

---

[1] Slavoj Žižek, "Living in the Time of Monsters", in M. Nikolakaki, ed., *Critical Pedagogy in the New Dark Ages: Challenges and Possibilities*, New York: Peter Lang Inc., 2012, p. 34.

[2] ICMA, The Price of Private Prisons", ICMA (Nov. 22, 2011), https://icma.org/blog-posts/price-private-prisons? gclid = CjwKCAiAl4WABhAJEiwATUnEF5qbBrXXOA4v_ 2JlPu8eDSh9195rfpg2Dquo7aXlqVWq9HNFeunJwhoCLvkQAvD_ BwE; Prison Policy Initiative, "Mass Incarceration: The Whole Pie 2020", Prison Policy Initiative (Aug. 11, 2020), https://www.prisonpolicy.org/reports/pie2020.html.

第六章 私营监狱公司滥用游说与竞选捐款：大规模监禁的腐败循环

负责经营移民关押系统中约80%的床位。[①] 诚然，现有的刑事司法系统和不同党派的施政是大规模监禁的结构性诱因，但也不能否认私营监狱的游说、竞选捐款活动和旋转门现象对该现状的推动作用，这无疑为国家权力的行使蒙上了阴影。无论如何，特殊利益团体不应从国家执法中获利，它们在代替国家行使刑罚权的同时，可能使国家的公正性受到折损。

[①] Nomaan Merchant, "Private Prison Companies Shower Campaign Cash on Trump and Republicans", People's World (Aug. 14, 2020), https://www.peoplesworld.org/article/private-prison-companies-shower-campaign-cash-on-trump-and-republicans/.

第七章 美国游说与竞选捐款反腐败前瞻：系统透明与配套技术

"腐败的影响，本身就是所有政治混乱的常年之源，它使国家失去活力，使议会失去智慧，让宪法中最古老的权威和信誉蒙上阴影。"[1] 腐败在美国当今的政治制度中提出了一系列法律问题：如果对腐败的了解仅限于非法，那么应如何应对所谓的系统性腐败？在"联合公民案"判决使得金钱受到与言论同等的保护以及现有竞选法律持续扩大匿名大捐款者影响力的情况下，政府或政党是否还能够，或者愿意改变这种状况？现代民主国家的立法机关已经作出了种种努力，包括为竞选活动支出和捐款设置上限，禁止某些资金来源等措施以遏制选举程序与民选官员可能陷入的腐败风险。但是，这些措施并不总是能够减轻竞选资金可能产生的负面影响，法律难免存在漏洞，执法机构也可能因为种种原因而缺乏执行力。此时，市民社会与媒体的公共监督力量变得越发重要。

这种监督力量的发挥需要透明度的提升，即能够以及时、可理解和可访问的方式向公众提供全面可靠的竞选财务数据和政府信息。对于联邦来说，更高的透明度要求制定更细致的法律，并保证联邦选举委员会、国税局甚至证券交易委员会等联邦机构协调行政资源，切实执行法律，以监督政党和候选人、捐款者和竞选服务提供者等竞选活动主体，如实报告竞选财务明细。对于政党来说，透明度意味着政党在内部建立问责制，要求使用内部账目和会计系统，并让政党成员充分了解财务情况，无论是接受公共补贴还是私人捐款，都必须对收到的资金进行审计。公众的义务或责任则在于更主动地要求公开有关竞选财务的全部信息，如一些美国公民社会组织通过将私人竞选捐款的数据与有利于特定捐款者

---

[1] Edmund Burke, "Speeches on the Independence of Parliament", *The Spectator*, May 26, 1855, p. 531.

的政策和政府合同批准进行比对联系，已经在竞选财务监管改革中发挥了重要作用。反腐败技术的构想也被首次提出：运用区块链和人工智能构建透明的政治选举和政府资金审查系统，以确保选举信息准确性和政治决策的可监控性，同时通过互联网社交媒体扩大选民政治参与维度。尽管没有能够一举消除巨额资金对选举腐蚀作用的全能策略，但一系列可行的改革措施可以协同运作，提高选举资金的透明度，防止政治选举和政府腐败，同时促进更大范围上的选民政治参与。

第一节 "联合公民案"时代竞选反腐败挑战

一 加密货币竞选捐款难以监管

近年来，以比特币为代表的加密货币越发广泛地参与了政治竞选财务活动。比特币作为一种严格数字化的货币，没有实物形式，无须通过银行等第三方，以点对点即 P2P 方式进行交易。截至 2023 年底，约有 17% 的美国人持有一种或以上的加密货币，[1] 至少 1/3 的中小型企业接受加密货币作为支付方式。[2] 公共廉政中心 2018 年发布的一项调查发现，已有 20 位候选人在各个级别的公职竞选中募集或接受了加密货币形式的捐款，2014 年以来，8 名候选人至少收到了 55 万美元的加密货币捐款。[3] 2020 年大选中，民主党总统候选人杨安泽（Andrew Yang）和加州众议员埃里

---

[1] Martynas Pupkevicius, "Key Cryptocurrency Statistics & Facts for 2023 and Beyond", Moneyzine（Dec. 5, 2023）, https：//moneyzine. com/personal-finance-resources/cryptocurrency-statistics/.

[2] Ron Shevlin, "The Coronavirus Cryptocurrency Craze：Who's Behind The Bitcoin Buying Binge?" Forbes（Jul. 27, 2020）, https：//www. forbes. com/sites/ronshevlin/2020/07/27/the-coronavirus-cryptocurrency-craze-whos-behind-the-bitcoin-buying-binge/? sh = 1ed8b6412abf; HSB, "One-Third of Small Businesses Accept Cryptocurrency", Munichre（Jan. 15, 2020）, https：//www. munichre. com/hsb/en/press-and-publications/press-releases/2020/2020-01-15-one-third-of-small-businesses-accept-cryptocurrency. html.

[3] Kristian Hernández, "Is Bitcoin Secretly Messing with the Midterms?" Politico Magazine（Oct. 26, 2018）, https：//www. politico. com/magazine/story/2018/10/26/is-bitcoin-secretly-messing-with-the-midterms-221915/.

克·斯沃威尔（Eric Swalwell）等人都接受了比特币捐款。① 迈阿密市长苏亚雷斯（Francis Suarez）和得州参议员特德·克鲁兹也相继宣布在2024年的竞选连任活动中接受加密货币捐款。②

比特币带来的风险在于其本质上是为匿名而设计的，而对竞选财务改革来说最重要的却是披露。尽管比特币交易记录储存在名为区块链的公共数字总账中，但用户不使用真实姓名，而是使用比特币地址，即看似随机的数字和字母字符串进行身份识别，因而得以保持匿名状态。这使得比特币捐款不仅受到反对政府干预其匿名捐款者的欢迎，还被洗钱者、有组织犯罪集团和试图将资金秘密转入选举的外国势力广泛使用。为了解决竞选活动中的比特币捐款问题，联邦选举委员会在2014年发布了一份咨询意见，要求加密货币捐款必须以实物捐赠的形式报告，③ 但委员会没有单独设立对加密货币捐款的追踪条目，只是推荐而非强制候选人在其竞选财务报告中对收到的加密货币捐款进行备注。④

这种对加密货币捐款的宽松监管态度无法应对一系列问题。一方面，实物捐赠的价值一般不会改变，而比特币的交易值常常剧烈波动。联邦选举委员会要求按照捐赠当天的比特币价格计算捐款，限额为100美元，但其价格在随后的提交报告日又很可能超出个人捐款限额。另一方面，许多加密货币本身就不可追溯来源。一些如门罗币（Monero）的加密货币本身就是以匿名且无法追踪的方式出售的"隐私硬币"。截至2023年12月，已有超过9000余种加密货币在国际市场中流通。⑤ 因此，除非监管机构确定参选者可以接受或禁止接受加密货币的特定种类，否则很难保证政治资

---

① Christine Stapleton, "Are Bitcoin Campaign Contributions a Fad or the Future of Fundraising?" *The Palm Beach Post*, Sep.17, 2020.

② Kelly Garrity, "Got Bitcoin? Now You can Donate It to This GOP Presidential Candidate", *Politico*, Aug.04, 2023; Teuta Franjkovic, "Bitcoin in the U.S. Election Race: What Role Will Crypto Play in Deciding Next President?" CNN (Nov.7, 2023), https://www.ccn.com/news/bitcoin-us-election-crypto-next-president/#:~:text=,several%20lawmakers%20hailing%20its%20significance.

③ FEC, "AO 2014 - 02 (Bitcoin contributions and disbursements)", FEC (May 08, 2014), https://www.fec.gov/files/legal/aos/2014-02/2014-02.pdf.

④ FEC, "How to Report Bitcoin Contributions", FEC (n.d.), https://www.fec.gov/help-candidates-and-committees/filing-reports/bitcoin-contributions/.

⑤ Raynor de Best, "Number of Cryptocurrencies Worldwide from 2013 to December 2023", Statista (Dec.5, 2023), https://www.statista.com/statistics/863917/number-crypto-coins-tokens/. 其中多数加密货币并不被普遍使用，主要的加密货币如以太币（Ethereum）、莱特币（Litecoin）和比特币等约占据了90%的市值。

第七章　美国游说与竞选捐款反腐败前瞻：系统透明与配套技术

金的可追踪性。尽管只有在捐款者提供姓名、地址和雇主并确认其是美国公民后，候选人或竞选委员会才能接受加密货币捐款，但研究表明，加密货币用户完全可以使用假名实施跨国转账，因为无须经过中介机构或银行的验证。[1] 这意味着捐款者可能建立多个假名账户，每个账户都捐到个人捐款上限。而且，目前尚无措施阻止外国人使用 VPN 获取美国 IP 地址进行捐款；居住在美国的非公民也可以通过伪造身份信息，使用加密货币捐款。与竞选活动历来依赖的现金或支票不同，公众显然无法轻易查询到某些加密货币的来源，这与选举透明的目标背道而驰。2024 年大选周期正式开始前，一个主要致力于加密货币捐款的超级政治行动委员会 Fairshake 就已经投入了 120 多万美元，用于支持众议院候选人的电视广告。[2] 尽管目前来看，Fairshake 投入资金的数额并不大，但整个加密货币行业在 2024 年大选周期中发挥的作用值得关注。

当然，适用于联邦候选人的加密货币规则也并不一定适用于州竞选人。2018 年开始，至少有 8 个州和华盛顿特区已经立法允许进行加密货币捐款，并各自在选举手册中增加了有关加密货币捐款的说明或对其进行限制，另有 8 个州出于对外国干预选举的忧虑，或缺乏足够资源和技术来监管比特币捐款等原因，已完全禁止加密货币捐款。[3] 这种考虑的原因之一是，州和地方选举中相关数据的缺乏会使得逐渐增加的加密货币变得更难以追踪。此外，加密货币还在加速流向 501 暗钱组织。2017 年，通过比特币收支平台 BitPay 向 501（c）（3）组织等非营利客户的捐款增加了一倍以上，743 个捐款者共捐出了 2600 万美元，每个捐款者的平均捐款从 2017 年的约 4700 美元上升到 2018 年的 3.5 万美元，一年间激增到原本的 7 倍多。[4] 目

---

[1] Tom Robinson, D. Phil & Yaya Fanusie, "Bitcoin Laundering: An Analysis of Illicit Flows into Digital Currency Services", Center on Sanctions & Illicit Finance (Jan. 12, 2018), https://info.elliptic.co/whitepaper-fdd-bitcoin-laundering.

[2] Jasper Goodman & Zachary Warmbrodt, "The New Crypto Campaign", Politico, Nov. 20, 2023.

[3] Kristian Hernández, "How Cryptocurrency is Senaking into State Elections", The Center for Public Integrity (Nov. 2, 2018), https://publicintegrity.org/politics/state-politics/how-cryptocurrency-is-sneaking-into-state-elections/. 各州立法情况详见 Bradley Coffey, "Cryptocurrency in Campaign Finance: The Future is Here", Multistate (Mar. 9, 2022), https://www.multistate.us/insider/2022/3/9/cryptocurrency-in-campaign-finance-the-future-is-here.

[4] Kristian Hernández, "How Cryptocurrency is Senaking into State Elections", The Center for Public Integrity (Nov. 2, 2018), https://publicintegrity.org/politics/state-politics/how-cryptocurrency-is-sneaking-into-state-elections/.

前，联邦、多数州和地方都未要求加密货币捐款者和接受捐款的候选人披露其唯一的钱包账号地址，因而这类交易实际尚未实现可追溯。

二 公司竞选支出权利被无限扩大

公司的竞选支出权利在"联合公民案"以前就已经得到了确立。尽管在"联合公民案"之前，已有 22 个州禁止公司支出来支持或反对选举候选人，但法律禁止公司竞选活动并不意味着公司不能合法地出资支持或反对候选人。相反，此前已有多种合法渠道允许公司在选举中投入大量资金。首先，公司可以自由参与所谓的"内部通讯"，即公司股东、执行和行政人员及其家人作出的竞选通讯。这些内部通讯不受资金的限制，其中可能包含明确提倡公司支持或反对某候选人的信息。其次，联邦法律允许公司无限制地在"旨在鼓励个人投票或登记投票的无党派活动"[①] 中花费，尽管此类活动内容必须是无党派的，但法律没有禁止公司协助与其支持相同候选人的团体进行投票宣传。再次，根据联邦法律，公司可以自由地使用其资源单独设立"用于政治目的的独立资金"[②] 即政治行动委员会，并为其支出。公司还可以支付股东、执行和行政人员及其家属为筹集捐款所花费的费用以及在某些情况下员工及其家属为政治行动委员会筹款而产生的花费。而政治行动委员会可以使用这些雇员的捐款进行竞选捐款或承担独立开支，以支持或反对候选人。即便公司的股东、执行人员、员工或家属每年可以向政治行动委员会捐款的上限为 5000 美元，政治行动委员会可以承担的独立支出金额却没有限制。不可否认的是，尽管"联合公民案"提到政治行动委员会是"独立于公司的协会"[③]，但在法律上它完全由创建它的公司所掌控。公司可以选择其管理人员及员工，还可以确定政治行动委员会所支持的候选人以及针对每个候选人的花费。尽管不允许公司动用自有财产向其捐款，但政治行动委员会的存在本身即公司被合法授权的竞选支出。最后，也是最重要的一点，对公司支出的限制仅适用于狭义定义的与选举相关的传播类别。该类别的确切范围随着时间的推移而变化，从最初的相对限制，到 2003—2007 年的有所放宽，再到"联合公民

---

① Id. § 431 (9) (B) (ii).
② Id. § 441b (b) (2) (C).
③ 130 S. Ct. 876, 897 (2010).

第七章 美国游说与竞选捐款反腐败前瞻：系统透明与配套技术

案"之前的几年，类别范围越来越有限。1976年巴克利诉瓦莱奥案将"竞选支出"的定义限制在候选人和政党以外所有团体表达主张的传播活动中，这些团体须使用所谓8个"魔法词"之一，以明确主张选举或击败特定的联邦政府候选人，而除此之外的其他所有活动都被归为"问题倡导"。事实证明，以是否使用8个"魔法词"为认定竞选支出的标准，极易使公司和其他竞选活动参与者逃避法律规制。竞选广告可以热烈地赞扬或严厉批评候选人，但只要避免在字面上明确呼吁选民选举或击败候选人，即使对候选人的性格、品质或私生活做出评价，都被视为"问题倡导"而非表达竞选主张。为了保证这类广告被认定为问题宣传而不是表达宣传，广告赞助者都会在广告下方加上小字说明，敦促观众或听众致电以获取更多信息，或者号召致电广告中所提到的候选人，以便知悉后者对相关议题的看法。由于此类倡导不被视为明示主张，这种标准划分却使得候选人实质上依赖于外围团体所播放的、不受竞选财务法规约束的广告。

由上可以明确的是，"联合公民案"以前的成文法和判例法实质上并不阻止真正想花钱支持或反对候选人的公司通过上述方式影响竞选。基于公司已享有的竞选影响力，"联合公民案"的直接影响无疑更为巨大。该判决意味着联邦最高法院一举推翻了其在过去至少20年中的竞选财务判例，并认定执行超过60年的限制公司竞选活动支出法律构成违宪，22个州的类似法规被一并废除。与2014年麦卡琴案的区别在于，"联合公民案"的判决并未影响对候选人或政党的捐款限额，而是放宽了公司和团体组织对竞选的支出。其判决允许公司、工会和个人无限制地捐款给超级政治行动委员会和非营利组织，后者又可以将钱花在攻击或赞美候选人的广告上。从竞选财务法的角度来看，在现今对腐败的狭窄定义下，由于这些团体被禁止与候选人协同，所以尚不构成一种法律意义上的腐败。总的来说，"联合公民案"还造成了目前竞选财务法律的一个明显缺陷：在2010年以前，企业和工会一直被禁止直接向政治行动委员会捐款，但他们的员工和工会成员被允许以个人名义向政治行动委员会捐赠，上限为5000美元。然而联合公民胜诉后，企业可以自由地将任意数额的政治活动资金转入与政党或候选人法律上无关联的超级政治行动委员会。这就导致在候选人完全由超级行动委员会资助的竞选方式下，没有竞选财务法律对其进行限制，而且捐款者的身份还保密。这种保护匿名的选举制度完全可能产生一名完全代表不具名利益集团的议员或总统，其是否会始终代表最普遍美国人民的共同利益，值得思考。

因为上述原因，该案被一些学者认为是"联邦最高法院对美国政治选举管制的放松"①，因为"钱已经能开口说话"②。2018年一项调查发现，有81%的被调查者支持修改宪法，推翻"联合公民案"的裁决。③ 同样作为保守派，极负盛名的第七巡回上诉法院前法官波斯纳对"联合公民案"的破坏性影响表示担忧："由于最高法院取消了基于第一修正案对竞选的捐款限制，我们的政治体系将面临全面腐败。"④ 布伦南司法中心甚至在其研究中指出："'联合公民案'的判决正在使美国回到水门事件之前贿赂制度合法存在的时代。"⑤ 尤其危险的是，"联合公民案"似乎在竞选财务法律和宪法第一修正案之外，还表明了一种对立法者动机的天然怀疑，还有天真又不切实际的经济自由主义，以及对政治腐败的盲目无视。这些因素累加，最终极大地改变了美国竞选政治格局。

即便如此，新的法案尚无可能推翻联邦最高法院判决以直接解决这一缺陷，只能间接通过提升选举活动中其他程序的透明性来预防腐败。2010年1月"联合公民案"前，至少有38个州和联邦政府要求所有捐款人披露全部或部分独立支出以及竞选通讯支出。⑥ 尽管如此，仍有暗钱等不明来源的资金可能对选民造成了影响。2012年3月，有地方法院裁定，凡在竞选通讯上花钱的团体都必须报告其所有捐款超过1000美元的捐款人，但该裁决在上诉中被推翻。此后，部分民主党议员分别在2010年、2014年和2019年试图在国会推动《披露法案》通过，法案提出公司、工会、超级政治行动委员会，以及活跃于政治的非营利组织都应披露竞选支出，

---

① Jeffery Toobin, "The John Roberts Project", *The New Yorker*, Apr. 7, 2014.
② Ronald K. L. Collins & David M. Skover, *When Money Speaks: The McCutcheon Decision, Campaign Finance Laws, and the First Amendment*, Oak Park: Top Five Books, LLC, 2014.
③ Americans Evaluate Campaign Finance Reform: A Survey of Voters Nationwide, School of Public Policy, University of Maryland, May, 2018, p.5.
④ Richard Posner, "Unlimited Campaign Spending-A Good Thing?" (*Becker-Posner Blog*) Apr. 8, 2012, https://www.becker-posner-blog.com/2012/04/unlimited-campaign-spendinga-good-thing-posner.html.
⑤ Adam Skaggs, "Buying Justice: The Impact of Citizens United on Judicial Elections", New York: Brennan Center for Justice (2010), https://www.brennancenter.org/our-work/research-reports/buying-justice-impact-citizens-united-judicial-elections.
⑥ Daniel Winik, Citizens Informed: Broader Disclosure and Disclaimer for Corporate Electoral Advocacy in the Wake of Citizens United, Yale Law School Legal Scholarship Repository, Page 625 footnote 13, Yale Law School, Jan.1, 2010.

并要求依据税法第501（c）（4）成立的团体组织披露1万美元或以上的选举支出捐款来源，该法案还计划对通过纳税中间公司和空壳公司规避披露的做法进行规制，以"纠正""联合公民案"造成的暗钱洪流。[1] 但法案遭到共和党人否决而未获通过。不仅是"联合公民案"，2014年麦卡琴案也为竞选财务规制开启了漏洞。麦卡琴的胜诉意味着，候选人可以通过被一种称为"联合筹款委员会"（Joint Fundraising Committee，简称JFC）的法人实体从数个捐款人处筹措大笔资金。联合筹款委员会可以由两个或两个以上的候选人、政治行动委员会或政党委员会成立，分担筹款成本并分配收益。尽管参与者从捐款者处获得的资金额度不能绕过直接捐款的上限，但这种方式可以让捐款者合法捐出巨额资金，因为在麦卡琴案判决后，捐款者给联合筹款委员会的支票总限额不存在了。换言之，涉及许多候选人或委员会的联合筹款委员会可以从单个捐款者处收取巨额捐款。这种巨型委员会在过去的几年中数量激增，像是一把保护伞，使得捐款者可以向其开出大额支票，然后由该团体按照捐款人的意愿将款项赠与受益人，从而形成一种系统性的腐败体系（见图7-1）。

统计表明，在"联合公民案"之后的选举周期里，利益团体的角力越来越集中到以超级政治行动委员会和暗钱非营利组织为首的外围支出组织中。[2] 空前数量的捐款被转换为不间断的电视和铺天盖地的网络政治广告，深度影响着选民的投票决定。在"联合公民案"后的数年中，各党领导人建立了超级政治行动委员会，通过将资金提供给对选民具有影响力的外部团体支持各自的候选人，从而模糊了超级政治行动委员会与候选人之间的界限，而候选人本不被允许与独立开支进行协调。在除去捐款限制的枷锁后，超级政治行动委员会很快就超越了全国政党委员会，成为支出最高的外围群体。自2010年起，这种每个新选举周期都能轻松打破上一个周期资金纪录的现象，往往就来源于外围支出的增加，而候选人则可以表示与外围支出毫无关系。2020年大选周期中，排名前三的外围支出团体仍全部

---

[1] Sheldon Whitehouse, "Senate Democrats Introduce Legislation to Crack Down on Secret Spending in Elections", United States Senator for Rhode Island (Jun. 24, 2014), https://www.whitehouse.senate.gov/news/release/senate-democrats-introduce-legislation-to-crack-down-on-secret-spending-in-elections.

[2] Karl Evers-Hillstrom, Raymond Arke & Luke Robinson, "A Look at the Impact of Citizens United on Its 9th Anniversary", Open Secrets (Jan. 21, 2019), https://www.opensecrets.org/news/2019/01/citizens-united/.

(亿美元)

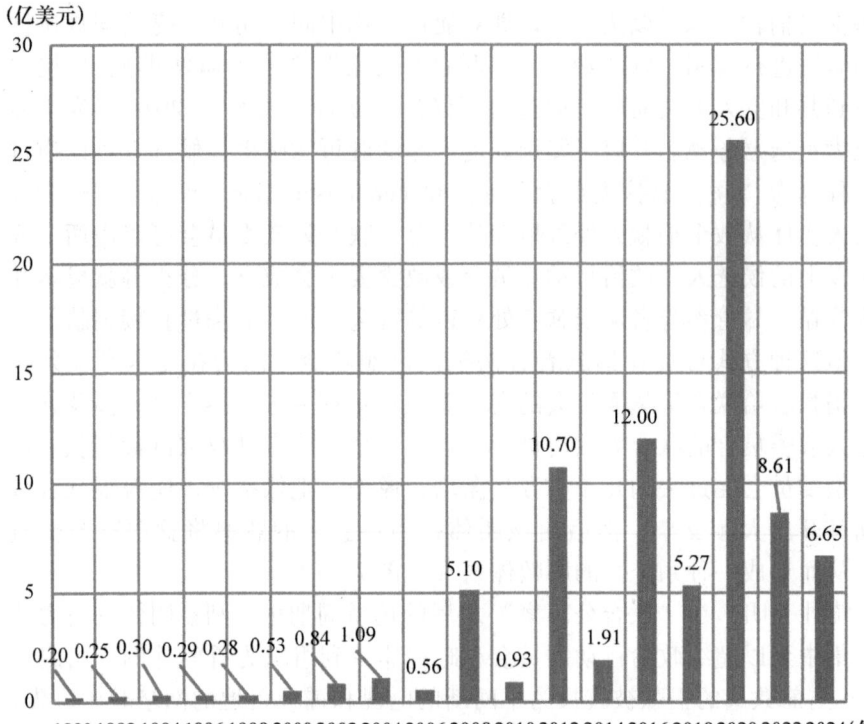

图 7－1 2010—2022 年联合筹款委员会所获捐款额

资料来源：Open Secrets, "Joint Fundraising Committees", Open Secrets (n. d.), https：//www.opensecrets.org/jfc/，数据截至 2024 年 3 月。

是背景势力雄厚的超级政治行动委员会：与前参议院多数党领袖米奇·麦康奈尔（Mitch McConnell）相关的参议院领导基金（Senate Leadership Fund）支出 2.93 亿美元；由前民主党参议员哈里·里德（Harry Reid）支持的"参议院多数"政治行动委员会（Senate Majority PAC）支出 2.33 亿美元；众议院共和党建立的"国会领导基金"（Congressional Leadership Fund）外围支出达 1.43 亿美元。[①] 长期来看，超级政治行动委员会的活跃意味着大捐款人的影响力在不断提高。2010 年，最大的个人捐款者向候选

[①] Open Secrets, "2020 Outside Spending, by Group", Open Secrets (n. d.), https：//www.opensecrets.org/outsidespending/summ.php?disp=O.

人和团体共捐出了 760 万美元。① 而麦卡琴案的裁决进一步帮助大捐款者挣脱了对单个捐款者在选举周期中捐赠数额的限制：2018 年和 2020 年，威尼斯人赌场的所有者阿德尔森家族向候选人和竞选团体组织分别捐献了 1.23 亿和 2.18 亿美元。② 对此，海尔曼教授曾针对 2010 年"联合公民案"与 1976 年巴克利诉瓦莱奥案的判决批评道："宪法权利并不包含花钱的权利。"并提出了进一步追问："金钱与政治言论的关系是什么？金钱与宪法所保护的权利有何关系？"她认为，不受限制的巨额外围支出资金分配，与言论自由权行使之间的激励关系，并不意味着限制某类支出的所有法律都需要进行最严格的宪法审查。③

三　旋转门法律催生隐形游说者

尽管旋转门不应被完全禁止，但现行法律也未能在其管制范围内发挥应有作用。包括《诚信领导和公开政府法》在内的主要游说法律不但未能有效防止旋转门的出现，其存在的漏洞反而让旋转门变换为其他更加难以受到法律监管的形式。这部曾被认为是"自水门事件以来最彻底的道德改革"的旋转门法律，已经禁止前议员和最高行政部门官员在结束国会工作后的一年至两年内参加相应的国会活动，奥巴马还以行政命令的形式将为期两年的游说禁令扩大至其就职后的所有行政部门雇员。但这并未起到预期的立法效果，现有法律并未在冷静期内暂停前国会议员及其助手的游说生涯，而只是导致其尽量避免注册为游说者，并将游说活动推向地下，从而形成了一种"隐形"游说文化。原因毫无疑问，旋转门法律和行政命令对"游说"和"游说者"的定义存在着明显漏洞：现行法律将游说者定义为前议员直接参与到游说活动中，并将其工作时间的 20% 以上用于服务同一位客户。因此许多前议员通过在多名客户身上均花费不到 20% 的总工作时间，或者提供所谓的"战略建议"和"历史参考"来规避冷静期禁令。并且，由于既没有针对前议员帮助游说活动的禁令，也没有禁止其成立游

---

① Open Secrets, "Who are the Biggest Donors?" Open Secrets (n.d.), https://www.opensecrets.org/elections-overview/biggest-donors? cycle = 2010&view = fc.
② Open Secrets, "Who are the Biggest Donors?" Open Secrets (n.d.), https://www.opensecrets.org/elections-overview/biggest-donors.
③ Deborah Hellman, "Money Talks but it Isn't Speech", *Minnesota Law Review*, No.95, 2011, pp. 953 – 1002.

说公司的禁令，即使处于冷静期，前议员和国会工作人员仍可以自由地在游说商店工作。2023年，国会议员的年薪为17.4万美元，是美国年收入中位数7.46万美元的2.3倍。[①] 尽管如此，很多议员抱怨在几乎没有涨薪的情况下很难同时在自己的家乡和昂贵的华盛顿特区体面定居。而如果他们加入游说公司，薪水将再翻数倍。具体来说，议员可于卸任后立即在游说公司和利益集团开展"法律顾问"和"战略顾问"的工作，只要他们在此期间不从事任何联邦游说活动即可。最鲜明的例子为克里斯·多德，他于2011年初结束了长达30年的民主党参议员生涯，10周后便上任好莱坞主要游说活动机构美国电影协会的主席兼首席执行官，[②] 但这并不意味着他成为法律意义上的游说者，因为他没有登记为说客，这些实质上的游说活动也完全游离于法律的监管之外。

即使在冷静期结束之后，许多参与游说活动的前国会议员和国会工作人员也从未注册为游说者。响应性政治中心和阳光基金会的联合研究表明，在2015年初刚刚结束"冷静期"的104名前国会议员和工作人员中，29名已被参与对政府游说活动的律师事务所雇佣为顾问或律师，而其中仅13人正式注册为游说者。[③] 自2007年《诚信领导和政府公开法》签署以来，华盛顿的注册游说者数量一直在稳步下降，[④] 但这并不意味着国会议员的游说旋转门已经停转，反而是现有旋转门法律规定浮于表面、更多的游说者潜伏于监管之外的证明。可以确定，这些前议员游说者正继续以"政策倡导者"等其他名义变相从事游说活动。旋转门和其他游说相关法

[①] Ida A. Brudnick, "Congressional Salaries and Allowances: In Brief", Congressional Research Service (Sep. 19, 2023), https://crsreports.congress.gov/product/pdf/RL/RL30064#: ~ : text = The%20compensation%20for%20most%20Senators, from%20Puerto%20Rico%20is%20%24174%2C000. &text = These%20levels%20have%20remained%20unchanged, March%202011%2C%202009)%2C%20P. L.; U. S. Census Bureau, "Income in the United States: 2022", Census Bureau (Sep, 2023), https://www.census.gov/content/dam/Census/library/publications/2023/demo/p60-279.pdf.

[②] Open Secrets, "Revolving Door: Christopher Dodd Employment Summary", Open Secrets (n. d.), https://www.opensecrets.org/revolving/rev_summary.php?id=76356.

[③] Open Secrets & Sunlight Foundation, "All Cooled Off: As Congress Convenes, Former Colleagues Will Soon be Calling From K Street", Sunlight Foundation (Jan. 6, 2015), https://sunlightfoundation.com/2015/01/06/coming-out-of-the-cool-as-congress-convenes-former-colleagues-will-soon-be-calling-from-k-street/.

[④] Michael Hiltzik, "The Revolving Door Spins Faster: Ex-Congressmen Become 'Stealth Lobbyists'", The Los Angeles Times, Jan. 6, 2015.

律对游说的定义流于形式，监管范围过于狭窄，只限于直接全职从事一线游说工作的说客，漏洞过多、无法形成有效监管。在旋转门的另一端转入变相的隐形游说后，反而使得旋转门现象几乎完全游离于现有法律的监管之外，游说行业也成为议员结束国会任期后公开兜售影响力的首选。

四　限制问题倡导引发争议

在巴克利诉瓦莱奥案中，最高法院判定政府只能规范那些明确主张支持或反对候选人的政治通讯。经过该案，第一修正案加强了对"不以明示用语提倡选举或击败已明确确定的候选人"言论的保护。法律仅对"表达倡导"（express advocacy）即独立支出进行规制，因此实际上许多形式的政治通讯都将完全不受约束。在《两党竞选改革法》颁布和麦康奈尔案之前，没有明确主张选举或击败明确身份的候选人的传播，即"问题倡导"（issue advocacy）是不受任何联邦竞选财务法规约束的，其宣传交流的形式和内容实际上可以是无限制的。在麦康奈尔案之后，最高法院维持了《两党竞选改革法》的联邦竞选通讯标准，国会有权针对特定选举日内联邦选举的某些类型的广播问题倡导进行规范。2007年的威斯康星州生命权案对与麦康奈尔案所涉及《两党竞选改革法》的同一条款提出了挑战，法院进一步缩小了联邦对广播宣传的监管范围。法院采用了"表达倡导"的狭义定义，认为联邦选举委员会不能根据宪法禁止在联邦大选前的特定期间使用公司自有资金为发行议题倡导广告提供资金。在威斯康星州生命权案后，受联邦监管的广播宣传范围仅限于表达倡导以及符合法院狭义的、与其功能等同的传播。这就意味着大量的问题倡导广告不会受到规制。

反对者则认为限制问题倡导与表达倡导只是一种污名化措施。竞选财务改革迄今为止不仅未能实现抗击特殊利益集团的目标，反而可能使得民主与自由付出沉重代价。因为政治支出可以帮助选民了解候选人，使选民在意识形态上有更明确的定位，并更好地认识政治议题和选举本身。因此，减少可能花费的捐款金额并限制其使用方式可能会损害政治言论的质量。竞选财务规制改革的反对者还提出，多年来竞选财务监管的倡导者一直在努力树立一种人设，使其看似扮演着国家的道德良心角色，与强大的特殊利益作斗争，从而在某种程度上成功地给反对者打上了拥护腐败系统的烙印。但对言论与表达的限制不仅仅会影响富裕的捐款者和寻求连任的候选人，缺乏社会广泛

游说、竞选捐款与美国政治腐败

支持的团体也是最依赖大捐款人而得以表达意见的团体。对少数族裔、性少数者、新移民和无家可归群体来说，很难找到足够多的支持者通过多笔小额捐款筹得所需资金，他们的发声和诉求也很容易被忽略。以乔治·索罗斯（George Soros）为例，其基金会对MoveOn.org的大量捐款使得该组织能够联系数百万美国人，并发展成为美国当代最成功的基层政治机器之一，这也说明了巨额政治支出不应该被不加以区分地污名化。

第二节　美国游说与竞选捐款反腐败的制度优化

美国人对政府权力的扩张有一种矛盾心理：一方面默认了一种大联邦政府，要求快速有效地对地方、国内尤其是国家间事务进行干预；另一方面又质疑联邦政府干预州政府事务、州政府侵犯公民权利，要求限制政府权力。这种矛盾心理在堕胎权上体现得尤为明显：2019年以来多个州立法禁止或限制妇女堕胎权利，2022年联邦最高法院在多布斯诉杰克逊妇女健康组织案[①]中，裁决认为宪法不赋予堕胎权，从而推翻了罗伊诉韦德案[②]和计划生育组织诉凯西案[③]等判例在过去50年中建立的一系列规则。另一个例子是2019年暴发的新冠病毒流行危机，政府在防疫工作中的权力界限问题引发了广泛的争论。这种矛盾心理也延伸至权力扩张下的游说和竞选捐款反腐败的规制中。因而尽管有许多方案被提出，但真正得到立法采纳却非易事。

一　精确披露执行规则

肯尼迪法官认为，革除对大公司不当影响选举的最佳手段是竞选财务披露。[④]但显然，现行的披露制度并没有起到应有的作用。[⑤]在"联合公

[①] Dobbs v. Jackson Women's Health Organization, 597 U.S. 215 (2022).
[②] Roe v. Wade, 410 U.S. 113 (1973).
[③] Planned Parenthood v. Casey, 505 U.S. 833 (1992).
[④] Citizens United, 130 S. Ct. p895.
[⑤] Paul Blumenthal, "Anthony Kennedy's Citizens United Disclosure Salve 'Not Working'", *The Huffington Post*, Nov. 2, 2015.

民案"后,可以接受无限制捐款的超级政治行动委员会已成为巨款流入选举的重要工具,其只需要在大选年每季度提交一次捐款者的信息(在奇数年则只需每半年提交一次),这显然延迟了披露制度的时效性;对于政治活跃的501(c)(4)社会福利团体等暗钱组织,国税局的现行规则并不要求其透露捐款者,因此其能够完全隔绝于公开范围运作,进而为候选人和超级政治行动委员会提供资金来匿名发挥影响力。显然,有效披露公司竞选支出可能需要更为复杂详细的规则——众多商业公司可能通过其他组织来筹集资金,因而披露的基本内容不仅要包含支出者,还必须包含为这些组织捐款的上游公司和其他捐款者。

透明化无疑是国会对联邦竞选披露执行规则的改革方向,但上述《披露法案》等种种提议仅仅为有效披露提供了一个框架,更有效的披露规则不仅意味着更频繁的披露周期,实现数据的即时在线化,还应体现在登记披露的细节方面,因而有必要进一步调整细化具体的执行规则。尽管现行法律对披露信息的项目做出了明确规定,但在执行时却可能打折扣。如媒体大亨可以将其职业登记为农民,仅仅因为他为参加赛马运动养了马;或者游说者仅将自己的身份登记为律师。[①] 还有,由于披露没有特定的格式,甚至连捐款者的名字也有可能出现不规范的情况:捐款者可以不登记中间名,或者只用缩写代替名字和中间名,只写出姓,那么同一个人的名字就有9种排列组合变化。这些技术性问题无疑加大了审查难度,因此,要求所有捐款均应以捐赠人的全名和其永久有效邮寄地址为准,将对披露工作的执行大有助益。这只是一个例子,无论如何,只有细致的规则才能真正保障联邦选举委员会等监督机构执行报告和披露法规,最终达到提高透明度的目的。

二 联邦证券交易委员会协助监管

在联邦选举委员会长期处于执法僵局和国税局监管错位的情况下,已有倡导选举信息公开的运动人士另辟蹊径,将改革目光投向了联邦证券交易委员会。2011年,来自哈佛大学等高校的9名学者联名建议证交

[①] Clyde Wilcox, "Transparency and Disclosure in Political Finance: Lessons from the United States", Paper prepared for presentation at the Democracy Forum for East Asia Conference on Political Finance, Sejong Institute, Seoul, Korea, 2011, p.32.

会制定新规则，要求上市公司就股东将公司资源用于政治活动的情况向公众披露。① 该请愿在证交会网站上收到了创纪录的一百万余条评论，还获得了近50位参众议员的支持。② 根据目前的证交会规定，上市公司必须提交8-K表格报告，以向股东公布重大利益事件。③ 而倡导全面披露制度的阳光基金会提议修订8-K表格，使报告囊括总支出达到1万美元的现金、实物捐赠，以及会费和从事政治活动组织的其他支出，并允许公众在线访问8-K系统，以公开获取竞选资金信息。④

此外，还可以考虑参照《证券交易法》的内幕交易标准，判定候选人是否与竞选委员会或竞选资金协调。尽管在一定程度上受到党派关系的束缚，联邦选举委员会仍有义务采取适当的执法措施，更积极地帮助选民、新闻工作者和研究人员实时了解大额资金对政治的影响，从而更广泛地实现问责。改善的第一步仍是细化和积极执行联邦协调规则，以确保所谓的独立支出与竞选活动在实质上没有关联。立法上应参考有关内幕交易行为的法律，此类法律禁止根据非公开信息进行股票关联交易。同样，当超级政治行动委员会的支出决策或竞选策略是基于非公开信息时，应将由此产生的行动视为与竞选人"协调"。以此为基础，联邦选举委员会可以积极执行反协调规则，从而使得超级政治行动委员会和候选人之间的独立关系受到真正监督，减少候选人向巨额资金腐败妥协的可能性。此时，超级政治行动委员会的支出对候选人的价值被降低，巨额资金流向超级政治行动委员会的动力也会随之降低。

三 推广竞选公共筹资

布鲁克斯曾在1910年构想了一种小额捐款竞选模式，即"由大量民

---

① Elizabeth M. Murphy & others, "Committee on Disclosure of Corporate Political Spending Petition for Rulemaking", SEC (Aug. 3, 2011), https://www.sec.gov/rules/petitions/2011/petn4-637.pdf.
② Leah M. Goodman, "As Dark Money Floods U. S. Elections, Regulators Turn a Blind Eye", Newsweek (Sep. 30, 2014), https://www.newsweek.com/2014/10/10/dark-money-floods-us-elections-regulators-turn-blind-eye-273951.html.
③ Sunlight Foundation, "A Comprehensive Disclosure Regime in the Wake of the Supreme Court's Decision in Citizens United v. Federal Election Commission", Sunlight Foundation (n. d.), https://sunlightfoundation.com/policy/documents/comprehensive-disclosure-regime-wake-supreme-court/.
④ 2013年，证券交易委员会宣布放弃考虑公司额外披露政治支出的计划。

第七章 美国游说与竞选捐款反腐败前瞻：系统透明与配套技术

众习惯性地向政党捐款，而每个人捐款额都相对较少"。[1] 他认为这样就可以杜绝竞选资金带来的问题。5年后，罗斯福总统提出了基于公共筹资的选举模型，允许符合一定条件的候选人获取足够的资金用于竞选活动，以帮助竞选者减轻对大捐款者及其中间人的依赖，减少腐败的诱惑与支配关系。为联邦选举提供公共资金，将可能改变金钱在政治中的运作模式。建立公共资金系统能够收集大量小额捐款，使得新的竞选者有资格获得足够资金来开展有效的竞选活动。通过税收抵免鼓励更多人参与，普通选民在选举中的影响力会得到加强，由公共资金支持的挑战者将有可能扭转行业资助者支配竞选结果的局面。同时，为符合一定条件的竞选人提供与小额捐款成比例的公共配套资金，将激励候选人专注于选民的小额捐款，而非游说者或其他狭隘利益集团的大笔捐款，候选人及其所代表的社会利益也会随之更加广泛和多样化。

20世纪80年代后期，一系列涉及大型竞选捐款和权力寻租的政府丑闻使得纽约市开始大胆改革其竞选财务系统：小额捐款以175美元为上限，选民每捐出1美元，市政府就向候选人配套捐款6美元，即100美元的小额捐款对候选人的实际价值为700美元。在过去的30年中，该公共资助计划显著了提高公民的参与度。根据市竞选财务委员会公布的数据，2009年选举中大多数捐款者都是首次捐款，这些新捐款者中绝大多数都是小额捐款，超过80%的单笔个人捐款不超过175美元。[2] 在2013年的市选举中，个人捐款者已成为市政选举候选人所获捐款的最大来源，超过90%的竞选经费来自个人捐款者，而在过去，纽约州选举所筹集的每1美元中，有近70美分来自如股份有限公司[3]、有限责任公司、政治行动委员会、工会或政党委员会等利益集团。纽约市的捐款者达到全州最多，该市

---

[1] Robert C. Brooks, *Corruption in America Politics and Life*, New York: Dodd, Mead & Co., 1910, p. 228.

[2] New York City Campaign Finance Board, "Why Do We Have Public Financing of NYC Elections?" NYCCFB (2012), http://www.nyccfb.info/PDF/press/WhyPublicFinancing.pdf?sm=press_21f.

[3] 股份有限公司与有限责任公司（LLC）二者的主要区别在于，股份有限公司可以永久存在，不因成员死亡或破产而解散，可以上市，也可以发行股票。而在有限责任公司中，股东的股权证明即是其出资证明书，根据股东身份的不同，出质转让受到时间与对象等诸多限制，不能随意转让，也不能流通，有限责任公司亦不能向社会公开募集资金。二者纳税税种也不同。但正如前文所述，某些州如特拉华对有限责任公司的注册信息几乎没有门槛，因而其可以作为隐瞒捐款者身份或从事其他非法活动的空壳公司。

· 255 ·

超过 2/3 的捐款单笔都在 175 美元以下。① 该实验还提升了公共资金支持的候选人在面对有大捐款者背书的候选人时的竞争力：尽管 2013 年选举中大量独立支出涌入纽约市，但外部资金支持的候选人不再总是稳操胜券，外围支出最高的 4 名市政委员会候选人全部落选。② 2019 年 9 月，纽约竞选财务委员会宣布计划投入 1 亿美元公共资金资助候选人的竞选活动，以期提高竞选的竞争性，减小巨额资金对竞选的影响。纽约竞选财务委员会计划降低纽约州竞选捐款上限并禁止游说者捐款，同时禁止寻求或正在与纽约州政府开展业务的公司，在相关业务期间前后的一年内向候选人捐款。该提案预计将在单个选举周期内为州长候选人提供高达 1800 万美元的公共资金，每名州议会候选人和参议院候选人也将分别获得 35 万和 75 万美元，而参与小额捐款的选民平均每人每天只花费不到 1 美分。③ 当捐款与公共配套资金相结合时，纽约选民便成为竞选中最大的"特殊利益集团"。截至 2018 年，已有 17 个州和多个城市制定了公共筹资制度。④ 目前，各州的选举公共筹资项目运作良好，不仅促进了选民参与，还在整体上提高了各参选人的竞争力。

公共资金匹配计划还应有强大的监督和执行机制支持，在确保资金得到负责任管理的同时，能够对候选人的公开信息进行选举前审核，以防止浪费和欺诈，为纳税人节省税金。显而易见，公共筹资在立法与行政机构选举中应得到更广泛的应用，⑤ 利用公共筹资部分取代商业筹资可使得竞

---

① New York City Campaign Finance Board, "Impact of Public Funds: New York City's Matching Funds Program Has Major, Positive Influences on New York City Elections", NYCCFB (n.d.), https://www.nyccfb.info/program/impact-of-public-funds/.

② New York City Campaign Finance Board, "Impact of Public Funds: New York City's Matching Funds Program Has Major, Positive Influences on New York City Elections", NYCCFB (n.d.), https://www.nyccfb.info/program/impact-of-public-funds/.

③ Michael J. Malbin & Brendan Glavin, "Small-Donor Matching Funds for New York State Elections: A Policy Analysis of the Potential Impact and Cost", Campaign Finance Institute (Feb. 13, 2019), https://www.followthemoney.org/research/institute-reports/cfi-small-donor-matching-funds-for-new-york-state-elections-a-policy-analysis-of-the-potential-impact-and-cost.

④ Wikipedia, "Publicly Funded Elections", https://en.wikipedia.org/wiki/Publicly_funded_elections.

⑤ 尽管大多数竞选支出都是私人募集的，但在初选和大选期间，符合一定条件的总统候选人也可以获得公共资助，同时也会因此受到一定的竞选支出限制。针对总统的公共筹资体系来自个人纳税申报单上的 3 美元退税（退税不会增加申报者的税收，而只是将政府资金中的 3 美元归入总统基金）。但由于 20 世纪 80 年代初以来使用支票的纳税人数量逐年下降，到 2006 年只有不到 8% 的纳税人将资金投入该基金，导致该基金长期缺乏资金运作。奥巴马在 2008 年初选时拒绝了联邦配套资金资助，因为他能够从私人捐款者那里筹集到足够竞选资金。详见维基百科 "Campaign finance in the United States" 词条。

选资金的来源更为透明和可追踪，在一定程度上减少政治利益分配与特殊利益集团之间的依赖关系以及双方日后建立"旋转门"进行利益输送的可能性，进而从竞选捐款的源头防止腐败。此外，还有学者进一步呼吁外围团体向候选人和政党提供代金券。[1] 更强大的政党与候选人将更有能力抵御与公共利益相悖的大捐款者及其资助的暗钱团体的金钱诱惑，同时减少对选举前30天内铺天盖地的广告背后超级政治行动委员会的"恐惧性依赖"，削弱此类超级资金组织在"联合公民案"时代主导选举舆论的趋势。[2] 2018年美国中期选举周期内，至少有124名竞选成功的国会议员公开表示支持公共融资。[3]

四 重塑公司反托拉斯监管

大公司的垄断地位并非一种偶然，而是和资本主义所处的发展阶段以及政府对反垄断/反托拉斯法律的执行力度密切相关。20世纪40—60年代，美国政府的反垄断干预较为频繁，但这种干预自20世纪80年代的里根经济改革起，便开始式微。在改革中，政府放松了对公司并购的管制，并购成本也随之大大降低。大公司通过发行公司债券与大型并购不断扩张，形成垄断地位，这种形势持续至今，并随着经济全球化政策在21世纪初期达到峰值（见图7-2）。而大公司背后的顶级富人，即1%人口中的1%人口，是大公司股价上升的直接受益者。在政府放松反托拉斯监管的情况下，顶级富人的巨额财富增长与经济增长几乎不成比例。自1978年以来，公司首席执行官的平均工资增长高达940%，而普

---

[1] Edward B. Foley, "Equal-Dollar-Per-Voter: A Constitutional Principle of Campaign Finance", *Columbia Law Review*, Vol. 94, No. 4, 1994, pp. 1204-1257; Bruce Ackerman & Ian Ayres, *Voting with Dollars: A New Paradigm for Campaign Finance*, New Haven, CT: Yale University Press, 2004, pp. 4-5.

[2] Adam Lioz & Blair Bowie, "Billion-Dollar Democracy: The Unprecedented Role of Money in the 2012 Elections", De͂mos (2013), https://www.demos.org/sites/default/files/publications/billion.pdf. 但透明国际的相关报告指出，公共筹资系统也并非完全理想，德国和西班牙的丑闻表明这种公共补贴模式并不是一种抗击腐败风险的普遍解决方案。

[3] Tim Lau, "A Bid to Counter Big Money in Politics Is Gaining Steam", Brennan Center for Justice (Jan. 15, 2019), https://www.brennancenter.org/our-work/analysis-opinion/bid-counter-big-money-politics-gaining-steam.

游说、竞选捐款与美国政治腐败

通工人的薪酬仅增长了12%。① 在当前的金融资本主义发展阶段，大公司有充分动机将经济权力转化为持续的政治影响，力图使政府保护其免于与下一代或外来资本家竞争，以维持当前不平等的收入分配模式。

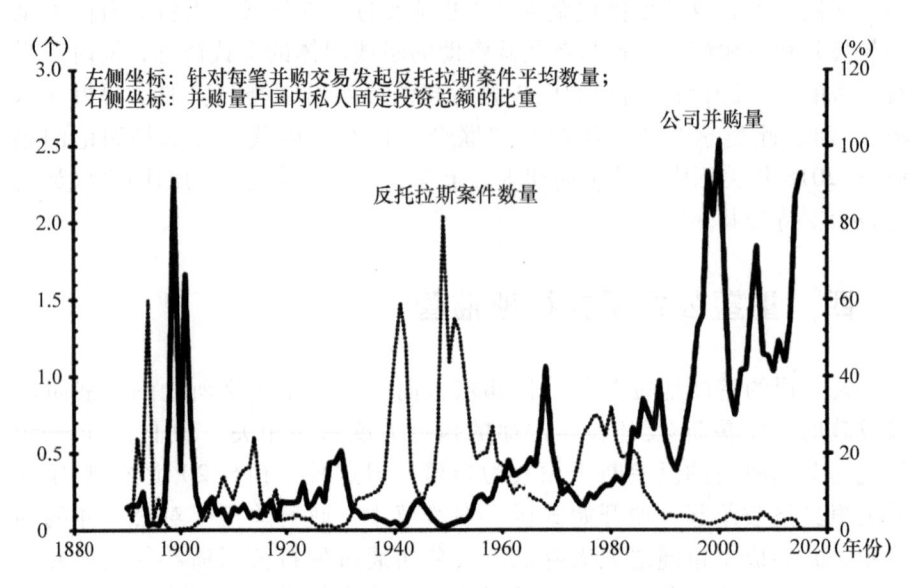

图7-2 政府托拉斯监管案件数量与美国公司并购规模

资料来源：Jonathan Tepper & Denise Hearn, *The Myth of Capitalism: Monopolies and the Death of Competition* (1st ed.), Hoboken, NJ: John Wiley & Sons, 2019, p.9.

占据垄断地位的大企业利用其财力为候选人购买媒体宣传，影响公众舆论，从而排除与大企业固有利益背道而驰的候选人，支持能为企业扩大利益者。多数情况下，形成行业巨头的托拉斯企业一般通过两种方式腐蚀美国政治的民主平等：一是通过竞选捐款、游说和旋转门招募，不当影响联邦政策；二是利用财力资助反托拉斯研究的经济学家做出对其有利的研究结论。但在2020年大选中，垄断社交媒体的巨头如"X"、脸书和油管似乎展示了第三种腐败影响方式。相比传统的行业托拉斯，主流社交媒体已经建立起了一种前所未有的全球性言论审查机制，它们利用《通信规范

---

① Lawrence Mishel & Julia Wolfe, "CEO Compensation Surged has Grown 940% Since 1978", Economic Policy Institute (Aug.14, 2019), https: //www. epi. org/publication/ceo-compensation-2018/.

第七章 美国游说与竞选捐款反腐败前瞻：系统透明与配套技术

法》第230条款[①]赋予的豁免空间掌控大选相关信息的话语权，对保守派言论进行大规模审查和封禁，如亚马逊关闭保守派社交媒体Parler服务器、脸书删除所有包含特朗普声音的内容等，都是更广泛意义上经济霸权垄断政治言论方向的腐败新范例。不仅如此，通过向选举倾注巨额资金，社交媒体巨头在现实空间也进一步释放着其巨大的政治影响力。脸书创始人扎克伯格以其名下的慈善组织为中介，在2020年选举周期中向各州和地方选举注入超过4亿美元。[②] 巨额资金对政治的短期和长期影响往往超过其表面所展示的力量，这种政治运作模式至少在某种程度上反映了现代民主制度时时都在商业托拉斯掌握下的事实。罗斯福在谈及特殊利益集团和大企业对美国政治和政府的控制权时说："有组织的金钱统治与有组织的暴民统治同样危险。"[③] 而当今的大型科技公司和跨国公司，有时在经济权力和政治影响力上甚至可以与国家政府相匹敌。腐败随时可能和前所未有的垄断相互作用，最终带来更大的社会经济危机。

可见，在对新的经济权力集中执行规范时，反托拉斯政策和对公司治理的监管变得更加重要。尽管特定的社会经济问题可能有多种解决方案，但在反托拉斯领域，诉诸法律和政府仍是市场控制的最有效工具。反托拉斯法律旨在保护竞争者，并保护作为经济体系调节者的自由竞争制度，从而使消费者利益免受企业任意定价的侵害，并在一定程度上避免民主制度被财富高度集中人群垄断的危险。这意味着政府需要在更普遍的范围上对公司治理进行深刻改革。方案之一是拆分大型社交网络巨头等行业托拉斯，约束其在某一领域的绝对话语权。通过建立完善行业机制，适当放宽市场准入，鼓励中小企业竞争，改造行业格局，使行业的后来者减轻对单一或特定法律法规政策的极度依赖而获得发展，间接分散财富的集中趋势，从而消解金钱侵蚀政治运行的动机。

总之，多维的透明度保障机制将遏制行业托拉斯的扩张。在公司内部治理等方面，应授权证交会要求上市公司向股东披露其政治支出，证交会强有力的执行机制更可能为大公司在选举中的政治财务活动公开带来积极

[①] 47 U.S.C. § 230.《通信规范法》的230条款为网络在线平台的言论审查行为提供了极大的豁免空间。

[②] AP news wire, "Mark Zuckerberg Donated $400M to Help Local Election Offices during Pandemic", The Independent（Nov.11, 2020）, https：//www.independent.co.uk/news/world/americas/mark-zuckerberg-donation-election-facebook-covid-b1721007.html.

[③] Paul Krugman, *The Conscience of a Liberal*, New York：W. W. Norton & Company, 2009, p.60.

变化。在外部监管方面，应进一步改革税法，明确501组织在税法中的定义与报告义务，令可能成为暗钱捐助主体的大公司、超级政治行动委员会、尤其是501组织等公开政治捐款去向，迫使国税局改变在其中不作为的现状。其他方面的税收改革也在可行措施之列，如对游说和竞选捐款，可视其公开披露程度适当以阶梯方式加重税率；在公平前提下对金融企业的征税结构进行改革，以堵塞其通过诸如501组织"避税"的同时又不当影响选举的双重法律漏洞。小捐款者的竞选融资方案尽管时有受挫，但也在不断摸索中取得了进展。最后，重塑对互联网科技巨头的反托拉斯监管，或可限制行业过度集中所带来的不成比例的金钱影响力，动摇垄断政治言论的网络审查霸权。

第三节　美国游说与竞选捐款反腐败的技术路径

政治反腐败不仅需要克服两党分歧，达成改革的一致意愿，构建可执行的立法配套制度，还需要相应的技术手段、媒体和社会公众监督。不同于以往由政府行政主导反腐败措施的情况，在21世纪互联网时代背景下，随着人工智能与区块链技术的运用以及网络社交媒体的高度发达，私人领域如市民、民间组织、公司企业在政治与政府反腐败中扮演的角色越发重要。透明、智能与高效已成为新技术对抗腐败的关键词，为传统的反腐败立法与执行政策提供了有力支持。

一　区块链构建透明选举系统

尽管在过去的一个世纪中，包括无记名投票权在内的隐私权已在美国社会思想中根深蒂固，匿名政治言论和匿名慈善捐赠也有着悠久的历史，[①]但在现今，透明公开已经成为监管游说、竞选捐款等政治活动中公认的核心要求。正如布兰代斯大法官在近一个世纪前所指出的："公开性是对社

---

① Bradly A. Smith, "The Strange Case of W. Spann, LLC", Institute for Free Speech（Aug. 5, 2011），https://www.ifs.org/blog/the-strange-case-of-w-spann-llc/.

第七章　美国游说与竞选捐款反腐败前瞻：系统透明与配套技术

会和行业顽疾的一种补救措施。阳光是最好的消毒剂，灯光是最高效的警察。"① 当立法者和游说者之间的互动被隐藏在门的另一侧、竞选捐款来源不明时，政府的公信力即受减损。提高透明度可以增进公众对政府选举和其他政治运作方式的理解，监督政府对其行为负责，最终促进更广泛和有效的公民政治参与。近年来，美国在提高政府透明度方面做出了诸多努力，在《信息自由法》等信息披露相关法律的敦促下，政府在数字化与在线发布行政活动记录方面已取得了重大进展，② 但不透明竞选捐款体系仍是竞选财务领域改革的首要障碍。③

区块链通过复杂的数学、先进的计算工具和加密技术所保障的数据真实性和公开性，使其成为防止信息伪造和腐败的有效工具。一方面，它提供了前所未有的信息安全性和记录完整性，消除了伪造的可能以及数据管理单点故障的相关风险。另一方面，它有助于克服传统官僚机构中的数据孤岛，使得公共实体之间得以彼此共享信息。区块链上的信息还易于获取，并能够被快速地交叉验证，执行成本很低，有助于更高效地预防和识别腐败。因此，以区块链为基础的公开政府机构信息系统将利用腐败行为的证据保留和责任可追溯性，营造一个极具威慑力的监督环境。具体来说，区块链可以应用于打击选举乃至政府腐败的三个方面：追踪竞选资金、防止选举欺诈和审查政府交易合同。

（一）区块链追踪竞选资金

区块链在政治进程中的首要应用是监管竞选资金。毫无疑问，在美国当前的政治制度中，竞选资金监管是一个重大问题。虽然法律规定候选人、政治竞选委员会与政党披露其捐款者和捐款数额，但仍有大量超级政治行动委员会和501非营利组织的资金来源不明。若能够建立一个政治资金系统，要求进行政治支出的组织使用一个公共的区块链来记录收支，使每一笔交易都可以被跟踪和查看，竞选资金系统的透明度将提升到一个新水平。因为在区

---

① Louis Brandeis, "What Publicity Can Do", *Harper's Weekly*: 10, Dec. 20, 1913.
② Michael Steinberg & Daniel Castro, "The State of Open Data Portals in Latin America", Center for Data Innovation (Jul. 2, 2017), https: //datainnovation.org/2017/07/the-state-of-open-data-portals-in-latin-america/.
③ 莱西格教授不同意此观点，他认为提高竞选经费的透明度并不能从根本上解决腐败问题，反而会将民众做出决策的过程不当暴露在外界审查之下，因而有言论自由被限制的危险。参见 Lawrence Lessig, *Lesterland: The Corruption of Congress and How to End It*, New York: Ted Conference, 2013.

块链创建的信息线索中，交易是按时间顺序记录的，以列表形式存储在加密的分类账上，由分散的群体进行维护和验证，从而形成了一个交易痕迹不可变的链，使每笔捐款交易的来源都具有完整的可追溯性。

作为捐款资金信息载体的区块链可能会改变腐败的运作方式。若一名腐败的参议员从亿万富翁那里接受暗钱，该参议员的竞选捐款将可以通过区块链的账本追溯到原始来源，此时暗钱与其他公开来源的资金没有区别。当然，在候选人或议员拒绝或回避使用区块链的情况下，条件交换式的贿赂和暗钱捐款仍然可能发生。此时选民可以决定不支持此类只靠少数公司或私人大笔资金支持的候选人，这本身就可能动摇寡头政治。研究表明，在政治环境没有受到有效监督的情况下，企业对政客的竞选捐款可以对自身的合同产生引导作用。[①] 作为捐款者的私人公司领域也可以用区块链系统进行自我监管和约束。由于目前法律不禁止完全由公司或团体资助的超级政治行动委员会，在私人领域进一步构建透明的、可追查来源的区块链登记公示系统十分必要。以区块链为代表的等分布式分类账技术可以实现在涉及政治竞选等公共利益的银行转账和合同中，对资产性质、登记情况和交易本身进行认证。如果公司将区块链运用到日常财务管理中，无论是股权交易、挪用公司款项，还是将资金输送到暗钱组织中资助政治竞选活动，或是跨国的销售交易，都将被记录在案。区块链可以防止公民或组织设置匿名离岸公司，将不法来源的财产用于洗钱或匿名竞选捐款。2017年，作为2/3世界500强公司注册地的特拉华州通过法律，允许公司利用区块链进行股票所有权的注册和转让。[②] 此类基于区块链的公司注册信息可以对公司最终实益所有者的身份进行认证，并允许联邦选举委员会、证券交易委员会、执法部门和税务管理部门更有效地执行监督。此时，确保区块链账本的访问自由和公开性将成为竞选财务监管的关键。

（二）区块链移动投票平台防止选举欺诈

近年来，选举舞弊和选民被剥夺选举权的情况显著增加，选举的廉洁

[①] Mihály Aazekas & others, "Institutional Quality, Campaign Contributions, and Favouritism in US Federal Government Contracting", Government Transparency Institutes（Aug.2018），http：//www.govtransparency.eu/wp-content/uploads/2018/08/Fazekas-et-al_DonationsPPcorr_US_GTI_WP_2018.pdf.

[②] Doneld G. Selkey, "Delaware Blockchain Law Goes into Effect", ［Morgan Lewis Blog］ Aug. 11, 2017, https：//www.morganlewis.com/blogs/sourcingatmorganlewis/2017/08/delaware-blockchain-law-goes-into-effect.

第七章　美国游说与竞选捐款反腐败前瞻：系统透明与配套技术

性受到质疑。如 2018 年的中期选举中，俄亥俄州辛辛那提市非裔选民密集的社区有 10% 的注册选民被从投票名单中删除，而这项数据在周边少数族裔人口较少的社区仅为 4%；[1] 北卡罗来纳州在发现缺席选民选票被用作舞弊后，该州众议院席位的竞选活动被宣告无效。[2] 特别是在 2020 年总统大选再次发生选举舞弊争议后，确保投票数据的安全与公正性已成为选举改革的首要目标之一。

区块链不仅可以追踪竞选资金，还可以通过提供"安全"这一关键属性，对选举产生巨大影响。如上所述，美国政治体系中的选举仍无法排除舞弊，无论是传统的本人亲自到投票站书写投票，还是邮寄投票和电子投票方式，都存在被伪造的风险。在法律改革陷入僵局的情况下，区块链技术可能成为保障选举公正的改革选项。区块链技术提供了一种替代方案，比纸质投票安全得多，同时又比邮寄投票和电子投票更方便，还有投票机器无法比拟的防篡改功能。与为加密货币搭建的系统类似，区块链技术提供的平台会创建一条高度分散、匿名而又可审核的数据链，在记录选票的同时防止各种类型的选举舞弊。由于区块链网络并不存在于某一个特定的地址，因此它不能被任何一方删除或关闭。不同于容易遭到黑客攻击的电子投票机，作为一种自我审计的生态系统，区块链透明且不可能存在腐败。其每隔十分钟便会将新产生的数据与其他数据协调，且存储在区块链上的数据库本身没有集中化的版本，这意味着没有任何漏洞可供黑客进行访问和破坏。换言之，区块链投票系统的运作方式与加密货币钱包类似，即确保投票人、其选票和选举结果之间有一个不可破解、不可更改的链。通过扫描 QR 二维码来核实自己的选票已计入官方结果，选民可以获知他们的选票已得到妥当记录。基于区块链的投票应用程序本身对与其相连接的互联网安全性也没有要求，因为黑客即使有权访问终端，也无法影响其他节点，故投票者无须担心设备接入的网络被侵入或监控。得益于加密和去中心化，选民可以在不向公众透露自己的身份或政治偏好的情况下有效地进行投票，同时存储在区块链

---

[1] Danielle Root & Adam Barclay, "Voter Suppression During the 2018 Midterm Elections", Center of American Progress（Nov. 20, 2018）, https：//www.americanprogress.org/issues/democracy/reports/2018/11/20/461296/voter-suppression-2018-midterm-elections/.

[2] Molly E. Reynolds, "Understanding the Election Scandal in North Carolina's 9th District", The Brookings Institution（Dec. 7, 2018）, https：//www.brookings.edu/blog/fixgov/2018/12/07/understanding-the-election-scandal-in-north-carolinas-9th-district/.

上的信息块向公众开放访问，每条记录都可以轻易得到验证。因而在增强数据可访问性的要求下，区块链投票技术所提供的安全性是双向的，更透明也更有利于保护选民隐私。

　　区块链投票技术的优越性还体现在选举的便捷性与经济性上。第一，区块链可以通过大大提升选举的便捷性，从而提高投票率。投票率往往是反映一国选举公信力的重要指标，尽管2020年大选的投票率创下了新高，但在全世界34个主要发达国家中，美国长期靠后，选民投票率仅排名第31位。[1] 区块链移动投票平台能够以极大的便捷性提升投票率：选民可在任何地方投票而无须排长队，在外州常住的选民也不需要请假长途跋涉回到家乡投票；投票将不受极端天气干扰；同时还能提高老年与残疾选民的投票率；在新冠疫情或类似情况下选用远程终端投票还可以避免人群聚集带来的交叉感染风险。同时，经济困难和少数族裔也将有更多机会平等地行使投票权。第二，区块链投票技术可以保证计票的准确性，避免计票争议相关的选举舞弊。系统能够确保每一张有效投票都被计入结果，没有非法废票或机器故障出错的可能，可以绝对确定统计票数，而不需要进行多次核算，投票结果将以更精确快捷的方式呈现。第三，区块链技术能直接削减竞选投票成本。在投票成本方面，目前每投出一张选票的成本为7—25美元，而区块链技术的预计花费为每票0.5美元。[2] 此外，美国政治竞选尤其是总统大选活动向来花费甚巨且逐年屡创新高，大量为特殊利益集团服务的资金不成比例地影响着选民所接收的竞选资讯。区块链投票将使得选民更有能力独立于庞大竞选支出所施加的影响，基于自己的认识和政治信仰投出选票，此时候选人的关注点也将由大公司和大捐款人转向选区选民，巨额竞选资金及其背后特殊利益集团的影响也会随之下降，选举公正性则进一步得到提升。

　　区块链投票软件的范例多种多样，它在未来选举中的推广应用不仅能促进选举的透明公正，还有望提升选民的政治参与度。目前，一些国家已经开始尝试基于区块链的选举投票。2018年11月，泰国历史最为悠久的

---

[1] Drew DeSilver, "In Past Elections, U. S. Trailed Most Developed Countries in Voter Turnout", Pew Research Center (Nov. 3, 2020), https: //www.pewresearch.org/fact-tank/2020/11/03/in-past-elections-u-s-trailed-most-developed-countries-in-voter-turnout/.

[2] Joe Liebkind, "How Blockchain Technology Can Prevent Voter Fraud", Investpedia (Dec. 9, 2020), https: //www.investopedia.com/news/how-blockchain-technology-can-prevent-voter-fraud/.

政党泰国民主党就首次使用区块链技术进行了初选。[1] Voatz, Votem 和 Smartmatic 等投票系统公司也正在尝试将区块链功能及其固有的安全保护引入美国的选举中。[2] 通过给投票者一个"钱包"进行用户标识,以及仅一次投票机会的"通证"(token),参与者可以从手机或电脑登录区块链进行投票,每张选票都构成一个投票链的一部分,因此没有人可以更改区块链上的任何数据。尽管联邦对区块链投票系统还有所保留,但部分州已为实施区块链投票系统启动了试点计划。在 2018 年的美国中期选举中,西弗吉尼亚州通过区块链系统成功记录了位于 31 个国家的 144 位美国公民的缺席选票;[3] 科罗拉多州丹佛市则在 2019 年市政选举中为所有海外选民、现役军人及其家属提供了基于区块链的智能手机应用,以方便其提交选票;[4] 犹他州部分居民则首次通过基于区块链的手机投票应用程序在 2020 年大选中投票选举总统。[5] 投票后,用户会收到一个唯一的 ID 号,随后可在区块链中查询该 ID 号以进行验证。[6] ID 号中不包含个人身份信息,任何人都可进行查询,以确保县级办公室正确地接受了投票。

(三)人工智能审查政府合同

人工智能技术已使对政府采购合同的腐败风险预警成为可能。由于腐败的风险是随机存在的,[7] 面对随机发生的政府与政治腐败行为,人工分析往往具有滞后性、非系统性与不完整性等缺陷。即使是经验丰富的数据

---

[1] Bitcoin Magazine, "Thailand Uses Blockchain – Supported Electronic Voting System in Primaries", Nasdaq (Nov. 13, 2018), https://www.nasdaq.com/articles/thailand-uses-blockchain-supported-electronic-voting-system-in-primaries-2018-11-13.

[2] Jeremy Owens, "The Promises and Pitfalls of Blockchain Politics", Medium (Aug. 16, 2019), https://medium.com/swlh/the-promises-and-pitfalls-of-blockchain-voting-11e738e5ed3a.

[3] Voatz, "The West Virginia Mobile Voting Pilot" (*Voatz Blog*), 2019, https://blog.voatz.com/wp-content/uploads/2019/02/West-Virginia-Mobile-Voting-White-Paper-NASS-Submission.pdf.

[4] Andrew Kenny, "Denver Will Allow Smartphone Voting for Thousands of People (but Probably Not You)", *The Denver Post*, Mar. 7, 2019.

[5] Hollie Mckay, "First Presidential Vote Cast Using Blockchain Technology", FoxNews (Oct. 16, 2020), https://www.foxnews.com/tech/first-presidential-vote-cast-using-blockchain-technology.

[6] Jed Pressgrove, "Utah County Puts Blockchain Voting to the Test in Live Audit", Government Technology (Sep. 4, 2019), https://www.govtech.com/products/Utah-County-Puts-Blockchain-Voting-to-the-Test-in-Live-Audit.html.

[7] 腐败广泛存在于社会的诸多领域是一个相对事实,一些假说认为,腐败的发生是依循特定条件的,故其有规律可循而并非随机发生,详见第二章脚注中对腐败空位链的描述。

分析师，也无法在识别多种变量的情况下高效处理海量的数据集。以欧盟委员会的阿拉克涅（Arachne）工具和韩国的政府投标指标分析系统（BRIAS）为代表，人工智能算法已开始被应用于识别监控公共合同承包等具有较高腐败风险的政府行为，在抗击腐败的斗争中逐渐发挥重要作用。阿拉克涅利用内部数据库中的合同、受益人和费用等内容，结合来自欧盟管理机构和外部数据库的股东、子公司和公司法人代表等信息，将其与事项涉及的从政者与制裁成员国名单进行交叉引用查询，可以在数亿个名称子集中评估筛选高腐败风险的交易或项目。[1] BRIAS 则旨在识别卡特尔垄断活动和公共采购中的操纵投标案例，通过从韩国电力采购系统中获取信息，检测公共承包过程中的异常情况，包括政府采购合同价格、数量和投标人等信息，对政府活动进行总体评分，如果分数超过一定阈值，则自动提交信息以供执法部门发起腐败调查。[2]

同时，人工智能技术亦开始与区块链结合，被交叉应用于采集政府信息的大型开放数据集中，以绘制腐败风险地图和追溯洗钱等非法资金流动，从而协助资源有限的执法监督机构防控腐败行为。2018 年，坦桑尼亚就利用区块链进行审计，清除了 1 万名在政府部门吃空饷的"幽灵公务员"，挽回了每月约 1.95 亿美元的损失。[3] 尼日利亚海关部门也使用区块链技术来存储金融交易信息，并运用人工智能在多个计算机网络之间共享这些交易，以追缴税款。[4] 此类技术与经验同样可以适用于美国。布什政府时期（2001—2009 年）的迪克·切尼副总统曾于 1995—2000 年担任哈里伯顿公司（Halliburton）高管。2003 年 3 月，哈里伯顿旗下的建筑与工程子公司未经招标就从五角大楼拿到了一份修复并运营伊拉克油井的合

---

[1] OECD, Fraud and Corruption in European Structural and Investment Funds, OECD, 2019, https://www.oecd.org/gov/ethics/prevention-fraud-corruption-european-funds.pdf.

[2] OECD, Country case: Korea's Bid Rigging Indicator Analysis System (BRIAS), OECD, 2016, https://www.oecd.org/governance/procurement/toolbox/search/korea-bid-rigging-indicator-analysis-system-brias.pdf.

[3] Halley E. Froehlich, "E-Governance in Africa and the World", in A. Froehlich & others, eds., *Space Supporting Africa. Volume 3: Security, Peace, and Development through Efficient Governance Supported by Space Applications*, Cham, Switzerland: Springer, 2020, p.83.

[4] Oracle, "Global Businesses Turn to Oracle Blockchain Service to Speed Transactions Securely", Oracle (Jul. 16, 2018), https://www.oracle.com/corporate/pressrelease/global-businesses-turn-to-oracle-blockchain-071618.html.

第七章　美国游说与竞选捐款反腐败前瞻：系统透明与配套技术

同，价值高达 70 亿美元。① 据统计，2001 年起的 10 年间，哈里伯顿公司及其子公司从联邦政府获得了约 395 亿美元的军事私有化合同，在同类承包商中排名第一。② 而自 2001 年起，切尼通过其从哈里伯顿购买的公司固定收益保险和股票期权中获利数百万美元。③ 上述例子所涉及政府采购合同中典型的利益冲突问题，完全可以通过人工智能预警系统进行评估和预警，减少政府做出腐败行为的裁量权空间。

由民间社团组织组成的类似网络通过挖掘算法和有针对性的数据分析，如对竞选融资活动和公共合同数据集进行交叉比对等，同样可能密切关注具备腐败风险的行为者，并跟踪政治资金对政府合同与议员行为的影响。2017 年，在世界经济论坛反腐败合作倡议（World Economic Forum's Partnering Against Corruption Initiative）下，美国发展银行、国际货币基金组织、万事达卡与普华永道会计师事务所（PWC）等多边组织和私营企业出资组成了联合数据共享的"科技为诚信"（Tech for Integrity）监督平台，监测包含竞选财务和政府公共合同之间的重叠部分，以推测腐败网络与政府行为之间的关联模式。④

在官方财务披露和公民信息自由领域的改革引导下，提升透明度已成为公共和私营部门治理不可阻挡的发展趋势。增进透明度的措施本身并非抑制公民投票权、禁止游说或竞选捐款等相关政治活动，而是制止可能被认为是不正当或不公平竞争的腐败操作。目前，将人工智能技术普遍运用于避免选举乃至政府活动中的腐败极具潜力，但仍可能面临一些障碍。技术上的障碍是，人工智能与大数据的交叉查询往往需要更透明开放的政府运作和政府内部跨部门的联网合作；可能面临的立法挑战则涉及信息的获取是否受到《信息自由法》的保护，因为凡涉及数据查询都可能受到侵犯

---

① CBS News, "Whistleblower Exposes $7 Billion No-bid Defense Department Contract", CBS (Jun. 30, 2019), https：//www.cbsnews.com/news/halliburton-whistleblower-on-exposing-7-billion-no-bid-defense-contract-2019-06-30/.

② Angelo Young, "Former Halliburton Subsidiary Received $39.5 Billion in Iraq-Related Contracts Over The Past Decade", Business Insider (Mar. 20, 2013), https：//www.businessinsider.com/halliburton-company-got-395billion-iraq-2013-3.

③ David E. Rosenbaum, "A Closer Look at Cheney and Halliburton", The New York Times, Sep. 28. 2004.

④ Maria F. P. Argüello & Tamar Ziff, "Hacking Corruption：Tech Tools to Fight Graft in the Americas", Atlantic Council (Jun. 18, 2019), https：//www.atlanticcouncil.org/in-depth-research-reports/report/hacking-corruption-tech-tools-to-fight-graft-in-the-americas/.

隐私权和商业秘密等方面的质疑。并且，尽管现代技术对公众承诺可以公开一切，但当代社会和政治组织总体上仍是不透明的，旨在降低交易成本的市场导向有时也可能与增强透明度的改革趋势发生冲突。此外，虚假网络信息对于人工智能与数据挖掘工具所得出的腐败风险评分也极具干扰性，因而对外部数据库的甄别也将是一大挑战。

二 互联网媒体扩展选民政治参与维度

如同当年的火车、飞机和广播、电视以及电话改变政治形式一样，互联网已成为21世纪政治活动的枢纽，为政治广告、竞选筹款乃至政治反腐败带来了意想不到的改变。谷歌、脸书、油管和亚马逊等科技巨头如今在经济格局中占据着主导地位，它们不仅构成了公共领域本身，还从根本上改变了政治竞选活动的运作方式。互联网带来的通信革命进一步打破了传统信息传递的地域阻碍和交互成本，改变了竞选筹款的传统格局，并以极其低廉的成本向大众提供丰富的定制化信息，极大地促进了选民政治参与的深度和广度。

（一）在线捐款平台凝聚小捐款者

通过在最大限度地减少竞选捐款交易成本的同时与尽量多的潜在捐款人接触，互联网已使得捐款额低于200美元的小额捐款者成为可能削弱大笔资金不当影响的民主新生力量。普通市民可以通过互联网分享政治观点，表达对候选人的看法并做出捐款。选民还可以运用互联网自发倡议支持某一候选人，为其发起竞选资金众筹，帮助候选人拒绝行业巨头及其游说者提供的大额赞助。现今的互联网最大限度地汇集了小额捐款者的力量。2004年布什和克里的竞选活动共计在互联网上筹集到1亿美元，其中大部分是小额捐款；2006年有候选人开始使用在线捐款平台筹集主要竞选资金，召开线上市镇会议，收集议题签名，并群发电子邮件号召支持者；同时各种组织团体利用互联网召集在线初选，动员支持者捐款；2008年奥巴马从小额捐款者处筹集到了大约24%的政治资金，在其竞选连任时，该比例上升至28%。[①]

2020年初暴发的新冠疫情进一步推动了这种趋势。防疫政策取消了传

---

① Richard H. Pildes, "Small-Donor-Based Campaign-Finance Reform and Political Polarization", *The Yale Law Journal Forum*, Vol.129, No.18, 2019, pp.150-170.

统竞选的实地拉票和筹资活动，使得竞选活动的组织形式由线下的户外广告、市政厅和其他公共场所集会宣讲大幅转至线上。隔离期间人们在社交媒体、新闻和娱乐流媒体服务上消磨更多的时间，也促使越来越多的竞选活动和政治行动委员会等其他竞选团体将预算大规模地转移到社交媒体和搜索广告上。同时，由于新冠疫情影响了大公司企业业绩，大额捐款不可避免地缩水，因而候选人比以往任何时候都更加依赖小捐款者的在线捐款，在线捐款平台一跃成为竞选活动的主要筹款工具。民主党人开始通过"蓝色行动"（ActBlue）众筹网站筹集资金，特朗普也有共和党的"红色必胜"（WinRed）网站，二者在2020年大选期间收到的捐款迅速增长，占特朗普和拜登在2020年竞选活动中所获捐款的57%。[1] 拜登还主持了多次虚拟筹款活动，同年6月举行的一次线上活动中，拜登的联合筹款委员会募集了400万美元。[2] 尤其在乔治·弗洛伊德（George Floyd）之死引发持续抗议后，拜登的在线捐款数量激增。

（二）社交网络促进选民监督

随着数字媒体时代的社交网络逐渐替代传统通信方式，成为政治信息的主流披露和监督渠道，以手机和其他电子设备为终端的公民网络生活开始在政治反腐败运动中发挥更强大的监督与引导作用。更便捷和广泛的政治网络参与显然能够增强候选人与普通选民的联系，从而使前者对后者的诉求有更直接的了解和回应。寻求竞选连任的候选人最担心的是持不同政见的当地选民和对其所接受竞选捐款的公开质疑者。选民利用脸书和"X"等互联网社交媒体工具组织起来，可以向国会议员发出公开信："请问您接受某公司5万美元捐款的原因是？您为他们做了什么？他们又要求您做什么？"竞选者则不得不公开其在大捐款人和普通民众的利益之间所选择的立场。

手机应用程序也发挥了不可忽视的作用。21世纪的前20年中，手机等智能移动终端的普及加速了科技应用程序的增长，打破了传统的信息壁垒，为市民提供并分享海量信息，疏通了对政府、从政者及其家庭成员腐

---

[1] Jackie Gu, "The Employees Who Gave Most to Trump and Biden", Bloomberg (Nov. 3, 2020), https://www.bloomberg.com/graphics/2020-election-trump-biden-donors/.

[2] Karl Evers-Hillstrom, "Political Donations Dropped off as Coronavirus Pandemic Peaked", Open Secrets (2020), https://www.opensecrets.org/news/2020/06/political-donations-dropped-off-as-coronavirus-pandemic-peaked/.

败行为的监督管道。2014年8月，响应性政治中心、阳光基金会和国家政治研究所利用所搜集的竞选捐款数据，发布了一款与"Bipartisan"即"两党"谐音的"Buypartisan"的智能手机应用。① 消费者登录此应用，用手机摄像头扫描超市中商品的条形码，便可查看该商品所属公司及其领导人的竞选捐款去向，以根据自身政治倾向做出消费选择（见图7-3）。

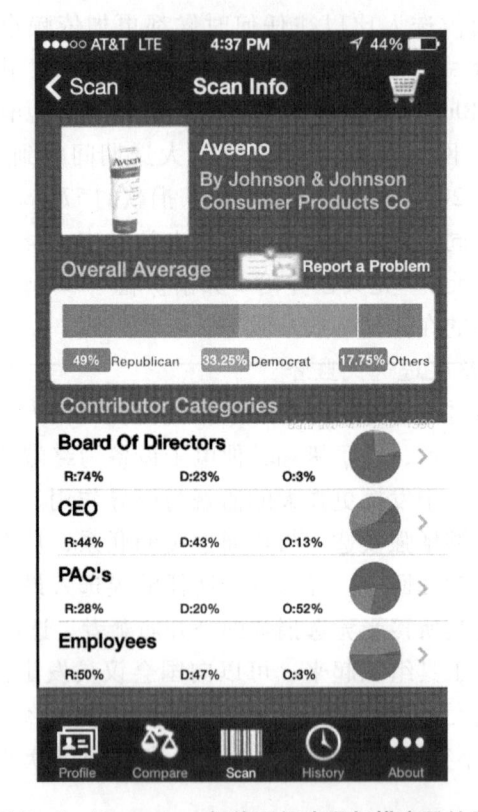

图7-3 Buypartisan智能手机应用扫描商品结果

资料来源：Al Kamen & Colby Itkowitz, "Want to Stop Enriching People Whose Politics You Hate? There's an App for That", *The Washington Post*, Aug. 12, 2014.

当然，丰富的互联网信息也为竞选监管带来了问题和挑战。一方面，通信成本极低的互联网政治广告挑战了限制和披露竞选资金以控制腐败的

---

① Al Kamen & Colby Itkowitz, "Want to Stop Enriching People Whose Politics You Hate? There's an App for That", *The Washington Post*, Aug. 12, 2014.

第七章 美国游说与竞选捐款反腐败前瞻：系统透明与配套技术

立法初衷。如前纽约市市长迈克·布隆博格2020年总统竞选期间在政治广告上花费了超过10亿美元，其中很大一部分用于数字广告：2020年的前6周内，面向美国脸书用户发布的24亿则总统竞选广告中，有16亿则由布隆博格发布。[1] 尽管最终退出竞选，布隆博格的确利用互联网扩大了自己的财富影响力，同时也淹没了其他财务上较为弱势的非主流竞争者的政治声音。与此同时，虚假或误导性的互联网信息泛滥成灾。无论是共和党人还是民主党人都定期建立网站，发布未经验证的有关对手的负面信息。而除付费政治广告外，此类互联网上的政治通讯并不受到竞选财务法律的监管。这也对选民在政治信息的甄别上提出了很高的要求。此外，互联网给竞选活动带来的影响还可能再次触及竞选财务披露与言论自由之间的微妙平衡，这也使得问题更趋复杂。

使用该应用程序对一款Aveeno品牌的护手霜进行扫描，显示其母公司为强生，该公司的竞选捐款有49%流向共和党，33%给了民主党，公司74%的董事会成员支持共和党候选人。

第四节　竞选财务制度改革的未来

即使经过多年的竞选财务改革，什么构成腐败或者何种情况下发生腐败，在竞选财务领域仍旧是个非常复杂的问题。美国公众对腐败的概念似乎远比任何法律定义都要广泛，但是要从法律上确定腐败，需要证明制定政策是为了换取捐款：潜在的捐款者寻求参与政府决策的通道，决策者则寻求捐款者的资金以资助其政党和竞选活动。这种双向的需求赋予了腐败巨大的诱惑力，同时证明难度也更大，因为从政者可以列举出许多其他合理理由来支持其决策，而大可不必是对竞选捐款者的报答。罗斯-艾克曼指出："民主政治制度必须找到一种方法，为政治竞选筹集资金，同时又不鼓励政客向捐款者兜售（影响力）。"[2] 这种目标既一针见血，又似乎蕴

---

[1] Julian Jaursch, "How to Write Rules for Fair Digital Campaigning", The Brookings Institution (2020), https://www.brookings.edu/techstream/how-to-write-rules-for-fair-digital-campaigning/.

[2] Susan Rose-Ackerman, *Corruption and Government: Causes, Consequences, and Reform*, Cambridge: Cambridge University Press, 1999, p.133.

含矛盾：作为两党相互竞争和妥协的产物，美国的竞选财务制度既包含限制腐败的目标，又张扬言论自由，从而在过去的一个世纪中，发展出了一套可接受和同时又不可接受的捐款规则和腐败行为界限。

一 竞选财务法律改革的局限性

在皮尤研究中心2018年的一项调查中，77%的公众表示"个人和组织可以用于政治竞选的金钱数额应受到限制"，只有20%的人支持言论自由相对无边界的观点，认为个人和组织的竞选支出不应受限；但相比于上述77%同意规制竞选经费的公众，仅有65%认为应该制定新的竞选财务法律以显著减小金钱在政治中的作用，而31%的受访者则坦言任何新法律都不会有效。① 最后一种观点看似武断，但也并非没有依据。整体来看，竞选资金监管似乎正在成为一种徒劳无益的努力。前联邦选举委员会主席也承认，在过去数十年中，"以限制竞选捐款和支出为主题的财务改革非但没有加强选举制度对民意的反映，反而为特殊利益和所谓的精英阶层提供了更强有力的支持，基层政治活动的机会也变得更有限"。②

（一）永无止境的漏洞与法律修改的滞后性

"联合公民案"的一份法庭之友意见书显示，联邦选举委员会已针对33种特定类型的政治言论和71种不同类型的"言论发布者"制定了法规。③ 这些法规与联邦选举委员会的其他附随法规总计超过800页。④ 自1975年成立至"联合公民案"前，委员会已在《联邦公报》（Federal Register）上发表了总计1278页的内容，以解释其决定，⑤ 此外还提供了1771个咨询意见。⑥ 与卷帙浩繁的法律法规形成对比的是，每一次重要的竞选

---

① Pew Research Center, "The Public, the Political System and American Democracy", Pew (Apr. 26, 2018), https://www.pewresearch.org/politics/2018/04/26/the-public-the-political-system-and-american-democracy/.

② Bradly A. Smith, *Unfree Speech: The Folly of Campaign Finance Reform*, Princeton, NJ: Princeton University Press, 2001, p. 66.

③ 130 S. Ct. at 895.

④ Bradly A. Smith, "Before the United States Senate Committee on the Judiciary: We the People? Corporate Spending in American Elections after Citizens United", Testimony of Bradley A. Smith, Mar. 10, 2010, p. 13.

⑤ 130 S. Ct. at 895.

⑥ 130 S. Ct. at 895.

改革似乎都在为竞选资金开辟新的不受法律监管的管道。竞选捐款或外围资金大量增加，从硬钱到软钱，从软钱到暗钱。具体例子是，当《联邦竞选法》规定了对大额捐款的限制时，政党和捐款者发现了软钱，将软钱作为不受管制的捐款渠道，用于所谓"政党建设"活动。这种政党建设活动很快还将"议题广告"囊括在内，或是攻击竞争者，或是盛赞自己支持的候选人，但它并没有敦促人们投票、支持或反对候选人。而当《两党竞选改革法》堵塞软钱的通道后，以民主党人为首的各党派继而将其多种的传统竞选职能转交给了激进主义团体。在《两党竞选改革法》试图通过禁止大选前60天之内的广告提及候选人以限制利益团体的议题广告时，各团体则选择通过在60天的窗口期以外投放广告来做出回应。还有全美步枪协会利用广播电视法中的例外规定，建立了自己的卫星广播站播放广告，联合公民组织则拍摄了关于竞选人的负面纪录片，计划于选举前30天内播放。再往前追溯，1947年《蒂尔曼法》将捐款主体限制扩大到工会时，工会和公司组成了第一个政治行动委员会，收集会员、股东和管理者的捐款以用于政治目的。种种现象表明，改革在实质上没能为选举中巨额资金的影响力和选举透明度带来预期程度的改变。在竞选财务改革伊始，法律法规就一直在追堵上述规避管制行为的漏洞，然而每一次改革都导致法律对基本权利施加更多更复杂的限制，不断引发侵犯言论自由、平等保护权等争议。这种努力的方向本身或许在一定程度上就是自欺欺人的，因为无论竞选法律法规何其全面庞杂，政治参与者总能在理论上找到法律漏洞，可以是税法，也可以是广播电视法或其他法律。就像麦迪逊所预料到的那样，每当一条政治参与途径被关闭时，活跃于政治领域的美国公民、公司和团体，无论出于何种动机，都会寻求下一个最有效的法律手段将自己对选举的影响最大化。

（二）改革沦为党派斗争工具

发起竞选财务改革的动机是认识竞选反腐败挑战的重要参照点。但即使以规制、披露竞选资金为主旨的反腐败法律最终在国会通过，竞选财务改革的目的也不能被简单理解为捍卫民主和反对金权政治腐败。

1894年举行的纽约制宪会议上，共和党人以利胡·罗脱呼吁立法禁止公司竞选捐款。尽管当时罗脱最终未能改变纽约的法律，但该倡议确实有效地发起了限制竞选捐款及其所购买言论的现代改革运动。讽刺的是，这场运动本身就指明了当时竞选财务法律改革的动机：其并非来自善政的崇高理想，而恰恰是出于党派利益。由于当时共和党人因接受来自商业界的贿赂而声誉不佳，罗脱此举的目的被认为是希望替共和党争取选民的再次支持。另一个例子是1907年《蒂尔曼法》，作为首个禁止公司向联邦候选人捐款的联邦法规，该法案的发起人本·蒂尔曼长期以种族隔离为其政治议程的核心，此种立场促进了他对控制公司支出的兴趣。① 当时许多公司反对种族隔离，因为商人们不愿为两套有轨电车系统埋单，更不想为不同种族的顾客分别建造单独的建筑入口、卫生间以及其他公共设施，并且希望雇佣非裔美国人以获得更廉价的劳动力。而蒂尔曼则设法将黑人排除于劳动力之外，种种分歧使其希望控制公司的政治影响力。上述例子也揭示了具有百年历史的竞选财务改革运动面临困境的根本原因之一：其初衷既非保护言论自由，也非监管特殊利益和维护民主，更不是限制政府权力。

但仅仅以立法者基于自身利益或政治信仰解释竞选财务法律改革所面临的困境，仍然可能低估了立法过程及其长期效果的复杂性。观察近几十年的竞选财务法律法规为选举带来的变化，不难发现限制竞选支出的每一步改革似乎最终都有利于提出改革的竞选方。以2002年的《两党竞选改革法》为例，和其他法律一样，其必须获得至少一党的多数支持和另一党一定数量的选票才能投票通过。由于当时民主党在规模日益增长的选举筹款活动中处于弱势，多数民主党人支持该法案，但其通过还需要来自共和党一定数量的选票。而调查发现，为《两党竞选改革法》投赞成票的共和党人大多在当时换届选举中可能面临落选。② 尽管民主党是该法案的最大受益者，但对于这些共和党议员来说，该法案对其现实利益的保护是不可抗拒的，反对法案者亦会被打上迎合竞选腐败的烙印。显然，竞选财务法律改革成为两党间斗争与党内竞争的武器。讽刺的是，这种武器并没有加剧竞争，而是削减了竞争。在这里，麦迪逊式的预言以一种迂回的形式实现了：政治家利用政治权力来实现自己的目标，而非公众利益。换言之，竞选财务法律可能已间接成为"腐败"的一种形式，而后果则是国会正在经历"1972年《联邦竞选法》通过以来选举竞争程度最大幅度的下降"③。

---

① Bradly A. Smith, "The Myth of Campaign Finance Reform", *National Affairs*, No. 6, Winter 2010.
② Bradly A. Smith, "The Myth of Campaign Finance Reform", *National Affairs*, No. 6, Winter 2010; John Samples, *The Fallacy of Campaign Finance Reform*, Chicago: The University of Chicago Press, 2006, p. 9.
③ John Samples, *The Fallacy of Campaign Finance Reform*, Chicago: The University of Chicago Press, 2006, p. 186.

这种结论绝非臆测，有研究表明，自《联邦竞选法》通过以来，众议院竞选中在任者与挑战者在平均支出比已从1.5∶1飙升至约4∶1。[1] 在任者在每个选举周期中都会获得更高的知名度，并与越来越多的捐款者建立联系，这使得竞选连任者无论是选择少数大捐款者还是通过更多人的少量捐款来筹集资金，也能够在同等条件下比其挑战者更容易筹到所需款项。因此，改革者所倡导的竞选法律改革最终仍最有利于寻求连任者，并且其进一步增强了特殊利益在选举中的既有干预能力，而非使二者的联系被削弱。

现实是，许多真正秉持彻底改革初衷，却与两党各自利益相悖的法案，往往最终只能停留在纸上。如多次在国会提出的、旨在终身禁止前议员参与对国会游说活动的《关闭旋转门法案》和《人民法案》等，一直都未能进入委员会投票程序。应当认识到，联邦竞选财务法律的诞生远非基于善政的崇高理想，而是从一开始就与党派优势竞争的动机挂钩，其发展变革是多方利益考量博弈的一系列结果的集合。因而联合公民时代所面临的竞选财务反腐败挑战，也只是当代美国政治现实的历史延续。

二 竞选财务法律改革趋势

（一）公司与披露仍为改革重点

在多种不确定因素下，美国竞选财务系统的未来改革仍阻碍重重。可以看到的趋势是，国会在不久的将来很可能通过新的立法进一步阻止外国资金轻易地流入竞选系统进而操控选举——该方向在竞选财务改革的选项中是争议最小、两党能够达成一致的。具体举措可能有：第一，对于国外资金流入美国境内的重要途径——空壳公司将逐渐以立法形式进行规管。众议院于2019年通过的《公司透明法案》和2020年提出的《滥用空壳公司法案》等都体现了这种趋势。第二，可能考虑将《外国代理人登记法》并入《游说披露法》，以应对大型跨国公司的政治影响。[2] 第三，未来可能会要求游说者对外国客户进行合理程度的尽职调查。第四，从安全的角度对

---

[1] Fred Wertheimer & Susan W. Manes, "Campaign Finance Reform: A Key to Restoring the Health of Our Democracy", *Columbia Law Review*, Vol.94, No.4, 1994, pp.1126-1159.

[2] Ben Judah & Nate Sibley, "The Enablers: How Western Professionals Import Corruption and Strengthen Authoritarianism", Hudson Institute (Sep., 2018), https://www.hudson.org/research/14520-the-enablers-how-western-professionals-import-corruption-and-strengthen-authoritarianism.

竞选资金进行更严密的监管，规范互联网上不明资金来源的竞选广告和竞选融资活动也将成为重点措施，互联网站点和掌握控制权的科技巨头公司将被要求承担更多的审查义务，以在网络竞选广告环节上增加外围竞选资金的透明度。具体法案如2019年的《诚实广告法案》等。但对于难以规制的旋转门现象，有人提议为国会议员及其工作者制定终身的冷静期禁令，并将禁令扩展至不得参与为外国政府与其控制的商业实体游说。但鉴于明显的利益冲突等原因，该提议在国会通过成为法律仍存在较大困难，未来的改革趋势或将集中于对倡导型游说者或其他隐形游说现象的间接规制。

而对于限制政治支出是否可能侵犯第一修正案言论自由权的争议，似乎仍将继续下去。对竞选捐款和支出的限制无疑会影响第一修正案的核心——言论、新闻和集会自由。但必须认识到，同对政府权力的限制一样，对《权利法案》所保障的自由加以限制同样具有正当性。无论是否承认这种正当性，对言论自由的此类限制都在实质上与竞选改革的目标密不可分。但现实是，尽管联邦最高法院从未认可"金钱就是言论"的观点，其也清楚地表达了，限制政治支出可以（通过限制公民表达政治观点和信息的能力）限制言论。实际上，在过去30年里列席联邦最高法院的19名法官中，只有史蒂文斯大法官曾明确表示，规制政治竞选活动和支出不应被视为对宪法第一修正案的侵犯。

值得庆幸的是，尽管在细节上一直存在争议，多年来对游说与竞选资金的公开仍至少在理念上获得了广泛支持。显然，及时有效的披露有助于执行竞选法规、控制腐败并增强问责制。同时，透明的体系反过来可以增强政府打击腐败动机的公信力。当然，并非所有违反竞选法律法规的行为都会构成腐败，也并非所有的政治腐败都涉及竞选财务，但反腐败与竞选财务披露都是民主政体的重要目标。随着互联网的普及，无论是新闻界、宣传团体、政治顾问、保障公众知情权益的相关团体还是其他研究机构所披露的信息或数据，都可能成为曝光问题的契机，隐瞒、掩盖资金来源也随之变得越发困难。联邦执法机构通常依据这些数据来找出违反竞选支出限额的情况，候选人则利用这些数据收集竞争对手的相关信息，类似的组织如公共竞选行动基金（Public Campaign Action Fund）则通过公开与竞选捐款有关的国会不当行为信息，推动"问责制"的改革工作。现今，公开竞选财务信息已被选民视为候选人良好声誉的象征，是竞选人的加分项。如在2000年和2004年的选举中，总统候选人均在CampaignWeb网站上公

第七章　美国游说与竞选捐款反腐败前瞻：系统透明与配套技术

开了他们收到的所有捐款。不仅如此，2020年选举周期中，已有超过50名国会议员，包括部分宣布参与总统大选的议员们都已作出象征性承诺，表明他们将拒绝公司政治行动委员会以及某些类型的超级政治行动委员会的竞选捐款。随着选举透明度的提升，此种行动将在未来选举中占据更重要的地位，也会成为越来越多的候选人争取选民的主流方式。

（二）推翻"联合公民案"存在立法与行政阻力

从判例法的实质角度分析，如果"联合公民案"不被推翻，大捐款人和大公司深度影响选举的现状就不会改变。由于"联合公民案"是基于宪法而非其他法律规定作出的判决，因此只能通过宪法修正案或最高法院本身的判决来修正或推翻。联邦最高法院在1803年马伯里诉麦迪逊案中[1]，为自身创设了对国会法律进行违宪性审查的权力，而在两个世纪后，罗伯茨大法官领导下的最高法院则使用这项权力剥夺了国会以及各州将巨额资金排除在政治选举之外的职能。尽管史蒂文斯大法官曾在"联合公民案"的反对意见中写道："公司本身并非'我们人民以及构建宪法的人民'中的一员。"[2] 绝大多数美国人也支持消除公司在选举中不成比例的影响，但由于特朗普政府已连续选任3名保守派大法官填补最高法院空缺，加之保守派一直在州选举中为公司友好型的法官提供竞选资金，短期内要推翻"联合公民案"，结束对大公司及其背后大捐款人对选举的资金控制仍有现实难度。

面对脆弱且缺乏执行力的竞选法律法规，竞选财务改革的支持者仍试图保障其现有规定的效力不受蚕食。许多法学教授、部分共和党和民主党官员，主张竞选的改革团体以及其他关心民主生存的美国人，都在以自己的方式努力尝试推翻"联合公民案"判决。如"竞选法律中心""民主21号组织""华盛顿公民责任与道德规范"以及"人民言论自由"等民间活动组织，都在持续不断地向联邦最高法院、联邦选举委员会、司法部、国税局、证交会和国会施加言论压力，要求终止大公司和特殊利益集团对选举的不当干预。[3] 包括加利福尼亚州、特拉华州、马萨诸塞州和康涅狄格

---

[1] Marbury v. Madison, 5 U.S.1 Cranch 137. 1803.

[2] U.S. Supreme Court, "Citizens United: Opinion of Stevens, J.", Supreme Court (n.d.), http://www.supremecourt.gov/opinions/09pdf/08-205.pdf.

[3] E. Rassweiler, "Corporate Control of Elections, Citizens United v. Federal Election Commission (2010) and Related Decisions: The History and Consequences", Corporate Control of Elections (2018), https://corporatecontrolofelections.com/#_edn21.

州在内的 22 个州、830 多个市镇和县议会已通过决议，要求国会通过宪法修正案以推翻"联合公民案"，其他州也在待决中。[①] 一些州也正在采取立法行动，将公司对其选举的控制限制在最小范围。如佛罗里达州圣彼得堡市议会于 2017 年 10 月投票对市政选举活动的公司捐款进行限制，禁止外资占比超过 5% 的公司向竞选出资，并要求披露其捐款。[②] 这是地方一级政府针对"联合公民案"的首次立法决议。联邦层面上，在 6 名大法官坐镇联邦最高法院的情况下，等待呈绝对优势的保守主义政治倾向发生扭转以及新的案例在上述恰当时机上诉至最高法院，从而形成推翻"联合公民案"的契机，仍只是一种受到多重变量影响的假设情况。

与此同时，众多旨在限制公司操控竞选的法案也在国会提出，但尚未有任何一个法案得到通过，来自反对者的挑战也从未减少。如和商界联系紧密、在美国立法和行政决策中具有重要影响的全美律师协会（ABA），也是限制公司竞选资金、提升匿名公司和组织来源资金透明度的强有力反对者之一。不过，全美律协在此议题上的立场并不完全取决于党派倾向，而是基于职业本能保护当事人的言论自由权和隐私。

此外，还存在一些消极的行政阻力因素。国税局通常是唯一要求非营利组织披露捐款者的联邦机构，但负责起诉与暗钱支出有关竞选财务违规行为的是司法部。"联合公民案"后，国税局面对突如其来的暗钱洪流不知所措，开始努力确定哪些组织将超过 50% 的年度预算支出用于政治活动，但又没有对"政治支出"的统一定义。并且国税局并没有监管选举中外国资金的义务，除非有法庭命令，其不会与司法部等其他联邦执法机构共享暗钱捐款者的名单。

（三）加密货币捐款逐渐增加

尽管不断增加的比特币竞选捐款引发了对于竞选资金透明度的担忧。但从美国机构政治维持现状的固有惯性来看，短期内加密货币还远远无法成为竞选融资的主流。接受加密货币捐款的政客数量仍然不多，加密货币捐款也只占其募集总捐款的一小部分。当然，部分倡导新技术的政客已经自然地将接受加密货币捐款作为其意识形态表达的一部分。在过去的 10

[①] D. Smith, "Dark Money: The Quixotic Quest to Clean up US Campaign Financing", *The Guardian*, Apr. 6, 2022.

[②] Charlie Frago, "St. Petersburg Council Acts to Limit Big Money in City Elections", *The Tampa Bay Times*, Oct. 6, 2017.

第七章　美国游说与竞选捐款反腐败前瞻：系统透明与配套技术

年中，一些联邦和州竞选人也倡导进一步放开对加密货币竞选资金的使用。① 就未来而言，加密货币在竞选财务中的地位取决于其在交易中的使用范围和可追踪性。由于加密货币捐款具有转账实时性，既快速又能够省去昂贵的转账费用，在一些国家已经成为政治反对者获取竞选捐款的重要途径之一。2019年10月联合国儿童基金会推出了加密货币基金，以接受比特币和以太币捐款，其他著名援助机构如美国红十字会和联合国世界粮食计划署也均已开始接受加密货币捐款。② 这些变化也正在改变加密货币往往是与非法交易有关的传统印象。如果越来越多的美国人开始使用加密货币来进行交易，并且政治竞选者被要求只能接受可追踪的加密货币种类，那么政治竞选最终也不会成为加密货币流通领域的例外。

（四）小额捐款人影响力上升

过去的2020年大选已经发生了一些积极的变化。尽管由于巨额暗钱的流入，此次大选打破了此前大选制造的开支纪录，成为美国历史上最昂贵的选举。根据白宫的预测，总统与参议院选举分别创下历史纪录，其中总统大选耗资达57亿美元，总竞选支出高达144亿美元，而在此前刷新当时最高纪录的2016年联邦竞选中，这两项支出分别约为23.8亿美元和65亿美元。③ 但竞选支出激增的源头首次发生了改变，竞选捐款频谱两端的捐款者共同推动了竞选支出的上升。一方面，亿万富翁们在"联合公民案"的庇护下，一如既往地向超级政治行动委员会开出了巨额支票；而另一方面，在本次竞选筹集资金总额中，有22%来自小额捐款者。④ 尤其是新冠疫情背景下数量急剧攀升的在线捐款者，在筹款活动中发挥着越来越重要的作用，捐款数突破总统竞选活动在2020年所获捐款总额的一半，这一比例是史无前例的。特朗普在此次竞选连任活动中筹集到了7.74亿

---

① Kirill Bryanov, "Bitcoin For America: Cryptocurrencies In Campaign Finance", CoinTelegraph (May 31, 2018), https://cointelegraph.com/news/bitcoin-for-america-cryptocurrencies-in-campaign-finance.

② Sritanshu Sinha, "Can Political Fundraising Through Crypto Find Mainstream Acceptance?" Coin Telegraph (Oct. 17, 2019), https://cointelegraph.com/news/can-political-fundraising-through-crypto-find-mainstream-acceptance.

③ Karl Evers-Hillstrom, "Most Expensive Ever: 2020 Election Cost $14.4 Billion", Open Secrets (Feb. 11, 2021), https://www.opensecrets.org/news/2021/02/2020-cycle-cost-14p4-billion-doubling-16/.

④ Shane Goldmacher, "The 2020 Campaign Is the Most Expensive Ever (By a Lot)", The New York Times, Oct. 28, 2020.

美元，其中亦有一半以上的资金来自捐款额小于200美元的小捐款者。[①] 此次大选表明，选举资金来源的两极结构正在形成："北极"是传统的、由联邦政府监管的个人捐款制度，经过不断的宣传呼吁，小额捐款者对选举的影响正在逐渐放大；而"南极"则是在很大程度上游离于披露监管之外的超级政治行动委员会和501免税组织，其代表着大公司及其背后大捐款人的巨额隐秘资金。这也为未来的美国竞选财务改革提供了更明晰的线索：在继续堵塞大公司和顶级富人滥用捐款规定漏洞的同时，应为小额捐款者提供更深入且党派中立的选举信息，帮助其充分决策，并提供更多的线上和线下捐款通道支持。

本章小结

在过去的10年中，各国政府几乎都在数字化或是接受数字创新以逐渐使其机构现代化，全球反腐败斗争规则也随之悄然改变。区块链和互联网技术使人们对政府改善公共服务和提升廉政的潜力抱有更高期望，政府与公民的关系亦有望以此为契机得到重塑。新技术不仅不会取代对法律改革和更强大执法机构的需求，还可能成为机构反腐败职能的强大辅助工具。信息化时代的互联网平台让具有同一优先利益的选民能够快速地联合起来，公民们越发强烈地意识到自身在民主进程中被赋予的话语权。即使是在大公司和暗钱蚕食民主政治的当下，公民及其个人投票仍然是不可忽视的强大力量。无论是对于大政府的焦虑，还是对各党派动机的怀疑和谴责，都可以通过广泛应用提升透明度的新技术，减少政府和私人商业领域在政治经济活动中可能危及民主的腐败风险。基于区块链的投票系统、互联网社交媒体和人工智能技术将在追踪政治资金、保障竞选公正和防范政府腐败方面发挥不可替代的作用，从而提高政治与政府透明度，重塑问责制，市民也将被允许更广泛且有深度地参与民主治理。此时，民主社会与政府的依存关系也将有望回归麦迪逊式的注解："公众观点为政府所设定

[①] Krystal Hur, "Small Donors Ruled 2020; Will That Change Post-Trump?" Open Secrets (Feb. 3, 2021), https://www.opensecrets.org/news/2021/02/small-donors-dominated-2020-will-that-change-in-midterms/.

的界限,方为每个自由政府的真正主权。"① 但这种扩大参与式的改革仍存在一定局限。一方面,作为美国人对民主文化的自我注解,"人民主权"(popular sovereignty)的内涵远比其他西方民主国家更为民粹主义,美国独特的"大众参与"和意识形态决定了,旨在赋予政治领导人权力的民主制度,只要发生任何变化,都将引起"人民"与"精英"之间的冲突;② 另一方面,脸书和"X"(原推特)这样的新社交媒体巨头正在利用其算法,决定公众所能了解到的事实,这种审查效应与通信革命带来的民主扩大参与叠加,无疑会进一步加剧社会内部意识形态的两极化和利益分歧。

---

① James Madison, "Public Opinion", *National Gazette*, Dec. 19, 1791.
② Richard H. Pildes, "Romanticizing Democracy, Political Fragmentation, and the Decline of American Government", *The Yale Law Journal*, No. 124, 2014, pp. 839–845.

结　论

美国宪法的起草者们确立了三权分立的宪政政府，并通过两院制代表人民行使政府权力。这种民主制度的设计意在实现许多不同的价值，游说、竞选捐款及其背后所代表的利益集团即为其衍生体，政治决策与改革的过程则展现了不同群体价值之间的冲突与权衡。回顾美国竞选改革的近代历史，联邦竞选财务制度的结构在一定程度上扭曲了立法机关的职能。由于只有一小部分的投票选民向竞选进行捐款，应对竞选成本不断攀升的立法者往往面临"双重选区"问题——其不仅必须对选民负责，还要对大捐款人做出回应。金钱在政治中的腐败影响早已突破了公开行贿的原始范畴，聚集在少数人手中的大量财富越来越多地以不为人知的方式渗透到选举中，不成比例地影响着竞选和立法结果，形成了实质上的利益交换。而在过去的20年中，金融资本主义阶段下的政治系统运转效率越来越低，党派分歧日益严重，就将反政治腐败的法案变为法律而言，国会正处于有史以来生产力最低的阶段。面对大公司和富人对宪法第一修正案、自由主义、平均主义和民主价值观的理解与取舍提出的挑战，"联合公民案"给出的回答不仅凸显了竞选财务法律规制的内在矛盾，也与美式民主问题的不可调和性相呼应——经济不平等正通过转变为公开的政治不平等延续，身份成为政治决策中利益的分割标准，一人一票的民主原则被破坏，普通选民在实质上丧失了平等选举权。

治理和预防游说、竞选捐款乃至更广泛政治活动中的腐败行为，其前提恰恰是承认美国代议制政府所特有的不平等和党派政治顽疾，而不能仅仅停留于抑制表面的游说活动和利益集团的竞选捐款。只有在该前提下，金钱在竞选捐款、政治广告和游说旋转门等政治活动中发挥的作用方能得到调整，民选代表才能主动避免利用民主代议制的缺陷，减少腐败的发生，此时革除内在腐败根源的努力才是合理的。因此竞选财务的改革目标，与其说是净化民主机制，不如说是设法克服其民主制度自身最严重的缺陷。并且，民主与经济制度的成熟发展从来不意味着国家政治与腐败绝缘，即使在法律高度发达的资本主义普通法社会中，各种礼物交换和招待行为与腐败之间的界限也并不总是十分清晰，界定与规制都存在操作上的困难。但越来越多的州和国会议员也正致力于推动法律改革，以促进选举与政治进程的安全与权利平等。在未来，竞选财务及反腐败法律政策的改革仍将以提升政治资金透明度为中心，逐步限制大公司对竞选的影响，切断外国竞选资金和提升小额捐款者的影响力。尽管改革措施不免存在局限性，许多细节问题也还有待实践进一步验证，但人民意见的充分表达与反馈、政治体制透明度的提高，仍然是防止民主意见表达转向多数人暴政的民粹主义以及回归公民权利与国家权力契约本质的根本途径。

值得注意的是，在美国社会民主思想极端分化的时代背景下，被过度理想化与抽象化的平等投票权、结社和言论自由等民主价值观念，对现有政治制度改革的推动作用十分有限。2020年伊始，引发剧烈社会震荡的新冠疫情与"黑人命贵"运动再次证明，这些理想观念往往因为脱离政府权力组织的事实经验，而使政府的有效治理及其权力合法性受损。因此，不应将一味扩大政治参与的改革视为治愈美式民主缺陷的灵药，而是需要更加谨慎地，在扩大公民参与政治和政府有效行使职能的局限性之间进行权衡。

参考文献

中文类

著作

林宏宇：《美国总统选举政治研究》，天津人民出版社2018年版。

周琪、袁征：《美国的政治腐败与反腐败——对美国反腐败机制的研究》，中国社会科学出版社2009年版。

［法］托克维尔：《论美国的民主》，高牧译，南海出版公司2007年版。

［美］C.赖特·米尔斯：《权力精英》，尹弘毅、法磊译，新华出版社2004年版。

［美］塞缪尔·亨廷顿：《美国政治：激荡于理想与现实之间》，先萌奇、景伟明译，新华出版社2017年版。

［美］苏珊·罗斯-阿克曼、邦妮·J.帕利夫卡：《腐败与政府：根源、后果与改革》，郑澜译，中信出版社2018年版。

［美］泽菲尔·提绍特：《美国的腐败——从富兰克林的鼻烟盒到联合公民胜诉案》，冯克利、苗晓枫译，中国方正出版社2015年版。

期刊

韦佳：《美国司法再投资改革实践检视》，《河南师范大学学报》（哲学社会科学版）2020年第1期。

徐彤武：《"外围团体"对2012年美国大选的影响》，《美国研究》2012年第3期。

网络资料

由检：《年赚300亿：特朗普背后的大金主，在美国监狱做成了一份大生意》，新浪网，http://k.sina.com.cn/article_6065395581_16986977d01900i8tg.html，2019年9月3日。

英文类

著作

Ackerman, B. & Ayres, I., *Voting with Dollars: A New Paradigm for Campaign Finance*, New Haven, CT: Yale University Press, 2004.

Anzalone, C. A., *Supreme Court Cases on Political Representation, 1787 – 2001*, New York: Routledge, 2002.

Austen-Smith, D., "Interest groups: Money, Information, and Influence", in D. C. Mueller, ed., *Perspectives on Public Choice: A Handbook*, New York: Cambridge University Press, 1997.

Ayres, I., "Disclosure Versus Anonymity in Campaign Finance", in I. Shapiro & S. Macedo, eds., *Designing Democratic Institutions*, New York: New York University Press, 2000.

Bartels, L., *Unequal Democracy: The Political Economy of the New Gilded Age*, Princeton, NJ: Princeton University Press, 2009.

Bauer, R. A., Sola Pool, I. de & Dexter, L. A., *American business and public policy*, New York: Atherton Press, 1963.

Baumgartner, F. R. & others, *Lobbying and Policy Change: Who Wins, Who Loses, and Why*, Chicago: University of Chicago Press, 2009.

Bennett, J. T., *Stifling Political Competition: How Government Has Rigged the System to Benefit Demopublicans and Exclude Third Parties*, New York: Springer, 2009.

Benson, G., *Political Corruption in America*, Lexington, MA: Lexington Books, 1978.

Berg, L. L., Hahn, H. & Schmidhauser, J. R., *Corruption in the American Political System*, Morristown, NJ: General Learning Press, 1976.

Berry, M., *Five Dollars and Porkchop Sandwich: Vote Buying and the Corruption of Democracy*, Boston, MA: Beacon Press, 2016.

Birnbaum, J., *The Lobbyists: How Influence Peddlers Get Their Way in Washington*, New York: Times Books, 1992.

Bordelon, G., "History and Evolution of Lobbying Regulation", in A. Handlin, ed., *Dirty Deals? An Encyclopedia of Lobbying, Political Influence, and Corruption*, Santa Barbara, CA: ABC-CLIO, LLC, 2014.

Braithwaite, J., *Corporate Crime in the Pharmaceutical Industry*, England: Routledge & Kegan Paul Books, 1984.

Bridenthal, R., *The Hidden History of Crime, Corruption, and States*, New York: Berghahn Books, 2013.

Brooks, R. C., *Corruption in America Politics and Life*, New York: Dodd, Mead & Co., 1910.

Caro, R., *The Years of Lyndon Johnson: Master of the Senate*, New York: Alfred A. Knopf, 2002.

Carter, D. T., *The Politics of Rage: George C. Wallace, the Origins of the New Conservatism, and the Transformation of American Politics*, New York: Simon & Schuster, 1995.

Cicero, M. T., *On the Commonwealth and on the Laws*, Cambridge: Cambridge University Press, 2017.

Clemens, E. S., *The People's Lobby: Organizational Innovation and the Rise of Interest-Group Politics in the United States, 1890 – 1925*, Chicago, IL: University of Chicago Press, 1997.

Collins, R. K. L. & Skover, D. M., *When Money Speaks: The McCutcheon Decision, Campaign Finance Laws, and the First Amendment*, Oak Park: Top Five Books, LLC, 2014.

Cost, J., *A Republic No More: Big Government and the Crisis of American Political Corruption*, New York: Encounter Books, 2015.

Cost, J., *The Price of Greatness: Alexander Hamilton, James Madison, and the Creation of American Oligarchy*, New York: Basic Books, 2018.

Dalberg-Action, J. E. E., "Letter to Bishop Mandell Creighton", in J. N. Figgis & R. V. Laurence, eds., *Historical Essays and Studies*, London: Macmillan, 1887.

Douglas, P. H., *Ethics in Government*, Cambridge, MA: Harvard University Press, 1952.

Drew, E., *Politics and Money, the New Road to Corruption*, New York: Macmillan Publishing Company, 1983.

Drew, E., *The Corruption of American Politics: What Went Wrong and Why*, Secaucus, NJ: Carol Publishing Group, 1999.

Dukes, G., Braithwaite, J. & Moloney, J. P., *Pharmaceuticals, Corporate Crime and Public Health*, Cheltenham, England: Edward Elgar, 2014.

Dye, T. R., *Politics in America*, Englewood Cliffs, NJ: Prentice Hall, 1995.

Falguera, E., Jones, S. & Ohman, M. eds., *Funding of Political Parties and Election Campaigns. A Handbook on Political Finance*, Stockholm: International Institute for Democracy and Electoral Assistance, 2014.

Ferguson, C. H., *Predator Nation: Corporate Criminals, Political Corruption, and the Hijacking of America*, New York: Crown Publishing Group, 2012.

Froehlich, A., "E-Governance in Africa and the World", in A. Froehlich & others eds., *Space Supporting Africa. Volume 3: Security, Peace, and Development through Efficient Governance Supported by Space Applications*, Cham, Switzerland: Springer, 2020.

Gardiner J. & Lyman, T., *Decisions for Sale, Corruption and Reform in Land-use and Building Regulations*, New York: Praeger, 1978.

Gardiner, J., *The Politics of Corruption: Organized Crime in an American City*, New York: Sage, 1970.

Gilens, M., *Affluence and Influence: Economic Inequality and Political Power in America*, Princeton, NJ: Princeton University Press, 2011.

Gore, A., *The Future: Six Drivers of Global Change*, New York: Random House Publishing Group, 2013.

Gottschalk, M., *Caught: The Prison State and the Lockdown of American Politics*, Princeton, NJ: Princeton University Press, 2016.

Green, P. & Ward, T., *State Crime: Governments, Violence and Corruption*, London: Pluto Press, 2004.

Grossman, G. & Helpman, E., *Special Interest Politics*, Cambridge, MA: MIT Press, 2001.

Hansen, J., *Gaining Access: Congress and the Farm Lobby, 1919 – 1981*, Chicago: University of Chicago Press, 1991.

Hasen, R. L., *Plutocrats United: Campaign Money, the Supreme Court, and the Distortion of American Elections*, New Haven, CT: Yale University Press, 2016.

Heinz, J. P. & others, *The Hollow Core: Private Interests in National Policy Making*, Cambridge, MA: Harvard University Press, 1993.

Hessenius, B., *Hardball Lobbying for Nonprofits: Real Advocacy for Nonprofits in the New Century*, New York: Palgrave Macmillan, 2007.

Holmes, L., *The End of Communist Power: Anti-Corruption Campaigns and Le-*

gitimation Crisis, Cambridge, England: Polity Press, 1993.

Hume, D., "Of the Independence of Parliament", in E. F. Miller, ed., Hume's Essays: Moral, Political and Literary, Indianapolis: Liberty Classics, 1985, (A) 1741 (8).

Žižek, S., "Living in the Time of Monsters", in M. Nikolakaki, ed., Critical Pedagogy in the New Dark Ages: Challenges and Possibilities, New York: Peter Lang Inc., 2012.

Johnson, D. W., Democracy for Hire: A History of American Political Consulting, New York: Oxford University Press, 2017.

Johnson, D. W., No Place for Amateurs: How Political Consultants Are Reshaping American Democracy, New York: Routledge, 2001.

Johnston, M., Political Corruption and Public Policy in America, Monterey, CA: Brooks/Cole Publishing, 1982.

Johnston, M., Syndromes of Corruption: Wealth, Power, and Democracy, Cambridge, UK: Cambridge University Press, 2005.

Johnston, M., "The Definitions Debate: Old Conflicts in New Guises", in A. K. Jain, ed., The Political Economy of Corruption, London: Routledge, 2001.

Josephon, M., The Robber Barons: Great American Capitalists, 1891 – 1901, New York: Harcourt, Brace and Company, 1934.

Kaiser, R. G., So Damn Much Money: The Triumph of Lobbying and the Corrosion of American Government (1st ed.), New York: Knopf, 2009.

Krugman, P., The Conscience of a Liberal, New York: W. W. Norton & Company, 2009.

Lessig, L., Lesterland: The Corruption of Congress and How to End It, New York: Ted Conference, 2013.

Lessig, L., Republic, Lost: How Money Corrupts Congress-and a Plan to Stop It, New York: Hatchette, 2011.

Link, W. A., Righteous Warrior: Jesse Helms and the Rise of Modern Conservatism, New York: St. Martin's Press, 2008.

Madison, J., "The House of Representatives from the New York Packet", The Federalist Papers: No. 52, Feb. 8, 1788, New York: Signet Classics, 2003.

Madison, J., "The Union as a Safeguard Against Domestic Faction and Insurrection from the New York Packet", The Federalist Papers, No. 10, Nov. 23, 1787, New York: Signet Classics, 2003.

Madison, J., "Vices of the Political System of the United States", in R. A. Rutland & W. M. E. Rachal, eds., *The Papers of James Madison*, Vol. 9, *April 1786 – 24 May 1787 and Supplement 1781 – 1784*, Chicago: The University of Chicago Press, 1975, pp. 345 – 358.

Mann, T. E. & Ornstein, N. J., *It's Even Worse than It Looks: How the American Constitutional System Collided with the New Politics of Extremism*, New York: Basic Books, 2016.

Mercer, L. J., "Railroad Land Grants", in K. L. Bryant, Jr., Ed., *Encyclopedia of American Business History and Biography: Railroads in the Age of Regulation, 1900 – 1980*, New York: Bruccoli Clark Layman, Inc. and Facts on File Publications, 1988.

Michael, M. J. & Gais, T. L., *The Day After Reform: Sobering Campaign Finance Lessons from the American States*, Albany: Rockefeller Institute Press, 1988.

Milbrath, L. W., *The Washington Lobbyists*, Chicago: Rand McNally, 1963.

Mintz, M. & Cohen, J. S., *America, Inc.: Who Owns and Operates the United States*, New York, NY: Dial Press, 1971.

Mitchell, J. L., Sebold, K. & others, *The Political Geography of Campaign Finance: Fundraising and Contribution Patterns in Presidential Elections, 2004 – 2012*, New York: Palgrave Macmillan, 2015.

Mueller, D. C. (1989). *Public Choice II: A Revised Edition of Public Choice*, Cambridge, MA: Cambridge University Press.

Myers, G., *History of the Supreme Court of the United States*, Chicago, IL: Charles H. Kerr & Company, 2015.

Myrdal, G., *An American Dilemma: The Negro Problem and Modern Democracy*, New York: Harper & Brothers Publishers, 1944.

Nownes, A. J. & Loomis, B. A., "Lobbying and the Balance of Power in American Politics", in A. J. Cigler, B. A. Loomis & A. J. Nownes, eds., *Interest Group Politics* (10th Ed.), Lanham, MA: Rowman & Littlefield, 2019.

Nownes, A. J., *Total Lobbying: What Lobbyists Want (and How They Try to Get It)*, New York: Cambridge University Press, 2006.

Olson, M., *The Logic of Collective Action: Public Goods and the Theory of Groups*, Cambridge, MA: Harvard University Press, 1965.

Overacker, L., *Money in Elections*, New York: MacMillan Company, 1932.

Persson, T. & Tabellini, G. , *Political Economics: Explaining Economic Policy*, Cambridge, MA: MIT Press, 2000.

Polybius, *The Histories of Polybius* (Vol. 1 & 2), London: MaCmillan and Co. , 1889.

Post, R. C. , *Citizens Divided: Campaign Finance Reform and the Constitution*, Cambridge, MA: Harvard University Press, 2014.

Reinsch, P. S. , *American Legislatures and Legislative Methods*, New York: Century Company, 1907.

Rose-Ackerman, S. , *Corruption and Government: Causes, Consequences, and Reform*, Cambridge: Cambridge University Press, 1999.

Rose-Ackerman, S. & Palifka, B. J. , *Corruption and Government: Causes, Consequences, and Reform*, Cambridge: Cambridge University Press, 2016.

Rose-Ackerman, S. , "Political Corruption and Democratic Structures", in A. K. Jain ed. , *The Political Economy of Corruption*, London: Routledge, 2001.

Rose-Ackerman, S. , *The Economics of Corruption: An Essay in Political Economy*, New York: Academic Press, 1978.

Rothstein, B. & Varraich, A. , *Making Sensing of Corruption*, New York: Cambridge University Press, 2017.

Sabato, L. J. & Simpson G. R. , *Dirty Little Secrets: The Persistence of Corruption in American Politics*, New York: Times Books, 1996.

Samples, J. , *The Fallacy of Campaign Finance Reform*, Chicago: The University of Chicago Press, 2006.

Schattschneider, E. E. , *The Semi-Sovereign People: A Realist's View of Democracy in America*, New York: Thomson Learning, 1975.

Schlozman, K. L. & Tierney, J. T. , *Organized Interests and American Democracy*, New York: Harper & Row, 1986.

Schlozman, K. L. , Verba, S. & Brady, H. E. , *The Unheavenly Chorus: Unequal Political Voice and the Broken Promise of American Democracy*, Princeton: Princeton University Press, 2012.

Scott, J. C. & Murphy, J. , *Comparative political corruption*, Englewood Cliffs: Prentice-Hall, 1972.

Selfa, L. , *The Democrats: A Critical History*, New York: Haymarket Books, 2008.

Sherrill, R. , *Why They Call It Politics* (2nd ed.), New York: Harcourt Brace

Jovanovich, 1974.

Sikes, E. R., *State and Federal Corrupt-Practices Legislation*, Durham, NC: Duke University Press, 1928.

Smith, B. A., *Unfree Speech: The Folly of Campaign Finance Reform*, Princeton, NJ: Princeton University Press, 2001.

Sorauf, F., *Money in American Elections*, Glenview, IL: Scott, Foresman, 1998.

Sussman, G., *Global Electioneering* (1st ed.), Lanham, MD: Rowman & Littlefield Publishing Group, 2005.

Sutherland, E. H., *White Collar Crime: The Uncut Version*, New Haven, CT: Yale University Press, 1983.

Teachout, Z., *Corruption in America-From Benjamin Franklin's Snuff Box to Citizens United*, Cambridge, MA: Harvard University Press, 2014.

Tepper, J. & Hearn, D., *The Myth of Capitalism: Monopolies and the Death of Competition* (1st ed.), Hoboken, NJ: John Wiley & Sons, 2019.

Tribe, L. & Matz, J., *Uncertain Justice: The Roberts Court and the Constitution*, New York: Picador, 2015.

Underkuffler, L. S., *Captured by Evil: The Idea of Corruption in Law*, New Haven, CT: Yale University Press, 2013.

Volcker, P. & Harper, C. (2018). *Keeping at It: The Request for Sound Money and Good Government*, New York: Public Affairs.

Wallis, J. J., "The Concept of Systematic Corruption in American History", in E. Glaeser & C. Goldin eds., *Corruption and Reform*, Chicago: University of Chicago Press, 2006.

Wolff, R. D. & Resnick, S. A., *Contending Economic Theories: Neo-classical, Keynesian, and Marxian*, Cambridge, MA: MIT Press, 2012.

Wright, J. R., *Interest Groups and Congress: Lobbying, Contributions, and Influence*, Needham Heights, MA: Allyn and Bacon, 1996.

期刊

Alexander, H. E. & Meyers, H. B., "A Financial Landslide for the G. O. P", *Fortune*, Mar. 1970.

Allard, N., "The Law of Lobbying: Lobbying Is an Honorable Profession: The Right to Petition and the Competition to Be Right", *Stanford Law & Policy Review*, No. 19, 2008.

Alschuler, A. W. & others, "Why Limits on Contributions to Super PACS

Should Survive Citizens United", *Fordham Law Review*, Vol. 86, No. 5, 2018.

Ansolabehere, S., Snyder, J. M. & Tripathi, M., "Are PAC Contributions and Lobbying Linked? New Evidence from the 1995 Lobby Disclosure Act", *Business and Politics*, Vol. 4, No. 2, 2002.

Austen-Smith, D. & Wright, J. R., "Competitive Lobbying for a Legislator's Vote", *Social Choice and Welfare*, Vol. 9, No. 3, 1992.

Austen-Smith, D. & Wright, J. R., "Counteractive lobbying", *American Journal of Political Science*, Vol. 38, No. 1, 1994.

Ayres, I. & Bulow, J., "The Donation Booth: Mandating Donor Anonymity to Disrupt the Market for Political Influence", *Stanford Law Review*, No. 50, 1998.

Baker, D., Issues in Trade Protectionism, *Report for the Center for Economic and Policy Research*, 2009.

Baker, P., Berry, M., Czitrom, D. & others, "Interchange: Corruption Has a History", *Journal of American History*, Vol. 105, No. 4, 2019.

Baron, D., "Electoral Competition with Informed and Uninformed Voters", *American Political Science Review*, No. 88, 1994.

Bassetti, T. & Pavesi, F., "Electoral Contributions and the Cost of Unpopularity", *Economic Inquiry*, Vol. 55, No. 4, 2017.

Bennedsen, M. & Feldmann, S. E., "Informational Lobbying and Political Contributions", *Journal of Public Economics*, Vol. 90, No. 4-5, 2006.

Bennedsen, M., "Vote Buying Through Resource Allocation in Government Controlled Enterprises", *Rivista di Politica Economica*, SIPI Spa, Vol. 93, No. 1, 1998.

BeVier, L., "Campaign Finance Reform: Specious Arguments, Intractable Dilemmas", *Columbia Law Review*, No. 94, 1994.

BeVier, L., "Money and Politics: A Perspective on the First Amendment and Campaign Finance Reform", *California Law Review*, No. 73, 1985.

Birnbaum, J., "The End of Legal Bribery How the Abramoff Case Could Change Washington", *Washington Monthly*, No. 38, 2006.

Blakely, C. R. & Bumphus, V. W., "Private and Public Sector Prisons-a Comparison of Select Characteristics", *Federal Probation*, Vol. 68, No. 1, 2004.

Blau, B. M., Brough, T. J. & Thomas, D. W., "Corporate Lobbying, Political Connections, and the Bailout of Banks", *Journal of Banking and Finance*, Vol. 37, No. 8, 2013.

Boas, T. C., Hidalgo, F. D. & Richardson, N. P., "The Spoils of Victory: Campaign Donations and Government Contracts in Brazil", *Journal of Politics*, Vol. 76, No. 2, 2014.

Boorstin, D., "Effects of Watergate", *The Congressional Quarterly*, 1973.

Brandeis, L., "What Publicity Can Do", *Harper's Weekly* 10, Dec. 20, 1913.

Brandenburg, B. & Schotland, R. A., "Keeping Courts Impartial Amid Changing Judicial Elections", *Dædalus*, Fall 2008, Fall.

Briffault, R., "Corporations, Corruption, and Complexity: Campaign Finance after Citizens United", *Cornell Journal of Law and Public Policy*, Vol. 20, No. 3, 2011.

Briffault, R., "Lobbying and Campaign Finance: Separate and Together", *Stanford Law & Policy Review*, No. 19, 2008.

Briffault, R., "The Anxiety of Influence: The Evolving Regulation of Lobbying", *Election Law Journal*, Vol. 13, No. 1, 2014.

Bronars, S. & Lott, Jr., J., "Do Campaign Donations Alter How a Politician Votes? Or, Do Donors Support Candidates Who Value the Same Things That They Do?" *Journal of Law and Economics*, Vol. 40, No. 2, 1997.

Brooks, R. C., "The Nature of Political Corruption", *Political Science Quarterly*, Vol. 24, No. 1, 1909.

Burke, E., Speeches on the Independence of Parliament, *The Spectator*, May 26, 1855.

Burke, T. F., "The Concept of Corruption in Campaign Finance Law", *Constitutional Commentary*, No. 1089, 1997.

Caiden, N., "Shortchanging the Public", *Public Administration Review*, Vol. 39, No. 3, 1979.

Cain, B. E., "Is 'Dependence Corruption' the Solution to America's Campaign Finance Problems?" *California Law Review*, Vol. 102, No. 1, 2014.

Campos, N. F. & Giovannoni, F., "Lobbying, Corruption and Political Influence", *Public Choice*, Vol. 131, No. 1/2, 2007.

Charron, N. & others, "Careers, Connections, and Corruption Risks: Investigating the Impact of Bureaucratic Meritocracy on Public Procurement Processes",

Journal of Politics, Vol. 79, No. 1, 2017.

Chirinko, R. S. & Wilson, D. J., "Can Lower Tax Rates Be Bought? Business Rent-Seeking and Tax Competition Among U. S. States", *National Tax Journal*, Vol. 63, No. 4, 2010.

Cooper, J., Gulen, H. & Ovtchinnikov, A., "Corporate Political Contributions and Stock Returns", *Journal of Finance*, Vol. 65, No. 2, 2010.

Correia, M., "Political Connections and SEC Enforcement", *Journal of Accounting and Economics*, Vol. 57, No. 2, 2014.

De Figueiredo, J. M., "Lobbying and Information in Politics", *Business and Politics*, No. 4, 2002.

DeMuth, C., "Our Corrupt Government", *Claremont Review of Books*, August 1, 2015.

Edwards, E. J., "Tammany: Early Spoilsment and the Reign of the Plug-Uglies", *McClure's Magazine*, Vol. 4, No. 1, 1985.

Florence, C. S. & others, "The Economic Burden of Prescription Opioid Overdose, Abuse, and Dependence in the United States, 2013", *Medical Care*, Vol. 54, No. 10, 2016.

Foley, E. B., "Equal-Dollar-Per-Voter: A Constitutional Principle of Campaign Finance", *Columbia Law Review*, Vol. 94, No. 4, 1994.

Foreman, C., "Money in Politics: Campaign Finance and Its Influence Over the Political Process and Public Policy", *UIC John Marshall Law Review*, Vol. 52, No. 185, 2018.

Fouirnaies, A. & Hall, A. B., "The Financial Incumbency Advantage: Causes and Consequences", *Journal of Politics*, Vol. 76, No. 3, 2014.

Gerber, Alan S. & others, "How Large and Long-Lasting are the Persuasive Effects of Televised Campaign Ads? Results from a Randomized Field Experiment", *American Political Science Review*, Vol. 105, No. 1, 2011.

Gerken, H. K. & Tausanovitch, A., "Lobbying, Campaign Finance, and the Privatization of Democracy", *Election Law Journal*, No. 13, 2014.

Gilens, M. & Page, B. I., "Testing Theories of American Politics: Elites, Interest Groups, and Average Citizens", *Perspectives on Politics*, Vol. 12, No. 3, 2014.

Goldstein, K., Schweidel, D. A. & Wittenwyler, M., "Lessons Learned: Political Advertising and Political Law", *Minnesota Law Review*, No. 96, 2012.

Grossman, G. & Helpman, E., "Electoral Competition and Special Interest Politics", *Review of Economic Studies*, No. 63, 1996.

Hall, R. L. & Deardorff, A. V., "Lobbying as Legislative Subsidy", *American Political Science Review*, Vol. 100, No. 1, 2006.

Harstad, B. & Svensson, J., "Bribes, Lobbying, and Development", *American Political Science Review*, Vol. 105, No. 1, 2011.

Hart, D. M., "Why Do Some Firms Give? Why Do Some Give a Lot?: High-Tech PACs, 1977 – 1996", *The Journal of Politics*, Vol. 63, No. 4, 2001.

Hasen, R. L., "Lobbying, Rent-Seeking, and the Constitution", *Stanford Law Review*, No. 64, 2012.

Hellman, D., "Money Talks but it Isn't Speech", *Minnesota Law Review*, No. 95, 2011.

Hill, M. D. & others, "Determinants and Effects of Corporate Lobbying", *Financial Management*, No. 42, 2013.

Hill, S. J. & Huber, G. A., "Representativeness and Motivations of the Contemporary Donorate: Results from Merged Survey and Administrative Records", *Political Behavior*, Vol. 39, No. 1, 2017.

Hojnacki, M. & others, "Studying Organizational Advocacy and Influence: Reexamining Interest Group Research", *Annual Review of Political Science*, No. 15, 2012.

Horwitz, M. J., "Republicanism and Liberalism in American Constitutional Thought", *William & Mary Law Review*, No. 29, 1987.

Johnston, M., "From Thucydides to Mayor Daley: Bad Politics, and a Culture of Corruption", *Political Science and Politics*, Vol. 39, No. 4, 2006.

Jorgensen, P., "Pharmaceuticals, Political Money, and Public Policy: A Theoretical and Empirical Agenda", *Journal of Law, Medicine & Ethics*, Vol. 41, No. 3, 2013.

Kalla, J. L. & Broockman, D. E., "Campaign Contributions Fcilitate Access to Congressional Officials: A Randomized Field Experiment", *American Journal of Political Science*, Vol. 60, No. 3, 2016.

Kang, M. S., "The End of Campaign Finance Law", *Virginia Law Review*, Vol. 98, No. 1, 2012.

Keene, D., "Big Pharma: The International Reach of the Opioid Crisis", Harvard Political Review (May 4, 2020), https://harvardpolitics.com/big-pharma/.

Lamm, C. B., "Let's Leave Politics Out of It", *ABA Journal*, Vol. 96, No. 3, 2010.

Langbein, L. I. , "Money and Access: Some Empirical Evidence", *The Journal of Politics*, Vol. 48, No. 4, 1986.

LaPira, T. M. & Thomas Ⅲ, H. F. , "Just How Many Newt Gingrich's Are There on K Street? Estimating the True Size and Shape of Washington's Revolving Door", *SSRN Electronic Journal*, Apr. , 2013.

Levinson, S. , "Electoral Regulation: Some Comments", *Hofstra Law Review*, No. 18, 1989.

Lin, D. H. , Lucas, E. & Murimi, I. B. , "Financial Conflicts of Interest and the Centers for Disease Control and Prevention's 2016 Guideline for Prescribing Opioids for Chronic Pain", *JAMA Internal Medicine*, Vol. 177, No. 3, 2017.

Lohmann, S. , "Information, Access, and Contributions: A Signaling Model of Lobbying", *Public Choice*, Vol. 85, No. 3 - 4, 1995.

Madison, J. , "Public Opinion", *National Gazette*, December 19, 1791.

McCoy, M. S. & Kanter, G. P. , "Campaign Contributions from Political Action Committees to Members of Congressional Committees Responding to the Opioid Crisis", *The Journal of the American Medical Association*, Vol. 320, No. 14, 2018.

McKay, A. M. , "Buying Amendments? Lobbyists' Campaign Contributions and Microlegislation in the Creation of the Affordable Care Act", *Legislative Studies Quarterly*, Vol. 45, No. 2, 2020.

Mukherjee, A. , "Impacts of Private Prison Contracting on Inmate Time Served and Recidivism", *American Economic Journal: Economic Policy*, Vol. 13, No. 2, 2021.

Murray, M. J. , "The Pharmaceutical Industry: A Study in Corporate Power", *International Journal of Health Services*, Vol. 4, No. 4, 1974.

Nagle, J. C. , "The Recusal Alternative to Campaign Finance Legislation", *Harvard Journal of Legislation*, No. 37, 2000.

Newmark, A. J. & Nownes, A. J. , "It's All Relative: Perceptions of Interest Group Influence", *Interest Groups & Advocacy*, Vol. 6, No. 1, 2016.

Nye, J. S. , "Corruption and Political Development: A Cost-Benefit Analysis", *American Political Science Review* No. 61, 1967.

O'Connor, A. , "The Privatized City", *Journal of Urban History*, Vol. 34, No. 2, 2008.

Page, B. I. , Bartels, L. M. & Seawright, J. , "Democracy and the Policy Preferences of Wealthy Americans", *Perspectives on Politics*, Vol. 11, No.

1, 2013.

Peters, J. G. & Welch, S., "Political Corruption in America: A Search for Definitions and a Theory, or If Political Corruption Is in the Mainstream of American Politics. Why Is It Not in the Mainstream of American Politics Research?" *American Political Science Review*, Vol. 72, No. 3, 1978.

Petrella, C. & Begley, J., "The Color of Corporate Corrections: The Overrepresentation of People of Color in the For-Profit Corrections Industry", *Radical Criminology*, No. 2, 2013.

Petrella, C., "The Color of Corporate Corrections, Part II: Contractual Exemptions and the Overrepresentation of People of Color in Private Prisons", *Radical Criminology*, No. 3, 2014.

Pildes, R. H., "Romanticizing Democracy, Political Fragmentation, and the Decline of American Government", *The Yale Law Journal*, No. 124, 2014.

Pildes, R. H., "Small-Donor-Based Campaign-Finance Reform and Political Polarization", *The Yale Law Journal Forum*, Vol. 129, No. 18, 2019.

Powell, L. W., "The Influence of Campaign Contributions on Legislative Policy", *The Forum: A Journal of Applied Research in Contemporary Politics*, Vol. 11, No. 3, 2013.

Richter, B. K., Samphantharak, K. & Timmons, J. F., "Lobbying and Taxes", *American Journal of Political Science*, Vol. 53, No. 4, 2009.

Riezman, R. & Wilson, J. D., "Political Reform and Trade Policy", *Journal of International Economics*, No. 42, 1997.

Robertson, C. & others, "The Appearance and the Reality of Quid Pro Quo Corruption: An Empirical Investigation", *Journal of Legal Analysis*, Vol. 8, No. 2, Winter 2016.

Rose-Ackerman, S., "Corruption & Purity", *Daedalus*, Vol. 147, No. 3, 2018.

Rundquist, B. S., Strom, G. S. & Peters, J. G., "Corrupt Politicians and Their Electoral Support: Some Theoretical and Empirical Observations", *American Political Science Review*, No. 71, 1977.

Seidman, L. M., "Can Free Speech Be Progressive?" *Columbia Law Review*, Vol. 118, No. 7, 2018.

Senturia, J. A., "Corruption, Political", *Encyclopedia of the Social Sciences*, No. 4, 1930.

Smith, B. A., "Faulty Assumptions and Undemocratic Consequences of Campaign Finance Reform", *The Yale Law Journal*, No. 105, 1996.

Smith, B. A., "The Myth of Campaign Finance Reform", *National Affairs*, No. 6, Winter 2010.

Smith, R. A., "Advocacy, Interpretation and Influence in the US Congress", *American Political Science Review*, No. 78, 1984.

Snyder, J. M., "On Buying Legislatures", *Economics and Politics*, No. 3, 1991.

Spivak, A. & Sharp, S., "Inmate Recidivism as a Measure of Private Prison Performance", *Crime and Delinquency*, Vol. 54, No. 3, 2008.

Stratmann, T., "Can Special Interests Buy Congressional Votes? Evidence from Financial Services Legislation", *Journal of Law & Economics*, Vol. 45, No. 2, 2002.

Stratmann, T., "The Market for Congressional Votes: Is Timing of Contributions Everything", *Journal of Law & Economics*, Vol. 41, No. 1, 1998.

Stratmann, T., "What Do Campaign Contributions Buy? Deciphering Causal Effects of Money and Votes", *Southern Economic Journal*, Vol. 57, No. 3, 1991.

Strauss, D. A., "Corruption, Equality, and Campaign Finance Reform", *Columbia Law Review*, No. 94, 1994.

Sullivan, K., "Two Concepts of Freedom of Speech", *Harvard Law Review*, No. 124, 2010.

Tahoun, A., "The Role of Stock Ownership by US Members of Congress on the Market for Political Favors", *Journal of Financial Economics*, Vol. 111, No. 1, 2014.

Tarullo, D. K., "Law and Politics in Twentieth Century Tariff History", *UCLA Law Review*, No. 34, 1986.

Taylor, A. J., "The Revolution in Federal Procurement, 1980-Present", *Business and Politics*, Vol. 21, No. 1, 2019.

Teachout, Z., Gifts, Offices, and Corruption", *Northwest University Law Review Colloquy*, Vol. 107, No. 30, 2012.

Thompson, D. F., "Theories of Institutional Corruption", *Annual Review of Political Science*, No. 21, 2018.

Thompson, D. F., "Two Concepts of Corruption", *George Washington Law Review, No. 73, 2005.

Tribe, L., "Dividing 'Citizens United': The Case v. The Controversy", *Constitutional Commentary*, Vol. 30, No. 2, 2015.

Van Zee, A., "The Promotion and Marketing of OxyContin: Commercial Triumph, Public Health Tragedy", *American Journal of Public Health*, Vol. 99, No. 2, 2009.

Wedel, J. R., "Rethinking Corruption in an Age of Ambiguity", *Annual Review of Law & Social Science*, No. 8, 2012.

Wertheimer, F. & Manes, S. W., "Campaign Finance Reform: A Key to Restoring the Health of Our Democracy", *Columbia Law Review*, Vol. 94, No. 4, 1994.

"Working Together for an Independent Expenditure: Candidate Assistance with Super PAC Fundraising", *Harvard Law Review*, No. 128, Mar., 2015.

Wouters, O. J., "Lobbying Expenditures and Campaign Contributions by the Pharmaceutical and Health Product Industry in the United States, 1999 – 2018", *JAMA Internal Medicine*, Vol. 180, No. 5, 2020.

Wright, J. R., "Contributions, Lobbying and Committee Voting in the US House of Representatives", *American Political Science Review*, No. 84, 1990.

政府和研究机构文件、报告

ACLU, "At America's Expense: The Mass Incarceration of the Elderly", ACLU (Jun., 2012), https://www.aclu.org/sites/default/files/field_document/elderlyprisonreport_20120613_1.pdf.

ACLU, "Banking on Bondage, Private Prisons and Mass Incarceration", ACLU (Nov., 2011), https://www.aclu.org/banking-bondage-private-prisons-and-mass-incarceration.

Ahmed, H., "How Private Prisons Are Profiting under the Trump Administration", American Progress (Aug. 9, 2019), https://cdn.americanprogress.org/content/uploads/2019/08/29100331/DrivingPrivatePrisons-Brief.pdf.

Alison, B. & Harkins, S., "Fixed Fortunes: Biggest Corporate Political Interests Spend Billions, Get Trillions", Sunlight Foundation (Nov. 17, 2014), https://sunlightfoundation.com/2014/11/17/fixed-fortunes-biggest-corporate-political-interests-spend-billions-get-trillions/.

Arizona Department of Corrections, "FY 2018 Operating Per Capita Cost Report", Arizona Department of Corrections (Jan., 2019), https://corrections. az. gov/sites/default/files/REPORTS/Operating_ Per_ Capita/adc-per-capcostreport_ fy2018-final. pdf.

Arizona Department of Corrections, "State versus Private Prison FY 2007 Cost Comparison", Arizona Department of Corrections (2009), www. azcorrections. gov/adc/reports/ADC_ FY2007_ cost_ comparison. pdf.

Balcerzak, A., "Surge in LLC Contributions Brings More Mystery about True Donors", Open Secrects (Apr. 27, 2017), https://www. opensecrets. org/news/2017/04/surge-in-llc-contributions-more-mystery/.

Barry, F., "Forget the Dictionary, Super PACs Aren't New", Bloomberg View (Mar. 21, 2021), https://www. bloomberg. com/opinion/articles/2014-03-21/forget-the-dictionary-super-pacs-aren-t-new.

Baumgart, A., "Companies that Funded Trump's Inauguration Came up Big in 2017", Open Secrets (Jan. 19, 2018), https://www. opensecrets. org/news/2018/01/companies-that-funded-trumps-inauguration/.

Beckel, M., "Dark Money Illuminated", Issue One (2018), https://www. issueone. org/wp-content/uploads/2018/09/Dark-Money-Illuminated-Report. pdf.

Beckel, M., "Drug Lobby Gave $750000 to Pro-Hatch Nonprofit in Utah's U. S. Senate Race", The Center for Public Integrity (Jun. 3, 2014), https://publicintegrity. org/politics/drug-lobby-gave-750000-to-pro-hatch-nonprofit-in-utahs-u-s-senate-race/.

Beckel, M., "Obama Bundlers Closely Tied to Influence Industry", The Center for Public Integrity (Mar. 8, 2013), http://www. publicintegrity. org/2013/03/08/12279/obama-bundlers-closely-tied-influence-industry.

Beckel, M. & Ratliff, A., "Mystery Money", Isssue One (Jul. 29, 2020), https://www. issueone. org/wp-content/uploads/2020/07/Mystery-Money-Report-Tipsheet. pdf.

Beckel, M., "The 'McCutcheon' Decision Explained-More Money to Pour into Political Process", The Center for Public Integrity (Apr. 22, 2014), https://www. publicintegrity. org/2014/04/22/14611/mccutcheon-decision-explained-more-money-pour-political-process.

Bentsen, K., "Money, Not Morals, Drives Marijuana Prohibition Movement", Open Secrets (Aug. 5, 2014), https://www. opensecrets. org/news/2014/08/money-not-morals-drives-marijuana-prohibition-movement/.

Biersack, B., "8 Years Later: How Citizens United Changed Campaign Finance", Open Secrets (Feb. 7, 2018), https://www.opensecrets.org/news/2018/02/how-citizens-united-changed-campaign-finance/.

Brady, J. S., "Remarks by President Trump on Delivering Lower Prescription Drug Prices for All Americans", The White House (Nov. 20, 2020), https://trumpwhitehouse.archives.gov/briefings-statements/remarks-president-trump-delivering-lower-prescription-drug-prices-americans/.

Brookings, "Event Summary: Political Corruption in the United States and Around the Globe", The Brookings Institution (Apr. 28, 2004), https://www.brookings.edu/opinions/event-summary-political-corruption-in-the-united-states-and-around-the-globe/.

Brudnick, I. A., "Congressional Salaries and Allowances: In Brief", Congressional Research Service (Sep. 19, 2023), https://crsreports.congress.gov/product/pdf/RL/RL30064#:~:text=The%20compensation%20for%20most%20Senators,from%20Puerto%20Rico%20is%20%24174%2C000.&text=These%20levels%20have%20remained%20unchanged,March%2011%2C%202009)%2C%20P.L.

California Secretary of State's Cal-Access Search, "Core Civic Lobbying Activity", California Secretary of Dr. Shirley N. Weber (2019), http://cal-access.sos.ca.gov/Lobbying/Employers/Detail.aspx?id=1145409&view=activity&session=2019.

California's Legislative Analyst's Office, "How much does it cost to incarcerate an inmate?" California's Legislative Analyst's Office (2019), https://lao.ca.gov/PolicyAreas/CJ/6_cj_inmatecost.

California's Legislative Analysts Office, "Proposition 6. Criminal Penalties and Laws. Public Safety Funding. Statute", California's Legislative Analysts Office (n.d.), http://www.lao.ca.gov/ballot/2008/6_11_2008.aspx.

California's Legislative Analyst's Office, "The California Legislature's Nonpartisan Fiscal and Policy Advisor Proposition 61", California's Legislative Analyst's Office (Nov. 08, 2016), https://lao.ca.gov/BallotAnalysis/Proposition?number=61&year=2016.

Canon, G., "Here's the Latest Evidence of How Private Prisons Are Exploiting Inmates for Profit", Mother Jones (Jun. 17, 2015), https://www.motherjones.com/crime-justice/2015/06/private-prisons-profit/.

Carson, E. A., "Prisoners in 2019", Bureau of Justice Statistics (Oct.,

2020), https://www.bjs.gov/content/pub/pdf/p19.pdf.

CDC, "2018 Annual Surveillance Report of Drug-Related Risks and Outcomes-United States Surveillance Special Report", CDC (Aug. 31, 2018), https://www.cdc.gov/drugoverdose/pdf/pubs/2018-cdc-drug-surveillance-report.pdf.

CDC, "Drug and Opioid-Involved Overdose Deaths-United States, 2013 – 2017", CDC (Jan., 2019), https://www.cdc.gov/mmwr/volumes/67/wr/mm675152e1.htm?s_cid=mm675152e1.

CDC, "Opioid Painkiller Prescribing", CDC (Sep. 26, 2017), https://www.cdc.gov/vitalsigns/opioid-prescribing/.

CDC, "Vital Signs: Overdoses of Prescription Opioid Pain Relievers-United States, 1999 – 2008", CDC (n.d.), https://www.cdc.gov/mmwr/preview/mmwrhtml/mm6043a4.htm.

Center for Responsive Politics, "Lobbying Corrections Corp of America-Bills 2010", Open Secrets (Feb., 2011), http://www.opensecrets.org/lobby/clientbills.php?id=D000021940&year=2010.

Center for Responsive Politics, "Lobbying Corrections Corp of America-Summary 2010", Open Secrets (Jun., 2011), www.opensecrets.org/lobby/clientsum.php?lname=Corrections+Corp+of+America&year=2010.

Centers for Medicare and Medicaid Services, "National Health Expenditure (NHE) Amounts by Type of Expenditure and Source of Funds: Calendar Years 1960 – 2028", Centers for Medicare and Medicaid Services (n.d.), https://www.cms.gov/Research-Statistics-Data-and-Systems/Statistics-Trends-and-Reports/NationalHealthExpendData/NationalHealthAccountsProjected.

Citizens For Ethics, "A Bitter Bill: How Big Pharma Lobbies to Keep Prescription Drug Prices High. Citizens for Responsibility and Ethics in Washington", Citizens For Ethics (Jun. 18, 2018), https://www.citizensforethics.org/a-bitter-pill-how-big-pharma-lobbies-to-keep-prescription-drug-prices-high/.

Congressional Research Service, Congressional Careers: Service Tenure and Patterns of Member Service, 1789 – 2019, Jan. 3, 2019, p. 13.

Democracy Project, "The Democracy Project: Reversing a Crisis of Confidence", Democracy Project (2018), https://www.democracyprojectreport.org/report.

Department of Health and Human Services, "Biden-Harris Administration Marks

Two Years of Advancements in HHS' Overdose Prevention Strategy with New Actions to Treat Addiction and Save Lives", HHS (Feb. 1, 2024), https://www.hhs.gov/about/news/2024/02/01/biden-harris-administration-marks-two-years-advancements-hhs-overdose-prevention-strategy-new-actions-treat-addiction-save-lives-press-release.html.

Department of Homeland Security, "U. S. Immigration and Customs Enforcement Budget Overview", Department of Homeland Security, (n. d.), https://www.dhs.gov/sites/default/files/publications/19_0318_MGMT_CBJ-Immigration-Customs-Enforcement_0.pdf.

Department of Justice., "Former Government Contractor Executives Indicted for Unlawful Campaign Contributions", DOJ (Feb. 20, 2022), https://www.justice.gov/opa/pr/former-government-contractor-executives-indicted-unlawful-campaign-contributions.

Department of Justice., "Former Interior Deputy Secretary Steven Griles Sentenced to 10 Months in Prison for Obstructing U. S. Senate Investigation into Abramoff Corruption Scandal", DOJ (Jun. 26, 2007), https://www.justice.gov/archive/opa/pr/2007/June/07_crm_455.html.

Department of Justice., "Italia Federici Sentenced for Evading Taxes and Obstructing Senate Investigation into Abramoff Corruption Scandal", DOJ (Dec. 14, 2007), https://www.justice.gov/archive/opa/pr/2007/December/07_crm_1005.html.

Department of Justice, "Opioid Manufacturer Purdue Pharma Pleads Guilty to Fraud and Kickback Conspiracies", DOJ (Nov. 24, 2020), https://www.justice.gov/opa/pr/opioid-manufacturer-purdue-pharma-pleads-guilty-fraud-and-kickback-conspiracies.

Department of Justice, "Review of the Drug Enforcement Administration's Regulatory and Enforcement Efforts to Control the Diversion of Opioids", Office of the Inspector General (2019), https://oig.justice.gov/reports/2019/e1905.pdf.

Department of the Treasury, Internal Revenue Service, "Guidance Under Section 6033 Regarding the Reporting Requirements of Exempt Organizations", *85 Federal Register 31959*, May 28, 2020.

DeSilver, D., "In Past Elections, U. S. Trailed Most Developed Countries in Voter Turnout", Pew Research Center (Nov. 3, 2020), https://www.pewresearch. org/fact-tank/2020/11/03/in-past-elections-u-s-trailed-most-developed-countries-in-voter-turnout/.

DeSilver, D. & Van Kessel, P., "As more Money Flows Into Campaigns, Americans Worry About Its influence", Pew Research Center (Dec. 7, 2015), https://www. pewresearch. org/fact-tank/2015/12/07/as-more-money-flows-into-campaigns-americans-worry-about-its- influence/.

Drutman, L., "The Political 1% of the 1% in 2012", Sunlight Fundation (Jun. 24, 2013), https://sunlightfoundation. com/2013/06/24/1pct_ of_ the_ 1pct/.

Dugan, A., "Majority of Americans See Congress as Out of Touch, Corrupt", Gallup (2015), https://news. gallup. com/poll/1600/Congress-Public. aspx.

Duwe, G. & Clark, V., "The Effects of Private Prison Confinement in Minnesota on Offender Recidivism", Minnesota Department of Corrections (Mar., 2013), https://mn. gov/doc/assets/MN_ Private_ Prison_ Evaluation_ Website_ Final_ tcm1089-272834. pdf.

Equal Justice Initiative, "Mass Incarceration Costs $182 Billion Every Year, Without Adding Much to Public Safety", EJI (Feb. 6, 2017), https://eji. org/news/mass-incarceration-costs-182-billion-annually.

Evers-Hillstrom, K., Arke, R. & Robinson, L., "A Look at the Impact of Citizens United on Its 9th Anniversary", Open Secrets (Jan. 21, 2019), https://www. opensecrets. org/news/2019/01/citizens-united/.

Evers-Hillstrom, K., "'Dark Money' Groups Funneled Millions to Powerful Super PACs During 2018 Midterms", Open Secrets (Jan. 3, 2019), Open Secrets,https://www. opensecrets. org/news/2019/01/dark-money/.

Evers-Hillstrom, K., "Most Expensive Ever: 2020 Election Cost $14.4 Billion", Open Secrets (Feb. 11, 2021), https://www. opensecrets. org/news/2021/02/2020-cycle-cost-14p4-billion-doubling-16/.

Evers-Hillstrom, K., "Pharma Lobby Poured Millions into 'Dark Money' Groups Influencing 2020", Open Secrets (Dec. 8. 2020), https://www. opensecrets. org/news/2020/12/pharma-lobby-poured-millions-into-darkmoney-groups.

Evers-Hillstrom, K., "Political Donations Dropped off as Coronavirus Pandemic Peaked", Open Secrets (2020), https://www. opensecrets. org/news/2020/06/political-donations-dropped-off-as-coronavirus-pandemic-peaked/.

Evers-Hillstrom, K., "Pro-Biden Super PAC Funds $100 Million Ad Campaign with 'Dark Money'", Open Secrets (Oct. 23, 2020), https://www.opensecrets.org/news/2020/10/pro-biden-super-pac-darkmon/.

Evers-Hillstrom, K. & Quinn, B., "Open Secrets Looks Back at 2020, a $14 Billion Year", Open Secrets (Dec. 22, 2020), https://www.opensecrets.org/news/2020/12/2020-opensecrets-year-in-review/.

Fang, L., "Disclosure Shows Private Prison Company Misled on Immigration Lobbying", The Nation (Jun. 4, 2013), https://www.thenation.com/article/archive/disclosure-shows-private-prison-company-misled-immigration-lobbying/.

Fazekas & others, "Institutional Quality, Campaign Contributions, and Favouritism in US Federal Government Contracting", Government Transparency Institutes (Aug. 2018), http://www.govtransparency.eu/wp-content/uploads/2018/08/Fazekas-et-al_DonationsPPcorr_US_GTI_WP_2018.pdf.

FDA, "Statement from FDA Commissioner Scott Gottlieb, M. D., on Agency's Efforts to Encourage the Development of and Broaden Access to Generic Versions of Opioid Analgesics that are Formulated to Deter Abuse", FDA (Jul. 20, 2018), https://www.fda.gov/news-events/press-announcements/statement-fda-commissioner-scott-gottlieb-md-agencys-efforts-encourage-development-and-broaden.

FEC, "Advisory Opinion 2011-12", FEC (Jun. 30, 2011), https://saos.fec.gov/saos/searchao;jsessionid=A07F1B8AF176F6344186DE1729A7D398?SUBMIT=continue&PAGE_NO=0.

FEC, "AO 2014-02 (Bitcoin contributions and disbursements)", FEC (May 08, 2014), https://www.fec.gov/files/legal/aos/2014-02/2014-02.pdf.

FEC., "FEC Provides Guidance Following U. S. District Court Decision in CREW v. FEC, 316 F. Supp. 3d 349 (D. D. C. 2018)", FEC (2018), https://www.fec.gov/updates/fec-provides-guidance-following-us-district-court-decision-crew-v-fec-316-f-supp-3d-349-ddc-2018/.

FEC, "How to Report Bitcoin Contributions", FEC (n. d.), https://www.fec.gov/help-candidates-and-committees/filing-reports/bitcoin-contributions/.

FEC, "OGC Enforcement Statistics For Fiscal Years 2003-2008", FEC (Jan., 2009), https://www.fec.gov/resources/cms-content/documents/

enforcestatsfy03-08. pdf.

FEC, "Schedule A: Reportable Bundled Contributions Forwarded by or Credited to Lobbyist/Registrants and Lobbyist/Registrant PACs", FEC (n. d.), https://docquery. fec. gov/cgi-bin/forms/C00000935/1224496/sa/3L.

FEC, "Status of Enforcement-Fiscal Year 2021, Second Quarter (01/01/21 - 03/31/21)", FEC (Apr., 2021), https://www. fec. gov/resources/cms-content/documents/2nd_ Quarter_ Status_ of_ Enforcement_ 2021. pdf.

Feldman, N., "Treat Millionaires Like They're Billionaires", Harvard University Weatherhead Center for International Affairs (Feb. 21, 2013), https://wcfia. harvard. edu/publications/treat-millionaires-they're-billionaires.

Felter, C., "The U. S. Opioid Epidemic", Council on Foreign Relations (Jul. 20, 2020), https://www. cfr. org/backgrounder/us-opioid-epidemic.

Fisher, G., "Limited Liability Donations: Corporate Dark Money Remains a Glaring Problem in the US", Sunlight Foundation (Aug. 5, 2014), https://sunlightfoundation. com/2014/08/05/limited-liability-donations-corporate-dark-money-remains-a-glaring-problem-in-the-us/.

Follow the Money, "Private Prisons: Hiding Behind a Veil of Democracy", Follow the Money (n. d.), https://www. followthemoney. org/assets/Uploads/Private-Prisons-Hiding-Behind-a-Veil-of-Democracy-Tylek. pdf.

Frago, C., "St. Petersburg Council Acts to Limit Big Money in City Elections", *The Tampa Bay Times*, Oct. 6, 2017.

Freedom for Immigrants, "Detention by the Numbers", Freedom for Immigrants (n. d.), https://www. freedomforimmigrants. org/detention-statistics/.

Friedman, M., "Just Facts: As Many Americans Have Criminal Records as College Diplomas", Brennan Center for Justice (Dec. 17, 2015), https://www. brennancenter. org/our-work/analysis-opinion/just-facts-many-americans-have-criminal-records-college-diplomas.

Garrett, R. S., "The State of Campaign Finance Policy: Recent Developments and Issues for Congress", Congressional Research Service (Sep. 12, 2023), https://crsreports. congress. gov/product/pdf/R/R41542.

Giorno, T., "Federal Lobbying Spending Reaches $4. 1 Billion in 2022 — The Highest Since 2010", Open Secrets (Jan. 26, 2023), https://www. opensecrets. org/news/2023/01/federal-lobbying-spending-reaches-4-1-billion-in-2022-the-highest-since-2010/.

Global Data, "Top 10 Pharma Companies in the US by Market Capitalization", Global Data (Sep. 30, 2023), https：//www.globaldata.com/companies/top-companies-by-sector/healthcare/us-companies-by-market-cap/#：~：text = Comprehensively%2C%20the%20top%2010%20Pharma, Inc%20is%20the%20lowest%20 (%24.

Gotsch, K. & Basti, V., "Capitalizing on Mass Incarceration：U.S Growth in Private Prisons", The Sentencing Project (Aug. 2, 2018), https：//www.sentencingproject.org/publications/capitalizing-on-mass-incarceration-u-s-growth-in-private-prisons/.

Gruberg, S., "How For-Profit Companies are Driving Immigration Detention Policies", Center for American Progress (Dec. 18, 2015), https：//www.americanprogress.org/issues/immigration/reports/2015/12/18/127769/how-for-profit-companies-are-driving-immigration-detention-policies/.

Gruberg, S. & Jawetz, T., "How the U.S. Department of Homeland Security Can End Its Reliance on Private Prisons", Center for American Progress (Sep. 14, 2016), https：//www.americanprogress.org/issues/immigration/news/2016/09/14/144160/how-the-u-s-department-of-homeland-security-can-end-its-reliance-on-private-prisons/.

Hadland, S. E., Rivera-Aguirre, A. & Marshall, B. D. L., "Association of Pharmaceutical Industry Marketing of Opioid Products with Mortality from Opioid-Related Overdoses", JAMA Network Open (Jan. 18, 2019), https：//jamanetwork.com/journals/jamanetworkopen/fullarticle/2720914.

Hannah, J., "Political Science Experts Team up for Book on Corruption", Wright State University News Room (Feb. 28, 2013), https：//webapp2.wright.edu/web1/newsroom/2013/02/28/political-science-experts-team-up-for-book-on-corruption/.

Hernández, K., "How Cryptocurrency is Senaking into State Elections", The Center for Public Integrity (Nov. 2, 2018), https：//publicintegrity.org/politics/state-politics/how-cryptocurrency-is-sneaking-into-state-elections/.

Hodai, B., "Marco Rubio, GEO Group, and a Legacy of Corruption", PR-Watch (Aug. 29, 2012), https：//www.prwatch.org/news/2012/08/11591/marco-rubio-geo-group-and-legacy-corruption.

Hupman, R. D., *Senate Election, Expulsion and Censure Cases from 1793 to 1972*, Washington：U.S. Government Printing Office, 1972.

Hur, K., "Small Donors Ruled 2020; Will That Change Post-Trump?" Open Secrets (Feb. 3, 2021), https://www.opensecrets.org/news/2021/02/small-donors-dominated-2020-will-that-change-in-midterms/.

ICMA, "The Price of Private Prisons", ICMA (Nov. 22, 2011), https://icma.org/blog-posts/price-private-prisons?gclid=CjwKCAiAl4WABhAJEiwATUnEF5qbBrXXOA4v_2JlPu8eDSh9195rfpg2Dquo7aXlqVWq9HNFeunJwhoCLvkQAvD_BwE.

In the Public Interest, "Buying Influence: How Private Prison Companies Expand Their Control of America's Criminal Justice System", In the Public Interest (Oct., 2016), https://www.inthepublicinterest.org/wp-content/uploads/ITPI_BuyingInfluence_Oct2016.pdf.

In the Public Interest, "Criminal: How Lockup Quotas and 'Low-Crime Taxes' Guarantee Profits for Private Prison Corporation", In the Public Interest (Sep., 2013), https://www.inthepublicinterest.org/wp-content/uploads/Criminal-Lockup-Quota-Report.pdf.

Issue One & R Street, "Why We Left Congress: How the Legislative Branch Is Broken and What We Can Do About It", Issue One (Dec., 2018), https://www.issueone.org/why-we-left/.

J. Baxter Olophant, "Top Tax Frustrations for Americans: The Feeling that Some Corporations, Wealthy People Don't Pay Fair Share", Pew Research Center (Apr. 7, 2023), https://www.pewresearch.org/short-reads/2023/04/07/top-tax-frustrations-for-americans-the-feeling-that-some-corporations-wealthy-people-dont-pay-fair-share/.

John Kennedy, "Sen. Kennedy's JACK Act Reveals Millions Paid to Lobbyists with Criminal Convictions", U.S. Senator for Louisiana (Feb. 20, 2020), https://www.kennedy.senate.gov/public/2020/2/sen-kennedy-s-jack-act-reveals-millions-paid-to-lobbyists-with-criminal-convictions.

Judah, B. & Sibley, N., "The Enablers: How Western Professionals Import Corruption and Strengthen Authoritarianism", Hudson Institute (Sep., 2018), https://www.hudson.org/research/14520-the-enablers-how-western-professionals-import-corruption-and-strengthen-authoritarianism.

Greenberg Quinlan Rosner, "Justice at Stake-State Judges Poll", Brennan Center for Justice (2001), http://www.justiceatstake.org/media/cms/JASJudgesSurveyResults_EA8838C0504A5.pdf.

Kang-Brown, J., Schattner-Elmaleh, E. & Hinds, O., "People in Prison in 2018", Vera Institute of Justice (Apr., 2019), https://www.vera.org/downloads/publications/people-in-prison-in-2018-updated.pdf.

Klobuchar, A., "Campaign Finance: Federal Framework, Agency Roles and Responsibilities, and Perspectives", U.S. Government Accountability Office (Feb. 3, 2020), https://www.gao.gov/assets/710/704228.pdf.

Kohler, J. C., "Corruption in the Pharmaceutical Sector: Diagnosing the Challenges", Transparency International (Jun., 2016), p. 17, https://www.transparency.org.uk/sites/default/files/pdf/publications/29-06-2016-Corruption_In_The_Pharmaceutical_Sector_Web-2.pdf.

Lambert, T., "Lobbying on Regulatory Enforcement Actions: Evidence from U.S. Commercial and Savings Banks", *Research Briefs in Economic Policy* (Jul. 13, 2018), https://www.cato.org/research-briefs-economic-policy/lobbying-regulatory-enforcement-actions-evidence-us-commercial?queryID=3d1e4dca7fddb5cd4c434a0b3e55636e.

Lau, T., "A Bid to Counter Big Money in Politics Is Gaining Steam", Brennan Center for Justice (Jan. 15, 2019), https://www.brennancenter.org/our-work/analysis-opinion/bid-counter-big-money-politics-gaining-steam.

Lessig, L., "McCutcheon v. FEC: Supreme Court Amicus Brief of Professor Lessig in Support of the FEC", Campaign Legal Center (2014), p. 12. https://campaignlegal.org/document/mccutcheon-v-fec-supreme-court-amicus-brief-professor-lessig-support-fec.

Liu, L., Pei, D. N. & Soto, P., "History of the Opioid Epidemic: How Did We Get Here?" Poison Control, National Capital Poison Center (n. d.), https://www.poison.org/articles/opioid-epidemic-history-and-prescribing-patterns-182.

Lobby Seven, "Campaign Finance: The Best Government Money Can Buy", Lobby Seven (Jul. 26, 2017), https://www.lobbyseven.com/single-post/2017/07/26/Volume-17-Campaign-Finance.

Lowery, D. & others, "Understanding the Relationship between Health PACs and Health Lobbying in the American States", *Publius*, No. 39, 2008, pp. 70-94.

Luan, L., "Profiting from Enforcement: The Role of Private Prisons in U.S. Immigration Detention", Migration Policy Institute (May 2, 2018), https://

www. migrationpolicy. org/article/profiting-enforcement-role-private-prisons-us-immigration-detention.

Malbin, M. J. & Glavin, B. , "Small-Donor Matching Funds for New York State Elections: A Policy Analysis of the Potential Impact and Cost", Campaign Finance Institute (Feb. 13, 2019), https://www. followthemoney. org/research/institute-reports/cfi-small-donor-matching-funds-for-new-york-state-elections-a-policy-analysis-of-the-potential-impact-and-cost.

Marcus, R. & Dunbar, J. , "Punishment for Coordination between Candidates and Outside Groups is Rare", The Center for Public Integrity (May 19, 2014), https://publicintegrity. org/federal-politics/rules-against-coordination-between-super-pacs-candidates-tough-to-enforce/.

Maskell, J. , *Lobbying Congress: An Overview of Legal Provisions and Congressional Ethics Rules*, CRS Report for Congress, Washington D. C: Library of Congress, 2007.

Mason, C. , "Too Good to be True: Private Prisons in America", The Sentencing Project (Jan. , 2012), https://sentencingproject. org/wp-content/uploads/2016/01/Too-Good-to-be-True-Private-Prisons-in-America. pdf.

Massoglia, A. , " 'Dark Money' Groups Find New Ways to Hide Donors in 2020 Election", Open Secrets (Oct. 30, 2020), https://www. opensecrets. org/news/2020/10/dark-money-2020-new-ways-to-hide-donors/.

Massoglia, A. & Evers-Hillstrom, K. , " 'Dark Money' Topped $1 Billion in 2020, Largely Boosting Democrats", Open Secrets (Mar. 17, 2021), https://www. opensecrets. org/news/2021/03/one-billion-dark-money-2020-electioncycle/.

Massoglia, A. & Evers-Hillstrom, K. , "Liberal 'Dark Money' Group Gets an Early Start Targeting GOP Senators ahead of 2020", Open Secrets (Jan. 31, 2019), https://www. opensecrets. org/news/2019/01/lib-dark-money-group-majority-forward-targeting-gop-senators-2020/.

Massoglia, A. , "State of Money in Politics: Billion-dollar 'Dark Money' Spending is Just the Tip of the Iceberg", Open Secrets (Feb. 21, 2019), https://www. opensecrets. org/news/2019/02/somp3-billion-dollar-dark-money-tip-of-the-iceberg/.

Mauer, M. , "The Changing Racial Dynamics of the War on Drugs", The Sentencing Project (Apr. , 2019), https://www. sentencingproject. org/wp-content/

uploads/2016/01/The-Changing-Racial-Dynamics-of-the-War-on-Drugs. pdf.

Meissner, D. & others, "Immigration Enforcement in the United States: The Rise of a Formidable Machinery", Migration Policy Institute (Jan., 2013), https://www.migrationpolicy.org/pubs/enforcementpillars.pdf.

Merchant, N., "Private Prison Companies Shower Campaign Cash on Trump and Republicans", People's World (Aug. 14, 2020), https://www.peoplesworld.org/article/private-prison-companies-shower-campaign-cash-on-trump-and-republicans/.

Miller, E., "Despite Some Big Losses, Top Spenders Won 88 Percent of 2020 Races", Open Secrets (Nov. 20, 2020).

Miller, E., "Outside Spending in 2020 Races Reaches Record $3.2 Billion", Open Secrets (Dec. 21, 2020), https://www.opensecrets.org/news/2020/12/outside-spending-reaches-record-in-2020.

Mishel, L. & Wolfe, J., "CEO Compensation Surged has Grown 940% Since 1978", Economic Policy Institute (Aug. 14, 2019), https://www.epi.org/publication/ceo-compensation-2018/.

Mulvihil, G. & Whyte, L. E., "Drugmakers Fought Domino Effect of Washington Opioid Limits", The Center for Public Integrity (Sep. 21, 2016), https://publicintegrity.org/state-politics/drugmakers-fought-domino-effect-of-washington-opioid-limits/.

Mumford, M., Schanzenbach, D. W. & Nunn R., "The Economics of Private Prisons", The Brookings Institution (2016), https://www.brookings.edu/wp-content/uploads/2016/10/es_20161021_private_prisons_economics.pdf.

Murphy, E. M. & others, "Committee on Disclosure of Corporate Political Spending Petition For Rulemaking", SEC (Aug. 3, 2011), https://www.sec.gov/rules/petitions/2011/petn4-637.pdf.

National Center for State Courts, "Judicial Selection and Retention", National Center for State Courts (n. d.), http://www.ncsconline.org/WC/CourTopics/FAQs.asp?topic=JudSel.

National Institute of Justice, "Measuring Recidivism", NIJ (Feb. 20, 2008), https://nij.ojp.gov/topics/articles/measuring-recidivism#statistics.

National Institute on Drug Abuse, "National Overdose Deaths from Select Prescription and Illicit Drugs", National Institute on Drug Abuse (Jan.,

2019), https：//www. drugabuse. gov/related-topics/trends-statistics/overdose-death-rates.

National Institute on Drug Abuse, "Overdose Death Rates", National Institute on Drug Abuse (Jun. 30, 2023), https：//www. drugabuse. gov/drug-topics/trends-statistics/overdose-death-rates.

National Women's Health Network, "Opioids and Women：From Prescription to Addiction", National Women's Health Network (n. d.), https：//www. nwhn. org/prescription-addiction-opioid-epidemic/.

Nellis, A., "Still Life：America's Increasing Use of Life and Long-Term Sentences", The Sentencing Project (May 3, 2017), https：//www. sentencingproject. org/publications/still-life-americas-increasing-use-life-long-term-sentences/.

New York City Campaign Finance Board, "Impact of Public Funds：New York City's Matching Funds Program Has Major, Positive Influences on New York City Elections", NYCCFB (n. d.), https：//www. nyccfb. info/program/impact-of-public-funds/.

New York City Campaign Finance Board, "Why Do We Have Public Financing of NYC Elections？" NYCCFB (2012), http：//www. nyccfb. info/PDF/press/WhyPublicFinancing. pdf？ sm = press_ 21f.

New York State Joint Commission on Public Ethics, "2012 Annual Report", 2013, https：//jcope. ny. gov/news/joint-commission-public-ethics-releases-2012-annual-report.

O'Dell, R. & Penzenstadler, N., "You Elected Them to Write New Laws. They're Letting Corporations Do It Instead", The Center for Public Integrity (Apr. 4, 2019), https：//publicintegrity. org/politics/state-politics/copy-paste-legislate/you-elected-them-to-write-new-laws-theyre-letting-corporations-do-it-instead/.

OECD, Country case：Korea's Bid Rigging Indicator Analysis System (BRIAS), OECD, 2016, https：//www. oecd. org/governance/procurement/toolbox/search/korea-bid-rigging-indicator-analysis-system-brias. pdf.

OECD, Fraud and Corruption in European Structural and Investment Funds, OECD, 2019, https：//www. oecd. org/gov/ethics/prevention- fraud-corruption-european-funds. pdf.

Olsen-Phillips, P., "State Legislatures Taking Aim at Dark Money, Disclosure", Sunlight Foundation (Mar. 17, 2015), https：//sunlightfoundation.

com/2015/03/17/state-legislatures-taking-aim-at-dark-money-disclosure/.

OpenCorporates, "The Open Company Data Index", OpenCorporates (n. d.), http：//registries. opencorporates. com.

Open Secrets, "2016 Outside Spending, by Super PAC", Open Secrets (n. d.), https：//www. opensecrets. org/outside-spending/super_pacs/2016? chrt = 2022&disp = O&type = S.

Open Secrets, "2016 Top Donors to Outside Spending Groups", Open Secrets (n. d.), https：//www. opensecrets. org/outsidespending/summ. php? disp = D.

Open Secrets, "2020 Outside Spending by Group", Open Secrets (n. d.), https：//www. opensecrets. org/outsidespending/summ. php? disp = O.

Open Secrets, "2022 Outside Spending, by Super PAC", Open Secrets (n. d.), https：//www. opensecrets. org/outside-spending/super_pacs.

Open Secrets, " '527s' Advocacy Group Spending", Center for Responsive Politics (n. d.), http：//www. OpenSecrets. org/527s.

Open Secrets, "Corrections Corp of America", Open Secrets (n. d.), https：//www. opensecrets. org/lobby/clientsum. php? id = D000021940&year = 2002.

Open Secrets, "Cost of Election", Open Secrets (n. d.), https：//www. opensecrets. org/overview/cost. php.

Open Secrets, "Dark Money Basics", Open Secrets (n. d.), https：//www. opensecrets. org/darkmoney/dark-money-basics. php.

Open Secrets, "Election Trends", Open Secrets (n. d.), https：//www. opensecrets. org/elections-overview/election-trends.

Open Secrets, "Former Members", Open Secrets (n. d.), https：//www. opensecrets. org/revolving/top. php? display = Z.

Open Secrets, "For-profit Prison", Open Secrets (Mar. 22, 2021), https：//www. opensecrets. org/industries. /indus. php? cycle = 2020&ind = G7000.

Open Secrets, "For-profit Prison Summary", Open Secrets (Feb. 2, 2024), https：//www. opensecrets. org/industries/indus? ind = G7000.

Open Secrets, "Industry Profile：Pharmaceuticals/Health Products", Open Secrets (n. d.), https：//www. opensecrets. org/federal-lobbying/industries/summary? id = H04.

Open Secrets, "Joint Fundraising Committees", Open Secrets (n. d.), https：//www. opensecrets. org/jfc/.

Open Secrets, "Outside Spending", Open Secrets (n. d.), https：//www.

opensecrets. org/outsidespending/.

Open Secrets, "Pharmaceutical Research & Manufacturers of America", Open Secrets (n. d.), https://www.opensecrets.org/lobby/clientsum.php? id = d000000504.

Open Secrets, "Pharmaceuticals/Health Product: Lobbying, 2021", Open Secrets (n. d.), https://www.opensecrets.org/industries/lobbying.php? cycle = 2016&ind = H04.

Open Secrets, "Pharmaceuticals / Health Products Background", Open Secrets (n. d.), https://www.opensecrets.org/industries/background? cycle = 2024&ind = H04.

Open Secrets, "Pharmaceuticals / Health Products: Money to Congress-Summary", Open Secrets (n. d.), https://www.opensecrets.org/industries/summary.php? ind = H04 + + .

Open Secrets, "Pharmaceuticals / Health Products: Money to Congress-Top 20 Member", Open Secrets (n. d.), https://www.opensecrets.org/industries/summary.php? ind = H04&cycle = All&recipdetail = M&sortorder = U.

Open Secrets, "Revolving Door: Christopher Dodd Employment Summary", Open Secrets (n. d.), https://www.opensecrets.org/revolving/rev_summary.php? id = 76356.

Open Secrets, "Revolving Door: Former Members of the 114th Congress", Open Secrets (n. d.), https://www.opensecrets.org/revolving/departing.php? cong = 114.

Open Secrets, "Sen. Charles E. Schumer-New York: Contributors 2007-2012", Open Secrets (n. d.), https://www.opensecrets.org/members-of-congress/contributors? type = C&cid = N00001093&newMem = N&cycle = 2012.

Open Secrets & Sunlight Foundation, "All Cooled Off: As Congress Convenes, Former Colleagues Will Soon be Calling From K Street", Sunlight Foundation (Jan. 6, 2015), https://sunlightfoundation.com/2015/01/06/coming-out-of-the-cool-as-congress-convenes-former-colleagues-will-soon-be-calling-from-k-street/.

Open Secrets, "Super PACs: How Many Donors Give", Open Secrets (n. d.), https://www.opensecrets.org/outside-spending/donor-stats/2016? type = B; https://www.opensecrets.org/outside-spending/donor-stats/2020? type = B.

Open Secrets, "Super PACs", Open Secrets (n. d.), https://www.opensecrets. org/outside-spending/super_ pacs/2020? chrt = 2022&disp = O&type = S.

Open Secrets, "Top Lobbying Spenders", Open Secrets (n. d.), www. opensecrets. org/lobby/top. php? showYear = 2018&indexType = s.

Open Secrets, "Top Organization Contributors", Open Secrets (n. d.), https://www. opensecrets. org/orgs/top-donors? topdonorcycle = 2020.

Open Secrets, "Top Spenders", Open Secrets (n. d.), https://www. opensecrets. org/federal-lobbying/top-spenders.

Open Secrets, "Who are the Biggest Donors?" Open Secrets (n. d.), https://www. opensecrets. org/elections-overview/biggest-donors? cycle = 2010&view = fc.

Open Serects, "Total Outside Spending by Election Cycle, Excluding Party Committees", Open Serects (n. d.), https://www. opensecrets. org/outsidespending/cycle_ tots. php (http://perma. cc/V4DH-4DUE).

Overby, P., "Beyond Quid Pro Quo: What Counts As Political Corruption?" NPR (May 4, 2015), https://www. npr. org/sections/itsallpolitics/2015/05/04/404052618/beyond-quid-pro-quo-what-counts-as-political-corruption.

Perrone, M. & Wieder, B., "Pro-Painkiller Echo Chamber Shaped Policy Amid Drug Epidemic", The Center for Public Integrity (Dec. 15, 2016), https://publicintegrity. org/state-politics/pro-painkiller-echo-chamber-shaped-policy-amid-drug-epidemic/.

Pew Research Center, "The Public, the Political System and American Democracy", Pew (Apr. 26, 2018), https://www. pewresearch. org/politics/2018/04/26/the-public-the-political-system-and-american-democracy/.

Pildes, R. H. supra note 1, 144 – 145.

Prison Policy Initiative, "Mass Incarceration: The Whole Pie 2020", Prison Policy Initiative (Aug. 11, 2020), https://www. prisonpolicy. org/reports/pie2020. html.

Prison Policy Initiative, "Mass Incarceration: The Whole Pie 2023", Prison Policy Initiative (Mar. 14, 2023), https://www. prisonpolicy. org/reports/pie2023. html.

Rahman, K. S. & Teachout, Z., "From Private Bads to Public Goods: Adapting Public Utility Regulation for Informational Infrastructure: Dismantling Surveillance-based Business Models", Knight First Amendment Institute at Columbia University (2020), https://knightcolumbia. org/content/from-private-bads-to-public-goods-adapting-public-utility-regulation-for-informational-infrastructure.

Raynor de Best, "Number of Cryptocurrencies Worldwide from 2013 to December 2023", Statista (Dec 5, 2023), https://www.statista.com/statistics/863917/number-crypto-coins-tokens/.

Reynolds, M. E., "Understanding the Election Scandal in North Carolina's 9th District", The Brookings Institution (Dec. 7, 2018), https://www.brookings.edu/blog/fixgov/2018/12/07/understanding-the-election-scandal-in-north-carolinas-9th-district/.

Root, D. & Barclay, A., "Voter Suppression During the 2018 Midterm Elections", Center of American Progress (Nov. 20, 2018), https://www.americanprogress.org/issues/democracy/reports/2018/11/20/461296/voter-suppression-2018-midterm-elections/.

Rosenberg, L., "U.S. Political Finance: Americans spend more on elections, but they lead from behind", Sunlight Foundation (Nov. 10, 2014), https://sunlightfoundation.com/2014/11/10/u-s-political-finance-americans-spend-more-on-elections-but-they-lead-from-behind/.

Ryan, L. C., "FY 2010 Operating Per Capita Cost Report: Cost Identification and Comparison of State and Private Contract Beds", Arizona Department of Corrections, Bureau of Planning, Budget, and Research (2011), https://static.prisonpolicy.org/scans/0904prison.pdf.

SEC, "Form 13F-HR Lazard Asset Management Llc", SEC (Aug. 13, 2013), https://sec.report/Document/0001207017-13-000157/.

Skaggs, A., "Buying Justice: The Impact of Citizens United on Judicial Elections", New York: Brennan Center for Justice (2010), https://www.brennancenter.org/our-work/research-reports/buying-justice-impact-citizens-united-judicial-elections.

Smith, B. A., "Before the United States Senate Committee on the Judiciary: We the People? Corporate Spending in American Elections after Citizens United", Testimony of Bradley A. Smith, March 10, 2010, p. 13.

Smith, B. A., "The Strange Case of W. Spann, LLC", Institute for Free Speech (Aug. 5, 2011), https://www.ifs.org/blog/the-strange-case-of-w-spann-llc/.

Solly, M., "U.S. Life Expectancy Drops for Third Year in a Row, Reflecting Rising Drug Overdoses Suicides", Smithsonian (Dec. 3, 2018), https://

www. smithsonianmag. com/smart-news/us-life-expectancy-drops-third-year-row-reflecting-rising-drug-overdose-suicide-rates-180970942/.

Sozan, M., "Solutions to Fight Private Prisons' Power Over Immigration Detention", Center for American Progress (Jul. 16, 2016), https://www.americanprogress.org/issues/democracy/reports/2018/07/16/453309/solutions-fight-private-prisons-power-immigration-detention/.

State of New Mexico Legislative Finance Committee, "Review of Private Prison Contracts Penalty Assessment", State of New Mexico Legislative Finance Committee (2010), http://www.privateci.org/private_pics/NMDOCstaffing.pdf.

Statista, "Leading Lobbying Industries in the United States in 2022, by Total Lobbying Spending", Statista (Nov. 3, 2023), https://www.statista.com/statistics/257364/top-lobbying-industries-in-the-us/.

Statista, "Pharmaceutical Spending Per Capita in Selected Countries as of 2018", Statista (2019), https://www.statista.com/statistics/266141/pharmaceutical-spending-per-capita-in-selected-countries/.

Statista, "Total Number of Registered Lobbyists in the United States from 2000 to 2022", Statista (Nov 3, 2023), https://www.statista.com/statistics/257340/number-of-lobbyists-in-the-us/.

Steinberg, M. & Castro, D., "The State of Open Data Portals in Latin America", Center for Data Innovation (Jul. 2. 2017), https://datainnovation.org/2017/07/the-state-of-open-data-portals-in-latin-america/.

Sunlight Foundation, "A Comprehensive Disclosure Regime in the Wake of the Supreme Court's Decision in Citizens United v. Federal Election Commission", Sunlight Foundation (n. d.), https://sunlightfoundation.com/policy/documents/comprehensive-disclosure-regime-wake-supreme-court/.

The Center for Public Integrity, "Pharma Lobbying Held Deep Influence Over Opioid Pilicies", The Center for Public Integrity (n. d.), https://publicintegrity.org/state-politics/pharma-lobbying-held-deep-influence-over-opioid-policies/.

The GEO Group, "2010 Annual Report", GEO (2011), https://www.annualreports.com/HostedData/AnnualReportArchive/t/NYSE_GEO_2010.pdf.

The GEO Group, "The GEO Group, Inc. Q4 2012 Earnings Conference Call Transcript", GEO (Feb. 21, 2013), http://conferencecalltranscripts.org/include?location=http://www.alacrastore.com/research/thomson-streetevents-Q4_ 2012_ The_ GEO_ Grerence_ Call-T5015529.

The Secretary of Health and Human Services, "American Patients First – The Trump Administration Blueprint to Lower Drug Prices and Reduce Out-of-Pocket Costs", HHS (May, 2018), https://www.hhs.gov/sites/default/files/AmericanPatientsFirst.pdf.

The Sentencing Project, "Private Prisons in the United States", The Sentencing Project (Aug. 2, 2018), https://www.sentencingproject.org/publications/private-prisons-united-states/.

Thompson, D. F., *Ethics in Congress: From Individual to Institutional Corruption*, Washington, DC: Brookings Institution, 1995, p. 117.

Torres-Spelliscy, C. (2020). *Dark Money in the 2020 Election*, Brennan Center for Juctice, https://www.brennancenter.org/our-work/analysis-opinion/dark-money-2020-election.

Torres-Spelliscy, C., "Got Corruption? Nixon's Milk Money", Brennan Center (Oct. 21, 2013), https://www.brennancenter.org/our-work/analysis-opinion/got-corruption-nixons-milk-money.

Torres-Spelliscy, C., "The History of Corporate Personhood", Brennan Center for Justice (Apr. 8, 2014), https://www.brennancenter.org/our-work/analysis-opinion/history-corporate-personhood.

U. S. Census Bureau, "Income in the United States: 2022", Census Bureau (Sep, 2023), https://www.census.gov/content/dam/Census/library/publications/2023/demo/p60-279.pdf.

U. S. Government Accountability Office, "2019 Lobbying Disclosure: Observations on Lobbyists' Compliance with Disclosure", Requirements (Jun., 2020), https://www.gao.gov/assets/710/705616.pdf.

U. S. Office of Special Counsel, "State, D. C., or Local Employee Hatch Act Information", Office of Special Counsel (n. d.), https://osc.gov/Services/Pages/HatchAct-StateLocal.aspx#tabGroup51.

U. S. Senate Committee on Homeland Security & Governmental Affairs, "Fueling an Epidemic (report two): Exposing the Financial Ties Between Opioid Manufacturers and Third Party Advocacy Groups", University of Pennsylvania (2018), https://www.law.upenn.edu/live/files/7738-report-fueling-an-epidemic-exposing-the-financial.

U. S. Supreme Court, "Citizens United: Opinion of Stevens, J.", Supreme

Court (n. d.), http://www.supremecourt.gov/opinions/09pdf/08-205.pdf.

U. S. Supreme Court, "Shaun McCutcheon, et al., Appellants v. FEC (2014), majority opinion: Opinion of Roberts, C. J.", Supreme Court (n. d.), http://www.supremecourt.gov/opinions/13pdf/12-536_ e1pf.pdf.

Vallas, R., "Removing Barriers to Opportunity for Parents With Criminal Records and Their Children", Center for American Progress (Dec. 10, 2015), https://www.americanprogress.org/issues/poverty/reports/2015/12/10/126902/removing-barriers-to-opportunity-for-parents-with-criminal-records-and-their-children/.

Vandewalker, I., "Shadow Campaigns: The Shift in Presidential Campaign Funding to Outside Groups", Brennan Center for Justice (2015), https://www.brennancenter.org/sites/default/files/analysis/Shadow_ Campaigns.pdf.

Wagner, P. & Rabuy, B., "Following the Money of Mass Incarceration", Prison Policy (Jan. 25, 2017), https://www.prisonpolicy.org/reports/money.html.

Walton, B., "The American Ruling Class", *Harvard Political Review*, *Harvard Politics*, Sep. 6, 2011, https://harvardpolitics.com/books-arts/the-american-ruling-class/.

Weiner, D. I. & Bacskai, O., "Owen Bacskai The FEC, Still Failing to Enforce Campaign Laws, Heads to Capitol Hill", Brennan Center for Justice (Sep. 15, 2023), https://www.brennancenter.org/our-work/analysis-opinion/fec-still-failing-enforce-campaign-laws-heads-capitol-hill.

Weiner, D. I., "Citizens United Five Years Later", Brennan Center for Justice (Jan. 15, 2015), https://www.brennancenter.org/our-work/research-reports/citizens-united-five-years-later.

Weiner, D. I. & Vandewalker, I., *Stronger Parties, Stronger Democracy: Rethinking Reform*, New York: Brennan Center, 2015, p. 2, https://www.brennancenter.org/sites/default/files/publications/Stronger _ Parties _ Stronger_ Democracy.pdf.

Wesleyan Media Project, "Digital Spending Dominates in Early 2020 Presidential Race: Candidates Have Spent $61 Million on Facebook and Google and Just $11 Million on TV", Wesleyan Media Project (Sep. 19, 2019), Wesleyan Media Project. http://mediaproject.wesleyan.edu/releases-091919/103018/.

West, G. & Baumgart, A., "Zero-tolerance' Immigration Policy is Big Money for Contractors, Nonprofits", Open Secrets (Jun. 21, 2018), https://www.opensecrets.org/news/2018/06/zero-tolerance-immigration-is-big-money-for-contractors-nonprofits/.

White, B., *Congressional Revolving Doors: The Journey from Congress to K Street*, Washington D. C. : Public Citizen's Congress Watch, 2005, p. 1 – 3.

White House Council of Economic Advisors, "Economic Perspectives on Incarceration and the Criminal Justice System", The White House (Apr., 2016), https://obamawhitehouse.archives.gov/sites/default/files/page/files/20160423_ cea_ incarceration_ criminal_ justice.pdf.

Whitehouse, S., "Senate Democrats Introduce Legislation to Crack Down on Secret Spending in Election", United States Senator for Rhode Island (Jun. 24, 2014), https://www.whitehouse.senate.gov/news/release/senate-democrats-introduce-legislation-to-crack-down-on-secret-spending-in-elections.

Whyte, L. E., Mulvihill, G. & Wieder, B., "Politics of Pain: Drugmakers Fought State Opioid Limits Amid Crisis", The Center for Public Integrity (Dec. 15, 2016), https://publicintegrity.org/state-politics/politics-of-pain-drugmakers-fought-state-opioid-limits-amid-crisis/.

Winter, R. K., *Money, Politics, and the First Amendment*, Washington, D. C. : American Enterprise Institute for Public Policy Research, 1971, p. 60.

Woodley, D., "Democracy Behind Bars: How Money in Politics, Felony Disenfranchisement and Prison Gerrymandering Fuel Mass Incarceration and Undermine Democracy", Democracy Behind Bars (Jul., 2018), https://democracybehindbars.org/wp-content/uploads/sites/9/2018/07/DemocracyBehindBarsWEB.pdf.

Yates, R., "Notes of the Secret Debates of the Federal Convention of 1787", Yale Law School (May 30, 1787), https://avalon.law.yale.edu/18th_century/yates.asp.

Zibel, A., "Revolving Congress: The revolving door class of 2019 flocks to K Street", Public Citizen (May 30, 2019), https://www.citizen.org/article/revolving-congress/.

报刊与其他网络资料

Alvarado, M. & others, " 'These People are Profitable': Under Trump, Private Prisons are Cashing in on ICE Detainees", USA Today (Dec. 21, 2019), https://www.usatoday.com/in-depth/news/nation/2019/12/19/ice-detention-private-prisons-expands-under-trump-administration/4393366002/.

AP news wire,"Mark Zuckerberg Donated $400M to Help Local Election Offices during Pandemic", The Independent (Nov. 11, 2020), https://www.independent.co.uk/news/world/americas/mark-zuckerberg-donation-election-facebook-covid-b1721007.html.

Archibold, R. C.,"Ex-Congressman Gets 8-Year Term in Bribery Case", *The New York Times*, Mar. 4, 2006.

Argüello, M. F. P. & Ziff, T.,"Hacking Corruption: Tech Tools to Fight Graft in the Americas", Atlantic Council (Jun. 18, 2019), https://www.atlanticcouncil.org/in-depth-research-reports/report/hacking-corruption-tech-tools-to-fight-graft-in-the-americas/.

Associated Press,"Audit: Private Prisons Cost More than State-run Prison", Associated Press (Jan. 2, 2019), https://apnews.com/article/af7177d9cce540ab9f2d873b99437154.

BallotPedia,"History of Campaign Finance Regulation", BallotPedia (n. d.), https://ballotpedia.org/History_of_campaign_finance_regulation.

Baumann, N.,"Cure for Campaign Finance Ruling?" Mother Jones (Feb. 11, 2020), https://www.motherjones.com/politics/2010/02/dems-reveal-response-citizens-united-decision/.

Beatty, J.,"A Sisyphean History of Campaign Finance Reform: A look at how we ended up back where we began", The Atlantic (Jul., 2007), https://www.theatlantic.com/magazine/archive/2007/07/a-sisyphean-history-of-campaign-finance-reform/306066/.

Beitsch, R.,"USDA's Perdue Fined for Violating Hatch Act while Promoting Food Boxes", The Hill (Oct. 08, 2020), https://thehill.com/homenews/administration/520240-usdas-perdue-fined-for-violating-hatch-act-while-promoting-food-boxes.

Bellware, K.,"Rod Blagojevich is Out of Prison Thanks to a Kind of Mercy He Rarely Showed as Governor", *The Washington Post*, Feb. 20, 2020.

Benson C. & McCormick, J.,"Gingrich Said to be Paid about $1.6 Million by Freddie Mac", *Bloomberg* (Nov. 17, 2011), https://www.bloomberg.com/news/articles/2011-11-16/gingrich-said-to-be-paid-at-least-1-6-million-by-freddie-mac.

Berens, M. & Shiffman, J.,"Thousands of U. S. Judges Who Broke Laws or

Oaths Remained on the Bench", Reuters (Jun. 30, 2020), https://www.reuters.com/investigates/special-report/usa-judges-misconduct/.

Berman, R., "An Exodus from Congress Tests the Lure of Lobbying", The Atlantic (May 1, 2018), https://www.theatlantic.com/politics/archive/2018/05/lobbying-the-job-of-choice-for-retired-members-of-congress/558851/.

Bertoni, S., "Billionaire Sheldon Adelson Says He Might Give $100M to Newt Gingrich or other Republican", Forbes (Feb. 21, 2012), https://www.forbes.com/sites/stevenbertoni/2012/02/21/billionaire-sheldon-adelson-says-he-might-give-100m-to-newt-gingrich-or-other-republican/.

Bitcoin Magazine, "Thailand Uses Blockchain-Supported Electronic Voting System in Primaries", Nasdaq (Nov. 13, 2018), https://www.nasdaq.com/articles/thailand-uses-blockchain-supported-electronic-voting-system-in-primaries-2018-11-13.

Bland, S., "Liberal Dark-money Behemoth Raised Nearly $140M Last Year", *Politico*, Nov. 20, 2020.

Blumenthal, P., "Anthony Kennedy's Citizens United Disclosure Salve 'Not Working'", *The Huffington Post*, Nov. 2, 2015.

Borger, J., "Industry that Stalks the US Corridors of Power", *The Guardian*, Feb. 13, 2001.

Bradley Coffey, "Cryptocurrency in Campaign Finance: The Future is Here", Multistate (Mar. 9, 2022), https://www.multistate.us/insider/2022/3/9/cryptocurrency-in-campaign-finance-the-future-is-here.

Briffault, R., "Statement of Richard Briffault", Columbia University, FEC "Forum: Corporate Political Spending and Foreign Influence" (Jun. 23, 2016), http://www.fec.gov/members/weintraub/CorporatePoliticalSpendingandForeignInfluence.shtml.

Brittain, A. & Harwell, D., "Private-prison Giant, Resurgent in Trump Era, Gathers at President's Resort", *The Washington Post*, Oct. 25, 2017.

Bronstein, S., Devine, C. & Griffin, D., "Whistleblower: EPA's Pruitt kept secret calendar to hide meetings", CNN (Jul. 3, 2018), https://edition.cnn.com/2018/07/02/politics/scott-pruitt-whistleblower-secret-calendar/index.html.

Bryanov, K., "Bitcoin For America: Cryptocurrencies in Campaign Finance", CoinTelegraph (May 31, 2018), https://cointelegraph.com/news/bitcoin-for-america-cryptocurrencies-in-campaign-finance.

Bryan S. M. , "New Mexico Faces Uphill Battle with Drug Abuse", The Journal (Sep. 22, 2016), https://nsr.the-journal.com/articles/2450.

Calabresi, S. G. , "Book Review: 'six Amendments' by John Paul Stevens-Justice Stevens argues that we need six new amendments. Among them: ending the death penalty and taking away the right to bear arms", The Wall Street Journal, Jul. 14, 2014.

Carlsen, L. , "With Immigration Reform Looming, Private Prisons Lobby to Keep Migrants Behind Bars", The Huffington Post, Mar. 5, 2013.

CBS News, "Whistleblower Exposes $7 Billion No-bid Defense Department Contract", CBS (Jun. 30, 2019), https://www.cbsnews.com/news/halliburton-whistleblower-on-exposing-7-billion-no-bid-defense-contract-2019-06-30/.

Clarke, M. , "Study Shows Private Prison Companies Use Influence to Increase Incarceration", Prison Legal News, Aug. 22, https://www.prisonlegalnews.org/news/2016/aug/22/study-shows-private-prison-companies-use-influence-increase-incarceration/.

Cline, S. , "Retiring Senators Lament Money in Politics: Senators Kerry, Harkin, and Levin All Decried the State of Campaign Finance in Retiring Remarks", U. S. NEWS (Mar. 8, 2013), https://www.usnews.com/news/articles/2013/03/08/retiring-senators-lament-money-in-politics.

Cohen, M. , "How For-profit Prisons Have Become the Biggest Lobby No One is Talking about", The Washington Post, Apr. 28, 2015.

Cohen, R. , "Germany's Lessons for China and America", The New York Times, May 22, 2020.

Confessore, N. , Cohen, S. & Yourish, K. , "Small Pool of Rich Donors Dominates Electing Giving", The New York Times, Aug. 1, 2015.

CoreCivic, "CoreCivic Reports Fourth Quarter and Full Year 2023 Financial Results", CoreCivic (Feb. 7, 2024), https://ir.corecivic.com/news-releases/news-release-details/corecivic-reports-fourth-quarter-and-full-year-2023-financial.

Costa, J. , "What's the Cost of a Seat in Congress?" Maplight (Mar. 10, 2013), https://maplight.org/story/whats-the-cost-of-a-seat-in-congress/.

Cost, J. , "The Swamp Isn't Easy to Drain: Corruption has been Inherent to American Government Since the Founding Fathers-and Acknowledge that is the First Step Toward Containing It", The Aclantic (Jul. 14, 2018), https://www.theatlantic.com/ideas/archive/2018/07/the-swamp-isnt-easy-to-drain/565151/.

Desert hope Treatment, "Who Are the Players in the Pharmaceutical Industry (Big Pharma)?" Desert hope Treatment (Oct. 2, 2019), https://deserthopetreatment.com/big-pharma/.

Diep, F., "Should We Blame Pharmaceutical Companies for America's Opioid Epidemic? Here's What the Science Says", Pacific Standard (Apr. 3, 2019), https://psmag.com/news/should-we-blame-pharmaceutical-companies-for-americas-opioid-epidemic.

Dixon, M., "Negron making $400K Annually as General Counsel for GEO Group", *Politico*, Mar. 15, 2019.

Duignan, B., "Citizens United v. Federal Election Commission", Britannica (Sep. 6, 2019), https://www.britannica.com/event/Citizens-United-v-Federal-Election-Commission.

Edsall, T. B., "After Citizens United, a Vicious Cycle of Corruption: Unconstrained Outside Spending on Elections is Corrosive to Our Democracy", *The New York Times*, Dec. 6, 2018.

Edsall, T. B., "The Shadow Lobbyist", *The New York Times*, Apr. 25, 2013.

Edsall, T. B., "Who Needs a Smoke-Filled Room?" *The New York Times*, Sep. 9, 2014.

Egan, M., "Record Inequality: The Top 1% Controls 38.6% of America's Wealth", CNN (Sep. 27, 2017), https://money.cnn.com/2017/09/27/news/economy/inequality-record-top-1-percent-wealth/index.html.

Eggen, D., "Post-Watergate Campaign Finance Limits Undercut by Changes", *The Washington Post*, Jun. 16, 2012.

Eggen, D., "Short-lived Firm's $1M Donation to GOP Fund Raises Concern Over Transparency", *The Washington Post*, Aug. 04, 2011.

Fortin, J., "D. E. A. Let Opioid Production Surge as Crisis Grew, Justice Dept. Says", *The New York Times*, Oct. 2, 2019.

Friedman, L., "The Investigations That Led to Scott Pruitt's Resignation", *The New York Times*, Jul. 13, 2018.

Froomkin, D., "Jack Abramoff, In New Book, Decries Endemic Corruption in Washington", *The Huffington Post*, Oct. 28, 2011.

Fuller, J., "From George Washington to Shaun McCutcheon: A Briefish History of Campaign Finance Reform", *The Washington Post*, Apr. 4, 2014.

Furtak, S., "Citizens United and Its Impact on Campaign Financing: A Brief Overview Current Events" [*HeinOnline Blog*], Mar. 8, 2018, https://home.heinonline.org/blog/2018/03/citizens-united-and-its-impact-on-campaign-financing-a-brief-overview/.

Galka, M., "The History of Campaign Spending", Metrocosm (Aug. 02, 2015), http://metrocosm.com/the-history-of-campaign-spending/.

Garrity, L., "Got Bitcoin? Now You can Donate It to This GOP Presidential Candidate", *Politico*, Aug. 04, 2023.

GEO Group, "The GEO Group Reports Fourth Quarter and Full Year 2023 Results", GEO Group (Feb. 15, 2024), https://investors.geogroup.com/news-releases/news-release-details/geo-group-reports-fourth-quarter-and-full-year-2023-results#:~:text=For%20the%20full%20year%202023,for%20the%20full%20year%202022.

Geraci, V. W., "Campaign Finance Reform Historical Timeline", Connecticut Network (n. d.), https://ct-n.com/civics/campaign_finance/Support%20Materials/CTN%20CFR%20Timeline.pdf.

Global Financial Integrity, "The Library Card Project: The Ease of Forming Anonymous Companies in the United States", Global Financial Integrity (Mar. 21, 2019), https://secureservercdn.net/50.62.198.97/34n.8bd.myftpupload.com/wp-content/uploads/2019/03/GFI-Library-Card-Project.pdf?time=1648218825.

Goldmacher, S., "The 2020 Campaign Is the Most Expensive Ever (By a Lot)", *The New York Times*, Oct. 28, 2020.

Gold, M., "Hedge Fund Manager S. Donald Sussman Gave $21 Million to Pro-Clinton Super PAC Priorities USA", *The Washington Post*, Oct, 20, 2016.

Gold, M., "Koch-backed Political Network, Built to Shield Donors, Raised $400 Million in 2012 Elections", *The Washington Post*, Jan. 5, 2014. https://www.washingtonpost.com/politics/koch-backed-political-network-built-to-shield-donors-raised-400-million-in-2012-elections/2014/01/05/9e7cfd9a-719b-11e3-9389-09ef9944065e_story.html.

Good Jobs First, "Discover Where Corporations are Getting Taxpayer Assistance Across the United States", Good Jobs First (n. d.), https://www.goodjobsfirst.org/subsidy-tracker.

Goodman, J. & Warmbrodt, Z. , "The New Crypto Campaign", *Politico*, Nov. 20, 2023.

Goodman, L. M. , "As Dark Money Floods U. S. Elections, Regulators Turn a Blind Eye", Newsweek (Sep. 30, 2014), https: //www. newsweek. com/2014/10/10/dark-money-floods-us-elections-regulators-turn-blind-eye-273951. html.

Govtrack, "Federal Legislation", Govtrack (May, 2011), www. govtrack. us/congress/legislation. xpd.

Grimaldi, J. V. & Schmidt, S. , "Lawmaker's Abramoff Ties Investigated", *The Washington Post*, Oct. 18, 2005, p. A01.

Grim, R. & Siddiqui, S. , "Call Time for Congress Shows How Fundraising Dominates Bleak Work Life", *The Huffington Post*, Dec. 06. 2017.

Gu, J. , "The Employees Who Gave Most to Trump and Biden", Bloomberg (Nov. 3, 2020), https: //www. bloomberg. com/graphics/2020-election-trump-biden-donors/.

Hacker, J. S. & Loewentheil, N. , "How Big Money Corrupts the Economy", Democracy Journal (Winter, 2013), https: //democracyjournal. org/magazine/27/how-big-money-corrupts-the-economy/.

Halpern, S. , "Filling the Empty Seats at the F. E. C. Won't Fix America's Corrupt Elections", *The New Yorker*, Aug. 4, 2011.

Harlan, C. , "Inside the Administration's $1 Billion Deal to Detain Central American Asylum Seekers", *The Washington Post*, Aug. 14, 2016.

Harris, G. , "Pfizer Pays $2. 3 Billion to Settle Marketing Case", *The New York Times*, Sep. 2, 2009.

Harris, P. , "America is Better Than This: Paralysis at the Top Leaves Voters Desperate for Change", The Guardian, Nov. 19, 2011.

Hassan, A. , "Doctor Who Prescribed 500000 Doses of Opioids Is Sent to Prison for 40 Years", *The New York Times*, Oct. 1, 2019.

Hennessey, K. , "White House Memo Fuels Debate on Whether Parks, Politics Mix", *Los Angeles Times*, Aug. 30, 2004.

Hernández, K. , "Is Bitcoin Secretly Messing with the Midterms?" Politico Magazine (Oct. 26, 2018), https: //www. politico. com/magazine/story/2018/10/26/is-bitcoin-secretly-messing-with-the-midterms-221915/.

Higham, S. & Bernstein, L. , "The Drug Industry's Triumph Over the DEA",

The Washington Post, Oct. 15, 2017.

Hiltzik, M., "The Revolving Door Spins Faster: Ex-Congressmen Become 'Stealth Lobbyists'", *The Los Angeles Times*, Jan. 6, 2015.

History Commons, "1896: Presidential Campaign Criticized as Corrupt, Public Begins Demanding Campaign Finance Reform", History Commons (n. d.), http://www.historycommons.org/context.jsp?item=a1896mckinleydouglas.

Hoffman, J., "Johnson & Johnson Ordered to Pay $572 Million in Landmark Opioid Trial", *The New York Times*, Aug. 26, 2019.

Hohmann, J., "The Daily 202: A Poll Commissioned by Bush and Biden Shows Americans Losing", *The Washington Post*, Jun. 26, 2018.

Holland, J., "Higher Profits Explain Why There Are More People of Color in Private Prisons", Moyers (Feb. 7, 2014), https://billmoyers.com/2014/02/07/higher-profits-explain-why-there-are-more-people-of-color-in-private-prisons/.

HSB, "One-Third of Small Businesses Accept Cryptocurrency", Munichre (Jan. 15, 2020), https://www.munichre.com/hsb/en/press-and-publications/press-releases/2020/2020-01-15-one-third-of-small-businesses-accept-cryptocurrency.html.

Jackman, M., "ALEC's Influence Over Lawmaking in State Legislatures", The Brookings Institute (2013), www.brookings.edu/articles/alecs-influence-over-lawmaking-in-state-legislatures/.

Jacobs, T., "Opioid Deaths Follow Where Big Pharma Spends Money on Marketing to Doctors", Pacific Standard (Jan. 18, 2019), https://psmag.com/social-justice/opioid-deaths-follow-where-big-pharma-spends-money-on-marketing-to-doctors.

Jaursch, J., "How to Write Rules for Fair Digital Campaigning", The Brookings Institution (2020), https://www.brookings.edu/techstream/how-to-write-rules-for-fair-digital-campaigning/.

Johnson, K., "Private Purchasing of Prisons Locks in Occupancy Rates", USA Today (Mar. 8, 2012), http://blog.wolfslaw.com/articles/Private%20purchasing%20of%20prisons%20locks%20in%20occupancy%20rates%20USATODAY.com.pdf.

Justice Policy Institute, "Gaming the System: How the Political Strategies of Private Prison Companies Promost Ineffective Incarceration Policies", Justice Policy Institute （Jun．, 2011）, http：//www. justicepolicy. org/uploads/justicepolicy/documents/gaming_ the_ system. pdf.

Kaiser Health News, "Pharma Racks up Huge Victory in Ohio as Voters Overwhelmingly Reject Drug Price Relief Act", Kaiser Health News （Nov. 08, 2017）, https：//khn. org/morning-breakout/pharma-racks-up-huge-victory-in-ohio-as-voters-overwhelmingly-reject-drug-price-relief-act/.

Kaiser, R. G. & Crites, A., "Citizen K Street：How lobbying became Washington's biggest business – Big money creates a new capital city. As lobbying booms, Washington and politics are transformed", *The Washington Post*, Sep. 6, 2011.

Kamen, A. & Itkowitz, C., "Want to Stop Enriching People Whose Politics You Hate? There's an App for That", *The Washington Post*, Aug. 12, 2014.

Kamisar, B., "Meet the Press Blog：Latest News, Analysis and Data Driving the Political Discussion", NBC News （Jan. 6, 2021）, https：//www. nbcnews. com/politics/meet-the-press/blog/meet-press-blog-latest-news-analysis-data-driving-political-discussion-n988541/ncrd1245783#blogHeader.

Kaplan, S. & Hoffman, J., "Mallinckrodt Reaches $1.6 Billion Deal to Settle Opioid Lawsuits", *The New York Times*, Feb. 25, 2020.

Kaplan, S. & Thomas, K., "Draft Order on Drug Prices Proposes Easing Regulation", *The New York Times*, Jun. 20, 2017, https：//www. nytimes. com/2017/06/20/health/draft-order-on-drug-prices-proposes-easing-regulations. html.

Katz, J. & Sanger-Katz, M., "'The Numbers Are So Staggering.' Overdose Deaths Set a Record Last Year", *The New York Times*, Nov. 29, 2018.

Kazin, M., "The Nation：One Political Constant", *The New York Times*, 2001, April 1.

Kelner, R. & others., "Congress Amends LDA Forms to Require Reporting of Lobbyist Convictions", Covington & Burling LLP （Apr. 8, 2019）, https：//www. insidepoliticallaw. com/2019/04/08/congress-amends-lda-forms-to-require-reporting-of-lobbyist-convictions/.

Kenny, A., "Denver Will Allow Smartphone Voting for Thousands of People （but probably not you）", *The Denver Post*, Mar. 7, 2019.

Kirkham, C., "Private Prisons Profit from Immigration Crackdown, Federal and Local Law Enforcement Partnerships", *The Huffington Post*, Aug.

6, 2012.

Kirzinger, A., Wu, B., Muñana, C. & Brodie, M., "Kaiser Health Tracking Poll-Late Summer 2018: The Election, Pre-Existing Conditions, and Surprises on Medical Bills", Kaiser Family Foundation (Sep. 5, 2018), https://www.kff.org/health-reform/poll-finding/kaiser-health-tracking-poll-late-summer-2018-the-election-pre-existing-conditions-and-surprises-on-medical-bills/.

Kitchenman, A., "New Jersey Tops Country in Prescribing Brand-Name Drugs", NJ Spotlight (Nov. 20, 2013), https://www.njspotlight.com/stories/13/11/19/new-jersey-tops-country-in-prescribing-brand-name-drugs/.

Klein, E., "The Most Depressing Graphic for Members of Congress", *The Washington Post*, Jan. 14, 2013.

Koerth-Baker, M., "How Money Affects Elections", FiveThirtyEight (Sep. 10, 2018), https://fivethirtyeight.com/features/money-and-elections-a-complicated-love-story/.

Kozlowska, H. & Karaian, J., "The First Big Winners of Donald Trump's Victory are Private Prison Companies, Whose Stocks are Soaring", Quartz (Nov. 9, 2016), https://qz.com/832775/election-2016-private-prison-company-stocks-cca-and-geo-group-are-surging.

Laflin, N., "Local Mother Tells Story of Son's Overdose Death in Newly Released Documentary", Koat (Feb. 7, 2020), https://www.koat.com/article/albuquerque-couple-featured-in-documentary-thats-getting-lots-of-attention-in-hollywood/30801047#.

Leary, A., "Behind Marco Rubio, a Powerful Ally: Private Prison Operator Geo Group", *Tampa Bay Times*, Aug. 25, 2016.

Lee, S., "By the Numbers: The U.S.'s Growing For-Profit Detention Industry", ProPublica (Jun. 20, 2012), https://www.propublica.org/article/by-the-numbers-the-u.s-growing-for-profit-detention-industry.

Lepore, J., "The Crooked and the Dead: Does the Constitution protect corruption?" *The New Yorker*, Aug. 18, 2014.

Liebkind, J., "How Blockchain Technology Can Prevent Voter Fraud", Investpedia (Dec. 9, 2020), https://www.investopedia.com/news/how-blockchain-technology-can-prevent-voter-fraud/.

Lioz, A. & Bowie, B., "Billion-Dollar Democracy: The Unprecedented Role of Money in the 2012 Elections", De⁻mos (2013), https://www.demos.org/sites/default/files/publications/billion.pdf.

Liptak, A., "How Conservatives Weaponized the First Amendment", *The New York Times*, Jun. 30, 2018.

Liptak, A., "Rendering Justice, With One Eye on Re-election", *The New York Times*, May 25, 2008.

Liptak, A. & Roberts, J., "Campaign Cash Mirrors a High Court's Rulings", *The New York Times*, Oct. 1, 2006.

Luo, M. & Zeleny, J., "Obama, in Shift, Says He'll Reject Public Funding", *The New York Times*, Jun. 20, 2008.

Lupkin, S., "A Look at How the Revolving Door Spins from FDA to Industry", National Public Radio (Sep. 28, 2016), https://www.npr.org/sections/health-shots/2016/09/28/495694559/a-look-at-how-the-revolving-door-spins-from-fda-to-industry.

Lu, W. & Dolan, P., "Former Price Aides Now Lobby Their Old Boss on Behalf of Tobacco, Big Pharm", CREW (Jul. 31, 2017), https://www.citizensforethics.org/reports-investigations/crew-investigations/revolving-door-former-price-aides-now-lobby-old-boss-behalf-tobacco-big-pharma/.

Macalister, T., "Pharma Overtakes Arms Industry to Top the League of Misbehaviour", *The Guardian*, Jul. 7, 2012.

Maraniss D. & Weisskopf M., "Speaker and His Directors Make the Cash Flow Right", *The Washington Post*, Nov. 27, 1995, Page A01.

Martinez, A., "Portrait of a Lobbyist: Power or Myth", *The Los Angeles Times*, May 26, 1974, p. 3.

Martynas Pupkevicius, "Key Cryptocurrency Statistics & Facts for 2023 and Beyond", Moneyzine (Dec. 5, 2023), https://moneyzine.com/personal-finance-resources/cryptocurrency-statistics/.

Mayer, J., "Covert Operations: The Billionaire Brothers Who are Waging a War Against Obama", *The New Yorker*, Aug. 23, 2010.

McElhatton, J., "Marshalls Service Nominee Answers Critics Conflict-of-Interest Charge", *The Washington Times*, Nov. 17, 2010.

McGreal, C., "How Big Pharma's Money- and its Politicians-Feed the US Opioid Crisis", *The Guardian*, Oct. 19, 2017.

McGreal, C., "Johnson & Johnson Opioid Ruling Explained – the Key Points",

The Guardian, Aug. 26, 2019.

Mckay, H., "First Presidential Vote Cast Using Blockchain Technology", FoxNews (Oct. 16, 2020), https://www.foxnews.com/tech/first-presidential-vote-cast-using-blockchain-technology.

Medvic, S. K., "The U. S. Political System is Flawed But not Corrupt", *The Washington Post*, May 5, 2017.

Meier, B., "In Guilty Plea, OxyContin Maker to Pay $600 Million", *The New York Times*, May 10, 2007.

Mounk, Y., "America Is Not a Democracy: How the United States Lost the Faith of its Citizens- and What It Can Do to Win Them Back", The Atlantic (Mar., 2018), https://www.theatlantic.com/magazine/archive/2018/03/america-is-not-a-democracy/550931/.

NCSL, "2017 Campaign Finance Enactments", NCSL (Jan. 3, 2018), https://www.ncsl.org/elections-and-campaigns/2017-campaign-finance-enactments.

Nichols J., "Teddy Roosevelt Was Right: Ban All Corporate Contributions", The Nation (Jan. 21, 2010), https://www.thenation.com/article/teddy-roosevelt-was-right-ban-all-corporate-contributions/.

Nieberg, P., "Three States Pass Amendments that 'Only Citizens' Can Vote", Associated Press (Nov. 7, 2020), https://apnews.com/article/alabama-local-elections-constitutions-florida-voting-rights-a28936630a24030df958092834f6b2c1.

Ogrysko, N., "Many Feds Do Care about the Hatch Act. But the Law Allows Others to Shrug It Off", Federal News Network (Aug. 31, 2020), https://federalnewsnetwork.com/mike-causey-federal-report/2020/08/many-feds-do-care-about-the-hatch-act-but-the-law-allows-others-to-shrug-it-off/.

Oracle, "Global Businesses Turn to Oracle Blockchain Service to Speed Transactions Securely", Oracle (Jul. 16, 2018), https://www.oracle.com/corporate/pressrelease/global-businesses-turn-to-oracle-blockchain-071618.html.

Owens, J., "The Promises and Pitfalls of Blockchain Politics", Medium (Aug. 16, 2019), https://medium.com/swlh/the-promises-and-pitfalls-of-blockchain-voting-11e738e5ed3a.

Parker, A., "Outside Money Drives a Deluge of Political Ads", *The New York Times*, Jul. 28, 2014.

Park, T., "Dirty Money: ALEC's Monopoly on American Law", The Byline

(Jun. 30, 2020), https://medium.com/thebyline/dirty-money-alecs-monopoly-on-american-law-2627ede1f2c.

Plan Against Pain, "An Analysis of the Impact of Opioid Overprescribing in America", Plan Against Pain (n.d.), https://www.planagainstpain.com/wp-content/uploads/2017/09/PlanAgainstPain_USND.pdf.

Posner, R., "Unlimited Campaign Spending – A Good Thing?" (*Becker-Posner Blog*) Apr. 8, 2012, https://www.becker-posner-blog.com/2012/04/unlimited-campaign-spendinga-good-thing-posner.html.

Pressgrove, J., "Utah County Puts Blockchain Voting to the Test in Live Audit", Government Technology (Sep. 4, 2019), https://www.govtech.com/products/Utah-County-Puts-Blockchain-Voting-to-the-Test-in-Live-Audit.html.

Rassweiler, E., "Corporate Control of Elections, Citizens United v. Federal Election Commission (2010) and Related Decisions: The History and Consequences", Corporate Control of Elections (2018), https://corporatecontrolofelections.com/#_edn21.

Reklaitis, V. & Marriner, K., "Newcomers? Congress is Still All About Long-timers-And One Party Has More of Them", Market Watch (Jan. 29, 2019), https://www.marketwatch.com/story/newcomers-congress-is-still-all-about-long-timers-and-one-party-has-more-of-them-2019-01-09.

Reuters Staff, "Maryland city approves letting non-citizens vote in local elections", Reuters (n.d.), https://www.reuters.com/article/us-usa-immigration-maryland/maryland-city-approves-letting-non-citizens-vote-in-local-elections-idUSKCN1BO242.

Robinson, T., Phil, D. & Fanusie, Y., "Bitcoin Laundering: An Analysis of Illicit Flows into Digital Currency Services", Center on Sanctions & Illicit Finance (Jan. 12, 2018), Center on Sanctions & Illicit Finance, https://info.elliptic.co/whitepaper-fdd-bitcoin-laundering.

Rosenbaum, D. E., "A Closer Look at Cheney and Halliburton", *The New York Times*, Sep. 28, 2004.

Rowen, B., "Campaign-Finance Reform: History and Timeline", InforPlease (n.d.), https://www.infoplease.com/history/us/campaign-finance-reform-history-and-timeline.

Sanchez, Y. W. & O'Dell, R., "What is ALEC? 'The Most Effective Organization' for Conservatives, Says Newt Gingrich", USA Today (Apr. 5, 2019), https://www.usatoday.com/story/news/investigations/2019/04/03/alec-american-legislative-exchange-council-model-bills-republican-conservative-devos-gingrich/3162357002/.

Sarlin, B., "San Francisco Allows Undocumented Immigrants to Vote in School Elections", NBC News (Jul. 21, 2018), https://www.nbcnews.com/politics/immigration/san-francisco-allows-undocumented-immigrants-vote-school-elections-n893221.

Satterfield, J., "Tennessee High Court Says Big Pharma Can be Held Liable in Opioid Epidemic", Knox News (Dec. 18, 2020), https://www.knoxnews.com/story/news/crime/2020/12/18/tennessee-high-court-big-pharma-can-held-liable-opioid-epidemic/3956216001/.

Schlozman, K. L., Verba, S. & Brady, H. E., "The People With No Lobby in Washington", Boston Globe (Aug. 26, 2012), https://www.bostonglobe.com/ideas/2012/08/25/the-people-with-lobby-washington/cJds8XhPRwgJUCt3MgUYhO/story.html.

Schmidt, S. & Grimaldi, J. V., "The Fast Rise and Steep Fall of Jack Abramoff", *The Washington Post*, p. A01.

Schouten, F., "Democrats Deride 'Dark' Money, but a New Analysis Shows it Helped Boost Joe Biden", CNN (Nov. 27, 2020), https://www.cnn.com/2020/11/27/politics/dark-money-democrats-joe-biden/index.html.

Schouten, F., "Private Prisons Back Trump and Could See Big Payoffs with New Policies", USA Today (Feb. 23, 2017), https://www.usatoday.com/story/news/politics/2017/02/23/private-prisons-back-trump-and-could-see-big-payoffs-new-policies/98300394/.

Selkey, D. G., "Delaware Blockchain Law Goes into Effect" [*Morgan Lewis Blog*], Aug. 11, 2017, https://www.morganlewis.com/blogs/sourcingatmorganlewis/2017/08/delaware-blockchain-law-goes-into-effect.

Selyukhn, A., "John McCain Predicts 'Huge Scandals' in the Super PAC Era", *The Huffington Post*, Mar. 27, 2012.

Serafini, M., "The Physicians' Quandary with Opioids: Pain versus Addiction", NEJM Catalyst (Apr. 26, 2018), https://catalyst.nejm.org/quandary-opioids-chronic-pain-addiction/.

Shenon, P., "Ney Is Sentenced to 30 Months in Prison", *The New York Times*,

Jan. 19, 2007.

Sherman, J. & Isenstadt, A., "Sheldon Adelson Kicks in $30M to Stop Democratic House Takeover: The Donation to the Congressional Leadership Fund is a Big Boost to Republicans Facing a Tough Midterm Environment", *Politico*, May 10, 2018.

Shevlin, R., "The Coronavirus Cryptocurrency Craze: Who's behind The Bitcoin Buying Binge?" Forbes (Jul. 27, 2020), https://www.forbes.com/sites/ronshevlin/2020/07/27/the-coronavirus-cryptocurrency-craze-whos-behind-the-bitcoin-buying-binge/? sh=1ed8b6412abf.

Sinha, S., "Can Political Fundraising through Cryp to Find Mainstream Acceptance?" Coin Telegraph (Oct. 17, 2019), https://cointelegraph.com/news/can-political-fundraising-through-crypto-find-mainstream-acceptance.

Smith, B. A., "President Wrong on Citizens United Case", National Review (Jan. 28, 2010), https://www.nationalreview.com/corner/president-wrong-citizens-united-case-bradley-smith/.

Smith, D., "Dark Money: The Quixotic Quest to Clean up US Campaign Financing", *The Guardian*, Apr., 6, 2022.

Solender, A., "Here's Why Trump Officials Rarely Face Penalties For Hatch Act Violations", Forbes (Aug. 26, 2020), https://www.forbes.com/sites/andrewsolender/2020/08/26/heres-why-trump-officials-rarely-face-penalties-for-hatch-act-violations/? sh=7a3ba64ca2d2.

Square, Z. P., "Do We Really Need Campaign Finance Reform?" Time (Jan. 19, 2016), https://time.com/4182502/campaign-finance-reform/.

Stapleton, C., "Are Bitcoin Campaign Contributions a Fad or the Future of Fundraising?" *The Palm Beach Post*, Sep. 17, 2020.

State Legislatures Magazine, "Blockchain Regulation, Campaign Finance Laws and Paid Family Leave", NCSL (Mar., 2018), https://www.ncsl.org/bookstore/state-legislatures-magazine/trends-blockchain-regulation-campaign-finance-laws-and-paid-family-leave.aspx.

Stiglitz, J. E., "Of the 1%, By the 1%, For the 1%", Vanity Fair (Mar. 31, 2011), http://www.vanityfair.com/news/2011/05/top-one-percent-201105.

Stoller, M., "Lobbying Used to Be Illegal: A Review of Zephyr Teachout's New Book on the Secret History of Corruption in America" [*Matt Stoller Blog*], Nov. 17, 2014, https://medium.com/@matthewstoller/in-america-lobbying-used-to-be-a-crime-a-review-of-zephyr-teachouts-new-book-cff14d1c0326.

Stout, D., "Ex-Louisiana Congressman Sentenced to 13 Years", *The New York Times*, Nov. 13, 2009.

Sullivan, K., "Judge Disciplined for Promoting Hillary Clinton's Immigration Plan", CNN (Sep. 18, 2019), https://www.cnn.com/2019/09/18/politics/immigration-judge-hatch-act-hillary-clinton/index.html.

Tankersley, J. & Tackett, M., "Trump Tax Cut Unlocks Millions for a Republican Election Blitz", *The New York Times*, Aug. 18, 2018.

Teuta Franjkovic, "Bitcoin in the U.S. Election Race: What Role Will Crypto Play in Deciding Next President?" CNN (Nov. 7, 2023), https://www.ccn.com/news/bitcoin-us-election-crypto-next-president/#:~:text=,several%20lawmakers%20hailing%20its%20significance.

Thomas, K., "the Opioid Drug Maker, to Pay $225 Million to Settle Fraud Charges", *The New York Times*, Jun. 5, 2019.

Toobin, J., "The John Roberts Project", *The New Yorker*, Apr. 7, 2014.

Urban, R. & Allison, B., "Prison Operators Could Cash in on Trump's 'Zero Tolerance' Immigration Policy", Bloomberg (Jun. 28, 2018), https://www.bloomberg.com/news/articles/2018-06-28/prison-operators-gain-as-u-s-immigration-detentions-surge.

Vittert, L., "The Cold Hard Facts about America's Private Prison System", Fox News (Dec. 19, 2018), https://www.foxnews.com/opinion/the-cold-hard-facts-about-americas-private-prison-system.

Voatz, "The West Virginia Mobile Voting Pilot" [*Voatz Blog*], 2019, https://blog.voatz.com/wp-content/uploads/2019/02/West-Virginia-Mobile-Voting-White-Paper-NASS-Submission.pdf.

Wachtel, K., "The Revolving Door: 29 People Who Went from Wall Street to Washington to Wall Street", Business Insider (Jul. 31, 2011), https://www.businessinsider.com/wall-street-washington-revolving-door-2011-4.

Wekipedia, "Duke Cunnningham", https://en.wikipedia.org/wiki/Duke_Cunningham.

Wertheimer, F., "How Chief Justice Roberts and Four Supreme Court Colleagues Gave the Nation a System of Legalized Bribery", *The Huffington Post*, Oct. 6, 2015.

Wikipedia, "Kids for Cash Scandal", https://en.wikipedia.org/wiki/Kids_

for_ cash_ scandal.

Wikipedia, "Publicly Funded Elections", https://en.wikipedia.org/wiki/Publicly_ funded_ elections.

Wikipedia, "Truth in Sentencing", https://en.wikipedia.org/wiki/Truth_ in_ sentencing#United_ States.

Wikipedia, "Turkish Lobby in the United States", https://en.wikipedia.org/wiki/Turkish_ lobby_ in_ the_ United_ States.

Wilson, D., "Merck to Pay $950 Million Over Vioxx", *The New York Times*, Nov. 22, 2011.

Yale Law School Legal Scholarship Repository, Advocacy in the Wake of Citizens United, Page 625 footnote 13, Yale Law School.

Young, A., "Former Halliburton Subsidiary Received $39.5 Billion in Iraq-Related Contracts Over The Past Decade", Business Insider (Mar. 20, 2013), https://www.businessinsider.com/halliburton-company-got-395billion-iraq-2013-3.

Zuesse, E., "Jimmy Carter Is Correct That the U.S. is No Longer a Democracy", *The Huffington Post*, Aug. 3, 2015.

会议、学位和其他论文

Americans Evaluate Campaign Finance Reform: A Survey of Voters Nationwide, School of Public Policy, University of Maryland, May, 2018.

Broms, R. & others, *Political Competition and Public Procurement Quality*, Gothenburg: QoG Working Paper Series No. 2017.

Burnham, W. D., *Democracy in Peril: The American Turnout Problem and the Path to Plutocracy*, Working Paper No. 5, The Roosevelt Institute, 2010.

Fung, Graham & Weil, D., *Disclosing Campaign Contributions to Reduce Corruption*, Ash Center for Democratic Government and Innovation, Harvard Kennedy School, 2007.

Hall, R. & Van Houweling, R. P., Campaign Contributions and Lobbying on the Medicare Modernization Act of 2003, Annual Meeting of the American Political Science Association, Philadelphia, PA, 2006.

Kim, S., Stuckat, J. & Wolters, L., Strategic and Sequential Links between Campaign Donations and Lobbying, MIT, 2020.

Page, B. I. & Seawright, J., What Do US Billionaires Want from Government? Paper presented at the annual meeting of the Midwest Political Science Association, 2014.

Ruiz, J. R., Lobbying, Campaign Contributions and Political Competition, Department of Economics Working Papers 55/16, University of Bath, Department of Economics, 2016.

Scoble, H., "Systemic Corruption", A paper presented at the annual meeting of the American Political Science Association, New Orleans, 1973.

Wilcox, C., "Transparency and Disclosure in Political Finance: Lessons from the United States", Paper prepared for presentation at the Democracy Forum for East Asia Conference on Political Finance, Sejong Institute, Seoul, Korea, 2011.

Wilson, A. J., *Comparative Political Corruption in the United States: The Florida Perspective*. M. A. Thesis, University of South Florida, 2013.

Winik, D., Citizens Informed: Broader Disclosure and Disclaimer for Corporate Electoral Advocacy in the Wake of Citizens United, Yale Law School Legal Scholarship Repository, Yale Law School, Jan. 1, 2010.

索 引

A

阿片危机　37,182,183,185,186,
188,192,193,199,202,204—206

B

保守主义　149,151—153,278

C

财务披露　35,64,106,110,172,
179,252,267,271,276

超级政治行动委员会　24,38,73,
86,101,107—109,111,113,116—
129,131,132,135,140—142,147,
149,159,162,164,170,176,179,
182,191,193,203,215,221,243,
245—248,253,254,257,260—262,
277,279,280

处方药　153,185,187,191,194,
196—202,204,205

D

大公司　4,18,24,29,42,57,62—
64,72,83,92,98,105,144,145,
148—153,180,183,206,252,257—
260,264,269,277,280,282,283

大规模监禁　37,208—212,221,
225,236,238,239

大捐款人　30,31,69,94,119,
125—127,143—145,173,215,248,
252,264,269,277,280,282

毒品　183,184,186,187,189,199,
208,225,226,236,238

堕胎　67,105,109,135,153,252

F

法律改革　21,38,175,176,179,
235,263,272—275,280,283

反腐败　3,6,17,18,21,23,36—
38,61,84,118,131,141,143,144,
148,153—156,158,172—176,180,
181,240,241,252,260,267—269,
273,275,276,280,283

非法移民　105,164,221,223,224,
226,228—230,236

芬太尼　183—186,198,199,204,
205

G

公共筹资　24,27,65,177,254—
257

国会议员　4,7,11,30,32,38,40,

索 引

42,46,48,53—57,76—79,82,84,
92—94,96,100—102,127,135,
154,158,159,161,163,166,167,
174,175,193,200,201,213,217,
232,249,250,257,269,276,277,
283

H

贿赂　4,7—9,13—15,19,20,22,
28—33,36,39,47,48,57,61,65,
74—85,93,94,96,105,135,155,
174,182,186—189,198,199,204,
206,246,262,274

J

加密货币捐款　38,180,241—244,
278,279
精英　3,36,38,47,92,95—97,
104,105,206,272,281
竞选财务法　17,21,22,24,27,31,
38,43,44,46,58,60,61,66—68,
71—75,79,82—84,107,112,120,
124,128,134,138—140,143—145,
149,154,159,168,176,179—181,
217,222,245,246,251,271—275,
282
竞选腐败　18,60,73,104,143,274
竞选捐款　1,3,5,6,8—10,12—
23,25,27—31,33—35,37—48,53,
58—68,71—77,79—90,93—99,
102,103,105,106,115,117,125,
132,141,143,145,147—150,153—
155,157,160—164,169,171,174,
182,183,188—194,196,197,199,
200,202,205,206,208,209,212—
217,221,222,225,228,230,232—
241,244,252,255—258,260—262,
267—273,276—279,282
竞选通讯　73,119,125,130,133,
146,147,159,168,169,173,176,
244,246,251
竞选资金监管　43,61,62,67,71,
145,261,272
拘留　210,211,218,220—224,
227—232,236—238

L

联邦选举委员会　5,22,29,43,
66—69,71,72,80,81,84,86,102,
108—110,113,115,117,118,120—
125,130,131,133,135,138—140,
142,145,147,148,152,154,155,
159,160,162,168—170,172,173,
176,179,183,222,225,240,242,
251,253,254,262,272,277
联邦证券交易委员会　94,159,253
联合公民　18,21—23,25—31,37,
38,60,72,73,81—84,87,93,102—
104,107,109,110,117,119,120,
125,127,129,131,132,136,137,
139,140,143—145,147—149,
151—153,158—161,174,179,182,
183,191,216,237,240,241,244,
247,249,252,257,272,273,275,
277—279,282

M

美国政治　1—3,6,7,17,18,31,
33,38—41,45,47,56,58,60,72,
84,88,89,93,95—97,99,105,106,

109,110,115,118,132,141,151,
225,237,246,258,259,263,264,
275

N

匿名捐款　107,117,136,242

Q

区块链　37,38,241,242,260—
266,280

R

人工智能　37,38,140,141,241,
260,265—268,280
软钱　24,25,67—69,71,72,81,
86,106—109,123,179,273

S

社交媒体　36,38,55,105,119,
142,203,241,258—260,269,280,
281
私营监狱　38,175,208—228,
230—239

T

特殊利益　2,3,5,14,15,20,32,
36—38,40,43,46,48,56,57,60,
73,83,89,92,94,96—100,103—
107,115,131,132,145,149,153,
174,213,216,235,239,251,256,
257,259,264,272,274,275,277
托拉斯　63,86,257—260

W

501 组织　72,111,115,116,119—
122,147,154,161,162,170,171,
195,260

X

刑事司法　34,84,157,160,185,
208—211,218,220,221,226,231,
236,237,239
旋转门　35,37,38,53—58,85,99,
106,154,165,166,174,201,204,
206,212,232,234,238,239,249—
251,257,258,275,276,282

Y

言论自由　5,7,17,18,23,29—31,
41,57,58,67,71—74,80,84,93,
98,105,143,145—148,150—153,
160,161,177,237,249,261,271—
274,276—278,283
药品监管　56,186,194—198,
202—204,206
游说　1,3,5,6,10—18,20,23,27,
29,30,32,33,36—58,74—77,79,
82—85,87—90,93—100,102,105,
106,112,115,132,134—136,149—
151,153—156,158,164—168,
171—176,182,183,188—209,212,
213,216,221,225—232,234—240,
249—253,255,256,258,260,261,
267,268,275,276,282

Z

政府合同　12,36,62,78,154,172,
212,213,215,217,218,220,225,
230,236,238,241,265,267
政治暗钱　37,107,110,118,137,

141,142

政治参与　7,10,39,51,58,62,85,89—92,144,241,261,264,268,273,283

政治腐败　1,3—10,17—21,23,25,28,29,33,36—39,51,56,58,61,65,67,74—76,79,81—85,92—95,99,106,149,175,180,209,246,265,273,276,282

政治选举　63,71,72,74,85,89,102,103,106,107,110,118,132,134,136,137,145,241,246,277

政治支出　24,27,42,53,71,112,117,123,129,133,134,144,159,162,169,183,251,252,254,259,261,276,278

制药巨头　182,188—190,193—198,200—205,208

案例索引

Adams v. East Boston Co., 127 N. E. 728, 631（Mass. 1920）
Austin v. Michigan Chamber of Commerce, 494 US 652, 660（1990）
Brown v. Socialist Workers' 74 Campaign Committee, 450 US 87（1982）
Buckley v. Valeo, 424 U. S. 1（1976）
Chesebrough v. Conover, 140 N. Y. 382, 387（1893）
Clippinger v. Hepbaugh, 5 Watts & Serg. 315, 320 – 321（Pa. 1843）
Citizens United v. FEC, 558 U. S. 08 – 205（2010）
Dobbs v. Jackson Women's Health Organization, 597 U. S. 215（2022）
FEC v. National Conservative PAC, 470 U. S. 480（1985）
FEC v. Wis. Right to Life, 551 U. S. 449（2007）
FEC v. Ted Cruz for Senate, 596 U. S. 289（2022）.
Marshall v. Baltimore & Ohio Railroad, 57 U. S. 314, 333 – 334（1853）
McCormick v. United States, 500 U. S. 257（1991）, p. 273
McCutcheon v. FEC, 572 U. S. 185（2014）
McDonnell v. United States 136 S. Ct. 2355（2016）
Newberry v. United States, 256 U. S. 232（1921）
Nixon v. Shrink Missouri Government PAC, 528 U. S. 377（2000）
Planned Parenthood v. Casey, 505 U. S. 833（1992）
Roe v. Wade, 410 U. S. 113（1973）
Rumely v. United States, 197 F. 2d 166, 173 – 174, 177（D. C. Cir. 1952）
Randall v. Sorrel, 548 U. S. 230（2006）
Santa Clara County v. Southern Pacific Railroad Company, 118 U. S. 394（1886）
Shelton v. Tucker, 364 U. S. 479（1960）
Steward Machine Co. v. Davis. 301 US 548, 57S. Ct. 883, 81 L. Ed. 1279-

Supreme Court, 1937

    Trist v. Child, 88 U. S. 441, 451 (1874)

    United States v. O'Brien, 391 U. S. 367 (1968)

    Virginia State Board of Pharmacy v. Virginia Citizens Consumer Council, Inc. 425 U. S. 748 (1976)

后　记

本书见证了我跨入 30 岁人生的新阶段。在写作的两年中，我重新认识了自己与世界，心智迈出了成熟的一大步。在中国社会科学院美国研究所工作期间，导师袁征教授对我的写作悉心指导，并真诚关心我的未来发展。袁老师为人正直、治学严谨，他的批评和鼓励一直鞭策着我进步。在我的学术与人生道路上，还有两位杰出的女性——天主教鲁汶大学法学院的 Letizia Paoli 教授，和乔治梅森大学恐怖主义、跨国犯罪与腐败研究中心主任 Louise Shelley 教授，也给予了我巨大帮助，她们是我一生学习的女性榜样。

我的父亲韦克平和母亲张小珍一直把我视为骄傲，包容我的不同寻常与任性，他们在我心里平凡又伟大。我的家人和来自中国、美国及欧洲的各位挚友，多年来无私的关心和支持，让我柔软的内心也长出了坚硬的内核，不再惧怕成长。

谨以此书，与所有在学术与实务界辛勤工作的女性共勉。

韦　佳
2024 年 6 月

第十一批《中国社会科学博士后文库》专家推荐表 1

《中国社会科学博士后文库》由中国社会科学院与全国博士后管理委员会共同设立，旨在集中推出选题立意高、成果质量高、真正反映当前我国哲学社会科学领域博士后研究最高学术水准的创新成果，充分发挥哲学社会科学优秀博士后科研成果和优秀博士后人才的引领示范作用，让《文库》著作真正成为时代的符号、学术的示范。

推荐专家姓名	袁征	电话	010-84083503
专业技术职务	研究员	研究专长	美国政治
工作单位	中国社会科学院美国研究所	行政职务	副所长
推荐成果名称	游说、竞选捐款与美国政治腐败		
成果作者姓名	韦佳		

（对书稿的学术创新、理论价值、现实意义、政治理论倾向及是否具有出版价值等方面做出全面评价，并指出其不足之处）

　　该博士后研究以近年来引发激烈讨论的暗钱渗透美国政治选举为背景，收集了大量的 2021 年选举周期最新统计数据，以及过去数十年美国选举与反腐败监管的立法资料，并穿插了法学与政治学的交叉研究分析。研究创新性地围绕加密货币与互联网新媒体在选举中所引发的争议，探讨了区块链与人工智能在选举乃至政治反腐败中的技术前景，具有较前沿的现实意义。尽管囿于研究者的法学学科背景，其在政治学理论方面的讨论尚欠深度，但其对所涉法律政策部分的深入分析，使得前述缺点得到一定平衡。政治理论倾向上方面，该研究立足于多方研究机构和非盈利组织提供的数据及文献，在事实分析、规律总结与结论发现上保持了较强的客观理性。总体上，该研究在理论研究与外交政策参考实务中均具有较高的学术与应用价值，兹推荐出版。

签字：袁征

2022 年 3 月 22 日

说明：该推荐表须由具有正高级专业技术职务的同行专家填写，并由推荐人亲自签字，一旦推荐，须承担个人信誉责任。如推荐书稿入选《文库》，推荐专家姓名及推荐意见将印入著作。

第十一批《中国社会科学博士后文库》专家推荐表 2

《中国社会科学博士后文库》由中国社会科学院与全国博士后管理委员会共同设立，旨在集中推出选题立意高、成果质量高、真正反映当前我国哲学社会科学领域博士后研究最高学术水准的创新成果，充分发挥哲学社会科学优秀博士后科研成果和优秀博士后人才的引领示范作用，让《文库》著作真正成为时代的符号、学术的示范。

推荐专家姓名	赵梅	电话	010-84083531
专业技术职务	研究员	研究专长	美国政治
工作单位	中国社会科学院美国研究所	行政职务	《美国研究》副主编
推荐成果名称	游说、竞选捐款与美国政治腐败		
成果作者姓名	韦佳		

（对书稿的学术创新、理论价值、现实意义、政治理论倾向及是否具有出版价值等方面做出全面评价，并指出其不足之处）

  研究者从自身专业特长与近年中美时事政治所关注议题出发，巧妙选取了美国大规模监禁与阿片危机的成因，作为竞选经费与游说腐败问题的两大代表性案例进行分析。研究视角新，同时具有较强的时事价值。该研究通过对一个世纪以来竞选经费法律的脉络梳理与规律总结，进一步完善了美国竞选经费制度中的理论研究，同时也为未来美国竞选经费制度的演变趋势提供了前瞻性预测，或在一定程度上为外交实践提供参考。由于研究者从事政治学研究时间较短，理论深度或有加强之空间，但研究总体在政治上客观中立，主观分析有理有据，写作及引用规范，仍具备较高的出版价值，谨荐贵社予以出版，望审核通过。

签字：（赵梅）

2022 年 3 月 22 日

说明：该推荐表须由具有正高级专业技术职务的同行专家填写，并由推荐人亲自签字，一旦推荐，须承担个人信誉责任。如推荐书稿入选《文库》，推荐专家姓名及推荐意见将印入著作。